ECON 1B03

Introduction to Microeconomics

McMaster University
Custom Textbook

NELSON / EDUCATION

COPYRIGHT © 2013 by Nelson Education Ltd.

Printed and bound in Canada
1 2 3 4 15 14 13 12

For more information contact Nelson Education Ltd., 1120 Birchmount Road, Toronto, Ontario, M1K 5G4. Or you can visit our Internet site at http://www.nelson.com

This textbook is a Nelson custom publication. Because your instructor has chosen to produce a custom publication, you pay only for material that you will use in your course.

ISBN-13: 978-0-17-666421-3
ISBN-10: 0-17-666421-1

Consists of Selections from:

Principles of Microeconomics 5th edition
N. Gregory Mankiw;
Ronald D. Kneebone;
Kenneth J. McKenzie;
Nicholas Rowe
ISBN 10: 0-17-650241-6, © 2012

Pinciples of Microeconomics Study Guide 5th edition
N. Gregory Mankiw;
Ronald D. Kneebone;
Kenneth J. McKenzie;
Shahram Manouchehri;
Peter Fortura
ISBN 10: 0-17-662294-2, © 2008

Cover Credit:

Shutterstock/nagib

Brief Contents

Tupungato/Shutterstock.com

INTRODUCTION

TEN PRINCIPLES OF ECONOMICS

Tupungato/Shutterstock.com

Learning Objectives

In this chapter, you will …

- Learn that economics is about the allocation of scarce resources
- Examine some of the tradeoffs that people face
- Learn the meaning of *opportunity cost*
- See how to use marginal reasoning when making decisions
- Discuss how incentives affect people's behaviour
- Consider why trade among people or nations can be good for everyone
- Discuss why markets are a good, but not perfect, way to allocate resources
- Learn what determines some trends in the overall economy

The word *economy* comes from the Greek word for "one who manages a household." At first, this origin might seem peculiar. But, in fact, households and economies have much in common.

A household faces many decisions. It must decide which members of the household do which tasks and what each member gets in return: Who cooks dinner? Who does the laundry? Who gets the extra dessert at dinner? Who gets to choose what TV show to watch? In short, the household must allocate its scarce resources among its various members, taking into account each member's abilities, efforts, and desires.

Like a household, a society faces many decisions. A society must decide what jobs will be done and who will do them. It needs some people to grow food, other people to make clothing, and still others to design computer software. Once society has allocated people (as well as land, buildings, and machines) to various jobs, it must also allocate the output of goods and services that they produce. It must decide who will eat caviar and who will eat potatoes. It must decide who will drive a Ferrari and who will take the bus.

scarcity
the limited nature
of society's resources

The management of society's resources (e.g., people, land, buildings, machinery) is important because resources are scarce. **Scarcity** means that society has limited resources and therefore cannot produce all the goods and services people wish to have. Just as a household cannot give every member everything he or she wants, a society cannot give every individual the highest standard of living to which he or she might aspire.

economics
the study of how society
manages its scarce resources

Economics is the study of how society manages its scarce resources. In most societies, resources are allocated not by a single central planner but through the combined actions of millions of households and firms. Economists therefore study how people make decisions: how much they work, what they buy, how much they save, and how they invest their savings. Economists also study how people interact with one another. For instance, they examine how the multitude of buyers and sellers of a good together determine the price at which the good is sold and the quantity that is sold. Finally, economists analyze forces and trends that affect the economy as a whole, including the growth in average income, the fraction of the population that cannot find work, and the rate at which prices are rising.

Although the study of economics has many facets, the field is unified by several central ideas. In the rest of this chapter, we look at ten principles of economics. Don't worry if you don't understand them all at first, or if you don't find them completely convincing. In the coming chapters we will explore these ideas more fully. The ten principles are introduced here just to give you an overview of what economics is all about. You can think of this chapter as a "preview of coming attractions."

HOW PEOPLE MAKE DECISIONS

There is no mystery to what an "economy" is. Whether we are talking about the economy of Vancouver, of Canada, or of the whole world, an economy is just a group of people interacting with one another as they go about their lives. Because the behaviour of an economy reflects the behaviour of the individuals who make up the economy, we start our study of economics with four principles of individual decision making.

Principle #1: People Face Tradeoffs

The first lesson about making decisions is summarized in the adage "There is no such thing as a free lunch." To get one thing that we like, we usually have to give up another thing that we like. Making decisions requires trading off one goal against another.

Consider a student who must decide how to allocate her most valuable resource—her time. She can spend all of her time studying economics; she can spend all of her time studying psychology; or she can divide her time between the two fields. For every hour she studies one subject, she gives up an hour she could have used studying the other. And for every hour she spends studying, she gives up an hour that she could have spent napping, bike riding, watching TV, or working at her part-time job for some extra spending money.

Or consider parents deciding how to spend their family income. They can buy food, clothing, or a family vacation. Or they can save some of the family income for retirement or the children's college or university education. When they choose to spend an extra dollar on one of these goods, they have one less dollar to spend on some other good.

When people are grouped into societies, they face different kinds of tradeoffs. The classic tradeoff is between "guns and butter." The more we spend on national defence (guns) to protect our shores from foreign aggressors, the less we can spend on consumer goods (butter) to raise our standard of living at home. Also important in modern society is the tradeoff between a clean environment and a high level of income. Laws that require firms to reduce pollution raise the cost of producing goods and services. Because of the higher costs, these firms end up earning smaller profits, paying lower wages, charging higher prices, or some combination of these three. Thus, while pollution regulations give us the benefit of a cleaner environment and the improved health that comes with it, they have the cost of reducing the incomes of the firms' owners, workers, and customers.

Another tradeoff society faces is between efficiency and equity. **Efficiency** means that society is getting the most it can from its scarce resources. **Equity** means that the benefits of those resources are distributed fairly among society's members. In other words, efficiency refers to the size of the economic pie, and equity refers to how the pie is divided. Often, when government policies are being designed, these two goals conflict.

efficiency
the property of society getting the most it can from its scarce resources

equity
the property of distributing economic prosperity fairly among the members of society

Consider, for instance, policies aimed at achieving a more equal distribution of economic well-being. Some of these policies, such as the welfare system or Employment Insurance, try to help those members of society who are most in need. Others, such as the individual income tax, ask the financially successful to contribute more than others to support the government. Although these policies have the benefit of achieving greater equity, they have a cost in terms of reduced efficiency. When the government redistributes income from the rich to the poor, it reduces the reward for working hard; as a result, people work less and produce fewer goods and services. In other words, when the government tries to cut the economic pie into more equal slices, the pie gets smaller.

Recognizing that people face tradeoffs does not by itself tell us what decisions they will or should make. A student should not abandon the study of psychology just because doing so would increase the time available for the study of economics. Society should not stop protecting the environment just because environmental regulations reduce our material standard of living. The poor should not be ignored just because helping them distorts work incentives. Nonetheless, acknowledging life's tradeoffs is important because people are likely to make good decisions only if they understand the options that they have available.

Principle #2: The Cost of Something Is What You Give Up to Get It

Because people face tradeoffs, making decisions requires comparing the costs and benefits of alternative courses of action. In many cases, however, the cost of some action is not as obvious as it might first appear.

Consider, for example, the decision whether to go to college or university. The benefit is intellectual enrichment and a lifetime of better job opportunities. But what is the cost? To answer this question, you might be tempted to add up the money you spend on tuition, books, room, and board. Yet this total does not truly represent what you give up to spend a year in college or university.

The first problem with this answer is that it includes some things that are not really costs of going to college or university. Even if you quit school, you would need a place to sleep and food to eat. Room and board are costs of going to college or university only to the extent that they are more expensive there than elsewhere. Indeed, the cost of room and board at your school might be less than the rent and food expenses that you would pay living on your own. In this case, the savings on room and board are a benefit of going to college or university.

The second problem with this calculation of costs is that it ignores the largest cost of going to college or university—your time. When you spend a year listening

IN THE NEWS

USING OPPORTUNITY COST TO SELL

Principle #2—the cost of something is what you give up to get it—is based on the concept of opportunity cost. The following newspaper article describes how retailers have used the concept to encourage otherwise hesitant buyers.

Opportunity Cost: Why Buy a Mercedes ... When You Can Get All This?

By Sarah Boesveld

You're in the local big-box electronics store, standing before a wall of flat-screen TVs. Dazed by the glowing scenes of *A Charlie Brown Christmas* and those fake-fireplace flames, your eyes dart between an $800 40-incher and a $1,000 46-incher until a store clerk saunters over and plants the seed of possibility.

"If you go with the $800 one," he tells you, "think of all the DVDs you could buy with the $200 you'll have left."

You rush to the cash and snap up the 40-inch TV. *Voilà!* You're the unwitting participant in a cunning salesman's trick: highlighting opportunity cost to close a deal.

It's a tool retailers use to land a sale rather than see a customer turn on her heel without buying anything. And it's one store clerks might be trying a little more frequently this season as shoppers try to stretch their dollars, experts say.

Most shoppers don't consider the other ways they could spend money without a few well-placed cues, a new study from the Yale School of Management has found.

If a customer shows interest in two items, a salesperson can likely land a sale

on the cheaper model by making her think about all the other Christmas gifts she'll be able to buy with the savings, says lead study author Shane Frederick, an associate professor of marketing at the Yale School of Management.

"I don't know that people very often think spontaneously, 'Here are the other five things I can buy for this price.'"

In a battery of experiments, Prof. Frederick and his colleagues had participants—students and people recruited via the Internet—respond to different purchasing scenarios and measured how and when they'd consider opportunity cost. Some of the experiments found explicit mentions of price difference made the cheaper option more

to lectures, reading textbooks, and writing papers, you cannot spend that time working at a job. For most students, the wages given up to attend school are the largest single cost of their education.

The **opportunity cost** of an item is what you give up to get that item. When making any decision, such as whether to attend college or university, decision makers should be aware of the opportunity costs that accompany each possible action. In fact, they usually are. College- or university-age athletes who can earn millions if they drop out of school and play professional sports are well aware that their opportunity cost of a postsecondary education is very high. It is not surprising that they often decide that the benefit is not worth the cost.

opportunity cost
whatever must be given up to obtain some item

appealing. Researchers also tested the purchasing "pain" of participants by using a "spendthrift-tightwad" scale and found tightwads were less influenced by cues.

"Different manipulations that would cue thoughts of outside expenditures would do one of two things," says Prof. Frederick, who was inspired to research this after being dealt the tactic by a Vancouver salesclerk. "It would make people buy the cheaper option, or it would deter people from some focal purchase, where the cheaper option is to buy nothing and save your money."

It's not just store clerks talking up cheaper items to make a sale. A recent IKEA ad shows two women standing in front of their new armoires—one expensive, the other cheap (and from IKEA). The pricey one holds just one pair of shoes, and the owner sports a scowl. The IKEA cabinet owner beams next to her cupboard overflowing with footwear.

Politicians and activists also raise the spectre of opportunity cost – think U.S. President Dwight Eisenhower's iconic costs-of-war speech from 1953, referenced by President Barack Obama last week as he tried to rally support for sending more troops to Afghanistan.

While the strategy works better for stores hawking lower-priced items, luxury jewellery retailer De Beers spun the idea on its head when it told consumers to put off pricey kitchen renovations in favour of a $20,000 (U.S.) pair of diamond earrings.

"It's not really that the kitchen renovation has been delayed by a year; the money is now gone and in the form of diamond earrings," says Prof. Frederick, who calls it a "genius" marketing move.

While his study didn't look at the recession's impact on opportunity cost, Prof. Frederick says shoppers are probably weighing their options more carefully now than two years ago.

"They're just more cautious generally, so every expenditure is more scrutinized," he says.

Laurence Ashworth, an associate professor of marketing at Queen's University business school, is more convinced of the recession's effects.

"The shoppers out there these days, with greater fear about the economic environment, are showing more signs of opportunity-cost consideration," he says. "One of the consequences of that is it's likely to push people toward cheaper alternatives within a certain product category."

Prof. Frederick suggests that shoppers should think of five other ways to spend their money when faced with a major purchase. "If you can still live without those other five things, then go out and purchase it."

Laura Stricker, a 23-year-old marketing student at George Brown College in Toronto, says she's always second-guessing her purchases. She doesn't need a slick salesclerk or an ad to sway her either way.

"I find it's more natural for me to always be looking out for better deals," she says. "But I think that for a lot of people I know, they tend to buy the first thing they see that they like. They're a lot more impulsive."

Source: Sarah Boesveld, "Opportunity cost: Why buy a Mercedes ... when you can get all this?" *The Globe and Mail*, December 7, 2009. © CTVglobemedia Publishing Inc. All Rights Reserved

Principle #3: Rational People Think at the Margin

rational people
people who systematically and purposefully do the best they can to achieve their objectives

Economists normally assume that people are rational. **Rational people** systematically and purposefully do the best they can to achieve their objectives, given the opportunities they have. As you study economics, you will encounter firms that decide how many workers to hire and how much of their product to manufacture and sell to maximize profits. You will encounter consumers who buy a bundle of goods and services to achieve the highest possible level of satisfaction, subject to their incomes and the prices of those goods and services.

Rational people know that decisions in life are rarely black and white, but usually involve shades of gray. At dinnertime, the decision you face is not between fasting or eating like a pig, but whether to take that extra spoonful of mashed potatoes. When exams roll around, your decision is not between blowing them off or studying 24 hours a day, but whether to spend an extra hour reviewing your notes instead of watching TV. Economists use the term **marginal changes** to describe small incremental adjustments to an existing plan of action. Keep in mind that "margin" means "edge," so marginal changes are adjustments around the edges of what you are doing.

marginal changes
small incremental adjustments to a plan of action

Rational people often make decisions by comparing *marginal benefits* and *marginal costs*. For example, consider an airline deciding how much to charge passengers who fly standby. Suppose that flying a 200-seat plane across the country costs the airline $100 000. In this case, the average cost of each seat is $100 000/200, which is $500. One might be tempted to conclude that the airline should never sell a ticket for less than $500. In fact, however, the airline can raise its profits by thinking at the margin. Imagine that a plane is about to take off with ten empty seats, and a standby passenger is waiting at the gate willing to pay $300 for a seat. Should the airline sell it to him? Of course it should. If the plane has empty seats, the cost of adding one more passenger is minuscule. Although the *average* cost of flying a passenger is $500, the *marginal* cost is merely the cost of the bag of peanuts and can of soda that the extra passenger will consume. As long as the standby passenger pays more than the marginal cost, selling him a ticket is profitable.

Marginal decision making can help explain some otherwise puzzling economic phenomena. Here is a classic question: Why is water so cheap, while diamonds are so expensive? Humans need water to survive, while diamonds are unnecessary; but, for some reason, people are willing to pay much more for a diamond than for a cup of water. The reason is that a person's willingness to pay for any good is based on the marginal benefit that an extra unit of the good will yield. The marginal benefit, in turn, depends on how many units a person already has. Although water is essential, the marginal benefit of an extra cup is small because water is plentiful. By contrast, no one needs diamonds to survive, but because diamonds are so rare, people consider the marginal benefit of an extra diamond to be large.

A rational decision maker takes an action if and only if the marginal benefit of the action exceeds the marginal cost. This principle can explain why airlines are willing to sell a ticket below average cost and why people are willing to pay more for diamonds than for water. It can take some time to get used to the logic of marginal thinking, but the study of economics will give you ample opportunity to practise.

Principle #4: People Respond to Incentives

An **incentive** is something (such as the prospect of a punishment or a reward) that induces a person to act. Because rational people make decisions by comparing costs and benefits, they respond to incentives. You will see that incentives play a central role in the study of economics. One economist went so far as to suggest that the entire field could be simply summarized: "People respond to incentives. The rest is commentary."

Incentives are crucial to analyzing how markets work. For example, when the price of an apple rises, people decide to eat more pears and fewer apples because the cost of buying an apple is higher. At the same time, apple orchards decide to hire more workers and harvest more apples because the benefit of selling an apple is also higher. As we will see, the effect of a good's price on the behaviour of buyers and sellers in a market—in this case, the market for apples—is crucial for understanding how the economy allocates scarce resources.

Public policymakers should never forget about incentives, because many policies change the costs or benefits that people face and, therefore, alter behaviour. A tax on gasoline, for instance, encourages people to drive smaller, more fuel-efficient cars. It also encourages people to take public transportation rather than drive, and to live closer to where they work. If the tax was large enough, people would switch to driving electric cars.

When policymakers fail to consider how their policies affect incentives, they often end up with results they did not intend. For example, consider public policy regarding auto safety. Today all cars have seat belts, but that was not true 50 years ago. In the 1960s, Ralph Nader's book *Unsafe at Any Speed* generated much public concern over auto safety. Parliament responded with laws requiring seat belts as standard equipment on new cars.

How does a seat belt law affect auto safety? The direct effect is obvious: When a person wears a seat belt, the probability of surviving a major auto accident rises. But that's not the end of the story, because the law also affects behaviour by altering incentives. The relevant behaviour here is the speed and care with which drivers operate their cars. Driving slowly and carefully is costly because it uses the driver's time and energy. When deciding how safely to drive, rational people compare the marginal benefit from safer driving to the marginal cost. They drive more slowly and carefully when the benefit of increased safety is high. It is no surprise, for instance, that people drive more slowly and carefully when roads are icy than when roads are clear.

Consider how a seat belt law alters a driver's cost–benefit calculation. Seat belts make accidents less costly because they reduce the likelihood of injury or death. In other words, seat belts reduce the benefits to slow and careful driving. People respond to seat belts as they would to an improvement in road conditions—by faster and less careful driving. The end result of a seat belt law, therefore, is a larger number of accidents. The decline in safe driving has a clear, adverse impact on pedestrians, who are more likely to find themselves in an accident but (unlike the drivers) don't have the benefit of added protection.

At first, this discussion of incentives and seat belts might seem like idle speculation. Yet, in a 1975 study, economist Sam Peltzman showed that the auto-safety laws have had many of these effects [Peltzman, Sam, 1975. "The Effects of Automobile Safety Regulation," *Journal of Political Economy*, University of Chicago Press, Vol. 83(4)]. According to Peltzman's evidence, these laws produce both fewer deaths per accident and more accidents. The net result is little change in the number of driver deaths and an increase in the number of pedestrian deaths.

incentive
something that induces a person to act

The Canadian Press/Kevin Frayer

Mick Jagger understood opportunity cost and incentives. In 1961, he became a scholarship student at the London School of Economics. In 1963, he abandoned a promising career as an economist, worked full-time on his music, and eventually earned millions of dollars with the Rolling Stones.

Peltzman's analysis of auto safety is an example of the general principle that people respond to incentives. When analyzing any policy, we must consider not only the direct effects but also the indirect effects that work through incentives. If the policy changes incentives, it will cause people to alter their behaviour.

QuickQuiz List and briefly explain the four principles of individual decision making.

HOW PEOPLE INTERACT

The first four principles discussed how individuals make decisions. As we go about our lives, many of our decisions affect not only ourselves but other people as well. The next three principles concern how people interact with one another.

Principle #5: Trade Can Make Everyone Better Off

You have probably heard on the news that the Americans are our competitors in the world economy. In some ways this is true, for Canadian and U.S. firms do produce many of the same goods. Blackberry and Apple compete for the same customers in the market for smart phones. Inniskillin and Gallo compete for the same customers in the market for wine.

Yet it is easy to be misled when thinking about competition among countries. Trade between Canada and the United States is not like a sports contest, where one side wins and the other side loses. In fact, the opposite is true: Trade between two countries can make each country better off.

To see why, consider how trade affects your family. When a member of your family looks for a job, he or she competes against members of other families who are looking for jobs. Families also compete against one another when they go shopping, because each family wants to buy the best goods at the lowest prices. So, in a sense, each family in the economy is competing with all other families.

Despite this competition, your family would not be better off isolating itself from all other families. If it did, your family would need to grow its own food, make its own clothes, and build its own home. Clearly, your family gains much from its ability to trade with others. Trade allows each person to specialize in the activities he or she does best, whether it is farming, sewing, or home building. By trading with others, people can buy a greater variety of goods and services at lower cost.

Countries as well as families benefit from the ability to trade with one another. Trade allows countries to specialize in what they do best and to enjoy a greater variety of goods and services. The Americans, as well as the French and the Egyptians and the Brazilians, are as much our partners in the world economy as they are our competitors.

Principle #6: Markets Are Usually a Good Way to Organize Economic Activity

The collapse of communism in the Soviet Union and Eastern Europe in the 1980s may be the most important change in the world during the past half-century. Communist countries worked on the premise that central planners in the government were in the best position to guide economic activity. These planners decided what goods and services were produced, how much was produced, and who produced and consumed these goods and services. The theory behind central planning was that only the government could organize economic activity in a way that promoted economic well-being for the country as a whole.

Today, most countries that once had centrally planned economies have abandoned this system and are trying to develop market economies. In a **market economy,** the decisions of a central planner are replaced by the decisions of millions of firms and households. Firms decide whom to hire and what to make. Households decide which firms to work for and what to buy with their incomes. These firms and households interact in the marketplace, where prices and self-interest guide their decisions.

At first glance, the success of market economies is puzzling. After all, in a market economy, no one is looking out for the economic well-being of society as a whole. Free markets contain many buyers and sellers of numerous goods and services, and all of them are interested primarily in their own well-being. Yet, despite decentralized decision making and self-interested decision makers, market economies have proven remarkably successful in organizing economic activity in a way that promotes overall economic well-being.

In his 1776 book *An Inquiry into the Nature and Causes of the Wealth of Nations,* economist Adam Smith made the most famous observation in all of economics: Households and firms interacting in markets act as if they are guided by an "invisible hand" that leads them to desirable market outcomes. One of our goals in this book is to understand how this invisible hand works its magic.

As you study economics, you will learn that prices are the instrument with which the invisible hand directs economic activity. In any market, buyers look at the price when determining how much to demand, and sellers look at the price when deciding how much to supply. As a result of the decisions that buyers and sellers make, market prices reflect both the value of a good to society and the cost to society of making the good. Smith's great insight was that prices adjust to guide these individual buyers and sellers to reach outcomes that, in many cases, maximize the welfare of society as a whole.

There is an important corollary to the skill of the invisible hand in guiding economic activity: When the government prevents prices from adjusting naturally to supply and demand, it impedes the invisible hand's ability to coordinate the millions of households and firms that make up the economy. This corollary explains why taxes adversely affect the allocation of resources: Taxes distort prices and thus the decisions of households and firms. It also explains the even greater harm caused by policies that directly control prices, such as rent control. And it explains the failure of communism. In communist countries, prices were not determined in the marketplace but were dictated by central planners. These planners lacked the information that is reflected in prices when prices are free to respond to market forces. Central planners failed because they tried to run the economy with one hand tied behind their backs—the invisible hand of the marketplace.

market economy
an economy that allocates resources through the decentralized decisions of many firms and households as they interact in markets for goods and services

ADAM SMITH AND THE INVISIBLE HAND

It may be only a coincidence that Adam Smith's great book *The Wealth of Nations* was published in 1776, the same year American revolutionaries signed the *Declaration of Independence*. But the two documents do share a point of view that was prevalent at the time—that individuals are usually best left to their own devices, without the heavy hand of government guiding their actions. This political philosophy provides the intellectual basis for the market economy, and for free society more generally.

Why do decentralized market economies work so well? Is it because people can be counted on to treat one another with love and kindness? Not at all. Here is Adam Smith's description of how people interact in a market economy:

Adam Smith

Man has almost constant occasion for the help of his brethren, and it is vain for him to expect it from their benevolence only. He will be more likely to prevail if he can interest their self-love in his favor, and show them that it is for their own advantage to do for him what he requires of them. . . . It is not from the benevolence of the butcher, the brewer, or the baker that we expect our dinner, but from their regard to their own interest. . . .

Every individual . . . neither intends to promote the public interest, nor knows how much he is promoting it. . . . He intends only his own gain, and he is in this, as in many other cases, led by an invisible hand to promote an end which was no part of his intention. Nor is it always the worse for the society that it was no part of it. By pursuing his own interest he frequently promotes that of the society more effectually than when he really intends to promote it.

Smith is saying that participants in the economy are motivated by self-interest and that the "invisible hand" of the marketplace guides this self-interest into promoting general economic well-being.

Many of Smith's insights remain at the centre of modern economics. Our analysis in the coming chapters will allow us to express Smith's conclusions more precisely and to analyze fully the strengths and weaknesses of the market's invisible hand.

Principle #7: Governments Can Sometimes Improve Market Outcomes

If the invisible hand of the market is so great, why do we need government? The study of economics will refine your view about the proper role and scope of government policy.

One reason we need government is that the invisible hand can work its magic only if the government enforces the rules and maintains the institutions that are key to a market economy. Most important, markets work only if **property rights** are enforced. A farmer won't grow food if he expects his crop to be stolen, a restaurant won't serve meals unless it is assured that customers will pay before they leave, and a music company won't produce CDs if too many potential customers avoid paying by making illegal copies. We all rely on government-provided police services and courts to enforce our rights over the things we produce—and the invisible hand counts on our ability to enforce our rights.

Yet there is another, more profound reason that we need government: The invisible hand is powerful, but it is not omnipotent. Although markets are often a good way to organize economic activity, this rule has some important exceptions. There are two broad reasons for a government to intervene in the economy and change the allocation of resources that people would choose on their own: to

property rights
the ability of an individual to own and exercise control over scarce resources

promote efficiency and to promote equity. That is, most policies aim either to enlarge the economic pie or to change how the pie is divided.

Consider first the goal of efficiency. Although the invisible hand usually leads markets to allocate resources efficiently, this is not always the case. Economists use the term **market failure** to refer to a situation in which the market on its own fails to produce an efficient allocation of resources. One possible cause of market failure is an **externality**, which is the impact of one person's actions on the well-being of a bystander. The classic example of an externality is pollution. Another possible cause of market failure is **market power**, which refers to the ability of a single person (or small group of people) to unduly influence market prices. For example, if everyone in town needs water but there is only one well, the owner of the well is not subject to the rigorous competition with which the invisible hand normally keeps self-interest in check. In the presence of externalities or market power, well-designed public policy can enhance economic efficiency.

The invisible hand may also fail to ensure that economic prosperity is distributed equitably. A market economy rewards people according to their ability to produce things that other people are willing to pay for. The world's best basketball player earns more than the world's best chess player simply because people are willing to pay more to watch basketball than chess. The invisible hand does not ensure that everyone has sufficient food, decent clothing, and adequate health care. Many public policies, such as the income tax and welfare systems, aim to achieve a more equitable distribution of economic well-being.

To say that the government *can* improve on market outcomes at times does not mean that it always *will*. Public policy is made not by angels but by a political process that is far from perfect. Sometimes policies are designed simply to reward the politically powerful. Sometimes they are made by well-intentioned leaders who are not fully informed. One goal of the study of economics is to help you judge when a government policy is justifiable to promote efficiency or equity, and when it is not.

QuickQuiz List and briefly explain the three principles concerning economic interactions.

market failure
a situation in which a market left on its own fails to allocate resources efficiently

externality
the impact of one person's actions on the well-being of a bystander

market power
the ability of a single economic actor (or small group of actors) to have a substantial influence on market prices

HOW THE ECONOMY AS A WHOLE WORKS

We started by discussing how individuals make decisions and then looked at how people interact with one another. All these decisions and interactions together make up "the economy." The last three principles concern the workings of the economy as a whole.

Principle #8: A Country's Standard of Living Depends on Its Ability to Produce Goods and Services

The differences in living standards around the world are staggering. In 2008, the average Canadian had an income of about $42 100. In the same year, the average Mexican earned $15 200, and the average citizen of Bangladesh earned $1600. Not surprisingly, this large variation in average income is reflected in various measures of the quality of life. Citizens of high-income countries have more TV sets, more cars, better nutrition, better health care, and longer life expectancy than citizens of low-income countries.

Changes in living standards over time are also large. In Canada, individuals' incomes have historically grown about 2 percent per year (after adjusting for changes in the cost of living). At this rate, average income doubles every 35 years. Over the past century, average income has risen about eightfold.

productivity
the quantity of goods and services produced from each hour of a worker's time

What explains these large differences in living standards among countries and over time? The answer is surprisingly simple. Almost all variation in living standards is attributable to differences in countries' **productivity**—that is, the amount of goods and services produced from each hour of a worker's time. In nations where workers can produce a large quantity of goods and services per unit of time, most people enjoy a high standard of living; in nations where workers are less productive, most people must endure a more meagre existence. Similarly, the growth rate of a nation's productivity determines the growth rate of its average income.

The fundamental relationship between productivity and living standards is simple, but its implications are far-reaching. If productivity is the primary determinant of living standards, other explanations must be of secondary importance. For example, it might be tempting to credit labour unions or minimum-wage laws for the rise in living standards of Canadian workers over the past century. Yet the real hero of Canadian workers is their rising productivity. As another example, some commentators have claimed that increased competition from Japan and other countries explained the slow growth in Canadian incomes during the 1970s and 1980s. Yet the real villain was not competition from abroad but flagging productivity growth in Canada.

The relationship between productivity and living standards also has profound implications for public policy. When thinking about how any policy will affect living standards, the key question is how it will affect our ability to produce goods and services. To boost living standards, policymakers need to raise productivity by ensuring that workers are well educated, have the tools needed to produce goods and services, and have access to the best available technology.

Principle #9: Prices Rise When the Government Prints Too Much Money

In Germany in January 1921, a daily newspaper cost 0.30 marks. Less than two years later, in November 1922, the same newspaper cost 70 000 000 marks. All other prices in the economy rose by similar amounts. This episode is one of history's most spectacular examples of **inflation,** an increase in the overall level of prices in the economy.

inflation
an increase in the overall level of prices in the economy

Although Canada has never experienced inflation even close to that in Germany in the 1920s, inflation has at times been an economic problem. During the 1970s, for instance, average inflation was 8 percent per year and the overall level of prices more than doubled. By contrast, inflation in the 1990s was about 2 percent per year; at this rate it would take 35 years for prices to double. Because high inflation imposes various costs on society, keeping inflation at a low level is a goal of economic policymakers around the world.

What causes inflation? In almost all cases of large or persistent inflation, the culprit turns out to be the same—growth in the quantity of money. When a government creates large quantities of the nation's money, the value of the money falls. In Germany in the early 1920s, when prices were on average tripling every month, the quantity of money was also tripling every month. Although less dramatic, the economic history of Canada points to a similar conclusion: The high inflation of the 1970s was associated with rapid growth in the quantity of money, and the low inflation of the 1990s was associated with slow growth in the quantity of money.

Principle #10: Society Faces a Short-Run Tradeoff between Inflation and Unemployment

Although a higher level of prices is, in the long run, the primary effect of increasing the quantity of money, the short-run story is more complex and more controversial. Most economists describe the short-run effects of monetary injections as follows:

* Increasing the amount of money in the economy stimulates the overall level of spending and thus the demand for goods and services.
* Higher demand may, over time, cause firms to raise their prices, but in the meantime, it also encourages them to increase the quantity of goods and services they produce and to hire more workers to produce those goods and services.
* More hiring means lower unemployment.

This line of reasoning leads to one final economy-wide tradeoff: a short-run tradeoff between inflation and unemployment.

Although some economists still question these ideas, most accept that society faces a short-run tradeoff between inflation and unemployment. This simply means that, over a period of a year or two, many economic policies push inflation and unemployment in opposite directions. Policymakers face this tradeoff regardless of whether inflation and unemployment both start out at high levels (such as the ones in the early 1980s), at low levels (such as the ones in the late 1990s), or somewhere in between. This short-run tradeoff plays a key role in the analysis of the **business cycle**—the irregular and largely unpredictable fluctuations in economic activity, as measured by the production of goods and services or the number of people employed.

business cycle
fluctuations in economic activity, such as employment and production

Policymakers can exploit the short-run tradeoff between inflation and unemployment using various policy instruments. By changing the amount that the government spends, the amount it taxes, and the amount of money it prints, policymakers can influence the combination of inflation and unemployment that the economy experiences. Because these instruments of monetary and fiscal policy are potentially so powerful, how policymakers should use these instruments to control the economy, if at all, is a subject of continuing debate.

QuickQuiz List and briefly explain the three principles that describe how the economy as a whole works.

HOW TO READ THIS BOOK

Economics is fun, but it can also be hard to learn. Our aim in writing this text is to make it as fun and easy as possible. But you, the student, also have a role to play. Experience shows that if you are actively involved as you study this book, you will enjoy a better outcome, both on your exams and in the years that follow. Here are a few tips about how best to read this book.

1. *Summarize, don't highlight.* Running a yellow marker over the text is too passive an activity to keep your mind engaged. Instead, when you come to the end of a section, take a minute and summarize what you just learned in your own words, writing your summary in the wide margins we've provided. When you've finished the chapter, compare your summary with the one at the end of the chapter. Did you pick up the main points?

2. *Test yourself.* Throughout the book, QuickQuizzes offer instant feedback to find out if you've learned what you are supposed to. Take the opportunity. Write your answer in the book's margin. The quizzes are meant to test your basic comprehension. If you aren't sure your answer is right, you probably need to review the section.

3. *Practise, practise, practise.* At the end of each chapter, Questions for Review test your understanding, and Problems and Applications ask you to apply and extend the material. Perhaps your instructor will assign some of these exercises as homework. If so, do them. If not, do them anyway. The more you use your new knowledge, the more solid it becomes.

4. *Study in groups.* After you've read the book and worked the problems on your own, get together with classmates to discuss the material. You will learn from each other—an example of the gains from trade.

5. *Don't forget the real world.* In the midst of all the numbers, graphs, and strange new words, it is easy to lose sight of what economics is all about. The Case Studies and In the News features sprinkled throughout this book should help remind you. Don't skip them. They show how the theory is tied to events happening in all of our lives. If your study is successful, you won't be able to read a newspaper again without thinking about supply, demand, and the wonderful world of economics.

TABLE 1.1

Ten Principles of Economics

How People Make Decisions		
	#1:	People face tradeoffs.
	#2:	The cost of something is what you give up to get it.
	#3:	Rational people think at the margin.
	#4:	People respond to incentives.
How People Interact		
	#5:	Trade can make everyone better off.
	#6:	Markets are usually a good way to organize economic activity.
	#7:	Governments can sometimes improve market outcomes.
How the Economy as a Whole Works		
	#8:	A country's standard of living depends on its ability to produce goods and services.
	#9:	Prices rise when the government prints too much money.
	#10:	Society faces a short-run tradeoff between inflation and unemployment.

CONCLUSION

You now have a taste of what economics is all about. In the coming chapters we will develop many specific insights about people, markets, and economies. Mastering these insights will take some effort, but it is not an overwhelming task. The field of economics is based on a few basic ideas that can be applied in many different situations.

Throughout this book we will refer back to the ten principles of economics highlighted in this chapter and summarized in Table 1.1. Whenever we do so, an icon will be displayed in the margin, as it is now. But even when that icon is absent, you should keep these principles in mind. Even the most sophisticated economic analysis is built using the ten principles introduced here.

SUMMARY

- The fundamental lessons about individual decision making are that people face tradeoffs among alternative goals, that the cost of any action is measured in terms of forgone opportunities, that rational people make decisions by comparing marginal costs and marginal benefits, and that people change their behaviour in response to the incentives they face.

- The fundamental lessons about interactions among people are that trade can be mutually beneficial, that markets are usually a good way of coordinating trade among people, and that the government can potentially improve market outcomes if there is some market failure or if the market outcome is inequitable.

- The fundamental lessons about the economy as a whole are that productivity is the ultimate source of living standards, that money growth is the ultimate source of inflation, and that society faces a short-run tradeoff between inflation and unemployment.

KEY CONCEPTS

scarcity, p. 4
economics, p. 4
efficiency, p. 5
equity, p. 5
opportunity cost, p. 7
rational people, p. 8

marginal changes, p. 8
incentive, p. 9
market economy, p. 11
property rights, p. 12
market failure, p. 13
externality, p. 13

market power, p. 13
productivity, p. 14
inflation, p. 14
business cycle, p. 15

QUESTIONS FOR REVIEW

1. Give three examples of important tradeoffs that you face in your life.
2. What is the opportunity cost of seeing a movie?
3. Water is necessary for life. Is the marginal benefit of a glass of water large or small?
4. Why should policymakers think about incentives?
5. Why isn't trade among countries like a game, with some winners and some losers?
6. What does the "invisible hand" of the marketplace do?
7. Explain the two main causes of market failure and give an example of each.
8. Why is productivity important?
9. What is inflation, and what causes it?
10. How are inflation and unemployment related in the short run?

PROBLEMS AND APPLICATIONS

1. Describe some of the tradeoffs faced by each of the following.
   a. a family deciding whether to buy a new car
   b. a member of Parliament deciding how much to spend on national parks
   c. a company president deciding whether to open a new factory
   d. a professor deciding how much to prepare for class
2. You are trying to decide whether to take a vacation. Most of the costs of the vacation (airfare, hotel, forgone wages) are measured in dollars, but the benefits of the vacation are psychological. How can you compare the benefits to the costs?
3. You were planning to spend Saturday working at your part-time job, but a friend asks you to go skiing. What is the true cost of going skiing? Now suppose that you had been planning to spend the day studying at the library. What is the cost of going skiing in this case? Explain.
4. You win $100 in a hockey pool. You have a choice between spending the money now or putting it away for a year in a bank account that pays 5 percent interest. What is the opportunity cost of spending the $100 now?
5. The company that you manage has invested $5 million in developing a new product, but the development is not quite finished. At a recent meeting, your salespeople report that the introduction of competing products has reduced the expected sales of your new product to $3 million. If it would cost $1 million to finish development and make the product, should you go ahead and do so? What is the most that you should pay to complete development?

6. Three managers of the Magic Potion Company are discussing a possible increase in production. Each suggests a way to make this decision.

   HARRY: We should examine whether our company's productivity—litres of potion per worker—would rise or fall.

   RON: We should examine whether our average cost—cost per worker—would rise or fall.

   HERMIONE: We should examine whether the extra revenue from selling the additional potion would be greater or smaller than the extra costs.

   Who do you think is right? Why?

7. The welfare system provides income for people who are very poor, with low incomes and few assets. If a recipient of welfare payments decides to work and earn some money, the amount he or she receives in welfare payments is reduced.
   a. How does the existence of the welfare system affect people's incentive to save money for the future?
   b. How does the reduction in welfare payments associated with higher earnings affect welfare recipients' incentive to work?

NEL

18

8. In 1997 the Government of Ontario reformed that province's welfare system. The reform reduced the amount of welfare payments to a person with no income, but also allowed welfare recipients to keep a larger part of their welfare payments if they did earn some income.
   a. How does this reform affect the incentive to work?
   b. How might this reform represent a tradeoff between equity and efficiency?

9. Your roommate is a better cook than you are, but you can clean more quickly than your roommate can. If your roommate did all of the cooking and you did all of the cleaning, would your chores take you more or less time than if you divided each task evenly? Give a similar example of how specialization and trade can make two countries both better off.

10. Suppose Canada adopted central planning for its economy, and you became the chief planner. Among the millions of decisions that you need to make for next year are how many compact discs to produce, what artists to record, and who should receive the discs.
    a. To make these decisions intelligently, what information would you need about the compact disc industry? What information would you need about each of the people in Canada?
    b. How would your decisions about CDs affect some of your other decisions, such as how many CD players to make or discs to produce? How might some of your other decisions about the economy change your views about CDs?

11. Nations with corrupt police and court systems typically have lower standards of living than nations with less corruption. Why might that be the case?

12. Explain whether each of the following government activities is motivated by a concern about equity or a concern about efficiency. In the case of efficiency, discuss the type of market failure involved.

    a. regulating cable TV prices
    b. providing some poor people with free prescription drugs
    c. prohibiting smoking in public places
    d. preventing mergers between major banks
    e. imposing higher personal income tax rates on people with higher incomes
    f. instituting laws against driving while intoxicated

13. Discuss each of the following statements from the standpoints of equity and efficiency.
    a. "Everyone in society should be guaranteed the best health care possible."
    b. "When workers are laid off, they should be able to collect unemployment benefits until they find a new job."

14. In what ways is your standard of living different from that of your parents or grandparents when they were your age? Why have these changes occurred?

15. Suppose Canadians decide to save more of their incomes. If banks lend this extra saving to businesses, which use the funds to build new factories, how might this lead to faster growth in productivity? Who do you suppose benefits from the higher productivity? Is society getting a free lunch?

16. Imagine that you are a policymaker trying to decide whether to reduce the rate of inflation. To make an intelligent decision, what would you need to know about inflation, unemployment, and the tradeoff between them?

17. Look at a newspaper or at the website of *The Economist* at http://www.economist.com to find three stories about the economy that have been in the news lately. For each story, identify one (or more) of the ten principles of economics discussed in this chapter that is relevant, and explain how it is relevant. Also, for each story, look through this book's table of contents and try to find a chapter that might shed light on the news event.

http://

For more study tools, please visit http://www.mankiw5e.nelson.com.

CHAPTER 1 Ten Principles of Economics

I. Chapter Overview

A. Context and Purpose

Chapter 1 is the first chapter in a three-chapter section that serves as the introduction to the text. Chapter 1 introduces ten fundamental principles on which the study of economics is based. In a broad sense, the rest of the text is an elaboration on these ten principles. Chapter 2 develops how economists approach problems, while Chapter 3 explains how individuals and countries gain from trade.

The purpose of Chapter 1 is to lay out ten economic principles that will serve as building blocks for the rest of the text. The ten principles can be grouped into three categories: how people make decisions, how people interact, and how the economy works as a whole. Throughout the text, references will repeatedly be made to these ten principles.

B. Helpful Hints

1. *Place yourself in the story.* Throughout the text, most economic situations will be composed of economic actors—buyers and sellers, borrowers and lenders, firms and workers, and so on. When you are asked to address how any economic actor would respond to economic incentives, place yourself in the story as the buyer or the seller, the borrower or the lender, the producer or the consumer. Do not think of yourself always as the buyer (a natural tendency) or always as the seller. You will find that your role playing will usually produce the right response once you learn to think like an economist—which is the topic of the next chapter.

2. *Trade is not a zero-sum game.* Some people see an exchange in terms of winners and losers. Their reaction to trade is that, after the sale, if the seller is happy, the buyer must be sad because the seller must have taken something from the buyer. That is, they view trade as a *zero-sum game* where what one gains the other must have lost. They fail to see that both parties to a voluntary transaction gain because each party is allowed to specialize in what it can produce most efficiently, and then trade for items that are produced more efficiently by others. Nobody loses, because trade is voluntary. Therefore, a government policy that limits trade reduces the potential gains from trade.

1

3. *An externality can be positive.* Because the classic example of an externality is pollution, it is easy to think of an externality as a cost that lands on a bystander. However, an externality can be positive in that it can be a benefit that lands on a bystander. For example, education is often cited as a product that emits a positive externality because when your neighbour educates herself, she is likely to be more reasonable, responsible, productive, and politically astute. In short, she is a better neighbour. Positive externalities, just as much as negative externalities, may be a reason for the government to intervene to promote efficiency.

II. Self-Testing Challenges

A. True/False Questions

_____1.   When the government redistributes income with taxes and welfare, the economy becomes more efficient.

_____2.   When economists say, "There is no such thing as a free lunch," they mean that all economic decisions involve tradeoffs.

_____3.   Adam Smith's "invisible hand" concept describes how corporate business reaches into the pockets of consumers like an "invisible hand."

_____4.   Rational people systematically and purposefully do the best they can to achieve their objectives.

_____5.   Canada will benefit economically if we eliminate trade with Asian countries because we will be forced to produce more of our own cars and clothes.

_____6.   When a jet flies overhead, the noise it generates is an externality.

_____7.   A tax on beer raises the price of beer and provides an incentive for consumers to drink more.

_____8.   An incentive is something that induces a person to act.

_____9.   Sue is better at cleaning and Bob is better at cooking. It will take fewer hours to eat and clean if Bob specializes in cooking and Sue specializes in cleaning than if they share the household duties evenly.

_____10.   High and persistent inflation is caused by moderate growth in the quantity of money in the economy.

_____11.   In the short run, a reduction in inflation tends to cause a reduction in unemployment.

_____12.   An auto manufacturer should continue to produce additional automobiles as long as the firm is profitable, even if the cost of the additional units exceeds the price received.

____13.   An individual farmer requires property rights to benefit from a market
            economy.

____14.   To a student, the opportunity cost of going to a basketball game would
            include the price of the ticket and the value of the time that could have
            been spent studying.

____15.   Workers in Canada have a relatively high standard of living because
            Canada has a relatively high minimum wage.

B. Multiple-Choice Questions

1. Which one of the following involve(s) a tradeoff faced by societies?
    a. buying a new car
    b. going to university
    c. watching a football game on Sunday afternoon
    d. guns and butter

2. Which one of the following is a reason that tradeoffs are required?
    a. because wants are unlimited and resources are efficient
    b. because wants are unlimited and resources are economical
    c. because wants are unlimited and resources are scarce
    d. because wants are unlimited and resources are unlimited

3. Which one of the following best defines what economics is the study of?
    a. how to avoid having to make tradeoffs
    b. how society manages its scarce resources
    c. how to fully satisfy our unlimited wants
    d. how to reduce our wants until we are satisfied

4. Which one of the following describes when a rational person will act?
    a. when the action is ethical
    b. when the action makes money for the person
    c. when the action produces marginal costs that exceed marginal benefits
    d. when the action produces marginal benefits that exceed marginal costs.

5. Which one of the following is an outcome of raising taxes and increasing welfare
    payments?
    a. improved equity at the expense of efficiency
    b. improved efficiency at the expense of equity
    c. reduced market power

6. Suppose Candace finds $20. If she chooses to use the $20 to go to a hockey game, which one of the following is her opportunity cost of going to the game?
   a. Nothing, because Candace found the money.
   b. $20 (because Candace could have used the $20 to buy other things).
   c. $20 (because Candace could have used the $20 to buy other things) plus the value of the time spent at the game.
   d. $20 (because Candace could have used the $20 to buy other things) plus the value of the time spent at the game, plus the cost of the dinner she consumed at the game.

7. Which one of the following best describes foreign trade?
   a. makes a country more equitable
   b. increases the scarcity of resources
   c. allows a country to avoid tradeoffs
   d. allows a country to have a greater variety of products at a lower cost than if it tried to produce everything at home

8. Because people respond to incentives, which one of the following would be expected to occur if the average salary of accountants increases by 50 percent while the average salary of teachers increases by 20 percent?
   a. Fewer students will attend university.
   b. Students will shift majors from education to accounting.
   c. Students will shift majors from accounting to education.

9. Which one of the following activities is **MOST** likely to produce an externality?
   a. A student reads a novel for pleasure.
   b. A student sits at home and watches television.
   c. A student has a party in her student residence room.
   d. A student eats a hamburger in the university cafeteria.

10. Which one of the following products would be **LEAST** capable of producing an externality?
    a. food
    b. cigarettes
    c. stereo equipment
    d. inoculations against disease

11. Which one of the following situations describes the **GREATEST** *market power*?
    a. Microsoft's impact on the price of desktop operating systems
    b. a farmer's impact on the price of corn
    c. Honda's impact on the price of autos
    d. a student's impact on university tuition

12. Which one of the following statements is true about a market economy?
    a. Taxes help prices communicate costs and benefits to producers and consumers.
    b. The strength of a market system is that it tends to distribute goods and services evenly across consumers.

    c.   Market participants act as if guided by an "invisible hand" to produce outcomes that maximize social welfare.

    d.   With a large enough computer, central planners could guide production more efficiently than markets could guide production.

13.   Which one of the following is true according to Adam Smith's "invisible hand"?
    a.   Markets work even in the absence of property rights.
    b.   Many buyers and sellers acting independently and out of self-interest can promote general economic well-being without even realizing it.
    c.   Individuals who are concerned about the public good will almost invisibly promote increased social welfare.
    d.   Government plays a behind-the-scenes role in making a market economy work efficiently.

14.   Which one of the following is a reason that workers in Canada enjoy a high standard of living?
    a.   because Canada has a high minimum wage
    b.   because unions in Canada keep the wage high
    c.   because workers in Canada are highly productive
    d.   because Canada has protected its industry from foreign competition

15.   Which one of the following is a cause of high and persistent inflation?
    a.   unions increasing wages too much
    b.   OPEC raising the price of oil too much
    c.   regulations raising the cost of production too much
    d.   governments increasing the quantity of money too much

16.   Which of the following statements occurs in the short run?
    a.   An increase in inflation temporarily increases unemployment.
    b.   A decrease in inflation temporarily increases unemployment.
    c.   Inflation and unemployment are unrelated in the short run.

17.   Which one of the following could be inferred by an increase in the price of beef?
    a.   It tells consumers to buy more beef.
    b.   It tells consumers to buy less pork.
    c.   It tells producers to produce more beef.
    d.   It provides no information because prices in a market system are managed by planning boards.

18.   Which one of the following is **NOT** part of the opportunity cost of going on vacation?
    1.   the money spent on food
    2.   the money spent on airplane tickets
    3.   the money spent on a Broadway show
    4.   the money that could have been earned by staying home and working

19. Which one of the following is a way that productivity can be increased?
    a. by raising union wages
    b. by raising minimum wage
    c. by improving the education of workers
    d. by restricting trade with foreign countries

C. Short-Answer Questions

1. Is air scarce? Is clean air scarce? _____
   _____
   _____

2. What is the opportunity cost when an employee saves some of her paycheque?
   _____
   _____

3. Why is there a tradeoff between equity and efficiency? _____
   _____
   _____

4. Water is necessary for life. Diamonds are not. Is the marginal benefit of an additional glass of water greater or less than the marginal benefit of an additional one-carat diamond? Why? _____
   _____
   _____

5. Tom's car needs to be repaired. He has already paid $800 to have the transmission fixed, but it still does not work properly. Tom can sell the car "as is" for $2000. If the car was fixed, Tom could sell it for $2500. The car can be fixed, with a guarantee, for another $300. Should Tom repair his car? Why or why not? _____
   _____
   _____

6. Why have automotive air bags reduced deaths from auto crashes less than we had hoped? _____
   _____
   _____

7. Suppose one country is better at producing agricultural products (because it has more fertile land) while another country is better at producing manufactured goods (it has a better educational system and more engineers). If each country produced its specialty and traded, would there be more or less total output than if each country produced enough of its own agricultural and manufactured goods to meet its own needs? Why? _____
   _____
   _____
   _____
   _____

8. In *The Wealth of Nations*, Adam Smith said, "It is not by the benevolence of the baker that you receive your bread." What did he mean?_____

_____

_____

9. If people save more and use it to build more physical capital, productivity will rise and people will have rising standards of living in the future. What is the opportunity cost of future growth?_____

_____

10. If the government printed twice as much money, what would happen to prices?_____

_____

_____

11. A goal for a society is to distribute resources equitably or fairly. How should resources be distributed if everyone were equally talented and worked equally hard? What if people had different talents and some people worked hard while others did not?_____

_____

_____

_____

_____

12. Why are property rights important to a market economy?_____

_____

_____

D. Practice Problems

1. People respond to incentives. Governments can alter incentives with public policy, and hence behaviour. However, sometimes public policy generates unintended consequences by producing results that were not anticipated. Describe one unintended consequence of each of the following public policies.

    a. To help the "working poor," the government raises the minimum wage to $25 per hour._____

    _____

    _____

    b. To help the homeless, the government places rent controls on apartments that restrict rent to $100 per month._____

    _____

    _____

    c. To limit the consumption of gasoline, the government raises the tax on gasoline by $2.00 per litre. _____

    _____

    _____

d. To reduce the consumption of drugs, the government makes drugs illegal.

_____

_____

_____

e. To raise the population of wolves, the government prohibits the killing of wolves._____

_____

2. Opportunity cost is what is given up to get an item. Because there is no such thing as a free lunch, what would likely be given up to obtain each of the items listed below?

a. Susan can work full time or go to university. She chooses university._____

_____

_____

_____

b. Susan can work full time or go to university. She chooses work

_____

_____

_____

_____

c. Farmer Jones has 100 hectares of land. He can plant corn, which yields 100 tonnes per hectare, or he can plant beans, which yield 40 tonnes per hectare. He chooses to plant corn. _____

_____

_____

d. Farmer Jones has 100 hectares of land. He can plant corn, which yields 100 tonnes per hectare, or he can plant beans, which yield 40 tonnes per hectare. He chooses to plant beans._____

_____

_____

e. In (a) and (b) above, and (c) and (d) above, which is the opportunity cost of which—university for work or work for university? Corn for beans or beans for corn?_____

_____

_____

E. Advanced Critical Thinking

Suppose the university decides to lower the cost of parking on campus by reducing the price of a parking permit from $300 per semester to $50 per semester.

1. What would happen to the number of students desiring to park their cars on campus?_____
    _____
    _____

2. What would happen to the amount of time it would take to find a parking place?_____
    _____
    _____

3. Thinking in terms of opportunity cost, would the lower price of a parking sticker necessarily lower the true cost of parking? _____
    _____
    _____

4. Would the opportunity cost of parking be the same for students with no outside employment and students with jobs earning $15 per hour?_____
    _____
    _____

III. Solutions

A. True/False Questions

1. F; the economy becomes less efficient because it decreases the incentive to work hard.
2. T
3. F; the "invisible hand" refers to how markets guide self-interested people to create desirable social outcomes.
4. T
5. F; all countries gain from voluntary trade.
6. T
7. F; higher prices reduce the quantity demanded.
8. T
9. T
10. F; high inflation is caused by excessive monetary growth.
11. F; a reduction in inflation tends to raise unemployment.
12. F; a manufacturer should produce as long as the marginal benefit exceeds the marginal cost.
13. T
14. T
15. F; workers in Canada have a high standard of living because they are productive.

B.   Multiple-Choice Questions

1. d	5. a	9. c	13. b	17. c
2. c	6. c	10. a	14. c	18. a
3. b	7. d	11. a	15. d	19. c
4. d	8. b	12. c	16. b	

C. Short-Answer Questions

1.   No, no need to give up anything to get it. Yes, it is not possible to have an unlimited amount without giving up something to get it (pollution equipment on cars, etc.).

2.   The items she could have enjoyed had she spent it (current consumption).

3.   Taxes and welfare make people more equal but reduce incentives for hard work, thus lowering total output.

4.   The marginal benefit of another glass of water is generally lower because the water supply is so large that one more glass is of little value. The opposite is true for diamonds.

5.   Yes, because the marginal benefit of fixing the car is $2500 − $2000 = $500 and the marginal cost is $300. The original repair payment is not relevant.

6.   The cost of an accident was lowered. This changed incentives, therefore people drive faster and have more accidents.

7.   There would be more total output if the countries specialize and trade because each country is doing what it does most efficiently.

8.   The baker produces the best bread possible, not out of kindness, but because it is in his best interest to do so. Self-interest can maximize social welfare.

9.   The opportunity cost of future growth is the need to give up consumption today.

10.   Prices would roughly double.

11.   Fairness would require that everyone get an equal share. Fairness would require that people not get an equal share.

12.   A farmer will not grow food if he expects his crop to be stolen. People rely on government to enforce their rights over the things they produce.

D. Practice Problems

1. a. Many would want to work at $25 per hour but few firms would want to hire low-productivity workers at this wage; therefore, it would create unemployment.

   b. Many renters would want to rent an apartment at $100 per month, but few landlords could produce an apartment at this price; therefore, this rent control would create more homelessness.

   c. Higher gas prices would reduce the number of kilometres driven. This would lower auto accidents, put less wear and tear on roads and cars, and reduce the demand for both cars and road repairs.

   d. This raises the price of drugs and makes selling them more profitable. This creates more drug sellers and increases violence as they fight to protect their turf.

   e. Restrictions on killing wolves reduce the population of animals upon which wolves may feed—e.g., rabbits, deer, etc.

2. a. She gives up income from work (and must pay tuition).

   b. She gives up a university degree and the increase in income throughout life that it would have brought her (but she does not have to pay tuition).

   c. He gives up 4000 tonnes of beans.

   d. He gives up 10 000 tonnes of corn.

   e. Each is the opportunity cost of the other because each decision requires giving something up.

E. Advanced Critical Thinking

1. More students would wish to park on campus.

2. It would take much longer to find a parking place.

3. No, because the value of the time spent looking for a parking place would have to be factored in.

4. No. Students who could be earning money working are giving up more while looking for a parking place than those with no outside employment. Therefore, their opportunity cost is higher.

THINKING LIKE AN ECONOMIST

Learning Objectives

In this chapter, you will ...

*   See how economists apply the methods of science
*   Consider how assumptions and models can shed light on the world
*   Learn two simple models— the circular flow and the production possibilities frontier
*   Distinguish between micro-economics and macroeconomics
*   Learn the difference between positive and normative statements
*   Examine the role of economists in making policy
*   Consider why economists sometimes disagree with one another

Every field of study has its own language and its own way of thinking. Mathematicians talk about axioms, integrals, and vector spaces. Psychologists talk about ego, id, and cognitive dissonance. Lawyers talk about venue, torts, and promissory estoppel.

Economics is no different. Supply, demand, elasticity, comparative advantage, consumer surplus, deadweight loss—these terms are part of the economist's language. In the coming chapters, you will encounter many new terms and some familiar words that economists use in specialized ways. At first, this new language may seem needlessly arcane. But, as you will see, its value lies in its ability to provide you with a new and useful way of thinking about the world in which you live.

The single most important purpose of this book is to help you learn the economist's way of thinking. Of course, just as you cannot become a mathematician, psychologist, or lawyer overnight, learning to think like an economist will take some time. Yet with a combination of theory, case studies, and examples of economics in the news, this book will give you ample opportunity to develop and practise this skill.

Before delving into the substance and details of economics, it is helpful to have an overview of how economists approach the world. This chapter, therefore, discusses the field's methodology. What is distinctive about how economists confront a question? What does it mean to think like an economist?

THE ECONOMIST AS SCIENTIST

Economists try to address their subject with a scientist's objectivity. They approach the study of the economy in much the same way as a physicist approaches the study of matter and a biologist approaches the study of life: They devise theories, collect data, and then analyze these data in an attempt to verify or refute their theories.

To beginners, it can seem odd to claim that economics is a science. After all, economists do not work with test tubes or telescopes. The essence of science, however, is the *scientific method*—the dispassionate development and testing of theories about how the world works. This method of inquiry is as applicable to studying a nation's economy as it is to studying the earth's gravity or a species' evolution. As Albert Einstein wrote in *Physics and Reality* (1936), "The whole of science is nothing more than a refinement of everyday thinking."

Although Einstein's comment is as true for social sciences such as economics as it is for natural sciences such as physics, most people are not accustomed to looking at society through the eyes of a scientist. Let's therefore discuss some of the ways in which economists apply the logic of science to examine how an economy works.

The Scientific Method: Observation, Theory, and More Observation

Isaac Newton, the famous seventeenth-century scientist and mathematician, allegedly became intrigued one day when he saw an apple fall from an apple tree. This observation motivated Newton to develop a theory of gravity that applies not only to an apple falling to the earth but to any two objects in the universe. Subsequent testing of Newton's theory has shown that it works well in many circumstances (although, as Einstein would later emphasize, not in all circumstances). Because Newton's theory has been so successful at explaining observation, it is still taught today in undergraduate physics courses around the world.

This interplay between theory and observation also occurs in the field of economics. An economist might live in a country experiencing rapid increases in prices and be moved by this observation to develop a theory of inflation. The theory might assert that high inflation arises when the government prints too much money. (As you may recall, this was one of the ten principles of economics in Chapter 1.) To test this theory, the economist could collect and analyze data on prices and money from many different countries. If growth in the quantity of money were not at all related to the rate at which prices are rising, the economist would start to doubt the validity of his theory of inflation. If money growth and inflation were strongly correlated in international data, as in fact they are, the economist would become more confident in his theory.

Although economists use theory and observation like other scientists, they do face an obstacle that makes their task especially challenging: Experiments are often difficult in economics. Physicists studying gravity can drop many objects in their laboratories to generate data to test their theories. By contrast, economists studying inflation are not allowed to manipulate a nation's monetary policy simply to generate useful data. Economists, like astronomers and evolutionary biologists, usually have to make do with whatever data the world happens to give them.

To find a substitute for laboratory experiments, economists pay close attention to the natural experiments offered by history. When a war in the Middle East interrupts the flow of crude oil, for instance, oil prices skyrocket around the world. For consumers of oil and oil products, such an event depresses living standards. For economic policymakers, it poses a difficult choice about how best to respond. But for economic scientists, it provides an opportunity to study the effects of a key natural resource on the world's economies, and this opportunity persists long after the wartime increase in oil prices is over. Throughout this book, therefore, we consider many historical episodes. These episodes are valuable to study because they give us insight into the economy of the past and, more important, because they allow us to illustrate and evaluate economic theories of the present.

The Role of Assumptions

If you ask a physicist how long it would take for a marble to fall from the top of a ten-storey building, she will answer the question by assuming that the marble falls in a vacuum. Of course, this assumption is false. In fact, the building is surrounded by air, which exerts friction on the falling marble and slows it down. Yet the physicist will correctly point out that friction on the marble is so small that its effect is negligible. Assuming that the marble falls in a vacuum greatly simplifies the problem without substantially affecting the answer.

Economists make assumptions for the same reason: Assumptions can simplify the complex world and make it easier to understand. To study the effects of international trade, for example, we may assume that the world consists of only two countries and that each country produces only two goods. Of course, the real world consists of dozens of countries, each of which produces thousands of different types of goods. But by assuming two countries and two goods, we can focus our thinking. Once we understand international trade in an imaginary world with two countries and two goods, we are in a better position to understand international trade in the more complex world in which we live.

The art in scientific thinking—whether in physics, biology, or economics—is deciding which assumptions to make. Suppose, for instance, that we were dropping a beach ball rather than a marble from the top of the building. Our physicist would realize that the assumption of no friction is far less accurate in this case: Friction exerts a greater force on a beach ball than on a marble because a beach ball is much larger. The assumption that gravity works in a vacuum is reasonable for studying a falling marble but not for studying a falling beach ball.

Similarly, economists use different assumptions to answer different questions. Suppose that we want to study what happens to the economy when the government changes the number of dollars in circulation. An important piece of this analysis, it turns out, is how prices respond. Many prices in the economy change infrequently; the newsstand prices of magazines, for instance, are changed only every few years. Knowing this fact may lead us to make different assumptions when studying the effects of the policy change over different time horizons. For studying the short-run effects of the policy, we may assume that prices do not change much. We may even make the extreme and artificial assumption that all prices are completely fixed. For studying the long-run effects of the policy, however, we may assume that all prices are completely flexible. Just as a physicist uses different assumptions when studying falling marbles and falling beach balls, economists use different assumptions when studying the short-run and long-run effects of a change in the quantity of money.

Economic Models

High-school biology teachers teach basic anatomy with plastic replicas of the human body. These models have all the major organs—the heart, the liver, the kidneys, and so on. The models allow teachers to show their students in a simple way how the important parts of the body fit together. Of course, these plastic models are not actual human bodies, and no one would mistake the model for a real person. These models are stylized, and they omit many details. Yet despite this lack of realism—indeed, because of this lack of realism—studying these models is useful for learning how the human body works.

Economists also use models to learn about the world, but instead of being made of plastic, they are most often composed of diagrams and equations. Like a biology teacher's plastic model, economic models omit many details to allow us to see what is truly important. Just as the biology teacher's model does not include all of the body's muscles and capillaries, an economist's model does not include every feature of the economy.

As we use models to examine various economic issues throughout this book, you will see that all the models are built with assumptions. Just as a physicist begins the analysis of a falling marble by assuming away the existence of friction, economists assume away many of the details of the economy that are irrelevant for studying the question at hand. All models—in physics, biology, or economics—simplify reality in order to improve our understanding of it.

Our First Model: The Circular-Flow Diagram

The economy consists of millions of people engaged in many activities—buying, selling, working, hiring, manufacturing, and so on. To understand how the economy works, we must find some way to simplify our thinking about all these activities. In other words, we need a model that explains, in general terms, how the economy is organized and how participants in the economy interact with one another.

circular-flow diagram
a visual model of the economy that shows how dollars flow through markets among households and firms

Figure 2.1 presents a visual model of the economy, called a **circular-flow diagram.** In this model, the economy is simplified to include only two types of decision makers—households and firms. Firms produce goods and services using inputs, such as labour, land (natural resources), and capital (buildings and machines). These inputs are called the *factors of production.* Households own the factors of production and consume all the goods and services that the firms produce.

Households and firms interact in two types of markets. In the *markets for goods and services,* households are buyers and firms are sellers. In particular, households buy the output of goods and services that firms produce. In the *markets for the factors of production,* households are sellers and firms are buyers. In these markets,

FIGURE 2.1

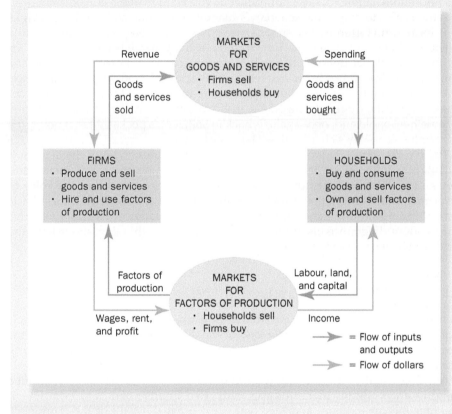

The Circular Flow

This diagram is a schematic representation of the organization of the economy. Decisions are made by households and firms. Households and firms interact in the markets for goods and services (where households are buyers and firms are sellers) and in the markets for the factors of production (where firms are buyers and households are sellers). The outer set of arrows shows the flow of dollars, and the inner set of arrows shows the corresponding flow of inputs and outputs.

households provide the inputs that the firms use to produce goods and services. The circular-flow diagram offers a simple way of organizing all the economic transactions that occur between households and firms in the economy.

The inner loop of the circular-flow diagram represents the flows of inputs and outputs. The households sell the use of their labour, land, and capital to the firms in the markets for the factors of production. The firms then use these factors to produce goods and services, which in turn are sold to households in the markets for goods and services. Hence, the factors of production flow from households to firms, and goods and services flow from firms to households.

The outer loop of the circular-flow diagram represents the corresponding flow of dollars. The households spend money to buy goods and services from the firms. The firms use some of the revenue from these sales to pay for the factors of production, such as the wages of their workers. What's left is the profit of the firm owners, who themselves are members of households. Hence, spending on goods and services flows from households to firms, and income in the form of wages, rent, and profit flows from firms to households.

Let's take a tour of the circular flow by following a dollar coin as it makes its way from person to person through the economy. Imagine that the dollar begins at a household, sitting in, say, your pocket. If you want to buy a cup of coffee, you take the dollar to one of the economy's markets for goods and services, such as your local Tim Hortons coffee shop. There you spend it on your favourite drink. When the dollar moves into the Tim Hortons cash register, it becomes revenue for the firm. The dollar doesn't stay at Tim Hortons for long, however, because the firm uses it to buy inputs in the markets for the factors of production. For instance, Tim Hortons might use the dollar to pay rent to its landlord for the space it occupies or to pay the wages of its workers. In either case, the dollar enters the income of some household and, once again, is back in someone's pocket. At that point, the story of the economy's circular flow starts once again.

The circular-flow diagram in Figure 2.1 is one simple model of the economy. It dispenses with details that, for some purposes, are significant. A more complex and realistic circular-flow model would include, for instance, the roles of government and international trade. Yet these details are not crucial for a basic understanding of how the economy is organized. Because of its simplicity, this circular-flow diagram is useful to keep in mind when thinking about how the pieces of the economy fit together.

Our Second Model: The Production Possibilities Frontier

Most economic models, unlike the circular-flow diagram, are built using the tools of mathematics. Here we consider one of the simplest such models, called the *production possibilities frontier,* and see how this model illustrates some basic economic ideas.

Although real economies produce thousands of goods and services, let's imagine an economy that produces only two goods—cars and computers. Together the car industry and the computer industry use all of the economy's resources, or factors of production. The **production possibilities frontier** is a graph that shows the various combinations of output—in this case, cars and computers—that the economy can possibly produce given the available factors of production and the available production technology that firms can use to turn these factors into output.

production possibilities frontier
a graph that shows the combinations of output that the economy can possibly produce given the available factors of production and the available production technology

Figure 2.2 is an example of a production possibilities frontier. In this economy, if all resources were used in the car industry, the economy would produce 1000 cars per year and no computers. If all resources were used in the computer industry, the economy would produce 3000 computers per year and no cars. The two endpoints of the production possibilities frontier represent these extreme possibilities. More likely, the economy divides its resources between the two industries, and this yields other points on the production possibilities frontier. For example, it can produce 600 cars and 2200 computers, shown in the figure by point A. Or by moving some of the factors of production to the car industry from the computer industry, the economy can produce 700 cars and 2000 computers, represented by point B.

Because resources are scarce, not every conceivable outcome is feasible. For example, no matter how resources are allocated between the two industries, the economy cannot produce the number of cars and computers represented by point C. Given the technology available for manufacturing cars and computers, the

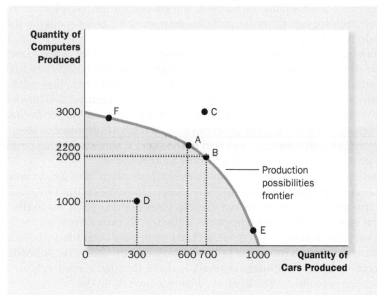

**The Production
Possibilities Frontier**

*The production possibilities frontier shows the
combinations of output—in this case, cars and
computers—that the economy can possibly produce. The
economy can produce any combination on or inside the
frontier. Points outside the frontier are not feasible given
the economy's resources.*

economy simply does not have enough of the factors of production to support that
level of output. With the resources it has, the economy can produce at any point
on or inside the production possibilities frontier, but it cannot produce at points
outside the frontier.

An outcome is said to be *efficient* if the economy is getting all it can from the
scarce resources it has available. Points on (rather than inside) the production possibilities frontier represent efficient levels of production. When the economy is
producing at such a point, say point A, there is no way to produce more of one
good without producing less of the other. Point D represents an *inefficient* outcome. For some reason, perhaps widespread unemployment, the economy is producing less than it could from the resources it has available: It is producing only
300 cars and 1000 computers. If the source of the inefficiency is eliminated, the
economy can increase its production of both goods. For example, if the economy
moves from point D to point A, its production of cars increases from 300 to 600,
and its production of computers increases from 1000 to 2200.

One of the ten principles of economics discussed in Chapter 1 is that people
face tradeoffs. The production possibilities frontier shows one tradeoff that society
faces. Once we have reached the efficient points on the frontier, the only way of
getting more of one good is to get less of the other. When the economy moves from
point A to point B, for instance, society produces 100 more cars, but at the expense
of producing 200 fewer computers.

This tradeoff helps us understand another of the ten principles of economics:
The cost of something is what you give up to get it. As we learned in Chapter 1,
this is called the *opportunity cost.* The production possibilities frontier shows the
opportunity cost of one good as measured in terms of the other good. When
society moves from point A to point B, it gives up 200 computers to get 100 additional cars. That is, at point A, the opportunity cost of 100 cars is 200 computers.

Put another way, the opportunity cost of each car is two computers. Notice that the opportunity cost of a car equals the slope of the production possibilities frontier. (If you don't recall what slope is, you can refresh your memory with the graphing appendix to this chapter.)

The opportunity cost of a car in terms of the number of computers is not a constant in this economy, but rather depends on how many cars and computers that the economy is producing. This is reflected in the shape of the production possibilities frontier. Because the production possibilities frontier in Figure 2.2 is bowed outward, the opportunity cost of a car is highest when the economy is producing many cars and fewer computers, such as at point E, where the frontier is steep. When the economy is producing few cars and many computers, such as at point F, the frontier is flatter, and the opportunity cost of a car is lower.

Economists believe that production possibilities frontiers often have this bowed shape. When the economy is using most of its resources to make computers, such as at point F, the resources best suited to car production, such as skilled autoworkers, are being used in the computer industry. Because these workers probably aren't very good at making computers, the economy won't have to lose much computer production to increase car production by one unit. The opportunity cost of a car in terms of computers is small, and the frontier is relatively flat. By contrast, when the economy is using most of its resources to make cars, such as at point E, the resources best suited to making cars are already being used in the car industry. Producing an additional car means moving some of the best computer technicians out of the computer industry and making them autoworkers. As a result, producing an additional car will mean a substantial loss of computer output. The opportunity cost of a car is high, and the frontier is quite steep.

The production possibilities frontier shows the tradeoff between the outputs of different goods at a given time, but the tradeoff can change over time. For example, suppose a technological advance in the computer industry raises the number of computers that a worker can produce per week. This advance expands society's set of opportunities. For any given number of cars, the economy can make more computers. If the economy does not produce any computers, it can still produce 1000 cars, so one endpoint of the frontier stays the same. But the rest of the production possibilities frontier shifts outward, as in Figure 2.3.

This figure illustrates economic growth. Society can move production from a point on the old frontier to a point on the new frontier. Which point it chooses depends on its preferences for the two goods. In this example, society moves from point A to point G, enjoying more computers (2300 instead of 2200) and more cars (650 instead of 600).

The production possibilities frontier simplifies a complex economy to highlight and clarify some basic but powerful ideas. We have used it to illustrate some of the concepts mentioned briefly in Chapter 1: scarcity, efficiency, tradeoffs, opportunity cost, and economic growth. As you study economics, these ideas will recur in various forms. The production possibilities frontier offers one simple way of thinking about them.

Microeconomics and Macroeconomics

Many subjects are studied on various levels. Consider biology, for example. Molecular biologists study the chemical compounds that make up living things.

FIGURE 2.3

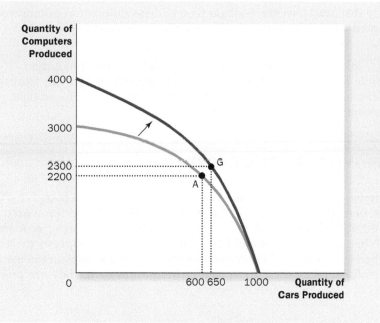

A Shift in the Production Possibilities Frontier

A technological advance in the computer industry enables the economy to produce more computers for any given number of cars. As a result, the production possibilities frontier shifts outward. If the economy moves from point A to point G, then the production of both cars and computers increases.

Cellular biologists study cells, which are made up of many chemical compounds and, at the same time, are themselves the building blocks of living organisms. Evolutionary biologists study the many varieties of animals and plants and how species change gradually over the centuries.

Economics is also studied on various levels. We can study the decisions of individual households and firms. Or we can study the interaction of households and firms in markets for specific goods and services. Or we can study the operation of the economy as a whole, which is just the sum of the activities of all these decision makers in all these markets.

The field of economics is traditionally divided into two broad subfields. **Microeconomics** is the study of how households and firms make decisions and how they interact in specific markets. **Macroeconomics** is the study of economy-wide phenomena. A microeconomist might study the effects of rent control on housing in Toronto, the impact of foreign competition on the Canadian auto industry, or the effects of compulsory school attendance on workers' earnings. A macroeconomist might study the effects of borrowing by the federal government, the changes over time in the economy's rate of unemployment, or alternative policies to raise growth in national living standards.

Microeconomics and macroeconomics are closely intertwined. Because changes in the overall economy arise from the decisions of millions of individuals, it is impossible to understand macroeconomic developments without considering the associated microeconomic decisions. For example, a macroeconomist might study the effect of a cut in the federal income tax on the overall production of goods and services. To analyze this issue, he or she must consider how the tax cut affects the decisions of households about how much to spend on goods and services.

microeconomics
the study of how households and firms make decisions and how they interact in markets

macroeconomics
the study of economy-wide phenomena, including inflation, unemployment, and economic growth

Despite the inherent link between microeconomics and macroeconomics, the two fields are distinct. However, because they address different questions, each field has its own set of models, which are often taught in separate courses.

QuickQuiz In what sense is economics like a science? • Draw a production possibilities frontier for a society that produces food and clothing. Show an efficient point, an inefficient point, and an infeasible point. Show the effects of a drought. • Define *microeconomics* and *macroeconomics*.

THE ECONOMIST AS POLICY ADVISER

Often economists are asked to explain the causes of economic events. Why, for example, is unemployment higher for teenagers than for older workers? Sometimes economists are asked to recommend policies to improve economic outcomes. What, for instance, should the government do to improve the economic well-being of teenagers? When economists are trying to explain the world, they are scientists. When they are trying to help improve it, they are policy advisers.

Positive versus Normative Analysis

To help clarify the two roles that economists play, we begin by examining the use of language. Because scientists and policy advisers have different goals, they use language in different ways.

For example, suppose that two people are discussing minimum-wage laws. Here are two statements you might hear:

POLLY: Minimum-wage laws cause unemployment.
NORMA: The government should raise the minimum wage.

Ignoring for now whether you agree with these statements, notice that Polly and Norma differ in what they are trying to do. Polly is speaking like a scientist: She is making a claim about how the world works. Norma is speaking like a policy adviser: She is making a claim about how she would like to change the world.

In general, statements about the world are of two types. One type, such as Polly's, is positive. **Positive statements** are descriptive. They make a claim about how the world *is*. A second type of statement, such as Norma's, is normative. **Normative statements** are prescriptive. They make a claim about how the world *ought to be*.

A key difference between positive and normative statements is how we judge their validity. We can, in principle, confirm or refute positive statements by examining evidence. An economist might evaluate Polly's statement by analyzing data on changes in minimum wages and changes in unemployment over time. By contrast, evaluating normative statements involves values as well as facts. Norma's statement cannot be judged using data alone. Deciding what is good or bad policy is not merely a matter of science. It also involves our views on ethics, religion, and political philosophy.

positive statements
claims that attempt to describe the world as it is

normative statements
claims that attempt to prescribe how the world should be

Positive and normative statements are fundamentally different, but they are often closely intertwined in a person's set of beliefs. In particular, positive views about how the world works affect normative views about what policies are desirable. Polly's claim that the minimum-wage laws cause unemployment, if true, might lead us to reject Norma's conclusion that the government should raise the minimum wage. Yet our normative conclusions cannot come from positive analysis alone; they involve value judgments as well.

As you study economics, keep in mind the distinction between positive and normative statements because it will help you stay focused on the task at hand. Much of economics is positive: It just tries to explain how the economy works. Yet those who use economics often have goals that are normative: They want to learn how to improve the economy. When you hear economists making normative statements, you know they have crossed the line from scientist to policy adviser.

Economists in Ottawa

U.S. President Harry Truman once said that he wanted to find a one-armed economist. When he asked his economists for advice, they always answered, "On the one hand, . . . On the other hand, ..."

Truman was right in realizing that economists' advice is not always straightforward. This tendency is rooted in one of the ten principles of economics in Chapter 1: People face tradeoffs. Economists are aware that tradeoffs are involved in most policy decisions. A policy might increase efficiency at the cost of equity. It might help future generations but hurt current generations. An economist who says that all policy decisions are easy is an economist not to be trusted.

The Government of Canada, like other governments, relies on the advice of economists. Economists at Finance Canada help design tax policy. Economists at Industry Canada help design and enforce Canada's competition laws. Economists at the department of Foreign Affairs and International Trade Canada help negotiate trade agreements with other countries. Economists at Human Resources and Skill Development Canada analyze data on workers and on those looking for work to help formulate labour-market policies. Economists at Environment Canada help design environmental regulations. The Canadian International Development Agency employs economists, both on staff and as consultants, to give advice on overseas development projects. Statistics Canada employs economists to collect the data analyzed by other economists and then give policy advice. The Bank of Canada, the quasi-independent institution that sets Canada's monetary policy, employs more than 200 economists to analyze financial markets and macroeconomic developments.

Economists outside the government also give policy advice. The C. D. Howe Institute, the Fraser Institute, the Institute for Research on Public Policy, the Canadian Centre for Policy Alternatives, and other independent organizations publish reports by economists that analyze current issues such as poverty, unemployment, and the deficit. These reports try to influence public opinion and give advice on government policies. Table 2.1 provides the URLs for the websites of some of these organizations; the URLs for all of them can be found in the Internet Resources section of our website at http://www.mankiw5e.nelson.com.

TABLE 2.1	
Websites of Some Major Economic Organizations	Here are the websites for two key government agencies that are responsible for collecting economic data and making economic policy. They are followed by the websites for just a few of the better-known organizations that employ economists and that are often thought to have an influence on government policy.

Department of Finance	http://www.fin.gc.ca
Bank of Canada	http://www.bankofcanada.ca
C. D. Howe Institute	http://www.cdhowe.org
Institute for Research on Public Policy	http://www.irpp.org
Canadian Centre for Policy Alternatives	http://www.policyalternatives.ca

The influence of economists on policy goes beyond their role as advisers: Their research and writings often affect policy indirectly. Economist John Maynard Keynes offered this observation:

> The ideas of economists and political philosophers, both when they are right and when they are wrong, are more powerful than is commonly understood. Indeed, the world is ruled by little else. Practical men, who believe themselves to be quite exempt from intellectual influences, are usually the slaves of some defunct economist. Madmen in authority, who hear voices in the air, are distilling their frenzy from some academic scribbler of a few years back.

Although these words were written in 1935, they remain true today. Indeed, the "academic scribbler" now influencing public policy is often Keynes himself, who, although deceased (1946), continues to impact economic thought through his many publications. His general theories about managing free markets on a global scale are considered to be the foundation of macroeconomics.

QuickQuiz Give an example of a positive statement and an example of a normative statement. • Name three parts of government that regularly rely on advice from economists.

SUPER BOWL ECONOMICS

Economists often offer advice to policymakers. Sometimes those policymakers are football coaches.

Incremental Analysis, With Two Yards to Go

By David Leonhardt

The academic paper that David Romer began writing two years ago did not look like something that could determine the outcome of a Super Bowl. Sure, it was an analysis of whether professional football teams punt more often than is rational, but it seemed intended mainly for the amusement of sports fans who happen to be professors.

Professor Romer, an economist at the University of California at Berkeley, used the phrases "Bellman equation" and "dynamic-programming analysis"—in the paper's title, no less. His footnotes cited work published in *Econometrica, Cognitive Science,* and other publications that are not exactly must-reads in N.F.L. locker rooms.

But when his conclusion—teams punt too much—began getting attention last summer, a reporter asked Bill Belichick, the coach of the New England Patriots, about the paper. "I read it," he said, according to *The Boston Herald.* "I don't know much of the math involved,

but I think I understand the conclusions and he has some valid points."

Upon hearing that, Professor Romer's jaw dropped, he said. His paper was available only on his Berkeley Internet site and the site of a group called the National Bureau of Economic Research. The article can be found at http://www.nber.org/papers/w9024.

But the most interesting development was yet to come. Two weeks ago, facing a fourth down in the Patriots' own territory on the very first drive of the game—a sure punting situation in the N.F.L.—Belichick decided to go for a first down and made it. The Patriots soon scored a touchdown and were on their way to today's Super Bowl, against the Carolina Panthers.

Football analysts immediately called the decision an instance of a coach's instinct triumphing over cold analysis. In fact, Professor Romer said last week, Belichick seemed to be "throwing gut instinct out the window and going on analysis." The information is right there in Figure 5 of the economist's paper: on fourth and 1 on your own 44-yard line, the potential benefit of keeping the drive

going outweighs the cost of giving the opponents good field position.

The coach may not have been thinking about Professor Romer's paper at that moment, but he has clearly adopted the methods of a social scientist in a way that few other sports coaches have. Belichick, who majored in economics at Wesleyan University, approaches his job much the way a financial analyst pores over a balance sheet. He seems to view every decision as a chance to perform better cost–benefit analysis than his peers do. Richard Miller, a Wesleyan economist with whom the coach remains in touch, calls the approach "incremental analysis." In plain English, it involves looking for subtle differences in one small area that can affect an entire system, whether that system is a company, a stock market, or a football game.

Source: David Leonhardt, "Ideas & Trends: Super Bowl Exonomics; Incremental Analysis, With Two Yards to Go." From *The New York Times*, February 1, 2004. Copyright © 2004 by The New York Times Co. Reprinted with permission. www.nytimes.com

Case Study

MR. MANKIW GOES TO WASHINGTON

One of the authors of the textbook you are now reading, Gregory Mankiw, admits to being a typical, nerdy university professor, more comfortable in the world of dusty books than in the world of glad-handing politicians. But from 2003 to 2005, he had the opportunity to leave the ivory tower and become the chairman of the U.S. Council of Economic Advisers (CEA) in the United States. For two years, he was President George W. Bush's chief economist. In what follows, he reports on his experiences.

* * * * * * * * * * * * * * * * * * * *

As chair of the CEA, I met with the President about twice a week. Some of these meetings were briefings on the state of the economy; most were discussions of current issues in economic policy. I worked closely with other members of the White House staff to analyze policy options and brief the President on a wide range of topics, such as tax policy, the federal budget, Social Security, and international trade. I also met regularly with economic officials outside the White House, such as Secretary of the Treasury John Snow and Federal Reserve Chairman Alan Greenspan, and with leaders of the business community.

For anyone used to the measured pace and quiet reflection of university life, taking such a job is exhilarating. Sitting in the Oval Office, flying on *Air Force One,* and spending the weekend with the President at Camp David are unforgettable experiences. Testifying as the President's representative before congressional committees, which include members who are usually partisan and sometimes hostile, is also an experience a person does not easily forget—no matter how hard one might try.

During my two years in Washington, I learned a lot about the process by which economic policy is made. It differs in many ways from the idealized policy process assumed in economics textbooks.

Throughout this text, whenever we discuss economic policy, we often focus on one question: What is the best policy for the government to pursue? We act as if policy were set by a benevolent king. Once the king figures out the right policy, he has no trouble putting his ideas into action.

In the real world, figuring out the right policy is only part of a leader's job, sometimes the easiest part. After the President hears from his economic advisers about what policy is best from their perspective, he turns to other advisers for related input. His communications advisers will tell him how best to explain the proposed policy to the public, and they will try to anticipate any misunderstandings that might arise to make the challenge more difficult. His press advisers will tell him how the news media will report on his proposal and what opinions will likely be expressed on the nation's editorial pages. His legislative affairs advisers will tell him how Congress will view the proposal, what amendments members of Congress will suggest, and the likelihood that Congress will pass some version of the President's proposal into law. His political advisers will tell him which groups will organize to support or oppose the proposed policy, how this proposal will affect his standing among different groups in the electorate, and whether it will affect support for any of the President's other policy initiatives. After hearing and weighing all this advice, the President then decides how to proceed.

My two years in Washington were a vivid reminder of an important lesson: Making economic policy in a representative democracy is a messy affair—and there are often good reasons presidents (and other politicians) do not advance the policies that economists advocate. Economists offer crucial input into the policy process, but their advice is only one ingredient of a complex recipe. ●

WHY ECONOMISTS DISAGREE

"If all economists were laid end to end, they would not reach a conclusion." This quip by George Bernard Shaw is revealing. Economists as a group are often criticized for giving conflicting advice to policymakers.

Why do economists so often appear to give conflicting advice to policymakers? There are two basic reasons:

- Economists may disagree about the validity of alternative positive theories about how the world works.
- Economists may have different values and, therefore, different normative views about what policy should try to accomplish.

Let's discuss each of these reasons.

Differences in Scientific Judgments

Several centuries ago, astronomers debated whether the earth or the sun was at the centre of the solar system. More recently, meteorologists have debated whether the earth is experiencing global warming and, if so, why. Science is a search for understanding about the world around us. It is not surprising that as the search continues, scientists can disagree about the direction in which truth lies.

Economists often disagree for the same reason. Economics is a young science, and there is still much to be learned. Economists sometimes disagree because they have different hunches about the validity of alternative theories or about the size of important parameters.

For example, economists disagree about whether the government should levy taxes based on a household's income or its consumption (spending). Advocates of a switch from the current income tax to a consumption tax believe that the change would encourage households to save more, because income that is saved would not be taxed. Higher saving, in turn, would lead to more rapid growth in productivity and living standards. Advocates of the current income tax system believe that household saving would not respond much to a change in the tax laws. These two groups of economists hold different normative views about the tax system because they have different positive views about the responsiveness of saving to tax incentives.

Differences in Values

Suppose that Peter and Paul both take the same amount of water from the town well. To pay for maintaining the well, the town taxes its residents. Peter has income of $50 000 and is taxed $5000, or 10 percent of his income. Paul has income of $10 000 and is taxed $2000, or 20 percent of his income.

Is this policy fair? If not, who pays too much and who pays too little? Does it matter whether Paul's low income is due to a medical disability or to his decision to pursue a career in acting? Does it matter whether Peter's high income is due to a large inheritance or to his willingness to work long hours at a dreary job?

These are difficult questions on which people are likely to disagree. If the town hired two experts to study how the town should tax its residents to pay for the well, we would not be surprised if they offered conflicting advice.

This simple example shows why economists sometimes disagree about public policy. As we learned earlier in our discussion of normative and positive analysis, policies cannot be judged on scientific grounds alone. Economists give conflicting advice sometimes because they have different values. Perfecting the science of economics will not tell us whether it is Peter or Paul who pays too much.

Perception versus Reality

Because of differences in scientific judgments and differences in values, some disagreement among economists is inevitable. Yet one should not overstate the amount of disagreement. In many cases, economists do offer a united view.

Table 2.2 contains ten propositions about economic policy. In a survey of economists in business, government, and academia, these propositions were endorsed

TABLE 2.2

Ten Propositions about Which Most Economists Agree

Source: Richard M. Alston, J.R. Kearl, and Michael B. Vaughn, "Is There Consensus among Economists in the 1990s?" *American Economic Review* (May 1992): 203–209. Reprinted by permission.

Proposition (and percentage of economists who agree)
1. A ceiling on rents reduces the quantity and quality of housing available. (93%)
2. Tariffs and import quotas usually reduce general economic welfare. (93%)
3. Flexible and floating exchange rates offer an effective international monetary arrangement. (90%)
4. Fiscal policy (e.g., tax cut and/or government expenditure increase) has a significant stimulative impact on a less than fully employed economy. (90%)
5. If the federal budget is to be balanced, it should be done over the business cycle rather than yearly. (85%)
6. Cash payments increase the welfare of recipients to a greater degree than do transfers-in-kind of equal cash value. (84%)
7. A large federal budget deficit has an adverse effect on the economy. (83%)
8. A minimum wage increases unemployment among young and unskilled workers. (79%)
9. The government should restructure the welfare system along the lines of a "negative income tax." (79%)
10. Effluent taxes and marketable pollution permits represent a better approach to pollution control than imposition of pollution ceilings. (78%)

by an overwhelming majority of respondents. Most of these propositions would fail to command a similar consensus among the general public.

The first proposition in the table is about rent control. For reasons we will discuss later, almost all economists believe that rent control adversely affects the availability and quality of housing and is a very costly way of helping the most needy members of society. Nonetheless, some provincial governments choose to ignore the advice of economists and place ceilings on the rents that landlords may charge their tenants.

The second proposition in the table concerns tariffs and import quotas, two policies that restrict trade among nations. For reasons we will discuss more fully in later chapters, almost all economists oppose such barriers to free trade. Nonetheless, over the years, Parliament has often chosen to restrict the import of certain goods.

Why do policies such as rent control and trade barriers persist if the experts are united in their opposition? The reason may be that economists have not yet convinced the general public that these policies are undesirable. One purpose of this book is to make you understand the economist's view of these and other subjects and, perhaps, to persuade you that it is the right one.

QuickQuiz Why might economic advisers to the prime minister disagree about a question of policy?

IN THE NEWS

ENVIRONMENTAL ECONOMISTS

Saving the planet with economics

Green Groups See Potent Tool in Economics

By Jessica E. Vascellaro

Many economists dream of getting high-paying jobs on Wall Street, at prestigious think tanks and universities or at powerful government agencies like the Federal Reserve.

But a growing number are choosing to use their skills not to track inflation or interest rates but to rescue rivers and trees. These are the "green economists," more formally known as environmental economists, who use economic arguments and systems to persuade companies to clean up pollution and to help conserve natural areas.

Working at dozens of advocacy groups and a myriad of state and federal environmental agencies, they are helping to formulate the intellectual framework behind approaches to protecting endangered species, reducing pollution and preventing climate change. They also are becoming a link between left-leaning advocacy groups and the public and private sectors.

"In the past, many advocacy groups interpreted economics as how to make a profit or maximize income," says Lawrence Goulden, a professor of environmental and resource economics at Stanford University in Stanford, Calif.

"More economists are realizing that it offers a framework for resource allocation where resources are not only labour and capital but natural resources as well.". . . .

The field of environmental economics began to take form in the 1960s when academics started to apply the tools of economics to the nascent green movement. The discipline grew more popular throughout the 1980s when the Environmental Protection Agency adopted a system of tradable permits for phasing out leaded gasoline. It wasn't until the 1990 amendment to the Clean Air Act, however, that most environmentalists started to take economics seriously.

The amendment implemented a system of tradable allowances for acid rain, a program pushed by Environmental Defense. Under the law, plants that can reduce their emissions more cost-effectively may sell their allowances to more heavy polluters. Today, the program has exceeded its goal of reducing the amount of acid rain to half its 1980 level and is celebrated as evidence that markets can help achieve environmental goals.

Its success has convinced its former critics, who at the time contended that environmental regulation was a matter of ethics, not economics, and favored installing expensive acid rain removal technology in all power plants instead.

Greenpeace, the international environmental giant, was one of the leading opponents of the 1990 amendment. But Kart Davies, research director for Greenpeace USA, said its success and the lack of any significant action on climate policy throughout [the] early 1990s brought the organization around to the concept. "We now believe that [tradable permits] are the most straightforward system of reducing emissions and creating the incentives necessary for massive reductions.". . . .

LET'S GET GOING

The first two chapters of this book have introduced you to the ideas and methods of economics. We are now ready to get to work. In the next chapter we start learning in more detail the principles of economic behaviour and economic policy.

As you proceed through this book, you will be asked to draw on many of your intellectual skills. You might find it helpful to keep in mind some advice from the great economist John Maynard Keynes in *Essays in Biography* (1933):

> The study of economics does not seem to require any specialized gifts of an unusually high order. Is it not . . . a very easy subject compared with the higher branches of philosophy or pure science? An easy subject, at which very few excel! The paradox finds its explanation, perhaps, in that the master-economist must possess a rare *combination* of gifts. He must be mathematician, historian, statesman, philosopher—in some degree. He must understand symbols and speak in words. He must contemplate the particular in terms of the general, and touch abstract and concrete in the same flight of thought. He must study the present in the light of the past for the purposes of the future. No part of man's nature or his institutions must lie entirely outside his regard. He must be purposeful and disinterested in a simultaneous mood; as aloof and incorruptible as an artist, yet sometimes as near the earth as a politician.

It is a tall order. But with practice, you will become more and more accustomed to thinking like an economist.

SUMMARY

- Economists try to address their subject with a scientist's objectivity. Like all scientists, they make appropriate assumptions and build simplified models in order to understand the world around them. Two simple economic models are the circular-flow diagram and the production possibilities frontier.

- The field of economics is divided into two subfields: microeconomics and macroeconomics. Microeconomists study decision making by households and firms and the interaction among households and firms in the marketplace. Macroeconomists study the forces and trends that affect the economy as a whole.

- A positive statement is an assertion about how the world *is*. A normative statement is an assertion about how the world *ought to be*. When economists make normative statements, they are acting more as policy advisers than scientists.

- Economists who advise policymakers offer conflicting advice either because of differences in scientific judgments or because of differences in values. At other times, economists are united in the advice they offer, but policymakers may choose to ignore it.

KEY CONCEPTS

circular-flow diagram, p. 24
production possibilities frontier, p. 26

microeconomics, p. 29
macroeconomics, p. 29

positive statements, p. 30
normative statements, p. 30

QUESTIONS FOR REVIEW

1. How is economics like a science?
2. Why do economists make assumptions?
3. Should an economic model describe reality exactly?
4. Draw and explain a production possibilities frontier for an economy that produces milk and cookies. What happens to this frontier if disease kills half of the economy's cow population?
5. Use a production possibilities frontier to describe the idea of "efficiency."

6. What are the two subfields into which economics is divided? Explain what each subfield studies.
7. What is the difference between a positive and a normative statement? Give an example of each.
8. What is the Bank of Canada?
9. Why do economists sometimes offer conflicting advice to policymakers?

PROBLEMS AND APPLICATIONS

1. Describe some unusual language used in one of the other fields that you are studying. Why are these special terms useful?

2. One common assumption in economics is that the products of different firms in the same industry are indistinguishable. For each of the following industries, discuss whether this is a reasonable assumption.
   a. steel
   b. novels
   c. wheat
   d. fast food

3. Draw a circular-flow diagram. Identify the parts of the model that correspond to the flow of goods and services and the flow of dollars for each of the following activities.
   a. Sam pays a storekeeper $1 for a litre of milk.
   b. Sally earns $7 per hour working at a fast-food restaurant.
   c. Serena spends $10 to see a movie.
   d. Stuart earns $10 000 from his 10 percent ownership of Acme Industrial.

4. Imagine a society that produces military goods and consumer goods, which we'll call "guns" and "butter."
   a. Draw a production possibilities frontier for guns and butter. Explain why it most likely has a bowed-out shape.
   b. Show a point that is impossible for the economy to achieve. Show a point that is feasible but inefficient.
   c. Imagine that the society has two political parties, called the Hawks (who want a strong military) and the Doves (who want a smaller military). Show a point on your production possibilities frontier that the Hawks might choose and a point the Doves might choose.
   d. Imagine that an aggressive neighbouring country reduces the size of its military. As a result, both the Hawks and the Doves reduce their desired production of guns by the same amount. Which party would get the bigger "peace dividend," measured by the increase in butter production? Explain.

5. The first principle of economics discussed in Chapter 1 is that people face tradeoffs. Use a production possibilities frontier to illustrate society's tradeoff between a clean environment and the quantity of industrial output. What do you suppose determines the shape and position of the frontier? Show what happens to the frontier if engineers develop an automobile engine with almost no emissions.

6. Classify the following topics as relating to microeconomics or macroeconomics.
   a. a family's decision about how much income to save
   b. the effect of government regulations on auto emissions
   c. the impact of higher national saving on economic growth
   d. a firm's decision about how many workers to hire
   e. the relationship between the inflation rate and changes in the quantity of money

7. Classify each of the following statements as positive or normative. Explain.
   a. Society faces a short-run tradeoff between inflation and unemployment.
   b. A reduction in the rate of growth of money will reduce the rate of inflation.
   c. The Bank of Canada should reduce the rate of growth of money.
   d. Society ought to require welfare recipients to look for jobs.
   e. Lower tax rates encourage more work and more saving.

8. Classify each of the statements in Table 2.2 as positive, normative, or ambiguous. Explain.

9. If you were prime minister, would you be more interested in your economic advisers' positive views or their normative views? Why?

10. The C. D. Howe Institute, the Fraser Institute, the Institute for Research on Public Policy, and the Canadian Centre for Policy Alternatives regularly publish reports containing economic commentary and policy recommendations. Find a recent publication from one of these organizations at your library (or on its website; see Table 2.1 or the Internet Resources section of this book's website) and read about an issue that interests you. Summarize the discussion of this issue and the author's proposed policy.

11. Who is the current governor of the Bank of Canada? Who is the current minister of Finance Canada? Who are the current ministers of Foreign Affairs Canada and International Trade Canada? Are any of these people economists? Does it matter?

12. Would you expect economists to disagree less about public policy as time goes on? Why or why not? Can their differences be completely eliminated? Why or why not?

13. Look up one of the websites listed in Table 2.1 or in the Internet Resources section of this book's website. What recent economic trends or issues are addressed there?

http://   For more study tools, please visit http://www.mankiw5e.nelson.com.

APPENDIX

Graphing: A Brief Review

Many of the concepts that economists study can be expressed with numbers—the price of bananas, the quantity of bananas sold, the cost of growing bananas, and so on. Often these economic variables are related to one another; for example, when the price of bananas rises, people buy fewer bananas. One way of expressing the relationships among variables is with graphs.

Graphs serve two purposes. First, when developing economic theories, graphs offer a way to visually express ideas that might be less clear if described with equations or words. Second, when analyzing economic data, graphs provide a way of finding how variables are in fact related in the world. Whether we are working with theory or with data, graphs provide a lens through which a recognizable forest emerges from a multitude of trees.

Numerical information can be expressed graphically in many ways, just as a thought can be expressed in words in many ways. A good writer chooses words that will make an argument clear, a description pleasing, or a scene dramatic. An effective economist chooses the type of graph that best suits the purpose.

In this appendix we discuss how economists use graphs to study the mathematical relationships among variables. We also discuss some of the pitfalls that can arise in the use of graphical methods.

Graphs of a Single Variable

Three common types of graphs are shown in Figure 2A.1. The *pie chart* in panel (a) shows how total income in Canada is divided among the sources of income, including wages and salaries, corporation profits, and so on. A slice of the pie represents each source's share of the total. The *bar graph* in panel (b) compares income for three countries. The height of each bar represents the average income in each country. The *time-series graph* in panel (c) traces the Canadian unemployment rate over time. The height of the line shows the unemployment rate in each month. You have probably seen similar graphs in newspapers and magazines.

Graphs of Two Variables: The Coordinate System

Although the three graphs in Figure 2A.1 are useful in showing how a variable changes over time or across individuals, such graphs are limited in how much they can tell us. These graphs display information only on a single variable. Economists are often concerned with the relationships between variables. Thus, they need to be able to display two variables on a single graph. The *coordinate system* makes this possible.

Suppose you want to examine the relationship between study time and grade point average. For each student in your class, you could record a pair of numbers: hours per week spent studying and grade point average. These numbers could then be placed in parentheses as an *ordered pair* and appear as a single point on the

Types of Graphs

The pie chart in panel (a) shows how national income is derived from various sources. The bar graph in panel (b) compares the average income in three countries. The time-series graph in panel (c) shows the unemployment rate in Canada from January 2000 to December 2009.

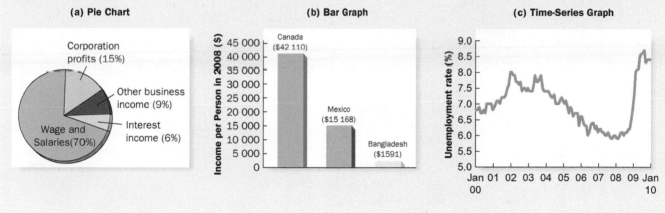

(a) Pie Chart

Corporation profits (15%)

Other business income (9%)

Interest income (6%)

Wage and Salaries(70%)

(b) Bar Graph

Income per Person in 2008 ($)

Canada ($42 110)

Mexico ($15 168)

Bangladesh ($1591)

(c) Time-Series Graph

Unemployment rate (%)

Jan 01 02 03 04 05 06 07 08 09 Jan
00   10

graph. Albert E., for instance, is represented by the ordered pair (25 hours/week, 3.5 GPA), while his "what-me-worry?" classmate Alfred E. is represented by the ordered pair (5 hours/week, 2.0 GPA).

We can graph these ordered pairs on a two-dimensional grid. The first number in each ordered pair, called the *x-coordinate*, tells us the horizontal location of the point. The second number, called the *y-coordinate*, tells us the vertical location of the point. The point with both an *x*-coordinate and a *y*-coordinate of zero is known as the *origin*. The two coordinates in the ordered pair tell us where the point is located in relation to the origin: *x* units to the right of the origin and *y* units above it.

Figure 2A.2 graphs grade point average against study time for Albert E., Alfred E., and their classmates. This type of graph is called a *scatterplot* because it plots scattered points. Looking at this graph, we immediately notice that points farther to the right (indicating more study time) also tend to be higher (indicating a better grade point average). Because study time and grade point average typically move in the same direction, we say that these two variables have a *positive correlation*. By contrast, if we were to graph party time and grades, we would likely find that higher party time is associated with lower grades; because these variables typically move in opposite directions, we would call this a *negative correlation*. In either case, the coordinate system makes the correlation between the two variables easy to see.

Curves in the Coordinate System

Students who study more do tend to get higher grades, but other factors also influence a student's grade. Previous preparation is an important factor, for

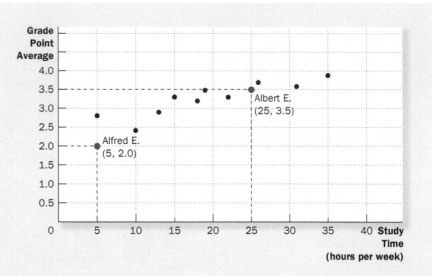

FIGURE 2A.2

Using the Coordinate System

Grade point average is measured on the vertical axis and study time on the horizontal axis. Albert E., Alfred E., and their classmates are represented by various points. We can see from the graph that students who study more tend to get higher grades.

instance, as are talent, attention from teachers, and even eating a good breakfast. A scatterplot like Figure 2A.2 does not attempt to isolate the effect that study has on grades from the effects of other variables. Often, however, economists prefer looking at how one variable affects another, holding everything else constant.

To see how this is done, let's consider one of the most important graphs in economics—the *demand curve*. The demand curve traces the effect of a good's price on the quantity of the good consumers want to buy. Before showing a demand curve, however, consider Table 2A.1, which shows how the number of novels that Emma buys depends on her income and on the price of novels. When novels are cheap, Emma buys them in large quantities. As they become more expensive, she borrows books from the library instead of buying them or chooses to go to the movies instead of reading. Similarly, at any given price, Emma buys more novels when she has a higher income. That is, when her income increases, she spends part of the additional income on novels and part on other goods.

We now have three variables—the price of novels, income, and the number of novels purchased—which is more than we can represent in two dimensions. To put the information from Table 2A.1 in graphical form, we need to hold one of the three variables constant and trace the relationship between the other two. Because the demand curve represents the relationship between price and quantity demanded, we hold Emma's income constant and show how the number of novels she buys varies with the price of novels.

Suppose that Emma's income is $30 000 per year. If we place the number of novels Emma purchases on the *x*-axis and the price of novels on the *y*-axis, we can graphically represent the middle column of Table 2A.1. When the points that represent these entries from the table—5 novels, $10; 9 novels, $9; and so on—are connected, they form a line. This line, pictured in Figure 2A.3, is known as Emma's demand curve for novels; it tells us how many novels Emma purchases at any

Price	Income		
	$20 000	$30 000	$40 000
$10	2 novels	5 novels	8 novels
9	6	9	12
8	10	13	16
7	14	17	20
6	18	21	24
5	22	25	28
	Demand curve, D_3	Demand curve, D_1	Demand curve, D_2

Novels Purchased by Emma

This table shows the number of novels Emma buys at various incomes and prices. For any given level of income, the data on price and quantity demanded can be graphed to produce Emma's demand curve for novels, as shown in Figures 2A.3 and 2A.4.

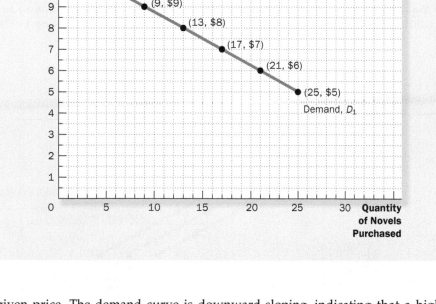

Demand Curve

The line D_1 shows how Emma's purchases of novels depend on the price of novels when her income is held constant. Because the price and the quantity demanded are negatively related, the demand curve slopes downward.

given price. The demand curve is downward sloping, indicating that a higher price reduces the quantity of novels demanded. Because the quantity of novels demanded and the price move in opposite directions, we say that the two variables are *negatively related*. (Conversely, when two variables move in the same direction, the curve relating them is upward sloping, and we say the variables are *positively related*.)

Now suppose that Emma's income rises to $40 000 per year. At any given price, Emma will purchase more novels than she did at her previous level of income. Just as earlier we drew Emma's demand curve for novels using the entries from the middle column of Table 2A.1, we now draw a new demand curve using the entries from the right-hand column of the table. This new demand curve (curve D_2) is pictured alongside the old one (curve D_1) in Figure 2A.4; the new curve is a similar line drawn farther to the right. We therefore say that Emma's demand curve for novels *shifts* to the right when her income increases. Likewise, if Emma's income was to fall to $20 000 per year, she would buy fewer novels at any given price and her demand curve would shift to the left (to curve D_3).

In economics, it is important to distinguish between *movements along a curve* and *shifts of a curve*. As we can see from Figure 2A.3, if Emma earns $30 000 per year and novels cost $8 apiece, she will purchase 13 novels per year. If the price of novels falls to $7, Emma will increase her purchases of novels to 17 per year. The demand curve, however, stays fixed in the same place. Emma still buys the same number of novels *at each price*, but as the price falls she moves along her demand curve from left to right. By contrast, if the price of novels remains fixed at $8 but her income rises to $40 000, Emma increases her purchases of novels from 13 to 16 per year. Because Emma buys more novels *at each price*, her demand curve shifts out, as shown in Figure 2A.4.

There is a simple way to tell when it is necessary to shift a curve. When a variable that is not named on either axis changes, the curve shifts. Income is on neither the x-axis nor the y-axis of the graph, so when Emma's income changes, her demand curve must shift. Any change that affects Emma's purchasing habits

FIGURE 2A.4

Shifting Demand Curves

The location of Emma's demand curve for novels depends on how much income she earns. The more she earns, the more novels she will purchase at any given price, and the farther to the right her demand curve will lie. Curve D_1 represents Emma's original demand curve when her income is $30 000 per year. If her income rises to $40 000 per year, her demand curve shifts to D_2. If her income falls to $20 000 per year, her demand curve shifts to D_3.

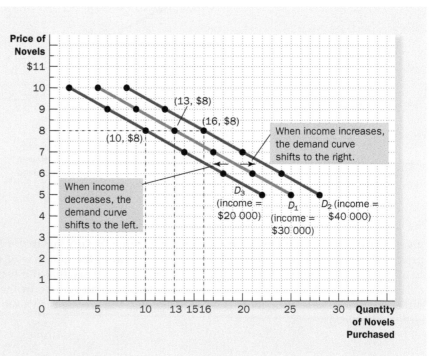

besides a change in the price of novels will result in a shift in her demand curve. If, for instance, the public library closes and Emma must buy all the books she wants to read, she will demand more novels at each price, and her demand curve will shift to the right. Or, if the price of movies falls and Emma spends more time at the movies and less time reading, she will demand fewer novels at each price, and her demand curve will shift to the left. By contrast, when a variable on an axis of the graph changes, the curve does not shift. We read the change as a movement along the curve.

Slope

One question we might want to ask about Emma is how much her purchasing habits respond to price. Look at the demand curve pictured in Figure 2A.5. If this curve is very steep, Emma purchases nearly the same number of novels regardless of whether they are cheap or expensive. If this curve is much flatter, Emma purchases many fewer novels when the price rises. To answer questions about how much one variable responds to changes in another variable, we can use the concept of *slope*.

The slope of a line is the ratio of the vertical distance covered to the horizontal distance covered as we move along the line. This definition is usually written out in mathematical symbols as follows:

$$\text{Slope} = \frac{\Delta y}{\Delta x}$$

Calculating the Slope of a Line

To calculate the slope of the demand curve, we can look at the changes in the x- and y-coordinates as we move from the point (21 novels, $6) to the point (13 novels, $8). The slope of the line is the ratio of the change in the y-coordinate (−2) to the change in the x-coordinate (+8), which equals −1/4.

where the Greek letter Δ (delta) stands for the change in a variable. In other words, the slope of a line is equal to the "rise" (change in y) divided by the "run" (change in x). The slope will be a small positive number for a fairly flat upward-sloping line, a large positive number for a steep upward-sloping line, and a negative number for a downward-sloping line. A horizontal line has a slope of zero because in this case the y-variable never changes; a vertical line is said to have an infinite slope because the y-variable can take any value without the x-variable changing at all.

What is the slope of Emma's demand curve for novels? First of all, because the curve slopes down, we know the slope will be negative. To calculate a numerical value for the slope, we must choose two points on the line. With Emma's income at $30 000, she will purchase 21 novels at a price of $6 or 13 novels at a price of $8. When we apply the slope formula, we are concerned with the change between these two points; in other words, we are concerned with the difference between them, which lets us know that we will have to subtract one set of values from the other, as follows:

$$\text{Slope} = \frac{\Delta y}{\Delta x} = \frac{\text{First } y\text{-coordinate} - \text{Second } y\text{-coordinate}}{\text{First } x\text{-coordinate} - \text{Second } x\text{-coordinate}} = \frac{6 - 8}{21 - 13} = -\frac{2}{8} = -\frac{1}{4}$$

Figure 2A.5 shows graphically how this calculation works. Try computing the slope of Emma's demand curve using two different points. You should get exactly the same result, $-\frac{1}{4}$. One of the properties of a straight line is that it has the same slope everywhere. This is not true of other types of curves, which are steeper in some places than in others.

The slope of Emma's demand curve tells us something about how responsive her purchases are to changes in the price. A small slope (a number close to zero) means that Emma's demand curve is relatively flat; in this case, she adjusts the number of novels she buys substantially in response to a price change. A larger slope (a number farther from zero) means that Emma's demand curve is relatively steep; in this case, she adjusts the number of novels she buys only slightly in response to a price change.

Cause and Effect

Economists often use graphs to advance an argument about how the economy works. In other words, they use graphs to argue about how one set of events *causes* another set of events. With a graph like the demand curve, there is no doubt about cause and effect. Because we are varying price and holding all other variables constant, we know that changes in the price of novels cause changes in the quantity Emma demands. Remember, however, that our demand curve came from a hypothetical example. When graphing data from the real world, it is often more difficult to establish how one variable affects another.

The first problem is that it is difficult to hold everything else constant when measuring how one variable affects another. If we are not able to hold variables constant, we might decide that one variable on our graph is causing changes in the other variable, when actually those changes are caused by a third *omitted variable* not pictured on the graph. Even if we have identified the correct two variables to look at, we might run into a second problem—*reverse causality*. In other words, we might decide that A causes B when in fact B causes A. The omitted-variable and reverse-causality traps require us to proceed with caution when using graphs to draw conclusions about causes and effects.

Omitted Variables   To see how omitting a variable can lead to a deceptive graph, let's consider an example. Imagine that the government, spurred by public concern about the large number of deaths from cancer, commissions an exhaustive study from Big Brother Statistical Services, Inc. Big Brother examines many of the items found in people's homes to see which of them are associated with the risk of cancer. Big Brother reports a strong relationship between two variables: the number of cigarette lighters that a household owns and the probability that someone in the household will develop cancer. Figure 2A.6 shows this relationship.

What should we make of this result? Big Brother advises a quick policy response. It recommends that the government discourage the ownership of cigarette lighters by taxing their sale. It also recommends that the government require warning labels: "Big Brother has determined that this lighter is dangerous to your health."

In judging the validity of Big Brother's analysis, one question is paramount: Has Big Brother held constant every relevant variable except the one under consideration? If the answer is no, the results are suspect. An easy explanation for Figure 2A.6 is that people who own more cigarette lighters are more likely to smoke cigarettes and that cigarettes, not lighters, cause cancer. If Figure 2A.6 does not hold constant the amount of smoking, it does not tell us the true effect of owning a cigarette lighter.

This story illustrates an important principle: When you see a graph being used to support an argument about cause and effect, it is important to ask whether the movements of an omitted variable could explain the results you see.

Reverse Causality   Economists can also make mistakes about causality by misreading its direction. To see how this is possible, suppose the Association of Canadian Anarchists commissions a study of crime in Canada and arrives at Figure 2A.7, which plots the number of violent crimes per thousand people in major cities against the number of police officers per thousand people. The

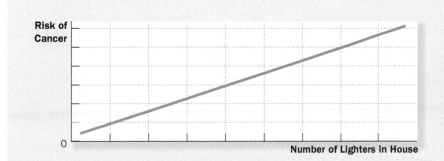

Graph with an Omitted Variable

The upward-sloping curve shows that members of households with more cigarette lighters are more likely to develop cancer. Yet we should not conclude that ownership of lighters causes cancer, because the graph does not take into account the number of cigarettes smoked.

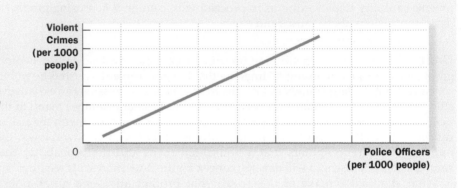

FIGURE 2A.7

Graph Suggesting Reverse Causality

The upward-sloping curve shows that cities with a higher concentration of police are more dangerous. Yet the graph does not tell us whether police cause crime or crime-plagued cities hire more police.

anarchists note the curve's upward slope and argue that because police increase rather than decrease the amount of urban violence, law enforcement should be abolished.

If we could run a controlled experiment, we would avoid the danger of reverse causality. To run an experiment, we would set the number of police officers in different cities randomly and then examine the correlation between police and crime. Figure 2A.7, however, is not based on such an experiment. We simply observe that more dangerous cities have more police officers. The explanation for this may be that more dangerous cities hire more police. In other words, rather than police causing crime, crime may cause an increase in police hiring. Nothing in the graph itself allows us to establish the direction of causality.

It might seem that an easy way to determine the direction of causality is to examine which variable moves first. If we see crime increase and then the police force expand, we reach one conclusion. If we see the police force expand and then crime increase, we reach the other. Yet there is also a flaw with this approach: Often people change their behaviour not in response to a change in their present conditions but in response to a change in their *expectations* of future conditions. A city that expects a major crime wave in the future, for instance, might well hire more police now. This problem is even easier to see in the case of babies and minivans. Couples often buy a minivan in anticipation of the birth of a child. The minivan comes before the baby, but we wouldn't want to conclude that the sale of minivans causes the population to grow!

There is no complete set of rules that says when it is appropriate to draw causal conclusions from graphs. Yet just keeping in mind that cigarette lighters don't cause cancer (omitted variable) and minivans don't cause larger families (reverse causality) will keep you from falling for many faulty economic arguments.

2 Thinking Like an Economist

I. Chapter Overview

A. Context and Purpose

Chapter 2 is the second chapter in a three-chapter section that serves as the introduction of the text. Chapter 1 introduced ten principles of economics that will be revisited throughout the text. Chapter 2 develops how economists approach problems, while Chapter 3 will explain how individuals and countries gain from trade.

The purpose of Chapter 2 is to become familiar with how economists approach economic problems. With practice, it is possible to approach similar problems in this dispassionate, systematic way. How economists employ the scientific method, the role of assumptions in model building, and the application of two specific economic models are explained. The important distinction between two roles economists can play—as scientists when they try to explain the economic world and as policymakers when they try to improve it—is clarified.

B. Helpful Hints

1. *Opportunity costs are not usually constant along a production possibilities frontier.* Notice that the production possibilities frontier shown in the following graph is bowed outward. It shows the production tradeoffs for an economy that produces only paper and pencils.

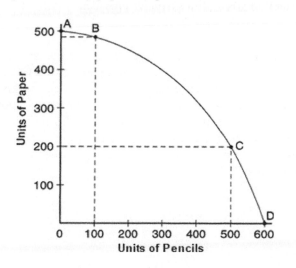

Starting at the point where the economy is using all of its resources to produce paper, the production of 100 units of pencils requires a tradeoff or an opportunity cost of only 25 units of paper (point A to point B). This is because when resources are moved from paper production to pencil production, the resources that are moved first are the ones best suited for pencil production and poorly suited for paper production. Therefore, pencil production increases

13

with very little decrease in paper production. However, if the economy were operating at point C, the opportunity cost of an additional 100 pencils (point C to D) is 200 units of paper. This is because the resources that would now be moved toward pencil production are the ones that were extremely well suited for paper production and poorly suited for pencil production. Therefore, as more and more of any particular good is produced, the opportunity cost per unit tends to rise because resources are specialized. That is, resources are not equally well suited for producing each output.

The argument above applies when moving either direction on the production possibilities frontier. For example, by starting at point D (maximum production of pencils) a small reduction in pencil production (100 units) releases enough resources to increase production of paper by a large amount (200 units). However, moving from point B to point A increases paper production by only 25 units.

2. *A production possibilities frontier shows only the choices available—not which point of production is best.* A common mistake made by students when using production possibilities frontiers is to look at a production possibilities frontier and suggest that a point somewhere near the middle "looks best." Students make this subjective judgment because the middle point appears to provide the biggest total number of units of production of the two goods. However, ask the following question: Using the production possibilities frontier in the previous graph, what production point would be best if paper were worth $10 per sheet and pencils were worth 1 cent per dozen? The resources would be moved toward paper production. What if paper was worth 1 cent per sheet and pencils were worth $50 each? We would move our resources toward pencil production. Clearly, what we actually choose to produce depends on the price of each good. Therefore, a production possibilities frontier provides only the choices available; it alone cannot determine which choice is best.

3. *Economic disagreement is interesting but economic consensus is more important.* Economists have a reputation for disagreeing with one another because they tend to highlight their differences. While their disagreements are interesting to them, the matters on which they agree are more important to students. There are a great number of economic principles for which there is near unanimous support from the economics profession. The aim of this text is to concentrate on the areas of agreement within the profession as opposed to the areas of disagreement.

II. Self-Testing Challenges

A. True/False Questions

_____1.   Economic models must mirror reality or they are of no value.

_____2.   Assumptions make the world easier to understand because they simplify reality and focus our attention.

_____3.   It is reasonable to assume that the world is composed of only one person when modeling international trade.

_____4.   When people act as scientists, they must try to be objective.

_____5.   If an economy is operating on its production possibilities frontier, it must be using its resources efficiently.

_____6.   If an economy is operating on its production possibilities frontier, it must produce less of one good if it produces more of another.

_____7.   Points outside the production possibilities frontier are attainable but inefficient.

_____8.   If an economy were experiencing substantial unemployment, the economy is producing inside the production possibilities frontier.

_____9.   The production possibilities frontier is bowed outward because the tradeoffs between the production of any two goods are constant.

_____10. An advance in production technology would cause the production possibilities curve to shift outward.

_____11. Macroeconomics is concerned with the study of how households and firms make decisions and how they interact in specific markets.

_____12. The statement, "An increase in inflation tends to cause unemployment to fall in the short run," is normative.

_____13. When economists make positive statements, they are more likely to be acting as scientists.

_____14. Positive statements can be refuted with evidence.

_____15. Most economists agree that tariffs and import quotas usually reduce economic welfare.

B. Multiple-Choice Questions

1. Which one of the following is essential to the scientific method?
    a. that the scientist be objective
    b. that only incorrect theories are tested
    c. that the scientist use precision equipment
    d. that the scientist use test tubes and have a clean lab

2. Which one of the following is **MOST** likely to produce scientific evidence about a theory?
    a. a radio talk-show host collecting data on how financial markets respond to taxation
    b. a lawyer employed by General Motors addressing the impact of air bags on passenger safety
    c. a tenured economist employed at a leading university analyzing the impact of proposed bank mergers
    d. an economist employed by the Canadian Auto Workers' union doing research on the impact of international trade

3. Which one of the following statements regarding the circular-flow diagram is true?
    a. The factors of production are owned by firms.
    b. The factors of production are owned by households.
    c. If Molson sells a case of beer, the transaction takes place in the market for factors of production.
    d. If Susan works for Bell Canada and receives a paycheque, the transaction takes place in the market for goods and services.

4. Which one of the following cases presents the **MOST** reasonable assumption?
    a. To address the benefits of trade, an economist assumes that there are two people and two goods.
    b. To estimate the speed at which a beach ball falls, a physicist assumes that it falls in a vacuum.
    c. To address the impact of money growth on inflation, an economist assumes that money is strictly coins.
    d. To address the impact of taxes on income distribution, an economist assumes that everyone earns the same income.

5. Which one of the following statements is true of economic models?
    a. built with assumptions
    b. useless if they are simple
    c. created to duplicate reality
    d. usually made of wood and plastic

6. Which one of the following is **NOT** a factor of production?
    a. land
    b. labour
    c. capital
    d. money

7.   Which one of the following refers to points on the production possibilities frontier?
      a. efficient
      b. inefficient
      c. unattainable
      d. normative

8.   Which one of the following will **NOT** shift a country's production possibilities frontier outward?
      a. an increase in the capital stock
      b. an advance in technology
      c. a reduction in unemployment
      d. an increase in the labour force

9.   Which one of the following is a depiction of economic growth?
      a. a movement from inside the curve toward the curve
      b. a shift in the production possibilities frontier outward
      c. a shift in the production possibilities frontier inward
      d. a movement along a production possibilities frontier toward capital goods

Use the following graph to answer questions 10–13.

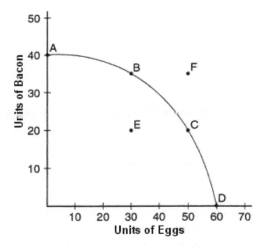

10.   If the economy is operating at point C, which one of the following is the opportunity cost of producing an additional 15 units of bacon?
      a. 10 units of eggs
      b. 20 units of eggs
      c. 30 units of eggs
      d. 40 units of eggs

11.   Which of the following is true if the economy is operating at point E?
      a. the opportunity cost of 20 additional units of eggs is 10 units of bacon.
      b. the opportunity cost of 20 additional units of eggs is 20 units of bacon.
      c. the opportunity cost of 20 additional units of eggs is 30 units of bacon.
      d. 20 additional units of eggs can be produced with no impact on bacon production.

12.   Which one of the following is represented by Point F?
        a. a combination of production that is inefficient because there are unemployed resources
        b. a combination of production that can be reached if we reduce the production of eggs by 20 units
        c. a combination of production that can be reached if there is a sufficient advance in technology

13.   Which one of the following statements represents the results of a move from point A to point D?
        a. the economy becomes more efficient
        b. the opportunity cost of eggs in terms of bacon falls
        c. the opportunity cost of eggs in terms of bacon rises
        d. the opportunity cost of eggs in terms of bacon is constant

14.   Which one of the following issues is related to microeconomics?
        a. the impact of money on inflation
        b. the impact of oil prices on auto production
        c. the impact of the government budget on saving
        d. the impact of globalization on unemployment in Canada

15.   Which one of the following statements about microeconomics and macroeconomics is **NOT** true?
        a. Microeconomics is a building block for macroeconomics.
        b. Macroeconomics is concerned with economy-wide phenomena.
        c. Microeconomics and macroeconomics each has its own set of models.
        d. The study of very large industries is a topic within macroeconomics.

16.   Which one of the following statements is normative?
        a. Printing too much money causes inflation.
        b. People work harder if the wage is higher.
        c. The unemployment rate should be lower.
        d. Large government deficits cause an economy to grow more slowly.

17.   In which one of the following statements made by an economist is the economist acting more like a scientist?
        a. The rate of inflation should be reduced because it robs the elderly of their savings.
        b. A reduction in employment insurance benefits will reduce the unemployment rate.
        c. The unemployment rate should be reduced because unemployment robs individuals of their dignity.
        d. The government should increase subsidies to universities because the future of our country depends on education.

18.   Which of the following most represents positive statements?
        a. microeconomic
        b. macroeconomic
        c. statements of description that can be tested
        d. statements of prescription that involve value judgments

19.   Suppose two economists are arguing about policies that deal with unemployment. One economist says, "The government should fight unemployment because it is the greatest social evil." The other economist responds, "Hogwash. Inflation is the greatest social evil." Which one of the following summarizes the positions of these two economists?
a.   They disagree because they have different values.
b.   They really do not disagree at all—it just looks that way.
c.   They disagree because at least one of them is incompetent.
d.   They disagree because they have different scientific judgments.

20.   Suppose two economists are arguing about policies that deal with unemployment. One economist says, "The government could lower unemployment by one percentage point if it would just increase government spending by 5 billion dollars." The other economist responds, "Hogwash. If the government spent an additional 5 billion dollars, it would reduce unemployment by only one-tenth of one percent, and that effect would only be temporary!" Which one of the following summarizes the positions of these two economists?
a.   They disagree because they have different values.
b.   They really do not disagree at all—it just looks that way.
c.   They disagree because at least one of them is incompetent.
d.   They disagree because they have different scientific judgments.

C. Short-Answer Questions

1.   Describe the scientific method._____
_____

2.   What is the role of assumptions in any science?_____
_____

3.   Is a more realistic model always better?_____
_____
_____

4.   Why does a production possibilities frontier have a negative slope (slope down and to the right)?_____
_____
_____

5.   Why is the production possibilities frontier bowed outward?_____
_____
_____

6.   What are the two subfields within economics? Which is more likely to be a building block of the other? Why? _____
_____
_____
_____

7.   When an economist makes a normative statement, is he or she more likely to be acting as a scientist or a policymaker? Why?_____

_____

_____

_____

8.   Which statements are testable: positive statements or normative statements? Why?_____

_____

9.   Provide two reasons why economists disagree._____

_____

_____

10.   Name two economic propositions on which more than 90 percent of economists agree. _____

_____

_____

D. Practice Problems

1.   Identify the parts of the circular-flow diagram immediately involved in the following transactions.

a.   Mary buys a car from General Motors for $25 000._____

_____

_____

_____

b.   General Motors pays Joe $5000 per month for work on the assembly line._____

_____

_____

_____

c.   Joe gets a $15 haircut._____

_____

_____

_____

_____

d.   Mary receives $10 000 of dividends on her General Motors stock._____

_____

_____

_____

_____

2. The following table provides information about the production possibilities frontier of Athletic Country.

Baseball Bats	Tennis Racquets
0	420
100	400
200	360
300	300
400	200
500	0

a. Plot and connect these points to create Athletic Country's production possibilities frontier.

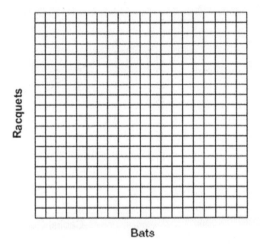

Racquets

Bats

b. If Athletic Country currently produces 100 baseball bats and 400 tennis racquets, what is the opportunity cost of an additional 100 bats?

_____

_____

c. If Athletic Country currently produces 300 baseball bats and 300 tennis racquets, what is the opportunity cost of an additional 100 bats?_____

_____

d. Why does the additional production of 100 bats in part (c) cause a greater tradeoff than the additional production of 100 bats in part (b)?_____

_____

_____

_____

e. Suppose Athletic Country is currently producing 200 baseball bats and 200 tennis racquets. How many additional bats could it produce without giving up any racquets? How many additional racquets could it produce without giving up any bats? _____

_____

_____

f. Is the production of 200 bats and 200 racquets efficient? Explain._____

_____

_____

3. The following production possibilities frontier shows the available tradeoffs between consumption goods and capital goods. Suppose two countries face the identical production possibilities frontier shown below.

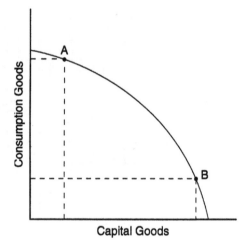

a. Suppose Party Country chooses to produce at point A while Parsimonious Country chooses to produce at point B. Which country will experience more growth in the future? Why? _____

_____

_____

b. In this model, what is the opportunity cost of future growth? _____

_____

c. Demonstrate the impact of economic growth on a production possibilities frontier such as the one shown above. Would the production possibilities frontier for Parsimonious Country shift more or less than that for Party Country? Why? _____

_____

d. Suppose there was an increase in technology that affected only the production of capital goods. Show the shift in the production possibilities curve.

e. Does the shift in part (d) above imply that all additional production must be in the form of capital goods? Why or why not? _____

_____

73

E. Advanced Critical Thinking

Kathy is watching *The National* on CBC. On the program, there is a discussion of the pros and cons of free trade (lack of obstructions to international trade). For balance, there are two economists present—one in support of free trade and one opposed. Kathy thinks to herself, "Those economists have no idea what's going on. They cannot agree on anything. One says free trade makes us rich. The other says it will drive us into poverty. If the experts do not know, how is the average person ever going to know whether free trade is best?"

1. Why might the economists be disagreeing on this issue?

_____
_____
_____
_____

2. Suppose that 93 percent of economists believe that free trade is generally best (which is the greatest agreement on any single issue). Is it now possible to give a more precise answer about why economists might disagree on this issue?_____

_____
_____
_____

3. What if it was later discovered that the economist opposed to free trade worked for a labour union. Would that help explain why there appears to be a difference of opinion on this issue?_____

_____
_____
_____

III. Solutions

A. True/False Questions

1. F; economic models are simplifications of reality.
2. T
3. F; there must be at least two individuals for trade.
4. T
5. T
6. T
7. F; points outside the production possibilities frontier cannot yet be attained.
8. T
9. F; it is bowed outward because the tradeoffs are not constant but are increasing.
10. T
11. F; macroeconomics is the study of economy-wide phenomena.
12. F; this statement is positive.
13. T
14. T
15. T

B. Multiple-Choice Questions

1. a	6. d	11. d	16. c
2. c	7. a	12. c	17. b
3. b	8. c	13. c	18. c
4. a	9. b	14. b	19. a
5. a	10. b	15. d	20. d

C. Short-Answer Questions

1. The dispassionate development and testing of theory by observing, testing, and observing again.

2. To simplify reality so that we can focus our thinking on what is actually important.

3. Not necessarily. Realistic models are more complex. They may be confusing and they may fail to focus on what is important.

4. Because if an economy is operating efficiently, production choices have opportunity costs. If we want more of one thing, we must have less of another.

5. Because resources are specialized and thus are not equally well suited for producing different outputs.

6. Microeconomics and macroeconomics. Microeconomics is more of a building block of macro because macro issues (for example, unemployment) are addressed; how individuals respond to work incentives such as wages and welfare needs to be considered.

7. As a policymaker, because normative statements are prescriptions about what ought to be and are somewhat based on value judgments.

8. Positive statements are statements of fact and are refutable by examining evidence.

9. Economists may have different scientific judgments. Economists may have different values.

10. A ceiling on rents reduces the quantity and quality of housing available. Tariffs and import quotas usually reduce general economic welfare.

D. Practice Problems

1. a. $25 000 of spending from households to market for goods and services. Car moves from market for goods and services to households. $25 000 of revenue from market for goods and services to firms, while car moves from firms to market for goods and services.

    b. $5000 of wages from firms to market for factors of production. Inputs move from market for factors of production to firms. Labour moves from households to market for factors of production, while $5000 income moves from market for factors of production to households.

    c. $15 of spending from households to market for goods and services. Service moves from market for goods and services to households. Service moves from firms to market for goods and services in return for $15 revenue.

    d. $10 000 of profit from firms to market for factors of production. Capital moves from market for factors of production to firms. Capital moves from households to market for factors of production in return for $10 000 income.

2. a.

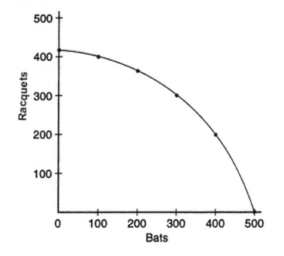

    b. 40 tennis racquets.

    c. 100 tennis racquets.

    d. Because as more baseball bats are produced, the resources best suited for making bats are already being used. Therefore, it takes even more resources to produce 100 bats and greater reductions in racquet production.
    e. 200 baseball bats. 160 tennis racquets.

    f. No. Resources were not used efficiently if production can be increased with no opportunity cost.

3. a.   Parsimonious Country. Capital (plant and equipment) is a factor of
          production and producing more of it now will increase future production.

    b.   Fewer consumption goods are produced now.

    c.

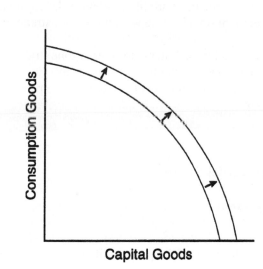

          The production possibilities curve will shift more for Parsimonious
          Country because it has experienced a greater increase in factors of
          production (capital).

    d.

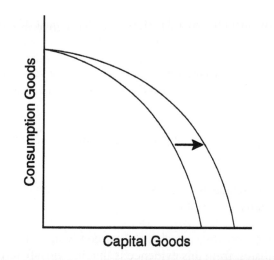

    e.   No, the outward shift improves choices available for both consumption and
          capital goods.

E. Advanced Critical Thinking

1. Economists may have different scientific judgments. Economists may have different values.

2. Those opposed to free trade are likely to have different values. There is not much disagreement on this issue within the mainstream economics profession.

3. Yes. It suggests that impediments to international trade may benefit some groups (unionized labour) but these impediments are unlikely to benefit the public in general. Those opposed to free trade are promoting their own interests.

IV. APPENDIX: Graphing: A Brief Review

A. True/False Questions

____1.   When graphing in the coordinate system, the x-coordinate tells us the horizontal location of the point while the y-coordinate tells us the vertical location of the point.

____2.   When a line slopes upward in the coordinate system, the two variables measured on each axis are positively related.

____3.   Price and quantity demanded for **MOST** goods are positively related.

____4.   If three variables are related, one of them must be held constant when graphing the other two in the coordinate system.

____5.   If three variables are related, a change in the variable not represented on the coordinate system will cause a movement along the curve drawn in the coordinate system.

____6.   The slope of a line is equal to the change in y divided by the change in x along the line.

____7.   When a line has negative slope, the two variables measured on each axis are positively related.

____8.   There is a positive correlation between lying down and death. If the conclusion from this evidence is that it is unsafe to lie down, then there is an omitted variable problem because critically ill people tend to lie down.

____9.   Reverse causality means that while people think A causes B, B may actually cause A.

____10.   Because people carry umbrellas to work in the morning and it rains later in the afternoon, carrying umbrellas must cause rain.

B. Practice Problems

1. The following ordered pairs of price and quantity demanded describe Joe's demand for cups of gourmet coffee:

2.

Price per cup of coffee	Quantity demanded of coffee
$5	2 cups
$4	4 cups
$3	6 cups
$2	8 cups
$1	10 cups

a. Plot and connect the ordered pairs on the graph provided below.

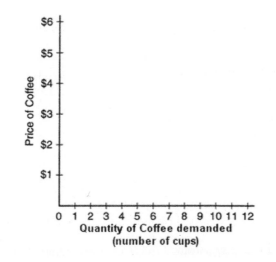

b. What is the slope of Joe's demand curve for coffee in the price range of $5 and $4? _____

c. What is the slope of Joe's demand curve for coffee in the price range of $2 and $1? _____

d. Are the price of coffee and Joe's quantity demanded of coffee positively related or negatively related? How can you tell?_____
    _____
    _____

e. If the price of coffee moves from $2 per cup to $4 per cup, what happens to the quantity demanded? Is this a movement along a curve or a shift in the curve?_____
    _____

f. Suppose Joe's income doubles from $20 000 per year to $40 000 per year. Now the following ordered pairs describe Joe's demand for gourmet coffee. Plot these ordered pairs on the graph provided in part (a) above.

Price per cup of coffee	Quantity demanded of coffee
$5	4 cups
$4	6 cups
$3	8 cups
$2	10 cups
$1	12 cups

g. Did the doubling of Joe's income cause a movement along his demand curve or a shift in his demand curve? Why?_____
_____
_____

3. An alien lands on earth and observes the following: On mornings when people carry umbrellas, it tends to rain later in the day. The alien concludes that umbrellas cause rain.

a. What error has the alien committed? _____

b. What role did *expectations* play in the alien's error? _____
_____
_____

c. If rain is truly caused by humidity, temperature, wind currents, and so on, what additional type of error has the alien committed when it decided that umbrellas cause rain? _____
_____
_____

V. Solutions for Appendix

A. True/False Questions

1. T
2. T
3. F; they are negatively related.
4. T
5. F; a change in a variable not represented on the graph will cause a shift in the curve.
6. T
7. F; negative slope implies a negative relation.
8. T
9. T
10. F; this is an example of reverse causation.

B. Practice Problems

1. a.

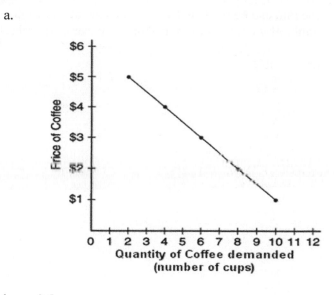

b. −0.5

c. −0.5

d. Negatively related. Because an increase in price is associated with a decrease in quantity demanded. That is, the demand curve slopes downward.

e. Decrease by 4 cups. Movement along curve.

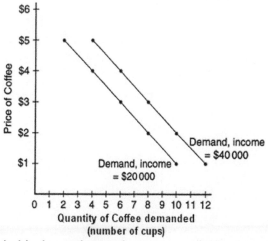

f. Shift in his demand curve because a variable changed (income) that is not measured on either axis.

2. a. Reverse causality.

    b. Because rain can be predicted, people's expectation of rain causes them to carry umbrellas before it rains, making it appear as if umbrellas cause rain.

    c. Omitted variables.

3

INTERDEPENDENCE AND THE GAINS FROM TRADE

Learning Objectives

In this chapter, you will ...

- Consider how everyone can benefit when people trade with one another
- Learn the meaning of *absolute advantage* and *comparative advantage*
- See how comparative advantage explains the gains from trade
- Apply the theory of comparative advantage to everyday life and national policy

Consider your typical day. You wake up in the morning, and you pour yourself juice from oranges grown in Florida and coffee from beans grown in Brazil. Over breakfast, you watch a news program broadcast from Toronto on your television set made in Japan. You get dressed in clothes made of cotton grown in Georgia and sewn in factories in Thailand. You drive to class in a car made of parts manufactured in more than a dozen countries around the world. Then you open up your economics textbook written by authors living in Massachusetts and Alberta, published by a company located in Ontario, and printed on paper made from trees grown in New Brunswick.

Every day you rely on many people from around the world, most of whom you do not know, to provide you with the goods and services that you enjoy. Such interdependence is possible because people trade with one another. Those people who provide you with goods and services are not acting out of generosity or concern for your welfare. Nor is some government agency directing them to make what you want and to give it to you. Instead, people provide you and other consumers with the goods and services they produce because they get something in return.

In subsequent chapters we will examine how our economy coordinates the activities of millions of people with varying tastes and abilities. As a starting point for this analysis, here we consider the reasons for economic interdependence. One of the ten principles of economics highlighted in Chapter 1 is that trade can make everyone better off. This principle explains why people trade with their neighbours and why nations trade with other nations. In this chapter we examine this principle more closely. What exactly do people gain when they trade with one another? Why do people choose to become interdependent?

NEL

51

A PARABLE FOR THE MODERN ECONOMY

To understand why people choose to depend on others for goods and services and how this choice improves their lives, let's look at a simple economy. Imagine that there are two goods in the world—meat and potatoes. And there are two people in the world—a cattle rancher and a potato farmer—each of whom would like to eat both meat and potatoes.

The gains from trade are most obvious if the rancher can produce only meat and the farmer can produce only potatoes. In one scenario, the rancher and the farmer could choose to have nothing to do with each other. But after several months of eating beef roasted, boiled, broiled, and grilled, the rancher might decide that self-sufficiency is not all it's cracked up to be. The farmer, who has been eating potatoes mashed, fried, baked, and scalloped, would likely agree. It is easy to see that trade would allow them to enjoy greater variety: Each could then have a steak with a baked potato.

Although this scenario illustrates most simply how everyone can benefit from trade, the gains would be similar if the rancher and the farmer were each capable of producing the other good, but only at great cost. Suppose, for example, that the potato farmer is able to raise cattle and produce meat, but that he is not very good at it. Similarly, suppose that the cattle rancher is able to grow potatoes, but that her land is not very well suited for it. In this case, it would be easy to show that the farmer and the rancher can each benefit by specializing in what he or she does best and then trading with the other.

The gains from trade are less obvious, however, when one person is better at producing *every* good. For example, suppose that the rancher is better at raising cattle *and* better at growing potatoes than the farmer. In this case, should the rancher or farmer choose to remain self-sufficient? Or is there still reason for them to trade with each other? To answer this question, we need to look more closely at the factors that affect such a decision.

Production Possibilities

Suppose that the farmer and the rancher each work 8 hours a day and can devote this time to growing potatoes, raising cattle, or a combination of the two. Table 3.1 shows the amount of time each person requires to produce 1 kg of each good. The farmer can produce a kilogram of potatoes in 15 minutes and a kilogram of meat in 60 minutes. The rancher, who is more productive in both activities, can produce a kilogram of potatoes in 10 minutes and a kilogram of meat in 20 minutes. The last two columns in Table 3.1 show the amounts of meat or potatoes the farmer and rancher can produce if they work an 8-hour day, producing only that good.

Panel (a) of Figure 3.1 illustrates the amounts of meat and potatoes that the farmer can produce. If the farmer devotes all 8 hours of his time to potatoes, he produces 32 kg of potatoes (measured on the horizontal axis) and no meat. If he devotes all his time to meat, he produces 8 kg of meat (measured on the vertical axis) and no potatoes. If the farmer divides his time equally between the two activities, spending 4 hours on each, he produces 16 kg of potatoes and 4 kg of meat. The figure shows these three possible outcomes and all others in between.

This graph is the farmer's production possibilities frontier. As we discussed in Chapter 2, a production possibilities frontier shows the various mixes of output that an economy can produce. It illustrates one of the ten principles of economics

TABLE 3.1

	Minutes Needed to Produce 1 kg of:		Amount of Meat or Potatoes Produced in 8 Hours	
	Meat	Potatoes	Meat	Potatoes
Farmer	60 min/kg	15 min/kg	8 kg	32 kg
Rancher	20 min/kg	10 min/kg	24 kg	48 kg

The Production Opportunities of the Farmer and the Rancher

FIGURE 3.1

(a) The Farmer's Production Possibilities Frontier

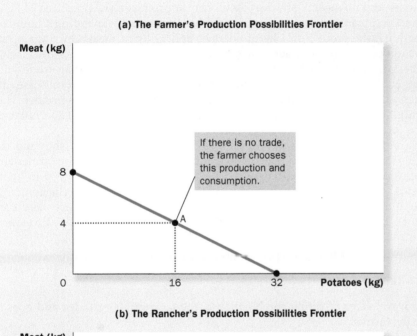

(b) The Rancher's Production Possibilities Frontier

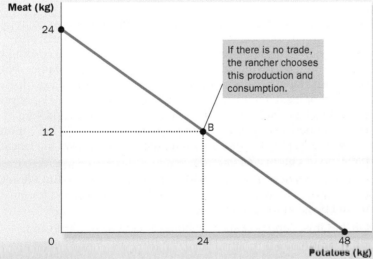

The Production Possibilities Frontier

Panel (a) shows the combinations of meat and potatoes that the farmer can produce. Panel (b) shows the combinations of meat and potatoes that the rancher can produce. Both production possibilities frontiers are derived from Table 3.1 and the assumption that the farmer and rancher each work 8 hours a day.

NEL

85

in Chapter 1: People face tradeoffs. Here the farmer faces a tradeoff between producing meat and producing potatoes. You may recall that the production possibilities frontier in Chapter 2 was drawn bowed out; in that case, the tradeoff between the two goods depended on the amounts being produced. Here, however, the farmer's technology for producing meat and potatoes (as summarized in Table 3.1) allows him to switch between one good and the other at a constant rate. Whenever the farmer spends 1 hour less producing meat and 1 hour more producing potatoes, he reduces his output of meat by 1 kg and raises his output of potatoes by 4 kg—and this is true regardless of how much he is already producing. As a result, the production possibilities frontier is a straight line.

Panel (b) of Figure 3.1 shows the production possibilities frontier for the rancher. If the rancher devotes all 8 hours of her time to potatoes, she produces 48 kg of potatoes and no meat. If she devotes all her time to meat, she produces 24 kg of meat and no potatoes. If the rancher divides her time equally, spending 4 hours on each activity, she produces 24 kg of potatoes and 12 kg of meat. Once again, the production possibilities frontier shows all the possible outcomes.

If the farmer and rancher choose to be self-sufficient, rather than trade with each other, then each consumes exactly what he or she produces. In this case, the production possibilities frontier is also the consumption possibilities frontier. That is, without trade, Figure 3.1 shows the possible combinations of meat and potatoes that the farmer and rancher can each consume.

Although these production possibilities frontiers are useful in showing the tradeoffs that the farmer and rancher face, they do not tell us what the farmer and rancher will actually choose to do. To determine their choices, we need to know the tastes of the farmer and the rancher. Let's suppose they choose the combinations identified by points A and B in Figure 3.1: The farmer produces and consumes 16 kg of potatoes and 4 kg of meat, while the rancher produces and consumes 24 kg of potatoes and 12 kg of meat.

Specialization and Trade

After several years of eating combination B, the rancher gets an idea and goes to talk to the farmer:

RANCHER: Farmer, my friend, have I got a deal for you! I know how to improve life for both of us. I think you should stop producing meat altogether and devote all your time to growing potatoes. According to my calculations, if you work 8 hours a day growing potatoes, you'll produce 32 kg of potatoes. If you give me 15 of those 32 kg, I'll give you 5 kg of meat in return. In the end, you'll get to eat 17 kg of potatoes and 5 kg of meat, instead of the 16 kg of potatoes and 4 kg of meat you now get. If you go along with my plan, you'll have more of *both* foods. [To illustrate her point, the rancher shows the farmer panel (a) of Figure 3.2.]

FARMER: *(sounding skeptical)* That seems like a good deal for me. But I don't understand why you are offering it. If the deal is so good for me, it can't be good for you too.

RANCHER: Oh, but it is! Suppose I spend 6 hours a day raising cattle and 2 hours growing potatoes. Then I can produce 18 kg of meat and 12 kg of potatoes. After I give you 5 kg of my meat in exchange for

NEL

FIGURE 3.2

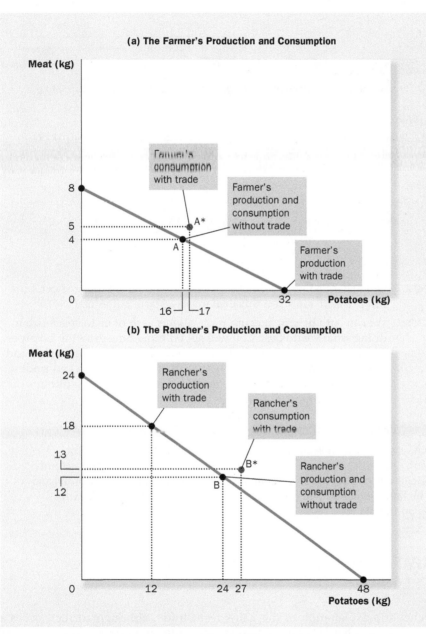

(a) The Farmer's Production and Consumption

Meat (kg)

Farmer's consumption with trade

Farmer's production and consumption without trade

A*

A

Farmer's production with trade

8

5

4

0   16   17   32   Potatoes (kg)

(b) The Rancher's Production and Consumption

Meat (kg)

Rancher's production with trade

Rancher's consumption with trade

B*

Rancher's production and consumption without trade

B

24

18

13

12

0   12   24 27   48   Potatoes (kg)

How Trade Expands the Set of Consumption Opportunities

The proposed trade between the farmer and the rancher offers each of them a combination of meat and potatoes that would be impossible in the absence of trade. In panel (a), the farmer gets to consume at point A* rather than point A. In panel (b), the rancher gets to consume at point B* rather than point B. Trade allows each to consume more meat and more potatoes.

15 kg of your potatoes, I'll end up with 13 kg of meat and 27 kg of potatoes. So I'll also consume more of both foods than I do now. [She points out panel (b) of Figure 3.2.]

FARMER: I don't know. . . . This sounds too good to be true.

RANCHER: It's really not as complicated as it seems at first. Here—I've summarized my proposal for you in a simple table. [The rancher hands the farmer a copy of Table 3.2.]

TABLE 3.2		Farmer		Rancher	
		Meat	Potatoes	Meat	Potatoes
Without Trade:					
Production and Consumption		4 kg	16 kg	12 kg	24 kg
With Trade:					
Production		0 kg	32 kg	18 kg	12 kg
Trade		Gets 5 kg	Gives 15 kg	Gives 5 kg	Gets 15 kg
Consumption		5 kg	17 kg	13 kg	27 kg
Gains from Trade:					
Increase in Consumption		+1 kg	+1 kg	+1 kg	+3 kg

The Gains from Trade: A Summary

FARMER: *(after pausing to study the table)* These calculations seem correct, but I'm puzzled. How can this deal make us both better off?

RANCHER: We can both benefit because trade allows each of us to specialize in doing what we do best. You will spend more time growing potatoes and less time raising cattle. I will spend more time raising cattle and less time growing potatoes. As a result of specialization and trade, each of us can consume more meat and more potatoes without working any more hours.

QuickQuiz Draw an example of a production possibilities frontier for Robinson Crusoe, a shipwrecked sailor who spends his time gathering coconuts and catching fish. Does this frontier limit Crusoe's consumption of coconuts and fish if he lives by himself? Does he face the same limits if he can trade with natives on the island?

COMPARATIVE ADVANTAGE: THE DRIVING FORCE OF SPECIALIZATION

The rancher's explanation of the gains from trade, although correct, poses a puzzle: If the rancher is better at both raising cattle and growing potatoes, how can the farmer ever specialize in doing what he does best? The farmer doesn't seem to do anything best. To solve this puzzle, we need to look at the principle of *comparative advantage.*

As a first step in developing this principle, consider the following question: In our example, who can produce potatoes at lower cost—the farmer or the rancher? There are two possible answers, and in these two answers lie the solution to our puzzle and the key to understanding the gains from trade.

Absolute Advantage

One way to answer the question about the cost of producing potatoes is to compare the inputs required by the two producers. Economists use the term **absolute advantage** when comparing the productivity of one person, firm, or nation to that of another. The producer that requires a smaller quantity of inputs to produce a good is said to have an absolute advantage in producing that good.

In our example, the rancher has an absolute advantage both in producing meat and in producing potatoes, because she requires less time than the farmer to produce a unit of either good. The rancher needs to input only 20 minutes to produce a kilogram of meat, whereas the farmer needs 60 minutes. Similarly, the rancher needs only 10 minutes to produce a kilogram of potatoes, whereas the farmer needs 15 minutes. Based on this information, we can conclude that the rancher has the lower cost of producing potatoes, if we measure cost in terms of the quantity of inputs.

absolute advantage
the comparison among producers of a good according to their productivity

Opportunity Cost and Comparative Advantage

There is another way to look at the cost of producing potatoes. Rather than comparing inputs required, we can compare the opportunity costs. Recall from Chapter 1 that the **opportunity cost** of some item is what we give up to get that item. In our example, we assumed that the farmer and the rancher each spend 8 hours a day working. Time spent producing potatoes, therefore, takes away from time available for producing meat. As the rancher and farmer reallocate time between producing the two goods, they move along their production possibility frontiers; they give up units of one good to produce units of the other. The opportunity cost measures the tradeoff between the two goods that each producer faces.

Let's first consider the rancher's opportunity cost. According to Table 3.1, producing 1 kg of potatoes takes her 10 minutes of work. When the rancher spends that 10 minutes producing potatoes, she spends 10 minutes less producing meat. Because the rancher needs 20 minutes to produce 1 kg of meat, 10 minutes of work would yield 0.5 kg of meat. Hence, the rancher's opportunity cost of producing 1 kg of potatoes is 0.5 kg of meat.

Now consider the farmer's opportunity cost. Producing 1 kg of potatoes takes him 15 minutes. Because he needs 60 minutes to produce 1 kg of meat, 15 minutes of work would yield 0.25 kg of meat. Hence, the farmer's opportunity cost of 1 kg of potatoes is 0.25 kg of meat.

Table 3.3 shows the opportunity costs of meat and potatoes for the two producers. Notice that the opportunity cost of meat is the inverse of the opportunity cost of potatoes. Because 1 kg of potatoes costs the rancher 0.5 kg of meat, 1 kg

opportunity cost
whatever must be given up to obtain some item

TABLE 3.3

The Opportunity Cost of Meat and Potatoes

	Opportunity Cost of:	
	1 kg of Meat	1 kg of Potatoes
Farmer	4 kg potatoes	0.25 kg meat
Rancher	2 kg potatoes	0.50 kg meat

comparative advantage
the comparison among producers
of a good according to their
opportunity cost

of meat costs the rancher 2 kg of potatoes. Similarly, because 1 kg of potatoes costs the farmer 0.25 kg of meat, 1 kg of meat costs the farmer 4 kg of potatoes.

Economists use the term **comparative advantage** when describing the opportunity cost of two producers. The producer who gives up less of other goods to produce good X has the smaller opportunity cost of producing good X and is said to have a comparative advantage in producing it. In our example, the farmer has a lower opportunity cost of producing potatoes than does the rancher: A kilogram of potatoes costs the farmer only 0.25 kg of meat, while it costs the rancher 0.50 kg of meat. Conversely, the rancher has a lower opportunity cost of producing meat than does the farmer: A kilogram of meat costs the rancher 2 kg of potatoes, while it costs the farmer 4 kg of potatoes. Thus, the farmer has a comparative advantage in growing potatoes, and the rancher has a comparative advantage in producing meat.

Although it is possible for one person to have an absolute advantage in both goods (as the rancher does in our example), it is impossible for one person to have a comparative advantage in both goods. Because the opportunity cost of one good is the inverse of the opportunity cost of the other, if a person's opportunity cost of one good is relatively high, his opportunity cost of the other good must be relatively low. Comparative advantage reflects the relative opportunity cost. Unless two people have exactly the same opportunity cost, one person will have a comparative advantage in one good, and the other person will have a comparative advantage in the other good.

Comparative Advantage and Trade

The gains from specialization and trade are based not on absolute advantage but rather on comparative advantage. When each person specializes in producing the good for which he or she has a comparative advantage, total production in the economy rises. This increase in the size of the economic pie can be used to make everyone better off.

In our example, the farmer spends more time growing potatoes, and the rancher spends more time producing meat. As a result, the total production of potatoes rises from 40 to 44 kg, and the total production of meat rises from 16 to 18 kg. The farmer and the rancher share the benefits of this increased production.

There is another way to look at the gains from trade—in terms of the price that each party pays the other. Because the farmer and the rancher have different opportunity costs, they can each think they are getting a bargain. That is, each benefits from trade by obtaining a good at a price that is lower than his or her opportunity cost of that good.

Consider the proposed deal from the viewpoint of the farmer. The farmer gets 5 kg of meat in exchange for 15 kg of potatoes. In other words, the farmer buys each kilogram of meat for a price of 3 kg of potatoes. This price of meat is lower than his opportunity cost for 1 kg of meat, which is 4 kg of potatoes. Thus, the farmer benefits from the deal because he gets to buy meat at a good price.

Now consider the deal from the rancher's viewpoint. The rancher buys 15 kg of potatoes for a price of 5 kg of meat. That is, the price of potatoes is one-third of a kilogram of meat. This price of potatoes is lower than her opportunity cost of 1 kg of potatoes, which is 0.5 kg of meat. The rancher benefits because she can buy potatoes at a good price.

THE LEGACY OF ADAM SMITH AND DAVID RICARDO

Economists have long understood the principle of comparative advantage. Here is how the great economist Adam Smith put the argument:

It is a maxim of every prudent master of a family, never to attempt to make at home what it will cost him more to make than to buy. The tailor does not attempt to make his own shoes, but buys them of the shoemaker. The shoemaker does not attempt to make his own clothes but employs a tailor. The farmer attempts to make neither the one nor the other, but employs those different artificers. All of them find it for their interest to employ their whole industry in a way in which they have some advantage over their neighbors, and to purchase with a part of its produce, or what is the same thing, with the price of part of it, whatever else they have occasion for.

This quotation is from Smith's 1776 book *An Inquiry into the Nature and Causes of the Wealth of Nations*, which was a landmark in the analysis of trade and economic interdependence.

Smith's book inspired David Ricardo, a millionaire stockbroker, to become an economist. In his 1817 book *Principles of Political Economy and Taxation*, Ricardo developed the principle of comparative advantage as we know it today. His defence of free trade was not a mere academic exercise. Ricardo put his economic beliefs to work as a member of the British Parliament, where he opposed the Corn Laws, which restricted the import of grain.

The conclusions of Adam Smith and David Ricardo on the gains from trade have held up well over time. Although economists often disagree on questions of policy, they are united in their support of free trade. Moreover, the central argument for free trade has not changed much in the past two centuries. Even though the field of economics has broadened its scope and refined its theories since the time of Smith and Ricardo, economists' opposition to trade restrictions is still based largely on the principle of comparative advantage.

David Ricardo

The Price of Trade

The principle of comparative advantage establishes that there are gains from specialization and trade, but it leaves open a couple of related questions: What determines the price at which trade takes place? How are the gains from trade shared between the trading parties? The precise answer to these questions is beyond the scope of this chapter, but we can state one general rule: *For both parties to gain from trade, the price at which they trade must lie between the two opportunity costs.*

In our example, the farmer and rancher agreed to trade at a rate of 3 kg of potatoes for each 1 kg of meat. This price is between the rancher's opportunity cost (2 kg of potatoes per 1 kg of meat) and the farmer's opportunity cost (4 kg of potatoes per 1 kg of meat). The price need not be exactly in the middle for both parties to gain, but it must be somewhere between 2 and 4.

To see why the price has to be in this range, consider what would happen if it was not. If the price of 1 kg of meat was below 2 kg of potatoes, both the farmer and the rancher would want to buy meat, because the price would be below their opportunity costs. Similarly, if the price of meat was above 4 kg of potatoes, both would want to sell meat, because the price would be above their opportunity costs. But there are only two members of this economy. They cannot both be buyers of meat, nor can they both be sellers. Someone has to take the other side of the deal.

A mutually advantageous trade can be struck at a price between 2 and 4. In this price range, the rancher wants to sell meat to buy potatoes, and the farmer wants to sell potatoes to buy meat. Each party can buy a good at a price that is lower than his or her opportunity cost. In the end, both of them specialize in the good for which he or she has a comparative advantage and are, as a result, better off.

QuickQuiz Robinson Crusoe can gather 10 coconuts or catch 1 fish per hour. His friend Friday can gather 30 coconuts or catch 2 fish per hour. What is Crusoe's opportunity cost of catching one fish? What is Friday's? Who has an absolute advantage in catching fish? Who has a comparative advantage in catching fish?

IN THE NEWS

HOW COMMITTED IS CANADA TO FREE TRADE?

Canada has removed many free trade restrictions over the past 20 years, especially with our NAFTA partners: the United States and Mexico. But as columnist Jeffrey Simpson explains in this article, one area in which Canada maintains trade restrictions is in the agricultural sector.

Canada Talks Boldly about Free Trade but Does Nothing to Achieve It

By Jeffrey Simpson

Pascal Lamy, the head of the World Trade Organization, was in Canada last week and displayed why he is one of the world's top diplomats.

Asked at a gala dinner in Toronto about Canada's supply-managed agricultural sector, he said some countries want free trade in agriculture, while others want protection. Canada has a foot in both camps. As such, he observed, Canada might be helpful in finding solutions.

They give gold medals at diplomacy schools for such adroitness. That he spoke in French meant most of his Toronto audience missed the verbal performance, but it was a beauty. Except, of course, that it was wrong.

Canada isn't looking to lead in the stalled world trade talks, just as it isn't trying to lead in next month's Copenhagen climate-change negotiations. In both cases, Canada is among the laggard countries, holding back change, hoping, actually, for very little progress in order not to upset domestic interests.

One of the best things that could happen to the sluggish world economy would be a world trade deal. It would not only spur trade but would improve productivity in the developed world, and give the developing countries a better shake in product areas where they might have a competitive advantage.

The major stumbling block remains agricultural subsidies, not just in the developed world but in countries such as India, which, with China, helped to torpedo agreement in the last negotiating push.

Farm subsidies are massive, both in absolute terms and in relation to the small number of farmers in the big developed countries. In Canada, there are farmers—such as those who raise

APPLICATIONS OF COMPARATIVE ADVANTAGE

The principle of comparative advantage explains interdependence and the gains from trade. Because interdependence is so prevalent in the modern world, the principle of comparative advantage has many applications. Here are two examples, one fanciful and one of great practical importance.

Should Mike Weir Mow His Own Lawn?

Mike Weir spends a lot of time walking around on grass. One of the most talented golfers in the PGA today, he can hit a drive and sink a putt in a way that most casual golfers only dream of doing. Most likely, he is talented at other activities too. For example, let's imagine that Weir can mow his lawn faster than anyone else. But just because he *can* mow his lawn fast, does this mean he *should*?

cattle and grow grain—who compete internationally and win. They want subsides reduced, especially in Europe.

But then there are the supply-managed farmers who hold in thrall Canadian politicians of every stripe. How much in thrall? Before the last WTO sessions, the House of Commons voted *unanimously* to instruct negotiators not to yield an inch so as to maintain the stratospheric tariff rates that protect dairy products, poultry, and eggs.

It's a racket that hurts Canadian consumers, especially low-income ones for whom food takes up a large share of total family income, and processors. But the merest hint of a lessening of the tariffs brings the supply-management lobby swarming over Ottawa, and to the international negotiating sessions, holding Canadian negotiators' feet to the fire.

As a result, Canada huddles in a corner with the agricultural protectionists such as South Korea, Japan, France and a few others, determined to scuttle progress. It's the same defensive posture that hurts Canada's efforts to negotiate bilateral free-trade deals that would generally be so helpful to a country with a small internal market that is so dependent on foreign trade.

Supply management arose in the 1970s as a direct response to the separatist threat in Quebec, where farmers are hugely consequential and exceedingly powerful. The Trudeau Liberals essentially tried to buy them off with supply management. Dairy, poultry, and egg farmers elsewhere immediately saw how helpful protectionism could be for them.

The Harper Conservatives, nominally free marketeers, ought to abhor supply management, except they have lots of rural Quebec and Ontario MPs. And remember that the government's principal political preoccupation was to tickle Quebec's tummy, at least until Quebeckers kicked them in the privates in the last election.

The Conservatives might hope to win in Quebec some day, but they always win in Alberta and Saskatchewan. These provinces form the party's core support. They are also major fossil fuel producers, with per capita greenhouse-gas emissions far above the national average.

With Stephen Harper and Environment Minister Jim Prentice both tied to Alberta, the government will do just about anything to protect the tar sands from being adversely affected by Copenhagen agreements or any bilateral deal with the United States.

Entering Copenhagen, the Canadian position is being mocked by experts at home and abroad, because no one outside the government's propaganda machine believes current policies will allow Canada to reduce emissions by 20 percent by 2020.

As a result, Canada's Copenhagen performance will be modelled on the one used at international trade negotiations: Talk boldly about wanting progress, while doing almost nothing to achieve it

Source: Jeffrey Simpson, "Canada talks boldly about free trade but does nothing to achieve it," *The Globe and Mail*, November 9, 2009. © CTVglobemedia Publishing Inc. All Rights Reserved.

To answer this question, we can use the concepts of opportunity cost and comparative advantage. Let's say that Weir can mow his lawn in 2 hours. In that same 2 hours, he could film a television commercial for Bell Canada and earn $10 000. By contrast, Forrest Gump, the boy next door, can mow Weir's lawn in 4 hours. In that same 4 hours, he could work at McDonald's and earn $20.

In this example, Weir's opportunity cost of mowing the lawn is $10 000 and Forrest's opportunity cost is $20. Weir has an absolute advantage in mowing lawns because he can do the work in less time. Yet Forrest has a comparative advantage in mowing lawns because he has the lower opportunity cost.

The gains from trade in this example are tremendous. Rather than mowing his own lawn, Weir should make the commercial and hire Forrest to mow the lawn. As long as Weir pays Forrest more than $20 and less than $10 000, both of them are better off.

Should Canada Trade with Other Countries?

Just as individuals can benefit from specialization and trade with one another, as the farmer and rancher did, so can populations of people in different countries. Many of the goods and services that Canadians enjoy are produced abroad, and many of the goods and services produced in Canada are sold abroad. Goods and services produced abroad and sold domestically are called **imports**. Goods and services produced domestically and sold abroad are called **exports**.

imports
goods and services produced abroad and sold domestically

exports
goods and services produced domestically and sold abroad

To see how countries can benefit from trade, suppose there are two countries, Canada and Japan, and two goods, food and cars. Imagine that the two countries produce cars equally well: A Canadian worker and a Japanese worker can each produce 1 car per month. By contrast, because Canada has more and better land, it is better at producing food: A Canadian worker can produce 2 tonnes of food per month, whereas a Japanese worker can produce only 1 tonne of food per month.

The principle of comparative advantage states that each good should be produced by the country that has the smaller opportunity cost of producing that good. Because the opportunity cost of a car is 2 tonnes of food in Canada but only 1 tonne of food in Japan, Japan has a comparative advantage in producing cars. Japan should produce more cars than it wants for its own use and export some of them to Canada. Similarly, because the opportunity cost of a tonne of food is 1 car in Japan but only $\frac{1}{2}$ car in Canada, Canada has a comparative advantage in producing food. Canada should produce more food than it wants to consume and export some of it to Japan. Through specialization and trade, both countries can have more food and more cars.

In reality, of course, the issues involved in trade among nations are more complex than this example suggests. Most important among these issues is that each country has many citizens with different interests. International trade can make some individuals worse off, even as it makes the country as a whole better off. When Canada exports food and imports cars, the impact on a Canadian farmer is not the same as the impact on a Canadian autoworker. Yet, contrary to the opinions sometimes voiced by politicians and political commentators, international trade is not like war, in which some countries win and others lose. Trade allows all countries to achieve greater prosperity.

QuickQuiz Suppose that the world's fastest typist happens to be trained in brain surgery. Should he do his own typing or hire a secretary? Explain.

CONCLUSION

You should now understand more fully the benefits of living in an interdependent economy. When Canadians buy tube socks from China, when residents of Manitoba drink apple juice from British Columbia, and when a homeowner hires the kid next door to mow the lawn, the same economics forces are at work. The principle of comparative advantage shows that trade can make everyone better off. But having seen why interdependence is desirable, you might naturally ask how it is possible. How do free societies coordinate the diverse activities of all the people involved in their economies? What ensures that goods and services will get from those who should be producing them to those who should be consuming them?

In a world with only two people, such as the rancher and the farmer, the answer is simple: These two people can directly bargain and allocate resources between themselves. In the real world with billions of people, the answer is less obvious. We take up this issue in the next chapter, where we see that free societies allocate resources through the market forces of supply and demand.

SUMMARY

- Each person consumes goods and services produced by many other people, both in our country and around the world. Interdependence and trade are desirable because they allow everyone to enjoy a greater quantity and variety of goods and services.

- There are two ways to compare the ability of two people in producing a good. The person who can produce the good with the smaller quantity of inputs is said to have an *absolute advantage* in producing the good. The person who has the

smaller opportunity cost of producing the good is said to have a *comparative advantage.* The gains from trade are based on comparative advantage, not absolute advantage.

- Trade makes everyone better off because it allows people to specialize in those activities in which they have a comparative advantage.

- The principle of comparative advantage applies to countries as well as to people. Economists use the principle of comparative advantage to advocate free trade among countries.

KEY CONCEPTS

absolute advantage, p. 57   comparative advantage, p. 58   exports, p. 62
opportunity cost, p. 57   imports, p. 62

QUESTIONS FOR REVIEW

1 Explain how absolute advantage and comparative advantage differ.

2. Give an example in which one person has an absolute advantage in doing something but another person has a comparative advantage.

3. Is absolute advantage or comparative advantage more important for trade? Explain your

reasoning using the example in your answer to question 2.

4. Will a nation tend to export or import goods for which it has a comparative advantage? Explain.

5. Why do economists oppose policies that restrict trade among nations?

PROBLEMS AND APPLICATIONS

1. Consider the farmer and the rancher from our example in this chapter. Explain why the farmer's opportunity cost of producing 1 kg of meat is 4 kg of potatoes. Explain why the rancher's opportunity cost of producing 1 kg of meat is 2 kg of potatoes.

2. Maria can read 20 pages of economics in an hour. She can also read 50 pages of sociology in an hour. She spends 5 hours per day studying.
   a. Draw Maria's production possibilities frontier for reading economics and sociology.
   b. What is Maria's opportunity cost of reading 100 pages of sociology?

3. Canadian and Japanese workers can each produce 4 cars per year. A Canadian worker can produce 10 tonnes of grain per year, whereas a Japanese worker can produce 5 tonnes of grain per year. To keep things simple, assume that each country has 100 million workers.
   a. For this situation, construct a table analogous to Table 3.1.
   b. Graph the production possibilities frontier of the Canadian and Japanese economies.
   c. For Canada, what is the opportunity cost of a car? Of grain? For Japan, what is the opportunity cost of a car? Of grain? Put this information in a table analogous to Table 3.3.
   d. Which country has an absolute advantage in producing cars? In producing grain?
   e. Which country has a comparative advantage in producing cars? In producing grain?
   f. Without trade, half of each country's workers produce cars and half produce grain. What quantities of cars and grain does each country produce?
   g. Starting from a position without trade, give an example in which trade makes each country better off.

4. Pat and Kris are roommates. They spend most of their time studying (of course), but they leave some time for their favourite activities: making pizza and brewing root beer. Pat takes 4 hours to brew 5 L of root beer and 2 hours to make a pizza. Kris takes 6 hours to brew 5 L of root beer and 4 hours to make a pizza.
   a. What is each roommate's opportunity cost of making a pizza? Who has the absolute advantage in making pizza? Who has the comparative advantage in making pizza?
   b. If Pat and Kris trade foods with each other, who will trade away pizza in exchange for root beer?
   c. The price of pizza can be expressed in terms of litres of root beer. What is the highest price at which pizza can be traded that would make both roommates better off? What is the lowest price? Explain.

5. Suppose that there are 10 million workers in Canada, and that each of these workers can produce either 2 cars or 30 tonnes of wheat in a year.
   a. What is the opportunity cost of producing a car in Canada? What is the opportunity cost of producing a tonne of wheat in Canada? Explain the relationship between the opportunity costs of the two goods.
   b. Draw Canada's production possibilities frontier. If Canada chooses to consume 10 million cars, how much wheat can it consume without trade? Label this point on the production possibilities frontier.
   c. Now suppose that the United States offers to buy 10 million cars from Canada in exchange for 20 tonnes of wheat per car. If Canada continues to consume 10 million cars, how much wheat does this deal allow Canada to consume? Label this point on your diagram. Should Canada accept the deal?

6. Consider a professor who is writing a book. The professor can both write the chapters and gather the needed data faster than anyone else at his university. Still, he pays a student to collect data at the library. Is this sensible? Explain.

7. England and Scotland both produce scones and sweaters. Suppose that an English worker can produce 50 scones per hour or 1 sweater per hour. Suppose that a Scottish worker can produce 40 scones per hour or 2 sweaters per hour.
   a. Which country has the absolute advantage in the production of each good? Which country has the comparative advantage?

b. If England and Scotland decide to trade, which commodity will Scotland trade to England? Explain.

c. If a Scottish worker could produce only 1 sweater per hour, would Scotland still gain from trade? Would England still gain from trade? Explain.

8. The following table describes the production possibilities of two cities.

	Red Sweaters per Worker per Hour	Blue Sweaters per Worker per Hour
Montreal	3	3
Toronto	2	1

a. Without trade, what is the price of blue sweaters (in terms of red sweaters) in Montreal? What is the price in Toronto?

b. Which city has an absolute advantage in the production of each colour of sweater? Which city has a comparative advantage in the production of each colour of sweater?

c. If the cities trade with each other, which colour of sweater will each export?

d. What is the range of prices at which trade can occur?

9. Suppose that all goods can be produced with fewer worker-hours in Germany than in France.

a. In what sense is the cost of all goods lower in Germany than in France?

b. In what sense is the cost of some goods lower in France?

c. If Germany and France traded with each other, would both countries be better off as a result? Explain in the context of your answers to parts (a) and (b).

10. Are the following statements true or false? Explain in each case.

a. "Two countries can achieve gains from trade even if one of the countries has an absolute advantage in the production of all goods."

b. "Certain very talented people have a comparative advantage in everything they do."

c. "If a certain trade is good for one person, it can't be good for the other one."

http:// For more study tools, please visit http://www.mankiw5e.nelson.com.

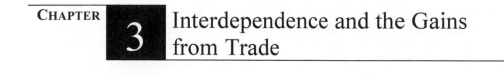

CHAPTER 3 — Interdependence and the Gains from Trade

I. Chapter Overview

A. Context and Purpose

Chapter 3 is the third chapter in the three-chapter section that serves as the introduction of the text. The first chapter introduced ten fundamental principles of economics. The second chapter developed how economists approach problems. This chapter shows how people and countries gain from trade (which is one of the ten principles discussed in Chapter 1).

The purpose of Chapter 3 is to demonstrate how everyone can gain from trade. Trade allows people to specialize in the production of things for which they have a comparative advantage and then exchange them for things that other people produce. Because of specialization, total output rises and through trade people are all able to share in the bounty. This is as true for countries as it is for individuals. Because everyone can gain from trade, restrictions on trade tend to reduce welfare.

B. Helpful Hints

1. *A step-by-step example of comparative advantage.* What follows is an example that will demonstrate most of the concepts discussed in Chapter 3. It will provide a pattern to follow when answering questions at the end of the chapter in the text and for the problems that follow in this Study Guide.

Suppose the following information about the productivity of industry in Japan and Korea is true.

Output

	Steel (units/h)	Televisions (no./h)
Japan	6	3
Korea	8	2

A Japanese worker can produce 6 units of steel or 3 units of televisions per hour. A Korean worker can produce 8 units of steel or 2 units of televisions per hour.

The production possibilities frontier for each country can be plotted, assuming each country has only one worker and the worker works only one hour. To plot the frontier, plot the end points and connect them with a line. For example, Japan can produce 6 units of steel with its worker or 3 units of televisions. It can also allocate one half hour to the production of each and get 3 units of steel and 1.5 televisions,

Any other proportion of the hour can be allocated to the two productive activities. The production possibilities frontier is linear in these cases because the labour resource can be moved from the production of one good to the other at a constant rate. The same can be done for Korea. Without trade, the production possibilities frontier is the consumption possibilities frontier, too.

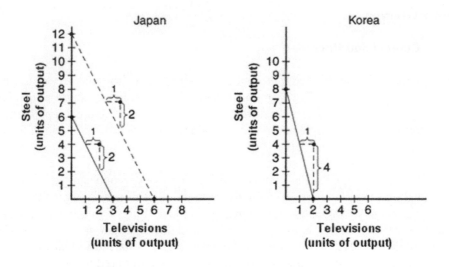

Comparative advantage determines specialization and trade. The opportunity cost of a television in Japan is 2 units of steel, which is shown by the slope of the production possibilities frontier in the previous graph. Alternatively, the opportunity cost of 1 unit of steel in Japan is one-half of a television. In Korea, the opportunity cost of a television is 4 units of steel and the cost of 1 unit of steel is one-quarter of a television. Because the opportunity cost of a television is lower in Japan, Japan has a comparative advantage in television production and should specialize in televisions. Because the opportunity cost of steel is lower in Korea, Korea has a comparative advantage in steel production and should specialize in steel.

What is the range of prices at which each country would be willing to exchange? If Japan specializes in television production and produces 3 televisions, it would be willing to trade televisions for steel as long as the price of steel is below one-half a television per unit of steel because that was the Japanese price for 1 unit of steel prior to trade. Korea would be willing to specialize in steel production and trade for televisions as long as the price of a television is less than 4 units of steel because that was the Korean price of a television prior to trade. In short, the final price must be between the original tradeoffs each faced in the absence of trade. One television will cost between 2 and 4 of units of steel. One unit of steel will cost between one-half and one-quarter of a television.

2. *Trade allows countries to consume outside their original production possibilities frontier.* Suppose that Japan and Korea settle on a trading price of 3 units of steel for 1 television (or one-third of a television for 1 unit of steel). (This price is provided. There is nothing in the problem that would permit the final trading price to be calculated. It is possible to calculate only the range in which it must lie.) This price is halfway between the two prices that each faces in the absence of trade. The range for the trading price is 4 units of steel for 1 television to 2 units of steel for 1 television.

If Japan specializes in television production, produces 3 televisions, and exports 1 television for 3 units of steel, Japan will be able to consume 2 televisions and 3 units of steel. When this point (2 televisions and 3 units of steel) is plotted on Japan's graph, it lies outside its production possibilities frontier. If Korea specializes, produces 8 units of steel, and exports 3 units for one television, Korea will be able to consume 5 units of steel and 1 television. When this point (5 units of steel and one television) is plotted on Korea's graph, it also lies outside its production possibilities frontier.

This is the gain from trade. Trade allows countries (and people) to specialize. Specialization increases world output. After trading, countries consume outside their individual production possibilities frontiers. In this way, trade is like an improvement in technology. It allows countries to move beyond their current production possibilities frontiers.

3. *Only comparative advantage matters—absolute advantage is irrelevant.* In the previous example, Japan had an absolute advantage in the production of televisions because it could produce 3 per hour while Korea could produce only 2. Korea had an absolute advantage in the production of steel because it could produce 8 units per hour compared to 6 for Japan.

To demonstrate that comparative advantage, not absolute advantage, determines specialization and trade, the previous example is altered such that Japan has an absolute advantage in the production of both goods. To this end, suppose Japan becomes twice as productive as in the previous table. That is, a worker can now produce 12 units of steel or 6 televisions per hour.

Output

	Steel (units/h)	Televisions (no./h)
Japan	12	6
Korea	8	2

Now Japan has an absolute advantage in the production of both goods. Japan's new production possibilities frontier is the dashed line in the previous graph. Will this change the analysis? Not at all. The opportunity cost of each good within Japan is the same—2 units of steel per television or one-half of a television per unit of steel (and Korea is unaffected). For this reason, Japan still has the identical comparative advantage as before and it will specialize in television production while Korea will specialize in steel. However, because productivity has doubled in Japan, its entire set of choices has improved and, thus, its material welfare has improved.

II. Self-Testing Challenges

A. True/False Questions

_____1.   If Japan has an absolute advantage in the production of an item, it must also have a comparative advantage in the production of that item.

_____2.   Comparative advantage, not absolute advantage, determines the decision to specialize in production.

_____3.   Absolute advantage is a comparison based on productivity.

_____4.   Self-sufficiency is the best way to increase one's material welfare.

_____5.   Comparative advantage is a comparison based on opportunity cost.

_____6.   If a producer is self-sufficient, the production possibilities frontier is also the consumption possibilities frontier.

_____7.   If a country's workers can produce five hamburgers per hour or ten bags of French fries per hour, absent trade, the price of one bag of fries is two hamburgers.

_____8.   If producers have different opportunity costs of production, trade will allow them to consume outside their production possibilities frontiers.

_____9.   If trade benefits one country, its trading partner must be worse off due to trade.

_____10.   Talented people who are the best at everything have a comparative advantage in the production of everything.

_____11.   The gains from trade can be measured by the increase in total production and consumption that comes from specialization.

_____12.   When a country removes a specific import restriction, it always benefits every worker in that country.

_____13.   If Germany's productivity doubles for everything it produces, this will not alter its prior pattern of specialization because it has not altered its comparative advantage.

_____14.   If an advanced country has an absolute advantage in the production of everything, it will benefit if it eliminates trade with less developed countries and becomes completely self-sufficient.

_____15.   If gains from trade are based solely on comparative advantage, and if all countries have the same opportunity costs of production, then there are no gains from trade

B. Multiple Choice Questions

1. Which one of the following situations is most likely for a nation that has an **absolute** advantage in the production of a good?
    a. It can benefit by restricting imports of that good.
    b. It will specialize in the production of that good and export it.
    c. It can produce that good using fewer resources than its trading partner.
    d. It can produce that good at a lower opportunity cost than its trading partner.

2. Which one of the following situations is most likely for a nation has a **comparative** advantage in the production of a good?
    a. It can benefit by restricting imports of that good.
    b. It must be the only country with the ability to produce that good.
    c. It can produce that good at a lower opportunity cost than its trading partner.
    d. It can produce that good using fewer resources than its trading partner.

3. Which one of the following statements about trade is true?
    a. People who are skilled at all activities cannot benefit from trade.
    b. Unrestricted international trade benefits every person in a country equally.
    c. Trade can benefit everyone in society because it allows people to specialize in activities in which they have an absolute advantage.
    d. Trade can benefit everyone in society because it allows people to specialize in activities in which they have a comparative advantage.

4. Which one of the following does the principle of comparative advantage state?
    a. Countries with a comparative advantage in the production of every good need not specialize.
    b. Countries should specialize in the production of goods that they enjoy consuming more than other countries enjoy consuming them.
    c. Countries should specialize in the production of goods for which they use fewer resources in production than do their trading partners.
    d. Countries should specialize in the production of goods for which they have a lower opportunity cost of production than do their trading partners.

5. Which one of the following statements is true?
    a. Self-sufficiency is the road to prosperity for most countries.
    b. A self-sufficient country consumes outside its production possibilities frontier.
    c. A self-sufficient country can, at best, consume on its production possibilities frontier.
    d. Only countries with an absolute advantage in the production of every good should strive to be self-sufficient.

6. Suppose a country's workers can produce 4 watches per hour or 12 rings per hour. Which one of the following is the domestic price of 1 ring if there is no trade?
    a. The domestic price of 1 ring is one-third of a watch.
    b. The domestic price of 1 ring is 3 watches.
    c. The domestic price of 1 ring is 4 watches.
    d. The domestic price of 1 ring is one-quarter of a watch.

7. Suppose a country's workers can produce 4 watches per hour or 12 rings per hour. Which one of the following is the opportunity cost of 1 watch if there is no trade?
    a. The opportunity cost of 1 watch is 3 rings.
    b. The opportunity cost of 1 watch is one-third of a ring.
    c. The opportunity cost of 1 watch is 4 rings.
    d. The opportunity cost of 1 watch is one-quarter of a ring.

The following table shows production data for Australia and Korea. Use this table for questions 8–15.

Output

	Food (no. units/worker/month)	Electronics (no. units/worker/month)
Australia	20	5
Korea	8	4

8. From the production data, which one of the following statements can be made about absolute advantage??
    a. Korea has an absolute advantage in the production of both food and electronics.
    b. Australia has an absolute advantage in the production of both food and electronics.
    c. Australia has an absolute advantage in the production of food while Korea has an absolute advantage in the production of electronics.
    d. Korea has an absolute advantage in the production of food while Australia has an absolute advantage in the production of electronics.

9. Which one of the following is the opportunity cost of 1 unit of electronics in Australia?
    a. 5 units of food
    b. one-fifth of a unit of food
    c. 4 units of food
    d. one-quarter of a unit of food

10. Which one of the following is the opportunity cost of 1 unit of electronics in Korea?
    a. 2 units of food
    b. one-half of a unit of food
    c. 4 units of food
    d. one-quarter of a unit of food

11.   Which one of the following is the opportunity cost of 1 unit of food in Australia?
      a.   5 units of electronics
      b.   one-fifth of a unit of electronics
      c.   4 units of electronics
      d.   one-quarter of a unit of electronics

12.   Which one of the following is the opportunity cost of 1 unit of food in Korea?
      a.   2 units of electronics
      b.   one-half of a unit of electronics
      c.   4 units of electronics
      d.   one-quarter of a unit of electronics

13.   Which one of the following statements can be made about comparative advantage?
      a.   Australia has a comparative advantage in the production of food while Korea has a comparative advantage in the production of electronics.
      b.   Korea has a comparative advantage in the production of food while Australia has a comparative advantage in the production of electronics.
      c.   Australia has a comparative advantage in the production of both food and electronics.
      d.   Korea has a comparative advantage in the production of both food and electronics.

14.   Which recommendation below would be the best for Korea?
      a.   specialize in food production, export food, and import electronics
      b.   specialize in electronics production, export electronics, and import food
      c.   produce both goods because neither country has a comparative advantage
      d.   produce neither good because it has an absolute disadvantage in the production of both goods

15.   Prices of electronics can be stated in terms of units of food. Which one of the following is the range of prices of electronics for which both countries could gain from trade?
      a.   The price must be greater than 4 units of food but less than 5 units of food.
      b.   The price must be greater than 2 units of food but less than 4 units of food.
      c.   The price must be greater than one-quarter of a unit of food but less than one-half of a unit of food.
      d.   The price must be greater than one-fifth of a unit of food but less than one-quarter of a unit of food.

16. Suppose the world consists of two countries—the United States and Canada. Further, suppose there are only two goods—food and clothing. Which one of the following statements best represents the situation?
   a. If the United States has an absolute advantage in the production of food, then Canada must have an absolute advantage in the production of clothing.
   b. If the United States has a comparative advantage in the production of food, Canada might also have a comparative advantage in the production of food.
   c. If the United States has a comparative advantage in the production of food, it must also have a comparative advantage in the production of clothing.
   d. If the United States has a comparative advantage in the production of food, then Canada must have a comparative advantage in the production of clothing.

Use the following production possibilities frontiers to answer questions 17–19. Assume each country has 20 workers and that each axis is measured in tonnes per month.

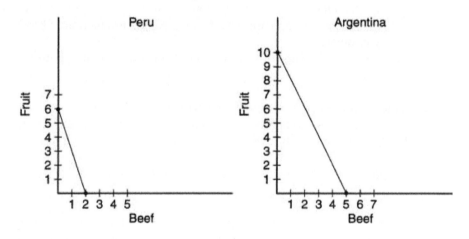

17. For which one of the following does Argentina have a comparative advantage in production?
   a. fruit
   b. beef
   c. both fruit and beef
   d. neither fruit nor beef

18. Which one of the following will Peru export?
   a. beef
   b. fruit
   c. both fruit and beef
   d. neither fruit nor beef

19. Which one of the following is the opportunity cost of producing a tonne of beef in Peru?
    a. one-third of a tonne of fruit
    b. 1 tonne of fruit
    c. 2 tonnes of fruit
    d. 3 tonnes of fruit

20. Joe is a tax accountant. He receives $100 per hour for preparing tax returns. He can type 5000 characters per hour into spreadsheets. He can hire an assistant who types 2500 characters per hour into spreadsheets. Which one of the following statements is the best recommendation?
    a. Joe should not hire an assistant because the assistant cannot type as fast as he can.
    b. Joe should hire the assistant as long as he pays the assistant less than $100 per hour.
    c. Joe should hire the assistant as long as he pays the assistant less than $50 per hour.

C. Short-Answer Questions

1. Why do people choose to become interdependent as opposed to self-sufficient?_____

2. Why is comparative advantage instead of absolute advantage important in determining trade?_____

3. What are the gains from trade? _____

4. Why is a restriction of trade likely to reduce economic welfare?_____

5. Suppose that a lawyer earning $200 per hour can also type at 200 words per minute. Should the lawyer hire a secretary who can type only 50 words per minute? Why or why not?_____

6. Evaluate this statement: A technologically advanced country, which is better than its neighbour at producing everything, would be better off if it closed its borders to trade because the less productive country is a burden to the advanced country.

D. Practice Problems

1. Angela is a college student. She takes a full load of classes and has only 5 hours per week for her hobby. Angela is artistic and can make 2 clay pots per hour or 4 coffee mugs per hour.

    a. Draw Angela's production possibilities frontier for pots and mugs based on the amount produced per week.

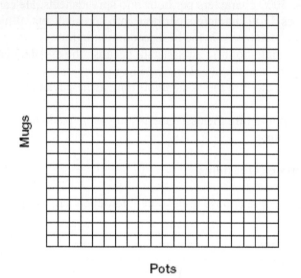

Pots

    b. What is Angela's opportunity cost of 1 pot? 10 pots? _____

    _____

    c. What is Angela's opportunity cost of 1 mug? 10 mugs?_____

    _____

    d. Why is her production possibilities frontier a straight line instead of bowed out like those presented in Chapter 2? _____

    _____

2. Suppose a worker in Germany can produce 15 computers or 5 tonnes of grain per month. Suppose a worker in Poland can produce 4 computers or 4 tonnes of grain per month. For simplicity, assume that each country has only one worker.

    a. Fill out the following table:

                        Output

	Computers (no./worker/month)	Grain (tonnes/worker/month)
Germany		
Poland		

b. Graph the production possibilities frontier for each country.

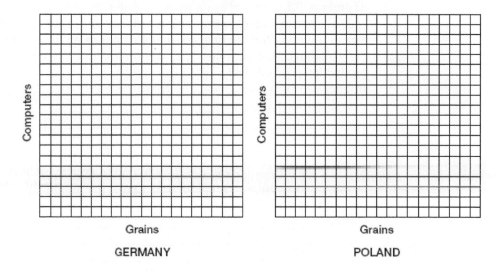

GERMANY   POLAND

c. What is the opportunity cost of 1 computer in Germany? What is the opportunity cost of 1 tonne of grain in Germany?_____

_____

d. What is the opportunity cost of 1 computer in Poland? What is the opportunity cost of 1 tonne of grain in Poland?_____

_____

e. Which country has the absolute advantage in producing computers? Grain?_____

_____

f. Which country has the comparative advantage in producing computers? Grain?_____

_____
_____
_____

g. Each country should tend toward specialization in the production of which good? Why?_____

_____
_____
_____

h. What are the range of prices for computers and grain for which both countries would benefit?_____

_____
_____

    i. Suppose Germany and Poland settle on a price of 2 computers for 1 tonne of grain or 0.5 tonnes of grain for a computer. Suppose each country specializes completely in production and they trade four computers for 2 tonnes of grain. Plot the final consumption points on the graphs made in part (b) above. Are these countries consuming inside or outside of their production possibilities frontier?_____

_____

_____

_____

    j. Suppose the productivity of a worker in Poland doubles so that a worker can produce 8 computers or 8 tonnes of grain per month. Which country has the absolute advantage in producing computers? Grain?_____

_____

_____

_____

    k. After the doubling of productivity in Poland, which country has a comparative advantage in producing computers? Grain? Has the comparative advantage changed? Has the economic welfare of either country changed?_____

_____

_____

_____

_____

    l. How would the analysis change if it was assumed, more realistically, that each country had 10 million workers?_____

_____

_____

_____

3. Suppose a worker in Canada can produce 4 cars or 20 computers per month while a worker in Russia can produce 1 car or 5 computers per month. Again, for simplicity, assume each country has only one worker.

    a. Fill out the following table:

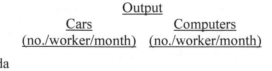

	Output	
	Cars (no./worker/month)	Computers (no./worker/month)
Canada		
Russia		

    b. Which country has the absolute advantage in the production of cars? Computers?_____

_____

_____

    c.   Which country has the comparative advantage in the production of cars? Computers?

_____

_____

_____

    d.   Are there any gains to be made from trade? Why or why not?_____

_____

_____

    e.   Does the answer in (d) above help pinpoint a source for gains from trade?_____

_____

_____

    f.   What might make two countries have different opportunity costs of production? (Use your imagination. This was not directly discussed in Chapter 3.)_____

_____

_____

_____

E. Advanced Critical Thinking

In an election debate a candidate says, "We need to stop the flow of foreign automobiles into our country. If we limit the importation of automobiles, our domestic auto production will rise and Canada will be better off."

1.   Is it likely that Canada will be better off if it limits auto imports? Explain._____

_____

_____

2.   Will anyone in Canada be better off if it limits auto imports? Explain._____

_____

_____

_____

3.   In the real world, does every person in the country gain when restrictions on imports are reduced? Explain._____

_____

_____

_____

III. Solutions

A. True/False Questions

1.   F; absolute advantage compares the quantities of inputs used in production while comparative advantage compares the opportunity costs.
2.   T
3.   T
4.   F; restricting trade eliminates gains from trade.
5.   T
6.   T
7.   F; the price of 1 bag of fries is one-half of a hamburger.
8.   T
9.   F; voluntary trade benefits both traders.
10. F; a low opportunity cost of producing one good implies a high opportunity cost of producing the other good.
11. T
12. F; it may harm those involved in that industry.
13. T
14. F; voluntary trade benefits all traders.
15. T

B.   Multiple-Choice Questions

1. c	6. a	11. d	16. d
2. c	7. a	12. b	17. b
3. d	8. b	13. a	18. b
4. d	9. c	14. b	19. d
5. c	10. a	15. b	20. c

C. Short-Answer Questions

1.   Because a consumer gets a greater variety of goods at a much lower cost than he or she could produce by himself or herself. That is, there are gains from trade.

2.   What is important in trade is how a country's costs without trade differ from another country's costs. This is determined by the relative opportunity costs across countries.

3.   The additional output and consumption that comes from countries with different opportunity costs of production specializing in the production of the item for which they have the lower domestic opportunity cost.

4.   Because it forces people to produce at a higher cost than they would pay when they trade.

5.   Yes, as long as the secretary earns less than $50 per hour, the lawyer is ahead.

6. This is not true. All countries can gain from trade if their opportunity costs of production differ. Even the least productive country will have a comparative advantage at producing something, and it can trade this good to the advanced country for less than the advanced country's opportunity cost.

D. Practice Problems

1. a.

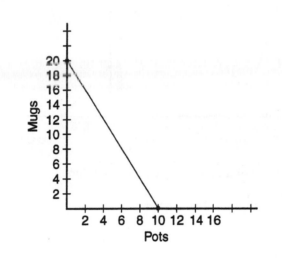

   b. 2 mugs. 20 mugs.

   c. One-half of a pot. 5 pots.

   d. Because her resources can be moved from the production of one good to another at a constant rate.

2. a.

	Output	
	Computers (no./worker/month)	Grain (no./worker/month)
Germany	15	5
Poland	4	4

b.

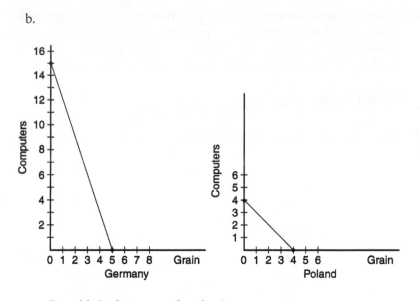

c. One-third of a tonne of grain. 3 computers.

d. 1 tonne of grain. 1 computer.

e. Germany because 1 worker can produce 15 compared to 4. Germany because 1 worker can produce 5 compared to 4.

f. Germany because a computer has the opportunity cost of only one-third of a tonne of grain compared to 1 tonne of grain in Poland. Poland because 1 tonne of grain has the opportunity cost of only 1 computer compared to 3 computers in Germany.

g. Germany should produce computers while Poland should produce grain because the opportunity cost of computers is lower in Germany and the opportunity cost of grain is lower in Poland. That is, each has a comparative advantage in those goods.

h. Grain must cost less than 3 computers to Germany. Computers must cost less than 1 tonne of grain to Poland.

i.

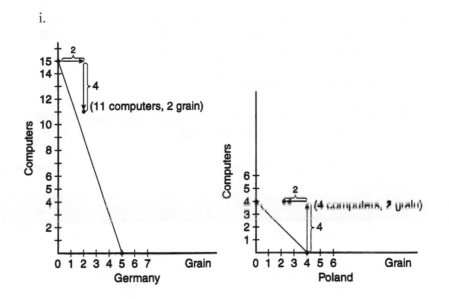

They are consuming outside their production possibilities frontier.

j. Germany because one worker can produce 15 compared to 8. Poland because one worker can produce 8 compared to 5.

k. Germany has comparative advantage in computers. Poland has comparative advantage in grain. No change in comparative advantage. Poland is better off, however, because it now has a larger set of choices.

l. It would not change absolute advantage or comparative advantage. It would change the scale in the previous two graphs by a factor of 10 million.

3. a.

Output

	Cars (no./worker/month)	Computers (no./worker/month)
Canada	4	20
Russia	1	5

b. Canada because 1 worker can produce 4 compared to 1. Canada because 1 worker can produce 20 compared to 5.

c. In both, the opportunity cost of 1 car is 5 computers. In both, the opportunity cost of 1 computer is one-fifth of a car. Therefore, neither has a comparative advantage in either good.

d. No. Each can get the same tradeoff between goods domestically.

e. Yes. There needs to be differences in opportunity costs of producing goods across countries for there to be gains from trade.

    f.   Resources or technology might be different across countries. That is, workers could be differently educated, land could be of different quality, or the available technology might be different.

E. Advanced Critical Thinking

1.   No. If Canada imports autos, it is because the opportunity cost of producing them elsewhere is lower than in Canada.

2.   Yes. Those associated with the domestic auto industry—shareholders (owners) of domestic auto producers and autoworkers.

3.   No. When we reduce restrictions on imports, the country gains from the increased trade but individuals in the affected domestic industry may lose.

© Jason Yoder/Dreamstime.com

SUPPLY AND DEMAND I:
HOW MARKETS WORK

2

THE MARKET FORCES OF SUPPLY AND DEMAND

Learning Objectives

In this chapter, you will ...

- Learn the nature of a competitive market

- Examine what determines the demand for a good in a competitive market

- Examine what determines the supply of a good in a competitive market

- See how supply and demand together set the price of a good and the quantity sold

- Consider the key role of prices in allocating scarce resources in market economies

When a cold snap hits Florida, the price of orange juice rises in supermarkets throughout Canada. When the weather turns warm in Quebec every summer, the price of hotel rooms in the Caribbean plummets. When a war breaks out in the Middle East, the price of gasoline in Canada rises and the price of a used SUV falls. What do these events have in common? They all show the workings of supply and demand.

Supply and *demand* are the two words that economists use most often—and for good reason. Supply and demand are the forces that make market economies work. They determine the quantity of each good produced and the price at which it is sold. If you want to know how any event or policy will affect the economy, you must think first about how it will affect supply and demand.

This chapter introduces the theory of supply and demand. It considers how buyers and sellers behave and how they interact with one another. It shows how supply and demand determine prices in a market economy and how prices, in turn, allocate the economy's scarce resources.

MARKETS AND COMPETITION

The terms *supply* and *demand* refer to the behaviour of people as they interact with one another in markets. Before discussing how buyers and sellers behave, let's first consider more fully what we mean by a "market" and the various types of markets we observe in the economy.

What Is a Market?

market
a group of buyers and sellers of a particular good or service

A **market** is a group of buyers and sellers of a particular good or service. The buyers as a group determine the demand for the product, and the sellers as a group determine the supply of the product.

Markets take many forms. Sometimes markets are highly organized, such as the markets for many agricultural commodities. In these markets, buyers and sellers meet at a specific time and place, where an auctioneer helps set prices and arrange sales.

More often, markets are less organized. For example, consider the market for ice cream in a particular town. Buyers of ice cream do not meet together at any one time. The sellers of ice cream are in different locations and offer somewhat different products. There is no auctioneer calling out the price of ice cream. Each seller posts a price for an ice-cream cone, and each buyer decides how much ice cream to buy at each store. Nonetheless, these consumers and producers of ice cream are closely connected. The ice-cream buyers are choosing from the various ice-cream sellers to satisfy their hunger, and the ice-cream sellers are all trying to appeal to the same ice-cream buyers to make their businesses successful. Even though it is not organized, the group of ice-cream buyers and ice-cream sellers forms a market.

What Is Competition?

The market for ice cream, like most markets in the economy, is highly competitive. Each buyer knows that there are several sellers from which to choose, and each seller is aware that his product is similar to that offered by other sellers. As a result, the price of ice cream and the quantity of ice cream sold are not determined by any single buyer or seller. Rather, price and quantity are determined by all buyers and sellers as they interact in the marketplace.

competitive market
a market in which there are many buyers and many sellers so that each has a negligible impact on the market price

Economists use the term **competitive market** to describe a market in which there are so many buyers and so many sellers that each has a negligible impact on the market price. Each seller of ice cream has limited control over the price because other sellers are offering similar products. A seller has little reason to charge less than the going price, and if he charges more, buyers will make their purchases elsewhere. Similarly, no single buyer of ice cream can influence the price of ice cream because each buyer purchases only a small amount.

In this chapter, we assume that markets are *perfectly competitive*. To reach this highest form of competition, a market must have two characteristics: (1) the goods offered for sale are all exactly the same, and (2) the buyers and sellers are so numerous that no single buyer or seller has any influence over the market price. Because buyers and sellers in perfectly competitive markets must accept the price the market determines, they are said to be *price takers*. At the market price, buyers can buy all they want, and sellers can sell all they want.

There are some markets in which the assumption of perfect competition applies perfectly. In the wheat market, for example, there are thousands of farmers who sell wheat and millions of consumers who use wheat and wheat products. Because no single buyer or seller can influence the price of wheat, each takes the price as given.

Not all goods and services, however, are sold in perfectly competitive markets. Some markets have only one seller, and this seller sets the price. Such a seller is called a *monopoly*. Your local cable television company, for instance, may be a monopoly. Residents of your town probably have only one cable company from which to buy this service. Some markets (covered in the study of microeconomics) fall between the extremes of perfect competition and monopoly.

Despite the diversity of market types we find in the world, assuming perfect competition is a useful simplification and, therefore, a natural place to start. Perfectly competitive markets are the easiest to analyze because everyone participating in the market takes the price as given by market conditions. Moreover, because some degree of competition is present in most markets, many of the lessons that we learn by studying supply and demand under perfect competition apply in more complicated markets as well.

QuickQuiz What is a market? • What are the characteristics of a competitive market?

DEMAND

We begin our study of markets by examining the behaviour of buyers. To focus our thinking, let's keep in mind a particular good—ice cream.

The Demand Curve: The Relationship between Price and Quantity Demanded

The **quantity demanded** of any good is the amount of the good that buyers are willing and able to purchase. As we will see, many things determine the quantity demanded of any good, but when analyzing how markets work, one determinant plays a central role—the price of the good. If the price of ice cream rose to $20 per scoop, you would buy less ice cream. You might buy frozen yogurt instead. If the price of ice cream fell to $0.20 per scoop, you would buy more. Because the quantity demanded falls as the price rises and rises as the price falls, we say that the quantity demanded is *negatively related* to the price. This relationship between price and quantity demanded is true for most goods in the economy and, in fact, is so pervasive that economists call it the **law of demand:** Other things equal, when the price of a good rises, the quantity demanded of the good falls, and when price falls, the quantity demanded rises.

The table in Figure 4.1 shows how many ice-cream cones Catherine buys each month at different prices of ice cream. If ice cream is free, Catherine eats 12 cones. At $0.50 per cone, Catherine buys 10 cones. As the price rises further, she buys fewer and fewer cones. When the price reaches $3.00, Catherine doesn't buy any ice cream at all. This table is a **demand schedule,** a table that shows the relationship between the price of a good and the quantity demanded, holding constant everything else that influences how much consumers of the good want to buy.

quantity demanded
the amount of a good that buyers are willing and able to purchase

law of demand
the claim that, other things equal, the quantity demanded of a good falls when the price of the good rises

demand schedule
a table that shows the relationship between the price of a good and the quantity demanded

Catherine's Demand Schedule and Demand Curve

The demand schedule shows the quantity demanded at each price. The demand curve, which graphs the demand schedule, shows how the quantity demanded of the good changes as its price varies. Because a lower price increases the quantity demanded, the demand curve slopes downward.

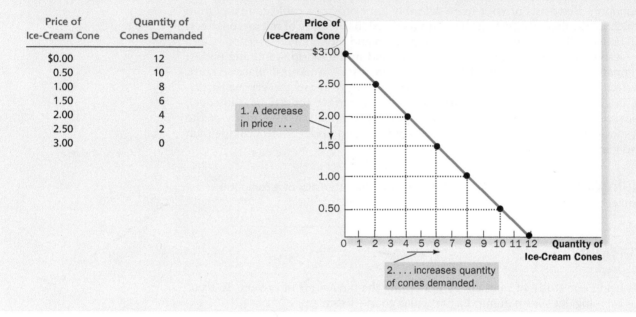

Price of Ice-Cream Cone	Quantity of Cones Demanded
$0.00	12
0.50	10
1.00	8
1.50	6
2.00	4
2.50	2
3.00	0

1. A decrease in price . . .

2. . . . increases quantity of cones demanded.

The graph in Figure 4.1 uses the numbers from the table to illustrate the law of demand. By convention, the price of ice cream is on the vertical axis, and the quantity of ice cream demanded is on the horizontal axis. The downward-sloping line relating price and quantity demanded is called the **demand curve.**

demand curve
a graph of the relationship between the price of a good and the quantity demanded

Market Demand versus Individual Demand

The demand curve in Figure 4.1 shows an individual's demand for a product. To analyze how markets work, we need to determine the *market demand,* which is the sum of all the individual demands for a particular good or service.

The table in Figure 4.2 shows the demand schedules for ice cream of two individuals—Catherine and Nicholas. At any price, Catherine's demand schedule tells us how much ice cream she buys, and Nicholas's demand schedule tells us how much ice cream he buys. The market demand at each price is the sum of the two individual demands.

The graph in Figure 4.2 shows the demand curves that correspond to these demand schedules. Notice that we sum the individual demand curves *horizontally* to obtain the market demand curve. That is, to find the total quantity demanded at any price, we add the individual quantities found on the horizontal axis of the individual demand curves. Because we are interested in analyzing how markets

FIGURE 4.2

Market Demand as the Sum of Individual Demands

The quantity demanded in a market is the sum of the quantities demanded by all the buyers at each price. Thus, the market demand curve is found by adding horizontally the individual demand curves. At a price of $2, Catherine demands 4 ice-cream cones, and Nicholas demands 3 ice-cream cones. The quantity demanded in the market at this price is 7 cones.

Price of Ice-Cream Cone	Catherine		Nicholas		Market
$0.00	12	+	7	=	19
0.50	10		6		16
1.00	8		5		13
1.50	6		4		10
2.00	4		3		7
2.50	2		2		4
3.00	0		1		1

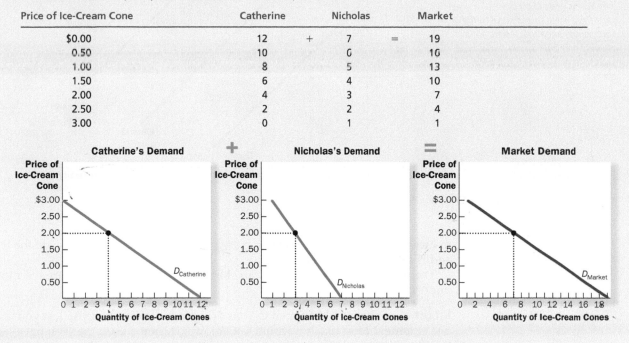

work, we will work most often with the market demand curve. The market demand curve shows how the total quantity demanded of a good varies as the price of the good varies, while all the other factors that affect how much consumers want to buy are held constant.

Shifts in the Demand Curve

The demand curve for ice cream shows how much ice cream people buy at any given price, holding constant the many other factors beyond price that influence consumers' buying decisions. As a result, this demand curve need not be stable over time. If something happens to alter the quantity demanded at any given price, the demand curve shifts. For example, suppose nutritionists discovered that people who regularly eat ice cream live longer, healthier lives. The discovery would raise the demand for ice cream. At any given price, buyers would now want to purchase a larger quantity of ice cream, and the demand curve for ice cream would shift.

Figure 4.3 illustrates shifts in demand. Any change that increases the quantity demanded at every price, such as our imaginary discovery by nutritionists, shifts the demand curve to the right and is called *an increase in demand.* Any change that

FIGURE 4.3

Shifts in the Demand Curve

Any change that raises the quantity that buyers wish to purchase at a given price shifts the demand curve to the right. Any change that lowers the quantity that buyers wish to purchase at a given price shifts the demand curve to the left.

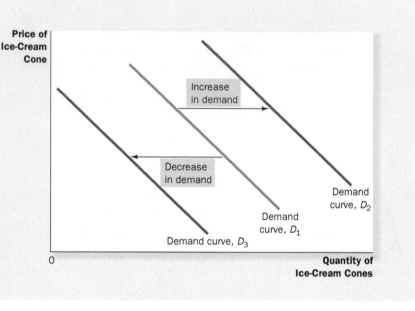

reduces the quantity demanded at every price shifts the demand curve to the left and is called *a decrease in demand*.

There are many variables that can shift the demand curve. Here are the most important:

Income What would happen to your demand for ice cream if you lost your job one summer? Most likely, it would fall. A lower income means that you have less to spend in total, so you would have to spend less on some—and probably most—goods. If the demand for a good falls when income falls, the good is called a **normal good.**

Not all goods are normal goods. If the demand for a good rises when income falls, the good is called an **inferior good.** An example of an inferior good might be bus rides. As your income falls, you are less likely to buy a car or take a cab, and more likely to ride the bus.

A related issue concerns the impact of wealth, as distinct from yearly income, on the demand for goods. For most individuals, the most important components of their wealth are the value of their home and the value of their savings. The value of both fell in conjunction with the recession that swept the world in 2008.

Canada was no exception. The Toronto Stock Exchange (TSX) index fell by almost 50 percent from its peak in January of 2008 to its low in March of 2009. Over the last three quarters of 2009, stock markets partly recovered, with the TSX index increasing by about 55 percent from its March low (although as of the beginning of 2010, the TSX index was still only about 80 percent of its 2009 high).

While there were significant regional variations, housing prices also fell in Canada during the recession. Over the last half of 2008, prices fell an average of about 7 percent in major Canadian cities. They have since largely recovered.

The impact of changes in wealth on both the amount and composition of goods that individuals consume is called the *wealth effect*. The size of the wealth

normal good
a good for which, other things equal, an increase in income leads to an increase in demand

inferior good
a good for which, other things equal, an increase in income leads to a decrease in demand

NEL

effect, if it even exists, is a matter of some dispute among economists. Some argue that the effect is significant, with the demand for some goods changing significantly with changes in wealth. Others argue that the effect is minimal. However, in principle, the wealth effect can shift the demand curve much like changes in income can.

Prices of Related Goods Suppose that the price of frozen yogurt falls. The law of demand says that you will buy more frozen yogurt. At the same time, you will probably buy less ice cream. Because ice cream and frozen yogurt are both cold, sweet, creamy desserts, they satisfy similar desires. When a fall in the price of one good reduces the demand for another good, the two goods are called **substitutes.** Substitutes are often pairs of goods that are used in place of each other, such as hot dogs and hamburgers, sweaters and sweatshirts, and movie tickets and video rentals.

Now suppose that the price of hot fudge falls. According to the law of demand, you will buy more hot fudge. Yet, in this case, you will buy more ice cream as well, because ice cream and hot fudge are often used together. When a fall in the price of one good raises the demand for another good, the two goods are called **complements.** Complements are often pairs of goods that are used together, such as gasoline and automobiles, computers and software, and peanut butter and jelly.

Tastes The most obvious determinant of your demand is your tastes. If you like ice cream, you buy more of it. Economists normally do not try to explain people's tastes because tastes are based on historical and psychological forces that are beyond the realm of economics. Economists do, however, examine what happens when tastes change.

Expectations Your expectations about the future may affect your demand for a good or service today. For example, if you expect to earn a higher income next month, you may be more willing to spend some of your current savings buying ice cream. As another example, if you expect the price of ice cream to fall tomorrow, you may be less willing to buy an ice-cream cone at today's price.

Number of Buyers Because market demand is derived from individual demands, it depends on all those factors that determine the demand of individual buyers, including buyers' incomes, tastes, expectations, and the prices of related goods. In addition, it depends on the number of buyers. If Peter, another consumer of ice cream, were to join Catherine and Nicholas, the quantity demanded in the market would be higher at every price and the demand curve would shift to the right.

Summary The demand curve shows what happens to the quantity demanded of a good when its price varies, holding constant all the other variables that influence buyers. When one of these other variables changes, the demand curve shifts. Table 4.1 lists all the variables that influence how much consumers choose to buy of a good.

If you have trouble remembering whether you need to shift or move along the demand curve, it helps to recall a lesson from the appendix to Chapter 2. A curve shifts when there is a change in a relevant variable that is not measured on either axis. Because the price is on the vertical axis, a change in price represents a movement along the demand curve. By contrast, income, the prices of related goods, tastes, expectations, and the number of buyers are not measured on either axis, so a change in one of these variables shifts the demand curve.

substitutes
two goods for which an increase in the price of one leads to an increase in the demand for the other

complements
two goods for which an increase in the price of one leads to a decrease in the demand for the other

TABLE 4.1

Variables That Influence Buyers

This table lists the variables that affect how much consumers choose to buy of any good. Notice the special role that the price of the good plays: A change in the good's price represents a movement along the demand curve, whereas a change in one of the other variables shifts the demand curve.

Variable	A Change in This Variable . . .
Price of the good itself	Represents a movement along the demand curve
Income	Shifts the demand curve
Prices of related goods	Shifts the demand curve
Tastes	Shifts the demand curve
Expectations	Shifts the demand curve
Number of buyers	Shifts the demand curve

Case Study

TWO WAYS TO REDUCE THE QUANTITY OF SMOKING DEMANDED

Public policymakers often want to reduce the amount that people smoke. There are two ways that policy can attempt to achieve this goal.

One way to reduce smoking is to shift the demand curve for cigarettes and other tobacco products. Public service announcements, mandatory health warnings on cigarette packages, and the prohibition of cigarette advertising on television are all policies aimed at reducing the quantity of cigarettes demanded at any given price. If successful, these policies shift the demand curve for cigarettes to the left, as in panel (a) of Figure 4.4.

Alternatively, policymakers can try to raise the price of cigarettes. If the government taxes the manufacture of cigarettes, for example, cigarette companies pass much of this tax on to consumers in the form of higher prices. A higher price encourages smokers to reduce the number of cigarettes they smoke. In this case, the reduced amount of smoking does not represent a shift in the demand curve. Instead, it represents a movement along the same demand curve to a point with a higher price and lower quantity, as in panel (b) of Figure 4.4.

How much does the amount of smoking respond to changes in the price of cigarettes? Economists have attempted to answer this question by studying what happens when the tax on cigarettes changes. They have found that a 10 percent increase in the price causes a 4 percent reduction in the quantity demanded. Teenagers are found to be especially sensitive to the price of cigarettes: A 10 percent increase in the price causes a 12 percent drop in teenage smoking.

A related question is how the price of cigarettes affects the demand for illicit drugs, such as marijuana. Opponents of cigarette taxes often argue that tobacco and marijuana are substitutes, so that high cigarette prices encourage marijuana use. By contrast, many experts on substance abuse view tobacco as a "gateway

What is the best way to stop this?

© image 100/Corbis

FIGURE 4.4

Shifts in the Demand Curve versus Movements along the Demand Curve

If warnings on cigarette packages convince smokers to smoke less, the demand curve for cigarettes shifts to the left. In panel (a), the demand curve shifts from D_1 to D_2. At a price of $10.00 per pack, the quantity demanded falls from 20 to 10 cigarettes per day, as reflected by the shift from point A to point B. By contrast, if a tax raises the price of cigarettes, the demand curve does not shift. Instead, we observe a movement to a different point on the demand curve. In panel (b), when the price rises from $10.00 to $20.00, the quantity demanded falls from 20 to 12 cigarettes per day, as reflected by the movement from point A to point C.

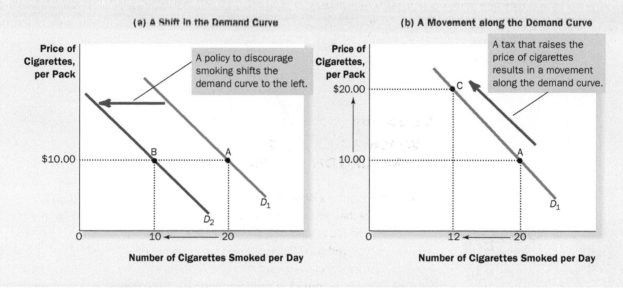

(a) A Shift in the Demand Curve

Price of Cigarettes, per Pack

A policy to discourage smoking shifts the demand curve to the left.

B   A

$10.00

D_2 D_1

0   10 ← 20

Number of Cigarettes Smoked per Day

(b) A Movement along the Demand Curve

Price of Cigarettes, per Pack

A tax that raises the price of cigarettes results in a movement along the demand curve.

$20.00   C

10.00   A

D_1

0   12 ← 20

Number of Cigarettes Smoked per Day

drug" leading the young to experiment with other harmful substances. Most studies of the data are consistent with this view: They find that lower cigarette prices are associated with greater use of marijuana. In other words, tobacco and marijuana appear to be complements rather than substitutes. ●

QuickQuiz Make up an example of a demand schedule for pizza, and graph the implied demand curve. ● Give an example of something that would shift this demand curve. ● Would a change in the price of pizza shift this demand curve?

SUPPLY

We now turn to the other side of the market and examine the behaviour of sellers. Once again, to focus our thinking, let's consider the market for ice cream.

The Supply Curve: The Relationship between Price and Quantity Supplied

The **quantity supplied** of any good or service is the amount that sellers are willing and able to sell. There are many determinants of quantity supplied, but once again

quantity supplied
the amount of a good that sellers are willing and able to sell

FIGURE 4.5

Ben's Supply Schedule and Supply Curve

The supply schedule shows the quantity supplied at each price. This supply curve, which graphs the supply schedule, shows how the quantity supplied of the good changes as its price varies. Because a higher price increases the quantity supplied, the supply curve slopes upward.

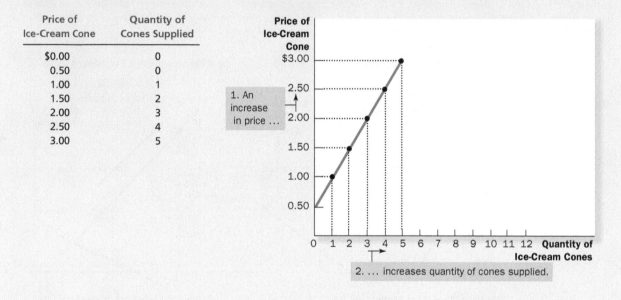

Price of Ice-Cream Cone	Quantity of Cones Supplied
$0.00	0
0.50	0
1.00	1
1.50	2
2.00	3
2.50	4
3.00	5

1. An increase in price ...

2. .... increases quantity of cones supplied.

law of supply
the claim that, other things equal, the quantity supplied of a good rises when the price of the good rises

supply schedule
a table that shows the relationship between the price of a good and the quantity supplied

supply curve
a graph of the relationship between the price of a good and the quantity supplied

price plays a special role in our analysis. When the price of ice cream is high, selling ice cream is profitable, and so the quantity supplied is large. Sellers of ice cream work long hours, buy many ice-cream machines, and hire many workers. By contrast, when the price of ice cream is low, the business is less profitable, and so sellers produce less ice cream. At a low price, some sellers may even choose to shut down, and their quantity supplied falls to zero. Because the quantity supplied rises as the price rises and falls as the price falls, we say that the quantity supplied is *positively related* to the price of the good. This relationship between price and quantity supplied is called the **law of supply:** Other things equal, when the price of a good rises, the quantity supplied of the good also rises, and when the price falls, the quantity supplied falls as well.

The table in Figure 4.5 shows the quantity supplied by Ben, an ice-cream seller, at various prices of ice cream. At a price below $1.00, Ben does not supply any ice cream at all. As the price rises, he supplies a greater and greater quantity. This is the **supply schedule,** a table that shows the relationship between the price of a good and the quantity supplied, holding constant everything else that influences how much producers of the good want to sell.

The graph in Figure 4.5 uses the numbers from the table to illustrate the law of supply. The curve relating price and quantity supplied is called the **supply curve.** The supply curve slopes upward because, other things equal, a higher price means a greater quantity supplied.

NEL

FIGURE 4.6

Market Supply as the Sum of Individual Supplies

The quantity supplied in a market is the sum of the quantities supplied by all the sellers at each price. Thus, the market supply curve is found by adding horizontally the individual supply curves. At a price of $2, Ben supplies 3 ice-cream cones, and Jerry supplies 4 ice-cream cones. The quantity supplied in the market at this price is 7 cones.

Price of Ice-Cream Cone	Ben		Jerry		Market
$0.00	0	+	0	=	0
0.50	0		0		0
1.00	1		0		1
1.50	2		2		4
2.00	3		4		7
2.50	4		6		10
3.00	5		8		13

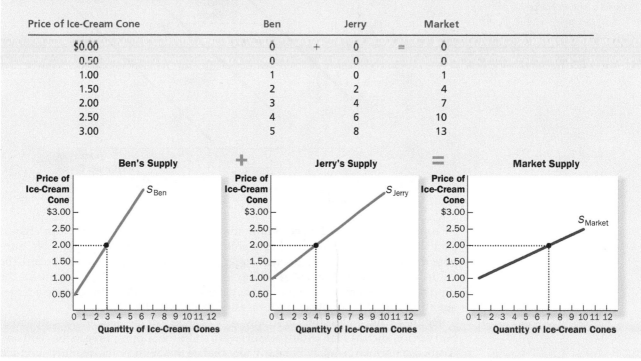

Market Supply versus Individual Supply

Just as market demand is the sum of the demands of all buyers, market supply is the sum of the supplies of all sellers. The table in Figure 4.6 shows the supply schedules for two ice-cream producers—Ben and Jerry. At any price, Ben's supply schedule tells us the quantity of ice cream Ben supplies, and Jerry's supply schedule tells us the quantity of ice cream Jerry supplies. The market supply is the sum of the two individual supplies.

The graph in Figure 4.6 shows the supply curves that correspond to the supply schedules. As with demand curves, we sum the individual supply curves *horizontally* to obtain the market supply curve. That is, to find the total quantity supplied at any price, we add the individual quantities found on the horizontal axis of the individual supply curves. The market supply curve shows how the total quantity supplied varies as the price of the good varies.

Shifts in the Supply Curve

The supply curve for ice cream shows how much ice-cream producers offer for sale at any given price, holding constant all the other factors beyond price that influ-

Shifts in the Supply Curve

Any change that raises the quantity that sellers wish to produce at a given price shifts the supply curve to the right. Any change that lowers the quantity that sellers wish to produce at a given price shifts the supply curve to the left.

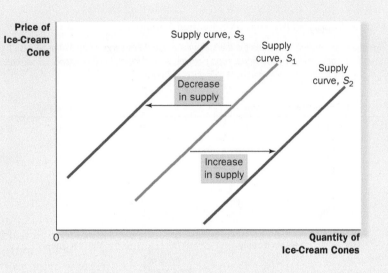

ence producers' decisions about how much to sell. This relationship can change over time, which is represented by a shift in the supply curve. For example, suppose the price of sugar falls. Because sugar is an input into producing ice cream, the fall in the price of sugar makes selling ice cream more profitable. This raises the supply of ice cream: At any given price, sellers are now willing to produce a larger quantity. Thus, the supply curve for ice cream shifts to the right.

Figure 4.7 illustrates shifts in supply. Any change that raises quantity supplied at every price, such as a fall in the price of sugar, shifts the supply curve to the right and is called *an increase in supply*. Similarly, any change that reduces the quantity supplied at every price shifts the supply curve to the left and is called *a decrease in supply*.

There are many variables that can shift the supply curve. Here are some of the most important:

Input Prices   To produce their output of ice cream, sellers use various inputs: cream, sugar, flavouring, ice-cream machines, the buildings in which the ice cream is made, and the labour of workers to mix the ingredients and operate the machines. When the price of one or more of these inputs rises, producing ice cream is less profitable, and firms supply less ice cream. If input prices rise substantially, a firm might shut down and supply no ice cream at all. Thus, the supply of a good is negatively related to the price of the inputs used to make the good.

Technology   The technology for turning the inputs into ice cream is yet another determinant of supply. The invention of the mechanized ice-cream machine, for example, reduced the amount of labour necessary to make ice cream. By reducing firms' costs, the advance in technology raised the supply of ice cream.

Expectations   The amount of ice cream a firm supplies today may depend on its expectations of the future. For example, if it expects the price of ice cream to rise in the future, it will put some of its current production into storage and supply less to the market today.

Variables That Influence Sellers

This table lists the variables that affect how much producers choose to sell of any good. Notice the special role that the price of the good plays: A change in the good's price represents a movement along the supply curve, whereas a change in one of the other variables shifts the supply curve.

Variable	A Change in This Variable . . .
Price of the good itself	Represents a movement along the supply curve
Input prices	Shifts the supply curve
Technology	Shifts the supply curve
Expectations	Shifts the supply curve
Number of sellers	Shifts the supply curve

Number of Sellers   Market supply depends on all those factors that influence the supply of individual sellers, such as the prices of inputs used to produce the good, the available technology, and expectations. In addition, the supply in a market depends on the number of sellers. If Ben or Jerry were to retire from the ice-cream business, the supply in the market would fall.

Summary   The supply curve shows what happens to the quantity supplied of a good when its price varies, holding constant all the other variables that influence sellers. When one of these other variables changes, the supply curve shifts. Table 4.2 lists all the variables that influence how much producers choose to sell of a good.

Once again, to help you remember whether you need to shift or move along the supply curve, keep in mind that a curve shifts only when there is a change in a relevant variable that is not named on either axis. The price is on the vertical axis, so a change in price represents a movement along the supply curve. By contrast, because input prices, technology, expectations, and the number of sellers are not measured on either axis, a change in one of these variables shifts the supply curve.

QuickQuiz Make up an example of a supply schedule for pizza, and graph the implied supply curve. • Give an example of something that would shift this supply curve. • Would a change in the price of pizza shift this supply curve?

SUPPLY AND DEMAND TOGETHER

Having analyzed supply and demand separately, we now combine them to see how they determine the quantity of a good sold in a market and its price.

Equilibrium

Figure 4.8 shows the market supply curve and market demand curve together. Notice that there is one point at which the supply and demand curves intersect. This point is called the market's **equilibrium**. The price at this intersection is called the **equilibrium price**, and the quantity is called the **equilibrium quantity**.

equilibrium
a situation in which the price has reached the level where quantity supplied equals quantity demanded

equilibrium price
the price that balances quantity supplied and quantity demanded

equilibrium quantity
the quantity supplied and the quantity demanded at the equilibrium price

FIGURE 4.8

**The Equilibrium
of Supply and Demand**

*The equilibrium is found where
the supply and demand curves
intersect. At the equilibrium price, the
quantity supplied equals the quantity
demanded. Here the equilibrium price
is $2: At this price, 7 ice-cream cones
are supplied, and 7 ice-cream cones
are demanded.*

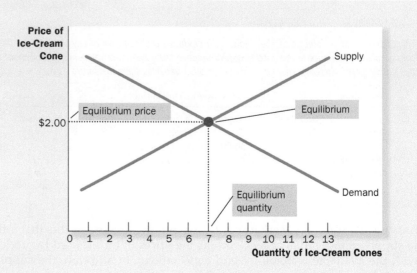

Here the equilibrium price is $2.00 per cone, and the equilibrium quantity is 7 ice-cream cones.

The dictionary defines the word *equilibrium* as a situation in which various forces are in balance—and this also describes a market's equilibrium. *At the equilibrium price, the quantity of the good that buyers are willing to buy exactly balances the quantity that sellers are willing to sell.* The equilibrium price is sometimes called the *market-clearing price* because, at this price, everyone in the market has been satisfied: Buyers can buy all they want to buy, and sellers can sell all they want to sell.

The actions of buyers and sellers naturally move markets toward the equilibrium of supply and demand. To see why, consider what happens when the market price is not equal to the equilibrium price.

Suppose first that the market price is above the equilibrium price, as in panel (a) of Figure 4.9. At a price of $2.50 per cone, the quantity of the good supplied (10 cones) exceeds the quantity demanded (4 cones). There is a **surplus** of the good: Suppliers are unable to sell all they want at the going price. A surplus is sometimes called a situation of *excess supply*. When there is a surplus in the ice-cream market, sellers of ice cream find their freezers increasingly full of ice cream they would like to sell but cannot. They respond to the surplus by cutting their prices. Falling prices, in turn, increase the quantity demanded and decrease the quantity supplied. Prices continue to fall until the market reaches the equilibrium.

Suppose now that the market price is below the equilibrium price, as in panel (b) of Figure 4.9. In this case, the price is $1.50 per cone, and the quantity of the good demanded exceeds the quantity supplied. There is a **shortage** of the good: Demanders are unable to buy all they want at the going price. A shortage is sometimes called a situation of *excess demand*. When a shortage occurs in the ice-cream market, buyers have to wait in long lines for a chance to buy one of the few cones

surplus
a situation in which quantity supplied is greater than quantity demanded

shortage
a situation in which quantity demanded is greater than quantity supplied

FIGURE 4.9

Markets Not in Equilibrium

In panel (a), there is a surplus. Because the market price of $2.50 is above the equilibrium price, the quantity supplied (10 cones) exceeds the quantity demanded (4 cones). Suppliers try to increase sales by cutting the price of a cone, and this moves the price toward its equilibrium level. In panel (b), there is a shortage. Because the market price of $1.50 is below the equilibrium price, the quantity demanded (10 cones) exceeds the quantity supplied (4 cones). With too many buyers chasing too few goods, suppliers can take advantage of the shortage by raising the price. Hence, in both cases, the price adjustment moves the market toward the equilibrium of supply and demand.

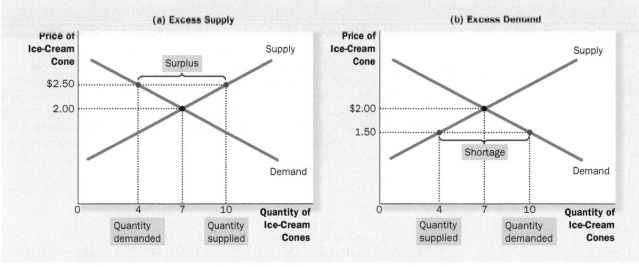

that are available. With too many buyers chasing too few goods, sellers can respond to the shortage by raising their prices without losing sales. As the price rises, quantity demanded falls, quantity supplied rises, and the market once again moves toward the equilibrium.

Thus, the activities of the many buyers and sellers automatically push the market price toward the equilibrium price. Once the market reaches its equilibrium, all buyers and sellers are satisfied, and there is no upward or downward pressure on the price. How quickly equilibrium is reached varies from market to market, depending on how quickly prices adjust. In most free markets, surpluses and shortages are only temporary because prices eventually move toward their equilibrium levels. Indeed, this phenomenon is so pervasive that it is called the **law of supply and demand:** The price of any good adjusts to bring the quantity supplied and quantity demanded for that good into balance.

law of supply and demand
the claim that the price of any good adjusts to bring the quantity supplied and the quantity demanded for that good into balance

Three Steps to Analyzing Changes in Equilibrium

So far we have seen how supply and demand together determine a market's equilibrium, which in turn determines the price of the good and the quantity of the good that buyers buy and sellers sell. Of course, the equilibrium price and

> ### TABLE 4.3
>
> A Three-Step Program for Analyzing Changes in Equilibrium
>
> 1. Decide whether the event shifts the supply or demand curve (or perhaps both).
> 2. Decide in which direction the curve shifts.
> 3. Use the supply-and-demand diagram to see how the shift changes the equilibrium price and quantity.

quantity depend on the position of the supply and demand curves. When some event shifts one of these curves, the equilibrium in the market changes. The analysis of such a change is called *comparative statics* because it involves comparing two unchanging situations—an initial equilibrium and a new equilibrium.

When analyzing how some event affects a market, we proceed in three steps. First, we decide whether the event shifts the supply curve, the demand curve, or in some cases, both curves. Second, we decide whether the curve shifts to the right or to the left. Third, we use the supply-and-demand diagram to compare the initial equilibrium and the new equilibrium, which shows how the shift affects the equilibrium price and quantity. Table 4.3 summarizes these three steps. To see how this recipe is used, let's consider various events that might affect the market for ice cream.

Example: A Change in Market Equilibrium Due to a Shift in Demand Suppose that one summer the weather is very hot. How does this event affect the market for ice cream? To answer this question, let's follow our three steps.

1. The hot weather affects the demand curve by changing people's taste for ice cream. That is, the weather changes the amount of ice cream that people want to buy at any given price. The supply curve is unchanged because the weather does not directly affect the firms that sell ice cream.
2. Because hot weather makes people want to eat more ice cream, the demand curve shifts to the right. Figure 4.10 shows this increase in demand as the shift in the demand curve from D_1 to D_2. This shift indicates that the quantity of ice cream demanded is higher at every price.
3. As Figure 4.10 shows, the increase in demand raises the equilibrium price from $2.00 to $2.50 and the equilibrium quantity from 7 to 10 cones. In other words, the hot weather increases the price of ice cream and the quantity of ice cream sold.

Shifts in Curves versus Movements along Curves Notice that when hot weather drives up the price of ice cream, the quantity of ice cream that firms supply rises, even though the supply curve remains the same. In this case, economists say there has been an increase in "quantity supplied" but no change in "supply."

FIGURE 4.10

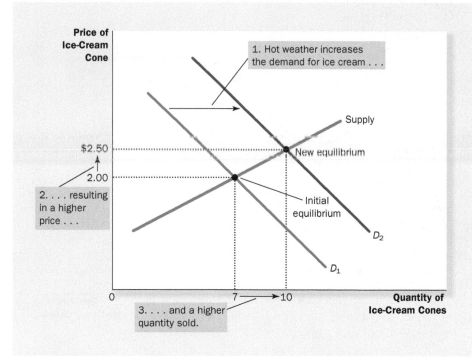

1. Hot weather increases the demand for ice cream . . .

Supply

New equilibrium

$2.50

2.00

2. . . . resulting in a higher price . . .

Initial equilibrium

D_2

D_1

Price of Ice-Cream Cone

0   7   10

3. . . . and a higher quantity sold.

Quantity of Ice-Cream Cones

How an Increase in Demand Affects the Equilibrium

An event that raises quantity demanded at any given price shifts the demand curve to the right. The equilibrium price and the equilibrium quantity both rise. Here, an abnormally hot summer causes buyers to demand more ice cream. The demand curve shifts from D_1 to D_2, which causes the equilibrium price to rise from $2.00 to $2.50 and the equilibrium quantity to rise from 7 to 10 cones.

"Supply" refers to the position of the supply curve, whereas the "quantity supplied" refers to the amount suppliers wish to sell. In this example, supply does not change, because the weather does not alter firms' desire to sell at any given price. Instead, the hot weather alters consumers' desire to buy at any given price and thereby shifts the demand curve. The increase in demand causes the equilibrium price to rise. When the price rises, the quantity supplied rises. This increase in quantity supplied is represented by the movement along the supply curve.

To summarize, a shift *in* the supply curve is called a "change in supply," and a shift *in* the demand curve is called a "change in demand." A movement *along* a fixed supply curve is called a "change in the quantity supplied," and a movement *along* a fixed demand curve is called a "change in the quantity demanded."

Example: A Change in Market Equilibrium Due to a Shift in Supply

Suppose that, during another summer, a hurricane destroys part of the sugar cane crop and drives up the price of sugar. How does this event affect the market for ice cream? Once again, to answer this question, we follow our three steps.

1. The change in the price of sugar, an input into making ice cream, affects the supply curve. By raising the costs of production, it reduces the amount of ice cream that firms want to produce and sell at any given price. The demand curve does not change, because the higher cost of inputs does not directly affect the amount of ice cream households wish to buy.

How a Decrease in Supply Affects the Equilibrium

An event that reduces quantity supplied at any given price shifts the supply curve to the left. The equilibrium price rises, and the equilibrium quantity falls. Here, an increase in the price of sugar (an input) causes sellers to supply less ice cream. The supply curve shifts from S_1 to S_2, which causes the equilibrium price of ice cream to rise from \$2.00 to \$2.50 and the equilibrium quantity to fall from 7 to 4 cones.

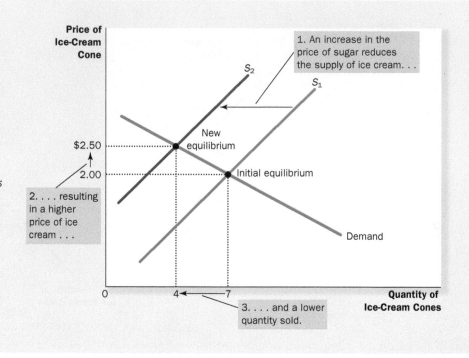

2. The supply curve shifts to the left because, at every price, the total amount that firms are willing to sell is reduced. Figure 4.11 illustrates this decrease in supply as a shift in the supply curve from S_1 to S_2.

3. As Figure 4.11 shows, the shift in the supply curve raises the equilibrium price from \$2.00 to \$2.50 and lowers the equilibrium quantity from 7 to 4 cones. As a result of the sugar price increase, the price of ice cream rises, and the quantity of ice cream sold falls.

Example: Shifts in Both Supply and Demand Now suppose that the heat wave and the hurricane occur during the same summer. To analyze this combination of events, we again follow our three steps.

1. We determine that both curves must shift. The hot weather affects the demand curve because it alters the amount of ice cream that households want to buy at any given price. At the same time, when the hurricane drives up sugar prices, it alters the supply curve for ice cream because it changes the amount of ice cream that firms want to sell at any given price.

2. The curves shift in the same directions as they did in our previous analysis: The demand curve shifts to the right, and the supply curve shifts to the left. Figure 4.12 illustrates these shifts.

3. As Figure 4.12 shows, there are three possible outcomes that might result, depending on the relative size of the demand and supply shifts. In both cases, the equilibrium price rises. In panel (a), where demand increases substantially while

FIGURE 4.12

A Shift in Both Supply and Demand

Here we observe a simultaneous increase in demand and decrease in supply. Three outcomes are possible. In panel (a), the equilibrium price rises from P_1 to P_2, and the equilibrium quantity rises from Q_1 to Q_2. In panel (b), the equilibrium price again rises from P_1 to P_2, but the equilibrium quantity falls from Q_1 to Q_2. Finally, in panel (c), the equilibrium price rises from P_1 to P_2, but the equilibrium quantity remains unchanged at Q_1.

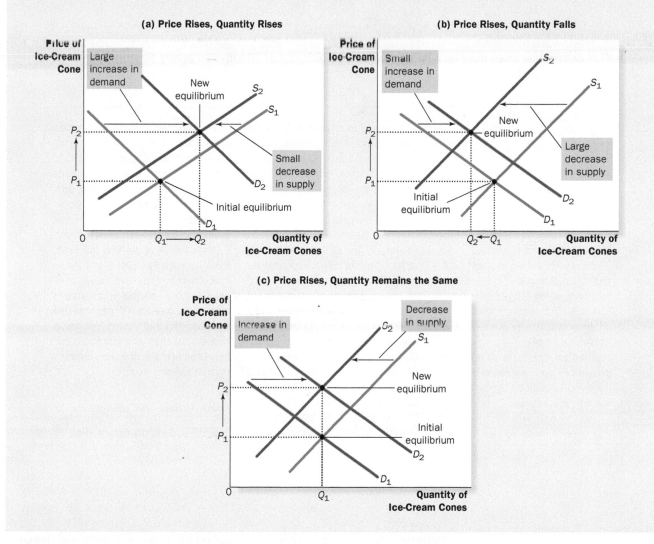

supply falls just a little, the equilibrium quantity also rises. By contrast, in panel (b), where supply falls substantially while demand rises just a little, the equilibrium quantity falls. In panel (c) supply and demand both change by the same magnitude such that the equilibrium quantity stays the same but the price rises. Thus, these events certainly raise the price of ice cream, but their impact on the amount of ice cream sold is ambiguous (that is, it could go either way).

IN THE NEWS

SUPPLY, DEMAND, AND TECHNOLOGY

This article discusses how technology (a supply shifter) and changes in tastes and preferences (a demand shifter) can have a big impact on the market for traditional goods, such as pulp and paper.

Analysts Say Pulp Mill Closure Signals Tougher Times Ahead

FREDERICTON (CP) — Forestry officials are warning of tough times ahead as technology and the rise of the Internet swing through the pulp and paper industry like an axe.

The axe fell earlier this month on the small town of Nackawic in western New Brunswick, where 400 jobs were lost and hundreds of other people were affected by the abrupt closure of the St. Anne-Nackawic pulp mill.

The New York-based owners of the mill blamed the rising cost of wood and the rising value of the loonie as major reasons for the closure.

Industry observers say it didn't help that the mill produced bleached hardwood pulp for use in products like photographic paper. David Chaundy, senior economist with the Atlantic Provinces Economic Council, said digital photography and the Internet are depressing demand for items like photographic paper and newsprint.

He said the Maritimes could see more closures in its all-important forestry sector. "There are definitely concerns that some of our mills are on the higher end of the cost curve and therefore are more vulnerable to reductions in commodity prices, or, if they're part of a multinational operation, to the closure of plants," Chaundy said. "That risk remains."

Analysts expect the demand for pulp, lumber and newsprint to be weaker over the next two to three years. Competition from countries in the southern hemisphere is hurting Canadian pulp and paper production. The strong Canadian dollar is also a factor in declining profits, since forest products such as lumber, pulp, and paper trade on world markets in U.S. dollars. It's estimated that each one-cent rise in the Canadian dollar drains about $500 million Cdn in revenues from the country's forest industry.

Yvon Poitras of the New Brunswick Forest Products Association said industries in New Brunswick feel the impact of volatile world markets more acutely because the province is so small. He said there are no other forestry closures in New Brunswick's immediate future. But he said all bets are off looking ahead to the next two or three years.

Source: Canadian Press, "Tough times seen for forestry industry," September 27, 2004. Copyright by The Canadian Press.

Summary We have just seen three examples of how to use supply and demand curves to analyze a change in equilibrium. Whenever an event shifts the supply curve, the demand curve, or perhaps both curves, you can use these tools to predict how the event will alter the amount sold in equilibrium and the price at which the good is sold. Table 4.4 shows the predicted outcome for any combination of shifts in the two curves. To make sure you understand how to use the tools of supply and demand, pick a few entries in this table and make sure you can explain to yourself why the table contains the prediction it does.

NEL

TABLE 4.4

What Happens to Price and Quantity When Supply or Demand Shifts?

As a quick quiz, make sure you can explain each of the entries in this table using a supply-and-demand diagram.

	No Change in Supply	An Increase in Supply	A Decrease in Supply
No Change in Demand	P same Q same	P down Q up	P up Q down
An Increase in Demand	P up Q up	P ambiguous Q up	P up Q ambiguous
A Decrease in Demand	P down Q down	P down Q ambiguous	P ambiguous Q down

QuickQuiz   On the appropriate diagram, show what happens to the market for pizza if the price of tomatoes rises. • On a separate diagram, show what happens to the market for pizza if the price of hamburgers falls.

CONCLUSION: HOW PRICES ALLOCATE RESOURCES

This chapter has analyzed supply and demand in a single market. Although our discussion has centred around the market for ice cream, the lessons learned here apply in most other markets as well. Whenever you go to a store to buy something, you are contributing to the demand for that item. Whenever you look for a job, you are contributing to the supply of labour services. Because supply and demand are such pervasive economic phenomena, the model of supply and demand is a powerful tool for analysis. We will be using this model repeatedly in the following chapters.

One of the ten principles of economics discussed in Chapter 1 is that markets are usually a good way to organize economic activity. Although it is still too early to judge whether market outcomes are good or bad, in this chapter we have begun to see how markets work. In any economic system, scarce resources have to be allocated among competing uses. Market economies harness the forces of supply and demand to serve that end. Supply and demand together determine the prices of the economy's many different goods and services; prices in turn are the signals that guide the allocation of resources.

For example, consider the allocation of beachfront land. Because the amount of this land is limited, not everyone can enjoy the luxury of living by the beach. Who gets this resource? The answer is: Whoever is willing to pay the price. The price of beachfront land adjusts until the quantity of land demanded exactly balances the quantity supplied. Thus, in market economies, prices are the mechanism for rationing scarce resources.

Similarly, prices determine who produces each good and how much is produced. For instance, consider farming. Because we need food to survive, it is crucial that some people work on farms. What determines who is a farmer and who is not? In a free society, there is no government planning agency making this decision and ensuring an adequate supply of food. Instead, the allocation of workers to farms is based on the job decisions of millions of workers. This decentralized system works well because these decisions depend on prices. The prices of food and the wages of farm workers (the price of their labour) adjust to ensure that enough people choose to be farmers.

If a person had never seen a market economy in action, the whole idea might seem preposterous. Economies are large groups of people engaged in many interdependent activities. What prevents decentralized decision making from degenerating into chaos? What coordinates the actions of the millions of people with their varying abilities and desires? What ensures that what needs to be done does in fact get done? The answer, in a word, is *prices*. If market economies are guided by an invisible hand, as Adam Smith famously suggested, then the price system is the baton that the invisible hand uses to conduct the economic orchestra.

SUMMARY

- Economists use the model of supply and demand to analyze competitive markets. In a competitive market, there are many buyers and sellers, each of whom has little or no influence on the market price.

- The demand curve shows how the quantity of a good demanded depends on the price. According to the law of demand, as the price of a good falls, the quantity demanded rises. Therefore, the demand curve slopes downward.

- In addition to price, other determinants of how much consumers want to buy include income, the prices of substitutes and complements, tastes, expectations, and the number of buyers. If one of these factors changes, the demand curve shifts.

- The supply curve shows how the quantity of a good supplied depends on the price. According to the law of supply, as the price of a good rises, the quantity supplied rises. Therefore, the supply curve slopes upward.

- In addition to price, other determinants of how much producers want to sell include input prices, technology, expectations, and the number of sellers. If one of these factors changes, the supply curve shifts.

- The intersection of the supply and demand curves determines the market equilibrium. At the equilibrium price, the quantity demanded equals the quantity supplied.

- The behaviour of buyers and sellers naturally drives markets toward their equilibrium. When the market price is above the equilibrium price, there is a surplus of the good, which causes the market price to fall. When the market price is below the equilibrium price, there is a shortage, which causes the market price to rise.

- To analyze how any event influences a market, we use the supply-and-demand diagram to examine how the event affects the equilibrium price and quantity. To do this we follow three steps. First, we decide whether the event shifts the supply curve or the demand curve (or both). Second, we decide which direction the curve shifts. Third, we compare the new equilibrium with the initial equilibrium.

- In market economies, prices are the signals that guide economic decisions and thereby allocate scarce resources. For every good in the economy, the price ensures that supply and demand are in balance. The equilibrium price then determines how much of the good buyers choose to purchase and how much sellers choose to produce.

KEY CONCEPTS

market, p. 70
competitive market, p. 70
quantity demanded, p. 71
law of demand, p. 71
demand schedule, p. 71
demand curve, p. 72
normal good, p. 74

inferior good, p. 74
substitutes, p. 75
complements, p. 75
quantity supplied, p. 77
law of supply, p. 78
supply schedule, p. 78
supply curve, p. 78

equilibrium, p. 81
equilibrium price, p. 81
equilibrium quantity, p. 81
surplus, p. 82
shortage, p. 82
law of supply and demand, p. 83

QUESTIONS FOR REVIEW

1. What is a competitive market? Briefly describe the types of markets other than perfectly competitive markets.

2. What are the demand schedule and the demand curve, and how are they related? Why does the demand curve slope downward?

3. Does a change in consumers' tastes lead to a movement along the demand curve or a shift in the demand curve? Does a change in price lead to a movement along the demand curve or a shift in the demand curve?

4. Popeye's income declines and, as a result, he buys more spinach. Is spinach an inferior or a normal good? What happens to Popeye's demand curve for spinach?

5. What are the supply schedule and the supply curve, and how are they related? Why does the supply curve slope upward?

6. Does a change in producers' technology lead to a movement along the supply curve or a shift in the supply curve? Does a change in price lead to a movement along the supply curve or a shift in the supply curve?

7. Define the equilibrium of a market. Describe the forces that move a market toward its equilibrium.

8. Beer and pizza are complements because they are often enjoyed together. When the price of beer rises, what happens to the supply, demand, quantity supplied, quantity demanded, and the price in the market for pizza?

9. Describe the role of prices in market economies.

PROBLEMS AND APPLICATIONS

1. Explain each of the following statements using supply-and-demand diagrams.
   a. When a cold snap hits Florida, the price of orange juice rises in supermarkets throughout Canada.
   b. When the weather turns warm in Quebec every summer, the prices of hotel rooms in Caribbean resorts plummet.
   c. When a war breaks out in the Middle East, the price of gasoline rises, while the price of a used SUV falls.

2. "An increase in the demand for notebooks raises the quantity of notebooks demanded, but not the quantity supplied." Is this statement true or false? Explain.

3. Consider the market for minivans. For each of the events listed below, identify which of the determinants of demand or supply are affected. Also indicate whether demand or supply is increased or decreased. Then show the effect on the price and quantity of minivans.
   a. People decide to have more children.
   b. A strike by steelworkers raises steel prices.
   c. Engineers develop new automated machinery for the production of minivans.
   d. The price of SUVs rises.
   e. A stock market crash lowers people's wealth.

4. Over the past 20 years, technological advances have reduced the cost of computer chips. How do you think this has affected the market for computers? For computer software? For typewriters?

5. Using supply-and-demand diagrams, show the effect of the following events on the market for sweatshirts.
   a. A hurricane in South Carolina damages the cotton crop.
   b. The price of leather jackets falls.
   c. All colleges require morning calisthenics in appropriate attire.
   d. New knitting machines are invented.

6. Suppose that in the year 2010, the number of births is temporarily high. How does this baby boom affect the price of baby-sitting services in 2015 and 2025? (Hint: Five-year-olds need baby-sitters, whereas fifteen-year-olds can be baby-sitters.)

7. Ketchup is a complement (as well as a condiment) for hot dogs. If the price of hot dogs rises, what happens to the market for ketchup? For tomatoes? For tomato juice? For orange juice?

8. Identify the flaws in this analysis. "If more Canadians go on a low-carb diet, the demand for bread will fall. The decrease in the demand for bread will cause the price of bread to fall. The lower price, however, will then increase the demand. In the new equilibrium, Canadians might end up consuming more bread than they did initially."

9. The market for pizza has the following demand and supply schedules:

Price	Quantity Demanded	Quantity Supplied
$4	135	26
5	104	53
6	81	81
7	68	98
8	53	110
9	39	121

Graph the demand and supply curves. What is the equilibrium price and quantity in this market? If the actual price in this market was *above* the equilibrium price, what would drive the market toward the equilibrium? If the actual price in this market was *below* the equilibrium price, what would drive the market toward the equilibrium?

10. Because bagels and cream cheese are often eaten together, they are complements.
    a. We observe that both the equilibrium price of cream cheese and the equilibrium quantity of bagels have risen. What could be responsible for this pattern—a fall in the price of flour or a fall in the price of milk? Illustrate and explain your answer.
    b. Suppose instead that the equilibrium price of cream cheese has risen but the equilibrium quantity of bagels has fallen. What could be responsible for this pattern—a rise in the price of flour or a rise in the price of milk? Illustrate and explain your answer.

11. Suppose that the price of hockey tickets at your school is determined by market forces. Currently, the demand and supply schedules are as follows:

Price	Quantity Demanded	Quantity Supplied
$4	10 000	8000
8	8 000	8000
12	6 000	8000
16	4 000	8000
20	2 000	8000

a. Draw the demand and supply curves. What is unusual about this supply curve? Why might this be true?
b. What are the equilibrium price and quantity of tickets?

c. Your school plans to increase total enrollment next year by 5000 students. The additional students will have the following demand schedule:

Price	Quantity Demanded
$4	4000
8	3000
12	2000
16	1000
20	0

Now add the old demand schedule and the demand schedule for the new students to calculate the new demand schedule for the entire school. What will be the new equilibrium price and quantity?

12. Consider the markets for DVD movies, TV screens, and tickets to movie theatres.
   a. For each pair, identify whether they are complements or substitutes:
      —DVDs and TV screens
      —DVDs and movie tickets
      —TV screens and movie tickets
   b. Suppose a technological advance reduces the cost of manufacturing TV screens. Draw a diagram to show what happens to the market for TV screens.
   c. Draw two more diagrams to show how the change in the market for TV screens affects the markets for DVDs and movie tickets

13. Market research has revealed the following information about the market for chocolate bars: The demand schedule can be represented by the equation $Q^D = 1600 - 300P$, where Q^D is the quantity demanded and P is the price. The supply schedule can be represented by the equation $Q^S = 1400 + 700P$, where Q^S is the quantity supplied.

   a. Calculate the equilibrium price and quantity in the market for chocolate bars.
   b. Say that in response to a major industry ad campaign, the demand schedule for chocolate bars shifted to the right, as represented by the equation $Q^D = 1800 - 300P$. What happens to the equilibrium price and quantity of chocolate bars in this case?
   c. Returning to the original demand schedule, say that the price of cocoa beans, a major ingredient in the production of chocolate bars, increased because of a drought in sub-Saharan Africa, a major producer of cocoa, changing the supply schedule to $Q^S = 1500 + 700P$. What happens to the equilibrium price and quantity in this case?

14. A survey shows an increase in drug use by young people. In the ensuing debate, two hypotheses are proposed:
   —Reduced police efforts have increased the availability of drugs on the street.
   —Cutbacks in educational efforts have decreased awareness of the dangers of drug addiction.
   a. Use supply-and-demand diagrams to show how each of these hypotheses could lead to an increase in the quantity of drugs consumed.
   b. How could information on what has happened to the price of drugs help us to distinguish between these explanations?

15. Consider the following events: Scientists reveal that consumption of oranges decreases the risk of diabetes and, at the same time, farmers use a new fertilizer that makes orange trees more productive. Illustrate and explain what effect these changes have on the equilibrium price and quantity of oranges.

http://   For more study tools, please visit http://www.mankiw5e.nelson.com.

Chapter 4
The Algebra of Supply and Demand

As we have seen, the competitive market is in equilibrium when supply and demand are equal. Since we have assumed, for simplicity, that supply and demand are linear functions, if we had the equations of these lines we could use basic algebra to solve for equilibrium price and quantity traded. In reality, economists often do estimate these equations for different industries, so it is not a giant leap for us to use equations, too.

Example 1

Suppose we are told that in the market for USB flash drives, demand is given by $Qd = 100 - 3P$ and supply is given by $Qs = 2P + 20$.

First of all, notice that the coefficient on Price in the demand equation is negative. It should be, since we know the demand curve is negatively sloped. Similarly, the coefficient on Price in the supply curve is positive, since the supply curve is positively sloped.

Second, notice that both equations are written in the form $Q = f(P)$. But when we graph supply and demand, P is on the y-axis. What we actually graph are the inverse demand and inverse supply curves. We can derive these inverse equations simply by rewriting them so that P is on the left-hand side.

For the inverse demand equation:

$$Qd = 100 - 3P$$

$$3P = 100 - Qd$$

$$P = 100/3 - Qd/3 \qquad \text{(notice the curve is still negatively sloped)}$$

For the inverse supply equation:

$$Qs = 2P + 20$$

$$2P = Qs - 20$$

$$P = Qs/2 - 10 \qquad \text{(notice the curve is still positively sloped)}$$

We can solve for equilibrium using either set of equations. The only difference is that if we use the Q = equations, we find equilibrium P first and then equilibrium quantity traded; if we use the inverse P = equations, we find equilibrium quantity traded first and then equilibrium P.

Now let's solve the original equations to find equilibrium P and Q:

In equilibrium, Qd = Qs (note that this is true only in equilibrium). Set Qd = Qs:

$$100 - 3P = 2P + 20$$

$$80 = 5P$$

$$P = 16 \quad \text{so equilibrium price is \$16.}$$

Now substitute P = 16 into either the demand or supply equation to get equilibrium Q. It doesn't matter which equation you pick because we set Qd = Qs so we'll get the same quantity either way.

If we substitute P = 16 into the demand equation:

$$Qd = 100 - 3(16)$$

$$Qd = 52$$

If we substitute P = 16 into the supply equation:

$$Qs = 2(16) + 20$$

$$Qs = 52$$

Since Qd = Qs is quantity traded in equilibrium, then equilibrium Q is 52 units of output.

Example 2

Let's use the same equations we used in the previous example.

Suppose that the market is not in equilibrium (we'll see more about this in Chapter 6). Suppose the current price in the market was $12. What is the quantity traded in the market?

At a price of $12, we need to calculate Qd and Qs separately because they will not be equal because the market is not in equilibrium. To do this, we just substitute P = 12 into both equations:

For quantity demanded:

$$Qd = 100 - 3(12)$$

$$Qd = 64$$

For quantity supplied:

$$Qs = 2(12) + 20$$

$$Qs = 44$$

Here, Qd > Qs resulting in a shortage.

What quantity will actually be traded in the market? The rule is that the short side dominates. This means that whichever is less, Qd or Qs, will be the amount traded. If Qd > Qs, effectively consumers can demand all they want but only the amount producers are willing to supply can be purchased. If Qs > Qd, suppliers can supply all they want but only the quantity consumers are willing to buy will be purchased. In our example, the quantity traded will be 44.

Practice Problems

1. Market demand is given as Qd = 200 – 3P. Market supply is given as Qs = 2P + 100. In a perfectly competitive equilibrium, what will be price and quantity traded in the market?
   a. price will be $140 and quantity will be 20
   b. price will be $20 and quantity will be 140
   c. price will be $60 and quantity will be 20
   d. price will be $120 and quantity will be 340

2. Market demand is given as Qd = 200 – 3P. Market supply is given as Qs = 2P + 100. What would result if the market price were $30?
   a. a shortage of 110
   b. a surplus of 110
   c. a surplus of 50
   d. a shortage of 50

3. Market demand is given as Qd = 200 – 3P. Market supply is given as Qs = 2P + 100. What would result if the market price were $15?
   a. a shortage of 25
   b. a surplus of 25
   c. a surplus of 130
   d. a shortage of 130

Answers: 1 b   2 c   3 a

4 The Market Forces of Supply and Demand

I. Chapter Overview

A. Context and Purpose

Earlier chapters provided an overview of the "economic way of thinking" in order to explain the operation of a market economy such as that of Canada. One of the cornerstones of a market economy is the interaction of supply and demand. Unfortunately, these terms are not well understood: A parrot can be taught to squawk "supply and demand" without any knowledge of the concepts. In reading the newspapers on any given day, examples of the misuse of supply and demand can be found. The terms take on a very specific meaning in economics that differs from their everyday use. This chapter explains what an economist means by supply and demand and shows how they interact to determine prices and quantities of goods and services. It also shows how various factors that change either supply or demand ultimately lead to changes in market prices and quantities.

B. Helpful Hints

1. *Supply means willingness to sell.* In everyday usage, supply often refers to physical stocks of a product or resource in the form of inventories available for sale. In economics, however, **supply** means *willingness to sell*. For example, the newspapers often report changes in global petroleum supplies, when really they mean inventories or petroleum reserves. The supply of petroleum is the willingness to sell those reserves, not the stock of petroleum itself.

2. *Demand means willingness to buy.* Demand is not simply consumer wants. Demand represents wants backed up by dollars and willingness to spend them.

3. *A market is a collection of buyers and sellers.* Markets are not physical locations; rather, they are the interaction of buyers and sellers. Such interaction *can* occur at a physical location: for example, an auction may represent a separate market. However, buyers and sellers can interact on a national or even global level, particularly as electronic communications grow. Money markets, for example, involve buyers and sellers around the world.

4. *"Demand" is the entire schedule or curve.* Demand refers to the whole demand schedule or demand curve, not just a point on the curve. It represents all of the price–quantity combinations that are acceptable to consumers. Because of this, increased sales that occur due to a price cut are not referred to as an increase in *demand*. There is, of course, an increase in the *quantity demanded*, but this is not an increase (or shift to the right) in demand itself.

5. *"Quantity demanded" is a point on the demand curve.* When there is a change in price, quantity demanded changes, but demand itself does not change.

6. *"Supply" is the entire schedule or curve.* Supply refers to the whole supply schedule or supply curve, not just a point on the curve. For supply to shift, the underlying factors that are held constant in plotting a supply curve must change. Changing the price simply means that we move to a new point on the existing supply curve, which represents a new quantity. Of course an increase in price encourages suppliers to sell more; however, this response to higher price is called an increase in *quantity supplied*, rather than an increase (or shift) in *supply*.

7. *"Quantity supplied" is a point on the supply curve.* When there is a change in price, the quantity supplied changes, even though the supply curve itself does not shift. The quantity supplied at a particular price is the amount that sellers are willing to sell at that price.

II. Self-Testing Challenges

A. True/False Questions

_____1. A decrease in the price of soft drinks will increase their demand (shift the curve to the right).

_____2. The supply of petroleum is fixed because there is only a finite amount in the ground.

_____3. At the equilibrium price, the amount that sellers are willing to sell is just equal to the amount that buyers are willing to buy.

_____4. An improvement in technology tends to reduce the supply (shift it to the left).

_____5. An increase in raw materials prices tends to reduce the supply (shift it to the left).

_____6. If sellers expect prices to rise in the future, this could cause prices to rise today by encouraging sellers to reduce their current supply in anticipation of a price hike.

_____7. A market refers to a physical location in which buyers and sellers interact.

_____8. A price that is below equilibrium results in excess supply.

_____9. Excess demand tends to drive price up until the market reaches equilibrium price and quantity.

_____10. An increase in supply tends to increase equilibrium price and quantity.

_____11. An equal increase in both supply and demand tends to increase equilibrium price and quantity.

_____12. An increase in supply accompanied by an equal decrease in demand tends to decrease equilibrium price while leaving equilibrium quantity unchanged.

_____13. The market supply curve is the vertical summation of all the individual supply curves.

_____14. Assuming that pizza and beer are complements, a decrease in the price of pizza would increase the demand for beer.

_____15. If pizza and hamburgers are substitutes for each other, a decrease in the price of pizza would increase the demand for hamburgers.

B. Multiple-Choice Questions

1. Which one of the following would decrease the demand (shift the curve to the left) for beer?
    a. The price of a substitute, wine, falls.
    b. The price of beer increases to $5.00 per bottle.
    c. Bars begin giving away spicy snacks to their customers.
    d. A new Health Canada study concludes that beer helps to reduce heart disease.

2. If buyers believe that the price of gasoline will rise soon, which one of the following is the **MOST** likely immediate result?
    a. an increase in the quantity demanded, due to the change in supply
    b. a decrease (shift to the left) in the demand for gasoline, due to a shift to substitutes
    c. a decrease (shift to the left) in the demand for gasoline, due to a change in tastes
    d. an increase (shift to the right) in the demand for gasoline, due to a change in expectations

3. A new technological breakthrough in genetic engineering makes it possible to grow twice as much corn per hectare as had been possible in the past. Which one of the following is the **MOST** likely outcome of this development?
    a. an increase in the demand for corn, due to the greatly reduced price
    b. an increase in quantity supplied, due to the increased willingness to sell corn
    c. an increase (shift to the right) in the supply of corn, due to the reduced cost of production
    d. a decrease (shift to the left) in the supply of corn, due to the increased costs associated with the new technology

149

4. A university student made the following statement to a friend at a university sporting event: "This football stadium is a good example of how unrealistic economics is: my economics professor claims that, according to a so-called 'Law of Supply,' supply varies directly with price, yet anybody can look around and see that the supply is fixed at 10 000 seats, no matter what the price is!" Which one of the following explains what is wrong with the student's statement?
   a. Supply is not fixed at 10 000 seats; it is quantity supplied that is fixed.
   b. This is simply an exception to the Law of Supply; it does not mean that it is not relevant for most cases.
   c. Supply is not the same thing as the physical stock of a good or service that is available; rather, supply is willingness to sell.

Use the following graph to answer questions 5–8:

The Market for Personal Sized Pizzas

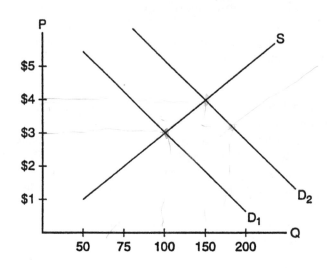

5. Referring to the graph above, which one of the following describes the initial equilibrium price and quantity?
   a. P = $2.00; Q = 75.
   b. P = $2.00; Q = 150.
   c. P = $3.00; Q = 100.
   d. P = $4.00; Q = 75.

6. Which one of the following would cause the demand for pizzas among university students to shift to the right?
   a. an increase in financial aid to university students
   b. half-price pizzas for anybody with a university ID
   c. an increase in the price of a complement, i.e., beer
   d. a decrease in the price of a substitute, i.e., hamburgers

150

7. After an increase in demand, which one of the following describes the new equilibrium price and quantity?
    a. P = $2.00; Q = 75.
    b. P = $2.00; Q = 150.
    c. P = $3.00; Q = 100.
    d. P = $4.00; Q = 150.

8. Which one of the following describes the effect of increase in demand on supply?
    a. It would first increase, then decrease over time.
    b. It would neither rise nor fall, although quantity supplied would increase.
    c. It would decrease (shift to the left).
    d. It would increase (shift to the right).

Use the following graph to answer questions 9–12:

The Market for Hand-Held Calculators

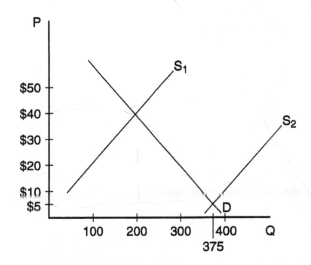

9. Referring to the graph above, which one of the following describes the initial equilibrium price and quantity?
    a. P = $5; Q = 375.
    b. P = $10; Q = 350.
    c. P = $20; Q = 100.
    d. P = $40; Q = 200.

10. Which one of the following is a factor that would cause an increase (shift to the right) in supply?
    a. improved technology
    b. higher labour costs
    c. lower number of sellers
    d. increased demand

11. Which choice below would be the new equilibrium price and quantity as a result of the increase in supply?
    a. P = $5; Q = 375.
    b. P = $10; Q = 350.
    c. P = $20; Q = 100.
    d. P = $30; Q = 250.

12. Suppose that the demand for calculators rose even more than the supply had increased. Which one of the following describes the changes in equilibrium price and quantity that would be the net effect of the two increases?
    a. an increase in price but a decrease in quantity
    b. an increase in quantity but a slight decrease in price
    c. decreases in both quantity and price
    d. increases in both quantity and price

13. Which one of the following describes what supply curves represent?
    a. inventories
    b. physical stocks
    c. total production
    d. willingness to sell

14. Which one of the following does a supply curve for a good or service show?
    a. the seller's target price.
    b. the seller's minimum acceptable price.
    c. the seller's maximum acceptable price.
    d. the seller's average acceptable price.

15. If equilibrium quantity rises but equilibrium price remains unchanged, which one of the following is the cause?
    a. an increase in both supply and demand
    b. a decrease in both demand and supply
    c. a decrease in demand and an increase in supply
    d. an increase in demand and a decrease in supply

16. If equilibrium price rises but equilibrium quantity remains unchanged, which one of the following is the cause?
    a. a decrease in demand and an increase in supply
    b. an increase in demand and a decrease in supply
    c. an increase in both supply and demand
    d. a decrease in both demand and supply

17. If equilibrium quantity and price rise, which one of the following is the cause?
    a. a decrease in both demand and supply.
    b. an increase in demand and decrease in supply.
    c. a decrease in demand and increase in supply.
    d. an increase in demand without a change in supply.

18. A freeze that destroys half of the coffee crop in South America would likely raise the price of coffee. Which one of the following would happen in turn?
    a. reduced demand for both coffee and tea
    b. reduced quantity demanded for both coffee and tea
    c. reduced demand for coffee and increased demand for tea
    d. reduced quantity demanded for coffee and increased demand for tea.

19. Which one of the following describes an inferior good?
    a. one for which demand rises as income rises
    b. one for which demand falls as income rises
    c. one for which demand is unrelated to income
    d. one for which demand is low because of the low quality of the good

20. Suppose that there is a shortage of parking spaces in downtown Toronto during weekdays. Which one of the following explains how the shortage can be eliminated?
    a. by lowering the price
    b. by decreasing the supply
    c. by allowing the price to rise
    d. by increasing the quantity demanded

C. Short-Answer Questions

1. What would happen to the demand for apples if consumers' incomes rose, and apples are a normal good? What if apples are an inferior good?

    _____
    _____
    _____
    _____

2. Explain why the price of a complement or a substitute can alter the demand for a good, even though the price of the good itself does not shift the demand.

    _____
    _____
    _____
    _____

D. Practice Problems

The supply and demand schedules below show hypothetical prices and quantities in the market for corn. The initial quantity supplied is shown by Q_s, and the quantity demanded is Q_d.

The Market for Corn
(in thousands of tonnes)

Price	Q_d	Q_s	$Q_{s'}$
$6.00	220	400	____
$5.50	240	360	____
$5.00	260	320	____
$4.50	280	280	____
$4.00	300	240	____
$3.50	320	200	____
$3.00	340	160	____

1. Plot the supply and demand curves for the initial supply and demand, Q_s and Q_d, on the graph that follows the questions.

   a. The equilibrium price of corn is $_____.

   b. The equilibrium quantity of corn is _____ thousand tonnes.

   c. At a price of $3.00 per tonne, there would be a (shortage, surplus) _____ of _____ thousand tonnes, and the price would tend to (fall, rise) _____.

   d. At a price of $5.00 per tonne, there would be a (shortage, surplus) _____ of _____ thousand tonnes, and the price would tend to (fall, rise) _____.

2. Suppose that the supply of corn increased by 60 thousand tonnes at every price. Show the new supply schedule as $Q_{s'}$ on the previous table.

   a. The new equilibrium price of corn is $_____.

   b. The new equilibrium quantity of corn is _____ thousand tonnes.

   c. Has the demand for corn changed as a result of this change in supply? Explain briefly._____
   _____
   _____

3. Give an example of a factor that could have caused such an increase in the supply of corn, and explain briefly._____
   _____
   _____

154

4. Notice that the increase in supply has resulted in a lower price and a higher quantity. Does this violate the Law of Supply, which states that the quantity of a good supplied increases as its price increases, all else being equal? Explain briefly.

_____

_____

_____

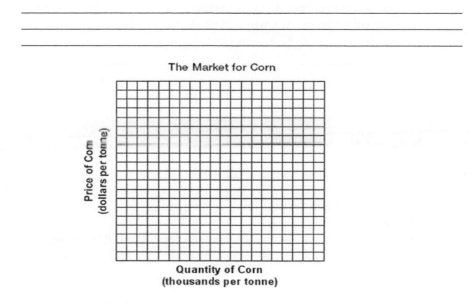

The Market for Corn

Price of Corn
(dollars per tonne)

**Quantity of Corn
(thousands per tonne)**

E. Advanced Critical Thinking

Consider the following editorial that appeared in a leading U.S. business publication following a freeze that destroyed much of the coffee crop in the late 1970s:

Coffee prices, it seems, are coming down again, after hitting a record high of $4.42 last year. An Agriculture Department economist, who had predicted $5-a-pound coffee this year, says he "underestimated the power of the U.S. consumer movement." Perhaps, or maybe, as with so many economists these days, he simply forgot his freshman economics, which has nothing to do with "movements." The coffee market is behaving the way the basic textbooks say a market behaves: Prices go up, demand falls, and prices come down.

— The Wall Street Journal, *November 30, 1977*

1. Suppose that coffee had started out at an equilibrium price of $1.00 per pound prior to the freeze.

   a. Show graphically the initial equilibrium, labelling supply and demand as S_1 and D_1, respectively. Use Q_1 to identify the original equilibrium quantity.

   b. Show graphically the effect of a freeze that destroys much of the coffee crop, labelling the new supply as S_2 and the new equilibrium quantity as Q_2. (The new equilibrium price is $4.42.)

c. Does the answer to part (b) show a change in demand? Why or why not?

_____

_____

d. Based on your analysis in parts (a–c), critique the *Wall Street Journal* editorial. What's wrong with its analysis? _____

_____

_____

_____

III. Solutions

A. True/False Questions

1. F; quantity demanded, not demand, will increase.
2. F; the physical stock of petroleum in the ground is fixed, but the supply is willingness to sell, which is not fixed.
3. T
4. F; technology tends to *increase* the supply (shift it to the right) by increasing productivity; that is, increasing output per unit of input.
5. T
6. T
7. F; a market need not be in a specific physical location; buyers and sellers can interact without being in the same location.
8. F; price below equilibrium results in excess demand, as buyers try to buy more than sellers are willing to sell at the low price.
9. T
10. F; increased supply moves the equilibrium to the right along the demand curve, resulting in a higher quantity and lower price.
11. F; an increase in both supply and demand will increase equilibrium quantity, but the effect on price depends on which curve shifts more; if they shift equally, price remains unchanged.
12. T
13. F; market supply is the horizontal summation of the individual supply curves; for each price, it represents the sum of all of the individual quantities supplied.
14. T
15. F; a decrease in the price of a good tends to decrease the demand for its substitutes.

B. Multiple-Choice Questions

1. a	6. a	11. a	16. b
2. d	7. d	12. d	17. d
3. c	8. b	13. d	18. d
4. c	9. d	14. b	19. b
5. c	10. a	15. a	20. c

C. Short-Answer Questions

1. An increase in consumer income increases the demand for normal goods and decreases the demand for inferior goods.

2. Prices of other goods are held constant in deriving a demand curve, even though they can affect consumption. When they change, the demand also changes (shifts right or left). The price of the good itself does not shift the demand, however, because price is already built into our definition of demand. Demand for a good includes all of the quantities that consumers are willing to buy at various prices of the good, thus holding other factors constant.

D. Practice Problems

1. a. $4.50

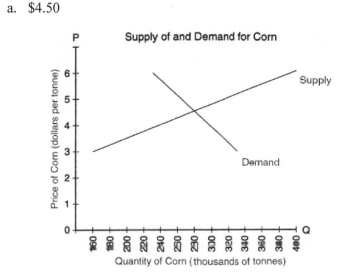

   b. 280

   c. Shortage, 180, rise

   d. Surplus, 60, fall

2. a. $4.00

   b. 300

   c. Demand has not changed. Supply increased, thus moving the equilibrium along the existing demand curve to a higher quantity and lower price.

3. Any of the factors that lower cost of production could shift the supply to the right, indicating increased willingness to sell at each price. For example, improvements in technology that increase productivity would lower cost and increase the supply.

4. No, this does not violate the Law of Supply. The Law of Supply holds other factors, such as technology, constant. The increase in supply represents a new supply curve, with an increased *willingness to sell*. Both the old and new supply curves follow the Law of Supply: as long as those other factors are constant, sellers will tend to be willing to sell more, but only at a higher price.

E. Advanced Critical Thinking

1. a   The original equilibrium should be at a price of $1.00, with the quantity simply labelled Q_1.

    b. The new equilibrium should be at a price of $4.42 and a quantity of Q_2, after a leftward shift in supply and a movement along the (unchanged) demand curve. Equilibrium price is higher and quantity is lower.

    c. Demand did not change; only the quantity demanded changed as the supply shifted left, thus moving along the existing demand curve. There were no changes in the factors that are held constant in deriving a demand curve.

    d. The newspaper's analysis was flawed. They confused (shifts in) demand with simple changes in quantity demanded in response to a price change. For the price to fall, one of the factors (other than price) affecting either supply or demand must have changed.

The Market for Coffee

ELASTICITY AND ITS APPLICATION

5

© Jason Yoder/Dreamstime.com

Learning Objectives

In this chapter, you will ...

- Learn the meaning of the elasticity of demand
- Examine what determines the elasticity of demand
- Learn the meaning of the elasticity of supply
- Examine what determines the elasticity of supply
- Apply the concept of elasticity in two very different markets

In 2007, when oil prices reached record high levels, gasoline prices in Canada skyrocketed, with average prices in Ontario, for example, increasing from about 75 cents per litre to just under $1.40. While prices have since dropped, an important question is: How did Canadian consumers respond to the higher price?

It is easy to answer this question in a broad fashion: Consumers bought less. That is simply the law of demand that we learned in the previous chapter. But you might want a precise answer: By how much did the consumption of gasoline fall? The answer to this question can be answered by using the concept of *elasticity*, which we develop in this chapter.

Elasticity is a measure of how much buyers and sellers respond to changes in market conditions. When studying how some event or policy affects a market, we can discuss not only the direction of the effects but their magnitude as well. Elasticity is useful in many applications, as we will see toward the end of the chapter.

Before proceeding, however, you might be curious about the answer to the gasoline consumption question. Many studies have examined consumers' response to gasoline prices, and they typically find that the quantity demanded responds more in the long run than it does in the short run. A 10 percent increase in the price of gasoline reduces gasoline consumption by about 2.5 percent after a year and about 6 percent after five years. About half of the long-run reduction in quantity demanded arises because people drive less and half because they switch to more fuel-efficient cars. Both responses are reflected in the demand curve and its elasticity.

THE ELASTICITY OF DEMAND

When we introduced demand in Chapter 4, we noted that consumers usually buy more of a good when its price is lower, when their incomes are higher, when the prices of substitutes for the good are higher, or when the prices of complements of the good are lower. Our discussion of demand was qualitative, not quantitative. That is, we discussed the direction in which quantity demanded moves, but not the size of the change. To measure how much consumers respond to changes in these variables, economists use the concept of **elasticity.**

elasticity
a measure of the responsiveness of quantity demanded or quantity supplied to one of its determinants

The Price Elasticity of Demand and Its Determinants

The law of demand states that a fall in the price of a good raises the quantity demanded. The **price elasticity of demand** measures how much the quantity demanded responds to a change in price. Demand for a good is said to be *elastic* if the quantity demanded responds substantially to changes in the price. Demand is said to be *inelastic* if the quantity demanded responds only slightly to changes in the price.

price elasticity of demand
a measure of how much the quantity demanded of a good responds to a change in the price of that good, computed as the percentage change in quantity demanded divided by the percentage change in price

The price elasticity of demand for any good measures how willing consumers are to move away from the good as its price rises. Thus, the elasticity reflects the many economic, social, and psychological forces that shape consumer tastes. Based on experience, however, we can state some general rules about what determines the price elasticity of demand.

Availability of Close Substitutes Goods with close substitutes tend to have more elastic demand because it is easier for consumers to switch from that good to others. For example, butter and margarine are easily substitutable. A small increase in the price of butter, assuming the price of margarine is held fixed, causes the quantity of butter sold to fall by a large amount. By contrast, because eggs are a food without a close substitute, the demand for eggs is less elastic than the demand for butter.

Necessities versus Luxuries Necessities tend to have inelastic demands, whereas luxuries have elastic demands. When the price of a visit to the dentist rises, people will not dramatically alter the number of times they go to the dentist, although they might go somewhat less often. By contrast, when the price of sailboats rises, the quantity of sailboats demanded falls substantially. The reason is that most people view dentist visits as a necessity and sailboats as a luxury. Of course, whether a good is a necessity or a luxury depends not on the intrinsic properties of the good but on the preferences of the buyer. For an avid sailor with little concern about his teeth, sailboats might be a necessity with inelastic demand and dentist visits a luxury with elastic demand.

Definition of the Market The elasticity of demand in any market depends on how we draw the boundaries of the market. Narrowly defined markets tend to have more elastic demand than broadly defined markets because it is easier to find close substitutes for narrowly defined goods. For example, food, a broad category, has a fairly inelastic demand because there are no good substitutes for food. Ice cream, a more narrow category, has a more elastic demand because it is easy to substitute other desserts for ice cream. Vanilla ice cream, a very narrow category, has a very elastic demand because other flavours of ice cream are almost perfect substitutes for vanilla.

Time Horizon   Goods tend to have more elastic demand over longer time horizons. As we saw in the introduction to this chapter, when the price of gasoline rises, the quantity of gasoline demanded falls only slightly in the first few months. Over time, however, people buy more fuel-efficient cars, switch to public transportation, or move closer to where they work. Within several years, the quantity of gasoline demanded falls substantially.

Computing the Price Elasticity of Demand

Now that we have discussed the price elasticity of demand in general terms, let's be more precise about how it is measured. Economists compute the price elasticity of demand as the percentage change in the quantity demanded divided by the percentage change in the price. That is,

$$\text{Price elasticity of demand} = \frac{\text{Percentage change in quantity demanded}}{\text{Percentage change in price}}$$

For example, suppose that a 10 percent increase in the price of an ice-cream cone causes the amount of ice cream you buy to fall by 20 percent. We calculate your elasticity of demand as

$$\text{Price elasticity of demand} = \frac{20 \text{ percent}}{10 \text{ percent}} = 2$$

In this example, the elasticity is 2, reflecting that the change in the quantity demanded is proportionately twice as large as the change in the price.

Because the quantity demanded of a good is negatively related to its price, the percentage change in quantity will always have the opposite sign as the percentage change in price. In this example, the percentage change in price is a *positive* 10 percent (reflecting an increase), and the percentage change in quantity demanded is a *negative* 20 percent (reflecting a decrease). For this reason, price elasticities of demand are sometimes reported as negative numbers. In this book we follow the common practice of dropping the minus sign and reporting all price elasticities as positive numbers. (Mathematicians call this the *absolute value.*) With this convention, a larger price elasticity implies a greater responsiveness of quantity demanded to price.

The Midpoint Method: A Better Way to Calculate Percentage Changes and Elasticities

If you try calculating the price elasticity of demand between two points on a demand curve, you will quickly notice an annoying problem: The elasticity from point A to point B seems different from the elasticity from point B to point A. For example, consider these numbers:

Point A: Price = $4   Quantity = 120

Point B: Price = $6   Quantity = 80

Going from point A to point B, the price rises by 50 percent, and the quantity falls by 33 percent, indicating that the price elasticity of demand is 33/50, or 0.66. By contrast, going from point B to point A, the price falls by 33 percent, and the quantity rises by 50 percent, indicating that the price elasticity of demand is 50/33, or 1.5.

One way to avoid this problem is to use the *midpoint method* for calculating elasticities. The standard way to compute a percentage change is to divide the change by the initial level. By contrast, the midpoint method computes a percentage change by dividing the change by the midpoint (or average) of the initial and final levels. For instance, $5 is the midpoint of $4 and $6. Therefore, according to the midpoint method, a change from $4 to $6 is considered a 40 percent rise because $(6 - 4)/5 \times 100 = 40$. Similarly, a change from $6 to $4 is considered a 40 percent fall.

Because the midpoint method gives the same answer regardless of the direction of change, it is often used when calculating the price elasticity of demand between two points. In our example, the midpoint between point A and point B is

Midpoint: Price = $5   Quantity = 100

According to the midpoint method, when going from point A to point B, the price rises by 40 percent and the quantity falls by 40 percent. Similarly, when going from point B to point A, the price falls by 40 percent and the quantity rises by 40 percent. In both directions, the price elasticity of demand equals 1.

We can express the midpoint method with the following formula for the price elasticity of demand between two points, denoted (Q_1, P_1) and (Q_2, P_2):

$$\text{Price elasticity of demand} = \frac{(Q_2 - Q_1)/[(Q_2 + Q_1)/2]}{(P_2 - P_1)/[(P_2 + P_1)/2]}$$

The numerator is the percentage change in quantity computed using the midpoint method, and the denominator is the percentage change in price computed using the midpoint method. If you ever need to calculate elasticities, you should use this formula.

In this book, however, we rarely perform such calculations. For most of our purposes, what elasticity represents—the responsiveness of quantity demanded to price—is more important than how it is calculated.

The Variety of Demand Curves

Economists classify demand curves according to their elasticity. Demand is *elastic* when the elasticity is greater than 1, so that quantity moves proportionately more than the price. Demand is *inelastic* when the elasticity is less than 1, so that quantity moves proportionately less than the price. If the elasticity is exactly 1, so that quantity moves the same amount proportionately as price, demand is said to have *unit elasticity*.

Because the price elasticity of demand measures how much quantity demanded responds to changes in the price, it is closely related to the slope of the demand curve. The following rule of thumb is a useful guide: The flatter the demand curve that passes through a given point, the greater the price elasticity of demand. The steeper the demand curve that passes through a given point, the smaller the price elasticity of demand.

Figure 5.1 shows five cases. In the extreme case of a zero elasticity shown in panel (a), demand is *perfectly inelastic,* and the demand curve is vertical. In this case, regardless of the price, the quantity demanded stays the same. As the elasticity rises, the demand curve gets flatter and flatter, as shown in panels (b), (c), and (d). At the opposite extreme shown in panel (e), demand is *perfectly elastic.* This occurs as the price elasticity of demand approaches infinity and the demand curve becomes horizontal, reflecting the fact that very small changes in the price lead to huge changes in the quantity demanded.

Finally, if you have trouble keeping straight the terms *elastic* and *inelastic,* here's a memory trick for you: *I*nelastic curves, such as in panel (a) of Figure 5.1, look like the letter *I.* *E*lastic curves, as in panel (e), look like the letter *E.* This is not a deep insight, but it might help on your next exam.

Total Revenue and the Price Elasticity of Demand

When studying changes in supply or demand in a market, one variable we often want to study is **total revenue,** the amount paid by buyers and received by sellers of the good. In any market, total revenue is $P \times Q$, the price of the good times the quantity of the good sold. We can show total revenue graphically, as in Figure 5.2. The height of the box under the demand curve is P, and the width is Q. The area of this box, $P \times Q$, equals the total revenue in this market. In Figure 5.2, where $P = \$4$ and $Q = 100$, total revenue is $\$4 \times 100$, or \$400.

total revenue (in a market) the amount paid by buyers and received by sellers of a good, computed as the price of the good times the quantity sold

How does total revenue change as one moves along the demand curve? The answer depends on the price elasticity of demand. If demand is inelastic, as in panel (a) of Figure 5.3, then an increase in the price causes an increase in total revenue. Here an increase in price from \$1 to \$3 causes the quantity demanded to fall only from 100 to 80, and so total revenue rises from \$100 to \$240. An increase in price raises $P \times Q$ because the fall in Q is proportionately smaller than the rise in P.

We obtain the opposite result if demand is elastic: An increase in the price causes a decrease in total revenue. In panel (b) of Figure 5.3, for instance, when the price rises from \$4 to \$5, the quantity demanded falls from 50 to 20, and so total revenue falls from \$200 to \$100. Because demand is elastic, the reduction in the quantity demanded is so great that it more than offsets the increase in the price. That is, an increase in price reduces $P \times Q$ because the fall in Q is proportionately greater than the rise in P.

Although the example in Figure 5.3 is extreme, it illustrates a general rule:

- When demand is inelastic (a price elasticity less than 1), price and total revenue move in the same direction.
- When demand is elastic (a price elasticity greater than 1), price and total revenue move in opposite directions.
- If demand is unit elastic (a price elasticity exactly equal to 1), total revenue remains constant when the price changes.

FIGURE 5.1

The Price Elasticity of Demand

The price elasticity of demand determines whether the demand curve is steep or flat. Note that all percentage changes are calculated using the midpoint method.

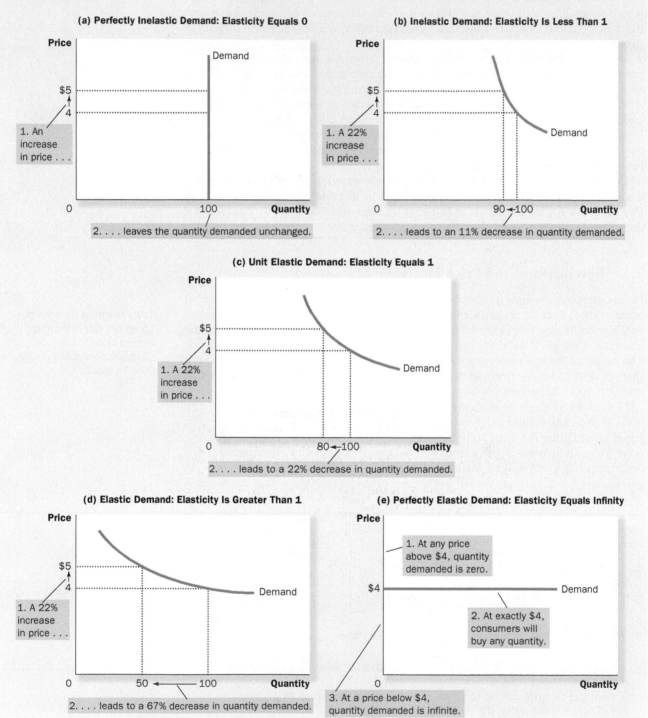

(a) Perfectly Inelastic Demand: Elasticity Equals 0

Price

Demand

$5

4

1. An increase in price . . .

0   100   Quantity

2. . . . leaves the quantity demanded unchanged.

(b) Inelastic Demand: Elasticity Is Less Than 1

Price

$5

4

1. A 22% increase in price . . .

Demand

0   90 100   Quantity

2. . . . leads to an 11% decrease in quantity demanded.

(c) Unit Elastic Demand: Elasticity Equals 1

Price

$5

4

1. A 22% increase in price . . .

Demand

0   80 100   Quantity

2. . . . leads to a 22% decrease in quantity demanded.

(d) Elastic Demand: Elasticity Is Greater Than 1

Price

$5

4

1. A 22% increase in price . . .

Demand

0   50   100   Quantity

2. . . . leads to a 67% decrease in quantity demanded.

(e) Perfectly Elastic Demand: Elasticity Equals Infinity

Price

1. At any price above $4, quantity demanded is zero.

$4   Demand

2. At exactly $4, consumers will buy any quantity.

0   Quantity

3. At a price below $4, quantity demanded is infinite.

FIGURE 5.2

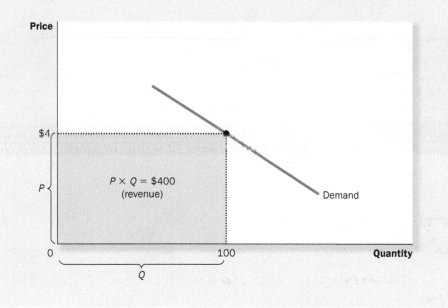

Total Revenue

The total amount paid by buyers, and received as revenue by sellers, equals the area of the box under the demand curve, P × Q. Here, at a price of $4, the quantity demanded is 100, and total revenue is $400.

Elasticity and Total Revenue along a Linear Demand Curve

Although some demand curves have an elasticity that is the same along the entire curve, that is not always the case. An example of a demand curve along which elasticity changes is a straight line, as shown in Figure 5.4. A linear demand curve has a constant slope. Recall that slope is defined as "rise over run," which here is the ratio of the change in price ("rise") to the change in quantity ("run"). This particular demand curve's slope is constant because each $1 increase in price causes the same 2-unit decrease in the quantity demanded.

Even though the slope of a linear demand curve is constant, the elasticity is not. The reason is that the slope is the ratio of *changes* in the two variables, whereas the elasticity is the ratio of *percentage changes* in the two variables. You can see this by looking at the table in Figure 5.4, which shows the demand schedule for the linear demand curve in the graph. The table uses the midpoint method to calculate the price elasticity of demand. At points with a low price and high quantity, the demand curve is inelastic. At points with a high price and low quantity, the demand curve is elastic.

The table also presents total revenue at each point on the demand curve. These numbers illustrate the relationship between total revenue and elasticity. When the price is $1, for instance, demand is inelastic, and a price increase to $2 raises total revenue. When the price is $5, demand is elastic, and a price increase to $6 reduces total revenue. Between $3 and $4, demand is exactly unit elastic, and total revenue is the same at these two prices.

FIGURE 5.3

The impact of a price change on total revenue (the product of price and quantity) depends on the elasticity of demand.

In panel (a), the demand curve is inelastic. In this case, an increase in the price leads to a decrease in quantity demanded that is proportionately smaller, so total revenue increases. Here, an increase in the price from $1 to $3 causes the quantity demanded to fall from 100 to 80. Total revenue rises from $100 to $240. In panel (b), the demand curve is elastic. In this case, an increase in the price leads to a decrease in quantity demanded that is proportionately larger, so total revenue decreases. Here, an increase in the price from $4 to $5 causes the quantity demanded to fall from 50 to 20. Total revenue falls from $200 to $100.

(a) The Case of Inelastic Demand

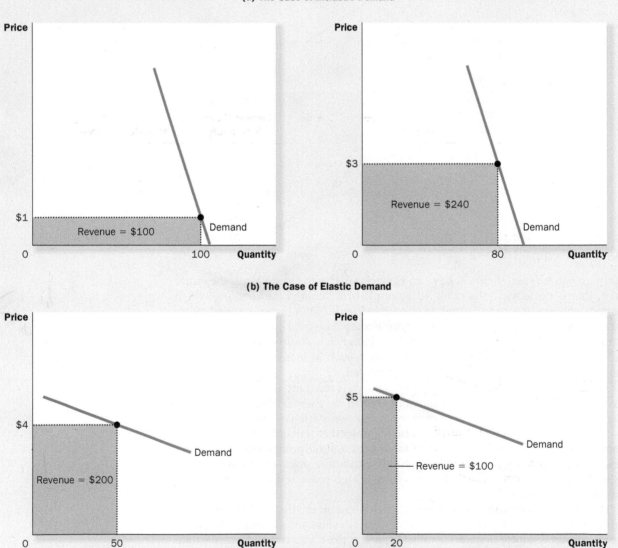

(b) The Case of Elastic Demand

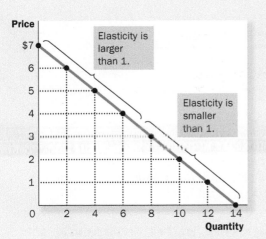

Elasticity of a Linear Demand Curve

The slope of a linear demand curve is constant, but its elasticity is not. The demand schedule in the table was used to calculate the price elasticity of demand by the midpoint method. At points with a low price and high quantity, the demand curve is inelastic. At points with a high price and low quantity, the demand curve is elastic.

Price	Quantity	Total Revenue (Price × Quantity)	Percent Change in Price	Percent Change in Quantity	Elasticity	Description
$7	0	$ 0				
			15	200	13.0	Elastic
6	2	12				
			18	67	3.7	Elastic
5	4	20				
			22	40	1.8	Elastic
4	6	24				
			29	29	1.0	Unit elastic
3	8	24				
			40	22	0.6	Inelastic
2	10	20				
			67	18	0.3	Inelastic
1	12	12				
			200	15	0.1	Inelastic
0	14	0				

Other Demand Elasticities

In addition to the price elasticity of demand, economists also use other elasticities to describe the behaviour of buyers in a market.

The Income Elasticity of Demand   The **income elasticity of demand** measures how the quantity demanded changes as consumer income changes. It is calculated as the percentage change in quantity demanded divided by the percentage change in income. That is,

$$\text{Income elasticity of demand} = \frac{\text{Percentage change in quantity demanded}}{\text{Percentage change in income}}$$

As we discussed in Chapter 4, most goods are *normal goods:* Higher income raises quantity demanded. Because quantity demanded and income move in the same direction, normal goods have positive income elasticities. A few goods, such as bus rides, are *inferior goods:* Higher income lowers the quantity demanded.

income elasticity of demand
a measure of how much the quantity demanded of a good responds to a change in consumers' income, computed as the percentage change in quantity demanded divided by the percentage change in income

IN THE NEWS

THE ELASTICITY OF CAFFEINE

This article describes an increase in the price of Tim Hortons and Starbucks coffee in Canada. According to both chains, prices went up more in Alberta than in the rest of the country because of higher wage costs. Can you think of other reasons? How elastic do you think the demand for coffee is to price changes?

Getting Your Caffeine Fix in Alberta Just Got a Little More Costly

Two major coffee-house chains hiked the price of a cuppa joe this week—the apparent result of the high cost of hiring and retaining staff.

Coffee and food items at Tim Hortons locations across the province cost about a dime more on Monday than they did the day before. On Tuesday, Starbucks outlets throughout Alberta increased their brewed coffee and tea prices by 10 cents a cup and their espresso and blended beverages by 15 cents.

The rise in the price of caffeinated black-gold seems to be yet another response to the province's oil boom: the Alberta price hikes are the highest in North America.

The only other province to see a Tim Hortons price increase on Monday was Quebec, while Starbucks announced a five-cent hike for all of the United States and Canada.

A medium double-double from Tim Hortons in Edmonton is now more expensive than in other major Canadian cities.

But Michael Percy, dean of the School of Business at the University of Alberta, doesn't think the extra dime will get between patrons and their caffeine fix. "Those types of (routine) purchases tend to be insensitive to those kinds of price increases," he said.

Moreover, he said, people are building expectations of higher prices because they're also making more money, creating an upward spiral of costs. Still, Percy said, retail businesses such as Tim Hortons and Starbucks have to strike a precarious balance in Alberta. They must pay their employees more to retain them, which forces them to hike up prices, he said. But they can't raise prices so high they'll lose patrons. "These businesses are put between a rock and a hard place," Percy said.

A TD Economics report released Tuesday showed fears that lower-income workers in non-resource jobs would suffer in Alberta's high-inflation environment were unfounded.

"In fact," the report said, "the greatest wage gains have occurred in the non-resources sector, which has led to a narrowing of the wage gap between the higher-paying and lower-paying industries."

A spokeswoman for Tim Hortons said she's confident customers will keep lining up. "As far as Tim Hortons is concerned, we still feel we provide a very good quality product at a very good price," Diane Slopek-Weber said.

She said Tim Hortons regularly reviews prices on a regional basis, focusing on factors such as the cost of energy, labour, garbage collection and gas. Based on those factors and others, Slopek-Weber said, price increases were specific to Alberta and Quebec.

A release from Starbucks suggests a similar logic, saying the larger Alberta price increase is due to regional factors, particularly rising costs within the business. Generally, prices went up across the board at Starbucks due to "our current environment of rising energy, fuel and supply chain costs," the release said.

BEAN COUNTER: What customers are paying for . . .

Tim Hortons (medium coffee in downtown location):

Vancouver:	$1.19
Edmonton:	$1.35
Toronto:	$1.24
Montreal:	$1.34
Halifax:	$1.24

Starbucks (tall coffee in downtown location):

Vancouver:	$1.75
Edmonton:	$1.80
Toronto:	$1.75
Montreal:	$1.88
Halifax:	$1.88

Source: Dominique Blain, "Our Java Prices Don't Jive with the Rest of Canada," *Edmonton Journal*, October 4, 2006. Material reprinted with the express permission of Edmonton Journal Group Inc., a Postmedia Network Partnership.

NEL

Because quantity demanded and income move in opposite directions, inferior goods have negative income elasticities.

Even among normal goods, income elasticities vary substantially in size. Necessities, such as food and clothing, tend to have small income elasticities because consumers, regardless of how low their incomes, choose to buy some of these goods. Luxuries, such as caviar and diamonds, tend to have large income elasticities because consumers feel that they can do without these goods altogether if their income is too low.

The Cross-Price Elasticity of Demand   The **cross-price elasticity of demand** measures how the quantity demanded of one good changes as the price of another good changes. It is calculated as the percentage change in quantity demanded of good 1 divided by the percentage change in the price of good 2. That is,

$$\text{Cross-price elasticity of demand} = \frac{\text{Percentage change in quantity demanded of good 1}}{\text{Percentage change in price of good 2}}$$

cross-price elasticity of demand
a measure of how much the quantity demanded of one good responds to a change in the price of another good, computed as the percentage change in quantity demanded of the first good divided by the percentage change in the price of the second good

Whether the cross-price elasticity is a positive or negative number depends on whether the two goods are substitutes or complements. As we discussed in Chapter 4, substitutes are goods that are typically used in place of one another, such as hamburgers and hot dogs. An increase in hot dog prices induces people to grill hamburgers instead. Because the price of hot dogs and the quantity of hamburgers demanded move in the same direction, the cross-price elasticity is positive. Conversely, complements are goods that are typically used together, such as computers and software. In this case, the cross-price elasticity is negative, indicating that an increase in the price of computers reduces the quantity of software demanded.

QuickQuiz   Define the price elasticity of demand. • Explain the relationship between total revenue and the price elasticity of demand.

THE ELASTICITY OF SUPPLY

When we introduced supply in Chapter 4, we noted that producers of a good offer to sell more of it when the price of the good rises, when their input prices fall, or when their technology improves. To turn from qualitative to quantitative statements about quantity supplied, we once again use the concept of elasticity.

The Price Elasticity of Supply and Its Determinants

The law of supply states that higher prices raise the quantity supplied. The **price elasticity of supply** measures how much the quantity supplied responds to changes in the price. Supply of a good is said to be *elastic* if the quantity supplied responds substantially to changes in the price. Supply is said to be *inelastic* if the quantity supplied responds only slightly to changes in the price.

price elasticity of supply
a measure of how much the quantity supplied of a good responds to a change in the price of that good, computed as the percentage change in quantity supplied divided by the percentage change in price

The price elasticity of supply depends on the flexibility of sellers to change the amount of the good they produce. For example, beachfront land has an inelastic supply because it is almost impossible to produce more of it. By contrast, manufactured goods, such as books, cars, and televisions, have elastic supplies because the firms that produce them can run their factories longer in response to a higher price.

In most markets, a key determinant of the price elasticity of supply is the time period being considered. Supply is usually more elastic in the long run than in the short run. Over short periods of time, firms cannot easily change the size of their factories to make more or less of a good. Thus, in the short run, the quantity supplied is not very responsive to the price. By contrast, over longer periods, firms can build new factories or close old ones. In addition, new firms can enter a market, and old firms can shut down. Thus, in the long run, the quantity supplied can respond substantially to price changes.

Computing the Price Elasticity of Supply

Now that we have some idea about what the price elasticity of supply is, let's be more precise. Economists compute the price elasticity of supply as the percentage change in the quantity supplied divided by the percentage change in the price. That is,

$$\text{Price elasticity of supply} = \frac{\text{Percentage change in quantity supplied}}{\text{Percentage change in price}}$$

For example, suppose that an increase in the price of milk from $2.85 to $3.15 per four-litre container raises the amount that dairy farmers produce from 9000 to 11 000 L per month. Using the midpoint method, we calculate the percentage change in price as

$$\text{Percentage change in price} = (3.15 - 2.85)/3.00 \times 100 = 10 \text{ percent}$$

Similarly, we calculate the percentage change in quantity supplied as

$$\text{Percentage change in quantity supplied} = (11\,000 - 9000)/10\,000 \times 100 = 20 \text{ percent}$$

In this case, the price elasticity of supply is

$$\text{Price elasticity of supply} = \frac{20 \text{ percent}}{10 \text{ percent}} = 2.0$$

In this example, the elasticity of 2 reflects the fact that the quantity supplied moves proportionately twice as much as the price.

The Variety of Supply Curves

Because the price elasticity of supply measures the responsiveness of quantity supplied to the price, it is reflected in the appearance of the supply curve. Figure 5.5 shows five cases. In the extreme case of a zero elasticity, as shown in

FIGURE 5.5

The Price Elasticity of Supply

The price elasticity of supply determines whether the supply curve is steep or flat. Note that all percentage changes are calculated using the midpoint method.

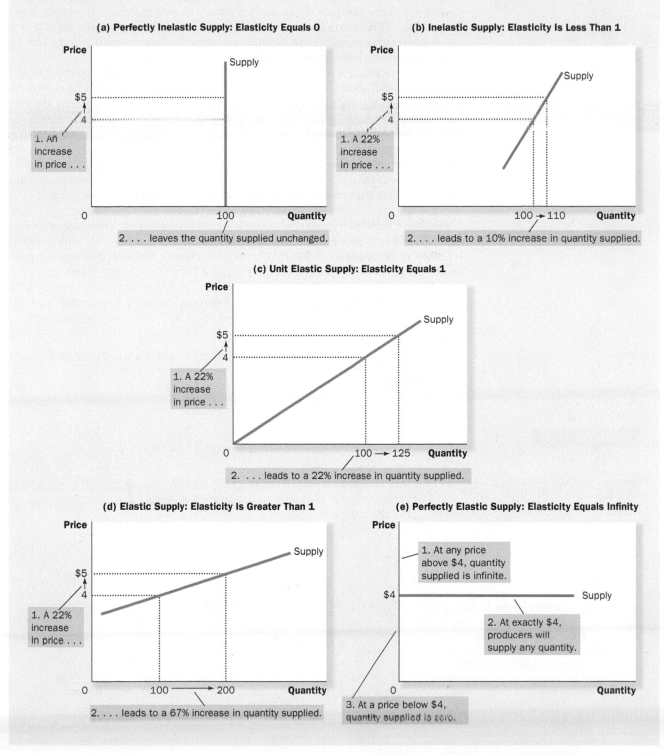

(a) Perfectly Inelastic Supply: Elasticity Equals 0

Price

Supply

$5

4

1. An increase in price . . .

0   100   Quantity

2. . . . leaves the quantity supplied unchanged.

(b) Inelastic Supply: Elasticity Is Less Than 1

Price

Supply

$5

4

1. A 22% increase in price . . .

0   100 → 110   Quantity

2. . . . leads to a 10% increase in quantity supplied.

(c) Unit Elastic Supply: Elasticity Equals 1

Price

Supply

$5

4

1. A 22% increase in price . . .

0   100 → 125   Quantity

2. . . . leads to a 22% increase in quantity supplied.

(d) Elastic Supply: Elasticity Is Greater Than 1

Price

Supply

$5

4

1. A 22% increase in price . . .

0   100 → 200   Quantity

2. . . . leads to a 67% increase in quantity supplied.

(e) Perfectly Elastic Supply: Elasticity Equals Infinity

Price

1. At any price above $4, quantity supplied is infinite.

$4 ————————— Supply

2. At exactly $4, producers will supply any quantity.

0   Quantity

3. At a price below $4, quantity supplied is zero.

panel (a), supply is *perfectly inelastic* and the supply curve is vertical. In this case, the quantity supplied is the same regardless of the price. As the elasticity rises, the supply curve gets flatter, which shows that the quantity supplied responds more to changes in the price. At the opposite extreme shown in panel (e), supply is *perfectly elastic.* This occurs as the price elasticity of supply approaches infinity and the supply curve becomes horizontal, meaning that very small changes in the price lead to very large changes in the quantity supplied.

In some markets, the elasticity of supply is not constant but varies over the supply curve. Figure 5.6 shows a typical case for an industry in which firms have factories with a limited capacity for production. For low levels of quantity supplied, the elasticity of supply is high, indicating that firms respond substantially to changes in the price. In this region, firms have capacity for production that is not being used, such as plants and equipment sitting idle for all or part of the day. Small increases in price make it profitable for firms to begin using this idle capacity. As the quantity supplied rises, firms begin to reach capacity. Once capacity is fully used, increasing production further requires the construction of new plants. To induce firms to incur this extra expense, the price must rise substantially, so supply becomes less elastic.

Figure 5.6 presents a numerical example of this phenomenon. When the price rises from $3 to $4 (a 29 percent increase, according to the midpoint method), the quantity supplied rises from 100 to 200 (a 67 percent increase). Because quantity supplied moves proportionately more than the price, the supply curve has elasticity greater than 1. By contrast, when the price rises from $12 to $15 (a 22 percent increase), the quantity supplied rises from 500 to 525 (a 5 percent increase). In this case, quantity supplied moves proportionately less than the price, so the elasticity is less than 1.

QuickQuiz Define the price elasticity of supply. • Explain why the price elasticity of supply might be different in the long run than in the short run.

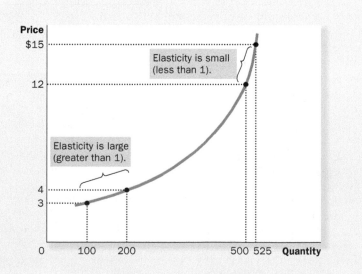

FIGURE 5.6

How the Price Elasticity of Supply Can Vary

Because firms often have a maximum capacity for production, the elasticity of supply may be very high at low levels of quantity supplied and very low at high levels of quantity supplied. Here, an increase in price from $3 to $4 increases the quantity supplied from 100 to 200. Because the increase in quantity supplied of 67 percent (computed using the midpoint method) is larger than the increase in price of 29 percent, the supply curve is elastic in this range. By contrast, when the price rises from $12 to $15, the quantity supplied rises only from 500 to 525. Because the increase in quantity supplied of 5 percent is smaller than the increase in price of 22 percent, the supply curve is inelastic in this range.

THREE APPLICATIONS OF SUPPLY, DEMAND, AND ELASTICITY

Can good news for farming be bad news for farmers? Why did the Organization of the Petroleum Exporting Countries (OPEC) fail to keep the price of oil high? Does drug interdiction increase or decrease drug-related crime? At first, these questions might seem to have little in common. Yet all three questions are about markets, and all markets are subject to the forces of supply and demand. Here we apply the versatile tools of supply, demand, and elasticity to answer these seemingly complex questions.

Can Good News for Farming Be Bad News for Farmers?

Imagine yourself as a Saskatchewan wheat farmer. Because you earn all of your income from selling wheat, you devote much effort to making your land as productive as possible. You monitor weather and soil conditions, check your fields for pests and disease, and study the latest advances in farm technology. You know that the more wheat you grow, the more you will have to sell after the harvest, and the higher your income and your standard of living will be.

One day, the University of Saskatchewan announces a major discovery. Researchers in its College of Agriculture and Bioresources have devised a new hybrid of wheat that raises by 20 percent the amount that farmers can produce from each hectare of land. How should you react to the news? Does this discovery make you better or worse off than you were before?

Recall from Chapter 4 that we answer such questions in three steps. First, we examine whether the supply or demand curve shifts. Second, we consider which direction the curve shifts. Third, we use the supply-and-demand diagram to see how the market equilibrium changes.

In this case, the discovery of the new hybrid affects the supply curve. Because the hybrid increases the amount of wheat that can be produced on each hectare of land, farmers are now willing to supply more wheat at any given price. In other words, the supply curve shifts to the right. The demand curve remains the same because consumers' desire to buy wheat products at any given price is not affected by the introduction of a new hybrid. Figure 5.7 shows an example of such a change. When the supply curve shifts from S_1 to S_2, the quantity of wheat sold increases from 100 to 110, and the price of wheat falls from \$3 to \$2.

But does this discovery make farmers better off? As a first cut at answering this question, consider what happens to the total revenue received by farmers. Farmers' total revenue is $P \times Q$, the price of the wheat times the quantity sold. The discovery affects farmers in two conflicting ways: The hybrid allows farmers to produce more wheat (Q rises), but now each tonne of wheat sells for less (P falls).

Whether total revenue rises or falls depends on the elasticity of demand. In practice, the demand for basic foodstuffs such as wheat is usually inelastic, for these items are relatively inexpensive and have few good substitutes. When the demand curve is inelastic, as it is in Figure 5.7, a decrease in price causes total revenue to fall. You can see this in the figure: The price of wheat falls substantially, whereas the quantity of wheat sold rises only slightly. Total revenue falls from

FIGURE 5.7

An Increase in Supply in the Market for Wheat

When an advance in farm technology increases the supply of wheat from S_1 to S_2, the price of wheat falls. Because the demand for wheat is inelastic, the increase in the quantity sold from 100 to 110 is proportionately smaller than the decrease in the price from $3 to $2. As a result, farmers' total revenue falls from $300 ($3 × 100) to $220 ($2 × 110).

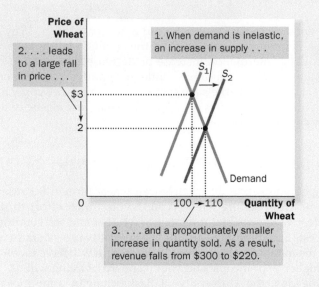

$300 to $220. Thus, the discovery of the new hybrid lowers the total revenue that farmers receive for the sale of their crops.

If farmers are made worse off by the discovery of this new hybrid, why do they adopt it? The answer to this question goes to the heart of how competitive markets work. Because each farmer is a small part of the market for wheat, he or she takes the price of wheat as given. For any given price of wheat, it is better to use the new hybrid in order to produce and sell more wheat. Yet when all farmers do this, the supply of wheat rises, the price falls, and farmers are worse off.

Although this example may at first seem only hypothetical, in fact it helps to explain a major change in the Canadian economy over the past century. Two hundred years ago, most Canadians lived on farms. Knowledge about farm methods was sufficiently primitive that most people had to be farmers to produce enough food. Yet, over time, advances in farm technology increased the amount of food that each farmer could produce. This increase in food supply, together with inelastic food demand, caused farm revenues to fall, which in turn encouraged people to leave farming.

A few numbers show the magnitude of this historic change. Two hundred years ago, about 75 percent of the Canadian labour force worked in agriculture and produced enough food to feed their own families and the families of the other 25 percent of the labour force. One hundred years ago, about 50 percent of the Canadian labour force worked on farms and each agricultural worker produced enough to feed his or her own family and one other family. As recently as 50 years ago, about 25 percent of the Canadian labour force worked on farms. In 2005, however, less than 3 percent of employed Canadians were employed in agriculture, which means that each agricultural worker produced enough food to feed about 35 workers and their families (and to export food as well). Since Canadians today eat at least as well as they did in the past, this decrease in the proportion of Canadians working in agriculture represents a tremendous increase in farm productivity.

This analysis of the market for farm products also helps to explain a seeming paradox of public policy: Certain farm programs try to help farmers by restricting the amount of milk and eggs that farmers are allowed to produce. Why do these programs do this? Their purpose is to reduce the supply of milk and eggs and thereby raise prices. Because demand is inelastic, farmers as a group receive greater total revenue if they supply a smaller amount of milk and eggs to the market. No single farmer would choose to restrict supply on his or her own, since each takes the market price as given. But if all farmers do so together, each of them can be better off.

When analyzing the effects of farm technology or farm policy, it is important to keep in mind that what is good for farmers is not necessarily good for society as a whole. Improvement in farm technology can be bad for farmers who become increasingly unnecessary, but it is surely good for consumers who pay less for food. Similarly, a policy aimed at reducing the supply of farm products may raise the incomes of farmers, but it does so at the expense of consumers.

Why Did OPEC Fail to Keep the Price of Oil High?

Many of the most disruptive events for the world's economies over the past several decades have originated in the world market for oil. In the 1970s, members of OPEC decided to raise the world price of oil in order to increase their incomes. These countries accomplished this goal by jointly reducing the amount of oil they supplied. From 1973 to 1974, the price of oil (adjusted for overall inflation) rose more than 50 percent. Then, a few years later, OPEC did the same thing again: From 1979 to 1981, the price of oil approximately doubled.

Yet OPEC found it difficult to maintain a high price. From 1982 to 1985, the price of oil steadily declined at about 10 percent per year. Dissatisfaction and disarray soon prevailed among the OPEC countries. In 1986 cooperation among OPEC members completely broke down, and the price of oil plunged 45 percent. In 1990 the price of oil (adjusted for overall inflation) was back to where it began in 1970, and it stayed at that low level throughout most of the 1990s.

As mentioned in the introduction to this chapter, the price of oil rose significantly again from 1999 to 2008, reaching historic levels (even adjusted for inflation), but it is generally agreed that the main driving force in this case was not OPEC supply restrictions but, rather, increased world demand, in part from a large and rapidly growing Chinese economy. Prices moderated after the 2008 recession as world demand fell.

The OPEC episode of the 1970s and 1980s shows how supply and demand can behave differently in the short run and in the long run. In the short run, both the supply and demand for oil are relatively inelastic. Supply is inelastic because the quantity of known oil reserves and the capacity for oil extraction cannot be changed quickly. Demand is inelastic because buying habits do not respond immediately to changes in price. Many drivers with old gas-guzzling cars, for instance, will just pay the higher price. Thus, as panel (a) of Figure 5.8 shows, the short-run supply-and-demand curves are steep. When the supply of oil shifts from S_1 to S_2, the price increase from P_1 to P_2 is large.

The situation is very different in the long run. Over long periods of time, producers of oil outside of OPEC respond to high prices by increasing oil exploration and by building new extraction capacity. Consumers respond with greater conservation, for instance by replacing old inefficient cars with newer efficient ones. Thus, as panel (b) of Figure 5.8 shows, the long-run supply-and-demand curves are more elastic. In the long run, the shift in the supply curve from S_1 to S_2 causes a much smaller increase in the price.

This analysis shows why OPEC succeeded in maintaining a high price for oil only in the short run. When OPEC countries agreed to reduce their production of oil, they shifted the supply curve to the left. Even though each OPEC member sold less oil, the price rose by so much in the short run that OPEC incomes rose. By contrast, in the long run when supply and demand are more elastic, the same reduction in supply, measured by the horizontal shift in the supply curve, caused a smaller increase in the price. Thus, OPEC's coordinated reduction in supply proved less profitable in the long run.

FIGURE 5.8

A Reduction in Supply in the World Market for Oil

When the supply of oil falls, the response depends on the time horizon. In the short run, supply and demand are relatively inelastic, as in panel (a). Thus, when the supply curve shifts from S_1 to S_2, the price rises substantially. By contrast, in the long run, supply and demand are relatively elastic, as in panel (b). In this case, the same size shift in the supply curve (S_1 to S_2) causes a smaller increase in the price.

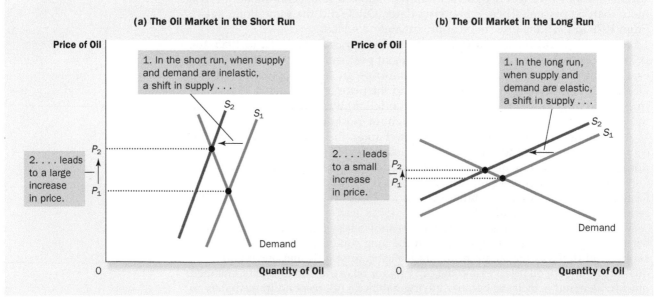

(a) The Oil Market in the Short Run

1. In the short run, when supply and demand are inelastic, a shift in supply . . .

2. . . . leads to a large increase in price.

(b) The Oil Market in the Long Run

1. In the long run, when supply and demand are elastic, a shift in supply . . .

2. . . . leads to a small increase in price.

OPEC still exists today, and it has from time to time succeeded at reducing supply and raising prices. But the price of oil (adjusted for overall inflation) has never returned to the peak reached in 1981. The cartel now seems to understand that raising prices is easier in the short run than in the long run.

Does Drug Interdiction Increase or Decrease Drug-Related Crime?

A persistent problem facing our society is the use of illegal drugs, such as heroin, cocaine, Ecstasy, and crack. Drug use has several adverse effects. One is that drug dependence can ruin the lives of drug users and their families. Another is that drug addicts often turn to robbery and other violent crimes to obtain the money needed to support their habit. To discourage the use of illegal drugs, Canadian governments devote millions of dollars each year to reducing the flow of drugs into the country. Let's use the tools of supply and demand to examine this policy of drug interdiction.

Suppose the government increases the number of officers devoted to the war on drugs. What happens in the market for illegal drugs? As usual, we answer this question in three steps. First, we consider whether the supply or demand curve shifts. Second, we consider the direction of the shift. Third, we see how the shift affects the equilibrium price and quantity.

Although the purpose of drug interdiction is to reduce drug use, its direct impact is on the sellers of drugs rather than on the buyers. When the government stops some drugs from entering the country and arrests more smugglers, it raises the cost of selling drugs and, therefore, reduces the quantity of drugs supplied at any given price. The demand for drugs—the amount buyers want at any given price—is not changed. As panel (a) of Figure 5.9 shows, interdiction shifts the supply curve to the left from S_1 to S_2 and leaves the demand curve the same. The equilibrium price of drugs rises from P_1 to P_2, and the equilibrium quantity falls from Q_1 to Q_2. The fall in the equilibrium quantity shows that drug interdiction does reduce drug use.

But what about the amount of drug-related crime? To answer this question, consider the total amount that drug users pay for the drugs they buy. Because few drug addicts are likely to break their destructive habits in response to a higher price, it is likely that the demand for drugs is inelastic, as it is drawn in the figure. If demand is inelastic, then an increase in price raises total revenue in the drug market. That is, because drug interdiction raises the price of drugs proportionately more than it reduces drug use, it raises the total amount of money that drug users pay for drugs. Addicts who already had to steal to support their habits would have an even greater need for quick cash. Thus, drug interdiction could increase drug-related crime.

Because of this adverse effect of drug interdiction, some analysts argue for alternative approaches to the drug problem. Rather than trying to reduce the supply of drugs, policymakers might try to reduce the demand by pursuing a policy of drug education. Successful drug education has the effects shown in panel (b) of Figure 5.9. The demand curve shifts to the left from D_1 to D_2. As a result, the equilibrium quantity falls from Q_1 to Q_2, and the equilibrium price falls from P_1 to P_2. Total revenue, which is price times quantity, also falls. Thus,

FIGURE 5.9

Policies to Reduce the Use of Illegal Drugs

Drug interdiction reduces the supply of drugs from S_1 to S_2, as shown in panel (a). If the demand for drugs is inelastic, then the total amount paid by drug users rises, even as the amount of drug use falls. By contrast, drug education reduces the demand for drugs from D_1 to D_2, as shown in panel (b). Because both price and quantity fall, the amount paid by drug users falls.

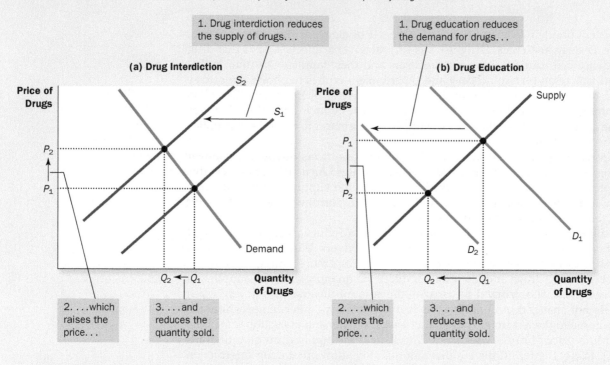

in contrast to drug interdiction, drug education can reduce both drug use and drug-related crime.

Advocates of drug interdiction might argue that the effects of this policy are different in the long run than in the short run because the elasticity of demand may depend on the time horizon. The demand for drugs is probably inelastic over short periods of time because higher prices do not substantially affect drug use by established addicts. But demand may be more elastic over longer periods of time because higher prices would discourage experimentation with drugs among the young and, over time, lead to fewer drug addicts. In this case, drug interdiction would increase drug-related crime in the short run while decreasing it in the long run.

QuickQuiz How might a drought that destroys half of all farm crops be good for farmers? If such a drought is good for farmers, why don't farmers destroy their own crops in the absence of a drought?

CONCLUSION

According to an old quip, even a parrot can become an economist simply by learning to say "supply and demand." These last two chapters should have convinced you that there is much truth in this statement. The tools of supply and demand allow you to analyze many of the most important events and policies that shape the economy. You are now well on your way to becoming an economist.

SUMMARY

- The price elasticity of demand measures how much the quantity demanded responds to changes in the price. Demand tends to be more elastic if close substitutes are available, if the good is a luxury rather than a necessity, if the market is narrowly defined, or if buyers have substantial time to react to a price change.

- The price elasticity of demand is calculated as the percentage change in quantity demanded divided by the percentage change in price. If the elasticity is less than 1, so that quantity demanded moves proportionately less than the price, demand is said to be inelastic. If the elasticity is greater than 1, so that quantity demanded moves proportionately more than the price, demand is said to be elastic.

- Total revenue, the total amount paid for a good, equals the price of the good times the quantity sold. For inelastic demand curves, total revenue rises as price rises. For elastic demand curves, total revenue falls as price rises.

- The income elasticity of demand measures how much the quantity demanded responds to changes in consumers' income. The cross-price elasticity of demand measures how much the quantity demanded of one good responds to changes in the price of another good.

- The price elasticity of supply measures how much the quantity supplied responds to changes in the price. This elasticity often depends on the time horizon under consideration. In most markets, supply is more elastic in the long run than in the short run.

- The price elasticity of supply is calculated as the percentage change in quantity supplied divided by the percentage change in price. If the elasticity is less than 1, so that quantity supplied moves proportionately less than the price, supply is said to be inelastic. If the elasticity is greater than 1, so that quantity supplied moves proportionately more than the price, supply is said to be elastic.

- The tools of supply and demand can be applied in many different kinds of markets. This chapter uses them to analyze the market for wheat, the market for oil, and the relationship of drug interdiction and the amount of drug-related crime.

KEY CONCEPTS

elasticity, p. 96
price elasticity of
   demand, p. 96
total revenue, p. 99

income elasticity of
   demand, p. 103
cross-price elasticity of
   demand, p. 105

price elasticity of supply, p. 105

QUESTIONS FOR REVIEW

1. Define the price elasticity of demand and the income elasticity of demand.

2. List and explain some of the determinants of the price elasticity of demand.

3. If the elasticity is greater than 1, is demand elastic or inelastic? If the elasticity equals 0, is demand perfectly elastic or perfectly inelastic?

4. On a supply-and-demand diagram, show equilibrium price, equilibrium quantity, and the total revenue received by producers.

5. If demand is elastic, how will an increase in price change total revenue? Explain.

6. What do we call a good whose income elasticity is less than 0?

7. How is the price elasticity of supply calculated? Explain what this measures.

8. What is the price elasticity of supply of Picasso paintings?

9. Is the price elasticity of supply usually larger in the short run or in the long run? Why?

10. What is the main advantage of using the midpoint method for calculating elasticity?

11. How did elasticity help explain why drug interdiction could reduce the supply of drugs, yet possibly increase drug-related crime?

PROBLEMS AND APPLICATIONS

1. For each of the following pairs of goods, which good would you expect to have more elastic demand and why?
   a. required textbooks or mystery novels
   b. Beethoven recordings or classical music recordings in general
   c. heating oil during the next six months or heating oil during the next five years
   d. root beer or water

2. Suppose that business travellers and vacationers have the following demand for airline tickets from Toronto to Montreal:

Price	Quantity Demanded (business travellers)	Quantity Demanded (vacationers)
$150	2100 tickets	1000 tickets
200	2000	800
250	1900	600
300	1800	400

   a. As the price of tickets rises from $200 to $250, what is the price elasticity of demand for (i) business travellers and (ii) vacationers? (Use the midpoint method in your calculations.)

   b. Why might vacationers have a different elasticity than business travellers?

3. Suppose that your demand schedule for compact discs is as follows:

Price	Quantity Demanded (income = $10 000)	Quantity Demanded (income = $12 000)
$ 8	40	50
10	32	45
12	24	30
14	16	20
16	8	12

   a. Use the midpoint method to calculate your price elasticity of demand as the price of compact discs increases from $8 to $10 if (i) your income is $10 000, and (ii) your income is $12 000.

   b. Calculate your income elasticity of demand as your income increases from $10 000 to $12 000 if (i) the price is $12, and (ii) the price is $16.

4. Emily has decided always to spend one-third of her income on clothing.
   a. What is her income elasticity of clothing demand?

b. What is her price elasticity of clothing demand?

c. If Emily's tastes change and she decides to spend only one-fourth of her income on clothing, how does her demand curve change? What are her income elasticity and price elasticity now?

5. *The Globe and Mail* (December 16, 1997) reported that milk consumption declined following price increases: "Since the early 1980s, the price of milk in Canada has increased 22 per cent. As prices rose, the demand for milk fell off. Total [consumption] of milk on a per capita basis dropped . . . to 2.62 hectolitres in 1995 from 2.92 hectolitres in 1986."

a. Use these data to estimate the price elasticity of demand for milk.

b. According to your estimate, what happens to milk producers' revenue when the price of milk rises?

c. Why might your estimate of the elasticity be unreliable? (Hint: Notice that *The Globe and Mail* is careless about the distinction between demand and quantity demanded.)

6. Two drivers—Tom and Jerry—each drive up to a gas station. Before looking at the price, each places an order. Tom says, "I'd like 40 litres of gas." Jerry says, "I'd like $40 worth of gas." What is each driver's price elasticity of demand?

7. You are the curator of a museum. The museum is running short of funds, so you decide to increase revenue. Should you increase or decrease the price of admission? Explain.

8. Consider public policy aimed at smoking.

a. Studies indicate that the price elasticity of demand for cigarettes is about 0.4. If a pack of cigarettes currently costs $10 and the government wants to reduce smoking by 20 percent, by how much should it increase the price?

b. If the government permanently increases the price of cigarettes, will the policy have a greater effect on smoking one year from now or five years from now?

c. Studies also find that teenagers have a higher price elasticity than do adults. Why might this be true?

9. Suppose that the price elasticity of demand for heating oil is 0.2 in the short run and 0.7 in the long run.

a. If the price of heating oil rises from $0.45 to $0.55 per litre, what happens to the quantity of heating oil demanded in the short run? In the long run? (Use the midpoint method in your calculations.)

b. Why might this elasticity depend on the time horizon?

10. Pharmaceutical drugs have an inelastic demand, and computers have an elastic demand. Suppose that technological advance doubles the supply of both products (that is, the quantity supplied at each price is twice what it was).

a. What happens to the equilibrium price and quantity in each market?

b. Which product experiences a greater change in price?

c. Which product experiences a greater change in quantity?

d. What happens to total consumer spending on each product?

11. Beachfront resorts have an inelastic supply, and automobiles have an elastic supply. Suppose that a rise in population doubles the demand for both products (that is, the quantity demanded at each price is twice what it was).

a. What happens to the equilibrium price and quantity in each market?

b. Which product experiences a greater change in price?

c. Which product experiences a greater change in quantity?

d. What happens to total consumer spending on each product?

12. Some years ago, flooding along the Red River in Manitoba destroyed thousands of hectares of wheat.

a. Farmers whose crops were destroyed by the floods were much worse off, but farmers whose crops were not destroyed benefited from the floods. Why?

b. What information would you need about the market for wheat to assess whether farmers as a group were hurt or helped by the floods?

13. Explain why the following might be true: A drought around the world raises the total revenue that farmers receive from the sale of grain, but a drought only in Alberta reduces the total revenue that Alberta farmers receive.

14. A price change causes the quantity demanded of a good to decrease by 30 percent, while the total revenue of that good increases by 15 percent. Is the demand curve elastic or inelastic? Explain.

15. The equilibrium price of coffee mugs rose sharply last month, but the equilibrium quantity was the same as ever. Three people tried to explain the situation. Which explanations could be right? Explain your logic.

BILLY: Demand increased, but supply was totally inelastic.

MARIAN: Supply increased, but so did demand

VALERIE: Supply decreased, but demand was totally inelastic.

16. You have the following information about good X and good Y:
    • Income elasticity of demand for good X: −3
    • Cross-price elasticity of demand for good X with respect to the price of good Y: 2

    Would an increase in income and a decrease in the price of good Y unambiguously decrease the demand for good X? Why or why not?

17. Suppose the demand curve for a product is $Q = 60/P$. Compute the quantity demanded at prices of $1, $2, $3, $4, $5, and $6. Graph the demand curve. Use the midpoint method to calculate the price elasticity of demand between $1 and $2 and between $5 and $6. How does this demand curve compare to the linear demand curve?

http://   For more study tools, please visit http://www.mankiw5e.nelson.com.

Chapter 5
The Algebra of Point Elasticity

Earlier in the textbook we learned how to calculate arc elasticity using the midpoint method. In truth, the only time anyone ever uses the midpoint method is in their introductory microeconomics course and then they never see it again. That's because we are more concerned with the impact of marginal changes in price on quantity demanded. In other words, if price changes by just a little, how much will quantity demanded change? We can answer this question by computing the **point elasticity** of demand.

We know that price elasticity = percentage change in Qd / percentage change in P. We can write this as:

$E(p) = \Delta Q/Q \ / \ \Delta P/P$

Rearranging, we get $E(p) = \Delta Q/\Delta P \ * \ P/Q$

But $\Delta Q/\Delta P$ is the rate of change in Qd with respect to price; it is the slope of the demand curve when it is written in the form Qd = f(P). So E(p) = slope of the demand curve * P/Q. Technically (for those who know some calculus), $E(p) = dQ/dP * P/Q$ for any demand curve. We will get a very precise determination of elasticity using this method.

In our first year course, all our demand curves are linear functions. This makes finding the slope easy – it is just the coefficient on P when demand is written in the form Qd = a – bP.

We have seen in our diagrams that elasticity is reflected in the slope of the demand curve - the flatter the demand curve, the more price elastic is the demand. Now we know why – it's because the slope of the demand curve is part of the equation for elasticity. Here's how this works:

The slope of our linear demand curve is constant, regardless of what price and quantity level we are at. When we graph our demand curve, we are graphing the inverse demand, so whatever value we get for dQ/ dP we are actually graphing a line with slope 1 / dQ/dP or dP/dQ.

Let's pick a point, any point, (Q, P). Now let's draw two demand curves going through the same point, one demand curve flatter than the other. P/Q is the same for both curves but the slopes are different. The bigger dQ/dP is, the more elastic is the demand curve. But a bigger dQ/dP means a smaller dP/dQ. So a bigger elasticity coefficient at (Q, P) means that we "see" a flatter demand curve when we graph it, like curve D1. Curve D2 is steeper, so dP/dQ is larger and therefore dQ/dP is smaller. A smaller dQ/dP means a smaller elasticity coefficient. That's why the flatter the demand curve, the more elastic is the demand curve and the steeper the demand curve, the more inelastic is the demand curve.

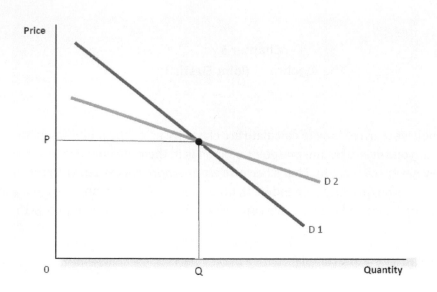

We have also seen that elasticity changes as we move up or down the demand curve. That's because for every P, there is a different corresponding Q so that P/Q is different at every point on the demand curve. Since the slope of our linear demand curve is constant, we will get a different coefficient of elasticity for every (P, Q) combination.

Example

Demand for gadgets is given by Qd = 100 − 4P.

At a price of $2, what is the point elasticity of demand?

First, we need to know what Qd is when P = 2. Substituting P = 2 into the demand equation yields Qd = 92.

The slope of our demand curve is simply − 4 (the slope coefficient on P from our equation). We know that price and quantity demanded are inversely related (from our Law of Demand), so we can ignore the minus sign.

E(p) = dQ/dP * P/Q = 4 * 2/92 = .087

Since .087 is less than 1, we know that at a price of $2, demand for gadgets is price inelastic.

What is the pointy elasticity of demand when price is $20?

When P = 20, Qd = 100 − 4(20) = 20.

E(p) = dQ/dP * P/Q = 4 * 20/20 = 4

184

Since 4 is greater than 1, we know that at a price of $20, demand for gadgets is price elastic.

Notice that at a higher price, demand is more elastic than at a lower price. This corresponds to our diagram that shows that as we move up and left along the demand curve, demand becomes more price elastic.

Practice Problems

1. Market demand is given as Qd = 200 – 3P. Market supply is given as Qs = 2P + 100. At a price of $25, what is the point price elasticity of demand?
   a. 1.4
   b. .7
   c. .6
   d. 2.3

2. Market demand is given as Qd = 200 – 3P. Market supply is given as Qs = 2P + 100. At a price of $40, what is the point price elasticity of demand?
   a. 1.5
   b. .8
   c. .6
   d. 2.1

3. Market demand is given as Qd = 200 – 3P. Market supply is given as Qs = 2P + 100. At a price of $10, what is the point price elasticity of demand?
   a. 3.7
   b. 5.0
   c. .18
   d. .9

Answers: 1 b   2 a   3 c

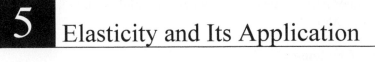

5 Elasticity and Its Application

I. Chapter Overview

A. Context and Purpose

This chapter extends the discussion of supply and demand, which was introduced in the previous chapter, to the exploration of consumer and producer responsiveness to changes in market conditions such as price. To measure this responsiveness, economists use the term *elasticity*. Consumers' (or producers') relative responsiveness to changes in any one of the determinants of demand (or supply) is known as elasticity of demand (or supply). Price elasticity of demand (or supply) measures the degree of response of quantity demanded (or quantity supplied) to any change in price. When consumers (or producers) are relatively more responsive to changes in price, their demand (or supply) is considered to be more elastic, just as a rubber band that is very elastic is highly responsive or stretchy. Knowledge of consumers' and producers' elasticity is useful to sellers, who need to know how price changes will affect sales and total revenues, as well as to government officials, who need to know how changes in taxes or other public policies will affect behaviour.

B. Helpful Hints

1. *Elasticity means responsiveness.* In its most general sense, elasticity is responsiveness, whether we are talking about rubber bands or people. In economics, we use various types of elasticity to measure people's responsiveness to changes in economic factors such as price or income. The price elasticity of demand is particularly important because it provides immediate information about the effect of a change in price upon total consumer spending on the product. To the seller, this spending represents revenue. If consumer demand is highly elastic, or responsive to price, sellers can raise total revenue by cutting price. Even though price falls, the increased quantity demanded (and sold) more than makes up for the drop in price as the dollar value of consumer spending (and revenue for the seller) rises. On the other hand, if demand is inelastic, cutting price will not generate enough additional sales to compensate, and total revenue will fall.

2. *Elasticity is not the same thing as slope.* Slope is constant along a straight-line demand curve, but price elasticity of demand varies with the point on the curve. This should be apparent if you keep in mind that slope is the steepness of the curve, which does not change along a straight-line demand curve; but the elasticity is the ratio of the relative changes in quantity and price, which depends on the starting point. Clearly a $1 change in price is a

63

bigger percentage change when the initial price is $1 than if the initial price is $1000!

II. Self-Testing Challenges

A. True/False Questions

_____ 1. The demand for Chevrolets is more elastic than the demand for automobiles in general.

_____ 2. The longer the time period, the more elastic the demand for a good or service, all else equal.

_____ 3. A normal good is one for which the income elasticity is greater than one.

_____ 4. A good perceived by the consumer to be a necessity will tend to have an elastic demand.

_____ 5. For a good with a price elasticity of demand of 0.8, an increase in price will cause total consumer spending on that good to rise.

_____ 6. The major problem facing agriculture in Canada today is the slow pace in implementing necessary technological changes in the production and distribution of food.

_____ 7. If Dennis allocates $24 as his monthly expenditure on beer, and he spends no more and no less, regardless of price, then his demand for beer is unit elastic.

_____ 8. Generally speaking, goods that are considered necessities tend to have inelastic demands.

_____ 9. The supply of land overlooking the Niagara River is highly price elastic.

_____ 10. If price elasticity of demand is zero, then any price change will also have a zero effect on total revenue.

B. Multiple-Choice Questions

1. All else equal, which of the following indicates when the price elasticity of demand tends to be higher?
    a. when the time period involved is shorter
    b. when the market is more broadly defined
    c. when there are more substitutes for the good or service
    d. when consumers perceive the good to be more of a necessity.

2. If a seller wants to increase total revenue, which one of the following describes what he should do?
    a. lower price if demand is inelastic
    b. raise price only if demand is elastic
    c. raise price only if demand is inelastic
    d. lower price if demand has unitary elasticity

3. Suppose the Minister of Health wants to reduce cigarette smoking by increasing tobacco taxes. Which one of the following describes why it will probably take a fairly large tobacco tax to make much of a difference?
    a. because price is irrelevant for consumers
    b. because supply of tobacco is relatively inelastic
    c. because demand for cigarettes is totally inelastic
    d. because demand for cigarettes is relatively inelastic

4. As income rises during economic upturns, consumption of potatoes declines, yet as income falls during economic downturns, consumption of potatoes rises. Which one of the following is the likely explanation for the changes in potato consumption?
    a. high income elasticity of demand
    b. very high price elasticity of supply
    c. very low price elasticity of demand
    d. negative income elasticity of demand

5. Which one of the following statements is true?
    a. When the price of meat rises, the supply of hamburgers falls.
    b. When the price of pencils falls, the quantity supplied of pencils rises.
    c. When the weather gets hotter, the quantity demanded for ice cream rises.
    d. A negative cross-price elasticity for two goods—Good A and Good B—would arise if A and B were complements.

6. Which one of the following is likely to have a high income elasticity of demand?
    a. fancy restaurant meals
    b. lunches at fast-food restaurants
    c. brown bag lunches from home

7. Which of the following is the income elasticity of demand for housing if people always spend 25% of their incomes on housing?
    a. 0.25
    b. 1.00
    c. 2.50
    d. 25.00

Use the following information to answer questions 8 and 9.
The city is considering a fare hike for its city bus service. At the current fare of $2.00, daily ridership is 2400 people. The city estimates that if it raises fares to $2.50, ridership will decline to 2100.

8. Using the midpoint method of calculating elasticity, which of the following is the price elasticity of demand?
    a. 0.0
    b. 0.6
    c. 1.0
    d. 6.0

9. Which of the following is recommended if the city wants to raise more revenue from its bus system?
    a. raise the price to $2.50
    b. keep the price at $2.00 and wait for demand to increase
    c. first lower the price to attract riders, then gradually increase price
    d. first raise price to get revenues, then lower price after the buses are paid off

10. Which one of the following is the likely outcome of the prevailing laws aimed at reducing the supply of illegal drugs?
    a. It reduces drug consumption but increases drug-related income and crime
    b. It reduces both drug consumption and drug-related income and crime
    c. It increases both drug consumption and drug-related income and crime
    d. It increases drug consumption but reduces drug-related income and crime

11. If the price elasticity of demand is 0.5, then which of the following will a 20% price hike lead to?
    a. 5% drop in quantity demanded
    b. 10% drop in quantity demanded
    c. 20% drop in quantity demanded
    d. 40% drop in quantity demanded

12.   If a 20% decline in price leads to a 30% decrease in quantity supplied, then which statement below is correct?
    a. price elasticity of demand is 1.5
    b. price elasticity of supply is 1.5
    c. price elasticity of demand is 3.0
    d. price elasticity of supply is 3.0

13.   Which one of the following is the **MAIN** reason that OPEC has been unable to keep oil prices high?
    a. Government regulations have prevented it.
    b. Supply tends to be more inelastic in the long run.
    c. Demand tends to become more elastic in the long run.
    d. Massive new petroleum discoveries have increased the supply.

14.   If price elasticity of supply tends to be higher, which one of the following will be the outcome?
    a. The time period will be longer.
    b. It will be easier for more new firms to enter the industry.
    c. The firms can be more adaptable to changing market conditions.
    d. The demand will also be higher.

15.   Suppose Bill buys one six-pack of beer each week, regardless of price, and he drinks it on Saturday night. Which one of the following statements is correct?
    a. price elasticity of demand is 0
    b. price elasticity of demand is 1
    c. price elasticity of demand is 6
    d. price elasticity of supply is greater than 1

16.   For a given increase in demand, which of the following indicates when price increases the **MOST**?
    a. supply is elastic
    b. supply is inelastic
    c. supply is unit elastic
    d. supply is perfectly elastic

17.   Which one of the following describes the elasticity of a straight-line (constant-slope) demand curve?
    a. elasticity remains constant along its length.
    b. elasticity increases as quantity demanded increases along its length.
    c. elasticity decreases as quantity demanded increases along its length.
    d. elasticity first increases and then decreases as quantity demanded increases.

18. Which one of the following is the cross-price elasticity of demand for orange golf balls with respect to any change in the price of white golf balls?
    a. positive and probably high
    b. negative and probably high
    c. positive and probably low
    d. negative and probably low

19. Which of the following is the cross elasticity of demand for bindings if, all else is equal, the demand for ski bindings falls by 40% when the price of skis increases by 20%?
    a. 0.5
    b. −0.5
    c. 2.0
    d. −2.0

20. Which one of the following describes a circumstance in which an increase in demand will not have any effect on price?
    a. where supply is unit elastic
    b. where supply is perfectly elastic
    c. where supply is perfectly inelastic
    d. where supply is a straight line through the origin

C. Short-Answer Questions

1. How could a good such as a new mid-priced car be both an inferior good and a normal good? _____
   _____
   _____
   _____

2. A 2004 study determined the following elasticities.

	Short run	Long run
Price elasticity of demand for fuel	0.25	0.64
Income elasticity of demand for fuel	0.40	1.00

Based on this information, assess whether the following statements are true or false. Explain your answers.

   a. If the price of fuel rises by 10% and stays at that level, the reduction in the volume of fuel consumed in the short run is more than that in the long run.

      _____
      _____
      _____

b. If the consumer's income goes up by 10%, the amount of fuel consumed will increase by 4% within a year and by 10% in the long run. These changes suggest that fuel is considered to be an inferior good. _____

_____

_____

_____

D. Practice Problems

1. The City Zoo is losing money. City Council is unwilling to contribute any tax dollars to support the zoo, asserting that the administration should simply raise prices in order to balance its budget. The price of admission is currently $4 per person, with average daily attendance of 600 people. City Council argues that the zoo needs to raise only one additional dollar per visitor to break even (the zoo is currently losing about $600 per day). The zoo management has hired a consultant to estimate the demand for admissions to the zoo and recommend a pricing policy.
The demand schedule that the consultant estimated is shown below:

Demand for Zoo Admissions

Price	Quantity of tickets demanded/day	Total revenue	% change in price	% change in quantity	Elasticity
$0	1200	$____	____%	____%	____
$1	1050	$____	____%	____%	____
$2	900	$____	____%	____%	____
$3	750	$____	____%	____%	____
$4	600	$____	____%	____%	____
$5	450	$____	____%	____%	____
$6	300	$____	____%	____%	____
$7	150	$____	____%	____%	____
$8	0	$____			

a. Fill in the blanks in the preceding table. (Use the midpoint method to calculate the percentage changes and elasticity.)

b. What should be the consultant's recommendation regarding pricing, given the zoo's budget crisis? Should they change the price from the current $4? Justify the position, based upon the estimate of the elasticity of demand. _____

_____

_____

_____

2. Consider the demand curve for sofas shown below. Use the midpoint method to calculate elasticity in the questions that follow.

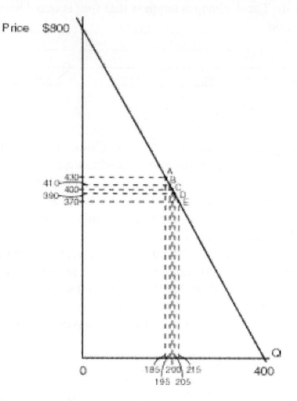

a. What is the slope of the demand curve for sofas? _____

b. What is the elasticity between points A and B? _____

c. What is the elasticity between points B and D? _____

d. What is the elasticity between points D and E? _____

e. In general, what happens to elasticity as quantity increases along a straight-line demand curve? Which part of the demand curve is elastic? Which part is inelastic? Explain. _____
    _____
    _____
    _____

E. Advanced Critical Thinking

BizExpress Airlines of Alberta must decide on a pricing policy for flights between Calgary and Edmonton. It has two types of travellers—business and leisure passengers—whose demand curves are D_B and D_L, respectively.

	Business travellers		Leisure travellers	
Price	D_B quantity demanded		Price	D_L quantity demanded
$400	200		$400	0
$300	300		$300	100
$200	400		$200	300
$100	500		$100	500

1. If BizExpress Airlines' goal is to maximize total revenue, and it has enough seats to satisfy all of the demand, what price should it charge business travellers? What about leisure travellers? Explain. Do airlines actually behave this way? How can an airline charge two different prices for essentially the same product (how do they separate the two markets)?

_____

_____

_____

_____

_____

2. Provide some other examples of real-world price discrimination—charging different prices to different people for the same product—based on differences in the price elasticity of demand between two (or more) groups of consumers.

_____

_____

_____

_____

III.   Solutions

A. True/False Questions

1. T
2. T
3. F; a normal good has an income elasticity greater than zero.
4. F; necessities tend to have inelastic demand curves.
5. T

6.   F; the major problem is inelastic demand, so that increased supply lowers total revenues.

7.   T

8.   T

9.   F; the supply of land overlooking the Niagara River is highly inelastic because it is almost impossible to produce more of it.

10.   F; if elasticity is less than one (including zero), then total revenue will move in the same direction as price. If elasticity is zero, then quantity does not change, and total revenue will change in proportion to the change in price.

B. Multiple-Choice Questions

1. c	5. d	9. a	13. c	17. c
2. c	6. a	10. a	14. a	18. a
3. d	7. b	11. b	15. a	19. d
4. d	8. b	12. b	16. b	20. b

C. Short-Answer Questions

1. Goods are not likely to have constant income elasticity's over all income ranges. Many products are normal goods initially, but as income rises, they often become inferior goods as people switch to more upscale products. For example, a mid-priced automobile tends to have fairly high income elasticity for most people, but above a certain income level, the income elasticity actually becomes negative, as people substitute more expensive automobiles for the mid-priced models. Even a luxury model could be an inferior good for some very high-income consumers.

2. a.   False. A 10% increase in the price of fuel reduces the volume of fuel consumed by 2.5% (= 0.25 × 10%) in the short run and 6.4% (= 0.64 × 10%) in the long run.

    b.   The first part of the statement is correct. The income elasticity's suggest that an increase in the consumer's income increases the demand for fuel by 4% (= 0.4 × 10%) in the short run and by 10% (= 1.0 × 10%) in the long run. The second part, however, is false. Fuel is a normal good because income elasticity's are positive.

D. Practice Problems

1. a.

Price	Quantity of tickets demanded/day	Total revenue	% change in price	% change in quantity	Elasticity
$0	1200	$0	200%	13%	0.07
$1	1050	$1050	67%	15%	0.22
$2	900	$1800	40%	18%	0.45
$3	750	$2250	29%	22%	0.76
$4	600	$2400	22%	29%	1.32
$5	450	$2250	18%	40%	2.22
$6	300	$1800	15%	67%	4.47
$7	150	$1050	13%	200%	15.38
$8	0	$0			

   b. The zoo should leave the price as it is. The demand is price elastic upwards, so if the zoo increased price, quantity demanded would fall more than enough to compensate for the increase, and total revenue would actually fall. The zoo is already gathering as much total revenue as it can, given its attractiveness to consumers; if it is to pay for itself, either costs must be cut, its attractiveness must be increased, or both.

2. a. The slope of the demand curve for sofas is −2.0. Remember: Slope = rise/run = Δprice/Δquantity, for any two points on this straight-line or constant slope demand curve. Even the end points will work: 800/400 = 2.

   b. The elasticity between points A and B is 1.1. Δquantity/quantity ÷ Δprice/price = 10/190 ÷ 20/420.

   c. The elasticity between points B and D is 1.0. Δquantity/quantity ÷ Δprice/price = 10/200 ÷ 20/400.

   d. The elasticity between points D and E is 0.9. Δquantity/quantity ÷ Δprice/price = 10/210 ÷ 20/380.

e. Elasticity falls as quantity increases along the straight-line demand curve. The upper part of the demand curve is always elastic, and the lower part is always inelastic. To see how this happens, consider points A, B, C, and D along the demand curve in the previous figure. Even though price and quantity change by constant amounts, the percentage changes also depend on the *levels* of price and quantity, which vary as we move along the demand curve. All straight-line demand curves behave this way: as price declines and quantity increases (down the demand curve), the elasticity declines, and as price increases and quantity declines (up the demand curve), elasticity increases.

E. Advanced Critical Thinking

1. BizExpress Airlines should sell 300 business tickets at $300 each, for total revenues of $90 000. It should sell 300 leisure tickets at $200 each, for total revenues of $60 000 from leisure travellers. This will maximize revenues from both groups. Of course the airline should make sure that it has enough seats first, so that it does not sell seats for $200 that it could have sold for $300 to business travellers. Airlines separate the leisure and business markets through restrictions such as advance purchase and Saturday-night layover requirements that business travellers are generally unwilling to meet. Leisure travellers, whose demand tends to be relatively elastic, are generally more willing than business travellers to accept such restrictions in order to get a low fare.

2. Any example of a product that is sold for different prices to different groups of people would work here, as long as the price differentials are not due to differences in cost of production. For example, senior citizen or student discounts for movie tickets or restaurants are used to lower the price for those people with higher elasticity of demand without cutting the price for everyone. Another example is "early bird" specials that restaurants use to cut the price for those who are willing to eat at a less popular time.

6

SUPPLY, DEMAND, AND GOVERNMENT POLICIES

© Jason Yoder/Dreamstime.com

Learning Objectives

In this chapter, you will ...

- Examine the effects of government policies that place a ceiling on prices

- Examine the effects of government policies that put a floor under prices

- Consider how a tax on a good affects the price of the good and the quantity sold

- Learn that taxes levied on buyers and taxes levied on sellers are equivalent

- See how the burden of a tax is split between buyers and sellers

Economists have two roles. As scientists, they develop and test theories to explain the world around them. As policy advisers, they use their theories to help change the world for the better. The focus of the preceding two chapters has been scientific. We have seen how supply and demand determine the price of a good and the quantity of the good sold. We have also seen how various events shift supply and demand and thereby change the equilibrium price and quantity.

This chapter offers our first look at policy. Here we analyze various types of government policy using only the tools of supply and demand. As you will see, the analysis yields some surprising insights. Policies often have effects that their architects did not intend or anticipate.

We begin by considering policies that directly control prices. For example, rent-control laws dictate a maximum rent that landlords may charge tenants. Minimum-wage laws dictate the lowest wage that firms may pay workers. Price controls are usually enacted when policymakers believe that the market price of a good or service is unfair to buyers or sellers. Yet, as we will see, these policies can generate inequities of their own.

After our discussion of price controls, we will consider the impact of taxes. Policymakers use taxes both to influence market outcomes and to raise revenue for public purposes. Although the prevalence of taxes in our economy is obvious, their effects are not. For example, when the government levies a tax on the amount that firms pay their workers, do the firms or the workers bear the burden of the tax? The answer is not at all clear—until we apply the powerful tools of supply and demand.

CONTROLS ON PRICES

To see how price controls affect market outcomes, let's look once again at the market for ice cream. As we saw in Chapter 4, if ice cream is sold in a competitive market free of government regulation, the price of ice cream adjusts to balance supply and demand: At the equilibrium price, the quantity of ice cream that buyers want to buy exactly equals the quantity that sellers want to sell. To be concrete, suppose the equilibrium price is $3 per cone.

Not everyone may be happy with the outcome of this free-market process. Let's say the Canadian Association of Ice-Cream Eaters complains that the $3 price is too high for everyone to enjoy a cone a day (their recommended diet). Meanwhile, the Canadian Organization of Ice-Cream Makers complains that the $3 price—the result of "cutthroat competition"—is too low and is depressing the incomes of its members. Each of these groups lobbies the government to pass laws that alter the market outcome by directly controlling the price of an ice-cream cone.

Because buyers of any good always want a lower price while sellers want a higher price, the interests of the two groups conflict. If the Ice-Cream Eaters are successful in their lobbying, the government imposes a legal maximum on the price at which ice cream can be sold. Because the price is not allowed to rise above this level, the legislated maximum is called a **price ceiling.** By contrast, if the Ice-Cream Makers are successful, the government imposes a legal minimum on the price. Because the price cannot fall below this level, the legislated minimum is called a **price floor.** Let us consider the effects of these policies in turn.

price ceiling
a legal maximum on the price at which a good can be sold

price floor
a legal minimum on the price at which a good can be sold

How Price Ceilings Affect Market Outcomes

When the government, moved by the complaints and campaign contributions of the Ice-Cream Eaters, imposes a price ceiling on the market for ice cream, two outcomes are possible. In panel (a) of Figure 6.1, the government imposes a price ceiling of $4 per cone. In this case, because the price that balances supply and demand ($3) is below the ceiling, the price ceiling is *not binding*. Market forces naturally move the economy to the equilibrium, and the price ceiling has no effect on the price or the quantity sold.

Panel (b) of Figure 6.1 shows the other, more interesting, possibility. In this case, the government imposes a price ceiling of $2 per cone. Because the equilibrium price of $3 is above the price ceiling, the ceiling is a *binding constraint* on the market. The forces of supply and demand tend to move the price toward the equilibrium price, but when the market price hits the ceiling, it can rise no further. Thus, the market price equals the price ceiling. At this price, the quantity of ice cream demanded (125 cones in the figure) exceeds the quantity supplied (75 cones). There is a shortage of ice cream, so some people who want to buy ice cream at the going price are unable to.

When a shortage of ice cream develops because of this price ceiling, some mechanism for rationing ice cream will naturally develop. The mechanism could be long lines: Buyers who are willing to arrive early and wait in line get a cone, while those unwilling to wait do not. Alternatively, sellers could ration

FIGURE 6.1

A Market with a Price Ceiling

In panel (a), the government imposes a price ceiling of $4. Because the price ceiling is above the equilibrium price of $3, the price ceiling has no effect, and the market can reach the equilibrium of supply and demand. In this equilibrium, quantity supplied and quantity demanded both equal 100 cones. In panel (b), the government imposes a price ceiling of $2. Because the price ceiling is below the equilibrium price of $3, the market price equals $2. At this price, 125 cones are demanded and only 75 are supplied, so there is a shortage of 50 cones.

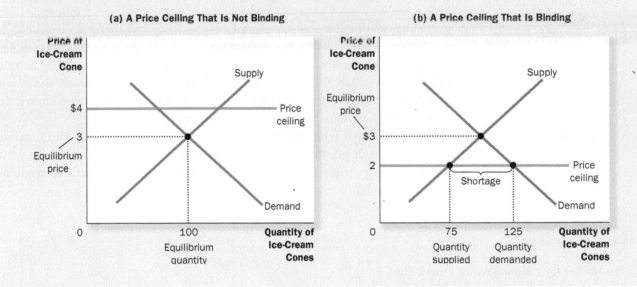

ice cream according to their own personal biases, selling it only to friends, relatives, or members of their own racial or ethnic group. Notice that even though the price ceiling was motivated by a desire to help buyers of ice cream, not all buyers benefit from the policy. Some buyers do get to pay a lower price, although they may have to wait in line to do so, but other buyers cannot get any ice cream at all.

This example in the market for ice cream shows a general result: *When the government imposes a binding price ceiling on a competitive market, a shortage of the good arises, and sellers must ration the scarce goods among the large number of potential buyers.* The rationing mechanisms that develop under price ceilings are rarely desirable. Long lines are inefficient, because they waste buyers' time. Discrimination according to seller bias is both inefficient (because the good does not necessarily go to the buyer who values it most highly) and potentially unfair. By contrast, the rationing mechanism in a free, competitive market is both efficient and impersonal. When the market for ice cream reaches its equilibrium, anyone who wants to pay the market price can get a cone. Free markets ration goods with prices.

Case Study
LINES AT THE GAS PUMP

As we discussed in the preceding chapter, in 1973 the Organization of the Petroleum Exporting Countries (OPEC) raised the price of crude oil in world oil markets. Because crude oil is the major input used to make gasoline, the higher oil prices reduced the supply of gasoline. In Canada the price of gas increased, but there were very few shortages. In the United States, it was very different. Long lines at gas stations became commonplace, and American motorists often had to wait for hours to buy only a few litres of gas.

What was responsible for the long gas lines? Most people blame OPEC. Surely, if OPEC had not raised the price of crude oil, the shortage of gasoline would not have occurred. Yet economists blame U.S. government regulations that limited the price that oil companies could charge for gasoline.

Figure 6.2 shows what happened. As shown in panel (a), before OPEC raised the price of crude oil, the equilibrium price of gasoline, P_1, was below the price ceiling. The price regulation, therefore, had no effect. When the price of crude oil

FIGURE 6.2

The Market for Gasoline with a Price Ceiling

Panel (a) shows the gasoline market when the price ceiling is not binding because the equilibrium price, P_1, is below the ceiling. Panel (b) shows the gasoline market after an increase in the price of crude oil (an input into making gasoline) shifts the supply curve to the left from S_1 to S_2. In an unregulated market, the price would have risen from P_1 to P_2. The price ceiling, however, prevents this from happening. At the binding price ceiling, consumers are willing to buy Q_D, but producers of gasoline are willing to sell only Q_S. The difference between quantity demanded and quantity supplied, $Q_D - Q_S$, measures the gasoline shortage.

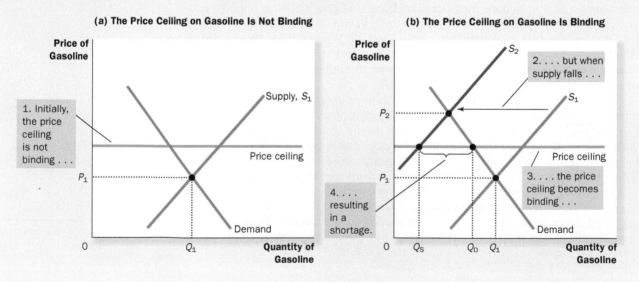

rose, however, the situation changed. The increase in the price of crude oil raised the cost of producing gasoline, and this reduced the supply of gasoline. As panel (b) shows, the supply curve shifted to the left, from S_1 to S_2. In an unregulated market, this shift in supply would have raised the equilibrium price of gasoline from P_1 to P_2, and no shortage would have resulted. Instead, the price ceiling prevented the price from rising to the equilibrium level. At the price ceiling, producers were willing to sell Q_S, and consumers were willing to buy Q_D. Thus, the shift in supply caused a severe shortage at the regulated price.

Eventually, the laws regulating the price of gasoline were repealed. Lawmakers came to understand that they were partly responsible for the many hours Americans lost waiting in line to buy gasoline. Today, when the price of crude oil changes, the price of gasoline can adjust to bring supply and demand into equilibrium. In Canada there were no price controls on gasoline in 1973, and so no long gas lines either. ●

Case Study
RENT CONTROL IN THE SHORT RUN AND LONG RUN

One common example of a price ceiling is rent control. In some provinces, the provincial government places a ceiling on rents that landlords may charge their tenants. The goal of this policy is to help the poor by making housing more affordable. Economists often criticize rent control, arguing that it is a highly inefficient way to help the poor raise their standard of living. One economist has called rent control "the best way to destroy a city, other than bombing."

The adverse effects of rent control are less apparent to the general population because these effects occur over many years. In the short run, landlords have a fixed number of apartments to rent, and they cannot adjust this number quickly as market conditions change. Moreover, the number of people searching for housing in a city may not be highly responsive to rents in the short run because people take time to adjust their housing arrangements. Therefore, the short-run supply and demand for housing are relatively inelastic.

Panel (a) of Figure 6.3 shows the short-run effects of rent control on the housing market. As with any binding price ceiling, rent control causes a shortage. Yet because supply and demand are inelastic in the short run, the initial shortage caused by rent control is small. The primary effect in the short run is to reduce rents.

The long-run story is very different because the buyers and sellers of rental housing respond more to market conditions as time passes. On the supply side, landlords respond to low rents by not building new apartments and by failing to maintain existing ones. On the demand side, low rents encourage people to find their own apartments (rather than living with their parents or sharing apartments with roommates) and induce more people to move into a city. Therefore, both supply and demand are more elastic in the long run.

Rent Control in the Short Run and in the Long Run

Panel (a) shows the short-run effects of rent control: Because the supply and demand for apartments are relatively inelastic, the price ceiling imposed by a rent-control law causes only a small shortage of housing. Panel (b) shows the long-run effects of rent control: Because the supply and demand for apartments are more elastic, rent control causes a large shortage.

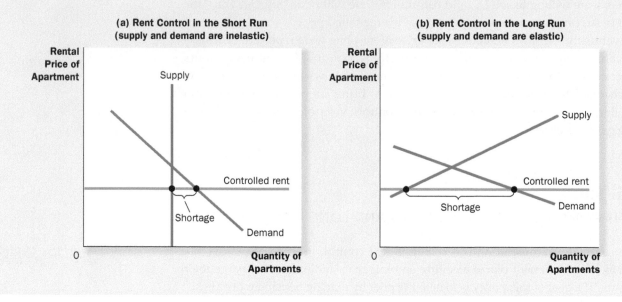

Panel (b) of Figure 6.3 illustrates the housing market in the long run. When rent control depresses rents below the equilibrium level, the quantity of apartments supplied falls substantially, and the quantity of apartments demanded rises substantially. The result is a large shortage of housing.

In provinces with rent control, landlords use various mechanisms to ration housing. Some landlords keep long waiting lists. Others give a preference to tenants without children. Still others discriminate on the basis of race. Sometimes, apartments are allocated to those willing to offer under-the-table payments to building superintendents. In essence, these bribes bring the total price of an apartment (including the bribe) closer to the equilibrium price.

To understand fully the effects of rent control, we have to remember one of the ten principles of economics from Chapter 1: People respond to incentives. In free markets, landlords try to keep their buildings clean and safe because desirable apartments command higher prices. By contrast, when rent control creates shortages and waiting lists, landlords lose their incentive to respond to tenants' concerns. Why should a landlord spend his money to maintain and improve his property when people are waiting to get in as it is? In the end, tenants get lower rents, but they also get lower-quality housing.

NEL

Policymakers often react to the effects of rent control by imposing additional regulations. For example, there are laws that make racial discrimination in housing illegal and require landlords to provide minimally adequate living conditions. These laws, however, are difficult and costly to enforce. By contrast, when rent control is eliminated and a market for housing is regulated by the forces of competition, such laws are less necessary. In a free market, the price of housing adjusts to eliminate the shortages that give rise to undesirable landlord behaviour. ●

How Price Floors Affect Market Outcomes

To examine the effects of another kind of government price control, let's return to the market for ice cream. Imagine now that the government is persuaded by the pleas of the Canadian Organization of Ice-Cream Makers. In this case, the government might institute a price floor. Price floors, like price ceilings, are an attempt by the government to maintain prices at other than equilibrium levels. Whereas a price ceiling places a legal maximum on prices, a price floor places a legal minimum.

When the government imposes a price floor on the ice-cream market, two outcomes are possible. If the government imposes a price floor of $2 per cone when the equilibrium price is $3, we obtain the outcome in panel (a) of Figure 6.4. In this case, because the equilibrium price is above the floor, the price floor is not

FIGURE 6.4

A Market with a Price Floor

In panel (a), the government imposes a price floor of $2. Because this is below the equilibrium price of $3, the price floor has no effect. The market price adjusts to balance supply and demand. At the equilibrium, quantity supplied and quantity demanded both equal 100 cones. In panel (b), the government imposes a price floor of $4, which is above the equilibrium price of $3. Therefore, the market price equals $4. Because 120 cones are supplied at this price and only 80 are demanded, there is a surplus of 40 cones.

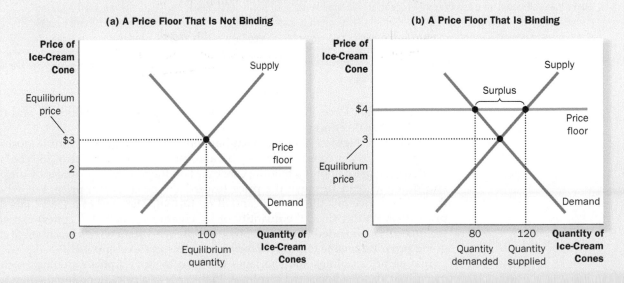

IN THE NEWS

DOES A DROUGHT NEED TO CAUSE A WATER SHORTAGE?

In drought-stricken rural Alberta, fighting-mad farmers like Don Bester are asking a provocative question: Why is Big Oil wasting so much freshwater when there are good alternatives? Big Oil's equally provocative answer: Because the province gives it as much as it wants—for free.

Water Fight

By Andrew Nikiforuk

The day Big Oil got the first warning that its water habits were about to be questioned came in the spring of 1999 on a patch of land just across from Don Bester's Alberta farmyard. That's when some consultants working for Petro-Canada proposed to sink a pipe in the same shallow freshwater aquifer that Bester used to quench the thirst of his 150 cows. The company not only wanted to remove millions of litres of freshwater every year (or enough to supply Bester's needs for 150 years), but it wanted to pump them all down an oil well. Petro-Canada, of course, had no idea its seemingly innocent request would touch off a

grassroots water rebellion in Alberta. Or, for that matter, open a big window on the little-known water habits of a $28-billion industry.

But, sure as rain, that's what happened. As a former oilpatch engineer, Bester, 55, knew what Petro-Canada was up to. Every year, the oilpatch gulps up billions of litres of freshwater to lubricate oilfields in Alberta, Saskatchewan and British Columbia in a process called "waterflooding." By injecting that water into constipated reservoirs, an oil company can push out more oil—not to mention more profits. In fact, more than 402 so-called water injectors dot the central Alberta landscape north of Bester's farm, which is located about a half hour's drive west of Red Deer. They

have been flooding oil pools since the 1960s.

Bester, however, wasn't much interested in seeing another "mistake" in the area. The feisty farmer promptly called together a bunch of his neighbours at the Butte Community Hall to set up a group to "protect Alberta's freshwater." Someone proposed they call themselves the Butte Advisory Committee, but Judy Winter, a 55-year-old farmer and part-time teacher, said no way: "I don't want to advise. I want to tell them."

Faced with the driest year since 1886, the newly minted Butte Action Committee (BAC) then posed a direct question: "Why are we even allowing this when there are alternatives?" Nobody had asked that before in oil-rich

binding. Market forces naturally move the economy to the equilibrium, and the price floor has no effect.

Panel (b) of Figure 6.4 shows what happens when the government imposes a price floor of $4 per cone. In this case, because the equilibrium price of $3 is below the floor, the price floor is a binding constraint on the market. The forces of supply and demand tend to move the price toward the equilibrium price, but when the market price hits the floor, it can fall no further. The market price equals the price floor. At this floor, the quantity of ice cream supplied (120 cones) exceeds the quantity demanded (80 cones). Some people who want to sell ice cream at the going price are unable to. *Thus, a binding price floor causes a surplus.*

Just as price ceilings and shortages can lead to undesirable rationing mechanisms, so can price floors and surpluses. In the case of a price floor, some sellers are unable to sell all they want at the market price. The sellers who appeal to the per-

Alberta and so far, good answers have eluded politicians and industry alike.

Ever since that first impertinent inquiry, BAC has brazenly fired dozens more at a succession of multibillion-dollar firms, including ConocoPhilips and Murphy Oil Corp. In the process of becoming a folk icon, or what one wag called "an aging bunch of hornets," the group has condemned waterfloods as "an irresponsible use of water." The oil industry, in turn, has accused BAC of irresponsible rhetoric and of being a threat to government revenues. But most water experts—and even some oilpatchers—concede that the group may have a point or two about the wisdom of using freshwater for waterfloods. They also think this very unusual water tale highlights Alberta's (and Canada's) cavalier attitude towards the conservation and pricing of water.

The issues are indeed big and hugely political. Each year Alberta Environment doles out water rights to agriculture and industry—all for free—from two sources: surfacewater (lakes and rivers) and groundwater (aquifers). The oilpatch not only soaks up great volumes of surfacewater for waterfloods, but also grabs 26% of the province's groundwater allocations, or almost as much

freshwater as rural Albertans drink every year. According to BAC, hydrologists estimate that pumping this freshwater into an oil well removes it from the water cycle for 80,000 years or longer. To BAC, that sounds like "forever."

Groundwater is the lifeblood of small farmers and small towns; nearly 500,000 Albertans and millions of cattle depend on it. When Petro-Canada initially came calling, Judy Winter, for one, couldn't believe the government would allow industry to use something as precious as potable water to recover oil. Winter called it false economics and compared the practice of waterflooding to paying someone a dollar to retrieve a dime in a sewage pool. "Water," she says, "is far more valuable than oil."

Freshwater flooding is an old, well-established practice in Alberta's oilfields. As every oilpatcher knows, conventional pumping only retrieves about 25% of the oil in any given reservoir. Waterflooding coaxes out another 5% to 10%. Even with that gain, the U.S. Department of Energy still regards waterflooding as an inefficient practice. If freshwater is accurately valued, natural gas, carbon dioxide, dirty water, salt water and chemicals can often get better returns. CO_2 is commonly used in west Texas. But in

Alberta, freshwater largely remains the flood of choice because, well, it's free.

A possible solution might involve true-blue capitalism. Giving away 230 billion litres of freshwater a year for oil production in a semi-arid province strikes most economists and policy experts as, well, very unbusinesslike. But Canadian industry has long been a champion of water gluttony. A 1995 Environment Canada report on industrial water use highlighted this theme: "The fact that water is cheaper than dirt is thought to explain why Canadian industries are relatively primitive in their water-using practices."

Michael M'Gonigle, a law professor at the University of Victoria and a water-resource expert, calls Alberta's waterflood giveaway "an obvious subsidy to industry." Free allocations, he adds, surrender an important policy lever to push industry to adopt smarter substitutes. Even charging a cent for every gallon would make a difference. "That doesn't strike me as a lot," says M'Gonigle, and it would, he points out, bring the government $61 million in revenues a year.

Source: Andrew Nikiforuk, "Water Fight," *Globe and Mail*, July 1, 2002.

sonal biases of the buyers, perhaps due to racial or familial ties, are better able to sell their goods than those who do not. By contrast, in a free market, the price serves as the rationing mechanism, and sellers can sell all they want at the equilibrium price.

Case Study
THE MINIMUM WAGE

An important example of a price floor is the minimum wage. Minimum-wage laws dictate the lowest price for labour that any employer may pay. Minimum wage rates differ by province and territory, as shown in Table 6.1. In 2010, minimum

NEL

TABLE 6.1

Minimum-Wage Rates across Canada

Jurisdiction	General Minimum-Wage Rate	Effective Date	Comments
British Columbia	$8.00	Nov. 1, 2001	Applies to workers with more than 500 hours worked; "first job/entry level" wage is $6.00.
Alberta	8.80	Apr. 1, 2009	Adjusted yearly according to average industrial wage growth
Saskatchewan	9.25	May 1, 2009	
Manitoba	9.50	Oct. 1, 2010	Also applies to residential construction and building maintenance workers; rates for workers in the heavy construction sector and industrial, commercial, and institutional construction vary by occupation
Ontario	10.25	Mar. 31, 2010	Students: $9.60; liquor servers: $8.90; homeworkers (for an employer): $11.28
Quebec	9.50	May 1, 2010	Workers getting tips: $8.25
New Brunswick	9.00	Sept. 1, 2010	To increase to $9.50 on Apr. 1, 2011, and to $10.00 on Sept. 1, 2011
Nova Scotia	9.65	Oct. 1, 2010	Inexperienced workers: $8.10
Prince Edward Island	9.00	Oct. 1, 2010	
Newfoundland & Labrador	10.00	July 1, 2010	
Northwest Territories	9.00	Apr. 1, 2010	To increase to $10.00 on April 1, 2011
Nunavut	10.00	Sept. 5, 2008	Applies to all employees in Nunavut.
Yukon	8.93	Apr. 1, 2010	Annual increases pegged to consumer price index

Note: For workers in federal jurisdiction industries, the minimum wage is the general adult minimum-wage rate of the province of territory where the work is performed.
Sources: Human Resources and Skills Development Canada: http://srv116.services.gc.ca/dimt-wid/sm-mw/rpt1.aspx?lang=eng and various provincial government Web pages.

wages ranged from a low of $8.00 per hour in British Columbia to a high of $10.25 in Ontario. In some provinces, lower rates apply for inexperienced workers and for restaurant and bar staff, who can earn tips to supplement their wages.

To examine the effects of a minimum wage, we must consider the market for labour. Panel (a) of Figure 6.5 shows the labour market, which, like all markets, is subject to the forces of supply and demand. Workers determine the supply of labour, and firms determine the demand. If the government doesn't intervene, the wage normally adjusts to balance labour supply and labour demand.

Panel (b) of Figure 6.5 shows the labour market with a minimum wage. If the minimum wage is above the equilibrium level, as it is here, the quantity of labour supplied exceeds the quantity demanded. The result is unemployment. Thus, the minimum wage raises the incomes of those workers who have jobs, but it lowers the incomes of those workers who cannot find jobs.

FIGURE 6.5

How the Minimum Wage Affects the Labour Market

Panel (a) shows a labour market in which the wage adjusts to balance labour supply and labour demand. Panel (b) shows the impact of a binding minimum wage. Because the minimum wage is a price floor, it causes a surplus: The quantity of labour supplied exceeds the quantity demanded. The result is unemployment.

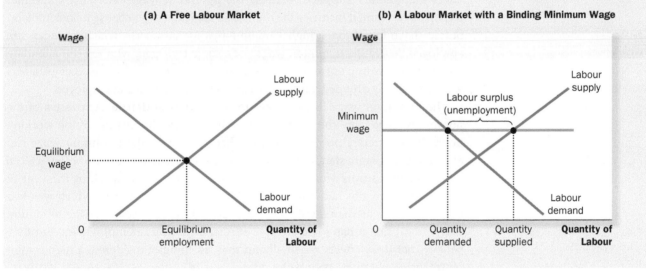

To fully understand the minimum wage, keep in mind that the economy contains not a single labour market, but many labour markets for different types of workers. The impact of the minimum wage depends on the skill and experience of the worker. Workers with high skills and much experience are not affected, because their equilibrium wages are well above the minimum. For these workers, the minimum wage is not binding.

The minimum wage has its greatest impact on the market for teenage labour. The equilibrium wages of teenagers are low because teenagers are among the least skilled and least experienced members of the labour force. In addition, teenagers are often willing to accept a lower wage in exchange for on-the-job training. (Some teenagers are willing to work as "interns" for no pay at all. Because internships pay nothing, however, the minimum wage does not apply to them. If it did, these jobs might not exist.) As a result, the minimum wage is more often binding for teenagers than for other members of the labour force.

Many economists have studied how minimum-wage laws affect the teenage labour market. These researchers compare the changes in the minimum wage over time with the changes in teenage employment. Although there is some debate about how much the minimum wage affects employment, the typical study finds that a 10 percent increase in the minimum wage depresses teenage employment between 1 and 3 percent. In interpreting this estimate, note that a 10 percent increase in the minimum wage does not raise the average wage of teenagers by 10 percent. A change in the law does not directly affect those teenagers who are already paid well above the minimum, and enforcement of minimum-wage laws is not perfect. Thus, the estimated drop in employment of 1 to 3 percent is significant.

In addition to altering the quantity of labour demanded, the minimum wage also alters the quantity supplied. Because the minimum wage raises the wage that teenagers can earn, it increases the number of teenagers who choose to look for jobs. Studies have found that a higher minimum wage influences which teenagers are employed. When the minimum wage rises, some teenagers who are still attending school choose to drop out and take jobs. These new dropouts displace other teenagers who had already dropped out of school and who now become unemployed.

The minimum wage is a frequent topic of political debate. Advocates of the minimum wage view the policy as one way to raise the income of the working poor. They correctly point out that workers who earn the minimum wage can afford only a meagre standard of living. For example, at a minimum wage of $7.00 per hour, two adults working 40 hours a week for every week of the year at minimum-wage jobs had a total annual income of only $41 600, which was less than half of the median family income in 2009. Many advocates of the minimum wage admit that it has some adverse effects, including unemployment, but they believe that these effects are small and that, all things considered, a higher minimum wage makes the poor better off.

Opponents of the minimum wage contend that it is not the best way to combat poverty. They note that a high minimum wage causes unemployment, encourages teenagers to drop out of school, and prevents some unskilled workers from getting the on-the-job training they need. Moreover, opponents of the minimum wage point out that the minimum wage is a poorly targeted policy. Not all minimum-wage workers are heads of households trying to help their families escape poverty. In fact, fewer than a third of minimum-wage earners are in families with incomes below the poverty line. Many are teenagers from middle-class homes working at part-time jobs for extra spending money. ●

Evaluating Price Controls

One of the ten principles of economics discussed in Chapter 1 is that markets are usually a good way to organize economic activity. This principle explains why economists usually oppose price ceilings and price floors. To economists, prices are not the outcome of some haphazard process. Prices, they contend, are the result of the millions of business and consumer decisions that lie behind the supply and demand curves. Prices have the crucial job of balancing supply and demand and, thereby, coordinating economic activity. When policymakers set prices by legal decree, they obscure the signals that normally guide the allocation of society's resources.

Another of the ten principles of economics is that governments can sometimes improve market outcomes. Indeed, policymakers are led to control prices because they view the market's outcome as unfair. Price controls are often aimed at helping the poor. For instance, rent-control laws try to make housing affordable for everyone, and minimum-wage laws try to help people escape poverty.

Yet price controls often hurt those they are trying to help. Rent control may keep rents low, but it also discourages landlords from maintaining their buildings and makes housing hard to find. Minimum-wage laws may raise the incomes of some workers, but they also cause other workers to be unemployed.

Helping those in need can be accomplished in ways other than controlling prices. For instance, the government can make housing more affordable by paying a fraction of the rent for poor families. Unlike rent control, such rent subsidies do not reduce the quantity of housing supplied and, therefore, do not lead to housing shortages. Similarly, wage subsidies raise the living standards of the working poor without discouraging firms from hiring them.

Although these alternative policies are often better than price controls, they are not perfect. Rent and wage subsidies cost the government money and, therefore, require higher taxes. As we see in the next section, taxation has costs of its own.

QuickQuiz   Define *price ceiling* and *price floor*, and give an example of each. Which leads to a shortage? Which leads to a surplus? Why?

TAXES

All governments—from the federal government in Ottawa to the local governments in small towns—use taxes to raise revenue for public projects, such as roads, schools, and national defence. Because taxes are such an important policy instrument, and because they affect our lives in many ways, the study of taxes is a topic to which we return several times throughout this book. In this section we begin our study of how taxes affect the economy.

To set the stage for our analysis, imagine that a local government decides to hold an annual ice-cream celebration—with a parade, fireworks, and speeches by town officials. To raise revenue to pay for the event, it decides to place a $0.50 tax on the sale of ice-cream cones. When the plan is announced, our two lobbying groups swing into action. The Canadian Organization of Ice-Cream Makers claims that its members are struggling to survive in a competitive market, and it argues that *buyers* of ice cream should have to pay the tax. The Canadian Association of Ice-Cream Eaters claims that consumers of ice cream are having trouble making ends meet, and it argues that *sellers* of ice cream should pay the tax. The town mayor, hoping to reach a compromise, suggests that half the tax be paid by the buyers and half be paid by the sellers.

To analyze these proposals, we need to address a simple but subtle question: When the government levies a tax on a good, who bears the burden of the tax? The people buying the good? The people selling the good? Or, if buyers and sellers share the tax burden, what determines how the burden is divided? Can the government simply legislate the division of the burden, as the mayor is suggesting, or is the division determined by more fundamental forces in the economy? Economists use the term **tax incidence** to refer to the distribution of a tax burden. As we will see, some surprising lessons about tax incidence arise just by applying the tools of supply and demand.

tax incidence
the manner in which the burden of a tax is shared among participants in a market

How Taxes on Buyers Affect Market Outcomes

We begin by considering a tax levied on buyers of a good. Suppose, for instance, that our local government passes a law requiring buyers of ice-cream cones to send $0.50 to the government for each ice-cream cone they buy. How does this law affect the buyers and sellers of ice cream? To answer this question, we can follow the three steps in Chapter 4 for analyzing supply and demand: (1) We decide whether the law affects the supply curve or demand curve. (2) We decide which way the curve shifts. (3) We examine how the shift affects the equilibrium.

Step One The initial impact of the tax is on the demand for ice cream. The supply curve is not affected because, for any given price of ice cream, sellers have the same incentive to provide ice cream to the market. By contrast, buyers now have to pay a tax to the government (as well as the price to the sellers) whenever they buy ice cream. Thus, the tax shifts the demand curve for ice cream.

Step Two We next determine the direction of the shift. Because the tax on buyers makes buying ice cream less attractive, buyers demand a smaller quantity of ice cream at every price. As a result, the demand curve shifts to the left (or, equivalently, downward), as shown in Figure 6.6.

We can, in this case, be precise about how much the curve shifts. Because of the $0.50 tax levied on buyers, the effective price to buyers is now $0.50 higher than the market price (whatever the market price happens to be). For example, if the market price of a cone happened to be $2.00, the effective price to buyers would be $2.50. Because buyers look at their total cost including the tax, they demand a quantity of

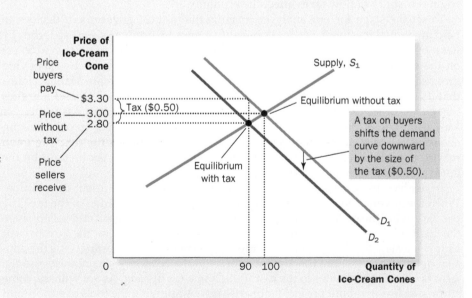

FIGURE 6.6

A Tax on Buyers

When a tax of $0.50 is levied on buyers, the demand curve shifts down by $0.50 from D_1 to D_2. The equilibrium quantity falls from 100 to 90 cones. The price that sellers receive falls from $3.00 to $2.80. The price that buyers pay (including the tax) rises from $3.00 to $3.30. Even though the tax is levied on buyers, buyers and sellers share the burden of the tax.

ice cream as if the market price were $0.50 higher than it actually is. In other words, to induce buyers to demand any given quantity, the market price must now be $0.50 lower to make up for the effect of the tax. Thus, the tax shifts the demand curve *downward* from D_1 to D_2 by exactly the size of the tax ($0.50).

Step Three   Having determined how the demand curve shifts, we can now see the effect of the tax by comparing the initial equilibrium and the new equilibrium. You can see in the figure that the equilibrium price of ice cream falls from $3.00 to $2.80 and the equilibrium quantity falls from 100 to 90 cones. Because sellers sell less and buyers buy less in the new equilibrium, the tax on ice cream reduces the size of the ice-cream market.

Implications   We can now return to the question of tax incidence: Who pays the tax? Although buyers send the entire tax to the government, buyers and sellers share the burden. Because the market price falls from $3.00 to $2.80 when the tax is introduced, sellers receive $0.20 less for each ice-cream cone than they did without the tax. Thus, the tax makes sellers worse off. Buyers pay sellers a lower price ($2.80), but the effective price including the tax rises from $3.00 before the tax to $3.30 with the tax ($2.80 + $0.50 = $3.30). Thus, the tax also makes buyers worse off.

To sum up, the analysis yields two lessons:

- Taxes discourage market activity. When a good is taxed, the quantity of the good sold is smaller in the new equilibrium.
- Buyers and sellers share the burden of taxes. In the new equilibrium, buyers pay more for the good, and sellers receive less.

How Taxes on Sellers Affect Market Outcomes

Now consider a tax levied on sellers of a good. Suppose the local government passes a law requiring sellers of ice-cream cones to send $0.50 to the government for each cone they sell. What are the effects of this law? Again, we apply our three steps.

Step One   In this case, the immediate impact of the tax is on the sellers of ice cream. Because the tax is not levied on buyers, the quantity of ice cream demanded at any given price is the same; thus, the demand curve does not change. By contrast, the tax on sellers makes the ice-cream business less profitable at any given price, so it shifts the supply curve.

Step Two   Because the tax on sellers raises the cost of producing and selling ice cream, it reduces the quantity supplied at every price. The supply curve shifts to the left (or, equivalently, upward).

Once again, we can be precise about the magnitude of the shift. For any market price of ice cream, the effective price to sellers—the amount they get to keep after paying the tax—is $0.50 lower. For example, if the market price of a cone happened to be $2.00, the effective price received by sellers would be $1.50. Whatever the market price, sellers will supply a quantity of ice cream as if the price were

$0.50 lower than it is. Put differently, to induce sellers to supply any given quantity, the market price must now be $0.50 higher to compensate for the effect of the tax. Thus, as shown in Figure 6.7, the supply curve shifts *upward* from S_1 to S_2 by exactly the size of the tax ($0.50).

Step Three   Having determined how the supply curve shifts, we can now compare the initial and the new equilibrium. The figure shows that the equilibrium price of ice cream rises from $3.00 to $3.30, and the equilibrium quantity falls from 100 to 90 cones. Once again, the tax reduces the size of the ice-cream market. And once again, buyers and sellers share the burden of the tax. Because the market price rises, buyers pay $0.30 more for each cone than they did before the tax was enacted. Sellers receive a higher price than they did without the tax, but the effective price (after paying the tax) falls from $3.00 to $2.80.

Implications   If you compare Figures 6.6 and 6.7, you will notice a surprising conclusion: *Taxes on buyers and taxes on sellers are equivalent.* In both cases, the tax places a wedge between the price that buyers pay and the price that sellers receive. The wedge between the buyers' price and the sellers' price is the same, regardless of whether the tax is levied on buyers or sellers. In either case, the wedge shifts the relative position of the supply and demand curves. In the new equilibrium, buyers and sellers share the burden of the tax. The only difference between taxes on buyers and taxes on sellers is who sends the money to the government.

   The equivalence of these two taxes is easy to understand if we imagine that the government collects the $0.50 ice-cream tax in a bowl on the counter of each

---

FIGURE 6.7

A Tax on Sellers

When a tax of $0.50 is levied on sellers, the supply curve shifts up by $0.50 from S_1 to S_2. The equilibrium quantity falls from 100 to 90 cones. The price that buyers pay rises from $3.00 to $3.30. The price that sellers receive (after paying the tax) falls from $3.00 to $2.80. Even though the tax is levied on sellers, buyers and sellers share the burden of the tax.

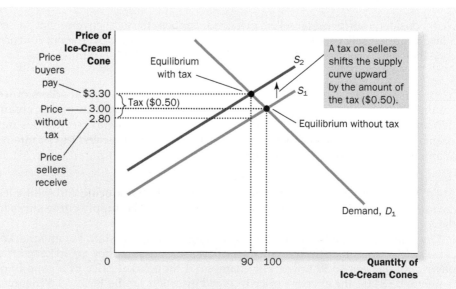

ice-cream store. When the government levies the tax on buyers, the buyer is required to place $0.50 in the bowl every time a cone is bought. When the government levies the tax on sellers, the seller is required to place $0.50 in the bowl after the sale of each cone. Whether the $0.50 goes directly from the buyer's pocket into the bowl, or indirectly from the buyer's pocket into the seller's hand and then into the bowl, does not matter. Once the market reaches its new equilibrium, buyers and sellers share the burden, regardless of how the tax is levied.

Case Study

CAN PARLIAMENT DISTRIBUTE THE BURDEN OF A PAYROLL TAX?

If you have ever received a paycheque, you probably noticed that taxes were deducted from the amount you earned. One of these taxes is called Employment Insurance (EI). The federal government uses the revenue from the EI tax to pay for benefits to unemployed workers, as well as for training programs and other policies. EI is an example of a payroll tax, which is a tax on the wages that firms pay their workers. In 2010, the total EI tax for the typical worker was about 4 percent of earnings.

Who do you think bears the burden of this payroll tax—firms or workers? When Parliament passed this legislation, it tried to mandate a division of the tax burden. According to the law, 58 percent of the tax is paid by firms, and 42 percent is paid by workers. That is, 58 percent of the tax is paid out of firm revenue, and 42 percent is deducted from workers' paycheques. The amount that shows up as a deduction on your pay stub is the worker contribution.

Our analysis of tax incidence, however, shows that lawmakers cannot so easily dictate the distribution of a tax burden. To illustrate, we can analyze a payroll tax as merely a tax on a good, where the good is labour and the price is the wage. The key feature of the payroll tax is that it places a wedge between the wage that firms pay and the wage that workers receive. Figure 6.8 shows the outcome. When a payroll tax is enacted, the wage received by workers falls, and the wage paid by firms rises. In the end, workers and firms share the burden of the tax, much as the legislation requires. Yet this division of the tax burden between workers and firms has nothing to do with the legislated division: The division of the burden in Figure 6.8 is not necessarily 58 percent–42 percent, and the same outcome would prevail if the law levied the entire tax on workers or if it levied the entire tax on firms.

This example shows that the most basic lesson of tax incidence is often overlooked in public debate. Lawmakers can decide whether a tax comes from the buyer's pocket or from the seller's, but they cannot legislate the true burden of a tax. Rather, tax incidence depends on the forces of supply and demand. ∎

FIGURE 6.8

A Payroll Tax

A payroll tax places a wedge between the wage that workers receive and the wage that firms pay. Comparing wages with and without the tax, you can see that workers and firms share the tax burden. This division of the tax burden between workers and firms does not depend on whether the government levies the tax on workers, levies the tax on firms, or divides the tax equally between the two groups.

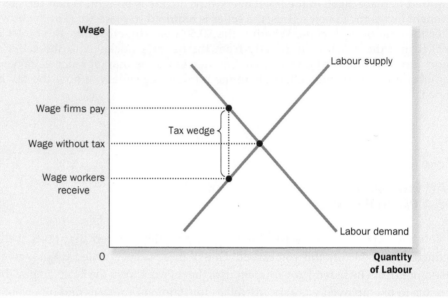

Elasticity and Tax Incidence

When a good is taxed, buyers and sellers of the good share the burden of the tax. But how exactly is the tax burden divided? Only rarely will it be shared equally. To see how the burden is divided, consider the impact of taxation in the two markets in Figure 6.9. In both cases, the figure shows the initial demand curve, the initial supply curve, and a tax that drives a wedge between the amount paid by buyers and the amount received by sellers. (Not drawn in either panel of the figure is the new supply or demand curve. Which curve shifts depends on whether the tax is levied on buyers or sellers. As we have seen, this is irrelevant for the incidence of the tax.) The difference in the two panels is the relative elasticity of supply and demand.

Panel (a) of Figure 6.9 shows a tax in a market with very elastic supply and relatively inelastic demand. That is, sellers are very responsive to changes in the price of the good (so the supply curve is relatively flat), whereas buyers are not very responsive (so the demand curve is relatively steep). When a tax is imposed on a market with these elasticities, the price received by sellers does not fall much, so sellers bear only a small burden. By contrast, the price paid by buyers rises substantially, indicating that buyers bear most of the burden of the tax.

Panel (b) of Figure 6.9 shows a tax in a market with relatively inelastic supply and very elastic demand. In this case, sellers are not very responsive to changes in the price (so the supply curve is steeper), while buyers are very responsive (so the demand curve is flatter). The figure shows that when a tax is imposed, the price paid by buyers does not rise much, while the price received by sellers falls substantially. Thus, sellers bear most of the burden of the tax.

The two panels of Figure 6.9 show a general lesson about how the burden of a tax is divided: *A tax burden falls more heavily on the side of the market that is less elastic.* Why is this true? In essence, the elasticity measures the willingness of buyers or sellers to leave the market when conditions become unfavourable. A small elas-

FIGURE 6.9

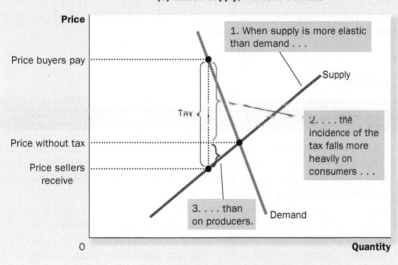

(a) Elastic Supply, Inelastic Demand

1. When supply is more elastic than demand . . .

Supply

Tax

2. . . . the incidence of the tax falls more heavily on consumers . . .

3. . . . than on producers.

Demand

Price buyers pay

Price without tax

Price sellers receive

Price

0

Quantity

How the Burden of a Tax Is Divided

In panel (a), the supply curve is elastic, and the demand curve is inelastic. In this case, the price received by sellers falls only slightly, while the price paid by buyers rises substantially. Thus, buyers bear most of the burden of the tax. In panel (b), the supply curve is inelastic, and the demand curve is elastic. In this case, the price received by sellers falls substantially, while the price paid by buyers rises only slightly. Thus, sellers bear most of the burden of the tax.

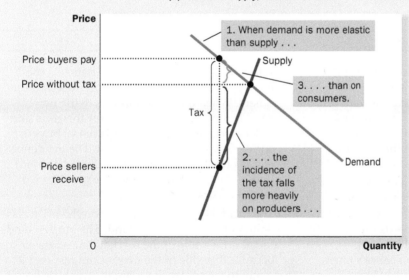

(b) Inelastic Supply, Elastic Demand

1. When demand is more elastic than supply . . .

Supply

3. . . . than on consumers.

Tax

2. . . . the incidence of the tax falls more heavily on producers . . .

Demand

Price buyers pay

Price without tax

Price sellers receive

Price

0

Quantity

ticity of demand means that buyers do not have good alternatives to consuming this particular good. A small elasticity of supply means that sellers do not have good alternatives to producing this particular good. When the good is taxed, the side of the market with fewer good alternatives cannot easily leave the market and must, therefore, bear more of the burden of the tax.

We can apply this logic to the payroll tax discussed in the previous case study. Most labour economists believe that the supply of labour is much less elastic than the demand. This means that workers, rather than firms, bear most of the burden of the payroll tax. In other words, the distribution of the tax burden is not at all close to the 58–42 split that lawmakers intended.

QuickQuiz In a supply-and-demand diagram, show how a tax on car buyers of $1000 per car affects the quantity of cars sold and the price of cars. In another diagram, show how a tax on car sellers of $1000 per car affects the quantity of cars sold and the price of cars. In both of your diagrams, show the change in the price paid by car buyers and the change in price received by car sellers.

CONCLUSION

The economy is governed by two kinds of laws: the laws of supply and demand and the laws enacted by governments. In this chapter we have begun to see how these laws interact. Price controls and taxes are common in various markets in the economy, and their effects are frequently debated in the press and among policymakers. Even a little bit of economic knowledge can go a long way toward understanding and evaluating these policies.

In subsequent chapters we will analyze many government policies in greater detail. We will examine the effects of taxation more fully, and we will consider a broader range of policies than we considered here. Yet the basic lessons of this chapter will not change: When analyzing government policies, supply and demand are the first and most useful tools of analysis.

SUMMARY

- A price ceiling is a legal maximum on the price of a good or service. An example is rent control. If the price ceiling is below the equilibrium price, the quantity demanded exceeds the quantity supplied. Because of the resulting shortage, sellers must in some way ration the good or service among buyers.

- A price floor is a legal minimum on the price of a good or service. An example is the minimum wage. If the price floor is above the equilibrium price, the quantity supplied exceeds the quantity demanded. Because of the resulting surplus, buyers' demands for the good or service must in some way be rationed among sellers.

- When the government levies a tax on a good, the equilibrium quantity of the good falls. That is, a tax on a market shrinks the size of the market.

- A tax on a good places a wedge between the price paid by buyers and the price received by sellers. When the market moves to the new equilibrium, buyers pay more for the good and sellers receive less for it. In this sense, buyers and sellers share the tax burden. The incidence of a tax (that is, the division of the tax burden) does not depend on whether the tax is levied on buyers or sellers.

- The incidence of a tax depends on the price elasticities of supply and demand. The burden tends to fall on the side of the market that is less elastic because that side of the market can respond less easily to the tax by changing the quantity bought or sold.

KEY CONCEPTS

price ceiling, p. 120 price floor, p. 120 tax incidence, p. 131

QUESTIONS FOR REVIEW

1. Give an example of a price ceiling and an example of a price floor.

2. Which causes a shortage of a good—a price ceiling or a price floor? Which causes a surplus?

3. What mechanisms allocate resources when the price of a good is not allowed to bring supply and demand into equilibrium?

4. Explain why economists usually oppose controls on prices.

5. What is the difference between a tax paid by buyers and a tax paid by sellers?

6. How does a tax on a good affect the price paid by buyers, the price received by sellers, and the quantity sold?

7. What determines how the burden of a tax is divided between buyers and sellers? Why?

PROBLEMS AND APPLICATIONS

1. Lovers of classical music persuade Parliament to impose a price ceiling of $40 per concert ticket. Does this policy get more or fewer people to attend classical music concerts?

2. The government has decided that the free-market price of cheese is too low.
   a. Suppose the government imposes a binding price floor in the cheese market. Use a supply-and-demand diagram to show the effect of this policy on the price of cheese and the quantity of cheese sold. Is there a shortage or surplus of cheese?
   b. Farmers complain that the price floor has reduced their total revenue. Is this possible? Explain.
   c. In response to farmers' complaints, the government agrees to purchase all of the surplus cheese at the price floor. Compared to the basic price floor, who benefits from this new policy? Who loses?

3. A recent study found that the demand and supply schedules for Frisbees are as follows:

Price per Frisbee	Quantity Demanded	Quantity Supplied
$11	1 million	15 million
10	2	12
9	4	9
8	6	6
7	8	3
6	10	1

a. What are the equilibrium price and quantity of Frisbees?

b. Frisbee manufacturers persuade the government that Frisbee production improves scientists' understanding of aerodynamics and thus is important for national security. A concerned Parliament votes to impose a price floor $2 above the equilibrium price. What is the new market price? How many Frisbees are sold?

c. Irate students march on Ottawa and demand a reduction in the price of Frisbees. An even more concerned Parliament votes to repeal the price floor and impose a price ceiling $1 below the former price floor. What is the new market price? How many Frisbees are sold?

4. Suppose the provincial government requires beer drinkers to pay a $2 tax on each case of beer purchased.
   a. Draw a supply-and-demand diagram of the market for beer without the tax. Show the price paid by consumers, the price received by producers, and the quantity of beer sold. What is the difference between the price paid by consumers and the price received by producers?
   b. Now draw a supply-and-demand diagram for the beer market with the tax. Show the price paid by consumers, the price received by producers, and the quantity of beer sold. What is the difference between the price paid by consumers and the price received

by producers? Has the quantity of beer sold increased or decreased?

5. An MP wants to raise tax revenue and make workers better off. A staff member proposes raising the payroll tax paid by firms and using part of the extra revenue to reduce the payroll tax paid by workers. Would this accomplish the MP's goal?

6. If the government places a $500 tax on luxury cars, will the price paid by consumers rise by more than $500, less than $500, or exactly $500? Explain.

7. Parliament decides that Canada should reduce air pollution by reducing its use of gasoline. It imposes a $0.50 tax for each litre of gasoline sold.
   a. Should it impose this tax on producers or consumers? Explain carefully, using a supply-and-demand diagram.
   b. If the demand for gasoline were more elastic, would this tax be more effective or less effective in reducing the quantity of gasoline consumed? Explain with both words and a diagram.
   c. Are consumers of gasoline helped or hurt by this tax? Why?
   d. Are workers in the oil industry helped or hurt by this tax? Why?

8. A case study in this chapter discusses the minimum-wage law.
   a. Suppose the minimum wage is above the equilibrium wage in the market for unskilled labour. Using a supply-and-demand diagram of the market for unskilled labour, show the market wage, the number of workers who are employed, and the number of workers who are unemployed. Also show the total wage payments to unskilled workers.
   b. Now suppose the provincial government proposes an increase in the minimum wage. What effect would this increase have on employment? Does the change in employment depend on the elasticity of demand, the elasticity of supply, both elasticities, or neither?
   c. What effect would this increase in the minimum wage have on unemployment? Does the change in unemployment depend

on the elasticity of demand, the elasticity of supply, both elasticities, or neither?
   d. If the demand for unskilled labour were inelastic, would the proposed increase in the minimum wage raise or lower total wage payments to unskilled workers? Would your answer change if the demand for unskilled labour were elastic?

9. Consider the following policies, each of which is aimed at reducing violent crime by reducing the use of guns. Illustrate each of these proposed policies in a supply-and-demand diagram of the gun market.
   a. a tax on gun buyers
   b. a tax on gun sellers
   c. a price floor on guns
   d. a tax on ammunition

10. The Canadian government administers two programs that affect the market for cigarettes. Health Canada media campaigns and labelling requirements are aimed at making the public aware of the dangers of cigarette smoking. At the same time, Agriculture and Agri-Food Canada imposes production quotas on tobacco farmers, which raise the price of tobacco above the equilibrium price.
   a. How do these two programs affect cigarette consumption? Use a graph of the cigarette market in your answer.
   b. What is the combined effect of these two programs on the price of cigarettes?
   c. Cigarettes are also heavily taxed. What effect does this tax have on cigarette consumption?

11. A subsidy is the opposite of a tax. With a $0.50 tax on the buyers of ice-cream cones, the government collects $0.50 for each cone purchased; with a $0.50 subsidy for the buyers of ice-cream cones, the government pays buyers $0.50 for each cone purchased.
   a. Show the effect of a $0.50 per cone subsidy on the demand curve for ice-cream cones, the effective price paid by consumers, the effective price received by sellers, and the quantity of cones sold.
   b. Do consumers gain or lose from this policy? Do producers gain or lose? Does the government gain or lose?

12. At the Pengrowth Saddledome, home of the Calgary Flames, seating is limited to about 17 000. Hence, the number of tickets issued is fixed at that figure. (Assume that all seats are equally desirable and are sold at the same price.) Seeing a golden opportunity to raise revenue, the City of Calgary levies a per-ticket tax of $5 to be paid by the hockey ticket buyer. Calgary sports fans, a famously civic-minded lot, dutifully send in the $5 per ticket. Draw a well-labelled graph showing the impact of the tax. On whom does the tax burden fall—the team's owners, the fans, or both? Why?

13. Say the demand schedule for ice-cream cones can be represented by the equation $Q^D = 160 - 3P$, where Q^D is the quantity demanded and P is the price. The supply schedule can be represented by $Q^S = 140 + 7P$, where Q^S is the quantity supplied.

   a. Calculate the equilibrium price and quantity in the market for ice-cream cones.

   b. Say the Canadian Association of Ice-Cream Eaters complains that the equilibrium price calculated in part (a) is too high, and their members cannot eat enough ice-cream cones at this price. They lobby the government to impose a price ceiling on ice-cream cones of $1. What is the quantity demanded at this price? The quantity supplied? Is there a shortage or surplus of ice cream? How big is it? What if a $2.50 price ceiling was imposed instead?

   c. Say instead that the Canadian Association of Ice-Cream Makers lobbies the government, arguing that the equilibrium price is too low for their members to make a decent living. They want a price floor of $3 per cone. What is the quantity demanded at this price? The quantity supplied? Is there a shortage or a surplus of ice cream? What is it? What if a price floor of $1.50 was imposed instead?

http:// For more study tools, please visit http://www.mankiw5e.nelson.com.

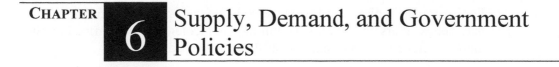

CHAPTER 6 Supply, Demand, and Government Policies

I. Chapter Overview

A. Context and Purpose

To provide a transition from the basics of supply and demand into the extended supply-and-demand discussion, this chapter broadens the analysis of supply and demand to include the role of government in a mixed market economy. In exploring the role of government, Chapter 6 considers the effects of price controls such as minimum-wage and rent-control laws. It also deals with questions of tax incidence; that is, who actually pays various taxes.

A. Helpful Hints

1. *Price ceilings and floors matter only if they are binding.* Remember that not all price ceilings and floors cause disturbances in markets. A price ceiling causes shortages only if it is *below* the equilibrium price (and is enforced). A ceiling, or maximum price, that is above the equilibrium price cannot prevent the market from reaching equilibrium. Similarly, a price floor causes surpluses only if it is *above* the equilibrium price and it is enforced. A price floor set below the equilibrium price will not prevent the market from reaching equilibrium.

2. *Taxes cause vertical shifts.* Even though economists normally look at supply-and-demand shifts in terms of left and right, it is useful in the case of tax incidence to look at the vertical shifts. A tax on buyers causes a vertical shift down in the demand curve that is just equal to the tax. For quantity demanded to stay the same, price must fall by the full amount of the tax that the buyer must pay. A tax on sellers causes a vertical shift up the price axis in the supply curve just equal to the tax. For quantity supplied to stay the same, price must increase by the full amount of the tax that the seller must pay.

3. *Taxes on buyers and taxes on sellers are equivalent.* Consider the case of a tax imposed in a market in which neither supply nor demand is totally elastic or totally inelastic. Although a tax on buyers shifts the demand curve, and a tax on sellers shifts the supply curve, the end result of either tax is reduced quantity sold, a higher price paid by buyers, and a lower price received by sellers. The difference between the prices paid and received is the tax, which introduces a wedge between buyers and sellers. Politically, it sometimes makes sense to switch a tax from buyers to sellers, or vice versa, but economically, it makes no sense; the result is the same.

For example Employment Insurance taxes by law are split 42–58% between workers and employers, but the tax incidence is determined by the market, after supply and demand shift and wages adjust.

II. Self-Testing Challenges

A. True/False Questions

_____1.   A price ceiling above equilibrium tends to cause shortages.

_____2.   A price floor above equilibrium tends to cause surpluses.

_____3.   A tax levied on buyers of a good or service shifts the demand curve up.

_____4.   A tax levied on sellers of a good or service shifts the supply curve up.

_____5.   A $1 per unit tax on sellers generally will raise price by $1.

_____6.   A $5 per unit tax on buyers generally will lower the equilibrium price by less than $5.

_____7.   A binding price ceiling on a competitive market causes a shortage in the market, and sellers must ration the scarce good among a large number of potential buyers.

_____8.   A $1 per unit tax on sellers is economically equivalent to a $1 per unit tax on buyers, except that the tax on sellers is more equitable for low-income buyers.

_____9.   Rent controls are least likely to cause large shortages of housing if the supply of housing is inelastic.

_____10.   The burden of a tax always falls on the side of the market with the smaller price elasticity.

B. Multiple-Choice Questions

1.   Which of the following describes the shift caused by a $500-per-automobile pollution tax on the manufacturers?
     a.   demand curve down by $500.
     b.   demand curve up by $500.
     c.   supply curve up by $500.
     d.   supply curve down by $500.

2. Which one of the following describes when a tax is **MOST** likely to be paid by the seller?
   a. when supply and demand are elastic
   b. when supply and demand are inelastic
   c. when demand is elastic and supply is inelastic
   d. when demand is inelastic and supply is elastic

3. Which one of the following is caused by a binding price ceiling?
   a. shortages
   b. excess supply
   c. quantity supplied greater than quantity demanded
   d. competition among buyers, driving price up to equilibrium

4. Which one of the following would **NOT** be predicted to result if the government impose a ceiling on the price of rental accommodation that is lower than the market equilibrium price??
   a. A shortage of rental units would develop.
   b. The existing stock of rental units would deteriorate.
   c. Those who obtain rental units at the controlled price would benefit.
   d. Construction of new rental accommodation would be encouraged.

5. Which one of the following describes when a tax would be split equally between buyers and sellers?
   a. when supply and demand are equal
   b. when supply and demand have equal elasticities
   c. when supply has a zero elasticity and demand has an infinite elasticity
   d. when supply has an infinite elasticity and demand has a zero elasticity.

6. Which one of the following will occur if the Government of Alberta imposes a $4 recycling fee on the buyer whenever a new tire is sold?
   a. It will move the demand curve down by $4.
   b. It will move the demand curve up by $ 4.
   c. It will move the supply curve up by $ 4.
   d. It will move the supply curve down by $ 4.

7. Which one of the following describes who will bear the burden of a sales tax imposed on a commodity with perfectly inelastic supply?
   a. It will be borne mostly by sellers.
   b. It will be borne completely by sellers.
   c. It will be borne mostly by buyers.
   d. It will be borne completely by buyers.

8. Which one of the following describes what economists mean when they say that a tax introduces a wedge in a market?
   a. It wedges money away from buyers.
   b. It wedges money away from sellers.
   c. It creates a wedge between the new and old equilibrium prices.
   d. It introduces a wedge between the price paid by the buyer and that received by the seller.

9. All else equal, which one of the following describes conditions under which a binding price ceiling will cause greater shortages?
   a. if both supply and demand are inelastic
   b. if both supply and demand are elastic
   c. if supply is elastic, but demand is inelastic
   d. if supply is inelastic, but demand is elastic

10. Which one of the following is a good way to distinguish shortage from scarcity?
    a. A shortage can be eliminated by raising price, but scarcity cannot be eliminated.
    b. Shortages result from price controls, but scarcity results from sellers holding back output.
    c. A shortage means that people cannot have all that they want at a zero price; scarcity means that people cannot have all they want at any price.
    d. At a high enough price, there is no scarcity, but shortages continue to exist even at high prices.

11. If the price of a commodity does not change after the government levies a sales tax on it, which one of the following is true?
    a. Supply of the commodity is more elastic than its demand.
    b. Demand for the commodity is more elastic than its supply.
    c. Supply of the commodity is perfectly elastic.
    d. Demand for the commodity is perfectly elastic.

12. All else equal, which one of the following describes when a binding price floor will cause **LESS** of a surplus?
    a. if both supply and demand are inelastic.
    b. if both supply and demand are elastic.
    c. if supply is elastic, but demand is inelastic.
    d. if supply is inelastic, but demand is elastic.

13. Which of the following statements about minimum-wage legislation is correct?
    a. effective only if the minimum wage is set below the market equilibrium wage
    b. has no effect on the quantity of labour hired
    c. is a price floor that creates unemployment
    d. is a price ceiling that creates a shortage of workers

14. Which one of the following will, in effect, occur with an increase in the demand in a market with a binding price ceiling?
    a. an increase the quantities bought and sold
    b. a decrease the quantities bought and sold
    c. no alteration of the quantities bought and sold
    d. an increase the amount of shortage

C. Short-Answer Questions

1.   The Employment Insurance (EI) contribution may be viewed as a tax on labour. In 2006, the EI rate was approximately 5% of gross income (subject to a contribution ceiling of $39 000), comprised of 2.1% (or 42% of the tax) contributed by employees and 2.9% (or 58% of the tax) contributed by employers. In other words, employers pay 1.4 times the employee rate. Suppose that conflicting pieces of legislation before Parliament would change the statutory or legal burden of the tax for a variety of alleged efficiency and equity reasons. One group would like to place the entire tax on employees, in order to provide an incentive for employers to create more jobs. An opposing group would like to place the entire tax on employers, in order to help workers who are facing a reduced standard of living.

Employment Insurance Taxes

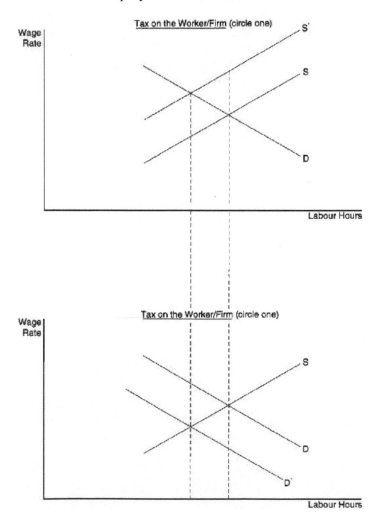

a. Show graphically the effects of the two proposals. Identify which curve shifts in each case (labour supply or demand for labour) by circling the appropriate response (worker or firm) in the subtitle above each diagram. On both diagrams, label the original wage as W_e and the equilibrium quantity of labour hired as L_e. Label the wage actually received by the workers (after the tax) as W_w. Label the wage actually paid (after a tax) by the firms as W_f. Label the resulting tax wedge between supply and demand. Show the effect on employment (number of hours of labour hired) as L_1.

b. What will happen to wages if the tax is levied against the employers? What if the tax is levied against the employees? What about employment (compare the results of the two proposals in terms of the effect on equilibrium hours worked)?

_____

_____

_____

c. Who are the winners and who are the losers (if any) if either of these proposals is enacted? Explain. _____

_____

_____

_____

2. Suppose that crude oil prices skyrocket because of a simultaneous failure in the Alberta oil patch and increased tension in the Middle East. As a result, gasoline prices rise by 50%. Parliament caves in to political pressure and places a 6-month price ceiling on gasoline at the previous year's level.

a. What will be the effect on quantity demanded of rolling back gasoline prices? Explain how this could happen. _____

_____

_____

b. What will be the effect on quantity supplied of rolling back gasoline prices? Explain.

_____

_____

_____

c. What will be the overall effect of this price ceiling?

_____

_____

_____

3. Minimum-wage laws dictate the lowest wage that employers must pay their employees. Such laws are enacted when policymakers believe that the market wage rate is unfair to workers, and their introduction is viewed as one way to raise the income of the working poor. How can the benefits received and the costs incurred of a minimum-wage law be measured? Should policymakers use minimum-wage laws as a tool to raise the income of the working poor and increase society's overall level of welfare?

_____

_____

_____

_____

D. Practice Problems

Use the table to answer the questions below. Note that Q_D is the initial quantity demanded and Q_S is the initial quantity supplied.

The Market for Widgets

Price	Q_D	Q_S	$Q_{S'}$	$Q_{D'}$
$1.00	1000	0	0	800
$1.50	900	100	0	700
$2.00	800	200	0	600
$2.50	700	300	100	500
$3.00	600	400	200	400
$3.50	500	500	300	300
$4.00	400	600	400	200
$4.50	300	700	500	100
$5.00	200	800	600	0

1. What are the initial equilibrium price and quantity? $P_1 = \$$ ___ ; $Q_{1=}$ ____

2. Suppose that the provincial government imposes a new $1 per unit tax on the sellers of widgets. The tax shifts the supply schedule from the original Q_S to the new $Q_{S'}$.

    a. The new equilibrium price and quantity are: $P_2 = \$$ ___ ; $Q_{2=}$ ____

    b. How much of the $1 tax is borne by the seller? _____

    c. How much of the tax is borne by the buyer? _____

d. Show graphically the old and new equilibria, labelling the original supply as S and the new supply as S$_1$. Label clearly the vertical shift in supply and the change in price and quantity as a result of the tax.

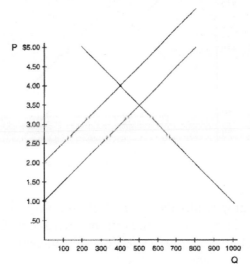

3. Suppose Ms. Malak, a provincial MLA in whose riding several widget factories are located, has proposed a new piece of legislation that would change the widget tax. Her bill would switch the tax from the seller to the buyer, under the rationale that the widget makers are losing money and cannot afford to pay the tax. If the bill passes the legislature, quantities supplied will change back from $Q_{S'}$ to Q_S, and quantities demanded will change from Q_D to $Q_{D'}$.

a. The new equilibrium price and quantity are: $P_3 = \$$ ____ ; $Q_3 =$ _____

b. How much of the $1 tax is borne by the seller?_____

c. How much of the tax is borne by the buyer?_____

d. Did the new legislation help the sellers? Why or why not?

_____

_____

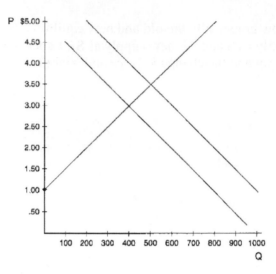

e. Show graphically the original (pre-tax) equilibrium and the new equilibrium, labelling the original demand as D and the new demand as D_1. Label clearly the vertical shift in demand and the change in price and quantity as a result of the tax.

4. Suppose the legislature has voted to abolish the widget tax; therefore price and quantity have returned to the original equilibrium. To help the widget makers in her province, Ms. Malak has proposed legislation that would enact a price floor of $4 in the market for widgets.

    a. As a result of her legislation:
        (i) The price will be $ _____.
        (ii) Quantity supplied will be $Q_S =$_____.
        (iii) Quantity demanded will be $Q_D =$ _____.
        (iv) And there will be (choose one)
                a) a shortage
                b) a surplus
                c) neither of the above
            _____ of _____.
        (v) The actual quantity sold will be_____.

    b. Who is helped and who is hurt by the price floors?
        _____
        _____
        _____
        _____

c. If the price floor had been enacted while the $1 tax on sellers was already in effect, what would have happened to price and quantity? Would there have been a shortage or surplus? _____

_____

_____

_____

5. Suppose that pressure from consumer groups leads to a reduction in the price floor from $4 to $3.

a. With the new price floor (and no tax), the price will be $ _____, quantity supplied will be Q_S = _____, and the quantity demanded will be Q_D = _____.

b. What is the effect of the new price floor at $3? Explain. _____

_____

_____

_____

c. Show graphically the effects of a price floor of $4 and $3, labelling clearly the equilibrium price and quantity, and any shortages or surpluses that result in each case. Label the $4 price floor as P_{F1} and the $3 price floor as P_{F2}.

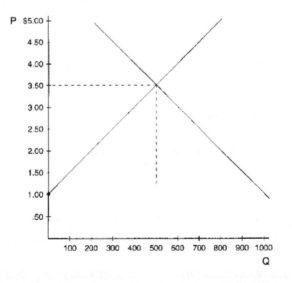

6. If the government had enacted a $3 price ceiling rather than a price floor, the result would have been: _____

_____

_____

_____

E. Advanced Critical Thinking

"Granny stunned by $400 rent hike," screamed the headlines of the *Edmonton Journal* on April 27, 2007. "Antonina Bielancska, 86, simply threw up her arms and said, 'Too much!'" Mrs. Bielancska had recently received a notice advising her that the monthly rent on her modest apartment would increase by $400 or 62%. The Letters to the Editor pages of Edmonton's newspapers were flooded with letters from outraged citizens. They suggested that it was simply landlords' greed and not the flawed logic of economics and the concept of scarcity that prevented everyone from having affordable housing. The outraged citizens provided statistics showing that the number of dwellings and number of families were roughly equal, which they felt provided proof that there was not a scarcity of housing. Consequently, the citizens argued for rent controls as a solution to the housing crisis in Edmonton. What's wrong with this thinking? Is it valid to argue that scarcity does not exist just by counting the number of dwellings? Are dwellings freely available at zero price? Suppose that rent controls forced the rent on a $1,050 apartment down to $650 per month. What would happen to new construction? To maintenance on existing apartments? What would happen to the quantity demanded? Write an economist's response to these critics of mainstream economics.

_____
_____
_____
_____
_____
_____

III. Solutions

A. True/False Questions

1. F; a ceiling (maximum price) above equilibrium has no effect, because the market will reach equilibrium before it reaches the legal maximum price.
2. T
3. F; a tax on buyers reduces their willingness to buy (the quantity demanded) at each price; which means that demand falls (shifts down).
4. T
5. F; normally demand has some nonzero elasticity that prevents sellers from passing the entire tax along to the buyer; price will normally go up, but by less than $1.
6. T
7. T
8. F; the two taxes are equivalent, even in terms of equity.
9. T
10. T

B. Multiple-Choice Questions

1. c	5. b	9. b	13. c
2. c	6. a	10. a	14. c
3. a	7. d	11. d	
4. d	8. d	12. a	

C. Short-Answer Questions

1.   a.   and b. (See the following graph.)

Employment Insurance Contribution (Taxes)

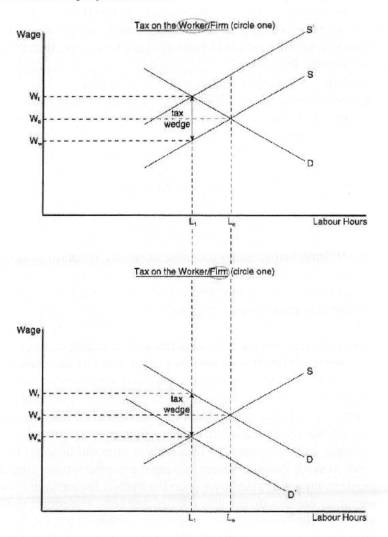

c. Neither the employers nor the employees gain or lose as a result of a change in the legal burden of the Employment Insurance contribution. The actual tax incidence depends on the relative elasticities of the supply of and demand for labour. A payroll tax like Employment Insurance contribution is a tax on the labour market. How the tax burden is actually allocated between workers and employers is determined by the market rather than by government. Of course, there may be political winners or losers. Politicians who supported one of these proposals would gain or lose, depending upon the popularity of the proposal.

2. a. When government rolls back gasoline prices, one result is an increase in quantity demanded. Buyers who would have carpooled or cut back on leisure driving, or taken mass transit will not make the effort when the price of gasoline is reduced. People respond to economic incentives.

    b. Sellers will respond to the lower gasoline prices by cutting back on the production of gasoline. To some extent, they will switch from gasoline production to other petroleum products. They will also cut back on petroleum production until the price goes back up by capping existing wells. If they expect the lower prices to continue, they will even cut back on exploration for new oil reserves.

    d. The result would be a shortage of gasoline, evidenced by long lines at gasoline stations. Buyers would try to get around the controls by offering bribes under the table to sellers. Because price will no longer work to ration scarce gasoline, the government may enact a rationing system to deal with the shortage. Otherwise, long waits may serve as the rationing device for gasoline.

3. It is difficult to measure the benefits and costs associated with the enactment of minimum-wage laws. Advocates of such laws point out that workers who earn the minimum wage can afford only a meager standard of living. One objective, therefore, is to help reduce the level of poverty among the working poor. However, opponents of such measures point to the fact that using minimum wage to fight poverty results in unemployment, encourages teenagers to drop out of school, and prevents some unskilled workers from getting the on-the-job training they need. The greatest impact of such laws is on the market for teenage labour, because teenagers are among the least skilled and least experienced members of the labour force. Relatively few of them are heads of households trying to help their families escape poverty. Minimum-wage laws, therefore, may raise the income of some workers, but they also cause other workers to be unemployed. It is not possible to make some workers better off without making others worse off. Policymakers should perhaps look for alternatives

to the minimum-wage laws. Wage subsidies, for example, raise the living standards of the working poor, without discouraging firms from hiring them.

D. Practice Problems

1. $P_1 = \$3.50$; $Q_1 = 500$

2. a. $P_2 = \$4$; $Q_2 = 400$

   b. $0.50

   c. $0.50

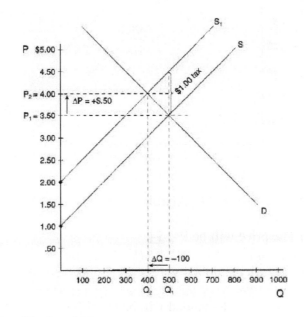

3. a. $P_3 = \$3$; $Q_3 = 400$.

   b. $0.50

   c. $0.50

237

d. No. The change in the legal burden did not help either the buyers or the sellers. The actual tax incidence after the market adjusts is identical. With either version of the tax, the quantity is 400 and buyers end up paying a total of $4 per widget, with sellers receiving only $3. The $1 gap is the tax that goes to the government. The only thing that changes is who actually writes the cheque to the government.

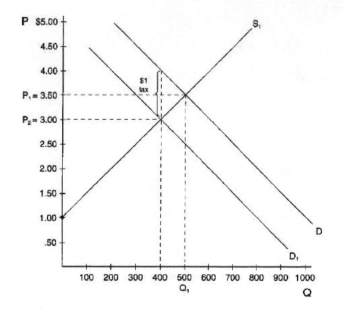

4. a. As a result of her legislation:

(i) The price will be P = $4.

(ii) Quantity supplied will be Q_S = 600.

(iii) Quantity demanded will be Q_D = 400.

(iv) And there will be a (surplus) of 200.

(v) The actual quantity sold will be 400.

b. Consumers are hurt by the price floor because they must pay an additional $0.50 per widget. Some sellers benefit by receiving higher prices for their product, but others are made worse off because they cannot find a market for all that they produce at $4.

c. With a $1 tax on sellers, the price already would have been at $4, so the floor would have had no effect on either price or quantity. It simply would have mandated a price that already existed. The price would stay at $4 and the quantity at 400. The market would clear, so there would be neither a shortage nor a surplus.

5. a. With the new price floor, the price will be $3.50, quantity supplied will be $Q_S = 500$, and the quantity demanded will be $Q_D = 500$.

    b. The new price floor is below the equilibrium price; therefore, it will have no effect on either price or quantity.

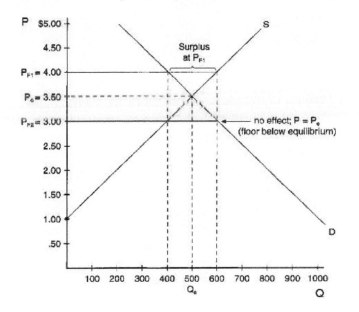

6. A shortage, or excess demand, of 200 units, because quantity demanded at $3 is 600, which is greater than the quantity supplied of 400.

E. Advanced Critical Thinking

Scarcity means that people cannot have everything they want at a zero price. People respond to economic incentives. If rent controls reduce the price of housing below the equilibrium level, quantity demanded will rise as people respond. Some buyers will choose to move into more spacious or luxurious housing; others may choose to move out of the family home and live on their own. All else equal, more people will also want to move into the area if housing is cheaper. On the supply side, however, nothing has happened to make more housing available to meet the demand. On the contrary, the seller (landlord) has an incentive to supply less housing. It may be tempting to think of the supply of housing as fixed; however, this view is not correct. Consider the extreme case: is it realistic to think that at a zero price, housing would still be available? Of course not! Particularly in the long run, the market will respond to below-equilibrium rents by building fewer housing units and allowing existing housing to deteriorate without repair or replacement. The stock of housing will shrink as quantity supplied responds to the lower price. It will benefit those buyers who are lucky enough to get housing at a reduced price. However, it will hurt those buyers who cannot get housing, even though they were willing to pay a higher price. It will also hurt sellers in general. The old saying is true: there really are no free lunches (or apartments).

© Richard Thomas/Dreamstime.com

SUPPLY AND DEMAND II:
MARKETS AND WELFARE

3

CONSUMERS, PRODUCERS, AND THE EFFICIENCY OF MARKETS

Learning Objectives

In this chapter, you will ...

- Examine the link between buyers' willingness to pay for a good and the demand curve

- Learn how to define and measure consumer surplus

- Examine the link between sellers' cost of producing a good and the supply curve

- Learn how to define and measure producer surplus

- See that the equilibrium of supply and demand maximizes total surplus in a market

When consumers go to grocery stores to buy their turkeys for a holiday dinner, they may be disappointed that the price of turkey is as high as it is. At the same time, when farmers bring to market the turkeys they have raised, they wish the price of turkey was even higher. These views are not surprising: Buyers always want to pay less, and sellers always want to be paid more. But is there a "right price" for turkey from the standpoint of society as a whole?

In previous chapters we saw how, in market economies, the forces of supply and demand determine the prices of goods and services and the quantities sold. So far, however, we have described the way markets allocate scarce resources without directly addressing the question of whether these market allocations are desirable. In other words, our analysis has been *positive* (what is) rather than *normative* (what should be). We know that the price of turkey adjusts to ensure that the quantity of turkey supplied equals the quantity of turkey demanded. But, at this equilibrium, is the quantity of turkey produced and consumed too small, too large, or just right?

welfare economics
the study of how the allocation of resources affects economic well-being

In this chapter we discuss **welfare economics,** the study of how the allocation of resources affects economic well-being. We begin by examining the benefits that buyers and sellers receive from taking part in a market. We then examine how society can make these benefits as large as possible. This analysis leads to a profound conclusion: The equilibrium of supply and demand in a market maximizes the total benefits received by buyers and sellers.

As you may recall from Chapter 1, one of the ten principles of economics is that markets are usually a good way to organize economic activity. The study of welfare economics explains this principle more fully. It also answers our question about the right price of turkey: The price that balances the supply and demand for turkey is, in a particular sense, the best one because it maximizes the total welfare of turkey consumers and turkey producers.

CONSUMER SURPLUS

We begin our study of welfare economics by looking at the benefits buyers receive from participating in a market.

Willingness to Pay

Imagine that you own a mint-condition recording of Elvis Presley's first album. Because you are not an Elvis Presley fan, you decide to sell it. One way to do so is to hold an auction.

Four Elvis fans show up for your auction: John, Paul, George, and Ringo. Each of them would like to own the album, but there is a limit to the amount that each is willing to pay for it. Table 7.1 shows the maximum price that each of the four possible buyers would pay. Each buyer's maximum is called his **willingness to pay,** and it measures how much that buyer values the good. Each buyer would be eager to buy the album at a price less than his willingness to pay, would refuse to buy the album at a price more than his willingness to pay, and would be indifferent about buying the album at a price exactly equal to his willingness to pay.

To sell your album, you begin the bidding at a low price, say $10. Because all four buyers are willing to pay much more, the price rises quickly. The bidding stops when John bids $80 (or slightly more). At this point, Paul, George, and Ringo

willingness to pay
the maximum amount that a buyer will pay for a good

TABLE 7.1

Four Possible Buyers' Willingness to Pay

Buyer	Willingness to Pay
John	$100
Paul	80
George	70
Ringo	50

have dropped out of the bidding because they are unwilling to bid any more than $80. John pays you $80 and gets the album. Note that the album has gone to the buyer who values the album most highly.

What benefit does John receive from buying the Elvis Presley album? In a sense, John has found a real bargain: He is willing to pay $100 for the album but pays only $80 for it. We say that John receives *consumer surplus* of $20. **Consumer surplus** is the amount a buyer is willing to pay for a good minus the amount the buyer actually pays for it.

Consumer surplus measures the benefit to buyers of participating in a market. In this example, John receives a $20 benefit from participating in the auction because he pays only $80 for a good he values at $100. Paul, George, and Ringo get no consumer surplus from participating in the auction because they left without the album and without paying anything.

Now consider a somewhat different example. Suppose that you had two identical Elvis Presley albums to sell. Again, you auction them off to the four possible buyers. To keep things simple, we assume that both albums are to be sold for the same price and that no buyer is interested in buying more than one album. Therefore, the price rises until two buyers are left.

In this case, the bidding stops when John and Paul bid $70 (or slightly higher). At this price, John and Paul are each happy to buy an album, and George and Ringo are not willing to bid any higher. John and Paul each receive consumer surplus equal to his willingness to pay minus the price. John's consumer surplus is $30, and Paul's is $10. John's consumer surplus is higher now than it was previously because he gets the same album but pays less for it. The total consumer surplus in the market is $40.

Using the Demand Curve to Measure Consumer Surplus

Consumer surplus is closely related to the demand curve for a product. To see how they are related, let's continue our example and consider the demand curve for this rare Elvis Presley album.

We begin by using the willingness to pay of the four possible buyers to find the demand schedule for the album. The table in Figure 7.1 shows the demand schedule that corresponds to Table 7.1. If the price is above $100, the quantity demanded in the market is 0 because no buyer is willing to pay that much. If the price is between $80 and $100, the quantity demanded is 1 because only John is willing to pay such a high price. If the price is between $70 and $80, the quantity demanded is 2 because both John and Paul are willing to pay the price. We can continue this analysis for other prices as well. In this way, the demand schedule is derived from the willingness to pay of the four possible buyers.

The graph in Figure 7.1 shows the demand curve that corresponds to this demand schedule. Note the relationship between the height of the demand curve and the buyers' willingness to pay. At any quantity, the price given by the demand curve shows the willingness to pay of the *marginal buyer*, the buyer who would leave the market first if the price was any higher. At a quantity of 4 albums, for instance, the demand curve has a height of $50, the price that Ringo (the marginal buyer) is willing to pay for an album. At a quantity of 3 albums, the demand curve has a height of $70, the price that George (who is now the marginal buyer) is willing to pay.

consumer surplus
a buyer's willingness to pay minus the amount the buyer actually pays

FIGURE 7.1

The Demand Schedule and the Demand Curve

The table shows the demand schedule for the buyers in Table 7.1. The graph shows the corresponding demand curve. Note that the height of the demand curve reflects buyers' willingness to pay.

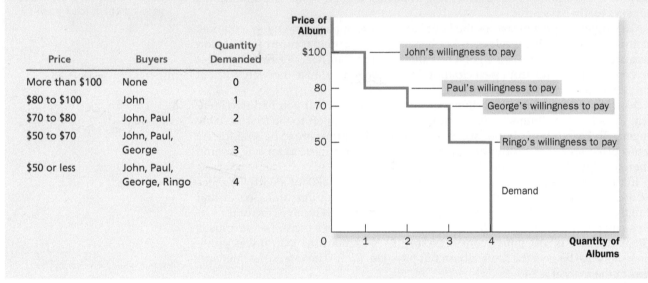

Price	Buyers	Quantity Demanded
More than $100	None	0
$80 to $100	John	1
$70 to $80	John, Paul	2
$50 to $70	John, Paul, George	3
$50 or less	John, Paul, George, Ringo	4

Because the demand curve reflects buyers' willingness to pay, we can also use it to measure consumer surplus. Figure 7.2 uses the demand curve to compute consumer surplus in our example. In panel (a), the price is $80 (or slightly above), and the quantity demanded is 1. Note that the area above the price and below the demand curve equals $20. This amount is exactly the consumer surplus we computed earlier when only 1 album is sold.

Panel (b) of Figure 7.2 shows consumer surplus when the price is $70 (or slightly above). In this case, the area above the price and below the demand curve equals the total area of the two rectangles: John's consumer surplus at this price is $30 and Paul's is $10. This area equals a total of $40. Once again, this amount is the consumer surplus we computed earlier.

The lesson from this example holds for all demand curves: *The area below the demand curve and above the price measures the consumer surplus in a market.* The reason is that the height of the demand curve measures the value buyers place on the good, as measured by their willingness to pay for it. The difference between this willingness to pay and the market price is each buyer's consumer surplus. Thus, the total area below the demand curve and above the price is the sum of the consumer surplus of all buyers in the market for a good or service.

How a Lower Price Raises Consumer Surplus

Because buyers always want to pay less for the goods they buy, a lower price makes buyers of a good better off. But how much does buyers' well-being rise in

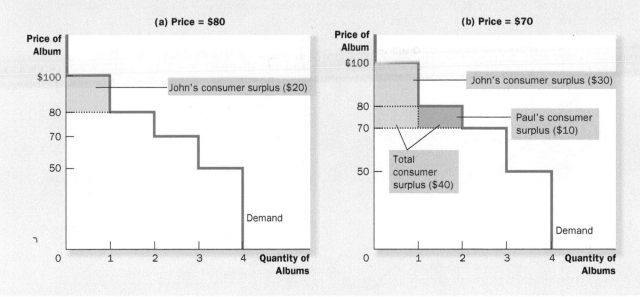

FIGURE 7.2

Measuring Consumer Surplus with the Demand Curve

In panel (a), the price of the good is $80, and the consumer surplus is $20. In panel (b), the price of the good is $70, and the consumer surplus is $40.

response to a lower price? We can use the concept of consumer surplus to answer this question precisely.

Figure 7.3 shows a typical downward-sloping demand curve. Although this demand curve appears somewhat different in shape from the steplike demand curves in our previous two figures, the ideas we have just developed apply nonetheless: Consumer surplus is the area above the price and below the demand curve. In panel (a), consumer surplus at a price of P_1 is the area of triangle ABC.

Now suppose that the price falls from P_1 to P_2, as shown in panel (b). The consumer surplus now equals area ADF. The increase in consumer surplus attributable to the lower price is the area BCFD.

This increase in consumer surplus is composed of two parts. First, those buyers who were already buying Q_1 of the good at the higher price P_1 are better off because they now pay less. The increase in consumer surplus of existing buyers is the reduction in the amount they pay; it equals the area of the rectangle BCED. Second, some new buyers enter the market because they are now willing to buy the good at the lower price. As a result, the quantity demanded in the market increases from Q_1 to Q_2. The consumer surplus these newcomers receive is the area of the triangle CEF.

What Does Consumer Surplus Measure?

Our goal in developing the concept of consumer surplus is to make normative judgments about the desirability of market outcomes. Now that you have seen

FIGURE 7.3

How the Price Affects Consumer Surplus

In panel (a), the price is P_1, the quantity demanded is Q_1, and consumer surplus equals the area of the triangle ABC. When the price falls from P_1 to P_2, as in panel (b), the quantity demanded rises from Q_1 to Q_2, and the consumer surplus rises to the area of the triangle ADF. The increase in consumer surplus (area BCFD) occurs in part because existing consumers now pay less (area BCED) and in part because new consumers enter the market at the lower price (area CEF).

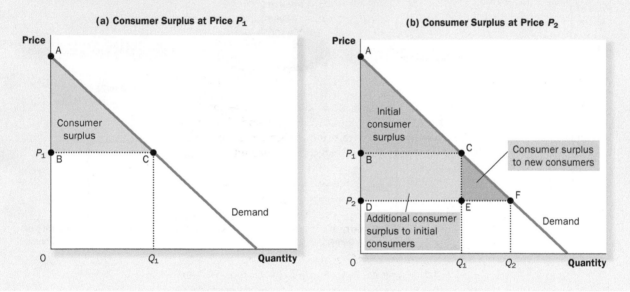

what consumer surplus is, let's consider whether it is a good measure of economic well-being.

Imagine that you are a policymaker trying to design a good economic system. Would you care about the amount of consumer surplus? Consumer surplus, the amount that buyers are willing to pay for a good minus the amount they actually pay for it, measures the benefit that buyers receive from a good *as the buyers themselves perceive it*. Thus, consumer surplus is a good measure of economic well-being if policymakers want to respect the preferences of buyers.

In some circumstances, policymakers might choose not to care about consumer surplus because they do not respect the preferences that drive buyer behaviour. For example, drug addicts are willing to pay a high price for heroin. Yet we would not say that addicts get a large benefit from being able to buy heroin at a low price (even though addicts might say they do). From the standpoint of society, willingness to pay in this instance is not a good measure of the buyers' benefit, and consumer surplus is not a good measure of economic well-being, because addicts are not looking after their own best interests.

In most markets, however, consumer surplus does reflect economic well-being. Economists normally presume that buyers are rational when they make decisions and that their preferences should be respected. In this case, consumers are the best judges of how much benefit they receive from the goods they buy.

QuickQuiz Draw a demand curve for turkey. In your diagram, show a price of turkey and the consumer surplus that results from that price. Explain in words what this consumer surplus measures.

PRODUCER SURPLUS

We now turn to the other side of the market and consider the benefits sellers receive from participating in a market. As you will see, our analysis of sellers' welfare is similar to our analysis of buyers' welfare.

Cost and the Willingness to Sell

Imagine now that you are a homeowner, and you need to get your house painted. You turn to four sellers of painting services: Mary, Frida, Georgia, and Grandma. Each painter is willing to do the work for you if the price is right. You decide to take bids from the four painters and auction off the job to the painter who will do the work for the lowest price.

Each painter is willing to take the job if the price she would receive exceeds her cost of doing the work. Here the term **cost** should be interpreted as the painters' opportunity cost: It includes the painters' out-of-pocket expenses (for paint, brushes, and so on) as well as the value that the painters place on their own time. Table 7.2 shows each painter's cost. Because a painter's cost is the lowest price she would accept for her work, cost is a measure of her willingness to sell her services. Each painter would be eager to sell her services at a price greater than her cost, and she would refuse to sell her services at a price less than her cost. At a price exactly equal to her cost, she would be indifferent about selling her services: She would be equally happy getting the job or walking away without incurring the cost.

When you take bids from the painters, the price might start off high, but it quickly falls as the painters compete for the job. Once Grandma has bid $600 (or slightly less), she is the sole remaining bidder. Grandma is happy to do the job for this price because her cost is only $500. Mary, Frida, and Georgia are unwilling to do the job for less than $600. Note that the job goes to the painter who can do the work at the lowest cost.

cost
the value of everything a seller must give up to produce a good

---

TABLE 7.2

The Costs of Four Possible Sellers

Seller	Cost
Mary	$900
Frida	800
Georgia	600
Grandma	500

producer surplus
the amount a seller is paid for a good minus the seller's cost

What benefit does Grandma receive from getting the job? Because she is willing to do the work for $500 but gets $600 for doing it, we say that she receives *producer surplus* of $100. **Producer surplus** is the amount a seller is paid minus the cost of production. Producer surplus measures the benefit to sellers of participating in a market.

Now consider a somewhat different example. Suppose that you have two identical houses that need painting. Again, you auction off the jobs to the four painters. To keep things simple, let's assume that no painter is able to paint both houses and that you will pay the same amount to paint each house. Therefore, the price falls until two painters are left.

In this case, the bidding stops when Georgia and Grandma each offer to do the job for a price of $800 (or slightly less). At this price, Georgia and Grandma are willing to do the work, and Mary and Frida are not willing to bid a lower price. At a price of $800, Grandma receives producer surplus of $300, and Georgia receives producer surplus of $200. The total producer surplus in the market is $500.

Using the Supply Curve to Measure Producer Surplus

Just as consumer surplus is closely related to the demand curve, producer surplus is closely related to the supply curve. To see how, let's continue our example.

We begin by using the costs of the four painters to find the supply schedule for painting services. The table in Figure 7.4 shows the supply schedule that corresponds to the costs in Table 7.2. If the price is below $500, none of the four painters

FIGURE 7.4

The Supply Schedule and the Supply Curve

The table shows the supply schedule for the sellers in Table 7.2. The graph shows the corresponding supply curve. Note that the height of the supply curve reflects sellers' costs.

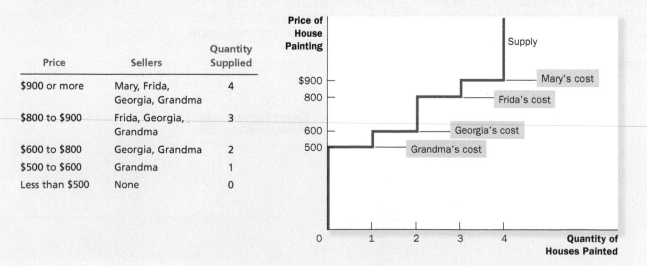

Price	Sellers	Quantity Supplied
$900 or more	Mary, Frida, Georgia, Grandma	4
$800 to $900	Frida, Georgia, Grandma	3
$600 to $800	Georgia, Grandma	2
$500 to $600	Grandma	1
Less than $500	None	0

NEL

is willing to do the job, so the quantity supplied is zero. If the price is between $500 and $600, only Grandma is willing to do the job, so the quantity supplied is 1. If the price is between $600 and $800, Grandma and Georgia are willing to do the job, so the quantity supplied is 2, and so on. Thus, the supply schedule is derived from the costs of the four painters.

The graph in Figure 7.4 shows the supply curve that corresponds to this supply schedule. Note that the height of the supply curve is related to the sellers' costs. At any quantity, the price given by the supply curve shows the cost of the *marginal seller*, the seller who would leave the market first if the price was any lower. At a quantity of 4 houses, for instance, the supply curve has a height of $900, the cost that Mary (the marginal seller) incurs to provide her painting services. At a quantity of 3 houses, the supply curve has a height of $800, the cost that Frida (who is now the marginal seller) incurs.

Because the supply curve reflects sellers' costs, we can use it to measure producer surplus. Figure 7.5 uses the supply curve to compute producer surplus in our example. In panel (a), we assume that the price is $600. In this case, the quantity supplied is 1. Note that the area below the price and above the supply curve equals $100. This amount is exactly the producer surplus we computed earlier for Grandma.

Panel (b) of Figure 7.5 shows producer surplus at a price of $800. In this case, the area below the price and above the supply curve equals the total area of the

FIGURE 7.5

Measuring Producer Surplus with the Supply Curve

In panel (a), the price of the good is $600, and the producer surplus is $100. In panel (b), the price of the good is $800, and the producer surplus is $500.

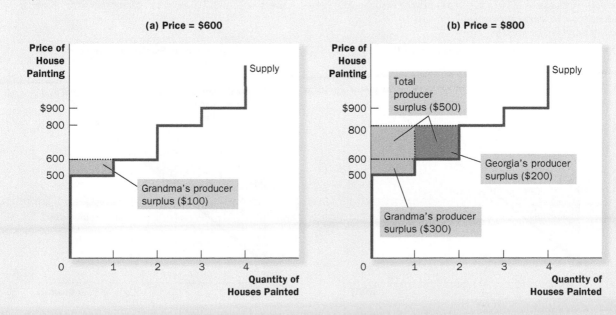

two rectangles. This area equals $500, the producer surplus we computed earlier for Georgia and Grandma when two houses needed painting.

The lesson from this example applies to all supply curves: *The area below the price and above the supply curve measures the producer surplus in a market.* The logic is straightforward: The height of the supply curve measures sellers' costs, and the difference between the price and the cost of production is each seller's producer surplus. Thus, the total area is the sum of the producer surplus of all sellers.

How a Higher Price Raises Producer Surplus

You will not be surprised to hear that sellers always want to receive a higher price for the goods they sell. But how much does sellers' well-being rise in response to a higher price? The concept of producer surplus offers a precise answer to this question.

Figure 7.6 shows a typical upward-sloping supply curve. Even though this supply curve differs in shape from the steplike supply curves in the previous figure, we measure producer surplus in the same way: Producer surplus is the area below the price and above the supply curve. In panel (a), the price is P_1, and producer surplus is the area of triangle ABC.

FIGURE 7.6

How the Price Affects Producer Surplus

In panel (a), the price is P_1, the quantity supplied is Q_1, and producer surplus equals the area of the triangle ABC. When the price rises from P_1 to P_2, as in panel (b), the quantity supplied rises from Q_1 to Q_2, and the producer surplus rises to the area of the triangle ADF. The increase in producer surplus (area BCFD) occurs in part because existing producers now receive more (area BCED) and in part because new producers enter the market at the higher price (area CEF).

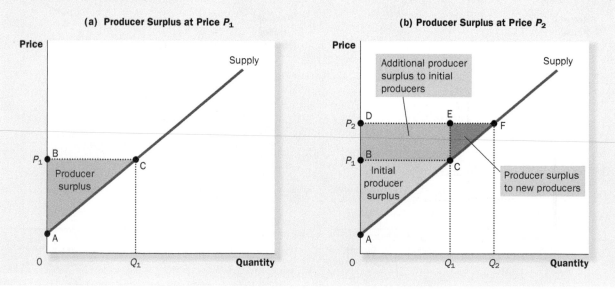

Panel (b) shows what happens when the price rises from P_1 to P_2. Producer surplus now equals area ADF. This increase in producer surplus has two parts. First, those sellers who were already selling Q_1 of the good at the lower price P_1 are better off because they now get more for what they sell. The increase in producer surplus for existing sellers equals the area of the rectangle BCED. Second, some new sellers enter the market because they are now willing to produce the good at the higher price, resulting in an increase in the quantity supplied from Q_1 to Q_2. The producer surplus of these newcomers is the area of the triangle CEF.

As this analysis shows, we use producer surplus to measure the well-being of sellers in much the same way as we use consumer surplus to measure the well-being of buyers. Because these two measures of economic welfare are so similar, it is natural to use them together. And, indeed, that is exactly what we do in the next section.

QuickQuiz Draw a supply curve for turkey. In your diagram, show a price of turkey and the producer surplus that results from that price. Explain in words what this producer surplus measures.

MARKET EFFICIENCY

Consumer surplus and producer surplus are the basic tools that economists use to study the welfare of buyers and sellers in a market. These tools can help us address a fundamental economic question: Is the allocation of resources determined by free markets in any way desirable?

The Benevolent Social Planner

To evaluate market outcomes, we introduce into our analysis a new, hypothetical character, called the benevolent social planner. The benevolent social planner is an all-knowing, all-powerful, well-intentioned dictator. This planner wants to maximize the economic well-being of everyone in society. What do you suppose this planner should do? Should he just leave buyers and sellers at the equilibrium that they reach naturally on their own? Or can he increase economic well-being by altering the market outcome in some way?

To answer this question, the benevolent social planner must first decide how to measure the economic well-being of a society. One possible measure is the sum of consumer and producer surplus, which we call *total surplus*. Consumer surplus is the benefit that buyers receive from participating in a market, and producer surplus is the benefit that sellers receive. It is therefore natural to use total surplus as a measure of society's economic well-being.

To better understand this measure of economic well-being, recall how we measure consumer and producer surplus. We define consumer surplus as

Consumer surplus = Value to buyers − Amount paid by buyers

Similarly, we define producer surplus as

Producer surplus = Amount received by sellers − Cost to sellers

When we add consumer and producer surplus together, we obtain

$$\text{Total surplus} = \text{Value to buyers} - \text{Amount paid by buyers} \\ + \text{Amount received by sellers} - \text{Cost to sellers}$$

The amount paid by buyers equals the amount received by sellers, so the middle two terms in this expression cancel each other. As a result, we can write total surplus as

$$\text{Total surplus} = \text{Value to buyers} - \text{Cost to sellers}$$

Total surplus in a market is the total value to buyers of the goods, as measured by their willingness to pay, minus the total cost to sellers of providing those goods.

efficiency
the property of a resource allocation of maximizing the total surplus received by all members of society

If an allocation of resources maximizes total surplus, we say that the allocation exhibits **efficiency**. If an allocation is not efficient, then some of the gains from trade among buyers and sellers are not being realized. For example, an allocation is inefficient if a good is not being produced by the sellers with lowest cost. In this case, moving production from a high-cost producer to a low-cost producer will lower the total cost to sellers and raise total surplus. Similarly, an allocation is inefficient if a good is not being consumed by the buyers who value it most highly. In this case, moving consumption of the good from a buyer with a low valuation to a buyer with a high valuation will raise total surplus.

equity
the fairness of the distribution of well-being among the members of society

In addition to efficiency, the social planner might also care about **equity**—the fairness of the distribution of well-being among the various buyers and sellers. In essence, the gains from trade in a market are like a pie to be distributed among the market participants. The question of efficiency is whether the pie is as big as possible. The question of equality concerns how the pie is sliced and how the portions are distributed among members of society.

In this chapter we concentrate on efficiency as the social planner's goal. Keep in mind, however, that real policymakers often care about equity as well. That is, they care about both the size of the economic pie and how the pie gets sliced and distributed among members of society.

Evaluating the Market Equilibrium

Figure 7.7 shows consumer and producer surplus when a market reaches the equilibrium of supply and demand. Recall that consumer surplus equals the area above the price and under the demand curve, and producer surplus equals the area below the price and above the supply curve. Thus, the total area between the supply and demand curves up to the point of equilibrium represents the total surplus in this market.

Is this equilibrium allocation of resources efficient? Does it maximize total surplus? To answer these questions, keep in mind that when a market is in equilibrium, the price determines which buyers and sellers participate in the market. Those buyers who value the good more than the price (represented by the segment AE on the demand curve) choose to buy the good; those buyers who value it less than the price (represented by the segment EB) do not. Similarly, those sellers whose costs are less than the price (represented by the segment CE on the supply curve) choose to produce and sell the good; those sellers whose costs are greater than the price (represented by the segment ED) do not.

FIGURE 7.7

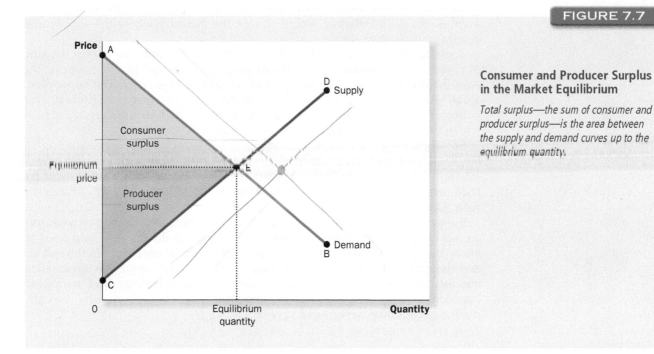

Consumer and Producer Surplus in the Market Equilibrium

Total surplus—the sum of consumer and producer surplus—is the area between the supply and demand curves up to the equilibrium quantity.

These observations lead to two insights about market outcomes:

1. Free markets allocate the supply of goods to the buyers who value them most highly, as measured by their willingness to pay.
2. Free markets allocate the demand for goods to the sellers who can produce them at least cost.

Thus, given the quantity produced and sold in a market equilibrium, the social planner cannot increase economic well-being by changing the allocation of consumption among buyers or the allocation of production among sellers.

But can the social planner raise total economic well-being by increasing or decreasing the quantity of the good? The answer is no, as stated in this third insight about market outcomes:

3. Free markets produce the quantity of goods that maximizes the sum of consumer and producer surplus.

Figure 7.8 illustrates why this is true. To interpret this figure, keep in mind that the demand curve reflects the value to buyers and the supply curve reflects the cost to sellers. At any quantity below the equilibrium level, such as Q_1, the value to the marginal buyer exceeds the cost to the marginal seller. As a result, increasing the quantity produced and consumed raises total surplus. This continues to be true until the quantity reaches the equilibrium level. Similarly, at any quantity beyond the equilibrium level, such as Q_2, the value to the marginal buyer is less than the cost to the marginal seller. In this case, decreasing the quantity raises total surplus, and this continues to be true until quantity falls to the equilibrium level. To maximize total surplus, the social planner would choose the quantity where the supply and demand curves intersect.

Together, these three insights tell us that the market outcome makes the sum of consumer and producer surplus as large as it can be. In other words, the equilibrium outcome is an efficient allocation of resources. The benevolent social planner can, therefore, leave the market outcome just as he finds it. This policy of leaving well enough alone goes by the French expression *laissez faire*, which literally translates to "allow them to do."

Society is lucky that the social planner doesn't need to intervene. Although it has been a useful exercise imagining what an all-knowing, all-powerful, well-intentioned dictator would do, let's face it: Such characters are hard to come by. Dictators are rarely benevolent, and even if we found someone so virtuous, he would lack crucial information.

Suppose our social planner tried to choose an efficient allocation of resources on his own, instead of relying on market forces. To do so, he would need to know the value of a particular good to every potential consumer in the market and the cost of every potential producer. And he would need this information not only for this market but for every one of the many thousands of markets in the economy. The task is practically impossible, which explains why centrally planned economies never work very well.

FIGURE 7.8

The Efficiency of the Equilibrium Quantity

At quantities less than the equilibrium quantity, such as Q1, the value to buyers exceeds the cost to sellers. At quantities greater than the equilibrium quantity, such as Q2, the cost to sellers exceeds the value to buyers. Therefore, the market equilibrium maximizes the sum of producer and consumer surplus.

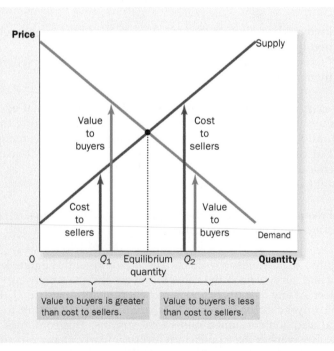

The planner's job becomes easy, however, once he takes on a partner: Adam Smith's invisible hand of the marketplace. The invisible hand takes all the information about buyers and sellers into account and guides everyone in the market to the best outcome as judged by the standard of economic efficiency. It is truly a remarkable feat. That is why economists so often advocate free markets as the best way to organize economic activity.

Case Study
SHOULD TICKET SCALPING BE ILLEGAL?

"Psssst . . . need a ticket?" We've all seen them at major sporting events, concerts, and even museum and art exhibit openings. Sometimes they lurk in the shadows, sometimes they market their wares blatantly. Perhaps you've even engaged in a business transaction with one of them.

"They," of course, are ticket scalpers. Whether or not ticket scalping is illegal depends on where you live. Twenty-two states and dozens of major cities in the United States have strict laws against ticket scalping, but in Canada, ticket scalping is illegal only in Alberta, Ontario, and Manitoba. In Alberta, for example, ticket scalping is covered under the provincial Amusements Act of 1957, which states: "No person shall sell, barter or exchange a ticket of admission to a place of amusement for a price or consideration greater than that paid or given for it to the owner of the place to which it authorizes admission." As well as the obvious venues of sporting arenas, stadiums, and concert halls, "place of amusement" includes "travelling picture shows, dance halls, circuses and menageries," and any place used to perform "burlesque, pantomime, [or] vaudeville." Sounds like they've got it covered.

Why is ticket scalping illegal? Some invoke equity arguments, claiming that it is fairer to let everyone stand in line than to let tickets go to the highest bidder. But this begs the question of why event tickets are different from other goods in this regard. Moreover, why is discriminating in favour of people who have more free (or less valuable) time fairer than discriminating in favour of people with more money? And why is it fairer to force everyone to stand in line and engage in unproductive activity? While there are some concerns about counterfeit tickets, scalping would seem to be the prototypical example of the victimless crime.

For the most part, economists argue that restrictions on scalping inconvenience the public, reduce the audience for cultural and sports events, waste police time, deprive the government of tax revenue, and actually drive up the cost of many tickets. Moreover, we have learned that one of the characteristics of market outcomes is that free markets allocate goods to the buyers who value them most highly. By restricting ticket scalping, some governments effectively introduce inefficiencies into the market for tickets.

Ticket brokers such as Canada's Ticketmaster are catching on. In 2009, Ticketmaster introduced a system that it calls "dynamic pricing." This involves reserving a batch of prime seats for each event that it then auctions off on its website. In this way, these tickets will go to those who value them most. And Ticketmaster and the artist get the money, rather than the scalper. ●

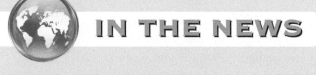

IN THE NEWS

SCALPING THEIR OWN TICKETS

When scalpers sell tickets, they keep the money. The biggest ticket broker in Canada has come up with a way to get a piece of the action.

Ticketmaster Creates Online Auction for Tickets

Long-established ticket seller Ticketmaster has set up an auction site to compete with online competitors who resell tickets. It plans to auction off tickets to some of the summer's hottest Canadian concerts, including Madonna, Bon Jovi, Roger Waters, and the Red Hot Chili Peppers.

Similar to auctions on eBay or classifieds sites craigslist or Kijiji, the Ticketmaster auction will have buyers bidding up the price of attractive seats to sellout shows. But unlike the private scalpers, who book blocks of tickets online and enrich themselves with the markup, Ticketmaster says it will split the proceeds with the artists themselves.

Scalping has come a long way from the enterprising high school kid and back alley deals just before a concert, the company says, estimating that billions of dollars are earned on black market ticket sales. "We felt that it was very important for us to build out an industry solution to an industry problem," Ticketmaster president Sean Moriarty told CBC Radio.

Arthur Fogel, tour producer for Madonna, says the singer decided to experiment with the auction for her summer tour. "There's a tremendous amount of revenue changing hands that the producer and the artist aren't sharing," he said.

For the Madonna show, the top face-value ticket price was $350, but auctioned tickets sold for $200 to $300 more, according to Fogel. The highest winning bid for a single ticket was $3,200.

Many concerts sell out in minutes online, and there is no recourse but scalpers for fans who want a seat. The Ticketmaster auction allows anyone to bid for a seat in a block set aside for auction. The auction is open for seven to ten days.

Moriarty said a portion of the money goes to the artists. "The folks who are putting all of the blood, sweat and tears into creating such great products and experiences are the ones who are compensated for their efforts," he said.

Poison fan Jay Matthews, who has stood in line at Ticketmaster for concerts from Alice Cooper to Judas Priest, sees it differently. "That's scalping to my eyes. That's scalping. That's not right," he said, as he waited in line for yet another concert.

Matthews didn't need an online auction to score tickets to Poison, whom he plans to see in Toronto in August. Lining up the old-fashioned way got him a pair of third-row floor tickets.

Source: CBC News, "Ticketmaster creates online auction for tickets," May 26, 2006. © CBC News.

QuickQuiz Draw the supply and demand for turkey. In the equilibrium, show producer and consumer surplus. Explain why producing more turkey would lower total surplus.

CONCLUSION: MARKET EFFICIENCY AND MARKET FAILURE

This chapter introduced the basic tools of welfare economics—consumer and producer surplus—and used them to evaluate the efficiency of free markets. We showed that the forces of supply and demand allocate resources efficiently. That is, even though each buyer and seller in a market is concerned only about his or her own welfare, they are together led by an invisible hand to an equilibrium that maximizes the total benefits to buyers and sellers.

A word of warning is in order. To conclude that markets are efficient, we made several assumptions about how markets work. When these assumptions do not hold, our conclusion that the market equilibrium is efficient may no longer be true. As we close this chapter, let's consider briefly two of the most important of these assumptions.

First, our analysis assumed that markets are perfectly competitive. In the world, however, competition is sometimes far from perfect. In some markets, a single buyer or seller (or a small group of them) may be able to control market prices. This ability to influence prices is called *market power*. Market power can cause markets to be inefficient because it keeps the price and quantity away from the equilibrium of supply and demand.

Second, our analysis assumed that the outcome in a market matters only to the buyers and sellers in that market. Yet, in the world, the decisions of buyers and sellers sometimes affect people who are not participants in the market at all. Pollution is the classic example of a market outcome that affects people not in the market. Such side effects, called *externalities*, cause welfare in a market to depend on more than just the value to the buyers and the cost to the sellers. Because buyers and sellers do not take these side effects into account when deciding how much to consume and produce, the equilibrium in a market can be inefficient from the standpoint of society as a whole.

Market power and externalities are examples of a general phenomenon called *market failure*—the inability of some unregulated markets to allocate resources efficiently. When markets fail, public policy can potentially remedy the problem and increase economic efficiency. Microeconomists devote much effort to studying when market failure is likely and what sorts of policies are best at correcting market failures. As you continue your study of economics, you will see that the tools of welfare economics developed here are readily adapted to that endeavour.

Despite the possibility of market failure, the invisible hand of the marketplace is extraordinarily important. In many markets, the assumptions we made in this chapter work well, and the conclusion of market efficiency applies directly. Moreover, our analysis of welfare economics and market efficiency can be used to shed light on the effects of various government policies. In the next two chapters we apply the tools we have just developed to study two important policy issues—the welfare effects of taxation and of international trade.

SUMMARY

- Consumer surplus equals buyers' willingness to pay for a good minus the amount they actually pay for it, and it measures the benefit that buyers receive from participating in a market. Consumer surplus can be computed by finding the area below the demand curve and above the price.

- Producer surplus equals the amount that sellers receive for their goods minus their costs of production, and it measures the benefit that sellers receive from participating in a market. Producer surplus can be computed by finding the area below the price and above the supply curve.

- An allocation of resources that maximizes the sum of consumer and producer surplus is said to be efficient. Policymakers are often concerned with the efficiency, as well as the equity, of economic outcomes.

- The equilibrium of supply and demand maximizes the sum of consumer and producer surplus. That is, the invisible hand of the marketplace leads buyers and sellers to allocate resources efficiently.

- Markets do not allocate resources efficiently in the presence of market failures such as market power or externalities.

KEY CONCEPTS

welfare economics, p. 146
willingness to pay, p. 146
consumer surplus, p. 147

cost, p. 151
producer surplus, p. 152
efficiency, p. 156

equity, p. 156

QUESTIONS FOR REVIEW

1. Explain how buyers' willingness to pay, consumer surplus, and the demand curve are related.

2. Explain how sellers' costs, producer surplus, and the supply curve are related.

3. In a supply-and-demand diagram, show producer and consumer surplus in the market equilibrium.

4. What is efficiency? Is it the only goal of economic policymakers?

5. What does the invisible hand do?

6. Name two types of market failure. Explain why each may cause market outcomes to be inefficient.

PROBLEMS AND APPLICATIONS

1. A drought in Nova Scotia reduces the apple harvest. What happens to consumer surplus in the market for apples? What happens to consumer surplus in the market for apple juice? Illustrate your answers with diagrams.

2. Suppose the demand for French bread rises. What happens to producer surplus in the market for French bread? What happens to producer surplus in the market for flour? Illustrate your answer with diagrams.

3. It is a hot day, and Bert is thirsty. Here is the value he places on a bottle of water:

Value of first bottle	$7
Value of second bottle	5
Value of third bottle	3
Value of fourth bottle	1

a. From this information, derive Bert's demand schedule. Graph his demand curve for bottled water.

b. If the price of a bottle of water is $4, how many bottles does Bert buy? How much consumer surplus does Bert get from his purchases? Show Bert's consumer surplus in your graph.

c. If the price falls to $2, how does quantity demanded change? How does Bert's consumer surplus change? Show these changes in your graph.

4. Ernie owns a water pump. Because pumping large amounts of water is harder than pumping small amounts, the cost of producing a bottle of water rises as he pumps more. Here is the cost he incurs to produce each bottle of water:

Cost of first bottle	$1
Cost of second bottle	3
Cost of third bottle	5
Cost of fourth bottle	7

a. From this information, derive Ernie's supply schedule. Graph his supply curve for bottled water.

b. If the price of a bottle of water is $4, how many bottles does Ernie produce and sell? How much producer surplus does Ernie get from these sales? Show Ernie's producer surplus in your graph.

c. If the price rises to $6, how does quantity supplied change? How does Ernie's producer surplus change? Show these changes in your graph.

5. Consider a market in which Bert from problem 3 is the buyer and Ernie from problem 4 is the seller.

a. Use Ernie's supply schedule and Bert's demand schedule to find the quantity supplied and quantity demanded at prices of $2, $4, and $6. Which of these prices brings supply and demand into equilibrium?

b. What are consumer surplus, producer surplus, and total surplus in this equilibrium?

c. If Ernie produced and Bert consumed one fewer bottle of water, what would happen to total surplus?

d. If Ernie produced and Bert consumed one additional bottle of water, what would happen to total surplus?

6. The cost of producing flat-screen TVs has fallen over the past several decades. Let's consider some implications of this fact.

a. Use a supply-and-demand diagram to show the effect of falling production costs on the price and quantity of flat-screen TVs sold.

b. In your diagram, show what happens to consumer surplus and producer surplus.

c. Suppose the supply of flat-screen TVs is very elastic. Who benefits most from falling production costs—consumers or producers of these TVs?

7. Four consumers are willing to pay the following amounts for haircuts:

Jerry: $7   Oprah: $2   Ricki: $8   Montel: $5

Four haircutting businesses have the following costs:

Firm A: $3   Firm B: $6   Firm C: $4   Firm D: $2

Each firm has the capacity to produce only one haircut. For efficiency, how many haircuts should be given? Which businesses should cut hair, and which consumers should have their hair cut? How large is the maximum possible total surplus?

8. Suppose a technological advance reduces the cost of making computers.

a. Use a supply-and-demand diagram to show what happens to price, quantity, consumer surplus, and producer surplus in the market for computers.

b. Computers and adding machines are substitutes. Use a supply-and-demand diagram to show what happens to price, quantity, consumer surplus, and producer surplus in the market for adding machines. Should adding machine producers be happy or sad about the technological advance in computers?

c. Computers and software are complements. Use a supply-and-demand diagram to show what happens to price, quantity, consumer surplus, and producer surplus in the market for software. Should software producers be happy or sad about the technological advance in computers?

d. Does this analysis help explain why software producer Bill Gates is one of the world's richest men?

9. Melissa buys an iPod for $120 and gets consumer surplus of $80.

a. What is her willingness to pay?

b. If she had bought the iPod on sale for $90, what would her consumer surplus have been?

c. If the price of an iPod was $250, what would her consumer surplus have been?

10. The supply and demand for broccoli are described by the following equations:

Supply: $Q^S = 4P - 80$

Demand: $Q^D = 100 - 2P$

Q is in bushels, and P is in dollars per bushel.

a. Graph the supply curve and the demand curve. What is the equilibrium price and quantity?

b. Calculate consumer surplus, producer surplus, and total surplus at the equilibrium.

c. If a dictator who hated broccoli was to ban the vegetable, who would bear the larger burden—the buyers or sellers of broccoli?

http://

For more study tools, please visit http://www.mankiw5e.nelson.com.

Chapter 7
The Algebra of Consumer and Producer Surplus

As we have seen in this chapter, Consumer Surplus (CS) is the area under the demand curve above the price consumers actually pay for the good. Similarly, Producer Surplus (PS) is the area under the price they actually receive for the good above the supply curve. In a competitive market equilibrium, total surplus is maximized.

CS and PS are the areas of triangles when we are in a competitive equilibrium. If we have the equations for demand and supply, we can easily find the areas of these triangles by finding equilibrium price and quantity and the values of the price intercepts for our demand and supply curves.

The area of a triangle is calculated as Area = ½ bh, where b is the length of the base of the triangle and h is the height of the triangle.

Consider the following diagram where we are in a competitive equilibrium:

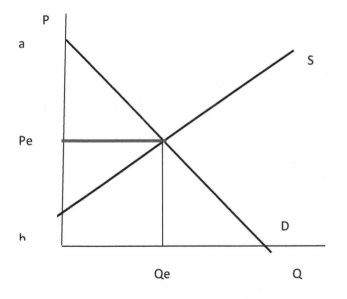

CS is the area under the demand curve above Pe. The base of this triangle is the length Qe. The height of this triangle is a – Pe. The area of this triangle is ½ Qe*(a-Pe), and that is the dollar value of CS.

PS is the area under Pe above the supply curve. The base of this triangle is the length Qe. The height of this triangle is Pe – b. The area of this triangle is ½ Qe*(Pe-b) and that is the dollar value of PS.

If we have the equations for demand and supply, we can find Pe and Qe and also find the values for the intercepts a and b. Then we can calculate a numerical value for CS and PS for our given market.

Example

Market demand for stuff is given by Qd = 80 – 2P and market supply for stuff is given by Qs = P – 10.

In equilibrium Qd = Qs:

80 – 2P = P – 10

$\qquad$ 90 = 3P

Pe = 30 and Qe = 20

Now we need the price intercepts for our demand and supply curves. To find these values, set Q = 0 in each equation.

For our demand curve, 0 = 80 – 2P so the P intercept is 40 (that would be a in our diagram).

For our supply curve, 0 = P – 10 so the P intercept is 10 (that would be b in our diagram).

For consumer surplus: the base of the triangle is 20 and the height is 40 – 30 = 10. CS = ½*20*10 = $100.

For producer surplus: the base of the triangle is 20 and the height is 30 – 10 = 20. PS = ½*20*20 = $200.

Total surplus (TS) is $100 + $200 = $300.

Here's what we did:

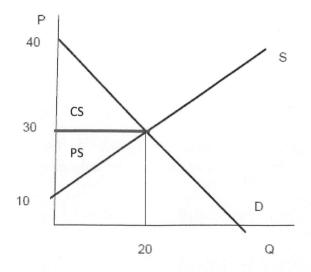

Practice Problems

1.   Market demand is given as Qd = 200 – 3P. Market supply is given as Qs = 2P + 100. In a perfectly competitive equilibrium, what will be the value of consumer surplus?
    a. $6538.00
    b. $3269.00
    c. $2800.00
    d. $1400.00

2.   Market demand is given as Qd = 200 – 3P. Market supply is given as Qs = 2P - 50. In a perfectly competitive equilibrium, what will be the value of producer surplus?
    a. $1250.00
    b. $625.00
    c. $416.75
    d. $833.50

Answers: 1 b   2 b

7 Consumers, Producers, and the Efficiency of Markets

I. Chapter Overview

A. Context and Purpose

Earlier chapters provided an overview of supply and demand as a way to set prices and determine how much to produce. This chapter looks at the question of whether or not supply and demand produce an outcome that is desirable from the standpoint of society. That is, does the market give people the maximum possible social well-being? The following two chapters will apply these results to policy questions regarding taxation and trade with other countries. In an economic sense, do people really know what's good for them? This section of three chapters will help to find the answers.

A. Helpful Hints

1. *Consumer surplus is the amount that a buyer is willing to pay for a good minus the amount actually paid.* That is, consumer surplus is the additional amount that the buyer would have willingly paid beyond the market price that he or she actually paid to get the product. Because the demand curve measures willingness to pay, the area under the demand curve but above the market price represents consumer surplus. As an example, suppose that Parminder is looking for cheap transportation; he will pay up to $3000 for a reliable used car that gets decent mileage. Luckily for Parminder, reliable, if not beautiful, cars are available for $2000. If Parminder buys at the market price of $2000, he will gain a consumer surplus of $1000 ($3000–$2000).

2. *Producer surplus, the mirror image of consumer surplus, is the amount a seller is paid, minus the cost of production.* That is, producer surplus is the excess that the seller receives beyond his or her opportunity cost of providing the good or service. As an example, suppose that Gladys is interested in selling her old car in order to buy a newer one. She is willing to unload it for $500, but luckily for her, the market values the car at $2000. If Gladys sells it, she will earn a producer surplus of $1500 ($2000–$500). The market price of $2000 was determined by the interaction of the marginal buyer (i.e., the buyer who would leave the market first if the price were any higher) and the marginal seller (i.e., the seller who would leave the market first if the price were any lower), each of whom valued the car at $2000.

93

3.   *Efficiency is the property of a resource allocation that maximizes the total surplus received by all members of society.* In the used-car example above, the total surplus is $2500 ($1000 + $1500).

4.   *Equity refers to the fairness of the distribution of well-being among the members of society, that is, the various buyers and sellers.* It requires normative judgments that go beyond positive economics.

5.   *Market failure refers to inefficient allocation of resources* and may occur where market power (the ability of a single buyer or seller, or a small group of them, to influence the price) or externalities (costs and benefits borne by those who are not participants in the market) are present.

6.   *A change in price alone simply reallocates the total surplus between consumers and producers.* It is very tempting to argue that price is directly responsible for differences in social welfare. For example, when sellers take advantage of inelastic demand to raise price, this directly lowers social welfare. Only if the quantity sold changes does the total surplus change. The used car example demonstrates that the total surplus can remain the same even when consumer surplus is either maximized or eliminated, as long as there is an offsetting change in producer surplus. People may feel that a certain outcome is unfair, but that is a separate question from the efficiency resulting from maximizing total welfare.

7.   *Remember that exchanges are voluntary.* Market exchanges make both the buyer and the seller better off because nobody is forced to trade if they do not want to. The more voluntary exchanges that occur, the more gains from trade there are.

II. Self-Testing Challenges

A. True/False Questions

_____1.   Consumer surplus measures the benefit that buyers receive from a good as the buyers themselves perceive it.

_____2.   Producer surplus refers to unsold inventories, due to a market price above equilibrium.

_____3.   When free markets work effectively, they maximize the sum of consumer and producer surplus.

_____4.   An efficient allocation of resources is one that maximizes the fairness of the outcome.

_____5.   Equity and efficiency are two economic goals that typically go together—usually an efficient outcome is an equitable outcome.

_____6.   Policymakers always want to respect the preferences of buyers in order to promote the economic well-being of society.

_____7.   The major advantage of using supply and demand to allocate resources is the inherent fairness of the outcome.

_____8.   Efficiency is an objective goal that can be judged on strictly positive grounds, but equity involves normative judgments that go beyond economics and delve into the realm of political philosophy.

_____9.   Competitive markets are efficient in that they allocate the demand for goods to the sellers who can produce them at the least cost, and they allocate the supply of goods to the buyers who value them most highly.

_____10.   From the standpoint of society, the willingness of drug addicts to pay a high price for heroin is a good measure of the buyers' benefit, and their consumer surplus is a good measure of economic well-being

B. Multiple-Choice Questions

1.   Which one of the following is maximized for economic efficiency?
    a.   total economic well-being
    b.   consumer surplus
    c.   producer surplus
    d.   total equity

2.   Which one of the following is producer surplus?
    a.   total cost to the sellers of participating in the market
    b.   difference between what the consumer offered and the actual price paid
    c.   inventories that could not be sold at the market price

3.   Which one of the following is the total economic well-being to society?
    a.   consumer surplus less the producer surplus
    b.   sum of consumer surplus plus producer surplus
    c.   ratio of consumer surplus to producer surplus

4. Which one of the following is consumer surplus?
    a. unused products that may be sold at auction
    b. the quantity of a good the consumer gets but did not have to pay for
    c. the amount that the consumer would have paid in excess of the actual price
    d. the total value of a good to a consumer

5. Which one of the following defines the term 'market failure'?
    a. income distribution is not equitable
    b. externalities are present in the economy
    c. the best attainable outcome has not been achieved
    d. the economy is not in equilibrium

6. Which choice below would be the most likely if less than the market's equilibrium quantity of diet colas was produced?
    a. resources must have had a higher valued alternative use producing something else
    b. consumer surplus will be higher than otherwise would be the case
    c. producer surplus will be higher than otherwise would be the case

7. Suppose that a technological breakthrough occurs in the production of cell phones. All else equal, the equilibrium price of cell phones will _____, the equilibrium quantity of cell phones sold will _____, consumer surplus will _____, and producer surplus will _____.
    a. increase, decrease, increase, decrease
    b. decrease, decrease, decrease, increase
    c. decrease, decrease, increase, increase
    d. decrease, increase, increase, increase

Use the following information to answer questions 8–10. Suppose that Cameron owns a classic Fender guitar. He has lost interest in it, and so it is worth only $50 to him. His friend, Juan, loves the guitar and would be willing to pay as much as $950 for it.

8. Which one of the following describes what would happen to social welfare if Cameron sells his guitar for $100?
    a. Social welfare decreases by $400.
    b. Social welfare remains unchanged.
    c. Social welfare rises by $50.
    d. It turns out that Juan is not the only friend who is interested in the guitar.

9. Ben also likes it and would pay $500, Sanam would pay $1200, and Bill would actually pay $2000! Which one of the following describes what Cameron should do in order to maximize this small society's well-being?
    a. He should sell the guitar to Juan, because Juan was the first to offer to buy it, but only if Juan matches Bill's offer.
    b. He should sell the guitar to Juan, even if Juan does not match Bill's offer.
    c. He should sell the guitar to Bill, but only if Bill pays $2000.
    d. He should sell the guitar to Bill, even if Bill pays no more than the others.

10. Judith is willing to sell her homemade brownies for $15 per box. She sells them and realizes a producer surplus of $12 per box. Which of the following indicates, in order, Judith's cost per box, and her sale price per box?
    a. $15, $12
    b. $12, $15
    c. $12, $27
    d. $15, $27

11. Medical care is vital to society's survival. From society's standpoint, under which one of the following conditions should people increase their spending on health care?
    a. as long as anyone is sick
    b. as long as total benefit increases when people increase their spending
    c. as long total cost is less than total benefit
    d. as long as an extra dollar of health-care spending generates at least a dollar in added benefits

12. Is an auction socially inefficient, efficient, equitable, or inequitable?
    a. inefficient, because goods go to those with the most money, rather than to those who want them the most
    b. efficient, because it allocates the units of the product to the buyers who value them the most, as evidenced by their willingness to pay
    c. equitable, because it is only fair for goods to go to those who are willing to pay for them
    d. inequitable, because not everyone can afford to keep up with the bidding

13. The price of a new car is $25 000. Consumers will continue to buy additional cars until the consumer surplus from the last car purchased is at which one of the following points?
    a. zero
    b. $25 000
    c. maximized
    d. minimized

14. In the previous question, **auto producers** will continue to supply additional cars until the producer surplus from the last car produced is at which one of the following points?
   a. zero
   b. $20 000
   c. maximized
   d. minimized

15. As a matter of public policy, people are not allowed to sell their organs. Which one of the following is a reason some economists believe that there would be large benefits to allowing a free market in organs?
   a. The shortage of organs for transplant would disappear.
   b. Sellers of organs would be worst off with less cash in their pockets.
   c. Buyers of organs would be better off having the quantity of organs available.
   d. Such a market would lead to a non-efficient outcome.

16. Which one of the following arguments would economists generally make about restricting ticket scalping?
   a. It increases the audience for events.
   b. It deprives the government of tax revenue and wastes police time.
   c. It increases the efficiency of ticket distribution.
   d. It eliminates the unfair price discrepancies.

17. Which of the following statements best represents externalities?
   a. they cause wealth in a market to depend on more than just the value to the buyers and the cost to the sellers
   b. they are side effects of production or consumption passed on to a party other than the sellers and buyers in the market
   c. they are examples of market success

C. Short-Answer Questions

1. Contrast the efficiency and equity goals in economic policymaking. How do they differ? _____
   _____
   _____
   _____

2. Economists tend to see ticket scalping as an example of how markets reach efficient outcomes. Why? _____
   _____
   _____
   _____
   _____
   _____

D. Practice Problems

1. There are five consumers looking for a particular used car in Farmville, Saskatchewan. Shayan is willing to pay $6000, Kathy would pay $5000, Fred would pay $4000, Gwen would pay $3000, and Camille would pay $2000. There are also five local dealers with cars that would satisfy the consumers: Bill's Beautiful Bargains has a car that cost Bill $6000, Al's Autos has one for which his opportunity cost was $5000, Cal's Classic Cars has one that cost $4000, Tim's Transportation has one that cost $3000, and Buy-A-Bomb has one that it is willing to sell for $2000. (Assume that all of the used cars are identical, except for the price charged.)

a. Plot the supply and demand diagrams for the used cars in the space below.

b. If the market moves to a single equilibrium price, how many autos will be sold, and at what price? Will this maximize efficiency? Explain.____

_____

_____

_____

_____

c. Label the consumer and producer surplus on your diagram. What is the dollar value of the consumer surplus? The producer surplus? The total surplus? Explain how the calculations were made.

_____

_____

_____

_____

d. It appears that each consumer could find a seller that would sell at a price that would coincide with the consumer's willingness to pay, if each buyer negotiated separately with a seller that matched his or her willingness to buy. For example, Bill is not very competitive, with a minimum price of $6000, but there is one buyer—Shayan—who would pay that much. Of course, for this to work, buyers and sellers would have to be unaware of the better options available elsewhere; otherwise, Shayan, for example, could do better buying from a lower-cost seller. Would it be more or less efficient for the buyers and sellers to be matched according to their willingness to buy and sell? (Hint: What would happen to total surplus, compared to the competitive solution?) _____

_____

_____

_____

2.   a. Explain how the free market maximizes total surplus. What assumptions are required for this result to occur?

_____

_____

_____

b. What happens to total surplus if production goes beyond the equilibrium? Explain. _____

_____

_____

c. What happens to total surplus if production stops short of equilibrium? Explain._____

_____

_____

_____

3.   a. Will a price ceiling always make consumers better off? How?____

_____

_____

_____

b. Will a price floor always make producers better off? How? _____

_____

_____

_____

E. Advanced Critical Thinking

Some groups argue for legalization of currently illegal drugs—perhaps even cocaine and heroin. They argue that free markets are inherently more efficient than government edicts in allocating resources, and that there is also the issue of freedom involved. Evaluate their arguments. What is the case for legalizing at least some currently illegal, controlled substances? What are the arguments against legalization? Do markets operate efficiently in the case of such controlled substances? _____

_____

_____

_____

III. Solutions

A. True/False Questions

1. T
2. F; producer surplus refers to the difference between market price and sellers' costs of production.
3. T
4. F; an efficient allocation of resources is one that maximizes total surplus.
5. F; equity and efficiency often conflict, because there is no reason for the mechanism that maximizes total surplus to also distribute it fairly.
6. F; in most markets, but not always. In some cases, policymakers might choose not to respect the preferences of buyers. For instance, a cocaine addict is willing to pay a high price for cocaine, but from society's point of view the willingness to pay, and hence consumer surplus, is not a good measure of economic well-being.
7. F; the major advantage of using supply and demand to allocate resources is the *efficiency* of the outcome, although it may be considered unfair.
8. T
9. T
10. F; because society believes that addicts do not look after their own best interests, neither their willingness to pay nor their consumer surplus are considered good measures.

B. Multiple-Choice Questions

1. a	5. c	9. d	13. a	17. b
2. c	6. c	10. d	14. a	
3. b	7. d	11. d	15. a	
4. c	8. d	12. b	16. b	

C. Short-Answer Questions

1. Efficiency means maximizing the total combined producer and consumer surplus from the market. It does not, however, guarantee any particular distribution of the resulting outcome. Efficiency is objectively measured as what is, but equity requires normative or value judgements about what ought to be.

2. If an economy is to allocate its scarce resources efficiently, goods must get to those consumers who value them most highly. Scalpers buy tickets to arts, entertainment, and sports events, and then resell them at a price above what they paid originally. By charging the highest prices the market will bear, scalpers help consumers with the greatest willingness to pay for the tickets to actually get them and, therefore, to increase the efficiency of ticket distribution.

D. Practice Problems

1. a.   Supply-and-demand diagrams for the used cars are plotted below.

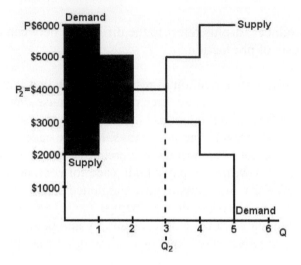

b. Market equilibrium would result in three cars sold at a price of $4000 each. It would leave out two buyers with low willingness to pay and two high-cost sellers, but it would maximize efficiency by maximizing total surplus (consumer surplus + producer surplus), as shown on the diagram.

c. The dollar value of consumer surplus is $3000 (Shayan gains $2000 at a price of $4000, and Kathy gains $1000 at that price). The producer surplus is also $3000 (Tim's gains $1000 at a price of $4000, and Buy-A-Bomb gains $2000). The total surplus is, therefore, $6000.

d. If the highest-cost seller sold to the highest-marginal-value consumer, and the lowest-cost seller sold to the consumer with the lowest marginal value, and so on, each auto would be sold and each consumer would have a car. However, it would be less efficient: there would be no consumer or producer surplus, because each buyer and seller would have broken even. Compared to the competitive solution, society would lose a $6000 total surplus.

2. a.   Free markets encourage the production of every good that adds more to benefits than it adds to cost. If decision makers take into account all of the social benefits and social costs of their actions when they choose, then their decisions will also maximize society's total surplus. This assumes that there is no market failure, due to, for example, externalities or concentration of market power.

b. If production occurs beyond equilibrium, then the additional units will have marginal costs greater than the marginal benefits from their production, resulting in a net loss of social well-being, because total surplus is reduced from its level at equilibrium.

c. Stopping short of equilibrium means that society is failing to produce some units of a good or service that have marginal benefits greater than the marginal cost. In this range, willingness to buy is higher than sellers cost of production, so society would gain from the additional output; that is, total surplus would rise.

3. a   Price ceilings will not always make consumers better off. If the supply curve is completely inelastic, a price ceiling will increase consumer surplus. If the demand is inelastic, price ceiling may result in a net loss of consumer surplus.

b. Price floors will not always make producers better off. If the demand curve is perfectly inelastic, a price floor will increase producer surplus. If the supply is inelastic, a price floor may result in a net loss of producer surplus.

E. Advanced Critical Thinking

It is true that free markets tend to be efficient in maximizing economic efficiency, by ensuring, at least under competition, that the market will provide every unit of output that adds more to society's benefits than it adds to its costs. One can also make the case that people should have the freedom to decide for themselves what is good for them. However, the counterargument is that there are external costs involved with the production and use of illegal drugs. The buyers and sellers of illegal drugs do not bear all of the costs of their actions. Increased crime rates, declining neighbourhoods, health costs, and other social costs are ignored by those in the market. (Of course, some of the external costs are a result of the illegality of the drugs, rather than the drugs themselves.) Such externalities result in market failure, leading to overproduction of those goods that have external costs.

APPLICATION: THE COSTS OF TAXATION

Learning Objectives

In this chapter, you will ...

- Examine how taxes reduce consumer and producer surplus

- Learn the meaning and causes of the deadweight loss of a tax

- Consider why some taxes have larger deadweight losses than others

- Examine how tax revenue and deadweight loss vary with the size of a tax

Taxes are often a source of heated political debate. In 1993, Jean Chrétien became prime minister of Canada in part because voters believed that he would scrap the Goods and Services Tax (GST) introduced by Brian Mulroney's government. On further reflection, however, the Chrétien government decided not to scrap the GST after all. In 2006, Stephen Harper promised to reduce the GST if he became prime minister. His Conservative Party formed a minority government largely on the basis of this promise, and he subsequently reduced the GST by two percentage points.

Because taxation has such a major impact on the modern economy, we return to the topic several times throughout this book as we expand the set of tools we have at our disposal. We began our study of taxes in Chapter 6. There we saw how a tax on a good affects its price and the quantity sold and how the forces of supply and demand divide the burden of a tax between buyers and sellers. In this chapter we extend this analysis and look at how taxes affect welfare, the economic well-being of participants in a market.

The effects of taxes on welfare might at first seem obvious. The government enacts taxes to raise revenue, and that revenue must come out of someone's pocket. As we saw in Chapter 6, both buyers and sellers are worse off when a good is taxed: A tax raises the price buyers pay and lowers the price sellers receive. Yet to understand fully how taxes affect economic well-being, we must compare the reduced welfare of buyers and sellers to the amount of revenue the government raises. The tools of consumer and producer surplus allow us to make this comparison. The analysis will show that the costs of taxes to buyers and sellers exceeds the revenue raised by the government.

While this chapter is devoted to discussing the costs of taxation, no one would deny that some level of taxation is necessary. One of the ten principles of economics in Chapter 1 is that governments can sometimes improve market outcomes. Taxes are one of the ways that governments can do this.

For example, governments must often provide goods and services such as roads, parks, police, and national defence, which are not well provided by the market; they need revenue to do this. We will discuss this in detail in Chapter 11. Also, sometimes governments can impose taxes to achieve a more efficient outcome when markets don't function properly, as in the case of so-called "corrective taxes," which will be discussed in Chapter 10. Finally, governments are also concerned with the distribution of income in society, and the tax system can play an important role in achieving equity objectives; we will pay some attention to this in Chapter 20.

The tax system thus plays an important and beneficial role in the economy. As Oliver Wendell Holmes, Jr., a member of the U.S. Supreme Court during the early 1900s, once said, "Taxes are what we pay for a civilized society." (These words are engraved on the U.S. Internal Revenue Service building in Washington, DC.) However, it is important to understand the nature of the costs associated with taxes.

THE DEADWEIGHT LOSS OF TAXATION

We begin by recalling one of the surprising lessons from Chapter 6: It does not matter whether a tax on a good is levied on buyers or sellers of the good. When a tax is levied on buyers, the demand curve shifts downward by the size of the tax; when it is levied on sellers, the supply curve shifts upward by that amount. In either case, when the tax is enacted, the price paid by buyers rises, and the price received by sellers falls. In the end, buyers and sellers share the burden of the tax, regardless of how it is levied.

Figure 8.1 shows these effects. To simplify our discussion, this figure does not show a shift in either the supply or demand curve, although one curve must shift. Which curve shifts depends on whether the tax is levied on sellers (the supply curve shifts) or buyers (the demand curve shifts). In this chapter, we can simplify the graphs by not bothering to show the shift. The key result for our purposes here is that the tax places a wedge between the price buyers pay and the price sellers receive. Because of this tax wedge, the quantity sold falls below the level that would be sold without a tax. In other words, a tax on a good causes the size of the market for the good to shrink. These results should be familiar from Chapter 6.

How a Tax Affects Market Participants

Let's use the tools of welfare economics to measure the gains and losses from a tax on a good. To do this, we must take into account how the tax affects buyers, sellers, and the government. The benefit received by buyers in a market is measured by consumer surplus—the amount buyers are willing to pay for the good minus the amount they actually pay for it. The benefit received by sellers in a market is measured by producer surplus—the amount sellers receive for the good minus their costs. These are precisely the measures of economic welfare we used in Chapter 7.

FIGURE 8.1

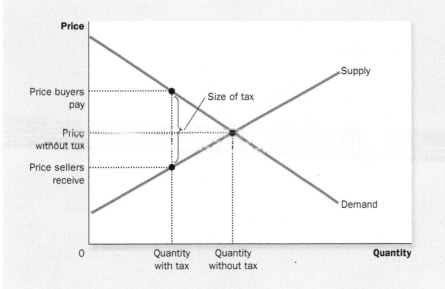

The Effects of a Tax

A tax on a good places a wedge between the price that buyers pay and the price that sellers receive. The quantity of the good sold falls.

What about the third interested party, the government? If T is the size of the tax and Q is the quantity of the good sold, then the government gets total tax revenue of $T \times Q$. It can use this tax revenue to provide services, such as roads, police, and public education, or to help the needy. Therefore, to analyze how taxes affect economic well-being, we use tax revenue to measure the government's benefit from the tax. Keep in mind, however, that this benefit actually accrues not to government but to those on whom the revenue is spent.

Figure 8.2 shows that the government's tax revenue is represented by the rectangle between the supply and demand curves. The height of this rectangle is the size of the tax, T, and the width of the rectangle is the quantity of the good sold, Q. Because a rectangle's area is its height times its width, this rectangle's area is $T \times Q$, which equals the tax revenue.

Welfare without a Tax   To see how a tax affects welfare, we begin by considering welfare before the government has imposed a tax. Figure 8.3 (p. 169) shows the supply-and-demand diagram and marks the key areas with the letters A through F.

Without a tax, the price and quantity are found at the intersection of the supply and demand curves. The price is P_1, and the quantity sold is Q_1. Because the demand curve reflects buyers' willingness to pay, consumer surplus is the area between the demand curve and the price, A + B + C. Similarly, because the supply curve reflects sellers' costs, producer surplus is the area between the supply curve and the price, D + E + F. In this case, because there is no tax, tax revenue equals zero.

Total surplus—the sum of consumer and producer surplus—equals the area A + B + C + D + E + F. In other words, as we saw in Chapter 7, total surplus is the area between the supply and demand curves up to the equilibrium quantity. The "Without Tax" column of the table in Figure 8.3 summarizes these conclusions.

FIGURE 8.2

Tax Revenue

The tax revenue that the government collects equals T × Q, the size of the tax T times the quantity sold Q. Thus, tax revenue equals the area of the rectangle between the supply and demand curves.

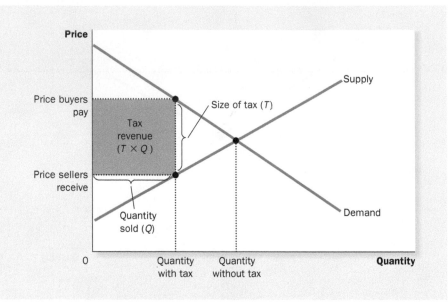

Welfare with a Tax   Now consider welfare after the tax is enacted. The price paid by buyers rises from P_1 to P_B, so consumer surplus now equals only area A (the area below the demand curve and above the buyer's price). The price received by sellers falls from P_1 to P_S, so producer surplus now equals only area F (the area above the supply curve and below the seller's price). The quantity sold falls from Q_1 to Q_2, and the government collects tax revenue equal to the area B + D.

To compute total surplus with the tax, we add consumer surplus, producer surplus, and tax revenue. Thus, we find that total surplus is area A + B + D + F. The "With Tax" column of the table provides a summary.

Changes in Welfare   We can now see the effects of the tax by comparing welfare before and after the tax is enacted. The last column in the table in Figure 8.3 shows the changes. The tax causes consumer surplus to fall by the area B + C and producer surplus to fall by the area D + E. Tax revenue rises by the area B + D. Not surprisingly, the tax makes buyers and sellers worse off and the government better off.

The change in total welfare includes the change in consumer surplus (which is negative), the change in producer surplus (which is also negative), and the change in tax revenue (which is positive). When we add these three pieces together, we find that total surplus in the market falls by the area C + E. *Thus, the losses to buyers and sellers from a tax exceed the revenue raised by the government.* The fall in total surplus that results when a tax (or some other policy) distorts a market outcome is called the **deadweight loss.** The area C + E measures the size of the deadweight loss.

deadweight loss
the fall in total surplus that results from a market distortion, such as a tax

To understand why taxes impose deadweight losses, recall one of the ten principles of economics in Chapter 1: People respond to incentives. In Chapter 7 we saw that markets normally allocate scarce resources efficiently. That is, the equilibrium of supply and demand maximizes the total surplus of buyers and sellers in a market. When a tax raises the price to buyers and lowers the price to sellers,

NEL

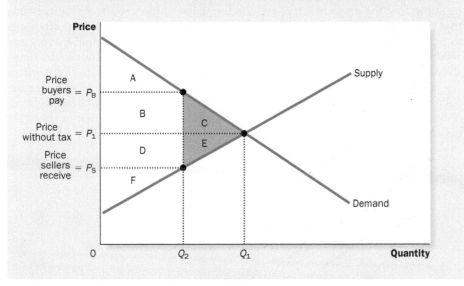

FIGURE 8.3

How a Tax Affects Welfare

A tax on a good reduces consumer surplus (by the area B + C) and producer surplus (by the area D + E). Because the fall in producer and consumer surplus exceeds tax revenue (area B + D), the tax is said to impose a deadweight loss (area C + E).

	Without Tax	With Tax	Change
Consumer Surplus	A + B + C	A	−(B + C)
Producer Surplus	D + E + F	F	−(D + E)
Tax Revenue	None	B + D	+(B + D)
Total Surplus	A + B + C + D + E + F	A + B + D + F	−(C + E)

The area C + E shows the fall in total surplus and is the deadweight loss of the tax.

however, it gives buyers an incentive to consume less and sellers an incentive to produce less than they otherwise would. As buyers and sellers respond to these incentives, the size of the market shrinks below its optimum. Thus, because taxes distort incentives, they cause markets to allocate resources inefficiently.

Deadweight Losses and the Gains from Trade

To gain some intuition for why taxes result in deadweight losses, consider an example. Imagine that Joe cleans Jane's house each week for $100. The opportunity cost of Joe's time is $80, and the value of a clean house to Jane is $120. Thus, Joe and Jane each receive a $20 benefit from their deal. The total surplus of $40 measures the gains from trade in this particular transaction.

Now suppose that the government levies a $50 tax on the providers of cleaning services. There is now no price that Jane can pay Joe that will leave both of them better off after paying the tax. The most Jane would be willing to pay is $120, but then Joe would be left with only $70 after paying the tax, which is less than his $80 opportunity cost. Conversely, for Joe to receive his opportunity cost of $80, Jane would need to pay $130, which is above the $120 value she places on a clean house. As a result, Jane and Joe cancel their arrangement. Joe goes without the income, and Jane lives in a dirtier house.

The tax has made Joe and Jane worse off by a total of $40 because they have lost this amount of surplus. At the same time, the government collects no revenue from Joe and Jane because they decide to cancel their arrangement. The $40 is pure deadweight loss: It is a loss to buyers and sellers in a market not offset by an increase in government revenue. From this example, we can see the ultimate source of deadweight losses: *Taxes cause deadweight losses because they prevent buyers and sellers from realizing some of the gains from trade.*

The area of the triangle between the supply and demand curves (area C + E in Figure 8.3) measures these losses. This loss can be seen most easily in Figure 8.4 by recalling that the demand curve reflects the value of the good to consumers and that the supply curve reflects the costs of producers. When the tax raises the price to buyers to P_B and lowers the price to sellers to P_S, the marginal buyers and sellers leave the market, so the quantity sold falls from Q_1 to Q_2. Yet, as the figure shows, the value of the good to these buyers still exceeds the cost to these sellers. As in our example with Joe and Jane, the gains from trade—the difference between buyers' value and sellers' cost—is less than the tax. Thus, these trades do not get made once the tax is imposed. The deadweight loss is the surplus lost because the tax discourages these mutually advantageous trades.

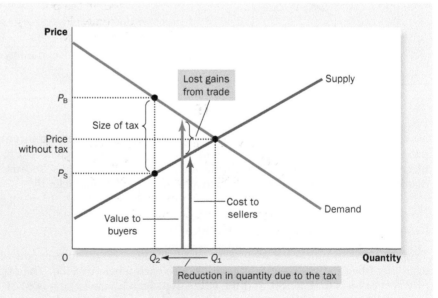

FIGURE 8.4

The Deadweight Loss

When the government imposes a tax on a good, the quantity sold falls from Q_1 to Q_2. As a result, some of the potential gains from trade among buyers and sellers do not get realized. These lost gains from trade create the deadweight loss.

QuickQuiz   Draw the supply and demand curves for cookies. If the government imposes a tax on cookies, show what happens to the quantity sold, the price paid by buyers, and the price paid by sellers. In your diagram, show the deadweight loss from the tax. Explain the meaning of the deadweight loss.

THE DETERMINANTS OF THE DEADWEIGHT LOSS

What determines whether the deadweight loss from a tax is large or small? The answer is the price elasticities of supply and demand, which measure how much the quantity supplied and quantity demanded respond to changes in the price.

Let's consider first how the elasticity of supply affects the size of the deadweight loss. In the top two panels of Figure 8.5, the demand curve and the size of the tax are the same. The only difference in these figures is the elasticity of the supply curve. In panel (a), the supply curve is relatively inelastic: Quantity supplied responds only slightly to changes in the price. In panel (b), the supply curve is relatively elastic: Quantity supplied responds substantially to changes in the price. Notice that the deadweight loss, the area of the triangle between the supply and demand curves, is larger when the supply curve is more elastic.

Similarly, the bottom two panels of Figure 8.5 show how the elasticity of demand affects the size of the deadweight loss. Here the supply curve and the size of the tax are held constant. In panel (c) the demand curve is relatively inelastic, and the deadweight loss is small. In panel (d) the demand curve is more elastic, and the deadweight loss from the tax is larger.

The lesson from this figure is easy to explain. A tax has a deadweight loss because it induces buyers and sellers to change their behaviour. The tax raises the price paid by buyers, so they consume less. At the same time, the tax lowers the price received by sellers, so they produce less. Because of these changes in behaviour, the size of the market shrinks below the optimum. The elasticities of supply and demand measure how much sellers and buyers respond to the changes in the price and, therefore, determine how much the tax distorts the market outcome. Hence, *the greater the elasticities of supply and demand, the greater the deadweight loss of a tax.*

Case Study
THE DEADWEIGHT LOSS DEBATE

Supply, demand, elasticity, deadweight loss—all this economic theory is enough to make your head spin. But believe it or not, these ideas go to the heart of a profound political question: How big should the government be? The debate hinges on these concepts because the larger the deadweight loss of taxation, the larger the cost of any government program. If taxation entails large deadweight losses, then these losses are a strong argument for a leaner government that does less and taxes less. But if taxes impose small deadweight losses, then government programs are less costly than they otherwise might be.

So how big are the deadweight losses of taxation? This is a question about which economists disagree. To see the nature of the disagreement, consider the

FIGURE 8.5

Tax Distortions and Elasticities

In panels (a) and (b), the demand curve and the size of the tax are the same, but the price elasticity of supply is different. Notice that the more elastic the supply curve, the larger the deadweight loss of the tax. In panels (c) and (d), the supply curve and the size of the tax are the same, but the price elasticity of demand is different. Notice that the more elastic the demand curve, the larger the deadweight loss of the tax.

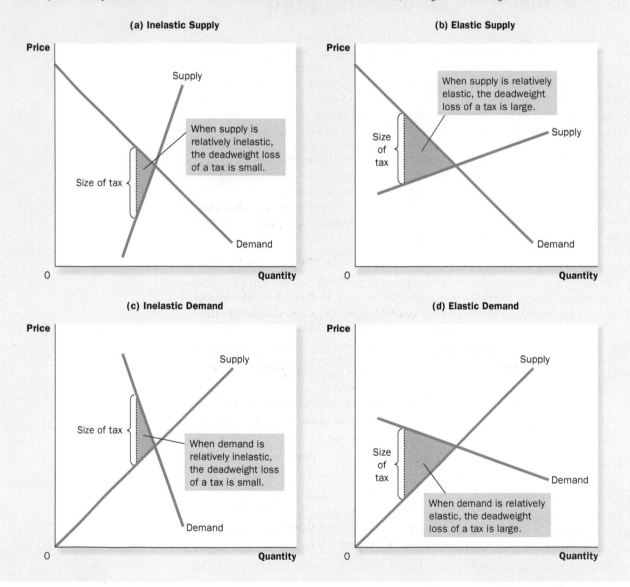

most important tax in the Canadian economy—the tax on labour. Employment Insurance contributions are a tax on labour. Both the federal and provincial income taxes are, to a large extent, labour taxes, because the source of most income is labour earnings. A labour tax places a wedge between the wage that firms pay and the wage that workers receive. If we add all forms of labour taxes together, the marginal tax rate on labour income—the tax on the last dollar of earnings—is over 50 percent for many workers.

Although the size of the labour tax is easy to determine, the deadweight loss of this tax is less straightforward. Economists disagree about whether this 50 percent labour tax has a small or a large deadweight loss. This disagreement arises because economists hold different views about the elasticity of labour supply.

Economists who argue that labour taxes are not very distorting believe that labour supply is fairly inelastic. Most people, they claim, would work full-time regardless of the wage. If so, the labour supply curve is almost vertical, and a tax on labour has a small deadweight loss.

Economists who argue that labour taxes are highly distorting believe that labour supply is more elastic. They admit that some groups of workers may supply their labour inelastically but claim that many other groups respond more to incentives. Here are some examples:

- Many workers can adjust the number of hours they work—for instance, by working overtime or by choosing jobs with longer or shorter hours. The higher the wage, the more hours they choose to work.
- Some families have second earners—often married women with children—with some discretion over whether to do unpaid work at home or paid work in the marketplace. When deciding whether to take a job, these second earners compare the benefits of being at home (including savings on the cost of child care) with the wages they could earn.
- Many of the elderly can choose when to retire, and their decisions are partly based on the wage. Once they are retired, the wage determines their incentive to work part-time.
- Some people consider engaging in illegal economic activity, such as the drug trade, or working at jobs that pay "under the table" to evade taxes. Economists call this the *underground economy*. In deciding whether to work in the underground economy or at a legitimate job, these potential criminals compare what they can earn by breaking the law with the wage they can earn legally.

In each of these cases, the quantity of labour supplied responds to the wage (the price of labour). Thus, the decisions of these workers are distorted when their labour earnings are taxed. Labour taxes encourage workers to work fewer hours, second earners to stay at home, the elderly to retire early, and the unscrupulous to enter the underground economy.

These two views of labour taxation persist to this day. Indeed, whenever you see two political candidates debating whether the government should provide more services or reduce the tax burden, keep in mind that part of the disagreement may rest on different views about the elasticity of labour supply and the deadweight loss of taxation. ●

HENRY GEORGE AND THE LAND TAX

Is there an ideal tax? Henry George, the nineteenth-century American economist and social philosopher, thought so. In his 1879 book *Progress and Poverty*, George argued that the government should raise all its revenue from a tax on land. This "single tax" was, he claimed, both equitable and efficient. George's ideas won him a large political following, and in 1886 he lost a close race for mayor of New York City (although he finished well ahead of Republican candidate Theodore Roosevelt).

George's proposal to tax land was motivated largely by a concern over the distribution of economic well-being. He deplored the "shocking contrast between monstrous wealth and debasing want" and thought landowners benefited more than they should from the rapid growth in the overall economy.

George's arguments for the land tax can be understood using the tools of modern economics. Consider first supply and demand in the market for renting land. As immigration causes the population to rise and technological progress causes incomes to grow, the demand for land rises over time. Yet because the amount of land is fixed, the supply is perfectly inelastic. Rapid increases in demand together with inelastic supply lead to large increases in the equilibrium rents on land, so that economic growth makes rich landowners even richer.

Henry George

Now consider the incidence of a tax on land. As we first saw in Chapter 6, the burden of a tax falls more heavily on the side of the market that is less elastic. A tax on land takes this principle to an extreme. Because the elasticity of supply is zero, the landowners bear the entire burden of the tax.

Consider next the question of efficiency. As we just discussed, the deadweight loss of a tax depends on the elasticities of supply and demand. Again, a tax on land is an extreme case. Because supply is perfectly inelastic, a tax on land does not alter the market allocation. There is no deadweight loss, and the government's tax revenue exactly equals the loss of the landowners.

Although taxing land may look attractive in theory, it is not as straightforward in practice as it may appear. For a tax on land not to distort economic incentives, it must be a tax on raw land. Yet the value of land often comes from improvements, such as clearing trees, providing sewers, and building roads. Unlike the supply of raw land, the supply of improvements has an elasticity greater than zero. If a land tax were imposed on improvements, it would distort incentives. Landowners would respond by devoting fewer resources to improving their land.

Today, few economists support George's proposal for a single tax on land. Not only is taxing improvements a potential problem, but the tax would not raise enough revenue to pay for the much larger government we have today. Yet many of George's arguments remain valid. Here is the assessment of the eminent economist Milton Friedman a century after George's book:

"In my opinion, the least bad tax is the property tax on the unimproved value of land, the Henry George argument of many, many years ago."

Quick Quiz The demand for beer is more elastic than the demand for milk. Would a tax on beer or a tax on milk have a larger deadweight loss? Why?

DEADWEIGHT LOSS AND TAX REVENUE AS TAXES VARY

Taxes rarely stay the same for long periods of time. Policymakers in local, provincial, territorial, and federal governments are always considering raising one tax or lowering another. Here we consider what happens to the deadweight loss and tax revenue when the size of a tax changes.

FIGURE 8.6

Deadweight Loss and Tax Revenue from Three Taxes of Different Sizes

The deadweight loss is the reduction in total surplus due to the tax. Tax revenue is the amount of the tax times the amount of the good sold. In panel (a), a small tax has a small deadweight loss and raises a small amount of revenue. In panel (b), a somewhat larger tax has a larger deadweight loss and raises a larger amount of revenue. In panel (c), a very large tax has a very large deadweight loss, but because it has reduced the size of the market so much, the tax raises only a small amount of revenue. Panels (d) and (e) summarize these conclusions. Panel (d) shows that as the size of the tax grows larger, the deadweight loss grows larger. Panel (e) shows that tax revenue first rises then falls. This relationship is sometimes called the Laffer curve.

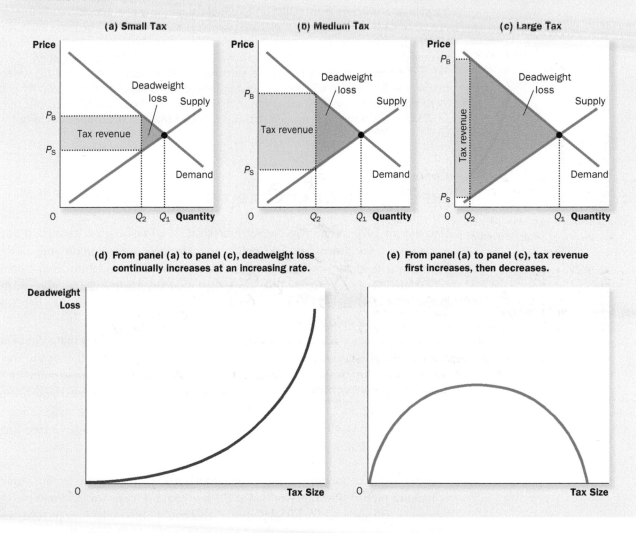

Figure 8.6 shows the effects of a small, medium, and large tax, holding constant the market's supply and demand curves. The deadweight loss—the reduction in total surplus that results when the tax reduces the size of a market below the optimum—equals the area of the triangle between the supply and demand curves. For the small tax in panel (a), the area of the deadweight loss triangle is quite small. But as the size of a tax rises in panels (b) and (c), the deadweight loss grows larger and larger.

Indeed, the deadweight loss of a tax rises even more rapidly than the size of the tax. The reason is that the deadweight loss is an area of a triangle, and an area of a triangle depends on the *square* of its size. If we double the size of a tax, for instance, the base and height of the triangle double, so the deadweight loss rises by a factor of 4. If we triple the size of a tax, the base and height triple, so the deadweight loss rises by a factor of 9.

The government's tax revenue is the size of the tax times the amount of the good sold. As Figure 8.6 shows, tax revenue equals the area of the rectangle between the supply and demand curves. For the small tax in panel (a), tax revenue is small. As the size of a tax rises from panel (a) to panel (b), tax revenue grows. But as the size of the tax rises further from panel (b) to panel (c), tax revenue falls because the higher tax drastically reduces the size of the market. For a very large tax, no revenue would be raised, because people would stop buying and selling the good altogether.

The last two panels of Figure 8.6 summarize these results. In panel (d) we see that as the size of a tax increases, its deadweight loss quickly gets larger. By contrast, panel (e) shows that tax revenue first rises with the size of the tax, but then, as the tax gets larger, the market shrinks so much that tax revenue starts to fall.

Case Study
THE LAFFER CURVE AND SUPPLY-SIDE ECONOMICS

One day in 1974, economist Arthur Laffer sat in a Washington restaurant with some prominent journalists and politicians. He took out a napkin and drew a figure on it to show how tax rates affect tax revenue. It looked much like panel (e) of our Figure 8.6. Laffer then suggested that the United States was on the downward-sloping side of this curve. Tax rates were so high, he argued, that reducing them would actually raise tax revenue.

Most economists were skeptical of Laffer's suggestion. The idea that a cut in tax rates could raise tax revenue was correct as a matter of economic theory, but there was more doubt about whether it would do so in practice. There was little evidence for Laffer's view that U.S. tax rates had in fact reached such extreme levels.

Nonetheless, the *Laffer curve* (as it became known) captured the imagination of Ronald Reagan. David Stockman, budget director in the first Reagan administration, offers the following story:

> [Reagan] had once been on the Laffer curve himself. "I came into the Big Money making pictures during World War II," he would always say. At that time the wartime income surtax hit 90 percent. "You could only make four pictures and then you were in the top bracket," he would continue. "So we all quit working after four pictures and went off to the country." High tax rates caused less work. Low tax rates caused more. His experience proved it.

When Reagan ran for president in 1980, he made cutting taxes part of his platform. Reagan argued that taxes were so high that they were discouraging hard work. He argued that lower taxes would give people the proper incentive to work, which would raise economic well-being and perhaps even tax revenue. Because the cut in tax rates was intended to encourage people to increase the quantity of labour they supplied, the views of Laffer and Reagan became known as *supply-side economics.*

Economists continue to debate Laffer's argument. Many believe that subsequent history refuted Laffer's conjecture that lower tax rates would raise tax revenue. Yet, because history is open to alternative interpretations, other economists view the events of the 1980s as more favourable to the supply-siders. To evaluate Laffer's hypothesis definitively, we would need to rerun history without the Reagan tax cuts and see if tax revenues were higher or lower. Unfortunately, that experiment is impossible.

Some economists take an intermediate position on this issue. They believe that while an overall cut in tax rates normally reduces revenue, some taxpayers at some times may find themselves on the wrong side of the Laffer curve. Other things equal, a tax cut is more likely to raise tax revenue if the cut applies to those taxpayers facing the highest tax rates. In addition, Laffer's argument may be more compelling when considering countries with much higher tax rates than the United States. In Sweden in the early 1980s, for instance, the typical worker faced a marginal tax rate of about 80 percent. Such a high tax rate provides a substantial disincentive to work. Studies have suggested that Sweden would indeed have raised more tax revenue if it had lowered its tax rates.

Economists disagree about these issues in part because there is no consensus about the size of the relevant elasticities. The more elastic that supply and demand are in any market, the more taxes in that market distort behaviour, and the more likely it is that a tax cut will raise tax revenue. There is no debate, however, about the general lesson: How much revenue the government gains or loses from a tax change cannot be computed just by looking at tax rates. It also depends on how the tax change affects people's behaviour. ●

QuickQuiz If the government doubles the tax on gasoline, can you be sure that revenue from the gasoline tax will rise? Can you be sure that the deadweight loss from the gasoline tax will rise? Explain.

CONCLUSION

In this chapter, we have used the tools developed in the previous chapter to further our understanding of taxes. One of the ten principles of economics discussed in Chapter 1 is that markets are usually a good way to organize economic activity. In Chapter 7, we used the concepts of producer and consumer surplus to make this principle more precise. Here, we have seen that when the government imposes taxes on buyers or sellers of a good, society loses some of the benefits of market efficiency. Taxes are costly to market participants, not only because taxes transfer resources from those participants to the government, but also because they alter incentives and distort market outcomes.

The analysis presented here and in Chapter 6 should give you a good basis for understanding the economic impact of taxes, but this is not the end of the story. Taxes play an important role in modern economies. Microeconomists study how best to design a tax system, including how to strike the right balance between equality and efficiency. Macroeconomists study how taxes influence the overall economy and how policymakers can use the tax system to stabilize economic activity and to achieve more rapid economic growth. So don't be surprised that, as you continue your study of economics, the subject of taxation comes up yet again.

SUMMARY

- A tax on a good reduces the welfare of buyers and sellers of the good, and the reduction in consumer and producer surplus usually exceeds the revenue raised by the government. The fall in total surplus—the sum of consumer surplus, producer surplus, and tax revenue—is called the *deadweight loss of the tax.*

- Taxes have deadweight losses because they cause buyers to consume less and sellers to produce less, and this change in behaviour shrinks the size

of the market below the level that maximizes total surplus. Because the elasticities of supply and demand measure how much market participants respond to market conditions, larger elasticities imply larger deadweight losses.

- As a tax grows larger, it distorts incentives more, and its deadweight loss grows larger. Tax revenue first rises with the size of a tax. Eventually, however, a larger tax reduces tax revenue because it reduces the size of the market.

KEY CONCEPTS

deadweight loss, p. 168

QUESTIONS FOR REVIEW

1. What happens to consumer and producer surplus when the sale of a good is taxed? How does the change in consumer and producer surplus compare to the tax revenue? Explain.

2. Draw a supply-and-demand diagram with a tax on the sale of the good. Show the deadweight loss. Show the tax revenue.

3. How do the elasticities of supply and demand affect the deadweight loss of a tax? Why do they have this effect?

4. Why do experts disagree about whether labour taxes have small or large deadweight losses?

5. What happens to the deadweight loss and tax revenue when a tax is increased?

PROBLEMS AND APPLICATIONS

1. The market for pizza is characterized by a downward-sloping demand curve and an upward-sloping supply curve.
   a. Draw the competitive market equilibrium. Label the price, quantity, consumer surplus,

   and producer surplus. Is there any deadweight loss? Explain.
   b. Suppose that the government forces each pizzeria to pay a $1 tax on each pizza sold. Illustrate the effect of this tax on the pizza

market, being sure to label the consumer surplus, producer surplus, government revenue, and deadweight loss. How does each area compare to the pre-tax case?

c. If the tax was removed, pizza eaters and sellers would be better off, but the government would lose tax revenue. Suppose that consumers and producers voluntarily transferred some of their gains to the government. Could all parties (including the government) be better off than they were with a tax? Explain using the labelled areas in your graph.

2. Nineteenth-century economist Henry George argued that the government should levy a sizable tax on land, the supply of which he took to be completely inelastic.

a. George believed that economic growth increased the demand for land and made rich landowners richer at the expense of the tenants, who made up the demand side of the market. Show this argument on an appropriately labelled diagram.

b. Who bears the burden of a tax on land—the owners of land or the tenants on the land? Explain.

c. Is the deadweight loss of this tax large or small? Explain.

d. Many cities and towns today levy taxes on the value of real estate. Why might the above analysis of George's land tax not apply to this modern tax?

3. Evaluate the following two statements. Do you agree? Why or why not?

a. "A tax that has no deadweight loss cannot raise any revenue for the government."

b. "A tax that raises no revenue for the government cannot have any deadweight loss."

4. Consider the market for rubber bands.

a. If this market has very elastic supply and very inelastic demand, how would the burden of a tax on rubber bands be shared between consumers and producers? Use the tools of consumer surplus and producer surplus in your answer.

b. If this market has very inelastic supply and very elastic demand, how would the burden

of a tax on rubber bands be shared between consumers and producers? Contrast your answer with your answer to part (a).

5. Suppose that the government imposes a tax on heating oil.

a. Would the deadweight loss from this tax likely be greater in the first year after it is imposed or in the fifth year? Explain.

b. Would the revenue collected from this tax likely be greater in the first year after it is imposed or in the fifth year? Explain.

6. After economics class one day, your friend suggests that taxing food would be a good way to raise revenue because the demand for food is quite inelastic. In what sense is taxing food a "good" way to raise revenue? In what sense is it not a "good" way to raise revenue?

7. U.S. Senator Daniel Patrick Moynihan once introduced a bill that would levy a 10 000 percent tax on certain hollow-tipped bullets.

a. Do you expect that this tax would raise much revenue? Why or why not?

b. Even if the tax would raise no revenue, what might be Senator Moynihan's reason for proposing it?

8. The government places a tax on the purchase of socks.

a. Illustrate the effect of this tax on equilibrium price and quantity in the sock market. Identify the following areas both before and after the imposition of the tax: total spending by consumers, total revenue for producers, and government tax revenue.

b. Does the price received by producers rise or fall? Can you tell whether total receipts for producers rise or fall? Explain.

c. Does the price paid by consumers rise or fall? Can you tell whether total spending by consumers rises or falls? Explain carefully. (Hint: Think about elasticity.) If total consumer spending falls, does consumer surplus rise? Explain.

9. Suppose the government currently raises $100 million through a $0.01 tax on widgets, and another $100 million through a $0.10 tax on gadgets. If the government doubled the tax rate on widgets and eliminated the tax on

gadgets, would it raise more money than today, less money, or the same amount of money? Explain.

10. Suppose the Canadian government decides that it needs to raise an additional $100 million in tax revenues. One Cabinet minister argues for a tax on all soft drinks. A second Cabinet minister argues for a tax on cola only, since this would give consumers a choice of paying the tax (by drinking cola) or avoiding it (by switching to another soft drink).

   a. Which market has the more elastic supply and demand curves: the market for cola, or the market for all soft drinks?

   b. To raise the same $100 million in revenue, which would require a higher rate: a tax on cola, or a tax on all soft drinks?

   c. Which would cause a larger deadweight loss: a tax on cola, or a tax on all soft drinks?

   d. Which would be the better tax? Explain.

11. Hotel rooms in Smalltown go for $100, and 1000 rooms are rented on a typical day.

   a. To raise revenue, the mayor decides to charge hotels a tax of $10 per rented room. After the tax is imposed, the going rate for hotel rooms rises to $108, and the number of rooms rented falls to 900. Calculate the amount of revenue this tax raises for Smalltown and the deadweight loss of the tax. (Hint: The area of a triangle is $\frac{1}{2} \times$ base $\times$ height.)

   b. The mayor now doubles the tax to $20. The price rises to $116, and the number of rooms rented falls to 800. Calculate tax revenue and deadweight loss with this larger tax. Do they double, more than double, or less than double? Explain.

12. This chapter analyzed the welfare effects of a tax on a good. Consider now the opposite policy. Suppose that the government *subsidizes* a good: For each unit of the good sold, the government pays $2 to the buyer. How does the subsidy affect consumer surplus, producer surplus, tax revenue, and total surplus? Does a subsidy lead to a deadweight loss? Explain.

13. Suppose that a market is described by the following supply and demand equations:

$$Q^S = 2P$$
$$Q^D = 300 - P$$

   a. Solve for the equilibrium price and the equilibrium quantity.

   b. Suppose that a tax of T is placed on buyers, so the new demand equation is

$$Q^D = 300 - (P + T)$$

   Solve for the new equilibrium. What happens to the price received by sellers, the price paid by buyers, and the quantity sold?

   c. Tax revenue is $T \times Q$. Use your answer to part (b) to solve for tax revenue as a function of T. Graph this relationship for T between 0 and 300.

   d. The deadweight loss of a tax is the area of the triangle between the supply and demand curves. Recalling that the area of a triangle is $\frac{1}{2} \times$ base $\times$ height, solve for deadweight loss as a function of T. Graph this relationship for T between 0 and 300.
   (Hint: Looking sideways, the base of the deadweight loss triangle is T, and the height is the difference between the quantity sold with the tax and the quantity sold without the tax.)

   e. The government now levies a tax on this good of $200 per unit. Is this a good policy? Why or why not? Can you propose a better policy?

http://

For more study tools, please visit http://www.mankiw5e.nelson.com.

Chapter 8
The Algebra of Taxation and Deadweight Losses

We have seen that whenever a unit sales tax is levied, regardless of whether it is levied on the consumer or on the producer, the consumer will pay a higher price and the firm will end up receiving a lower price than the equilibrium outcome (as long as both curves have elasticity greater than 0 and less than infinity). Now we can use algebra for our analysis.

First suppose that we are only told there has been a tax levied and all we are given are the original demand and supply equations and a new after – tax equation (for either demand or supply, depending on whom the tax was levied). We solve for the new, after – tax equilibrium. Let's do an example:

The market for pizzas is represented by the following equations for demand and supply:

$$Qd = 20 - 2P$$

$$Qs = P - 1$$

In eqm, $\quad$ Qd =Qs

$$20 - 2P = P - 1$$

$$P = \$7$$

$$Q = 6$$

Now suppose a tax on trans fats results in a $3 tax per pizza for pizza firms.

The new supply curve is

$$Qs = P - 4$$

For consumers, P_c is determined where the new Qs = Qd

$$P - 4 = 20 - 2P$$

$$P = \$8$$

Since the firm has to pay the tax, it will end up with $5 for each pizza sold (the consumer pays them $8 and the firm has to send $3 of that to the government for the tax).

To find Q, substitute P = 8 into either the new Qs or Qd: (I'll use the new Qs)

$$Qs = P - 4$$

$Q_s = 4$

So, with the tax, only 4 pizzas are traded in the market.

The government's tax revenue is $3 * 4 = $12

Here's what it looks like:

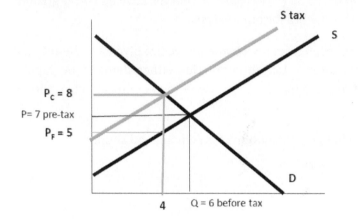

Now consider that we have current demand and supply equations and are told the amount of the unit tax. Let t = the amount of the per unit tax. If the tax is placed on the consumer, the price the consumer will pay will be $p_c = p_f + t$ (the price the firm receives plus the tax). We substitute this into the demand curve. The firm will receive p_f. We use p_f in the supply curve. Now we solve for equilibrium Q and p_f. Just add the tax, t, to p_f and that is what the consumer pays. The government's tax revenue is $t * Q$.

If the tax is placed on the firm, the firm will end up with $p_f = p_c - t$ (the price the consumer pays minus the tax which it must remit to the government). We substitute this into the supply curve. The consumer will just pay p_c and we use this in the demand curve. Now we solve for equilibrium Q and p_c. Just subtract the tax, t, from p_c and that is what the firm ends up receiving.

Example

In a competitive market, market supply for a good is $Q = 3p$ and market demand is given as $Q = 10 - 2p$.

In equilibrium, $3p = 10 - 2p$ so p = 2 and equilibrium quantity is Q = 6.

Now the government imposes a $0.50 per unit tax on consumers of the good.

The consumer pays $p_c = p_f + .50$ (the price the firm receives plus the tax).

The firm receives p_f.

The new equilibrium is $3p_f = 10 - 2 (p_f + .50)$

$$3 p_f = 10 - 2 p_f - 1$$

$$5 p_f = 9$$

$$p_f = 1.80$$

So the firm receives $1.80 and the consumer pays $1.80 + the .50 tax = $2.30.

Now, let's reverse it and place the tax on firms.

The firm will end up with $p_f = p_c - .50$ (the price the consumer pays minus the tax which it must remit to the government).

The new equilibrium is $3(p_c - .50) = 10 - 2 p_c$

$$3p_c - 1.50 = 10 - 2 p_c$$

$$5 p_c = 11.50$$

$$p_c = 2.30$$

So the consumer pays $2.30 and the firm remits the .50 tax to the government for a net take of $1.80, the same as before.

Deadweight Loss

Compared to the perfectly competitive outcome, whenever output is less than the competitive level of output, there will be a loss in total surplus. Since after - tax output is less than the competitive output, there will be a deadweight loss in surplus due to the tax.

Let's return to the first example, the pizza market. Here's what the deadweight loss looks like:

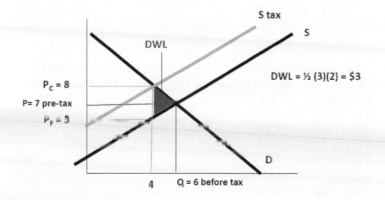

So all we need is the price consumers pay, price the firm receives, pre-tax equilibrium Q and after-tax Q to find the area of the DWL triangle.

Practice Problems

1. Market demand is given as Qd = 200 − 3P. Market supply is given as Qs = 2P + 100. The government imposes a sales tax on consumers. The new, after-tax demand is given as Qd$_{tax}$ = 191 -3P. How much do consumers pay after the tax is levied?
   a. $23.00
   b. $18.20
   c. $21.20
   d. $17.00

2. Market demand is given as Qd = 200 − 3P. Market supply is given as Qs = 2P + 100. The government imposes a sales tax on consumers. The new, after-tax demand is given as Qd$_{tax}$ = 191 -3P. How much do producers receive after the tax is levied?
   a. $23.00
   b. $18.20
   c. $21.20
   d. $17.00

3. Market demand is given as Qd = 200 − 3P. Market supply is given as Qs = 2P + 100. The government imposes a sales tax on consumers. The new, after-tax demand is given as Qd$_{tax}$ = 191 -3P. What is the amount of the tax?
   a. $2.00
   b. $3.00
   c. $5.00
   d. $8.00

4. Market demand is given as Qd = 200 − 3P. Market supply is given as Qs = 2P + 100. The government imposes a sales tax on consumers. The new, after-tax demand is given as Qd$_{tax}$ = 191 -3P. What is the consumer's burden of the tax?
   a. $2.25
   b. $3.10
   c. $1.20
   d. $1.80

5. Market demand is given as Qd = 200 − 3P. Market supply is given as Qs = 2P + 100. The government imposes a sales tax on consumers. The new, after-tax demand is given as Qd$_{tax}$ = 191 -3P. What is the producer's burden of the tax?
   a. $2.25
   b. $3.10
   c. $1.20

d. $1.80

6.   Market demand is given as Qd = 200 – 3P. Market supply is given as Qs = 2P + 100. The government imposes a sales tax on consumers. The new, after-tax demand is given as Qd_{tax} = 191 -3P. What is the government's revenue from the tax?
   a. $409.20
   b. $420.00
   c. $2482.48
   d. $2968.00

7.   Market demand is given as Qd = 200 – 3P. Market supply is given as Qs = 2P + 100. The government imposes a sales tax on consumers. The new, after-tax demand is given as Qd_{tax} = 191 -3P. What is the deadweight loss due to the tax?
   a. $10.80
   b. $5.40
   c. $210.00
   d. $420.00

8.   Market demand is given as Qd = 200 – 3P. Market supply is given as Qs = 2P + 100. The government imposes a $1.50 sales tax on consumers. What is the price consumers now pay for the good?
   a. $19.10
   b. $21.20
   c. $20.60
   d. $23.00

9.   Market demand is given as Qd = 200 – 3P. Market supply is given as Qs = 2P + 100. The government imposes a $5.00 sales tax on producers. What is the price firms now receive for the good after the tax has been remitted?
   a. $22.00
   b. $21.00
   c. $19.00
   d. $17.00

   Answers: 1 c   2 b   3 b   4 c   5 d   6 a   7 b   8 c   9 d

299

8 Application: The Costs of Taxation

I. Chapter Overview

A. Context and Purpose

The previous chapter provided a foundation for welfare economics by looking at the net social gain from production at the competitive equilibrium. That chapter explained that maximizing society's total surplus requires production up to but not beyond the point at which the marginal benefit of another unit of output equals its marginal cost. This chapter applies that analysis to policy questions about the efficiency effects of taxation. Specifically, how does taxation distort behaviour and cause a deadweight loss to society in excess of the actual taxes paid?

A. Helpful Hints

1. *Deadweight loss of taxation arises because taxes introduce a wedge between the price paid by buyers and the price received by sellers.* The tax wedge decreases the quantity sold below the socially optimal level that would have resulted under the pre-tax competitive market. As a result, the tax costs the buyers and sellers more than the actual tax paid; it also costs them a loss of total surplus because of the distortion of behaviour that results in underproduction relative to the outcome of the pre-tax competitive market.

2. *The size of deadweight loss depends on the elasticities of demand and supply.* As elasticity increases, the responsiveness to the incentive effect of taxation increases and, as a result, the deadweight loss will be greater. On a supply-and-demand diagram, the triangle of welfare loss is greater when the curves are more elastic.

3. *Deadweight loss and tax revenues vary as tax rates change.* Deadweight loss actually changes more than proportionately when the tax rates change. Further, as tax rates rise, tax revenues first rise, then eventually fall as the tax reduces the quantity sold so much that even higher rates cannot raise additional revenues.

4. *Taxes do more than raise revenue; they also influence people's behaviour.* Sometimes that is desirable, for example, when cigarette taxes are used to discourage smoking. Other times, however, the distortion caused by taxation is undesirable and represents the loss of well-being to society.

5.   *If taxes did not alter behaviour, there would be no net loss of well-being to society.* Even though taxpayers would be worse off in terms of the amount of the taxes paid, the recipients of those revenues would be better off, and the net effect would be zero, because the gains and losses would cancel each other out.

II. Self-Testing Challenges

A. True/False Questions

___1.   Higher tax rates always lead to higher tax revenues, although the outcome may be inefficient.

___2.   A tax that raises no tax revenue cannot have a deadweight loss.

___3.   If labour supply is fairly inelastic, then the deadweight loss associated with a labour tax will be small and not very distorting.

___4.   Taxes cause deadweight losses because they prevent buyers and sellers from realizing some of the gains from trade.

___5.   A subsidy (negative tax) tends to cause deadweight loss by encouraging overproduction of a good, beyond the point at which the marginal benefit equals the marginal cost to society.

___6.   If policymakers desire to minimize deadweight loss from taxation, they should tax goods and services that have relatively close substitutes.

___7.   The less elastic the supply and demand in a market, the less taxes will distort behaviour in that market, and the more likely it is that a tax hike will raise tax revenue.

___8.   Most economists agree that Canada would raise more revenue under the individual income tax if tax rates were lowered.

___9.   The greater the elasticities of demand and supply, the greater the deadweight loss of a tax.

___10.   A tax on producers tends to distort output decisions and result in higher deadweight losses than a tax on buyers.

B. Multiple-Choice Questions

1.   Which one of the following is a reason that taxes cause deadweight losses?
      a. because they reduce taxpayers' incomes
      b. because they are used to support government programs, which are less valuable than private spending to society
      c. because they prevent buyers and sellers from realizing some of the gains from trade
      d. because they redistribute income from productive to unproductive members of society

Use the following information to answer questions 2 and 3.

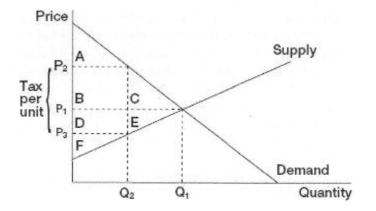

2.   If a tax is levied on *buyers* of the good, which one of the following is the price the sellers receive after tax and the deadweight loss to society?
      a. P_1; A + B + D + F
      b. P_2; C + E
      c. P_3; B + D + C + E
      d. P_3; C + E

3.   If a tax is levied on *sellers* of the good, which one of the following is the price buyers pay after tax and the deadweight loss to society?
      a. P_1; A + B + D + F
      b. P_2; C + E
      c. P_2; B + D + C + E
      d. P_3; C + E

4.   Which one of the following describes when deadweight loss from taxation is likely to be the **GREATEST?**
      a. if supply is elastic and demand is inelastic
      b. if both supply and demand are elastic
      c. if supply is inelastic and demand is elastic
      d. if both supply and demand are inelastic

5.   Which one of the following is **MORE** likely to increase the deadweight loss of income taxes on labour?
     a. if workers have no control over their hours of work, because the work week is standardized
     b. if retirement age is mandated by law or custom
     c. if the underground economy becomes more widespread
     d. if parliament shifts the legal burden of the income tax to the employer

6.   Suppose cigarette taxes are cut in order to reduce smuggling. Cigarette manufacturers argue that the tax revenue losses would be small because more cigarettes would be legally purchased. Anti-smoking groups argue that the revenue losses would be larger. Based on this information, which one of the following can be presumed?
     a. anti-smoking groups believe that the demand for legally purchased cigarettes is less elastic than the manufacturers believe
     b. anti-smoking groups believe that the demand for legally purchased cigarettes is more elastic than the manufacturers believe
     c. anti-smoking groups believe that the supply of smuggled cigarettes is equal to what the manufacturers believe
     d. anti-smoking groups believe that the supply of smuggled cigarettes is more elastic than the manufacturers believe

7.   Which one of the following taxes would be **LEAST** likely to result in a deadweight loss?
     a. a tax on labour
     b. a tax on housing
     c. a tax on automobiles
     d. a tax on the unimproved value of land

8.   Which one of the following **BEST** describes the implication of the Laffer Curve?
     a. Policymakers should consider the relevant market elasticities.
     b. Policymakers should consider whether a reduction in the tax rate would increase or decrease tax revenues.
     c. Policymakers should consider whether raising taxes would discourage foreign investment.
     d. Policymakers should consider whether lowering taxes would encourage immigration.

9.   Suppose that beer is taxed at a very low rate. Which one of the following describes what will happen to tax revenues if the government gradually increases the tax rate on beer?
     a. revenues fall
     b. revenues rise
     c. revenues rise initially, then eventually fall
     d. revenues fall initially, then eventually rise

10. Which one of the following describes the effect of raising tax rates on deadweight loss?
    a. Deadweight loss increases more than proportionately.
    b. Deadweight loss increases less than proportionately.
    c. Deadweight loss decreases less than proportionately.
    d. Deadweight loss decreases more than proportionately.

11. Imposing a sales tax on a product will _____ consumer surplus and _____ producer surplus.
    a. decrease, increase
    b. increase, decrease
    c. decrease, decrease
    d. increase, increase

Questions 12–15 refer to the graph below, which shows a market both before and after a tax.

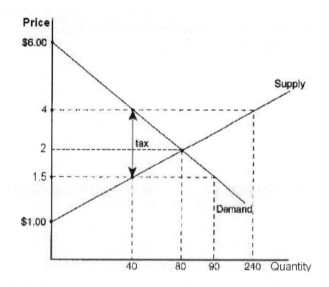

12. Which one of the following describes the effect the tax will have on output?
    a. Output will increase from 40 to 80.
    b. Output will increase from 80 to 90.
    c. Output will decrease from 80 to 40.
    d. Output will decrease from 90 to 40.

13. Which one of the following will be the deadweight loss from the tax?
    a. $50
    b. $80
    c. $100
    d. $150

14. Which one of the following describes the output if the tax is increased to $5?
    a. Output will drop to zero, as will tax revenues.
    b. Output will decrease, but tax revenues will rise.
    c. Output will decrease (but not to zero), along with tax revenues.
    d. Output will increase, but tax revenues will fall.

15. With the $5 tax, which one of the following will be the deadweight loss?
    a. zero
    b. $50
    c. $100
    d. $200

C. Short-Answer Questions

1. Often taxes that promote economic efficiency have negative effects on equity, especially if equity is perceived to require progressive taxes (taxes with a higher average tax rate on those with higher incomes). Why would this goal conflict with efficiency? _____

   _____
   _____
   _____
   _____

2. An old and long-standing debate over the appropriate size of government hinges on the relative size of the deadweight loss of taxation and the cost of any government program. How big should the government be? Evaluate this question considering the tax on labour—the most important tax in Canada. _____

   _____
   _____
   _____

3. Sales taxes cause markets to allocate resources inefficiently because they distort incentives. How? _____

   _____
   _____
   _____

D. Practice Problems

1. The following graph shows the market for gasoline both before and after the imposition of a gasoline tax.

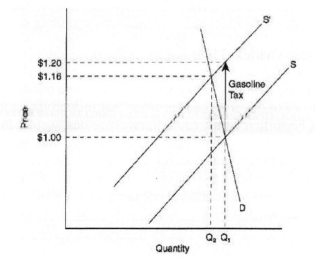

a. How much is the gasoline tax, and by how much does the price of gasoline rise in response to the tax? Explain. By law, is this a tax on the buyer or the seller? How can you tell? _____

_____

_____

_____

b. Label the area of deadweight loss on the diagram and explain. What would happen to the total deadweight loss if demand were more elastic? Why?_____

_____

_____

_____

c. What would happen to the market for gasoline if the tax were switched to the other side of the market, but at the same tax rate? Does it matter whether the buyer or the seller is responsible for the tax? Would the equilibrium quantity change if the tax is switched? Would there be any change in the deadweight loss? Explain. _____

_____

_____

_____

_____

d. Who really pays the tax? The consumer? The seller? Both? How is it possible to tell? What caused this result?_____

_____

_____

_____

_____

E. Advanced Critical Thinking

In recent years, proposals to increase the cigarette tax drastically have gained strength. Critics of the proposed tax argue that such an increase would be undesirable, because it would cause tremendous deadweight loss to society. They also argue that it would be unproductive in reducing smoking, because the demand for cigarettes is inelastic. Is this argument consistent? If the demand is inelastic, will the tax have a large impact on total surplus? Is the notion of deadweight loss even appropriate when the goal is to distort behaviour away from smoking? Discuss. _____

_____

_____

_____

_____

_____

III. Solutions

A.   True/False Questions

1.   F; higher tax rates tend to lead to higher tax revenues initially, but after a point, revenue falls.
2.   F; a tax that raises no tax revenue can have a large deadweight loss, if it destroys the market for a product.
3.   T
4.   T
5.   T
6.   F; if policymakers tax goods and services that have relatively close substitutes, deadweight loss is likely to be greater, because people are more likely to change their behaviour in response to the tax.
7.   T
8.   F; most economists would agree that Canadian tax rates are not so high that they would reduce revenue, if rates were lowered.
9.   T
10. F; taxes on producers (supply) have the same effects as taxes on the buyers (demand); the market adjusts price and output to compensate.

B. **Multiple-Choice Questions**

1. c	5. c	9. c	13. a
2. d	6. a	10. a	14. a
3. b	7. d	11. c	15. d
4. b	8. b	12. c	

C. **Short-Answer Questions**

1. There is no reason for equity and efficiency to go together. One (efficiency) is objective and the other (equity) depends on our values—our sense of what is fair. In fact, taxes that do not alter behaviour are most likely to be efficient, yet they are more likely to be lump-sum taxes or taxes on necessities that tend to be more burdensome to the poor.

2. If taxation entails small deadweight losses, then government programs financed by these taxes are less costly and there would be a strong argument for a larger government. However, taxation accompanied by large deadweight losses would be an argument for a smaller government.

   Advocates of a leaner government argue that deadweight losses of labour tax are large because labour supply is rather elastic—the quantity of labour supplied responds to the wage. The decisions of these workers, therefore, are distorted when their earnings are taxed.

   Those who argue that labour taxes are not very distorting believe that labour supply is rather inelastic and a tax results in a small deadweight loss.

3. A sales tax raises the price to buyers and lowers the price to sellers, thereby giving buyers an incentive to consume less and sellers an incentive to produce less than they otherwise would.

D. **Practice Problems**

1. The graph on the next page shows the market for gasoline before and after the imposition of a gasoline tax. Use the graph to answer the following questions.

   a. The gasoline tax rate is $0.20, as shown by the $0.20 vertical shift in supply. This shows that willingness to sell has shifted, requiring an additional $0.20 for any given quantity to be supplied. The equilibrium price rises by $0.16, from $1.00 to $1.16, indicating that the buyer is paying most of the tax. The legal burden is on the seller, as shown by the shift in supply, rather than demand.

b. The deadweight loss is the shaded triangle shown, which is the area between the supply (willingness to sell) and demand (willingness to buy), and between the new equilibrium output (Q_2) and the old output before the tax (Q_1). It represents the lost total surplus due to the loss of output. If demand were more elastic, then the tax would cause a greater loss of output, as quantity demanded falls more dramatically, resulting in a greater deadweight loss (a larger triangle of lost surplus).

c. The effect would be the same if the tax were switched to the buyer instead of the seller. Output would still drop to Q_2, and the consumer would still be stuck with $0.16 of the $0.20 tax. However, the graph would look different, because demand would shift by $0.20, rather than supply. The drop in demand would lower the price to $0.96, plus the $0.20 tax, for a total cost to the consumer of $1.16, which is the same as before. The deadweight loss would be the same.

d. Eighty percent of the tax ($0.16 of the $0.20) is borne by the consumer; the rest of the tax is borne by the seller, as shown by the effect on market price. When demand is less elastic than supply, the consumer is less adaptable and will be stuck with a larger share of the tax. If demand is relatively more elastic, then the seller will bear more of the burden of the tax.

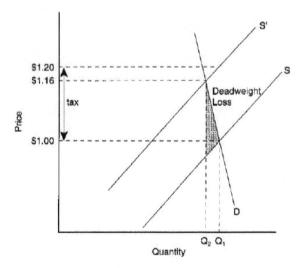

E.   Advanced Critical Thinking

The usual notion of deadweight loss is not appropriate for evaluating the cigarette tax. Normally, distortion of behaviour is an undesirable effect of taxation. However, in the case of cigarettes, a major reason for the tax is to discourage consumption, because the free-market equilibrium is not considered to be efficient. There are externalities involved that smokers do not take into account (the health costs of second-hand smoke, for example), and to the extent that cigarettes may be addictive, it is not clear that truly voluntary exchange results from the free market. As a result, the deadweight loss from reducing production and consumption of cigarettes may actually be a social gain. Ironically, the inelastic demand means that even if the distortion of behaviour is positive, it is also relatively slight, unless the tax rate is quite high.

APPLICATION: INTERNATIONAL TRADE

Learning Objectives

In this chapter, you will ...

- Consider what determines whether a country imports or exports a good

- Examine who wins and who loses from international trade

- Learn that the gains to winners from international trade exceed the losses to losers

- Analyze the welfare effects of tariffs and import quotas

- Examine the arguments people use to advocate trade restrictions

If you check the labels on the clothes you are now wearing, you will probably find that some of your clothes were made in another country. A century ago the textiles and clothing industry was a major part of the Canadian economy, but that is no longer the case. Faced with foreign competitors that could produce quality goods at low cost, many Canadian firms found it increasingly difficult to produce and sell textiles and clothing at a profit. As a result, they laid off their workers and shut down their factories. Today, much of the textiles and clothing that Canadians consume are imported from abroad.

The story of the textiles industry raises important questions for economic policy: How does international trade affect economic well-being? Who gains and who loses from free trade among countries, and how do the gains compare to the losses?

Chapter 3 introduced the study of international trade by applying the principle of comparative advantage. According to this principle, all countries can benefit from trading with one another because trade allows each country to specialize in doing what it does best. But the analysis in Chapter 3 was incomplete. It did not explain how the international marketplace achieves these gains from trade or how the gains are distributed among various economic participants.

We now return to the study of international trade and take up these questions. Over the past several chapters, we have developed many tools for analyzing how markets work: supply, demand, equilibrium, consumer surplus, producer surplus, and so on. With these tools we can learn more about the effects of international trade on economic well-being.

THE DETERMINANTS OF TRADE

Consider the market for textiles. The textile market is well suited to examining the gains and losses from international trade: Textiles are made in many countries around the world, and there is much world trade in textiles. Moreover, the textile market is one in which policymakers often consider (and sometimes implement) trade restrictions to protect domestic producers from foreign competitors. We examine here the textile market in the imaginary country of Isoland.

The Equilibrium without Trade

As our story begins, the Isolandian textile market is isolated from the rest of the world. By government decree, no one in Isoland is allowed to import or export textiles, and the penalty for violating the decree is so large that no one dares try.

Because there is no international trade, the market for textiles in Isoland consists solely of Isolandian buyers and sellers. As Figure 9.1 shows, the domestic price adjusts to balance the quantity supplied by domestic sellers and the quantity demanded by domestic buyers. The figure shows the consumer and producer surplus in the equilibrium without trade. The sum of consumer and producer surplus measures the total benefits that buyers and sellers receive from participating in the textile market.

FIGURE 9.1

The Equilibrium without International Trade

When an economy cannot trade in world markets, the price adjusts to balance domestic supply and demand. This figure shows consumer and producer surplus in an equilibrium without international trade for the textile market in the imaginary country of Isoland.

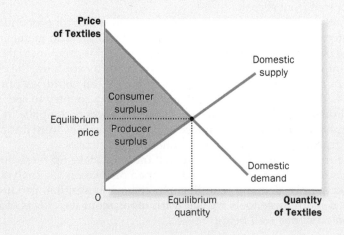

Now suppose that, in an election upset, Isoland elects a new president. The president campaigned on a platform of "change" and promised the voters bold new ideas. Her first act is to assemble a team of economists to evaluate Isolandian trade policy. She asks them to report back on three questions:

1. If the government allowed Isolandians to import and export textiles, what would happen to the price of textiles and the quantity of textiles sold in the domestic textile market?
2. Who would gain from free trade in textiles and who would lose, and would the gains exceed the losses?
3. Should a tariff (a tax on textile imports) or an import quota (a limit on textile imports) be part of the new trade policy?

After reviewing supply and demand in their favourite textbook (this one, of course), the Isolandian economics team begins its analysis.

The World Price and Comparative Advantage

The first issue our economists take up is whether Isoland is likely to become a textile importer or a textile exporter. In other words, if free trade was allowed, would Isolandians end up buying or selling textiles in world markets?

To answer this question, the economists compare the current Isolandian price of textiles to the price of textiles in other countries. We call the price prevailing in world markets the **world price.** If the world price of textiles is higher than the domestic price, then Isoland would become an exporter of textiles once trade is permitted. Isolandian textile producers would be eager to receive the higher prices available abroad and would start selling their textiles to buyers in other countries. Conversely, if the world price of textiles is lower than the domestic price, then Isoland would become an importer of textiles. Because foreign sellers offer a better price, Isolandian textile consumers would quickly start buying textiles from other countries.

world price
the price of a good that prevails in the world market for that good

In essence, comparing the world price and the domestic price before trade indicates whether Isoland has a comparative advantage in producing textiles. The domestic price reflects the opportunity cost of textiles: It tells us how much an Isolandian must give up to get one unit of textiles. If the domestic price is low, the cost of producing textiles in Isoland is low, suggesting that Isoland has a comparative advantage in producing textiles relative to the rest of the world. If the domestic price is high, then the cost of producing textiles in Isoland is high, suggesting that foreign countries have a comparative advantage in producing textiles.

As we saw in Chapter 3, trade among nations is ultimately based on comparative advantage. That is, trade is beneficial because it allows each nation to specialize in doing what it does best. By comparing the world price and the domestic price before trade, we can determine whether Isoland is better or worse at producing textiles than the rest of the world.

QuickQuiz The country Autarka does not allow international trade. In Autarka, you can buy a wool suit for 3 ounces of gold. Meanwhile, in neighbouring countries, you can buy the same suit for 2 ounces of gold. If Autarka was to allow free trade, would it import or export suits?

THE WINNERS AND LOSERS FROM TRADE

To analyze the welfare effects of free trade, the Isolandian economists begin with the assumption that Isoland is a small economy compared to the rest of the world. This small-economy assumption means that Isoland's actions have little effect on world markets. Specifically, any change in Isoland's trade policy will not affect the world price of textiles. The Isolandians are said to be *price takers* in the world economy. That is, they take the world price of textiles as given. They can sell textiles at this price and be exporters or buy textiles at this price and be importers.

The small-economy assumption is not necessary to analyze the gains and losses from international trade. But the Isolandian economists know from experience (and from reading Chapter 2 of this book) that making simplifying assumptions is a key part of building a useful economic model. The assumption that Isoland is a small economy simplifies the analysis, and the basic lessons do not change in the more complicated case of a large economy.

The Gains and Losses of an Exporting Country

Figure 9.2 shows the Isolandian textile market when the domestic equilibrium price before trade is below the world price. Once free trade is allowed, the domestic price rises to equal the world price. No seller of textiles would accept less than the world price, and no buyer would pay more than the world price.

With the domestic price now equal to the world price, the domestic quantity supplied differs from the domestic quantity demanded. The supply curve shows the quantity of textiles supplied by Isolandian sellers. The demand curve shows the quantity of textiles demanded by Isolandian buyers. Because the domestic quantity supplied is greater than the domestic quantity demanded, Isoland sells textiles to other countries. Thus, Isoland becomes a textile exporter.

Although domestic quantity supplied and domestic quantity demanded differ, the textile market is still in equilibrium because there is now another participant in the market: the rest of the world. One can view the horizontal line at the world price as representing the demand for textiles from the rest of the world. This demand curve is perfectly elastic because Isoland, as a small economy, can sell as many textiles as it wants at the world price.

Now consider the gains and losses from opening up trade. Clearly, not everyone benefits. Trade forces the domestic price to rise to the world price. Domestic producers of textiles are better off because they can now sell textiles at a higher price, but domestic consumers of textiles are worse off because they have to buy textiles at a higher price.

To measure these gains and losses, we look at the changes in consumer and producer surplus. Before trade is allowed, the price of textiles adjusts to balance domestic supply and domestic demand. Consumer surplus, the area between the demand curve and the before-trade price, is area A + B. Producer surplus, the area between the supply curve and the before-trade price, is area C. Total surplus before trade, the sum of consumer and producer surplus, is area A + B + C.

After trade is allowed, the domestic price rises to the world price. Consumer surplus is area A (the area between the demand curve and the world price). Producer surplus is area B + C + D (the area between the supply curve and the world price). Thus, total surplus with trade is area A + B + C + D.

FIGURE 9.2

International Trade in an Exporting Country

Once trade is allowed, the domestic price rises to equal the world price. The supply curve shows the quantity of textiles produced domestically, and the demand curve shows the quantity consumed domestically. Exports from Isoland equal the difference between the domestic quantity supplied and the domestic quantity demanded at the world price. Sellers are better off (producer surplus rises from C to B + C + D), and buyers are worse off (consumer surplus falls from A + B to A). Total surplus rises by an amount equal to area D, indicating that trade raises the economic well-being of the country as a whole.

	Before Trade	After Trade	Change
Consumer Surplus	A + B	A	−B
Producer Surplus	C	B + C + D	+(B + D)
Total Surplus	A + B + C	A + B + C + D	+D

The area D shows the increase in total surplus and represents the gains from trade.

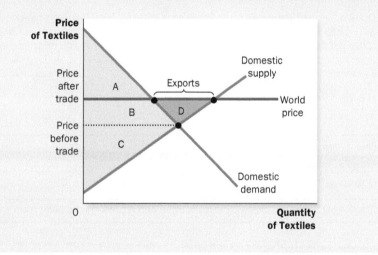

These welfare calculations show who wins and who loses from trade in an exporting country. Sellers benefit because producer surplus increases by the area B + D. Buyers are worse off because consumer surplus decreases by the area B. Because the gains of sellers exceed the losses of buyers by the area D, total surplus in Isoland increases.

This analysis of an exporting country yields two conclusions:

1. When a country allows trade and becomes an exporter of a good, domestic producers of the good are better off, and domestic consumers of the good are worse off.
2. Trade raises the economic well-being of a nation in the sense that the gains of the winners exceed the losses of the losers.

The Gains and Losses of an Importing Country

Now suppose that the domestic price before trade is above the world price. Once again, after free trade is allowed, the domestic price must equal the world price. As Figure 9.3 shows, the domestic quantity supplied is less than the domestic quantity demanded. The difference between the domestic quantity demanded and the domestic quantity supplied is bought from other countries, and Isoland becomes a textile importer.

In this case, the horizontal line at the world price represents the supply of the rest of the world. This supply curve is perfectly elastic because Isoland is a small economy and, therefore, can buy as many textiles as it wants at the world price.

FIGURE 9.3

International Trade in an Importing Country

Once trade is allowed, the domestic price falls to equal the world price. The supply curve shows the amount produced domestically, and the demand curve shows the amount consumed domestically. Imports equal the difference between the domestic quantity demanded and the domestic quantity supplied at the world price. Buyers are better off (consumer surplus rises from A to A + B + D), and sellers are worse off (producer surplus falls from B + C to C). Total surplus rises by an amount equal to area D, indicating that trade raises the economic well-being of the country as a whole.

	Before Trade	After Trade	Change
Consumer Surplus	A	A + B + D	+(B + D)
Producer Surplus	B + C	C	−B
Total Surplus	A + B + C	A + B + C + D	+D

The area D shows the increase in total surplus and represents the gains from trade.

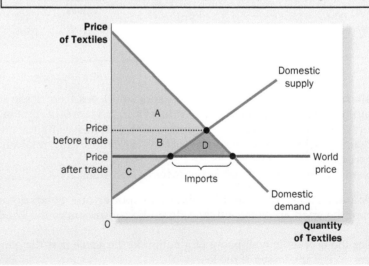

Now consider the gains and losses from trade. Once again, not everyone benefits. When trade forces the domestic price to fall, domestic consumers are better off (they can now buy textiles at a lower price), and domestic producers are worse off (they now have to sell textiles at a lower price). Changes in consumer and producer surplus measure the size of the gains and losses, as shown in the graph and table in Figure 9.3. Before trade, consumer surplus is area A, producer surplus is area B + C, and total surplus is area A + B + C. After trade is allowed, consumer surplus is area A + B + D, producer surplus is area C, and total surplus is area A + B + C + D.

These welfare calculations show who wins and who loses from trade in an importing country. Buyers benefit because consumer surplus increases by the area B + D. Sellers are worse off because producer surplus falls by the area B. The gains of buyers exceed the losses of sellers, and total surplus increases by the area D.

This analysis of an importing country yields two conclusions parallel to those for an exporting country:

1. When a country allows trade and becomes an importer of a good, domestic consumers of the good are better off, and domestic producers of the good are worse off.
2. Trade raises the economic well-being of a nation in the sense that the gains of the winners exceed the losses of the losers.

Having completed our analysis of trade, we can better understand one of the ten principles of economics in Chapter 1: Trade can make everyone better off. If Isoland opens up its textile market to international trade, that change will create winners and losers, regardless of whether Isoland ends up exporting or importing textiles. In either case, however, the gains of the winners exceed the losses of the losers, so the winners could compensate the losers and still be better off. In this sense, trade *can* make everyone better off. But *will* trade make everyone better off? Probably not. In practice, compensation for the losers from international trade is rare. Without such compensation, opening up to international trade is a policy that expands the size of the economic pie, while perhaps leaving some participants in the economy with a smaller slice.

We can now see why the debate over trade policy is so often contentious. Whenever a policy creates winners and losers, the stage is set for a political battle. Nations sometimes fail to enjoy the gains from trade simply because the losers from free trade have more political clout than the winners. The losers lobby for trade restrictions, such as tariffs and import quotas.

The Effects of a Tariff

The Isolandian economists next consider the effects of a **tariff**—a tax on imported goods. The economists quickly realize that a tariff on textiles will have no effect if Isoland becomes a textile exporter. If no one in Isoland is interested in importing textiles, a tax on textile imports is irrelevant. The tariff matters only if Isoland becomes a textile importer. Concentrating their attention on this case, the economists compare welfare with and without the tariff.

Figure 9.4 shows the Isolandian market for textiles. Under free trade, the domestic price equals the world price. A tariff raises the price of imported textiles above the world price by the amount of the tariff. Domestic suppliers of textiles,

tariff
a tax on goods produced abroad and sold domestically

FIGURE 9.4

The Effects of a Tariff

A tariff reduces the quantity of imports and moves a market closer to the equilibrium that would exist without trade. Total surplus falls by an amount equal to area D + F. These two triangles represent the deadweight loss from the tariff.

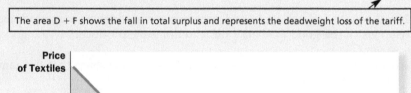

	Before Tariff	After Tariff	Change
Consumer Surplus	A + B + C + D + E + F	A + B	−(C + D + E + F)
Producer Surplus	G	C + G	+C
Government Revenue	None	E	+E
Total Surplus	A + B + C + D + E + F + G	A + B + C + E + G	−(D + F)

The area D + F shows the fall in total surplus and represents the deadweight loss of the tariff.

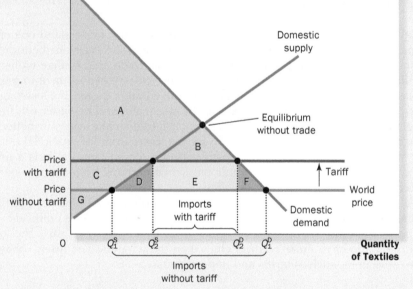

who compete with suppliers of imported textiles, can now sell their textiles for the world price plus the amount of the tariff. Thus, the price of textiles—both imported and domestic—rises by the amount of the tariff and is, therefore, closer to the price that would prevail without trade.

The change in price affects the behaviour of domestic buyers and sellers. Because the tariff raises the price of textiles, it reduces the domestic quantity demanded from Q_1^D to Q_2^D and raises the domestic quantity supplied from Q_1^S to Q_2^S. *Thus, the tariff reduces the quantity of imports and moves the domestic market closer to its equilibrium without trade.*

Now consider the gains and losses from the tariff. Because the tariff raises the domestic price, domestic sellers are better off and domestic buyers are worse off. In addition, the government raises revenue. To measure these gains and losses, we look at the changes in consumer surplus, producer surplus, and government revenue. These changes are summarized in the table in Figure 9.4.

Before the tariff, the domestic price equals the world price. Consumer surplus, the area between the demand curve and the world price, is area A + B + C + D + E + F. Producer surplus, the area between the supply curve and the world price, is area G. Government revenue equals zero. Total surplus—the sum of consumer surplus, producer surplus, and government revenue—is area A + B + C + D + E + F + G.

Once the government imposes a tariff, the domestic price exceeds the world price by the amount of the tariff. Consumer surplus is now area A + B. Producer surplus is area C + G. Government revenue, which is the quantity of after-tariff imports times the size of the tariff, is area E. Thus, total surplus with the tariff is area A + B + C + E + G.

To determine the total welfare effects of the tariff, we add the change in consumer surplus (which is negative), the change in producer surplus (positive), and the change in government revenue (positive). We find that total surplus in the market decreases by the area D + F. This fall in total surplus is called the *deadweight loss* of the tariff.

A tariff causes a deadweight loss simply because a tariff is a type of tax. Like most taxes, it distorts incentives and pushes the allocation of scarce resources away from the optimum. In this case, we can identify two effects. First, when the tariff raises the domestic price of textiles above the world price, it encourages domestic producers to increase production from Q_1^S to Q_2^S. Even though the cost of making these incremental units exceeds the cost of buying them at the world price, the tariff makes it profitable for domestic producers to manufacture them nonetheless. Second, when the tariff raises the price that domestic textile consumers have to pay, it encourages them to

IMPORT QUOTAS: ANOTHER WAY TO RESTRICT TRADE

Beyond tariffs, another way that nations sometimes restrict international trade is by putting limits on how much of a good can be imported. In this book, we will not analyze such a policy, other than to point out the conclusion: Import quotas are much like tariffs. Both tariffs and import quotas reduce the quantity of imports, raise the domestic price of the good, decrease the welfare of domestic consumers, increase the welfare of domestic producers, and cause deadweight losses.

There is only one difference between these two types of trade restriction: A tariff raises revenue for the government, whereas an import quota creates surplus for those who get the licences to import. The profit for the holder of an import licence is the difference between the domestic price (at which the licence holder sells the imported good) and the world price (at which the licence holder buys it).

Tariffs and import quotas are even more similar if the government charges a fee for the import licences. Suppose the government sets the licence fee equal to the difference between the domestic price and the world price. In this case, all of the profit of licence holders is paid to the government in licence fees, and the import quota works exactly like a tariff. Consumer surplus, producer surplus, and government revenue are precisely the same under the two policies.

IN THE NEWS

CANADA, THE UNITED STATES, AND SOFTWOOD LUMBER

In 2006, Canada and the United States struck a new deal on the importation of softwood lumber from Canada to the United States. The op-ed piece below, written by an economist at the University of Western Ontario, discusses the merits of tariffs versus import quotas. The deal ultimately struck combined elements of both.

Why Quotas Are an Inferior System: An Export Tax Lets Markets Work and Is Easier to Remove

By Ron Wonnacott

News reports suggest Canada and the United States are on the brink of a soft-wood-lumber agreement that would include a "voluntary" export-restraint system that would impose a quota or market-sharing agreement on Canadian exporters. This is not the best idea.

Under a quota system, Canada would get a fixed share (its historical one-third?) of the U.S. market, with this in turn divided up as quotas among Canadian exporting firms. The benefits would go to Canadian exporting firms holding the valuable quota rights; they would be able to sell in the United States at the higher price resulting from the scarcity generated by the export limits.

A quota arrangement might be polit-ically attractive. It avoids the problem created by an alternative Canadian export tax, such as deciding what to do with tax receipts. Should they go to the federal treasury, to the provinces, or to victimized firms (and risk triggering U.S. retaliation)?

Otherwise, however, the quota system is inferior. Even if the initial Canadian share of the American market can be appropriately negotiated (and there is a strong argument that the present one-third being considered is too restrictive), how can this share be changed later if producers on one side of the border become more efficient than on the other? Behind the protection they receive, will U.S. producers be under less pressure to innovate and otherwise increase efficiency?

reduce consumption of textiles from Q_1^D to Q_2^D. Even though domestic consumers value these incremental units at more than the world price, the tariff induces them to cut back their purchases. Area D represents the deadweight loss from the overproduction of textiles, and area F represents the deadweight loss from the underconsumption. The total deadweight loss of the tariff is the sum of these two triangles.

The Lessons for Trade Policy

The team of Isolandian economists can now write to the new president:

Dear Madam President,

You asked us three questions about opening up trade. After much hard work, we have the answers.

Within Canada, how is the total Canadian export share to be allocated as quotas to Canadian firms? How are Canadian exporters' quotas to be monitored to ensure compliance? When should a new Canadian entrant be granted an export quota, and at whose expense? The longer the time frame, the greater the potential protectionist drift as the quota system becomes increasingly unable to keep up with changing conditions on both sides of the border.

In contrast, a Canadian export tax deals with these problems (albeit imperfectly) by simply changing the price signal and then letting each firm respond to market changes resulting from, for example, new technology and timber availability. This enhances efficiency and generates higher long-term income.

Whereas an export tax allows each firm to decide on its production volume in response to a market price, a quota dictates the maximum each firm can produce. In the face of perceived injustice, a firm has an incentive to exercise its political influence on the government

to increase its quota, with large, wealthy incumbent firms having an advantage.

Under either a quota or export tax regime, Canadian firms may complain they are being treated unfairly relative to U.S. competitors. But the government can rightly point to the existence of an international agreement; break that and you will again face the damaging and uncertain pre 2006 situation.

However, under a quota system alone, there will be additional complaints by Canadian firms of being unfairly treated relative to other Canadian firms. Under a tax regime, the government's reply would be: Blame the market. In short, under a quota system there will be more complaints that are harder to respond to.

The message is not that we should reject a mutually beneficial agreement because it includes a quota system. The point is that an export tax is strongly preferred, especially since the objective is an agreement that will prevent protectionist drift and will last over time.

Moreover, an export tax is easier to transform into an open border—if and

when the U.S. government shifts its focus from the narrow interests of one industry to the economy as a whole. Canadian firms victimized by past U.S. trade action can also be most directly and transparently compensated by the substantial return of past U.S. duty collections.

To conclude: If a mutually beneficial agreement cannot be struck without Canada providing some protection for the U.S. industry, it is important for it to be in the form of an export tax. If quota provisions cannot be avoided, there should be an agreed-upon route and timetable to phase them soon into an export tax.

There should also be a renewed commitment to rely on NAFTA's dispute-settlement mechanism, and to improve its operation to ensure that disputes are resolved quickly, instead of being allowed to fester until interests become so politically and financially entrenched that a side negotiation is necessary to break the impasse.

Source: Ronald Wonnacott, "Why Quotas Are an Inferior System: An Export Tax Lets Markets Work and Is Easier to Remove." Reprinted with the permission of the author.

Question: If the government allowed Isolandians to import and export textiles, what would happen to the price of textiles and the quantity of textiles sold in the domestic textile market?

Answer: Once trade is allowed, the Isolandian price of textiles would be driven to equal the price prevailing around the world.

If the world price is now higher than the Isolandian price, our price would rise. The higher price would reduce the amount of textiles Isolandians consume and raise the amount of textiles that Isolandians produce. Isoland would, therefore, become a textile exporter. This occurs because, in this case, Isoland would have a comparative advantage in producing textiles.

Conversely, if the world price is now lower than the Isolandian price, our price would fall. The lower price would raise the amount of textiles that Isolandians consume and lower the amount of textiles that Isolandians produce. Isoland would, therefore, become a textile importer. This occurs because, in this case, other countries would have a comparative advantage in producing textiles.

Question: Who would gain from free trade in textiles and who would lose, and would the gains exceed the losses?

Answer: The answer depends on whether the price rises or falls when trade is allowed. If the price rises, producers of textiles gain, and consumers of textiles lose. If the price falls, consumers gain, and producers lose. In both cases, the gains are larger than the losses. Thus, free trade raises the total welfare of Isolandians.

Question: Should a tariff or an import quota be part of the new trade policy?

Answer: A tariff, like most taxes, has deadweight losses: The revenue raised would be smaller than the losses to the buyers and sellers. In this case, the deadweight losses occur because the tariff would move the economy closer to our current no-trade equilibrium. An import quota works much like a tariff and would cause similar deadweight losses. The best policy, from the standpoint of economic efficiency, would be to allow trade without a tariff or an import quota.

We hope you find these answers helpful as you decide on your new policy.

Your faithful servants,
Isolandian Economics Team

QuickQuiz Draw the supply and demand curves for wool suits in the country of Autarka. When trade is allowed, the price of a suit falls from 3 to 2 ounces of gold. In your diagram, what is the change in consumer surplus, the change in producer surplus, and the change in total surplus? How would a tariff on suit imports alter these effects?

Other Benefits of International Trade

The conclusions of the Isolandian economics team are based on the standard analysis of international trade. Their analysis uses the most fundamental tools in the economist's toolbox: supply, demand, and producer and consumer surplus. It shows that there are winners and losers when a nation opens itself up to trade, but the gains to the winners exceed the losses of the losers.

The case for free trade can be made even stronger, however, because there are several other economic benefits of trade beyond those emphasized in the standard analysis. Here, in a nutshell, are some of these other benefits:

- **Increased variety of goods.** Goods produced in different countries are not exactly the same. German beer, for instance, is not the same as Canadian beer. Free trade gives consumers in all countries greater variety from which to choose.
- **Lower costs through economies of scale.** Some goods can be produced at low cost only if they are produced in large quantities—a phenomenon called *economies of scale*. A firm in a small country cannot take full advantage of economies of scale if it can sell only in a small domestic market. Free trade gives firms access to larger world markets and allows them to realize economies of scale more fully.

- **Increased competition.** A company shielded from foreign competitors is more likely to have market power, which in turn gives it the ability to raise prices above competitive levels. This is a type of market failure. Opening up trade fosters competition and gives the invisible hand a better chance to work its magic.
- **Enhanced flow of ideas.** The transfer of technological advances around the world is often thought to be linked to the trading of the goods that embody those advances. The best way for a poor agricultural nation to learn about the computer revolution, for instance, is to buy some computers from abroad rather than trying to make them domestically.

Thus, free international trade increases variety for consumers, allows firms to take advantage of economies of scale, makes markets more competitive, and facilitates the spread of technology. If the Isolandian economists also took these effects into account, their advice to their president would be even more forceful.

THE ARGUMENTS FOR RESTRICTING TRADE

The letter from the economics team persuades the new president of Isoland to consider opening up trade in textiles. She notes that the domestic price is now high compared to the world price. Free trade would, therefore, cause the price of textiles to fall and hurt domestic textile producers. Before implementing the new policy, she asks Isolandian textile companies to comment on the economists' advice.

Not surprisingly, the textile companies are opposed to free trade in textiles. They believe that the government should protect the domestic textile industry from foreign competition. Let's consider some of the arguments they might give to support their position and how the economics team would respond.

The Jobs Argument

Opponents of free trade often argue that trade with other countries destroys domestic jobs. In our example, free trade in textiles would cause the price of textiles to fall, reducing the quantity of textiles produced in Isoland and thus reducing employment in the Isolandian textile industry. Some Isolandian textileworkers would lose their jobs.

Yet free trade creates jobs at the same time that it destroys them. When Isolandians buy textiles from other countries, those countries obtain the resources to buy other goods from Isoland. Isolandian workers would move from the textile industry to those industries in which Isoland has a comparative advantage. Although the transition may impose hardship on some workers in the short run, it allows Isolandians as a whole to enjoy a higher standard of living.

Opponents of trade are often skeptical that trade creates jobs. They might respond that *everything* can be produced more cheaply abroad. Under free trade, they might argue, Isolandians could not be profitably employed in any industry. As Chapter 3 explains, however, the gains from trade are based on comparative advantage, not absolute advantage. Even if one country is better than another country at producing everything, each country can still gain from trading with the other. Workers in each country will eventually find jobs in the industry in which that country has a comparative advantage.

The National-Security Argument

When an industry is threatened with competition from other countries, opponents of free trade often argue that the industry is vital for national security. For example, if Isoland was considering free trade in steel, domestic steel companies might point out that steel is used to make guns and tanks. Free trade would allow Isoland to become dependent on foreign countries to supply steel. If a war later broke out, Isoland might be unable to produce enough steel and weapons to defend itself.

Economists acknowledge that protecting key industries may be appropriate when there are legitimate concerns over national security. Yet they fear that this argument may be used too quickly by producers eager to gain at consumers' expense. One should be wary of the national-security argument when it is made by representatives of industry rather than the defence establishment. Companies have an incentive to exaggerate their role in national defence to obtain protection from foreign competition. A nation's generals may see things very differently. Indeed, when the military is a consumer of an industry's output, it would benefit from imports. Cheaper steel in Isoland, for example, would allow the Isolandian military to accumulate a stockpile of weapons at lower cost.

The Infant-Industry Argument

New industries sometimes argue for temporary trade restrictions to help them get started. After a period of protection, the argument goes, these industries will mature and be able to compete with foreign competitors. Similarly, older industries sometimes argue that they need temporary protection to help them adjust to new conditions. Canada's "National Policy," started by Sir John A. Macdonald in 1878, could be seen as an attempt to protect the infant Canadian manufacturing sector from foreign (especially U.S.) competition. This protection from foreign competition lasted for 110 years, until the Canada–U.S. Free Trade Agreement of 1989.

Economists are often skeptical about such claims. The primary reason is that the infant-industry argument is difficult to implement in practice. To apply protection successfully, the government would need to decide which industries will eventually be profitable and decide whether the benefits of establishing these industries exceed the costs to consumers of protection. Yet "picking winners" is extraordinarily difficult. It is made even more difficult by the political process, which often awards protection to those industries that are politically powerful. And once a powerful industry is protected from foreign competition, the "temporary" policy is hard to remove.

In addition, many economists are skeptical about the infant-industry argument even in principle. Suppose, for instance, that the Isolandian textile industry is young and unable to compete profitably against foreign rivals. Yet there is reason to believe that the industry can be profitable in the long run. In this case, the owners of the firms should be willing to incur temporary losses to obtain the eventual profits. Protection is not necessary for an industry to grow. Firms in various industries—such as many Internet firms today—incur temporary losses in the hope of growing and becoming profitable in the future. And many of them succeed, even without protection from foreign competition.

The Unfair-Competition Argument

A common argument is that free trade is desirable only if all countries play by the same rules. If firms in different countries are subject to different laws and regulations, then it is unfair (the argument goes) to expect the firms to compete in the international marketplace. For instance, suppose that the government of Neighbourland subsidizes its textile industry by giving textile companies large tax breaks. The Isolandian textile industry might argue that it should be protected from this foreign competition because Neighbourland is not competing fairly.

Would it, in fact, hurt Isoland to buy textiles from another country at a subsidized price? Certainly, Isolandian textile producers would suffer, but Isolandian textile consumers would benefit from the low price. Moreover, the case for free trade is no different: The gains of the consumers from buying at the low price would exceed the losses of the producers. Neighbourland's subsidy to its textile industry may be a bad policy, but it is the taxpayers of Neighbourland who bear the burden. Isoland can benefit from the opportunity to buy textiles at a subsidized price.

The Protection-as-a-Bargaining-Chip Argument

Another argument for trade restrictions concerns the strategy of bargaining. Many policymakers claim to support free trade but, at the same time, argue that trade restrictions can be useful when we bargain with our trading partners. They claim that the threat of a trade restriction can help remove a trade restriction already imposed by a foreign government. For example, Isoland might threaten to impose a tariff on textiles unless Neighbourland removes its tariff on wheat. If Neighbourland responds to this threat by removing its tariff, the result can be freer trade.

The problem with this bargaining strategy is that the threat may not work. If it doesn't work, the country has a difficult choice. It can carry out its threat and implement the trade restriction, which would reduce its own economic welfare. Or it can back down from its threat, which would cause it to lose prestige in international affairs. Faced with this choice, the country would probably wish that it had never made the threat in the first place.

Case Study
TRADE AGREEMENTS AND THE WORLD TRADE ORGANIZATION

A country can take one of two approaches to achieving free trade. It can take a *unilateral* approach and remove its trade restrictions on its own. This is the approach that Great Britain took in the nineteenth century and that Chile and South Korea have taken in more recent years. Alternatively, a country can take a *multilateral* approach and reduce its trade restrictions while other countries do the same. In other words, it can bargain with its trading partners in an attempt to reduce trade restrictions around the world.

One important example of the multilateral approach is the North American Free Trade Agreement (NAFTA), which in 1993 lowered trade barriers among the United States, Mexico, and Canada. Another is the General Agreement on Tariffs

IN THE NEWS

A RETHINK OF CANADA'S TRADE FOCUS

Canada is, and always has been, a trading country closely linked to the United States. This article argues for a different approach.

Look beyond the U.S.

America's pre-eminence is in decline. If Canada is to prosper, we must seek new foreign trade partners.

By Jack M. Mintz

At the beginning of this decade, elite opinion held that our priority for trade should be to deepen our relationship with the United States, our most important trading partner. Having ended this decade, it is far from clear that this is the best approach for Canada. The U.S. is a waning star. We need to branch out to other countries where growth will be more pronounced as well as to strengthen our bargaining position

with an increasingly protectionist partner.

Our past trade strategy focused on the United States, especially after the terrorist attacks that resulted in 3,000 deaths in New York and Washington, D.C. Canadians debated whether we should pursue a "Big Idea," a term coined by U of T's Wendy Dobson, such as a common market, a custom union or just some new trade partnership to reduce regulatory, tax and other barriers with the United States. Sure, we looked at some new trade deals with Chile and Israel but most attention was paid to our relationship with the United States, and secondarily to Mexico, our other NAFTA partner.

We are now in a different world. The United States is on the precipice of decline as it struggles with a sick housing market, excessive public and private debt loads, an antiquated tax system, anti-growth regulatory policies, falling productivity with an aging population and increasing isolationism. It is hard to see the U.S. growing at its historical 3% over the coming decade. With high unemployment and distrust of the benefits from globalization, U.S. trade policy is becoming more inward with trade agreement initiatives being replaced by "Buy American" provisions.

The U.S. share of world GDP (about a fifth) will continue to fall this coming

and Trade (GATT), which is a continuing series of negotiations among many of the world's countries with the goal of promoting free trade. Canada helped to found GATT after World War II in response to the high tariffs imposed during the Great Depression of the 1930s. Many economists believe that the high tariffs contributed to the economic hardship during that period. GATT has successfully reduced the average tariff among member countries from about 40 percent after World War II to about 5 percent today.

The rules established under GATT are now enforced by an international institution called the World Trade Organization (WTO). The WTO was established in 1995 and has its headquarters in Geneva, Switzerland. As of July 2008, 153 countries have joined the organization, accounting for 97 percent of world trade. The functions of the WTO are to administer trade agreements, provide a forum for negotiations, and handle disputes that arise among member countries.

decade as emerging and developing countries almost double their size. By 2030, China will be the second largest economy in the world, rivaling the U.S. for economic domination. Other emerging economies, including Brazil, India and Indonesia with growth rates double that of the U.S., could be major markets for Canadian exporters. It would be a mistake for Canada to ignore markets beyond North America.

The Australians have been particularly adept at growing international markets for their products and services, heavily dominated by mining. In 2008, Australian exports to Japan were $51-billion, followed by China ($33-billion), Korea ($18.5-billion), India ($15.4-billion) and the United States ($11.4-billion). Which country will grow faster in the future—Canada or Australia? Not a hard question to answer.

In our relations with the U.S. elephant, we have little leverage to negotiate trade improvements since we have no credible threat to turn elsewhere. A good example is energy exports to the U.S. market. If the U.S. wishes to penalize consumption of our oil sand production, we have little

room to manoeuvre. But if we export to Asia and other markets, we improve our negotiating position significantly.

The same could be argued for lumber, minerals, manufactured products and services. Trade with the U.S. is economical because of lower transport costs and cultural similarity. However, as the U.S. increases its protectionism, Canada may simply turn to other markets where tariffs, regulations, and other costs are eased relative to the United States.

So what would a new trade strategy look like? First principle: Don't throw out the baby with the bath water. Given our good trading relationship with the U.S., we should try to negotiate better terms that would reduce trade barriers by pursuing policies that harmonize regulations, reduce cross-border withholding taxes and ease congestion at the border. We should also seek exemptions from U.S. protectionist legislation—it has worked before and may again.

Second principle: Develop new markets for Canadian exporters, especially with growing parts of the world. In some countries, Canadians are highly respected (the Chinese still talk about Norman

Bethune). And we can leverage our multicultural business communities who have good contacts elsewhere. Our goal should be to establish new free trade agreements with large countries such as Brazil, China, Europe, Korea, India and Japan so that we can develop new markets elsewhere.

Third principle: Continue pursuing competitiveness and innovation so that we can benefit from greater world-wide trade. This is the policy framework of the federal government in recent years and, despite the recession, there is no need to change course. Competition, taxation, regulation and innovation policies should be reformed to encourage a more dynamic economy with successful businesses competing abroad. If we have a successful economy, our exchange rate will rise but this only means that Canadians are becoming richer as we more easily buy goods and services imported from abroad.

There is a big world out there beyond the U.S. and it is getting even bigger.

Source: Jack Mintz, "Look Beyond the U.S.," *National Post*, January 14, 2010. Material reprinted with the express permission of The National Post Company, a CanWest Partnership.

What are the pros and cons of the multilateral approach to free trade? One advantage is that the multilateral approach has the potential to result in freer trade than a unilateral approach because it can reduce trade restrictions abroad as well as at home. If international negotiations fail, however, the result could be more restricted trade than under a unilateral approach.

In addition, the multilateral approach may have a political advantage. In most markets, producers are fewer and better organized than consumers—and thus wield greater political influence. Reducing the Isolandian tariff on textiles, for example, may be politically difficult if considered by itself. The textile companies would oppose free trade, and the users of textiles who would benefit are so numerous that organizing their support would be difficult. Yet suppose that Neighbourland promises to reduce its tariff on wheat at the same time that Isoland reduces its tariff on textiles. In this case, the Isolandian wheat farmers, who are also politically powerful, would back the agreement. Thus, the multilateral approach to free trade can sometimes win political support when a unilateral reduction cannot. ●

QuickQuiz The textile industry of Autarka advocates a ban on the import of wool suits. Describe five arguments its lobbyists might make. Give a response to each of these arguments.

CONCLUSION

Economists and the general public often disagree about free trade. In 1988, for example, Canada faced the question of whether to sign the Canada–U.S. Free Trade Agreement, which reduced trade restrictions between Canada and the United States. Opinion polls showed the general public in Canada to be about evenly split on the issue. Prime Minister Brian Mulroney campaigned for the free trade agreement and won re-election, but with a minority of the popular vote. Opponents viewed free trade as a threat to job security and the Canadian standard of living. By contrast, economists overwhelmingly supported the agreement. They viewed free trade as a way of allocating production efficiently and raising living standards in both countries.

Economists see the benefits of trade between countries in the same way that they see the benefits of trade between provinces, or between cities, or between people. Individuals would have a much lower standard of living if they had to produce all their own food, clothing, and housing. So would a city. So would a province. The United States has always had unrestricted trade among the states, and the country as a whole has benefited from the specialization that trade allows in such a large market. With a few exceptions, Canada, too, has free trade among the provinces: Ontario builds cars, Alberta pumps oil, British Columbia saws lumber, and so on. The world could similarly benefit from free trade among countries.

To better understand economists' view of trade, let's continue our parable. Suppose that the country of Isoland ignores the advice of its economics team and decides not to allow free trade in textiles. The country remains in the equilibrium without international trade.

Then, one day, some Isolandian inventor discovers a new way to make textiles at very low cost. The process is quite mysterious, however, and the inventor insists on keeping it a secret. What is odd is that the inventor doesn't need traditional inputs such as cotton or wool. The only material input he needs is wheat. And even more oddly, to manufacture textiles from wheat, he hardly needs any labor input at all.

The inventor is hailed as a genius. Because everyone buys clothing, the lower cost of textiles allows all Isolandians to enjoy a higher standard of living. Workers who had previously produced textiles do suffer when their factories close, but eventually they find work in other industries. Some become farmers and grow the wheat that the inventor turns into textiles. Others enter new industries that emerge as a result of higher Isolandian living standards. Everyone understands that the displacement of these workers is an inevitable part of progress and economic growth.

NEL

After several years, a newspaper reporter decides to investigate this mysterious new textile process. She sneaks into the inventor's factory and learns that the inventor is a fraud. The inventor has not been making textiles at all. Instead, he has been smuggling wheat abroad in exchange for textiles from other countries. The only thing that the inventor had discovered was the gains from international trade.

When the truth is revealed, the government shuts down the inventor's operation. The price of textiles rises, and workers return to jobs in textile factories. Living standards in Isoland fall back to their former levels. The inventor is jailed and held up to public ridicule. After all, he was no inventor. He was just an economist.

SUMMARY

- The effects of free trade can be determined by comparing the domestic price without trade to the world price. A low domestic price indicates that the country has a comparative advantage in producing the good and that the country will become an exporter. A high domestic price indicates that the rest of the world has a comparative advantage in producing the good and that the country will become an importer.

- When a country allows trade and becomes an exporter of a good, producers of the good are better off, and consumers of the good are worse off. When a country allows trade and becomes an importer of a good, consumers are better off, and producers are worse off. In both cases, the gains from trade exceed the losses.

- A tariff—a tax on imports—moves a market closer to the equilibrium that would exist without trade and, therefore, reduces the gains from trade. Although domestic producers are better off and the government raises revenue, the losses to consumers exceed these gains.

- There are various arguments for restricting trade: protecting jobs, defending national security, helping infant industries, preventing unfair competition, and responding to foreign trade restrictions. Although some of these arguments have some merit in some cases, economists believe that free trade is usually the better policy.

KEY CONCEPTS

world price, p. 183   tariff, p. 187

QUESTIONS FOR REVIEW

1. What does the domestic price that prevails without international trade tell us about a nation's comparative advantage?

2. When does a country become an exporter of a good? An importer?

3. Draw the supply-and-demand diagram for an importing country. What is consumer surplus and producer surplus before trade is allowed? What is consumer surplus and producer surplus with free trade? What is the change in total surplus?

4. Describe what a tariff is, and describe its economic effects.

5. List five arguments often given to support trade restrictions. How do economists respond to these arguments?

6. What is the difference between the unilateral and multilateral approaches to achieving free trade? Give an example of each.

PROBLEMS AND APPLICATIONS

1. Canada represents a small part of the world apple market.
   a. Draw a diagram depicting the equilibrium in the Canadian apple market without international trade. Identify the equilibrium price, equilibrium quantity, consumer surplus, and producer surplus.
   b. Suppose that the world apple price is below the Canadian price before trade, and that the Canadian apple market is now opened to trade. Identify the new equilibrium price, quantity consumed, quantity produced domestically, and quantity imported. Also show the change in the surplus of domestic consumers and producers. Has domestic total surplus increased or decreased?

2. The world price of wine is below the price that would prevail in Canada in the absence of trade.
   a. Assuming that Canadian imports of wine are a small part of total world wine production, draw a graph for the Canadian market for wine under free trade. Identify consumer surplus, producer surplus, and total surplus in an appropriate table.
   b. Now suppose that an unusual shift of the Gulf Stream leads to an unseasonably cold summer in Europe, destroying much of the grape harvest there. What effect does this shock have on the world price of wine? Using your graph and table from part (a), show the effect on consumer surplus, producer surplus, and total surplus in Canada. Who are the winners and losers? Is Canada as a whole better off or worse off?

3. Suppose that Parliament imposes a tariff on imported clothes to protect the Canadian clothing industry from foreign competition. Assuming that Canada is a price taker in the world clothing market, show on a diagram (a) the change in the quantity of imports, (b) the loss to Canadian consumers, (c) the gain to Canadian manufacturers, (d) government revenue, and (e) the deadweight loss associated with the tariff. The loss to consumers can be decomposed into three pieces: a transfer to domestic producers, a transfer to the government, and a deadweight loss. Use your diagram to identify these three pieces.

4. Most Canadian dairy farmers oppose free trade, and most Canadian lumber producers support it. For simplicity, assume that Canada is a small country in the markets for both milk and lumber, and that without free trade, Canada would not trade these goods internationally. (Both of these assumptions are false, but they do not affect the qualitative responses to the following questions.)
   a. Based on who opposes and who supports free trade, do you think the world milk price is above or below the Canadian no-trade milk price? Do you think the world lumber price is above or below the Canadian no-trade lumber price? Now analyze the welfare consequences of free trade for both markets.
   b. Considering both markets together, would free trade make Canadian producers as a group better off or worse off? Would it make Canadian consumers as a group better off or worse off? Does it make Canada as a whole better off or worse off?

5. Imagine that winemakers in British Columbia petitioned the provincial government to tax wines imported from Ontario. They argue that this tax would both raise tax revenue for the provincial government and raise employment in the BC wine industry. Do you agree with these claims? Is it a good policy?

6. The nation of Textilia does not allow imports of clothing. In its equilibrium without trade, a T-shirt costs $20 and the equilibrium quantity is 3 million T-shirts. One day, after reading Adam Smith's *The Wealth of Nations* while on vacation, the president decides to open the Textilian market to international trade. The market price of a T-shirt falls to the world price of $16. The number of T-shirts consumed in Textilia rises to 4 million, while the number of T-shirts produced declines to 1 million.
   a. Illustrate in a graph the situation just described. Your graph should show all of the numbers.
   b. Calculate the change in consumer surplus, producer surplus, and total surplus that results from opening up trade. (Hint: Recall that the area of a triangle is $\frac{1}{2} \times$ base $\times$ height.)

7. Assume that Canada is an importer of televisions and that there are no trade restrictions. Canadian consumers buy 1 million televisions per year, of which 400 000 are produced domestically and 600 000 are imported.
   a. Suppose that a technological advance among Japanese television manufacturers causes the world price of televisions to fall by $100. Draw a graph to show how this change affects the welfare of Canadian consumers and Canadian producers and how it affects total surplus in Canada.
   b. After the fall in price, consumers buy 1.2 million televisions, of which 200 000 are produced domestically and 1 million are imported. Calculate the change in consumer surplus, producer surplus, and total surplus from the price reduction.
   c. If the government responded by putting a $100 tariff on imported televisions, what would this do? Calculate the revenue that would be raised and the deadweight loss. Would it be a good policy from the standpoint of Canadian welfare? Who might support the policy?
   d. Suppose that the fall in price is attributable not to technological advance but to a $100 per television subsidy from the Japanese government to Japanese industry. How would this affect your analysis?

8. Consider a small country that exports steel. Suppose that a "pro-trade" government decides to subsidize the export of steel by paying a certain amount for each tonne sold abroad. How does this export subsidy affect the domestic price of steel, the quantity of steel produced, the quantity of steel consumed, and the quantity of steel exported? How does it affect consumer surplus, producer surplus, government revenue, and total surplus? (Hint: The analysis of an export subsidy is similar to the analysis of a tariff.)

9. Consider the arguments for restricting trade.
   a. Assume you are a lobbyist for timber, an established industry suffering from low-priced foreign competition. Which two or three of the five arguments do you think would be most persuasive to the average member of Parliament as to why he or she

should support trade restrictions? Explain your reasoning.
   b. Now assume you are an astute student of economics (hopefully not a hard assumption). Although all the arguments for restricting trade have their shortcomings, name the two or three arguments that seem to make the most economic sense to you. For each, describe the economic rationale for and against these arguments for trade restrictions.

10. China is a major producer of grains, such as wheat, corn, and rice. In 2008, the Chinese government, concerned that grain exports were driving up food prices for domestic consumers, imposed a tax on grain exports. Draw the graph that describes the market for grain in an exporting country. Use this graph as the starting point to answer the following questions.
    a. How does an export tax affect domestic grain prices?
    b. How does it affect the welfare of domestic consumers, the welfare of domestic producers, and government revenue?
    c. What happens to total welfare in China, as measured by the sum of consumer surplus, producer surplus, and tax revenue?

11. Consider a country that imports a good from abroad. For each of the following statements, say whether it is true or false. Explain your answer.
    a. "The greater the elasticity of demand, the greater the gains from trade."
    b. "If demand is perfectly inelastic, there are no gains from trade."
    c. "If demand is perfectly inelastic, consumers do not benefit from trade."

12. Kawmin is a small country that produces and consumes jellybeans. The world price of jellybeans is $1 per bag, and Kawmin's domestic demand and supply for jellybeans are governed by the following equations:

Demand: $Q^D = 8 - P$
Supply: $Q^S = P$

where P is in dollars per bag and Q is in bags of jellybeans.
    a. Draw a well-labelled graph of the situation in Kawmin if the nation does not allow trade. Calculate the following (recalling that

the area of a triangle is $\frac{1}{2} \times$ base $\times$ height): the equilibrium price and quantity, consumer surplus, producer surplus, and total surplus.

b. Kawmin then opens the market to trade. Draw another graph to describe the new situation in the jellybean market. Calculate the equilibrium price, quantities of consumption and production, imports, consumer surplus, producer surplus, and total surplus.

c. After awhile, the czar of Kawmin responds to the pleas of jellybean producers by placing a $1 per bag tariff on jellybean imports. On a graph, show the effects of this tariff. Calculate the equilibrium price, quantities of consumption and production, imports, consumer surplus, producer surplus, government revenue, and total surplus.

d. What are the gains from opening up trade? What are the deadweight losses from restricting trade with the tariff? Give numerical answers.

For more study tools, please visit http://www.mankiw5e.nelson.com.

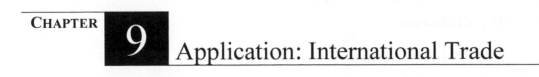

CHAPTER 9 Application: International Trade

I. Chapter Overview

A. Context and Purpose

The previous chapter provided an application of welfare economics to the efficiency effects of taxation. This chapter adds another application of welfare economics, but in this case to international trade. The chapter identifies the winners and losers from free trade, as well as the welfare effects of protectionism.

A. Helpful Hints

1. *The determinants of trade involve world price.* When the price of a good within a country differs from the world price, then there is an incentive for that country to enter the international market for the good. If the world price is higher than the domestic price, then domestic producers will have an incentive to export the good. If the world price is lower than the domestic price, then domestic consumers will have an incentive to import the good from abroad.

2. *Exporting a good causes the domestic price to rise, which hurts domestic consumers but helps domestic producers.* However, the gains of the sellers are greater than the losses of the buyers, and total surplus rises. Similarly, importing a good causes the domestic price to fall, hurting domestic producers but helping domestic consumers. The gains for the consumers are greater than the losses by the producers, causing total surplus to rise. As a result, both imports and exports cause a net gain in total surplus, and the country's economic well-being rises.

3. *Countries do not trade, people do.* When someone in Canada buys from someone in Mexico, both parties benefit, just as surely as if both the buyer and seller had been in Canada.

4. *There are winners and losers from international trade.* It is this fact that accounts for much of the resistance to free trade. The losers tend to be more vocal than the winners, who are more diffused and less visible.

117

II. Self-Testing Challenges

A. True/False Questions

_____ 1.   The main problem with the argument that tariffs are needed to protect domestic jobs is that such trade restrictions never really save jobs.

_____ 2.   Free international trade raises the economic well-being of all trading nations in the sense that the gains of the winners exceed the losses of the losers.

_____ 3.   International trade creates jobs.

_____ 4.   When a country allows trade and becomes an exporter of a good, domestic consumers of a good are better off and domestic producers of the good are worse off.

_____ 5.   Free trade makes the nation better off, even though it may not make everyone in the country better off.

_____ 6.   A country whose price of steel is less than the world price must be subsidizing its steel industry.

_____ 7.   If a government imposes a tariff on an imported good, it increases the country's gain from trade.

_____ 8.   According to the infant-industry argument, new small industries may need temporary trade restrictions to help them get started.

_____ 9.   An increased variety of goods, lower costs through economies of scale, increased competition, and enhanced flow of ideas are all benefits that make the case for free international trade.

_____ 10. The difference between a tariff and an import quota is that while the former raises revenue for the government, the latter creates surplus for those who get the licences to import.

B. Multiple-Choice Questions

1.   Which one of the following describes the outcomes when a country allows trade and becomes an importer of a good?
    a.   Domestic consumers of the good are better off, and domestic producers of the good are worse off.
    b.   Domestic consumers of the good are worse off, and domestic producers of the good are better off.

c. Both domestic consumers and domestic producers are better off.
d. Both domestic consumers and domestic producers are worse off.

2. Which one of the following describes the outcomes when a country allows trade and becomes an importer of a good?
    a. Both the price paid by domestic consumers and the price received by domestic producers of the good rise.
    b. The price paid by domestic consumers rises, but the price received by domestic producers falls.
    c. The price paid by domestic consumers falls, but the price received by domestic producers rises.
    d. Both the price paid by domestic consumers and the price received by domestic producers fall.

3. Which one of the following occurs when a country allows trade and becomes an importer of a good?
    a. The economic well-being of everyone in the country rises.
    b. The economic well-being of everyone in the country falls.
    c. The gains of the producers exceed the losses of the consumers.
    d. The gains of the consumers exceed the losses of the producers.

4. Which one of the following would occur if a tariff was placed on imported steel in Canada?
    a. It would raise the total surplus in the Canadian market for steel.
    b. It would lower the total surplus in the Canadian market for steel.
    c. It would raise the total surplus of foreign exporters and consumers of steel.
    d. It would raise the Canadian standard of living at the expense of the exporting country.

The graph below shows the market for good Y in a small country, along with the world price for Y. Use the information provided to answer questions 5–7.

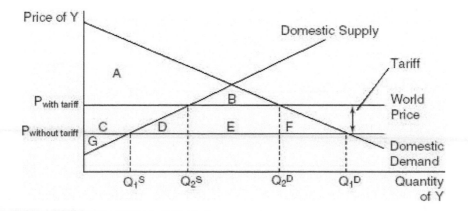

5.   Which one of the following is represented by Area E?
    a.   government revenues as a result of tariff
    b.   gain in welfare of domestic consumers as a result of tariff
    c.   deadweight loss from underconsumption as a result of tariff
    d.   gain in welfare of domestic producers as a result of the tariff
6.   Which one of the following is represented by Area D?
    a.   government revenues as a result of tariff
    b.   gain in welfare of domestic consumers as a result of tariff
    c.   deadweight loss from overproduction as a result of tariff
    d.   gain in welfare of domestic producers as a result of tariff

7.   Which one of the following is represented by Area F?
    a.   government revenues as a result of tariff
    b.   gain in welfare of domestic consumers as a result of tariff
    c.   deadweight loss from underconsumption as a result of tariff
    d.   gain in welfare of domestic producers as a result of tariff

8.   Which one of the following is the main difference between a tariff and a quota?
    a.   A tariff generates added revenue for the government, but revenue generated from a quota is received by the industry.
    b.   A quota harms consumers, but a tariff harms producers.

    c.   A quota increases the volume of imports, but a tariff decreases volume of imports.

The graph below shows the market for good Z in the small country of Alphaland. Use the information to answer questions 9–11.

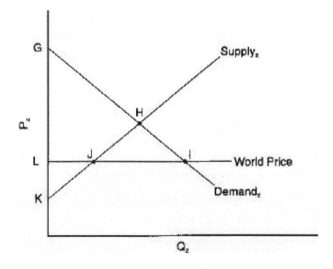

9. Which one of the following explains what Alphaland should do in order to maximize total surplus?
   a. It should increase exports of good Z until the domestic price falls to the world price.
   b. It should increase exports of good Z until the world price rises to the domestic price.
   c. It should increase imports of good Z until the world price rises to the domestic price.
   d. It should increase imports of good Z until the domestic price falls to the world price.

10. After trade, total surplus will increase by which one of the following graph areas?
    a. GHK
    b. GIJK
    c. HIJ
    d. LJK

11. Which one of the following describes the status of good Z's consumers and producers in Alphaland, as a result of trade?
    a. Consumers will be better off, but the producers will be worse off.
    b. Consumers will be worse off, but the producers will be better off.
    c. Consumers and producers will be worse off.
    d. Consumers and producers will be better off.

12. Which of the following statements is supported by the infant-industry argument?
    a. new industries should be discouraged because they cannot compete with established firms
    b. protecting a new industry from foreign competition may be desirable in the short term in order to give it time to become competitive
    c. new industries may require permanent subsidies from the government in order to be competitive with established foreign firms
    d. protecting industries that produce products for young children can be a worthwhile investment in the nation's human capital

13. Which of the following is the best response if Mexico subsidizes its textile production, making it impossible for Canadian producers to compete?
    a. a high tariff on textiles would improve economic well-being in Canada
    b. Canada's most appropriate response would be to retaliate with an identical subsidy
    c. the ideal response would be to threaten retaliation without actually following through on the threat
    d. Canada would maximize its economic well-being by purchasing the subsidized textiles from Mexico

14.   Some opponents of free trade argue that when Canadians buy shirts from Bangladesh, Canadian workers lose their jobs. Which one of the following is a good counterargument?
   a.   The jobs lost as a result of free trade pay salaries below the poverty line.
   b.   Free trade creates jobs, many of which pay more than the jobs lost.
   c.   Imports from Bangladesh create more handling and distributing jobs than they lose.
   d.   The jobs lost are concentrated in restricted geographic areas.

Use the following table to answer question 15.

Good	Canada	Japan
X	5	4
Z	10	5

15.   Which one of the following is the best advice?
   a.   Japan should produce good Z and Canada should produce good X, and they should trade with each other.
   b.   Japan should produce good X and Canada should produce good Z, and they should trade with each other.
   c.   Japan should produce both X and Z and export them to Canada.

16.   Which one of the following is the advantage held by Japan?
   a.   an absolute advantage in producing good X only
   b.   an absolute advantage in producing good Z only
   c.   an absolute advantage, but not a comparative advantage, in producing both goods
   d.   a comparative advantage, but not an absolute advantage, in producing both goods

17.   Which one of the following describes how Japan's combined consumer and producer surplus will be maximized?
   a.   if Japan specializes according to its comparative advantage
   b.   if Japan specializes according to its absolute advantage
   c.   if Japan uses tariffs to protect its domestic industries
   d.   if Japan subsidizes good Z, which requires 25% more labour than good X to produce

C. Short-Answer Questions

1. Suppose that Alphaland and Utopia can provide widgets and frinzels according to the following production possibilities.

Daily Output Per Worker

Country	Widgets	Frinzels
Alphaland	20	20
Utopia	40	80

a. Which country is the lower opportunity cost producer of widgets? Of frinzels? Explain. _____

_____
_____
_____
_____
_____

b. Alphaland seems to be generally less productive than Utopia in terms of both goods. How can Alphaland hope to compete internationally with Utopia? _____

_____
_____
_____
_____

2. International trade *can* make everyone better off, but will it?

_____
_____
_____
_____

3. Rebut the following claim.
Imposing tariffs on imported goods will increase employment, and hence income, in Canada. There is a double advantage here. If the tariff moves production to Canada, there will be a reduction in unemployment and an increase in government revenue. If, on the other hand, production is not moved to Canada, the government still gets revenue from tax on imported goods. _____

_____
_____
_____
_____
_____

341

D. Practice Problems

1. The graph below shows a country before and after the imposition of a tariff.

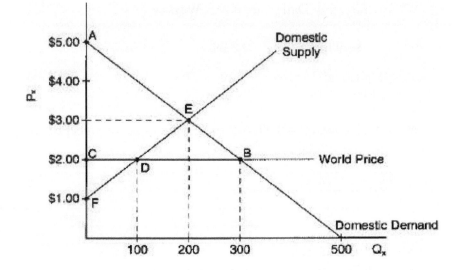

   a. Show graphically and calculate the actual change in consumer surplus and producer surplus as a result of the tariff. (Hint: Remember that the area of a triangle = 0.5 × base × height.) What is the change in the total surplus? How was the result calculated? _____

   _____
   _____
   _____
   _____

   b. Why did total surplus change in response to the tariff?

   _____
   _____
   _____
   _____

2. Economists are generally critical of tariffs and quotas, even though such trade restrictions are often popular with the general public.

   a. Who wins and who loses from tariffs and other trade restrictions?

   _____
   _____
   _____
   _____

b. What effect does a tariff have on economic well-being? Why?

_____

_____

_____

c. In light of the answer to part (b) above, why are trade restrictions so popular?

_____

_____

_____

_____

d. List the arguments for trade restrictions and evaluate each briefly.

1. _____

_____

_____

2. _____

_____

_____

3. _____

_____

_____

4. _____

_____

_____

5. _____

_____

E. Advanced Critical Thinking

Recently, a representative of the Canadian Auto Workers' union said, in support of protection for the Canadian auto industry, "we want free trade, but we want fair trade." He argued that Japanese automakers are subsidized by their government, and therefore should not be allowed free entry into the Canadian auto market.

a.   Given the large number of Canadian autoworkers who have lost their jobs in recent decades due to foreign competition, should Canada act to reduce the number of imported cars if other countries are creating artificial advantages for their industries? Who would win and who would lose? What would happen to society's overall economic well-being? Explain. What if another country subsidized every industry? Could they put Canada out of business? _____

_____
_____
_____
_____
_____
_____

b.   In the supply and demand diagram below, fill in the world price, and label the equilibrium quantity and the price with free international trade, as well as after import restrictions eliminate all imported cars.

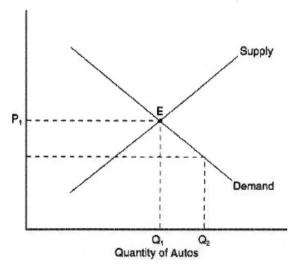

III. Solutions

A. True/False Questions

1. F; tariffs save some domestic jobs (those in competition with imports) at the expense of other domestic jobs (those in export industries).
2. T
3. F; international trade redistributes jobs from less productive to more productive uses.
4. F; domestic producers of a good are better off while domestic consumers are worse off.
5. T
6. F; if a country has a price of steel that is less than the world price, this indicates that the country has a comparative advantage in steel.
7. F; any trade restriction, including a tariff, reduces gains from trade.
8. T
9. T
10. T

B. Multiple-Choice Questions

1. a	5. a	9. d	13. d	17. a
2. d	6. c	10. c	14. b	
3. d	7. c	11. a	15. a	
4. b	8. a	12. b	16. c	

C. Short-Answer Questions

1. Alphaland and Utopia can provide widgets and frinzels according to the following production possibilities.

Daily Output Per Worker

Country	Widgets	Frinzels
Alphaland	20	20
Utopia	40	80

a. Alphaland is the lower opportunity cost producer of widgets, even though its workers are only half as productive as Utopia's (20 per day vs. 40 per day). This is because Alphaland's opportunity cost of producing widgets is the frinzels that it could have produced instead. At a ratio of 20:20, the opportunity cost of a widget is one frinzel. In Utopia, the ratio is 40:80, for an opportunity cost of 2 frinzels per widget. Utopia, however, is the lower opportunity cost producer of frinzels (80 frinzels to 40 widgets, or 2 frinzels to 1 widget) vs. 20 frinzels to 20 widgets or 1 frinzel for 1 widget in Alphaland. As a result, even though Utopia has an absolute advantage in either good, it has a comparative advantage only in producing frinzels. Alphaland has the comparative advantage in widgets. Both countries gain if they specialize according to their comparative advantages.

   b. Even though Utopia has an absolute advantage in producing both goods, it nevertheless gives up more to produce widgets than if it produces frinzels and trades them for Alphaland's widgets at any relative price less than 2:1. Similarly, Alphaland would gain at any relative price greater than 1:1. At any relative price between 1 and 2 frinzels per widget, both countries gain.

2.   Trade will probably *not* make everyone better off. Compensation for those who lose as a result of trade is rare. In the absence of such compensation, trade expands the size of the economic pie, but might leave some groups in the economy with a smaller slice.

3.   Imposition of tariffs will raise the price of goods to consumers but will not necessarily increase employment, and hence income, to compensate for this increased cost. Countries affected by the tariff may retaliate by imposing their own protective measures against Canadian exports, which may lead to more unemployment and less government revenue.

D. Practice Problems

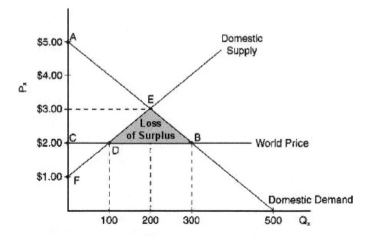

1.   a. Total surplus falls from $500 to $400. With trade, the equilibrium is at point B, with a price of $2 and consumption (including imports) of 300. Of this quantity of 300, 100 are produced by domestic firms and 200 are imported. The original surplus, with trade, is the area ABC, representing consumer surplus, plus area CDF, which is producer

surplus. Numerically, this surplus is ½ ($5–$2)(300) + ½ ($2–$1)(100) = $500. After eliminating trade, the equilibrium shifts to point E, at a price of $3 and a total domestic output of 200. The total surplus is triangle AEF, or ½ ($5–$1)(200) = $400. Thus, the total surplus falls by $100, which is also the area of triangle DEB = ½ ($3–$2)(300–100).

b. Total surplus falls because buyers and sellers are prevented from making all of the exchanges that are in their best interests. Cutting consumption of good X back from 300 to 200 units means that consumers will not be able to buy 100 units that had a marginal value (or benefit) to society which exceeded the marginal cost of producing it.

2. a. Winners include domestic producers, who face less competition, and foreign consumers, who have more of their products left to consume at home. Losers include domestic consumers, who face a restricted supply, and foreign producers, whose foreign markets are restricted by tariffs.

b. A tariff lowers overall economic well-being by reducing the sum of producer and consumer surplus, just as any other tax would do—by distorting behaviour and reducing output below the competitive market equilibrium.

c. The winners from trade restrictions are highly visible and tend to be quite vocal in their opposition to free trade. The losers—the general public—are more diffused and harder to identify. If consumers in general pay slightly higher prices, it may not be obvious that trade restrictions are the cause, even though the total loss is great.

d. 1. Trade restrictions can protect some jobs in industries that compete with imports, but at the expense of others that are in export-related industries. Canada's imports provide the dollars that our trading partners use to buy our exports.

2. Trade restrictions can also provide temporary protection for new or "infant" industries until they get established, but the problem is that infant industries never want to grow up.

3. National security is another possibly valid argument, but every industry tries to claim that it is vital.

4. Retaliation against unfair competition is another argument, but retaliation ends up hurting the economic welfare of the retaliating country.

5. The threat of protectionism can be used to encourage trading partners to reduce their trade barriers, but it can also backfire and lead to trade wars that make both trading partners worse off.

E. Advanced Critical Thinking

a. Although it would be politically popular to protect autoworkers, it would actually reduce our total surplus from automobiles. It would help autoworkers and auto companies in Canada, but it would hurt Canadian auto buyers and foreign auto producers. It would also help foreign consumers of automobiles, who would find that more of their supply would stay at home, thus holding down the price they pay. Most industries seem to make the claim that imports are subsidized, but it is not possible for another country to subsidize everything and drive all industries out of business. When a country subsidizes one industry and makes it more competitive internationally, it makes it harder for its other industries to compete. Jobs are not created, but merely redistributed from less subsidized to more subsidized industries.

b.

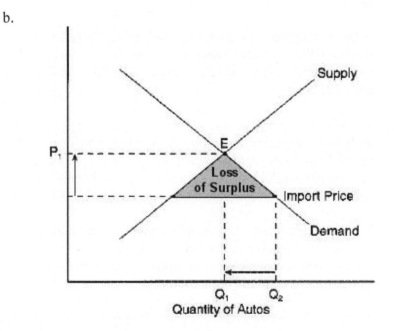

© Beverley Lu/GetStock.com

4

THE ECONOMICS OF
THE PUBLIC SECTOR

EXTERNALITIES

Learning Objectives

In the chapter, you will ...

- Learn the nature of an externality

- See why externalities can make market outcomes inefficient

- Examine how people can sometimes solve the problem of externalities on their own

- Consider why private solutions to externalities sometimes do not work

- Examine the various government policies aimed at solving the problem of externalities

Firms that make and sell paper also create, as a byproduct of the manufacturing process, a chemical called *dioxin*. Scientists believe that once dioxin enters the environment, it raises the population's risk of cancer, birth defects, and other health problems.

Is the production and release of dioxin a problem for society? In Chapters 4 through 9 we examined how markets allocate scarce resources with the forces of supply and demand, and we saw that the equilibrium of supply and demand is typically an efficient allocation of resources. To use Adam Smith's famous metaphor, the invisible hand of the marketplace leads self-interested buyers and sellers in a market to maximize the total benefit that society derives from that market. This insight is the basis for one of the ten principles of economics in Chapter 1: Markets are usually a good way to organize economic activity. Should we conclude, therefore, that the invisible hand prevents firms in the paper market from emitting too much dioxin?

Markets do many things well, but they do not do everything well. In this chapter we begin our study of another of the ten principles of economics: Governments can sometimes improve market outcomes. We examine why markets sometimes fail to allocate resources efficiently, how government policies can potentially improve the market's allocation, and what kinds of policies are likely to work best.

externality
the uncompensated impact of one person's actions on the well-being of a bystander

The market failures examined in this chapter fall under a general category called *externalities*. An **externality** arises when a person engages in an activity that influences the well-being of a bystander and yet neither pays nor receives any compensation for that effect. If the impact on the bystander is adverse, it is called a *negative externality*; if it is beneficial, it is called a *positive externality*. In the presence of externalities, society's interest in a market outcome extends beyond the well-being of buyers and sellers who participate in the market; it also includes the well-being of bystanders who are affected indirectly. Because buyers and sellers neglect the external effects of their actions when deciding how much to demand or supply, the market equilibrium is not efficient when there are externalities. That is, the equilibrium fails to maximize the total benefit to society as a whole. The release of dioxin into the environment, for instance, is a negative externality. Self-interested paper firms will not consider the full cost of the pollution they create and, therefore, will emit too much pollution unless the government prevents or discourages them from doing so.

Externalities come in many varieties, as do the policy responses that try to deal with the market failure. Here are some examples:

* The exhaust from automobiles is a negative externality because it creates smog that other people have to breathe. As a result of this externality, drivers tend to pollute too much. The federal government attempts to solve this problem by setting emission standards for cars. It also taxes gasoline to reduce the amount that people drive.
* Restored historic buildings convey a positive externality because people who walk or ride by them can enjoy their beauty and the sense of history that these buildings provide. Building owners do not get the full benefit of restoration and, therefore, tend to discard older buildings too quickly. Many local governments respond to this problem by regulating the destruction of historic buildings and by providing tax breaks to owners who restore them.
* Barking dogs create a negative externality because neighbours are disturbed by the noise. Dog owners do not bear the full cost of the noise and, therefore, tend to take too few precautions to prevent their dogs from barking. Local governments address this problem by making it illegal to "disturb the peace."
* Research into new technologies provides a positive externality because it creates knowledge that other people can use. Because inventors cannot capture the full benefits of their inventions, they tend to devote too few resources to research. The federal government addresses this problem partially through the patent system, which gives inventors exclusive rights to their inventions for a period of time.
* A large body of scientific research suggests that carbon dioxide and other greenhouse gas emissions associated with the use of fossil fuels contributes to global warming. This in turn is thought to be associated with changes in ocean levels, weather patterns, and other climate-related changes. Individuals do not take full account of these externalities when consuming energy and therefore tend to consume too much. Governments around the world have addressed this by imposing taxes on carbon emissions as well as by implementing cap-and-trade systems with tradable permits.

In each of these cases, some decision maker fails to take account of the external effects of his or her behaviour. The government responds by trying to influence this behaviour to protect the interests of bystanders.

NEL

EXTERNALITIES AND MARKET INEFFICIENCY

In this section we use the tools from Chapter 7 to examine how externalities affect economic well-being. The analysis shows precisely why externalities cause markets to allocate resources inefficiently. Later in the chapter we examine various ways in which private actors and public policymakers may remedy this type of market failure.

Welfare Economics: A Recap

We begin by recalling the key lessons of welfare economics from Chapter 7. To make our analysis concrete, we will consider a specific market—the market for aluminum. Figure 10.1 shows the supply and demand curves in the market for aluminum.

As you should recall from Chapter 7, the supply and demand curves contain important information about costs and benefits. The demand curve for aluminum reflects the value of aluminum to consumers, as measured by the prices they are willing to pay. At any given quantity, the height of the demand curve shows the willingness to pay of the marginal buyer. In other words, it shows the value to the consumer of the last unit of aluminum bought. Similarly, the supply curve reflects the costs of producing aluminum. At any given quantity, the height of the supply curve shows the cost of the marginal seller. In other words, it shows the cost to the producer of the last unit of aluminum sold.

In the absence of government intervention, the price adjusts to balance the supply and demand for aluminum. The quantity produced and consumed in the market equilibrium, shown as Q_{MARKET} in Figure 10.1, is efficient in the sense that it maximizes the sum of producer and consumer surplus. That is, the market allocates resources in a way that maximizes the total value to the consumers who buy and use aluminum minus the total costs to the producers who make and sell aluminum.

FIGURE 10.1

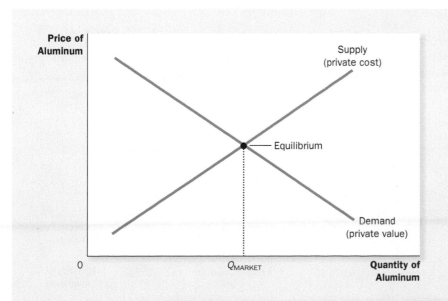

The Market for Aluminum

The demand curve reflects the value to buyers, and the supply curve reflects the costs of sellers. The equilibrium quantity, Q_{MARKET}, maximizes the total value to buyers minus the total costs of sellers. In the absence of externalities, therefore, the market equilibrium is efficient.

Negative Externalities

Now let's suppose that aluminum factories emit pollution: For each unit of aluminum produced, a certain amount of smoke enters the atmosphere. Because this smoke creates a health risk for those who breathe the air, it is a negative externality. How does this externality affect the efficiency of the market outcome?

Because of the externality, the cost to *society* of producing aluminum is larger than the cost to the aluminum producers. For each unit of aluminum produced, the *social cost* includes the private costs of the aluminum producers plus the costs to those bystanders affected adversely by the pollution. Figure 10.2 shows the social cost of producing aluminum. The social-cost curve is above the supply curve because it takes into account the external costs imposed on society by aluminum producers. The difference between these two curves reflects the cost of the pollution emitted.

What quantity of aluminum should be produced? To answer this question, we once again consider what a benevolent social planner would do. The planner wants to maximize the total surplus derived from the market—the value to consumers of aluminum minus the cost of producing aluminum. The planner understands, however, that the cost of producing aluminum includes the external costs of the pollution.

The planner would choose the level of aluminum production at which the demand curve crosses the social-cost curve. This intersection determines the optimal amount of aluminum from the standpoint of society as a whole. Below this level of production, the value of the aluminum to consumers (as measured by the height of the demand curve) exceeds the social cost of producing it (as measured by the height of the social-cost curve). The planner does not produce more than this level because the social cost of producing additional aluminum exceeds the value to consumers.

FIGURE 10.2

Pollution and the Social Optimum

In the presence of a negative externality, such as pollution, the social cost of the good exceeds the private cost. The optimal quantity, $Q_{OPTIMUM}$, is therefore smaller than the equilibrium quantity, Q_{MARKET}.

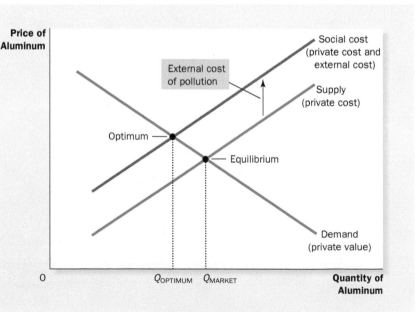

NEL

Note that the equilibrium quantity of aluminum, Q_{MARKET}, is larger than the socially optimal quantity, $Q_{OPTIMUM}$. The reason for this inefficiency is that the market equilibrium reflects only the private costs of production. In the market equilibrium, the marginal consumer values aluminum at less than the social cost of producing it. That is, at Q_{MARKET} the demand curve lies below the social-cost curve. Thus, reducing aluminum production and consumption below the market equilibrium level raises total economic well-being.

We can measure the value of this increase in economic well-being using the concept of *deadweight loss* introduced in Chapters 8 and 9. In those chapters the deadweight loss was the reduction in total surplus that resulted from the imposition of a tax or tariff. The same approach can be used to measure the reduction in total surplus associated with the inefficient allocation of resources due to the presence of an externality.

Figure 10.3 shows how we use the concepts of consumer and producer surplus to determine the deadweight loss of the externality caused by the aluminum factory emitting pollution. The equilibrium is determined by the intersection of the supply curve, which reflects the private cost of producing aluminum, and the demand curve. The equilibrium quantity is Q_{MARKET} and the price is P_{MARKET}.

At the equilibrium level of aluminum production, Q_{MARKET}, and the corresponding market price, P_{MARKET}, consumer surplus is measured in the usual way as the area between the demand curve and the equilibrium price, A + B + C + D. The measure of producer surplus is slightly more complicated but follows the same logic used in Chapters 8 and 9. We showed in Chapter 7 that in the absence of a market failure, producer surplus is simply the amount received by sellers less the cost to those sellers. In the presence of an externality, the basic idea is the same. However, rather than using the private cost to sellers of producing aluminum, as

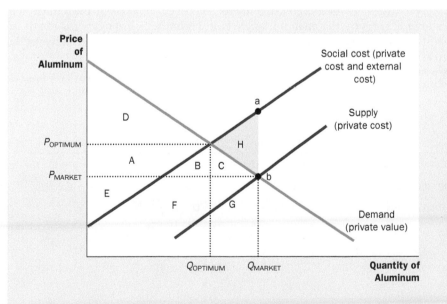

FIGURE 10.3

Deadweight Loss of a Negative Externality

A negative externality means that the social-cost curve lies above the demand curve at the market equilibrium quantity, Q_{MARKET}. Compared with the social optimum, $Q_{OPTIMUM}$, consumer surplus at the market equilibrium is higher by area A + B + C, and producer surplus measured using the social-cost curve is lower by A + B + C + H. The net effect is a reduction in total surplus, shown by deadweight loss triangle H.

measured by the height of the supply or private-cost curve, we use the *social cost* of producing aluminum, as measured by the height of the social-cost curve.

The social-cost curve includes both the private costs of the aluminum producers and the external costs imposed on bystanders affected by the pollution. In Figure 10.3, the cost to society of producing the quantity of aluminum sold is the area between the social-cost curve and the market quantity, Q_{MARKET}, area F + G + B + C + H. The amount received by the sellers is simply the quantity of aluminum sold, Q_{MARKET}, times the market price of aluminum, P_{MARKET}, which is given by area E + F + G. So, producer surplus measured using the social cost of producing aluminum is the amount received by sellers less the social cost to society, or (E + F + G) – (F + G + B + C + H), which simplifies to E – (B + C + H).

Total surplus at the market equilibrium level of aluminum production then consists of consumer surplus (A + B + C + D) plus producer surplus [E – (B + C + H)]. The "At Q_{MARKET}" column of Table 10.1 summarizes these conclusions.

Now consider economic welfare measured at the socially optimal level of aluminum production, $Q_{OPTIMUM}$. The price of aluminum that would generate this socially optimal level of production is $P_{OPTIMUM}$. We will discuss below ways in which this price might be achieved. For now, let's say that the social planner simply imposes this price on the market. At this price, consumers will demand $Q_{OPTIMUM}$ units of aluminum, and consumer surplus is reduced to D. Producer surplus measured using the social-cost curve is the amount received by sellers at price $P_{OPTIMUM}$, the area of rectangle A + E + F + B, less the social cost of producing $Q_{OPTIMUM}$ units of aluminum, area F + B. This gives a producer surplus of A + E. These conclusions are summarized in the "At $Q_{OPTIMUM}$" column of Table 10.1.

We can now see the change in economic welfare associated with moving from the market equilibrium level of aluminum production, Q_{MARKET}, to the socially optimal level of aluminum production, $Q_{OPTIMUM}$. The "Change" column of Table 10.1 shows that moving from Q_{MARKET} to $Q_{OPTIMUM}$ causes consumer surplus to fall by area A + B + C, and producer surplus to rise by area A + B + C + H. In the case of a negative externality in production, the increase in producer surplus of moving from Q_{MARKET} to $Q_{OPTIMUM}$, measured using the social-cost curve, exceeds the reduction in consumer surplus by the area of triangle H in Figure 10.3. Triangle H is the deadweight loss to society, or reduction in total surplus, caused by the externality (pollution) associated with producing aluminum.

TABLE 10.1

Deadweight Loss of a Negative Production Externality

This table refers to the areas marked in Figure 10.3 to show how a negative externality generates a deadweight loss in the economy.

	At Q_{MARKET}	At $Q_{OPTIMUM}$	Change
Consumer surplus	A + B + C + D	D	–(A + B + C)
Producer surplus	E – (B + C + H)	A + E	A + B + C + H
Total surplus	D + A + E – H	D + A + E	H

Another way of understanding the nature of the market failure arising from an externality and determining the deadweight loss triangle is to consider the difference between the social-cost curve and the demand curve for aluminum at the equilibrium level of production, Q_{MARKET}. In Chapter 7 we saw that the height of the demand curve at a given level of demand measures the value that buyers place on the last unit of the good demanded, as measured by their willingness to pay for it. We also saw that the height of the private supply curve at a particular level of production measures the cost to the seller of producing the last unit of the good produced.

The height of the social-cost curve in the presence of a negative production externality incorporates the seller's private costs of production plus the costs imposed on others due to the negative externality. At Q_{MARKET}, the social-cost curve lies above the demand curve. This means that at Q_{MARKET} the social cost of the last unit of aluminum produced exceeds the value placed on that unit by buyers. Total surplus would therefore be higher if this unit of aluminum was not produced at all. In fact, the social cost of production exceeds the value placed on aluminum by the buyers for all units of aluminum produced in excess of $Q_{OPTIMUM}$. The loss in total surplus of producing Q_{MARKET} units of aluminum rather than $Q_{OPTIMUM}$ units is equal to the area of the triangle formed by the social-cost curve and the demand curve between $Q_{OPTIMUM}$ and Q_{MARKET}. This is the deadweight loss associated with the negative production externality.

How can the social planner achieve the socially optimal level of aluminum production and eliminate the deadweight loss associated with the externality? One way would be to tax aluminum producers for each tonne of aluminum sold. The tax would shift the supply curve for aluminum up by the size of the tax. If the tax accurately reflects the social cost of pollution, the new supply curve coincides with the social-cost curve. In the new market equilibrium, aluminum producers would produce the socially optimum quantity of aluminum.

The use of such a tax is called **internalizing the externality** because it gives buyers and sellers in the market an incentive to take into account the external effects of their actions. Aluminum producers would, in essence, take the costs of pollution into account when deciding how much aluminum to supply because the tax would make them pay for these external costs. And, because the market price would reflect the tax on producers, consumers of aluminum would have an incentive to use a smaller quantity. The policy is based on one of the ten principles of economics: People respond to incentives. Later in this chapter, we consider in more detail how policymakers can deal with externalities.

internalizing the externality
alter incentives so that people take account of the external effects of their actions

Positive Externalities

Although some activities impose costs on third parties, others yield benefits. For example, consider education. To a large extent, the benefit of education is private: The consumer of education becomes a more productive worker and thus reaps much of the benefit in the form of higher wages. Beyond these private benefits, however, education also yields positive externalities. One externality is that a more educated population leads to more informed voters, which means better government for everyone. Another externality is that a more educated population tends to mean lower crime rates. A third externality is that a more educated population may encourage the development and dissemination of technological advances, leading to higher productivity and wages for everyone. Because of these three positive externalities, a person may prefer to have neighbours who are well educated.

The analysis of positive externalities is similar to the analysis of negative externalities. As Figure 10.4 shows, the demand curve does not reflect the value to society of the good. Because the social value is greater than the private value, the social-value curve lies above the demand curve. The optimal quantity is found where the social-value curve and the supply curve (which represents costs) intersect. Hence, the socially optimal quantity is greater than the quantity determined by the private market.

Once again, the government can correct the market failure by inducing market participants to internalize the externality. The appropriate response in the case of positive externalities is exactly the opposite to the case of negative externalities. To move the market equilibrium closer to the social optimum, a positive externality requires a subsidy. In fact, that is exactly the policy the government follows: Education is heavily subsidized through public schools and government scholarships.

To summarize: *Negative externalities lead markets to produce a larger quantity than is socially desirable. Positive externalities lead markets to produce a smaller quantity than is socially desirable. To remedy the problem, the government can internalize the externality by taxing goods that have negative externalities and subsidizing goods that have positive externalities.*

FIGURE 10.4

Education and the Social Optimum

In the presence of a positive externality, the social value of the good exceeds the private value. The optimal quantity, $Q_{OPTIMUM}$, is therefore larger than the equilibrium quantity, Q_{MARKET}.

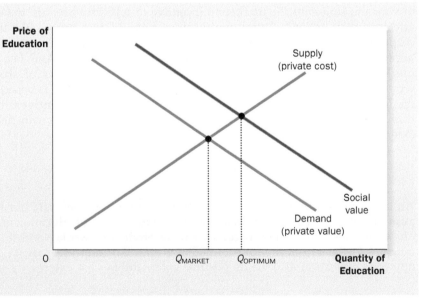

NEL

Case Study

TECHNOLOGY SPILLOVERS AND INDUSTRIAL POLICY

A potentially important type of positive externality is called a *technology spillover*—the impact of one firm's research and production efforts on other firms' access to technological advance. For example, consider the market for industrial robots. Robots are at the frontier of a rapidly changing technology. Whenever a firm builds a robot, there is some chance that the firm will discover a new and better design. This new design will benefit not only this firm but society as a whole because the design will enter society's pool of technological knowledge. That is, the new design may have positive externalities for other producers in the economy.

In this case, the government can internalize the externality by subsidizing the production of robots. If the government paid firms a subsidy for each robot produced, the supply curve would shift down by the amount of the subsidy, and this shift would increase the equilibrium quantity of robots. To ensure that the market equilibrium equals the social optimum, the subsidy should equal the value of the technology spillover.

How large are technology spillovers, and what do they imply for public policy? This is an important question, because technological progress is the key to why living standards rise over time. Yet it is also a difficult question on which economists often disagree.

Some economists believe that technology spillovers are pervasive and that the government should encourage those industries that yield the largest spillovers. For instance, these economists argue that if making computer chips yields greater spillovers than making potato chips, then the government should use the tax laws to encourage the production of more computer chips relative to potato chips. The Canadian tax code does this in a limited way by offering special tax breaks for expenditures on research and development. Some other nations go further by subsidizing specific industries that supposedly offer large technology spillovers. Government intervention in the economy that aims to promote technology-enhancing industries is sometimes called *industrial policy*.

Other economists are skeptical about industrial policy. Even if technology spillovers are common, the success of an industrial policy requires that the government be able to measure the size of the spillovers from different markets. This measurement problem is difficult at best. Moreover, without precise measurements, the political system may end up subsidizing those industries with the most political clout, rather than those that yield the largest positive externalities.

Another way to deal with technology spillovers is patent protection. The patent laws protect inventors by giving them exclusive rights to their inventions for a period of time. When a firm makes a technological breakthrough, it can patent the idea and capture much of the economic benefit for itself. The patent is said to internalize the externality by giving the firm a *property right* over its invention. If other firms want to use the new technology, they would have to obtain permission from the inventing firm and pay it some royalty. Thus, the patent system gives firms a greater incentive to engage in research and other activities that advance technology. ●

QuickQuiz   Give an example of a negative externality and a positive externality.
● Explain why market outcomes are inefficient in the presence of externalities.

PUBLIC POLICIES TOWARD EXTERNALITIES

We have discussed why externalities lead markets to allocate resources inefficiently but have mentioned only briefly how this inefficiency can be remedied. In practice, both public policymakers and private individuals respond to externalities in various ways. All of the remedies share the goal of moving the allocation of resources closer to the social optimum.

This section considers governmental solutions. As a general matter, the government can respond to externalities in one of two ways. *Command-and-control policies* regulate behaviour directly. *Market-based policies* provide incentives so that private decision makers will choose to solve the problem on their own.

Command-and-Control Policies: Regulation

The government can remedy an externality by making certain behaviours either required or forbidden. For example, it is a crime to dump poisonous chemicals into the water supply. In this case, the external costs to society far exceed the benefits to the polluter. The government therefore institutes a command-and-control policy that prohibits this act altogether.

In most cases of pollution, however, the situation is not this simple. Despite the stated goals of some environmentalists, it would be impossible to prohibit all polluting activity. For example, virtually all forms of transportation—even the horse—produce some undesirable polluting byproducts. But it would not be sensible for the government to ban all transportation. Thus, instead of trying to eradicate pollution altogether, society has to weigh the costs and benefits to decide the kinds and quantities of pollution it will allow. In Canada, environmental policy is shared among all three levels of government—federal, provincial and territorial, and municipal. At the federal level, Environment Canada is the department responsible for developing and enforcing regulations aimed at protecting the environment.

Environmental regulations can take many forms. Sometimes Environment Canada dictates a maximum level of pollution that a factory may emit. Other times Environment Canada requires that firms adopt a particular technology to reduce emissions. In all cases, to design good rules, the government regulators need to know the details about specific industries and about the alternative technologies that those industries could adopt. This information is often difficult for government regulators to obtain.

Market-Based Policy 1: Corrective Taxes and Subsidies

Instead of regulating behaviour in response to an externality, the government can use market-based policies to align private incentives with social efficiency. For instance, as we saw earlier, the government can internalize the externality by imposing taxes on activities that have negative externalities and subsidizing activities that have positive externalities. Taxes enacted to deal with the effects of negative externalities are called **corrective taxes**. They are also called *Pigovian taxes* after economist Arthur Pigou (1877–1959), an early advocate of their use. An ideal corrective tax would equal the external cost from an activity with negative externalities, and an ideal corrective subsidy would equal the external benefit from an activity with positive externalities.

For example, consider again Figure 10.3 (p. 209), which considered an externality in the aluminum market. In Figure 10.3, the corrective tax is the difference between the social-cost curve and the private-supply curve. In the diagram, this is equal to the distance between a and b, which is the difference between the social and private cost of producing an additional unit of aluminum.

Economists usually prefer corrective taxes over regulations as a way to deal with pollution because such taxes can reduce pollution at a lower cost to society. To see why, let us consider an example.

Suppose that two factories—a paper mill and a steel mill—are each dumping 500 tonnes of glop into a river each year. Environment Canada decides that it wants to reduce the amount of pollution. It considers two solutions:

1. Regulation: Environment Canada could tell each factory to reduce its pollution to 300 tonnes of glop per year.
2. Corrective tax: Environment Canada could levy a tax on each factory of $50 000 for each tonne of glop it emits.

The regulation would dictate a level of pollution, whereas the tax would give factory owners an economic incentive to reduce pollution. Which solution do you think is better?

Most economists would prefer the tax. They would first point out that a tax is just as effective as a regulation in reducing the overall level of pollution. Environment Canada can achieve whatever level of pollution it wants by setting the tax at the appropriate level. The higher the tax, the larger the reduction in pollution. Indeed, if the tax is high enough, the factories will close down altogether, reducing pollution to zero.

Although regulation and corrective taxes are both capable of reducing pollution, the tax accomplishes this goal more efficiently. The regulation requires each factory to reduce pollution by the same amount, but an equal reduction is not necessarily the least expensive way to clean up the water. It is possible that the paper mill can reduce pollution at lower cost than the steel mill. If so, the paper mill would respond to the tax by reducing pollution substantially to avoid the tax, whereas the steel mill would respond by reducing pollution less and paying the tax.

In essence, the corrective tax places a price on the right to pollute. Just as markets allocate goods to those buyers who value them most highly, a corrective tax allocates pollution to those factories that face the highest cost of reducing it. Whatever the level of pollution Environment Canada chooses, it can achieve this goal at the lowest total cost using a tax.

corrective taxes
taxes enacted to correct the effects of negative externalities

"If the gas tax was any larger, I'd take the bus."

Economists also argue that corrective taxes are better for the environment. Under the command-and-control policy of regulation, the factories have no reason to reduce emission further once they have reached the target of 300 tonnes of glop. By contrast, the tax gives the factories an incentive to develop cleaner technologies, because a cleaner technology would reduce the amount of tax the factory has to pay.

Corrective taxes are unlike most other taxes. As we discussed in Chapter 8, most taxes distort incentives and move the allocation of resources away from the social optimum. The reduction in economic well-being—that is, in consumer and producer surplus—exceeds the amount of revenue the government raises, resulting in a deadweight loss. By contrast, when externalities are present, society also cares about the well-being of the bystanders who are affected. Corrective taxes alter incentives to account for the presence of externalities and thereby move the allocation of resources closer to the social optimum. Thus, while corrective taxes raise revenue for the government, they also enhance economic efficiency.

Case Study
WHY IS GASOLINE TAXED SO HEAVILY?

In many nations, gasoline is among the most heavily taxed goods. The gas tax can be viewed as a corrective tax aimed at three negative externalities associated with driving:

1. *Congestion:* If you have ever been stuck in bumper-to-bumper traffic, you have probably wished that there were fewer cars on the road. A gasoline tax keeps congestion down by encouraging people to take public transportation, carpool more often, and live closer to work.
2. *Accidents:* Whenever a person buys a large car or a sport utility vehicle, he makes himself safer, but he puts his neighbours at risk. A person driving a typical car is much more likely to die if hit by a sport utility vehicle than if hit by another car. The gas tax is an indirect way of making people pay when their large, gas-guzzling vehicles impose risk on others, which in turn makes them take account of this risk when choosing what vehicle to purchase.
3. *Pollution:* The burning of fossil fuels such as gasoline is widely believed to be the cause of global warming. Experts disagree about how dangerous this threat is, but there is no doubt that the gas tax reduces the risk by reducing the use of gasoline.

So the gas tax, rather than causing deadweight losses like most taxes, could actually make the economy work better. It means less traffic congestion, safer roads, and a cleaner environment.

How high should the tax on gasoline be? Taxes on gasoline vary throughout the world. Most European countries impose gasoline taxes that are much higher than

NEL

those in Canada, while the United States imposes much lower taxes. A 2007 study published in the *Journal of Economic Literature* summarized the research on the size of the various externalities associated with driving. It concluded that the optimal corrective tax on gasoline was about 55 cents per litre. Gasoline taxes vary across Canada, but on average are about 35 percent of the price. At a price of 90 cents per litre, taxes are thus about 31 cents. This is lower than the optimal corrective tax of 55 cents.

The tax revenue from a higher gasoline tax could be used to lower other taxes that distort incentives and cause deadweight losses. This type of "environmental tax shift" has been advocated by many economists. In addition, some of the burdensome government regulations that require automakers to produce more fuel-efficient cars would prove unnecessary. This idea, however, has never proven politically popular. ●

Market-Based Policy 2: Tradable Pollution Permits

Returning to our example of the paper mill and the steel mill, let us suppose that, despite the advice of its economists, Environment Canada adopts the regulation and requires each factory to reduce its pollution to 300 tonnes of glop per year. Then one day, after the regulation is in place and both mills have complied, the two firms go to Environment Canada with a proposal. The steel mill wants to increase its emission of glop by 100 tonnes. The paper mill has agreed to reduce its emission by the same amount if the steel mill pays it $5 million. Should Environment Canada allow the two factories to make this deal?

From the standpoint of economic efficiency, allowing the deal is good policy. The deal must make the owners of the two factories better off because they are voluntarily agreeing to it. Moreover, the deal does not have any external effects because the total amount of pollution remains the same. Thus, social welfare is enhanced by allowing the paper mill to sell its right to pollute to the steel mill.

The same logic applies to any voluntary transfer of the right to pollute from one firm to another. If Environment Canada allows firms to make these deals, it will, in essence, have created a new scarce resource: pollution permits. A market to trade these permits will eventually develop, and that market will be governed by the forces of supply and demand. The invisible hand will ensure that this new market efficiently allocates the right to pollute. The firms that can reduce pollution only at high cost will be willing to pay the most for the pollution permits. The firms that can reduce pollution at low cost will prefer to sell whatever permits they have.

One advantage of allowing a market for pollution permits is that the initial allocation of pollution permits among firms does not matter from the standpoint of economic efficiency. Those firms that can reduce pollution most easily would be willing to sell whatever permits they get, and those firms that can reduce pollution only at high cost would be willing to buy whatever permits they need. As long as there is a free market for the pollution rights, the final allocation will be efficient whatever the initial allocation.

Although reducing pollution using pollution permits may seem quite different from using corrective taxes, in fact the two policies have much in

FIGURE 10.5

The Equivalence of Corrective Taxes and Pollution Permits

In panel (a), Environment Canada sets a price on pollution by levying a corrective tax, and the demand curve determines the quantity of pollution. In panel (b), Environment Canada limits the quantity of pollution by limiting the number of pollution permits, and the demand curve determines the price of pollution. The price and quantity of pollution are the same in the two cases.

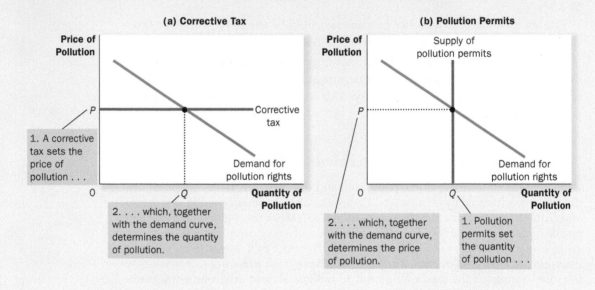

(a) Corrective Tax

Price of Pollution

P ———— Corrective tax

1. A corrective tax sets the price of pollution . . .

Demand for pollution rights

0   Q   Quantity of Pollution

2. . . . which, together with the demand curve, determines the quantity of pollution.

(b) Pollution Permits

Price of Pollution

Supply of pollution permits

P

1. Pollution permits set the quantity of pollution . . .

Demand for pollution rights

0   Q   Quantity of Pollution

2. . . . which, together with the demand curve, determines the price of pollution.

common. In both cases, firms pay for their pollution. With corrective taxes, polluting firms must pay a tax to the government. With pollution permits, polluting firms must pay to buy the permit. (Even firms that already own permits must pay to pollute: The opportunity cost of polluting is what they could have received by selling their permits on the open market.) Both corrective taxes and pollution permits internalize the externality of pollution by making it costly for firms to pollute.

The similarity of the two policies can be seen by considering the market for pollution. Both panels in Figure 10.5 show the demand curve for the right to pollute. This curve shows that the lower the price of polluting, the more firms will choose to pollute. In panel (a), Environment Canada uses a corrective tax to set a price for pollution. In this case, the supply curve for pollution rights is perfectly elastic (because firms can pollute as much as they want by paying the tax), and the position of the demand curve determines the quantity of pollution. In panel (b), Environment Canada sets a quantity of pollution by issuing pollution permits. In this case, the supply curve for pollution rights is perfectly inelastic (because the quantity of pollution is fixed by the number of permits), and the position of the demand curve determines the price of pollution. Hence, for any given demand curve for pollution, Environment Canada can achieve any point on the demand curve either by setting a price with a corrective tax or by setting a quantity with pollution permits.

In some circumstances, however, selling pollution permits may be better than levying a corrective tax. Suppose Environment Canada wants no more than 600 tonnes of glop to be dumped into the river. But, because Environment Canada does not know the demand curve for pollution, it is not sure what size tax would achieve that goal. In this case, it can simply auction off 600 pollution permits. The auction price would yield the appropriate size of the corrective tax.

The idea of the government auctioning off the right to pollute may at first sound like a figment of some economist's imagination. And, in fact, that is how the idea began. But increasingly pollution permits, like corrective taxes, are now widely viewed as a cost-effective way to keep the environment clean.

Emission permit trading systems (also known as *cap and trade*) are common throughout the world. For example, the European Union Emission Trading Scheme for greenhouse gas emissions is the largest emissions trading scheme in the world. Policy discussions on climate change policy in Canada have focused on developing a North American permit trading system.

Objections to the Economic Analysis of Pollution

Many environmentalists object to the use of pollution permits and other market-based solutions to pollution on the grounds that it is simply not right to allow someone to pollute for a fee. Clean air and clean water, they argue, are fundamental human rights that should not be debased by considering them in economic terms. How can you put a price on clean air and clean water? The environment is so important, they claim, that we should protect it as much as possible, regardless of the cost.

Economists have little sympathy with this type of argument. To economists, good environmental policy begins by acknowledging the first of the ten principles of economics in Chapter 1: People face tradeoffs. Certainly, clean air and clean water have value. But their value must be compared to their opportunity cost—that is, to what one must give up to obtain them. Eliminating all pollution is impossible. Trying to eliminate all pollution would reverse many of the techno-logical advances that allow us to enjoy a high standard of living. Few people would be willing to accept poor nutrition, inadequate medical care, or shoddy housing to make the environment as clean as possible.

Economists argue that some environmental activists hurt their own cause by not thinking in economic terms. A clean environment is a good like other goods. Like all normal goods, it has a positive income elasticity: Rich countries can afford a cleaner environment than poor ones and, therefore, usually have more rigorous environmental protection. In addition, like most other goods, clean air and water obey the law of demand: The lower the price of environmental protection, the more the public will want. The economic approach of using pollution permits and corrective taxes reduces the cost of environmental protection and should, there-fore, increase the public's demand for a clean environment.

QuickQuiz   A glue factory and a steel mill emit smoke containing a chemical that is harmful if inhaled in large amounts. Describe three ways the town government might respond to this externality. What are the pros and cons of each of your solutions?

IN THE NEWS

ECONOMIC POLICY AND CLIMATE CHANGE

In the fall of 2006, former World Bank chief economist Nicholas Stern released to the British government a long-awaited report on climate change. The following op-ed piece by a McGill University economist discusses one of the key features of the report—tradable permits.

For Efficient Carbon Reduction, Permit Me

By William Watson

Apart from being a formidable politician, Margaret Thatcher must have been a great teacher. How else do you explain that post-Thatcher Britain is such a thoroughly market-oriented place?

A case in point is Gordon Brown, the chancellor of the exchequer, currently playing Paul Martin to Tony Blair's Jean Chrétien. He's supposed to be more Old Labour than Mr. Blair, but even he is miles ahead of the most forward-thinking Canadian politicians.

The latest example is Sir Nicholas Stern's recent report on global warming, which you can find on Chancellor Brown's website. Sir Nicholas, referred to on the website as "Nick"—if New Labour likes you, they call you by your diminutive—was formerly chief economist at the World Bank. The headlines his report generated focused on how global warming could cause damage as high as 25 per cent of world GDP but could be largely controlled at a cost of just one per cent of world GDP, which looks like a pretty good deal.

Expert reaction to the report has focused on whether the 25-per-cent number is much too high (I've read a lot who say it is) and the one-per-cent number much too low (ditto). Reading these debates gives me the same queasy feeling that prompted me to drop out of university chemistry. We economists are hard-wired against definitive predictions concerning the future behaviour of fiendishly complicated "general-equilibrium" systems, be they national

PRIVATE SOLUTIONS TO EXTERNALITIES

Although externalities tend to cause markets to be inefficient, government action is not always needed to solve the problem. In some circumstances, people can develop private solutions.

The Types of Private Solutions

Sometimes, the problem of externalities is solved with moral codes and social sanctions. Consider, for instance, why most people do not litter. Although there are laws against littering, these laws are not vigorously enforced. Most people do not litter just because it is the wrong thing to do. The Golden Rule taught to most children is "Do unto others as you would have them do unto you." This moral injunction tells us to take account of how our actions affect other people. In economic terms, it tells us to internalize externalities.

economies or world ecospheres. Besides, "Nick" Stern isn't a chemist either (though Margaret Thatcher was).

What does ring true, though, is his endorsement of tradeable carbon-dioxide permits as a means of controlling carbon outputs.

How does it work? A central agency determines the ecosystem's capacity to absorb the emission you're worried about. Suppose it's one million tonnes a year. The agency issues one million one-tonne permits. For every permit you've got, you can emit one tonne of bad stuff. But you can't emit more than you've got permits for. If you do, there are heavy fines or other ways of making you co-operate.

If, on a business-as-usual basis, people want to emit more than one million tonnes, then the permits will be scarce: They'll cost something in a newly emerging market for permits (for you're allowed, even encouraged, to buy and sell them).

At that point the beautiful efficiency of the market takes over. Anyone considering emitting bad stuff will need a permit. But permits now cost money. So would-be emitters can save money by reducing their emissions. The higher the market takes the permit price, the greater the incentive to reduce.

Who will reduce and who will buy permits and carry on as before? People whose costs of cleaning up their emission acts are low can profit by cleaning up and selling their permits to those whose clean-up costs are high and who therefore need permits in order to continue on as before—though even they'll probably do some cleaning up, too.

What's lovely about this system is that, except for the policing and the initial decision about how many permits to issue, governments don't have to inform themselves about who has the easiest clean-ups. It all happens automatically.

If a permit system goes worldwide, which countries will clean up most? Those whose clean-up costs are lowest. The Stern Report suggests that in many cases they will be developing countries.

They'll sell their permits to developed countries that, because of their industrial make-up or because they've already done all the easy cleaning up, face high costs for further clean-ups.

Here's where ideological objections intrude. Though a permit system would get the world to the right overall amount of emissions it might well involve rich countries buying permits from poor countries in order to continue emissions. The poor countries would get the rich countries' money in return, but those who see clean-up as a quasi-religious obligation consider letting people "buy the right to pollute" a sort of eighth deadly sin.

The British, even British Labourites, have got over such concerns. Canadians still seem a long way from understanding, let alone buying into a tradeable permit system. If only one of our political leaders were a bull-headed chemist.

Source: William Watson, "For Efficient Carbon Reduction, Permit Me." Reprinted with the permission of the author.

Another private solution to externalities is charities, many of which are established to deal with externalities. For example, Greenpeace, whose goal is to protect the environment, is a nonprofit organization funded with private donations. As another example, colleges and universities receive gifts from alumni, corporations, and foundations in part because education has positive externalities for society. The government encourages this private solution to externalities through the tax system by allowing an income tax deduction for charitable donations.

The private market can often solve the problem of externalities by relying on the self-interest of the relevant parties. Sometimes the solution takes the form of integrating different types of businesses. For example, consider an apple grower and a beekeeper who are located next to each other. Each business confers a positive externality on the other: By pollinating the flowers on the trees, the bees help the orchard produce apples. At the same time, the bees use the nectar they get from the apple trees to produce honey. Nonetheless, when the apple grower is deciding how many trees to plant and the beekeeper is deciding how many bees to keep, they neglect the positive externality. As a result, the apple grower plants too few trees and the beekeeper keeps too few bees. These externalities could be internalized if the beekeeper bought the apple orchard or if the apple grower bought the beehives: Both activities would then take place within the same firm, and this single firm could choose the optimal number of trees and bees. Internalizing externalities is one reason that some firms are involved in more than one type of business.

Another way for the private market to deal with external effects is for the interested parties to enter into a contract. In the forgoing example, a contract between the apple grower and the beekeeper can solve the problem of too few trees and too few bees. The contract can specify the number of trees, the number of bees, and perhaps a payment from one party to the other. By setting the right number of trees and bees, the contract can solve the inefficiency that normally arises from these externalities and make both parties better off.

The Coase Theorem

Coase theorem
the proposition that if private parties can bargain without cost over the allocation of resources, they can solve the problem of externalities on their own

How effective is the private market in dealing with externalities? A famous result, called the **Coase theorem** after economist Ronald Coase, suggests that it can be very effective in some circumstances. According to the Coase theorem, if private parties can bargain without cost over the allocation of resources, then the private market will always solve the problem of externalities and allocate resources efficiently.

To see how the Coase theorem works, consider an example. Suppose that Dick owns a dog named Spot. Spot barks and disturbs Jane, Dick's neighbour. Dick gets a benefit from owning the dog, but the dog confers a negative externality on Jane. Should Dick be forced to send Spot to the pound, or should Jane have to suffer sleepless nights because of Spot's barking?

Consider first what outcome is socially efficient. A social planner, considering the two alternatives, would compare the benefit that Dick gets from the dog to the cost that Jane bears from the barking. If the benefit exceeds the cost, it is efficient for Dick to keep the dog and for Jane to live with the barking. Yet if the cost exceeds the benefit, then Dick should get rid of the dog.

According to the Coase theorem, the private market will reach the efficient outcome on its own. How? Jane can simply offer to pay Dick to get rid of the dog. Dick will accept the deal if the amount of money Jane offers is greater than the benefit of keeping the dog.

By bargaining over the price, Dick and Jane can always reach the efficient outcome. For instance, suppose that Dick gets a $500 benefit from the dog and Jane bears an $800 cost from the barking. In this case, Jane can offer Dick $600 to get rid of the dog, and Dick will gladly accept. Both parties are better off than they were before, and the efficient outcome is reached.

It is possible, of course, that Jane would not be willing to offer any price that Dick would accept. For instance, suppose that Dick gets a $1000 benefit from the dog and Jane bears an $800 cost from the barking. In this case, Dick would turn down any offer below $1000, while Jane would not offer any amount above $800. Therefore, Dick ends up keeping the dog. Given these costs and benefits, however, this outcome is efficient.

So far, we have assumed that Dick has the legal right to keep a barking dog. In other words, we have assumed that Dick can keep Spot unless Jane pays him enough to induce him to give up the dog voluntarily. How different would the outcome be, on the other hand, if Jane had the legal right to peace and quiet?

According to the Coase theorem, the initial distribution of rights does not matter for the market's ability to reach the efficient outcome. For instance, suppose that Jane can legally compel Dick to get rid of the dog. Although having this right works to Jane's advantage, it probably will not change the outcome. In this case, Dick can offer to pay Jane to allow him to keep the dog. If the benefit of the dog to Dick exceeds the cost of the barking to Jane, then Dick and Jane will strike a bargain in which Dick keeps the dog.

Although Dick and Jane can reach the efficient outcome regardless of how rights are initially distributed, the distribution of rights is not irrelevant: It determines the distribution of economic well-being. Whether Dick has the right to a barking dog or Jane the right to peace and quiet determines who pays whom in the final bargain. But, in either case, the two parties can bargain with each other and solve the externality problem. Dick will end up keeping the dog only if the benefit exceeds the cost.

To sum up: *The Coase theorem says that private economic actors can solve the problem of externalities among themselves. Whatever the initial distribution of rights, the interested parties can always reach a bargain in which everyone is better off and the outcome is efficient.*

Why Private Solutions Do Not Always Work

Despite the appealing logic of the Coase theorem, private actors on their own often fail to resolve the problems caused by externalities. The Coase theorem applies only when the interested parties have no trouble reaching and enforcing an agreement. In the real world, however, bargaining does not always work, even when a mutually beneficial agreement is possible.

Sometimes the interested parties fail to solve an externality problem because of **transaction costs,** the costs that parties incur in the process of agreeing to and following through on a bargain. In our example, imagine that Dick and Jane speak different languages so that, to reach an agreement, they will need to hire a translator. If the benefit of solving the barking problem is less than the cost of the translator, Dick and Jane might choose to leave the problem unsolved. In more realistic examples, the transaction costs are the expenses not of translators but of the lawyers required to draft and enforce contracts.

At other times, bargaining simply breaks down. The recurrence of wars and labour strikes shows that reaching agreement can be difficult and that failing to reach agreement can be costly. The problem is often that each party tries to hold out for a better deal. For example, suppose that Dick gets a $500 benefit from the dog, and Jane bears an $800 cost from the barking. Although it is efficient for Jane to pay Dick to get rid of the dog, there are many prices that could lead to this outcome. Dick might demand $750, and Jane might offer only $550. As they haggle over the price, the inefficient outcome with the barking dog persists.

Reaching an efficient bargain is especially difficult when the number of interested parties is large because coordinating everyone is costly. For example, consider a factory that pollutes the water of a nearby lake. The pollution confers a negative externality on the local fishermen. According to the Coase theorem, if the pollution is inefficient, then the factory and the fishermen could reach a bargain in which the fishermen pay the factory not to pollute. If there are many fishermen, however, trying to coordinate them all to bargain with the factory may be almost impossible.

transaction costs
the costs that parties incur in the process of agreeing and following through on a bargain

When private bargaining does not work, the government can sometimes play a role. The government is an institution designed for collective action. In this example, the government can act on behalf of the fishermen, even when it is impractical for the fishermen to act for themselves. In the next section, we examine how the government can try to remedy the problem of externalities.

QuickQuiz Give an example of a private solution to an externality. • What is the Coase theorem? • Why are private economic actors sometimes unable to solve the problems caused by an externality?

CONCLUSION

The invisible hand is powerful but not omnipotent. A market's equilibrium maximizes the sum of producer and consumer surplus. When the buyers and sellers in the market are the only interested parties, this outcome is efficient from the standpoint of society as a whole. But when there are external effects, such as pollution, evaluating a market outcome requires taking into account the well-being of third parties as well. In this case, the invisible hand of the marketplace may fail to allocate resources efficiently.

In some cases, people can solve the problem of externalities on their own. The Coase theorem suggests that the interested parties can bargain among themselves and agree on an efficient solution. Sometimes, however, an efficient outcome cannot be reached, perhaps because the large number of interested parties makes bargaining difficult.

When people cannot solve the problem of externalities privately, the government often steps in. Yet, even now, society should not abandon market forces entirely. Rather, the government can address the problem by requiring decision makers to bear the full costs of their actions. Corrective taxes on emissions and pollution permits, for instance, are designed to internalize the externality of pollution. More and more, they are the policy of choice for those interested in protecting the environment. Market forces, properly redirected, are often the best remedy for market failure.

SUMMARY

- When a transaction between a buyer and seller directly affects a third party, the effect is called an *externality*. Negative externalities, such as pollution, cause the socially optimal quantity in a market to be less than the equilibrium quantity. Positive externalities, such as technology spillovers, cause the socially optimal quantity to be greater than the equilibrium quantity.

- Governments pursue various policies to remedy the inefficiencies caused by externalities. Sometimes the government prevents socially inefficient activity by regulating behaviour. Other

times it internalizes an externality using corrective taxes. Another public policy is to issue permits. For instance, the government could protect the environment by issuing a limited number of pollution permits. The end result of this policy is largely the same as imposing corrective taxes on polluters.

- Those affected by externalities can sometimes solve the problem privately. For instance, when one business confers an externality on another business, the two businesses can internalize the externality by merging. Alternatively, the interested parties can solve the problem by negotiating a contract. According to the Coase theorem, if people can bargain without cost, then they can always reach an agreement in which resources are allocated efficiently. In many cases, however, reaching a bargain among the many interested parties is difficult, so the Coase theorem does not apply.

KEY CONCEPTS

externality, p. 206
internalizing the externality, p. 211

corrective taxes, p. 215
Coase theorem, p. 222

transaction costs, p. 223

QUESTIONS FOR REVIEW

1. Give an example of a negative externality and an example of a positive externality.

2. Draw a supply-and-demand diagram to explain the effect of a negative externality in production.

3. In what way does the patent system help society solve an externality problem?

4. List some of the ways that the problems caused by externalities can be solved without government intervention.

5. Imagine that you are a nonsmoker sharing a room with a smoker. According to the Coase theorem, what determines whether your roommate smokes in the room? Is this outcome efficient? How do you and your roommate reach this solution?

6. What are corrective taxes? Why do economists prefer them over regulations as a way to protect the environment from pollution?

PROBLEMS AND APPLICATIONS

1. There are two ways to protect your car from theft. The Club makes it difficult for a car thief to take your car. LoJack makes it easier for the police to catch a car thief. Which of these types of protection conveys a negative externality on other car owners? Which conveys a positive externality? Do you think there are any policy implications of your analysis?

2. Do you agree with the following statements? Why or why not?
   a. "The benefits of corrective taxes as a way to reduce pollution have to be weighed against the deadweight losses that these taxes cause."
   b. "When deciding whether to levy a corrective tax on consumers or producers, the government should be careful to levy the tax on the side of the market generating the externality."

3. Consider the market for fire extinguishers.
   a. Why might fire extinguishers exhibit positive externalities?
   b. Draw a graph of the market for fire extinguishers, labelling the demand curve, the social-value curve, the supply curve, and the social-cost curve.
   c. Indicate the market equilibrium level of output and the efficient level of output. Give an intuitive explanation for why these quantities differ.
   d. If the external benefit is $10 per extinguisher, describe a government policy that would result in the efficient outcome.

4. Ringo loves playing rock-and-roll music at high volume. Luciano loves opera and hates rock and roll. Unfortunately, they are next-door

neighbours in an apartment building with paper-thin walls.

a. What is the externality here?

b. What command-and-control policy might the landlord impose? Could such a policy lead to an inefficient outcome?

c. Suppose the landlord lets the tenants do whatever they want. According to the Coase theorem, how might Ringo and Luciano reach an efficient outcome on their own? What might prevent them from reaching an efficient outcome?

5. It is rumoured that the Swiss government subsidizes cattle farming, and that the subsidy is larger in areas with more tourist attractions. Can you think of a reason why this policy might be efficient?

6. Greater consumption of alcohol leads to more motor vehicle accidents and, thus, imposes costs on people who do not drink and drive.

a. Illustrate the market for alcohol, labelling the demand curve, the social-value curve, the supply curve, the social-cost curve, the market equilibrium level of output, and the efficient level of output.

b. On your graph, shade the area corresponding to the deadweight loss of the market equilibrium. (Hint: The deadweight loss occurs because some units of alcohol are consumed for which the social cost exceeds the social value.) Explain.

7. Many observers believe that the levels of pollution in our society are too high.

a. If society wishes to reduce overall pollution by a certain amount, why is it efficient to have different amounts of reduction at different firms?

b. Command-and-control approaches often rely on uniform reductions among firms. Why are these approaches generally unable to target the firms that should undertake larger reductions?

c. Economists argue that appropriate corrective taxes or tradable pollution rights will result in efficient pollution reduction. How do these approaches target the firms that should undertake larger reductions?

8. The Pristine River has two polluting firms on its banks. Acme Industrial and Creative Chemicals each dump 100 tonnes of glop into the river each year. The cost of reducing glop emissions per tonne equals $10 for Acme and $100 for Creative. The local government wants to reduce overall pollution from 200 tonnes to 50 tonnes.

a. If the government knew the cost of reduction for each firm, what reductions would it impose to reach its overall goal? What would be the cost to each firm and the total cost to the firms together?

b. In a more typical situation, the government would not know the cost of pollution reduction at each firm. If the government decided to reach its overall goal by imposing uniform reductions on the firms, calculate the reduction made by each firm, the cost to each firm, and the total cost to the firms together.

c. Compare the total cost of pollution reduction in parts (a) and (b). If the government does not know the cost of reduction for each firm, is there still some way for it to reduce pollution to 50 tonnes at the total cost you calculated in part (a)? Explain.

9. Figure 10.5 (p. 218) shows that for any given demand curve for the right to pollute, the government can achieve the same outcome either by setting a price with a corrective tax or by setting a quantity with pollution permits. Suppose there is a sharp improvement in the technology for controlling pollution.

a. Using graphs similar to those in Figure 10.5, illustrate the effect of this development on the demand for pollution rights.

b. What is the effect on the price and quantity of pollution under each regulatory system? Explain.

10. Suppose that the government decides to issue tradable permits for a certain form of pollution.

a. Does it matter for economic efficiency whether the government distributes or auctions the permits? Does it matter in any other ways?

b. If the government chooses to distribute the permits, does the allocation of permits among firms matter for efficiency? Does it matter in any other ways?

11. A local drama company proposes a new neighbourhood theatre in Vancouver. Before approving the permit, the city planner completes a study of the theatre's impact on the surrounding community.

a. One finding of the study is that theatres attract traffic, which adversely affects the community. The city planner estimates that the cost to the community from the extra traffic is $5 per ticket. What kind of an externality is this? Why?

b. Graph the market for theatre tickets, labelling the demand curve, the social-value curve, the supply curve, the social-cost curve, the market equilibrium level of output, and the efficient level of output. Also show the per-unit amount of the externality.

c. On further review, the city planner uncovers a second externality. Rehearsals for the plays tend to run until late at night, with actors, stagehands, and other theatre members coming and going at various hours. The planner has found that the increased foot traffic improves the safety of the surrounding streets, an estimated benefit to the community of $2 per ticket. What kind of externality is this? Why?

d. On a new graph, illustrate the market for theatre tickets in the case of these two externalities. Again, label the demand curve, the social-value curve, the supply curve, the social-cost curve, the market equilibrium level of output, the efficient level of output, and the per-unit amount of both externalities.

e. Describe a government policy that would result in an efficient outcome.

12. There are three industrial firms in Happy Valley.

Firm	Initial Pollution Level	Cost of Reducing Pollution by 1 Unit
A	70 units	$20
B	80	25
C	50	10

The government wants to reduce pollution to 120 units, so it gives each firm 40 tradable pollution permits.

a. Who sells permits and how many do they sell? Who buys permits and how many do they buy? Briefly explain why the sellers and buyers are each willing to do so. What is the total cost of pollution reduction in this situation?

b. How much higher would the costs of pollution reduction be if the permits could not be traded?

13. The market for a particular chemical, called Negext, is described by the following equations. Demand is given by

$$Q^D = 100 - 5P$$

Supply is given by

$$Q^S = 5P$$

where Q is measured as units of Negext and P is price in dollars per unit.

a. Find the equilibrium price and quantity. Compute consumer surplus, producer surplus, and total surplus in the market equilibrium.

b. For each unit of Negext produced, 4 units of pollution are emitted, and each unit of pollution imposes a cost on society of $1. Compute the total cost of pollution when the market for Negext is in equilibrium. What is total surplus from this market after taking into account the cost of pollution?

c. Would banning Negext increase or decrease welfare? Why?

d. Suppose that the government restricts emissions to 100 units of pollution. Graph the Negext market under this constraint. Find the new equilibrium price and quantity and show them on your graph. Compute how this policy affects consumer surplus, producer surplus, and the cost of pollution. Would you recommend this policy? Why?

e. Suppose that instead of restricting pollution, the government imposes a tax on producers equal to $4 for each unit of chemical produced.

Calculate the new equilibrium price and quantity, as well as consumer surplus, producer surplus, tax revenue, and the cost of pollution. What is total surplus now? Would you recommend this policy? Why?

f. New research finds the social cost of pollution is really higher than $1. How would that change the optimal policy response? Is there some cost of pollution that would make it sensible to ban Negext? If so, what is it?

http://   For more study tools, please visit http://www.mankiw5e.nelson.com.

CHAPTER 10 Externalities

I. Chapter Overview

A. Context and Purpose

Markets do many things well, but they do not do everything well; at times markets fail. This chapter considers the situation in which the market does not perform efficiently—when decision makers do not bear all of the costs or realize all of the benefits of their actions. The chapter also looks at the role of government in correcting such market imperfections.

B. Helpful Hints

1. *Externality* refers to a positive or negative effect on a third party as a result of a transaction between a buyer and a seller.

2. *Internalizing an externality* means altering incentives (through a tax or other market-based schemes or regulations) so that people take account of the external effects of their actions.

3. *Transactions costs* refer to the costs of negotiating and implementing an agreement between buyers and sellers.

4. The *Coase theorem* states that for any initial distribution of property rights, if transactions costs are relatively small, the affected parties can negotiate to internalize the externality and reach a bargain that will make everyone better off.

5. *Corrective* or *Pigovian taxes* are taxes set equal to the external cost of pollution in order to internalize the negative externality.

6. *You really can have too much of a good thing.* We live life at the margin, so even if people put a high value on a clean environment, at some point they are likely to decide that a little more cleanup costs more than it is worth (at the margin). Suppose that Canadians choose to clean up 99% of the air pollution that results from producing paper. Even though Canadians put a high value on a clean environment, they may choose to leave the remaining 1% if it is discovered that eliminating the last 1% of air pollution will cost as much to clean up as the first 99% did. That is, the marginal cost exceeds the marginal benefit for the final 1%.

131

7.   *It is difficult to identify the most efficient level of environmental cleanup because many of the benefits are hard to measure.* For example, how much value is put on a life saved through pollution control? The typical reaction is that each life has an infinite value, but people do not behave that way. Rational people take risks with their lives every day as they drive cars, eat, work, and play. The economic value of a human life is difficult to measure, but it is nevertheless a real factor to consider in evaluating environmental cleanup or other government programs.

II. Self-Testing Challenges

A. True/False Questions

_____1.   Because buyers and sellers neglect the external effects of their actions when deciding how much to demand or supply, the market equilibrium is not efficient.

_____2.   Tradeable pollution permits have the same effects on output and the level of pollution as a Pigovian tax on polluters.

_____3.   "Do unto others as you would have them do unto you," tells people to internalize externalities.

_____4.   A corrective or Pigovian tax reduces economic efficiency by distorting taxpayer behaviour.

_____5.   A disadvantage of market-based policies designed to clean up the environment is that they treat the environment as if it were a commodity rather than a priceless resource.

_____6.   If studded snow tires do an estimated $10 damage to the highways per vehicle each year, then the most efficient outcome for society would be to ban the use of studded snow tires.

_____7.   According to the Coase theorem, negative externalities require government action because the market fails to take into account external social costs.

_____8.   When correcting for a negative externality, command-and-control policies are preferable because they are more efficient.

_____9.   Patent protection internalizes technology spillovers by giving the inventors property rights over their inventions.

_____10.   Positive externalities lead markets to produce a smaller quantity than is socially desirable and to charge a price that is too low to be optimal.

B.   Multiple-Choice Questions

1.   Which one of the following describes when private solutions to negative externalities are **LEAST** likely to be effective?
     a.   when the costs of pollution are high
     b.   when the costs of pollution cleanup are high
     c.   when property rights are clearly assigned to one party
     d.   when transactions costs are high

2.   Pulp and paper mills not only produce paper but they also create dioxin, a byproduct of the manufacturing process. Therefore, which one of the following can be said about this market?
     a.   equilibrium price and equilibrium output are too high to be socially desirable
     b.   equilibrium price and equilibrium output are too low to be socially desirable
     c.   equilibrium price is too low and equilibrium output is too high to be socially desirable
     d.   equilibrium price is too high and equilibrium output is too low to be socially desirable

3.   A market economy has a tendency to _____ goods with positive externality and _____ goods with negative externality.
     a.   overproduce, underconsume
     b.   overproduce, underproduce
     c.   underproduce, overproduce

4.   Which of the following is supported by the Coase theorem?
     a.   The market can internalize external costs and benefits, and achieve efficiency, if private parties can negotiate solutions to the externalities.
     b.   Government can improve upon the operation of the market by using environmental controls.
     c.   The market can internalize externalities if all parties involved have roughly equal bargaining power.
     d.   Correcting externalities through the market can work, but only if the innocent third parties have clearly established and enforceable property rights.

5.   Which one of the following is **NOT** a plausible example of market failure due to externalities?
     a.   a beekeeper who benefits from being next to an apple orchard
     b.   the high salaries of professional hockey players
     c.   long traffic jams every day on Whitemud Drive in Edmonton
     d.   the production of a lighthouse

6.   Which one of the following negative externalities would be a target for correction by a gasoline tax, which is a waste tax?
    a.   construction
    b.   accidents
    c.   pollution
    d.   pedestrian safety

7.   Relative to market-based pollution control policies, which one of the following statements can be made about direct regulation?
    a.   requires less detailed information to set the pollution limits
    b.   provides more of an incentive to develop better technology to clean up beyond the minimum
    c.   allows polluters to pollute at no charge, up to the limits set by the government
    d.   makes it easier to fine-tune regulations for different situations

8.   Which one of the following is the essential problem with the existence of externalities?
    a.   a discrepancy between private and social cost
    b.   a discrepancy between private benefit and social cost
    c.   a discrepancy between private cost and social benefit
    d.   government failure

9.   Many goods with negative externalities are overproduced, relative to the socially optimal level. Which one of the following is this an example of?
    a.   market failure
    b.   government failure
    c.   producer failure

10.   Which one of the following is an example of internalizing an externality?
    a.   The municipal government offers subsidies to homeowners to offset the cost of beautifying their front yards.
    b.   A restaurant no longer serves imported wine, having decided to offer only domestic wine.
    c.   A beekeeper buys extra hives to expand the business.

11.   Which of the following describes when a deadweight loss from pollution cleanup occurs?
    a.   whenever pollution cleanup imposes costs on society
    b.   whenever society puts a price tag on pollution, thus providing a "licence to pollute"
    c.   when government gets involved
    d.   whenever some units of pollution cleanup cost more than their marginal benefit to society

12. Suppose the last unit of output produced at a paper mill has a value to society of $10 and a social cost of $15, but the private cost to the company is $10, and the current price is $10. Which one of the following is true?
    a. Market is in equilibrium, but a lower output would make society better off.
    b. Market is in equilibrium, but a higher output would make society better off.
    c. Output is too low, and price is too high, for equilibrium.
    d. Output is too high, and price is too low, for equilibrium.

13. In the presence of technology spillovers, the market tends to _____ and _____ the product relative to society's best interest.
    a. overproduce, underprice
    b. overproduce, overprice
    c. underproduce, underprice
    d. underproduce, overprice

14. Which one of the following is an example of a private solution to the problem of externalities?
    a. Greenpeace Canada
    b. Canadian National Parks
    c. Canada Post
    d. Natural Resources Canada

15. Which one of the following would be achieved by the **MOST** efficient pollution control system?
    a. It would ensure that each polluter cleans up to the point where total social benefits are maximized.
    b. It would ensure that each polluter cleans up just to the point where that the polluter's last unit of cleanup has a social value exactly equal to its social cost.
    c. It would ensure that each polluter meets exactly the same pollution standards as all the other polluters.
    d. It would ensure that each polluter cleans up to the maximum level that is technically feasible.

16. Heavy trucks travelling on the Trans-Canada Highway cause noise pollution in nearby neighbourhoods. Which one of the following is an efficient policy to deal with this?
    a. Rely on the "invisible hand" to take care of the problem.
    b. Provide a subsidy to each trucking company, depending on the total amount of noise its trucks create in the affected neighbourhoods.
    c. Impose a tax on each trucking company, depending on the total amount of noise its trucks create in the affected neighbourhoods.
    d. Subsidize trucking companies that install noise-abatement devices.

17. Which one of the following is an important question to address in defining an anti-pollution policy?
    a. How do we reduce pollution to the appropriate level?
    b. How do we eliminate pollution?
    c. How do we learn to live with pollution, rather than worry about its growth?
    d. How do we design a policy, not to be used today, but instead when it is needed later in the decade?

18. Which one of the following outcomes is supported by the Coase theorem when transaction costs are low and property rights exist?
    a. deadweight losses result due to positive externalities
    b. deadweight losses result due to negative externalities
    c. private transactions cannot be efficient
    d. private transactions are efficient

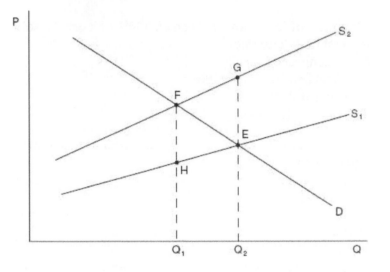

Refer to the above figure to answer questions 19 and 20. In the above figure, D represents the demand curve; S_1 represents the supply curve and indicates private marginal cost at each level of output, and S_2 indicates the marginal cost to society at each level of output when the marginal external cost of the pollution created by the production of this good is taken into account.

19. Which one of the following is demonstrated in the above figure?
    a. A competitive industry will produce Q_2 units of this good, and the efficiency loss to society is given by area EFH.
    b. A competitive industry will produce Q_2 units of this good, and the efficiency loss to society is given by area EFG.
    c. A competitive industry will produce Q_2 units of this good, and the efficiency loss to society is given by area EHFG.

20.   Given the conditions described by the above figure, which one of the following is the appropriate government policy to pursue?
a.   Levy a tax on this good equal to FH per unit.
b.   Levy a tax on this good equal to EG per unit.
c.   Levy a tax on this good equal to FG per unit.

C.   **Short-Answer Questions**

1.   According to the Coase theorem, the market can often solve problems of negative externalities on its own.

a.   What conditions must hold for the market solution to work?

_____
_____
_____

b.   When the private parties involved can negotiate a solution to a negative externality, does it matter for economic efficiency who pays whom? For example, if the problem is water pollution, does it matter whether the polluter is penalized for polluting or the victim subsidizes the polluter for not polluting? Or, if government is involved, will a pollution tax have a different effect than a subsidy to polluters to not pollute? Include an explanation of how such different assignments of property rights to the environment affect the opportunity cost to the polluter of continuing to pollute.

_____
_____
_____
_____
_____

2.   Reducing pollution using pollution permits is quite different from using Pigovian taxes. Would an economist agree? Why or why not?

_____
_____
_____
_____

3.   Because positive externalities harm no one, there is no need for government intervention. Would an economist agree? Explain.

_____
_____
_____
_____

4. Critics argue that carbon credits look like a good idea at first glance, but there are several reasons why they are not likely to work. (1) It would be very difficult to decide who should get them because some firms with older factories may not be able to clean up as much as newer firms. (2) Credits would give firms a licence to pollute, thus putting a dollar value on a priceless resource. (3) Some firms might make money by selling their credits rather than using them themselves. How would an economist respond? Are these criticisms valid for explaining why such a system would not be efficient for society?_____

_____

_____

_____

_____

_____

_____

_____

D.   Practice Problems

An economics consultant has been hired by the city of Sydney, Nova Scotia. The city is faced with a massive cleanup bill for benzopyrene, which has been found in the town's drinking water. A local manufacturer dumped solvents into a pit on its property for a number of years because it cost the firm less than proper disposal. The firm has gone out of business, leaving contamination with an estimated cleanup cost of $6.5 million. The Nova Scotia Department of Environment (NSDOE) has presented the following options: (a) do nothing—live with the problem or move out; (b) boil water for drinking and otherwise avoid contact with water; (c) drill new water wells and cap the old, contaminated wells; or (d) find the source of contamination and clean it up completely. The following table shows estimated costs and benefits of each cleanup option. The cost is the cost of cleanup, not the cost of pollution itself. The benefit is the reduction in the damage due to the contamination. Note that the maximum potential benefit is $6.5 million, which represents total elimination of the damage from benzopyrene. Fill in the missing blanks.

NSDOE Cleanup Options for Sydney, Nova Scotia

Option	Total cost (millions)	Total benefit (millions)	Marginal cost (millions)	Marginal benefit (millions)	Net benefit (millions)
a. Do nothing	0	0	$____	$____	$____
b. Boil water	$1	$4	$____	$____	$____
c. Drill new wells	$2	$5.5	$____	$____	$____
d. Complete cleanup	$5	$6.5	$____	$____	$____

Note: All benefits and costs are social rather than private. Specifically: marginal cost = the marginal cost to society of one additional level of cleanup; marginal benefit = the marginal benefit to society (social value) of one additional level of cleanup; and net benefit = total benefit − total cost (to society). Total benefit is the reduction in pollution damage, up to the point of complete elimination of the $6.5 million in damage from benzopyrene contamination.

1.   Based on these numbers, what level of cleanup should the economics consultant recommend and why?

_____

_____

_____

2.   How might an economics consultant interpret the total benefit column? That is, what kinds of benefits would be included here? What kinds of problems would be anticipated in measuring the benefits of such an environmental cleanup project?

_____

_____

_____

_____

_____

3.   What would be the dollar value of the deadweight loss from total cleanup (option d)? Why would total cleanup result in a deadweight loss to society even though the people would like to have a clean environment?

_____

_____

_____

_____

4.   If total cleanup (option d) were the only alternative to doing nothing (option a), would the economics consultant recommend it? Explain why or why not. _____

_____

_____

_____

5.   The economics consultant has just discovered that the polluter could have disposed of the solvent properly for $1 million, and thus would have avoided all contamination of the water supply.

    a.   Why did the market not take care of the problem before the contamination occurred? Would that not have been more efficient?

_____

_____

b. What conditions would have been required to achieve a market solution so that the victims and the polluters could have avoided this problem? _____

_____

_____

_____

c. Would the contamination have occurred if the polluter had also owned the Sydney Water Company? Why or why not? _____

_____

_____

_____

E. Advanced Critical Thinking

The Optimal Level of Crime Prevention: How Many Robberies Are Too Many?

A public official recently argued that society's goal should be to eliminate crime that society should not stop until there is not a single occurrence of a robbery or murder. His assertion is that even one robbery is one too many. Even if society has enough resources to make it feasible to eliminate crime, would it make sense? Or is this bad economics? Is it possible to make an analogy with pollution control? Write a short essay explaining what is wrong with this way of thinking.

_____
_____
_____
_____
_____
_____
_____
_____
_____
_____
_____
_____

In order to answer these and other questions, consider the hypothetical case study of the small town of Dry Coulee, Manitoba. The number of robberies has increased over the past decade, and the town council is under pressure from the voting public to clean up crime. The town has hired a consultant to estimate the economic effects of forming a professional police department instead of relying on a volunteer who works part-time when he is not working at his regular job as a clerk at the local hardware store. The council has just received the consultant's report and must decide how many police officers to hire.

According to the consultant, the projected social cost of crime without any police protection at all is $200 000 per year. This includes explicit costs such as property loss, medical costs, and lost earnings due to injuries, as well as intangible costs such as loss of peace of mind or reduced quality of life due to the higher crime rate. The benefit from each additional police officer hired is the estimated reduction in the total social cost of crime in the village; therefore, the maximum possible benefit from crime prevention is $200 000, which represents the total elimination of crime (and its social costs) in the village. The consultant has found that the village can hire police officers at an annual cost of $30 000 each, including salary and fringe benefits.

The consultant's estimates of costs and benefits follow. Fill in the missing numbers and answer the questions that follow. The first line is already filled in.

Consultant's Report: Annual Costs and Benefits of Various Levels of Police Protection for Dry Coulee, Manitoba

Number of police officers	Total social cost	Marginal social cost	Total social benefit	Marginal social benefit	Net social benefit
0	$0	$ —	$0	$ —	$0
1	$30 000	$____	$30 000	$____	$____
2	$60 000	$____	$70 000	$____	$____
3	$90 000	$____	$105 000	$____	$____
4	$120 000	$____	$134 000	$____	$____
5	$150 000	$____	$160 000	$____	$____
6	$180 000	$____	$180 000	$____	$____
7	$210 000	$____	$190 000	$____	$____
8	$240 000	$____	$196 000	$____	$____
9	$270 000	$____	$200 000	$____	$____
10	$300 000	$____	$200 000	$____	$____

1. Some people argue that the town should hire enough police officers to eliminate crime. Based on the consultant's report, how should the town respond? How many police officers should the town hire and why?

2. Plot marginal social cost (MSC) and marginal social benefit (MSB) on the graph below, and label the socially optimal amount of crime prevention. Plot the total cost (TC) and total benefit (TB) on the graph on the next page, and identify the point that maximizes net benefit (TB – TC). (This point should coincide with your answer to question 1.)

Marginal Social Cost (MSC) and Marginal Social Benefit (MSB) of Crime Prevention

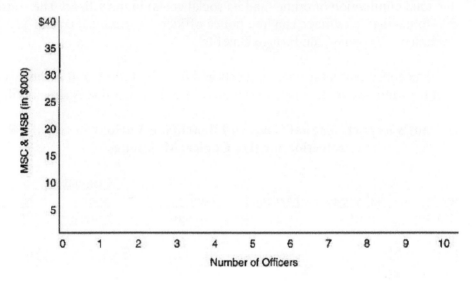

Total Cost (TC), Total Benefits (TB), and Net Benefits (TB–TC) of Crime Prevention

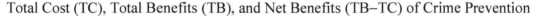

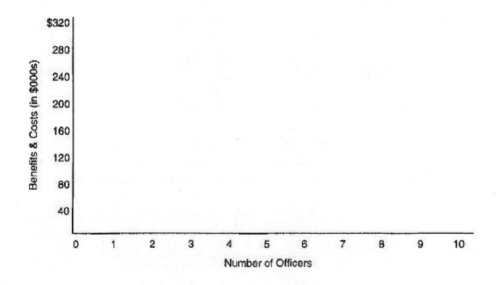

III. Solutions

A. True/False Questions

1. T
2. T
3. T
4. F; it improves efficiency by eliminating a distortion of behaviour caused by not pricing a scarce resource.
5. F; an advantage of market-based policies is that they put a price on a scarce resource that had previously been treated as a free good.
6. F; even if the studded snow tires do $10 in damage to the highways, it is efficient to use them if their benefit exceeds their cost, including the $10 in external cost to society. A $10 tax would let the market determine whether or not they were worth their full cost to society.
7. F; according to the Coase theorem, the market may be able to internalize externalities when negotiating costs are not excessive.
8. F; market-based policies such as a corrective tax or a Pigovian tax internalize an externality more efficiently.
9. T
10. T

B. Multiple-Choice Questions

1. d	5. b	9. a	13. d	17. a
2. c	6. c	10. a	14. a	18. d
3. c	7. c	11. d	15. b	19. b
4. a	8. a	12. a	16. c	20. a

C. Short-Answer Questions

1. a. The affected parties must be able to negotiate a settlement. For this to happen, the transactions costs must be low enough to make it worthwhile. As a result, the market is more likely to work efficiently when the affected population is small. With a large population, it is difficult to identify everyone and work out a settlement.

   b. According to the Coase theorem, if the affected parties can negotiate a solution to an externality, the result will be the same improvement in economic efficiency regardless of who pays whom. If the victims of pollution own the property rights to the environment, they can charge the polluter for using their scarce resource. If the polluter owns the rights, the victims can subsidize the polluter in order to cut back on pollution. Either way, the polluter will internalize the pollution cost. Losing a subsidy has the same opportunity cost as paying an equivalent pollution charge.

2. Disagree, because the two policies have much in common. In both cases, polluting firms pay for the pollution they generate. In the case of pollution permits, firms must pay to buy the permit. Even for those firms that already own permits, there is an opportunity cost of polluting that exists in terms of what they could have received by selling their permits. With Pigovian taxes, firms must pay a levy to the government based on the amount of pollution they generate. The pollution permits and Pigovian taxes both internalize the externality of pollution by making it costly for firms to pollute.

3. Positive externalities lead markets to produce a smaller quantity and charge a lower price than is socially desirable. Therefore, government intervention will internalize this externality.

4. These arguments are invalid. First, if newer factories can clean up more easily than older factories, then it is more efficient for the new factories to clean up relatively more. A cleanup should be undertaken wherever it can be done at the lower cost. Second, credits put a price on a scarce resource that had been underpriced (free to the user) in the past, which encouraged overconsumption. Prices are put on other scarce resources, so why exclude this one? Third, if some firms sell their credits, it means that other firms put a higher value on them. As long as the total number of credits issued equals the amount of pollution that society will accept, why not let the firms decide who can clean up at the lowest cost?

D. Practice Problems

NSDOE Cleanup Options for Sydney, Nova Scotia

	Option	Total cost (millions)	Total benefit (millions)	Marginal cost (MC) (millions)	Marginal benefit (MB) (millions)	Net benefit (millions)
a.	Do nothing	$0	$0	—	—	$0
b.	Boil water	$1	$4	$1	$4	$3
c.	Drill new wells	$2	$5.5	$1	$1.5	$3.5
d.	Complete cleanup	$5	$6.5	$3	$1	$1.5

Note: All benefits and costs are social rather than private. Specifically: marginal cost = marginal cost to society; marginal benefit = marginal benefit to society (social value); and net benefit = total benefit – total cost (to society)

1. The most efficient level of cleanup is option (c):, drill new wells. To maximize social well-being, every action that has a marginal benefit greater than the marginal cost should be taken. This means that option (c) is the best choice: its marginal benefit is $1.5 million while its marginal cost is only $1 million. Society gains another $0.5 million (MB − MC) by moving from option (b) to (c). Even though society would like to have total cleanup—option (d)—it is not worth the cost to society. Option (d) has a marginal cost of $3 million, which exceeds its marginal benefit of $1 million to society.

2. The total benefit from pollution cleanup is actually the reduction in the cost of pollution to society. In this example, the total benefit from eliminating the source of pollution is $6.5 million, which represents the benefits from avoiding the damage by the pollutant. These benefits would include such factors as reduced risk to property or human health, including lost hours of work and medical bills, as well as pain and suffering. Measurement of the factors is difficult because the health effects are uncertain and likely to be long term. Even if the health effects are known, it is difficult to estimate the full dollar value of pain and suffering and other intangible health costs.

3. Total cleanup would reduce net benefits from $3.5 million to $1.5 million, making society $2 million worse off. Another way to see this is to look at the marginal benefit and marginal cost of option (d); at that point, the marginal cost of $3 million exceeds the MB of $1 million by $2 million. This $2 million shortfall reduces the net benefit of the cleanup program by $2 million relative to the previous option.

4. If the choice were all or nothing, then total cleanup would make sense because the net benefit is positive. A $1.5 million net benefit is better than nothing.

5. a. To the polluter, dumping the chemical was costless even though it imposed a $6.5 million cost on society. Clearly, it would have been more efficient to spend $1 million to avoid a $6.5 million cost rather than spending much more later without even being able to clean things up completely. The problem is that the $6.5 million is an external cost, leading to excessive pollution. If the polluter had been paying the full social cost of pollution, it would have paid the $1 million to avoid contamination rather than $6.5 million in environmental damage.

   b. If property rights to the environment had been defined clearly, and if the victims had been identified, then the victims could have negotiated with polluters not to pollute. The cost of pollution would have been internalized, and the polluters would have paid the $1 million to avoid contamination rather than bearing the full $6.5 million in environmental damage.

c. If the same company owned both the polluter and the water supply, then the company would have had an incentive to pay the $1 million in disposal costs for the benzopyrene rather than do $6.5 million in damage to a resource that it owned. This would have internalized the cost, i.e., which is similar to the answer to 5(b) above.

E. Advanced Critical Thinking

This is bad economics. Because society cannot have everything it wants, society has to make choices. Marginalist thinking says that no matter how much people value something, they should still stop at the point at which the next unit provides an additional benefit that is less than its cost. People would like to stop crime, but society should never use more resources to prevent an additional crime than that prevention is worth to society. The cure should never cost more than the problem being solved. Pollution is similar to crime: in both cases, society would like less of the activity, but society does not want to spend $100 000, for example, to save $10 000 in social costs.

Consultant's Report: Annual Costs and Benefits of Various Levels of Police Protection for Dry Coulee, Manitoba

Number of police officers	Total social cost	Marginal social cost	Total social benefit	Marginal social benefit	Net social benefit
0	$0	—	$0	—	$0
1	$30 000	$30 000	$30 000	$30 000	$0
2	$60 000	$30 000	$70 000	$40 000	$10 000
3	$90 000	$30 000	$105 000	$35 000	$15 000
4	$120 000	$30 000	$134 000	$29 000	$14 000
5	$150 000	$30 000	$160 000	$26 000	$10 000
6	$180 000	$30 000	$180 000	$20 000	$0
7	$210 000	$30 000	$190 000	$10 000	($20 000)
8	$240 000	$30 000	$196 000	$6 000	($44 000)
9	$270 000	$30 000	$200 000	$4 000	($70 000)
10	$300 000	$30 000	$200 000	$0	($100 000)

1. The town should hire police officers as long as the last officer hired costs no more than the estimated value of that officer to the town. That is, keep hiring as long as MB > MC, and stop hiring when MB = MC. This means hiring three officers because the first three officers have marginal benefits greater than the $30 000 marginal cost, but even one additional officer would have a marginal benefit to the town of less than the $30 000 marginal cost. Note that hiring three officers also maximizes the net benefit to society.

2. Marginal Social Cost (MSC) and Marginal Social Benefit (MSB) of Crime Prevention

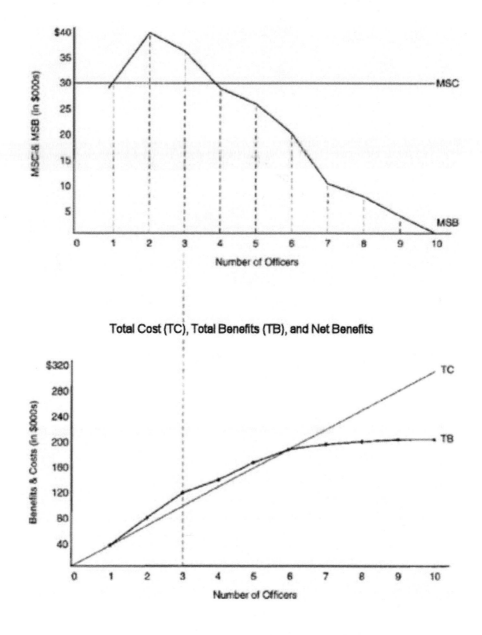

Learning Objectives

In this chapter, you will ...

- Learn the defining characteristics of public goods and common resources

- Examine why private markets fail to provide public goods

- Consider some of the important public goods in our economy

- See why the cost–benefit analysis of public goods is both necessary and difficult

- Examine why people tend to use common resources too much

- Consider some of the important common resources in our economy

An old song lyric maintains that "the best things in life are free." A moment's thought reveals a long list of goods that the songwriter could have had in mind. Nature provides some of them, such as rivers, mountains, beaches, lakes, and oceans. The government provides others, such as playgrounds, parks, and parades. In each case, people do not pay a fee when they choose to enjoy the benefit of the good.

Goods without prices provide a special challenge for economic analysis. Most goods in our economy are allocated in markets, where buyers pay for what they receive and sellers are paid for what they provide. For these goods, prices are the signals that guide the decisions of buyers and sellers. When goods are available free of charge, however, the market forces that normally allocate resources in our economy are absent.

In this chapter we examine the problems that arise for goods without market prices. Our analysis will shed light on one of the ten principles of economics in Chapter 1: Governments can sometimes improve market outcomes. When a good does not have a price attached to it, private markets cannot ensure that the good is produced and consumed in the proper amounts. In such cases, government policy can potentially remedy the market failure and raise economic well-being.

THE DIFFERENT KINDS OF GOODS

How well do markets work in providing the goods that people want? The answer to this question depends on the good being considered. As we discussed in Chapter 6, we can rely on the market to provide the efficient number of ice-cream cones: The price of ice-cream cones adjusts to balance supply and demand, and this equilibrium maximizes the sum of producer and consumer surplus. Yet, as we discussed in Chapter 10, we cannot rely on the market to prevent aluminum manufacturers from polluting the air we breathe: Buyers and sellers in a market typically do not take account of the external effects of their decisions. Thus, markets work well when the good is ice cream, but they work badly when the good is clean air.

In thinking about the various goods in the economy, it is useful to group them according to two characteristics:

excludability
the property of a good whereby a person can be prevented from using it

1. Is the good **excludable?** Can people be prevented from using the good?
2. Is the good **rival in consumption?** Does one person's use of the good diminish another person's ability to use it?

rival in consumption
the property of a good whereby one person's use diminishes other people's use

Using these two characteristics, Figure 11.1 divides goods into four categories:

private goods
goods that are both excludable and rival

1. **Private goods** are both excludable and rival in consumption. Consider an ice-cream cone, for example. An ice-cream cone is excludable because it is possible to prevent someone from eating an ice-cream cone—you just don't give it to him. An ice-cream cone is rival in consumption because if one person eats an ice-cream cone, another person cannot eat the same cone. Most goods in the economy are private goods like ice-cream cones. When we analyzed supply and demand in Chapters 4, 5, and 6 and the efficiency of markets in Chapters 7, 8, and 9, we implicitly assumed that goods were both excludable and rival in consumption.

FIGURE 11.1

Four Types of Goods

Goods can be grouped into four categories according to two questions: (1) Is the good excludable? That is, can people be prevented from using it? (2) Is the good rival in consumption? That is, does one person's use of the good diminish other people's use of it? This diagram gives examples of goods in each of the four categories.

| | Rival in Consumption? | |
	Yes	No
Excludable? Yes	**Private Goods** • Ice-cream cones • Clothing • Congested toll roads	**Natural Monopolies** • Fire protection • Cable TV • Uncongested toll roads
Excludable? No	**Common Resources** • Fish in the ocean • The environment • Congested nontoll roads	**Public Goods** • Tornado siren • National defence • Uncongested nontoll roads

2. **Public goods** are neither excludable nor rival in consumption. That is, people cannot be prevented from using a public good, and one person's use of a public good does not reduce another person's ability to use it. For example, national defence is a public good. Once the country is defended from foreign aggressors, it is impossible to prevent any single person from enjoying the benefit of this defence. Moreover, when one person enjoys the benefit of national defence, he or she does not reduce the benefit to anyone else.

3. **Common resources** are rival in consumption but not excludable. For example, fish in the ocean are a rival good: When one person catches fish, there are fewer fish for the next person to catch. Yet these fish are not an excludable good because, given the vast size of an ocean, it is difficult to stop fishermen from taking fish out of it.

4. When a good is excludable but not rival in consumption, it is an example of a *natural monopoly*. For instance, consider fire protection in a small town. It is easy to exclude people from using this good: The fire department can just let their houses burn down. Yet fire protection is not rival in consumption. Firefighters spend much of their time waiting for a fire, so protecting an extra house is unlikely to reduce the protection available to others. In other words, once a town has paid for the fire department, the additional cost of protecting one more house is small. In Chapter 15 we give a more complete definition of natural monopolies and study them in some detail.

Although Figure 11.1 offers a clean separation of goods into four categories, the boundary between the categories is sometimes fuzzy. Whether goods are excludable or rival in consumption is often a matter of degree. Fish in an ocean may not be excludable because monitoring fishing is so difficult, but a large enough Coast Guard could make fish at least partly excludable. Similarly, although fish are generally rival in consumption, this would be less true if the population of fishermen was small relative to the population of fish. (Think of North American fishing waters before the arrival of European settlers.) For purposes of our analysis, however, it will be helpful to group goods into these four categories.

In this chapter, we examine goods that are not excludable: public goods and common resources. Because people cannot be prevented from using these goods, they are available to everyone free of charge. The study of public goods and common resources is closely related to the study of externalities. For both of these types of goods, externalities arise because something of value has no price attached to it. If one person was to provide a public good, other people would be better off. They would receive a benefit without paying for it—a positive externality. Similarly, when one person uses a common resource such as the fish in the ocean, other people are worse off because there are fewer fish to catch. They suffer a loss but are not compensated for it—a negative externality. Because of these external effects, private decisions about consumption and production can lead to an inefficient allocation of resources, and government intervention can potentially raise economic well-being.

public goods
goods that are neither excludable nor rival

common resources
goods that are rival but not excludable

QuickQuiz Define *public goods* and *common resources*, and give an example of each.

PUBLIC GOODS

To understand how public goods differ from other goods and what problems they present for society, let's consider an example: a fireworks display. This good is not excludable because it is impossible to prevent someone from seeing fireworks, and it is not rival in consumption because one person's enjoyment of fireworks does not reduce anyone else's enjoyment of them.

The Free-Rider Problem

The citizens of Smalltown, Canada, like seeing fireworks on Canada Day. Each of the town's 500 residents places a $10 value on the experience. The cost of putting on a fireworks display is $1000. Because the $5000 of benefits exceed the $1000 of costs, it is efficient for Smalltown residents to have a fireworks display on Canada Day.

Would the private market produce the efficient outcome? Probably not. Imagine that Ellen, a Smalltown entrepreneur, decided to put on a fireworks display. Ellen would surely have trouble selling tickets to the event because her potential customers would quickly figure out that they could see the fireworks even without a ticket. Because fireworks are not excludable, people have an incentive to be free riders. A **free rider** is a person who receives the benefit of a good but avoids paying for it. In Ellen's case, because people would have an incentive to be free riders rather than ticket buyers, the market would fail to produce an efficient outcome.

One way to view this market failure is that it arises because of an externality. If Ellen did put on the fireworks display, she would confer an external benefit on those who saw the display without paying for it. When deciding whether to put on the display, Ellen ignores these external benefits. Even though a fireworks display is socially desirable, it is not privately profitable. As a result, Ellen makes the socially inefficient decision not to put on the display.

Although the private market fails to supply the fireworks display demanded by Smalltown residents, the solution to Smalltown's problem is obvious: The local government can sponsor a Canada Day celebration. The town council can raise everyone's taxes by $2 and use the revenue to hire Ellen to produce the fireworks. Everyone in Smalltown is better off by $8—the $10 in value from the fireworks minus the $2 tax bill. Ellen can help Smalltown reach the efficient outcome as a public employee even though she could not do so as a private entrepreneur.

The story of Smalltown is simplified, but it is also realistic. In fact, many local governments in Canada do pay for fireworks on Canada Day. Moreover, the story shows a general lesson about public goods: Because public goods are not excludable, the free-rider problem prevents the private market from supplying them. The government, however, can potentially remedy the problem. If the government decides that the total benefits exceed the costs, it can provide the public good and pay for it with tax revenue, making everyone better off.

Some Important Public Goods

There are many examples of public goods. Here we consider three of the most important.

free rider
a person who receives the benefit of a good but avoids paying for it

National Defence   The defence of the country from foreign aggressors is a classic example of a public good. Once the country is defended, it is impossible to prevent any single person from enjoying the benefit of this defence, which makes it nonexcludable. Moreover, when one person enjoys the benefit of national defence, he does not reduce the benefit of anyone else, which makes it nonrival.

National defence in Canada falls under the control of the federal government. In 2009 the federal government spent about $19 billion on national defence, or around $560 per person. While this is a lot of money, other countries spend even more. In 2007 the U.S. federal government spent a total of US$553 billion, or about US$1800 per person, on national defence. People disagree about whether this amount is too small or too large, but almost no one doubts that some government spending for national defence is necessary. Even economists who advocate for small government agree that national defence is a public good that government should provide.

Basic Research   Knowledge is created through research. In evaluating the appropriate public policy toward knowledge creation, it is important to distinguish general knowledge from specific technological knowledge. Specific technological knowledge, such as the invention of a longer-lasting battery, a smaller microchip, or a better digital music player, can be patented. The patent gives the inventor the exclusive right to the knowledge he or she has created for a period of time. Anyone else who wants to use the patented information must pay the inventor for the right to do so. In other words, the patent makes the knowledge created by the inventor excludable.

By contrast, general knowledge is a public good. For example, a mathematician cannot patent a theorem. Once a theorem is proved, the knowledge is not excludable: The theorem enters society's general pool of knowledge that anyone can use without charge. The theorem is also not rival in consumption: One person's use of the theorem does not prevent any other person from using the theorem.

Profit-seeking firms spend a lot on research trying to develop new products that they can patent and sell, but they do not spend much on basic research. Their incentive, instead, is to free-ride on the general knowledge created by others. As a result, in the absence of any public policy, society would devote too few resources to creating new knowledge.

The government tries to provide the public good of general knowledge in various ways. Federal government agencies, such as the Natural Sciences and Engineering Research Council of Canada and the Social Sciences and Humanities Research Council of Canada, subsidize basic research in medicine, mathematics, physics, chemistry, biology, and even economics. Determining the appropriate level of governmental support for basic research is difficult because the benefits are hard to measure. Morover, members of Parliament who determine the funding for these sorts of programs have little expertise in science and, therefore, are not in the best position to judge what lines of research will produce the largest benefits. So, while basic research is surely a public good, we should not be surprised if the public sector fails to pay for the right amount and the right kinds.

Fighting Poverty   Many government programs are aimed at helping poor people. The welfare programs administered by the provinces and territories provide some income for low income individuals. Many municipalities provide subsidized housing for low-income families. Other benefits to low-income individuals are delivered through the tax system by means of refundable tax credits, the value of which declines as a person's income increases.

Economists disagree among themselves about what role the government should play in fighting poverty. Although we discuss this debate more fully in Chapter 20, here we note one important argument: Advocates of antipoverty programs claim that fighting poverty is a public good. Even if everyone prefers living in a society without poverty, fighting poverty is not a "good" that private actions will adequately provide.

To see why, suppose someone tried to organize a group of wealthy individuals to try to eliminate poverty. They would be providing a public good. This good would not be rival in consumption: One person's enjoyment of living in a society without poverty would not reduce anyone else's enjoyment of it. The good would not be excludable: Once poverty is eliminated, no one can be prevented from taking pleasure in this fact. As a result, there would be a tendency for people to free-ride on the generosity of others, enjoying the benefits of poverty elimination without contributing to the cause.

Because of the free-rider problem, eliminating poverty through private charity will probably not work. Yet government action can solve this problem. Taxing the wealthy to raise the living standards of the poor can potentially make everyone better off. The poor are better off because they now enjoy a higher standard of living, and those paying the taxes are better off because they enjoy living in a society with less poverty.

Case Study
ARE LIGHTHOUSES PUBLIC GOODS?

Some goods can switch between being public goods and being private goods depending on the circumstances. For example, a fireworks display is a public good if performed in a town with many residents. Yet if performed at a private amusement park such as Canada's Wonderland, a fireworks display is more like a private good because visitors to the park pay for admission.

Another example is a lighthouse. Economists have long used lighthouses as an example of a public good. Lighthouses are used to mark specific locations so that passing ships can avoid treacherous waters. The benefit that the lighthouse provides to the ship captain is neither excludable nor rival in consumption, so each captain has an incentive to free-ride by using the lighthouse to navigate without paying for the service. Because of this free-rider problem, private markets usually fail to provide the lighthouses that ship captains need. As a result, most lighthouses today are operated by the government.

In some cases, however, lighthouses may be closer to private goods. On the coast of England in the nineteenth century, some lighthouses were privately owned and operated. Instead of trying to charge ship captains for the service, however, the owner of the lighthouse charged the owner of the nearby port. If the port owner did not pay, the lighthouse owner turned off the light, and ships avoided that port.

What kind of good?

NEL

In deciding whether something is a public good, one must determine the number of beneficiaries and whether these beneficiaries can be excluded from using the good. A free-rider problem arises when the number of beneficiaries is large and exclusion of any one of them is impossible. If a lighthouse benefits many ship captains, it is a public good. Yet if it primarily benefits a single port owner, it is more like a private good. ●

The Difficult Job of Cost–Benefit Analysis

So far we have seen that the government provides public goods because the private market on its own will not produce an efficient quantity. Yet deciding that the government must play a role is only the first step. The government must then determine what kinds of public goods to provide and in what quantities.

Suppose that the government is considering a public project, such as building a new highway. To judge whether to build the highway, it must compare the total benefits of all those who would use it to the costs of building and maintaining it. To make this decision, the government might hire a team of economists and engineers to conduct a study, called a **cost–benefit analysis,** the goal of which is to estimate the total costs and benefits of the project to society as a whole.

Cost–benefit analysts have a tough job. Because the highway will be available to everyone free of charge, there is no price with which to judge the value of the highway. Simply asking people how much they would value the highway is not reliable: Quantifying benefits is difficult using the results from a questionnaire, and respondents have little incentive to tell the truth. Those who would use the highway have an incentive to exaggerate the benefit they receive to get the highway built. Those who would be harmed by the highway have an incentive to exaggerate the costs to them to prevent the highway from being built.

The efficient provision of public goods is, therefore, intrinsically more difficult than the efficient provision of private goods. Private goods are provided in the market. Buyers of a private good reveal the value they place on it by the prices they are willing to pay. Sellers reveal their costs by the prices they are willing to accept. By contrast, cost–benefit analysts do not observe any price signals when evaluating whether the government should provide a public good. Their findings on the costs and benefits of public projects are, therefore, rough approximations at best.

cost–benefit analysis
a study that compares the costs and benefits to society of providing a public good

Case Study
HOW MUCH IS A LIFE WORTH?

Imagine that you have been elected to serve as a member of your local town council. The town engineer comes to you with a proposal: The town can spend $10 000 to build and operate a traffic light at a town intersection that now has only a stop sign. The benefit of the traffic light is increased safety. The engineer estimates, based on data from similar intersections, that the traffic light would reduce the risk of a fatal traffic accident over the lifetime of the traffic light from 1.6 to 1.1 percent. Should you spend the money for the new light?

To answer this question, you turn to cost–benefit analysis. But you quickly run into an obstacle: The costs and benefits must be measured in the same units if you are to compare them meaningfully. The cost is measured in dollars, but the benefit—the possibility of saving a person's life—is not directly monetary. To make your decision, you have to put a dollar value on a human life.

At first, you may be tempted to conclude that a human life is priceless. After all, there is probably no amount of money that you could be paid to voluntarily give up your life or that of a loved one. This suggests that a human life has an infinite dollar value.

For the purposes of cost–benefit analysis, however, this answer leads to non-sensical results. If we truly placed an infinite value on human life, we should be placing traffic lights on every street corner. Similarly, we should all be driving large cars with all the latest safety features, instead of smaller ones with fewer safety features. Yet traffic lights are not at every corner, and people sometimes choose to buy small cars without side-impact air bags or antilock brakes. In both our public and private decisions, we are at times willing to risk our lives to save some money.

Once we have accepted the idea that a person's life does have an implicit dollar value, how can we determine what that value is? One approach, sometimes used by courts to award damages in wrongful-death suits, is to look at the total amount of money a person would have earned if he or she had lived. Economists are often critical of this approach. It has the bizarre implication that the life of a retired or disabled person has no value.

A better way to value human life is to look at the risks that people are voluntarily willing to take and how much they must be paid for taking them. Mortality risk varies across jobs, for example. Construction workers in high-rise buildings face greater risk of death on the job than office workers do. By comparing wages in risky and less risky occupations, controlling for education, experience, and other determinants of wages, economists can get some sense about what value people put on their own lives. Studies using this approach conclude that the value of a human life is about $10 million.

We can now return to our original example and respond to the town engineer. The traffic light reduces the risk of fatality by 0.5 percentage points. Thus, the expected benefit from having the traffic light is 0.005 × $10 million, or $50 000. This estimate of the benefit well exceeds the cost of $10 000, so you should approve the project. ●

QuickQuiz What is the *free-rider problem?* • Why does the free-rider problem induce the government to provide public goods? • How should the government decide whether to provide a public good?

COMMON RESOURCES

Common resources, like public goods, are not excludable: They are available free of charge to anyone who wants to use them. Common resources are, however, rival in consumption: One person's use of the common resource reduces other people's ability to use it. Thus, common resources give rise to a new problem. Once the good is provided, policymakers need to be concerned about how much it is used. This problem is best understood from the classic parable called the **Tragedy of the Commons.**

The Tragedy of the Commons

Consider life in a small medieval town. Of the many economic activities that take place in the town, one of the most important is raising sheep. Many of the town's families own flocks of sheep and support themselves by selling the sheep's wool, which is used to make clothing.

As our story begins, the sheep spend much of their time grazing on the land surrounding the town, called the Town Common. No family owns the land. Instead, the town residents own the land collectively, and all the residents are allowed to graze their sheep on it. Collective ownership works well because land is plentiful. As long as everyone can get all the good grazing land they want, the Town Common is not a rival good, and allowing residents' sheep to graze for free causes no problems. Everyone in town is happy.

As the years pass, the population of the town grows, and so does the number of sheep grazing on the Town Common. With a growing number of sheep and a fixed amount of land, the land starts to lose its ability to replenish itself. Eventually, the land is grazed so heavily that it becomes barren. With no grass left on the Town Common, raising sheep is impossible, and the town's once prosperous wool industry disappears. Many families lose their source of livelihood.

What causes the tragedy? Why do the shepherds allow the sheep population to grow so large that it destroys the Town Common? The reason is that social and private incentives differ. Avoiding the destruction of the grazing land depends on the collective action of the shepherds. If the shepherds acted together, they could reduce the sheep population to a size that the Town Common can support. Yet no single family has an incentive to reduce the size of its own flock because each flock represents only a small part of the problem.

In essence, the Tragedy of the Commons arises because of an externality. When one family's flock grazes on the common land, it reduces the quality of the land available for other families. Because people neglect this negative externality when deciding how many sheep to own, the result is an excessive number of sheep.

If the tragedy had been foreseen, the town could have solved the problem in various ways. It could have regulated the number of sheep in each family's flock, internalized the externality by taxing sheep, or auctioned off a limited number of sheep-grazing permits. That is, the medieval town could have dealt with the problem of overgrazing in the way that modern society deals with the problem of pollution.

In the case of land, however, there is a simpler solution. The town can divide up the land among town families. Each family can enclose its parcel of land with a fence and then protect it from excessive grazing. In this way, the land becomes a

Tragedy of the Commons
a parable that illustrates why common resources get used more than is desirable from the standpoint of society as a whole

private good rather than a common resource. This outcome in fact occurred during the enclosure movement in England in the seventeenth century.

The Tragedy of the Commons is a story with a general lesson: When one person uses a common resource, that person diminishes other people's enjoyment of it. Because of this negative externality, common resources tend to be used excessively. The government can solve the problem by reducing use of the common resource through regulation or taxes. Alternatively, the government can sometimes turn the common resource into a private good.

This lesson has been known for thousands of years. The ancient Greek philosopher Aristotle pointed out the problem with common resources: "What is common to many is taken least care of, for all men have greater regard for what is their own than for what they possess in common with others."

IN THE NEWS

SOLUTIONS TO ROAD CONGESTION

Road congestion is a growing problem in large Canadian cities. This article explores several market-based solutions.

How to Cut Commuting Times in the GTA
By Matti Siemiatycki

It is little wonder that in recent years, commuting times and road congestion have occupied an increasing amount of public attention. According to a recently released Statistics Canada report, Canadians spend an average of 63 minutes per day commuting between home and work—an increase of 9 minutes since 1992. In the Greater Toronto Area (GTA), the city with the longest average commuting times in the country, the average round-trip commute was 79 minutes—equivalent to two weeks a year.

As gas prices rise, longer commuting times are no longer merely an inconvenience. They translate into a growing financial burden on the majority of city residents who commute by car, and businesses face the pinch of paying more for moving goods. As well, a growing body of research has found that longer time spent in cars is associated with rising rates of obesity that can contribute to health problems.

With time, money, and personal health at stake, what was once a mundane part of the typical daily routine is now front-page news. Commuters, businesses and their political representatives are beginning to wonder aloud what alternatives are available to cut daily travel times.

A variety of solutions are often suggested to cut commuting times. These focus primarily on linking land-use densification with major improvements to public transit infrastructure, creating the preconditions for more users to conveniently commute by streetcar, bus and subway rather than by car.

However, linking transit infrastructure investments with more dense development is only one part of successfully

Some Important Common Resources

There are many examples of common resources. In almost all cases, the same problem arises as in the Tragedy of the Commons: Private decision makers use the common resource too much. Governments often regulate behaviour or impose fees to mitigate the problem of overuse.

Clean Air and Water As we discussed in Chapter 10, markets do not adequately protect the environment. Pollution is a negative externality that can be remedied with regulations or with corrective taxes on polluting activities. One can view this market failure as an example of a common-resource problem. Clean air and clean water are common resources like open grazing land, and excessive pollution is like excessive grazing. Environmental degradation is a modern Tragedy of the Commons.

reducing commuting times. In heavily congested cities such as Toronto, aggressive complementary strategies are necessary to support transit use and raise funds for new investments, while encouraging more efficient use of existing road space.

Complementary strategies that support commuting options can take a variety of forms, including:

Congestion Charging: Road-tolling initiatives have been the most effective measure to rapidly reduce congestion. In London, when a $12 toll was instituted to enter the central city in 2003, weekday inner-city congestion dropped by 20 per cent almost immediately. Money collected from the toll was reinvested in improving public transit and keeping fare prices stable, which made transit a viable option to a growing number of commuters. A recently implemented toll in Stockholm achieved similar reductions in traffic.

Carpooling: While transit is an ideal commuting option for trips originating in and destined for dense urban areas, it may be less suitable for trips in lower density suburban areas. In these instances, programs that encourage increased occupancy in each car through carpooling can contribute to reducing road congestion. Programs that support carpooling include the development of online databases to match commuters who make similar trips, and high occupancy vehicle lanes on highways.

Parking Cash-Out: Businesses provide a cash rebate to employees for not using their parking spot for a given period, a policy predicated on the idea that a firm can save money if they do not have to lease as many parking spaces. In California, a study of eight companies that implemented parking cash-out programs found that the share of solo occupancy vehicle commuters decreased by 17 per cent, while carpooling increased by 14 per cent and transit usage increased by 50 per cent.

Pay-As-You-Go Auto Insurance: At present, insurance is charged as a flat fee, meaning that once it is paid drivers have no incentive to use the car less. However, by charging for insurance based on distance travelled, the Victoria Transport Policy Institute has estimated that total vehicle mileage would be reduced by 10 per cent. Britain, Australia and the state of Texas are currently experimenting with pay-as-you-go auto insurance.

When implemented in combination with improved transit infrastructure and land use densification, strategies that encourage a range of commuting options provide an effective approach to reducing congestion and travel times in Toronto, as has been the case in cities around the world.

Of course, the upfront costs and necessary behavioural change associated with many of these strategies make them appear unpalatable in the short term, and thus politically difficult to implement. Yet the alternative of increasing road congestion and growing commuting times is a far worse option, as it has pernicious impacts on economic efficiency, personal finances, air quality and health.

Source: Matti Siemiatycki, "How to Cut Commuting Times in the GTA." Reprinted with the permission of the author.

Congested Roads   Roads can be either public goods or common resources. If a road is not congested, then one person's use does not affect anyone else. In this case, use is not rival in consumption, and the road is a public good. Yet if a road is congested, then use of that road yields a negative externality. When one additional person drives on the road, it becomes more crowded, and other people must drive more slowly. In this case, the road is a common resource.

One way for the government to address the problem of road congestion is to charge drivers a toll. A toll is, in essence, a corrective tax on the externality of congestion. Often, as in the case of local roads, tolls are not a practical solution because the cost of collecting them is too high.

Sometimes congestion is a problem only at certain times of day. If a bridge is heavily travelled only during rush hour, for instance, the congestion externality is larger during this time than during other times of day. The efficient way to deal with these externalities is to charge higher tolls during rush hour. This toll would provide an incentive for drivers to alter their schedules and would reduce traffic when congestion is greatest.

Another policy that responds to the problem of road congestion, discussed in a case study in the previous chapter, is the tax on gasoline. Gasoline is a complementary good to driving: An increase in the price of gasoline tends to reduce the quantity of driving demanded. Therefore, a gasoline tax reduces road congestion. A gasoline tax, however, is an imperfect solution to road congestion. The problem is that the gasoline tax affects other decisions besides the amount of driving on congested roads. For example, the gasoline tax discourages driving on noncongested roads, even though there is no congestion externality for these roads.

Fish, Whales, and Other Wildlife   Many species of animals are common resources. Fish and whales, for instance, have commercial value, and anyone can go to the ocean and catch whatever is available. Each person has little incentive to maintain the species for the next year. Just as excessive grazing can destroy the Town Common, excessive fishing and whaling can destroy commercially valuable marine populations.

The ocean remains one of the least regulated common resources. Two problems prevent an easy solution. First, many countries have access to the oceans, so any solution would require international cooperation among countries that hold different values. Second, because the oceans are so vast, enforcing any agreement is difficult. As a result, fishing rights have been a frequent source of international tension among normally friendly countries.

In Canada, various laws aim to protect fish and other wildlife. For example, the government charges for fishing and hunting licences, and it restricts the lengths of the fishing and hunting seasons. Fishermen are often required to throw back small fish, and hunters can kill only a limited number of animals. All these laws reduce the use of a common resource and help maintain animal populations.

Case Study
THE COLLAPSE OF THE ATLANTIC COD FISHERY

The Atlantic Ocean off the shores of Newfoundland was once so full of cod that in 1497 explorer John Cabot marvelled that they actually blocked his ship. In the centuries to follow, boats from fishing nations around the world flocked to Canada's east coast to exploit the abundance of northern cod. Five hundred years later, the cod are virtually gone. What happened?

The population of northern cod had yielded an overall annual catch of about 250 000 tonnes for more than a century prior to the mid-1950s. Until then, most of the fishing took place mainly in small craft in waters relatively close to shore, using traditional techniques that involved fishing from dories or small trawlers.

In the mid-1950s, Newfoundland's dories were displaced by a new breed of factory fishing vessel. These new "factory trawlers," or "draggers," came from Germany, Great Britain, Spain, Portugal, Poland, the Soviet Union, Cuba, and even East Asia, and legally fished to within 20 kilometres of the eastern Canadian coast. They set and hauled enormous baglike nets that plowed and scraped the ocean bottom, quickly processing and deep-freezing the fish on board. Catches of northern cod increased substantially throughout the late 1950s and early 1960s as fishing vessels from around the world enjoyed essentially unencumbered access to the north Atlantic fishery off Canada's east coast. With no meaningful regulation of the resource, the catch peaked at just over 800 000 tonnes in the late 1960s.

The distant-water fleet, new technology, and virtually unlimited access to the common property resource subjected the northern cod to intense pressure, and by 1975 the declining northern cod population was yielding just 300 000 tonnes annually. Concerned that stocks were being reduced to almost nothing, Canada passed legislation in 1976 to extend their national jurisdictions over marine resources to 370 kilometres, prohibiting foreign boats from fishing within this limit.

In recognition of the overfishing that resulted from unregulated access to the fish stocks, Canada also initiated a quota system for fishing the northern cod, by implementing total allowable catch (TAC) limits based on the concept of maximum sustainable yield (MSY)—the maximum amount of fish that could be taken from a stock without depleting it. Unfortunately, when setting TAC limits the government considered short-term economic and political factors as well as biological ones in establishing its quota, which meant that TACs figures were set too high.

Although the 370-kilometre limit and a new regulatory regime were intended to conserve and restore fish stocks, they actually resulted in a larger Canadian fishing fleet to replace foreign fishers, as throughout the 1980s the Canadian government promoted more and more investment in the Atlantic fishery. In the mid-1980s, scientists began warning that the stock was declining and recommended the TAC limits be cut in half. Instead of acting immediately and reducing catch quotas at the first signs of overfishing, the federal government delayed conservation action and implemented only moderate reductions in the TAC limits, fearing the massive unemployment that would have resulted from shutting down the industry.

In 1992, the biomass estimate for northern cod was the lowest ever measured and the Canadian minister of Fisheries and Oceans had no choice but to declare a ban on fishing northern cod. Over 40 000 people lost their jobs, and the marine ecosystem is still in a state of collapse.

The collapse of the cod fishery is a prototypical example of what can go wrong with a common property resource, even in the presence of the government's attempt to manage the resource. While Canada finally introduced measures that in principle could have preserved the fish stocks and protected them from the Tragedy of the Commons, the government acted too slowly and based quotas on short-term political and economic considerations. This provides an example of how ill-conceived government intervention might not ultimately address market failures and improve market outcomes. ●

QuickQuiz Why do governments try to limit the use of common resources?

CONCLUSION: THE IMPORTANCE OF PROPERTY RIGHTS

In this chapter and the previous one, we have seen there are some "goods" that the market does not provide adequately. Markets do not ensure that the air we breathe is clean or that our country is defended from foreign aggressors. Instead, societies rely on the government to protect the environment and to provide for national defence.

Although the problems we considered in these chapters arise in many different markets, they share a common theme. In all cases, the market fails to allocate resources efficiently because *property rights* are not well established. That is, some item of value does not have an owner with the legal authority to control it. For example, although no one doubts that the "good" of clean air or national defence is valuable, no one has the right to attach a price to it and profit from its use. A factory pollutes too much because no one charges the factory for the pollution it emits. The market does not provide for national defence because no one can charge those who are defended for the benefit they receive.

When the absence of property rights causes a market failure, the government can potentially solve the problem. Sometimes, as in the sale of pollution permits, the solution is for the government to help define property rights and thereby unleash market forces. Other times, as in the restriction on hunting seasons, the solution is for the government to regulate private behaviour. Still other times, as in the provision of national defence, the solution is for the government to supply a good that the market fails to supply. In all cases, if the policy is well planned and well run, it can make the allocation of resources more efficient and thus raise economic well-being.

SUMMARY

- Goods differ in whether they are excludable and whether they are rival in consumption. A good is excludable if it is possible to prevent someone from using it. A good is rival in consumption if one person's use of the good reduces other people's ability to use the same unit of the good. Markets work best for private goods, which are both excludable and rival in consumption. Markets do not work as well for other types of goods.

- Public goods are neither rival in consumption nor excludable. Examples of public goods include fireworks displays, national defence, and the creation of fundamental knowledge. Because

people are not charged for their use of the public good, they have an incentive to free-ride when the good is provided privately. Therefore, governments provide public goods, making their decision about the quantity based on cost–benefit analysis.

- Common resources are rival in consumption but not excludable. Examples include common grazing land, clean air, and congested roads. Because people are not charged for their use of common resources, they tend to use them excessively. Therefore, governments try to limit the use of common resources.

KEY CONCEPTS

excludability, p. 230
rival in consumption, p. 230
private goods, p. 230

public goods, p. 231
common resources, p. 231
free rider, p. 232

cost–benefit analysis, p. 235
Tragedy of the Commons, p. 237

QUESTIONS FOR REVIEW

1. Explain what is meant by a good being "excludable." Explain what is meant by a good being "rival in consumption." Is a pizza excludable? Is it rival in consumption?

2. Define and give an example of a public good. Can the private market provide this good on its own? Explain.

3. What is cost–benefit analysis of public goods? Why is it important? Why is it hard?

4. Define and give an example of a common resource. Without government intervention, will people use this good too much or too little? Why?

PROBLEMS AND APPLICATIONS

1. Both public goods and common resources involve externalities.
   a. Are the externalities associated with public goods generally positive or negative? Use examples in your answer. Is the free-market quantity of public goods generally greater or less than the efficient quantity?
   b. Are the externalities associated with common resources generally positive or negative? Use examples in your answer. Is the free-market use of common resources generally greater or less than the efficient use?

2. Think about the goods and services provided by your local government.
   a. Using the classification in Figure 11.1 (p. 230), explain into which category each of the following goods falls:
      • police protection
      • snowplowing
      • education
      • rural roads
      • city streets
   b. Why do you think the government provides items that are not public goods?

3. Charlie loves watching *Teletubbies* on his local public TV station, but he never sends any

money to support the station during its fundraising drives.
   a. What name do economists have for Charlie?
   b. How can the government solve the problem caused by people like Charlie?
   c. Can you think of ways the private market can solve this problem? How does the existence of cable TV alter the situation?

4. Some economists argue that private firms will not undertake the efficient amount of basic scientific research.
   a. Explain why this is so. In your answer, classify basic research in one of the categories shown in Figure 11.1.
   b. What sort of policy has Canada adopted in response to this problem?
   c. It is often argued that this policy increases the technological capability of Canadian producers relative to that of foreign firms. Is this argument consistent with your classification of basic research in part (a)? (Hint: Can excludability apply to some potential beneficiaries of a public good and not others?)

5. Why is there litter along most highways but rarely in people's yards?

6. Highway 407 in Toronto has one of the most modern toll systems in the world. Tolls are determined electronically, and vary both by the time of day and by the type of vehicle. Why is this a good idea?

7. Timber companies in Canada cut down many trees on publicly owned land and many trees on privately owned land. Discuss the likely efficiency of logging on each type of land in the absence of government regulation. How do you think the government should regulate logging on publicly owned lands? Should similar regulations apply to privately owned land?

8. High-income people are willing to pay more than lower-income people to avoid the risk of death. For example, they are more likely to pay for safety features on cars. Do you think cost–benefit analysts should take this fact into account when evaluating public projects? Consider, for instance, a rich town and a poor town, both of which are considering the installation of a traffic light. Should the rich town use a higher dollar value for a human life in making this decision? Why or why not?

9. Four roommates are planning to spend the weekend in their dorm room watching old movies, and they are debating how many to watch. The following table shows their willingness to pay for each film.

	Orson	Alfred	Woody	Ingmar
First film	$7	$5	$3	$2
Second film	6	4	2	1
Third film	5	3	1	0
Fourth film	4	2	0	0
Fifth film	3	1	0	0

a. Within the dorm room, is the showing of a movie a public good? Why or why not?

b. If it costs $8 to rent a movie, how many movies should the roommates rent to maximize total surplus?

c. If they choose the optimal number from part (b) and then split the cost of renting the movies equally, how much surplus does each person obtain from watching the movies?

d. Is there any way to split the cost to ensure that everyone benefits? What practical problems does this solution raise?

e. Suppose they agree in advance to choose the efficient number and to split the cost of the movies equally. When Orson is asked his willingness to pay, will he have an incentive to tell the truth? If so, why? If not, what will he be tempted to say?

f. What does this example teach you about the optimal provision of public goods?

10. The village of Ectenia has ten residents. Villagers can earn income by either weaving baskets or fishing. Because the lake has a limited number of fish, the more that villagers fish, the less each catches. In particular, if n households fish in the lake, then each fishing household makes an amount

$$I_f = 12 - 2n$$

where I_f is daily income measured in dollars. The income that a household makes by weaving baskets is $2 a day.

a. Assume that each household independently makes the decision of whether to weave baskets or fish in the lake. How many households do you expect to see fishing each day? How many households do you expect to see weaving baskets? (Hint: Think about opportunity cost.) Calculate the total income of the village in this equilibrium.

b. Show that when 3 households fish in the lake, the total income of the village is larger than the one you found in part (a). What prevented the villagers from reaching this higher income allocation of resources when they acted independently?

c. If the villagers together decided to achieve the allocation in part (b), what kinds of rules would they need to institute? If they wanted everyone to benefit equally in the new system, what kind of tax and transfer system would they need?

d. What type of good is the fishery? What characteristics make it that type of good?

http:// For more study tools, please visit http://www.mankiw5e.nelson.com.

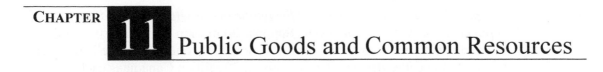

I. Chapter Overview

A. Context and Purpose

The market works well at allocating resources when everyone bears the costs and benefits of their actions. Unfortunately, this restriction does not always hold, which leads to imperfections in the market. Chapters 10–12 analyze the role of government in correcting for such market imperfections.

The previous chapter investigated the role of government in correcting the problems that externalities cause for the market. The next chapter covers the tax system. This chapter extends the analysis of the role of government to cover public goods and common resources, which are those goods that are consumed simultaneously by multiple users, even by those who do not pay for the goods.

A. Helpful Hints

1. *Excludable and rival goods.* An excludable good is one that others can be prevented from using. A rival good is a good of which one person's consumption takes away from another's enjoyment.

2. *Private goods.* These are goods that are both excludable and rival, such as hamburgers.

3. *Public goods.* These are goods that are neither excludable nor rival, such as national defence.

4. *Common resources.* These are goods that are rival but not easily excludable, such as fish in the ocean.

5. *Natural monopoly.* This is the market for a good that is excludable but not rival, such as cable television signals.

6. *Not all public goods are provided by government, and not all private goods are provided by markets.* However, in those cases where markets provide public goods, finding an efficient way to pay for the good can be tricky. Consider commercial television as an example. Exclusion is not feasible with present technology, and consumption is nonrival. In short, a commercial television signal is a public good. Because of the difficulty in excluding free riders, the broadcast companies have turned to another way to generate revenues: they sell advertising.

149

7. *It is possible to satisfy the demand for public goods without providing a separate good for each consumer.* Suppose 30 million Canadians would like to have one nuclear submarine for protection. Only one submarine is required to satisfy the entire demand. Conversely, if 30 million Canadians each demand a private good such as one hamburger, then 30 million hamburgers are required to satisfy the market demand. Because of the nonrival nature of consumption, Canadians can "pass the hat" or ask everyone to contribute toward the purchase of a public good for the group. Because of the free-rider problem, that "contribution" may have to be mandatory in the form of taxes.

8. *Some essentially private goods share characteristics with public goods.* The same logic about "passing the hat" to pay for a public good applies to some goods that are neither purely public nor purely private. Suppose that a few friends would like to rent a new video. As long as everyone wants to see the same movie, only one copy needs to be rented in order to meet everyone's demand. Up to the point that the room gets crowded, the video rental behaves in part like a public good in that it has nonrival consumption. One more person viewing the film does not take away from the enjoyment of the other viewers.

9. *Public goods differ from private goods not because of who provides them, but because of innate characteristics of the goods themselves.* Government may provide goods that are essentially private (excludable and rival), such as a congested provincial campground. Similarly, markets may provide goods that are essentially public (nonexcludable and nonrival). Commercial television signals, for example, are essentially public goods, with infeasible exclusion (without using different broadcast technology) and nonrival consumption (additional viewers do not detract from others' enjoyment). To avoid the free-rider problem, broadcasters use commercial advertising to pay for the good.

10. *Common resources tend to be overproduced and overconsumed.* If it seems unlikely that common pools of petroleum would lead to overproduction and consumption of oil, consider two children who must share a box of popcorn or a soft drink at the movies. Granted, drilling for oil is a bit more difficult than sipping pop through a straw, but the basic analysis is the same. In each case, property rights are not assigned clearly, causing the parties involved to use the resource at a faster than desirable rate. With the popcorn, one child might prefer to eat slowly, making the popcorn last for the entire movie. However, if he waits, the other child may finish off the popcorn. Both eat faster to make sure that they get their share. Similarly with oil, companies that choose to leave oil in the ground for later use will be left out as others drill the wells dry.

II. Self-Testing Challenges

A. True/False Questions

_____1. Private decisions about consumption and production of nonexcludable goods lead to an efficient allocation of resources.

_____2. Contrary to what the musicians maintain, downloading music from the Internet is not a free-rider problem.

_____3. An uncongested road is a common resource.

_____4. To avoid inefficient exclusion, the government often provides excludable, but not rival, goods and services.

_____5. A good or service that is excludable and rival is known as a private good and is most efficiently provided by the market.

_____6. The main weakness of national defence as an example of a public good is that defence is actually provided privately in a market economy through aerospace companies and other defence contractors.

_____7. Human life is priceless.

_____8. The socially optimal price for admission to our national parks is zero.

_____9. A private good is one that is always provided by the market.

_____10. General knowledge, as opposed to specific technological knowledge, is an excludable good.

B. Multiple-Choice Questions

1. Which one of the following are sidewalks an example of?
   a. public good
   b. private good
   c. common resource
   d. public or private good depending on who provides it

2. The whaling industry has hunted some species of whales nearly to extinction. Cattle, however, continue to thrive on farms throughout the world. Which one of the following is the major reason for this difference between cattle and whales?
   a. Whales are a common resource and cattle are private property.
   b. Whales are more valuable than cattle, and whalers are simply responding to economic incentives.
   c. The technology for harvesting whales has improved faster than that for cattle.
   d. Whaling is an international industry but cattle are raised locally.

3. Which one of the following is a reason that more litter occurs along highways than in private driveways?
   a. because there is more traffic on highways
   b. because nobody cares about litter along highways
   c. because highways are a common resource
   d. because there are not enough tax dollars to clean the highways

4. Which one of the following are flood control dams?
   a. public goods
   b. private goods
   c. natural monopolies
   d. common resources

5. Which one of the following is the **BEST** example of the Tragedy of the Commons?
   a. an AIDS epidemic
   b. overconsumption when McDonald's misjudges and underprices its basic hamburger
   c. when tomatoes in a community garden are picked before they are fully ripe
   d. the failure of communism and the downfall of the Soviet Union

6. Which one of the following describes a good that is neither rival nor excludable?
   a. it generates positive externality
   b. it generates negative externality
   c. It is a public good
   d. It is a private good

7. The free-rider problem is associated with _____ and is a consequence of their consumption being _____.
   a. public goods, excludable.
   b. public goods, not excludable.
   c. private goods, excludable.
   d. private goods, not excludable.

8. Which of the following statements can be made about public goods?
   a. cost nothing to produce.
   b. can be consumed by additional people without additional cost once they are produced.
   c. tend to be overconsumed from the standpoint of society.
   d. are overproduced by the market.

9. Which one of the following explains why private firms are **NOT** likely to fund the socially optimal amount of basic research?
   a. because basic research has no payoff
   b. because basic research yields benefits that cannot be measured in dollars
   c. because basic research provides long-term but not short-term benefits
   d. because basic research produces benefits to society as a whole, including those who do not pay for it

10. Which of the following occurs when someone consumes a common resource, (unlike the case with public goods)? ,?
    a. engages in rival consumption
    b. increase the benefits received by other consumers
    c. tends to underconsume it from the standpoint of society
    d. does not impose a negative externality on others

11. Which one of the following refers to the provision of an education in a public school?
    a. it is excludable and rival
    b. it is nonexcludable but rival
    c. it is excludable but nonrival
    d. it is nonexcludable and nonrival

12. Which one of the following explains why markets are **NOT** likely to produce a public good?
    a. because of the cost of producing the public good
    b. because the technology is too expensive for private firms to produce the public good
    c. because of the negative externalities associated with these goods
    d. because it is almost impossible to prevent a person not willing to pay for the good from receiving benefits from the good

13. Which one of the following features does a common good share with a private good?
    a. rival consumption
    b. excludability
    c. efficient provision by the market
    d. nonrival consumption

14. Which one of the following features is common to both private goods and natural monopolies?
    a. they are both excludable
    b. they are both nonrival
    c. they are both produced efficiently by the market
    d. they are both consumable by additional users without making existing users worse off

15. Which one of the following is an example of the Tragedy of the Commons?
    a. a crime is committed in a public place
    b. a common resource becomes rival in consumption
    c. law enforcement in public places is enhanced
    d. property rights are ignored
    e. common resources are divided equally among their users.

16. Which one of the following explains why cost benefit analysis is difficult?
    a. because analysts cannot estimate the explicit cost of a project that has not been completed
    b. because analysts do not have access to information about typical cost overruns
    c. because analysts do not typically observe prices when evaluating the benefits of a public good
    d. because analysts are not able to consider the opportunity cost of resources

17. Many species of animals with commercial value are threatened with extinction. Which one of the following explains why the cow, a valuable source of food, does not face this threat?
    a. because cows are a common resource
    b. because cows are privately owned
    c. because veterinary practices have protected cows from diseases
    d. because their hides fetch less money than other species

18. Which one of the following is the simplest way to solve the problem of congested roads?
    a. build more roads
    b. offer more public transportation
    c. levy a gasoline tax
    d. institute tolls

C. Short-Answer Questions

1. From 1850 to 1950, the annual average catch of northern cod, a population of cod located on the eastern shores of Newfoundland and Labrador, was 250 000 tonnes. By 1968, the size of the annual catch reached a peak of 800 000 tonnes, but the stock of northern cod was not large enough to support this level of fishing. The federal government set a limit of 120 000 tonnes on the catch of the species in 1991 and closed this fishery in 1992. In 1999, the federal government reopened it with a limit of 7000 tonnes, only to halt it again later. Why did the government limit and/or halt the size of the catch? Would it not be rational for fishers to cut back voluntarily on the quantity of fish they catch, when it is obvious that everyone benefits if they all agree to some restraint in order to avoid exhaustion of this resource? _____

_____

_____

_____

_____

2. A lighthouse is often given as an example of a public good. Why? (How does it satisfy the criteria for a public good?) Are there any reasons why a lighthouse might fail to meet the test for a public good? Explain. __

_____

_____

_____

_____

3. Food is more of a basic necessity than highways, yet governments build roads for the general public and normally do not provide food for everyone. Why?

_____

_____

_____

_____

D. Practice Problems

1. Consider the following goods and services. Identify their characteristics in terms of rivalry and excludability, then categorize each as either private, public, natural monopoly, or common resource. Explain the answers.
    a. Commercial television signals. _____

_____

_____

_____

b. Congested city streets. _____

_____

_____

_____

c. A poem. _____

_____

_____

_____

d. General medical research on the relationship between lifestyle and heart disease.

_____

_____

_____

e. A congested public swimming pool. _____

_____

_____

_____

f. An uncongested private swimming pool. _____

_____

_____

_____

2. The following table shows four possible categories of goods according to degree of rivalness and excludability.

a. Label the four types as either public goods, private goods, common resources, or natural monopolies.

b. Give an example not already used in the text of a good in each category.

c. Explain briefly under each example why it belongs in the category.

Categories of Good

RIVAL?

	YES	NO
YES	TYPE: _____ EXAMPLE: _____ EXPLAIN: _____ _____ _____ _____ _____ _____ _____ _____ _____	TYPE: _____ EXAMPLE: _____ EXPLAIN: _____ _____ _____ _____ _____ _____ _____ _____ _____
NO	TYPE: _____ EXAMPLE: _____ EXPLAIN: _____ _____ _____ _____ _____ _____ _____ _____ _____	TYPE: _____ EXAMPLE: _____ EXPLAIN: _____ _____ _____ _____ _____ _____ _____ _____ _____

EXCLUDABLE?

3. Why does free access to a common resource generate an inefficient solution?

_____
_____
_____

E. Advanced Critical Thinking

1. According to the late Jacques Cousteau, "our goal for the environment should be total cleanup: We should not stop until all effluent should be drinkable and all smokestack gases should be breathable."

    a. Do you agree? If we had achieved 99.9% cleanup, would you agree that our goal should be to eliminate the final 0.1% pollution? Would it change your opinion if there were clear evidence that cleaning up the final 0.1% residual pollution would save 10 lives per year? What if the cost to society for the final 0.1% cleanup were $1 trillion? Write a critique of Cousteau's statement, explaining clearly why you agree or disagree. _____
    _____
    _____
    _____
    _____
    _____
    _____

    b. In what sense is the environment a common resource? Does this help to explain why achieving the optimal level of environmental cleanup tends to require government action? _____
    _____
    _____
    _____
    _____
    _____
    _____

2. Irving Kristol, in a *Wall Street Journal* article entitled "The Hidden Cost of Regulation," wrote that environmental cleanup is an "economically unproductive expenditure" because it does not contribute to profit. Kristol argued that "cleaner water is a 'free social asset' to the population in the neighbourhood." He also argued that environmental regulations "render . . . economic costs invisible." Write a critique of Kristol's statement, in the form of a Letter to the Editor of a major newspaper, explaining clearly the ways in which you agree or disagree. Include a discussion of whether or not environmental cleanup is a "productive expenditure." Could it be productive for society overall but not for the individual firm? What is Kristol assuming about the property rights to the environment? In what sense is he right that regulation renders costs invisible? In what sense does environmental regulation have the opposite effect, i.e., in making explicit some existing costs that had been invisible to polluters?

III. Solutions

A. True/False Questions

1. F; such decisions regarding nonexcludable goods lead to an inefficient allocation of resources due to externalities—something of value has no price attached to it.

2. F; downloading music from the Internet is not excludable and the musicians are not paid for their creations; downloaders get a free ride.

3. F; an uncongested road is not a common resource because the consumption is not rival; rather, if exclusion is not practical, it is a public good (until it becomes crowded).

4. T

5. T

6. F; this is irrelevant: nonrivalness and nonexclusion make national defence a public good, which would be true even if an aerospace firm ran the military as a private company.

7. F; at least in an economic sense, society does not put an infinite value on life; people take risks with human life every day in a variety of ways.

8. F; at a zero price, Canada's national parks would be hopelessly overcrowded, indicating that the price is too low for equilibrium; price serves to ration scarce resources efficiently, including space in national parks.
9. F; private goods are sometimes provided by government (surplus food, for example); some goods are private because of their innate characteristics of rivalness and excludability.
10. F; general knowledge is a public good; one person's use of an item of general knowledge does not prevent any other person from using the same knowledge.

B. Multiple-Choice Questions

1. a	5. c	9. d	13. a	17. b
2. a	6. c	10. a	14. a	18. d
3. c	7. b	11. a	15. b	
4. c	8. b	12. d	16. c	

C. Short-Answer Questions

1. Because northern cod is a common resource, there is a tendency toward overfishing, and it illustrates an important example of an externality. Even if every fisher would like to cut back in order to maintain the cod stocks over time, this will not happen without collective action such as regulation. If a fisher tries to conserve the stock by leaving the cod in the ocean, someone else will probably catch that cod. Although there will be fewer fish to catch in the future, the cost will be borne by all. Without enforceable property rights and in the absence of regulations, there is no incentive for rational people to conserve. Or, in other words, there is an incentive to overfish.

2. Traditionally, a lighthouse has been used as an example of a public good. Consumption is nonrival in the sense that the light is available for everyone simultaneously; additional users do not diminish the value received by others. Supposedly it is also very difficult to exclude those who refuse to pay. However, the claim of nonexclusion may be overstated: it is certainly possible for a lighthouse owner to contract with ship owners to turn on the light only when their ships are passing, while leaving the light off at other times to avoid free riders.

3. Food is a private good subject to rival consumption and easy exclusion of nonpayers. As such, food lends itself easily to efficient provision by the market. Highways, however, are nonrival, at least during uncongested periods, and exclusion is difficult for other than limited-access highways. Although there are some strong arguments for pricing roads to ration their usage during congested periods, it is still more challenging to price roads than to price food.

D. Practice Problems

1. a.   Commercial television signals. This good is nonrival because an additional viewer does not reduce the strength of the signal received by other viewers. Nonexcludable (with current equipment) because anyone with a tuner can receive the signal without paying. This makes it a public good even though it is provided privately.

   b.   Congested city streets. This good is rival because additional users impose costs on other drivers by increasing the congestion. Nonexcludable because it would be very difficult to charge tolls on city streets with virtually unlimited access. This is a common resource that tends to be overconsumed.

   c.   A poem. This good is nonrival because many people can enjoy the same poem at the same time. Nonexcludable because users can read the poem or even memorize it and enjoy it without paying for it. As such, it is a classic case of a public good.

   d.   General medical research on the relationship between lifestyle and heart disease. Consumption is nonrival because the same research can benefit one or one billion people simultaneously. It is also nonexcludable because once knowledge is gained, it is virtually impossible to keep it away from people who do not pay for it. Basic research is a public good.

   e.   A congested public swimming pool. This good is rival because of the crowding. More users clearly will detract from the benefits received by existing users. It is also excludable because it is very easy to admit only those who buy an admission ticket. It meets both criteria for a private good even though it is publicly provided.

   f.   An uncongested private swimming pool. This good is nonrival because it is not crowded. As long as it is not crowded, additional swimmers do not impose costs on other users. It is also excludable, not because it is privately owned, but because it is easy to require the purchase of a ticket for admission. Therefore, it meets the requirements for a natural monopoly. The fact that it is privately owned is irrelevant.

2.

Categories of Goods
RIVAL?

	YES	NO
YES	TYPE: Private EXAMPLE: sirloin steak EXPLAIN: My consumption of a steak prevents you from consuming it, and those who do not pay can be excluded (any similar example would work here).	TYPE: Natural Monopoly EXAMPLE: a nearly empty theatre EXPLAIN: Because it is not crowded, consumption is nonrival, yet exclusion is still possible (those who do not buy tickets are not admitted)
NO	TYPE: Common Resource EXAMPLE: wild mushrooms EXPLAIN: People who pick wild mushrooms tend to pick all that they can find because they know that if they leave any to regenerate, someone else will come along and pick them anyway. The pickers would be more likely to do a controlled harvest if they could keep the mushroom patch to themselves.	TYPE: Public Good EXAMPLE: a song EXPLAIN: A song can be enjoyed by additional people without taking away enjoyment by others. It is also very difficult to exclude nonpayers from enjoying it, although copyright owners try to collect royalties from public use (an action that is not always successful).

EXCLUDABLE? (row label spanning YES/NO)

3. Common resources are rival but nonexcludable. As a result, the use of these resources by one consumer reduces the amount available for others, and externalities associated with the use of common resources are generally negative. Because these resources are not priced (P = 0), people tend to overuse and, as a result, the socially optimal quantity is less than the actual quantity consumed.

E. Advanced Critical Thinking

1. a. Although the goal is noble, it is impractical and would actually make society worse off. Even without factories, cars, furnaces, or even campfires, human beings themselves cannot even meet the standard of zero effluent. Zero tolerance on the environment would mean cleaning up every vestige of pollution, even if the residual pollution were trivial, yet would cost billions of dollars to correct. Even if society had the technology, society would be worse off by cleaning up pollution beyond the point at which the last dollar spent provided a dollar's worth of benefit to society. Even when lives are involved, costs and benefits need to be weighed. Suppose that society could eliminate the residual pollution and save 10 lives per year at a social cost of $1 trillion per year. More lives could be saved each year by reallocating that $1 trillion to other lifesaving activities, such as making highways safer or medical research. The $1 trillion has to come from somewhere; nothing is free. If the alternative is other lifesaving activities, then spending the $1 trillion on the environment may actually cost lives!

    b. Unless property rights to the environment are established, clean air and water are owned by nobody, and, therefore, they tend to be treated as free goods. If the marginal cost of using the environment is zero to the individual, then in the absence of restrictions, he or she will use it as long as an additional unit has any positive marginal benefit. Although rational for the individual, it is overconsumption from the standpoint of society.

2. Kristol makes a valid point that environmental cleanup is not free; it takes resources away from other uses. To call it unproductive, however, suggests that it has no value. He glosses over the distinction between private and public benefits. Certainly, a clean environment has benefits to society, even if cleanup does not add to profit. The fact that pollution is a negative externality is, of course, the rationale for government intervention: the individual polluter does not consider the social good in making a decision about environmental cleanup. Kristol argues that regulation hides some costs to society in the sense that, unless forced to do so by law, regulators will not measure the costs of their regulations to business and society as a whole. However, the purpose of environmental

policy is to make explicit some costs that polluters traditionally ignored because they were able to shift those costs to others. When regulators internalize negative externalities, they actually make visible to the polluter some costs that had been invisible. Kristol apparently treats the property rights to the environment as "first come, first served." Otherwise, it makes no sense to state that when a polluter cleans up after itself, it is providing a "free social asset" to the community. Only if one accepts the argument that the polluter owns the environment does it follow that restoring it to its original state is somehow a gift to the victims of pollution.

© Chad Mcdermott/Dreamstime.com

FIRM BEHAVIOUR AND THE ORGANIZATION OF INDUSTRY

THE COSTS OF PRODUCTION

© Chad Mcdermott/Dreamstime.com

The economy is made up of thousands of firms that produce the goods and services you enjoy every day: General Motors produces automobiles, General Electric produces light bulbs, and General Mills produces breakfast cereals. Some firms, such as these three, are large; they employ thousands of workers and have thousands of shareholders who share in the firms' profits. Other firms, such as the local barbershop or candy store, are small; they employ only a few workers and are owned by a single person or family.

In previous chapters we used the supply curve to summarize firms' production decisions. According to the law of supply, firms are willing to produce and sell a greater quantity of a good when the price of the good is higher, and this response leads to a supply curve that slopes upward. For analyzing many questions, the law of supply is all you need to know about firm behaviour.

In this chapter and the ones that follow, we examine firm behaviour in more detail. This topic will give you a better understanding of what decisions lie behind the supply curve in a market. In addition, it will introduce you to a part of economics called *industrial organization*—the study of how firms' decisions regarding prices and quantities depend on the market conditions they face. The town in which you live, for instance, may have several pizzerias but only one cable television company. How does this difference in the number of firms affect the prices in these markets and the efficiency of the market outcomes? The field of industrial organization addresses exactly this question.

Before we turn to these issues, however, we need to discuss the costs of production. All firms, from Bell Canada Enterprises to your local deli, incur costs as they make the goods and services that they sell. As we will see in the coming chapters, a firm's costs are a key determinant of its production and pricing decisions. In this chapter, we define some of the variables that economists use to measure a firm's costs, and we consider the relationships among them.

A word of warning: This topic can seem dry and technical. To be honest, some might even call it boring. But it provides a crucial foundation for the fascinating topics that follow.

WHAT ARE COSTS?

We begin our discussion of costs at Hungry Helen's Cookie Factory. Helen, the owner of the firm, buys flour, sugar, chocolate chips, and other cookie ingredients. She also buys the mixers and ovens, and hires workers to run this equipment. She then sells the resulting cookies to consumers. By examining some of the issues that Helen faces in her business, we can learn some lessons about costs that apply to all firms in the economy.

Total Revenue, Total Cost, and Profit

We begin with the firm's objective. To understand what decisions a firm makes, we must understand what it is trying to do. It is conceivable that Helen started her firm because of an altruistic desire to provide the world with cookies or, perhaps, out of love for the cookie business. More likely, Helen started her business to make money. Economists normally assume that the goal of a firm is to maximize profit, and they find that this assumption works well in most cases.

What is a firm's profit? The amount that the firm receives for the sale of its output (cookies) is called its **total revenue.** The amount that the firm pays to buy inputs (flour, sugar, workers, ovens, etc.) is called its **total cost.** Helen gets to keep any revenue that is not needed to cover costs. **Profit** is a firm's total revenue minus its total cost. That is,

$$\text{Profit} = \text{Total revenue} - \text{Total cost}$$

Helen's objective is to make her firm's profit as large as possible.

To see how a firm goes about maximizing profit, we must consider fully how to measure its total revenue and its total cost. Total revenue is the easy part: It equals the quantity of output the firm produces times the price at which it sells its output. If Helen produces 10 000 cookies and sells them at $2 a cookie, her total revenue is $20 000. By contrast, the measurement of a firm's total cost is more subtle.

Costs as Opportunity Costs

When measuring costs at Hungry Helen's Cookie Factory or any other firm, it is important to keep in mind one of the ten principles of economics from Chapter 1: The cost of something is what you give up to get it. Recall that the *opportunity cost* of an item refers to all those things that must be forgone to acquire that item. When economists speak of a firm's cost of production, they include all the opportunity costs of making its output of goods and services.

total revenue (for a firm)
the amount a firm receives for the sale of its output

total cost
the market value of the inputs a firm uses in production

profit
total revenue minus total cost

A firm's opportunity costs of production are sometimes obvious and sometimes less so. When Helen pays $1000 for flour, that $1000 is an opportunity cost because Helen can no longer use that $1000 to buy something else. Similarly, when Helen hires workers to make the cookies, the wages she pays are part of the firm's costs. Because these costs require the firm to pay out some money, they are called **explicit costs.** By contrast, some of a firm's opportunity costs, called **implicit costs,** do not require a cash outlay. Imagine that Helen is skilled with computers and could earn $100 per hour working as a programmer. For every hour that Helen works at her cookie factory, she gives up $100 in income, and this forgone income is also part of her costs.

This distinction between explicit and implicit costs highlights an important difference between how economists and accountants analyze a business. Economists are interested in studying how firms make production and pricing decisions. Because these decisions are based on both explicit and implicit costs, economists include both when measuring a firm's costs. By contrast, accountants have the job of keeping track of the money that flows into and out of firms. As a result, they measure the explicit costs but often ignore the implicit costs.

The difference between economists and accountants is easy to see in the case of Hungry Helen's Cookie Factory. When Helen gives up the opportunity to earn money as a computer programmer, her accountant will not count this as a cost of her cookie business. Because no money flows out of the business to pay for this cost, it never shows up on the accountant's financial statements. An economist, however, will count the forgone income as a cost because it will affect the decisions that Helen makes in her cookie business. For example, if Helen's wage as a computer programmer rises from $100 to $500 per hour, she might decide that running her cookie business is too costly and choose to shut down the factory to become a full-time computer programmer.

The Cost of Capital as an Opportunity Cost

An important implicit cost of almost every business is the opportunity cost of the financial capital that has been invested in the business. Suppose, for instance, that Helen used $300 000 of her savings to buy her cookie factory from the previous owner. If Helen had instead left this money deposited in a savings account that pays an interest rate of 5 percent, she would have earned $15 000 per year. To own her cookie factory, therefore, Helen has given up $15 000 per year in interest income. This forgone $15 000 is one of the implicit opportunity costs of Helen's business.

As we have already noted, economists and accountants treat costs differently, and this is especially true in their treatment of the cost of capital. An economist views the $15 000 in interest income that Helen gives up every year as a cost of her business, even though it is an implicit cost. Helen's accountant, however, will not show this $15 000 as a cost because no money flows out of the business to pay for it.

To further explore the difference between economists and accountants, let's change the example slightly. Suppose now that Helen did not have the entire $300 000 to buy the factory but, instead, used $100 000 of her own savings and borrowed $200 000 from a bank at an interest rate of 5 percent. Helen's accountant, who measures only explicit costs, will now count the $10 000 interest paid on the bank loan every year as a cost because this amount of money now flows out of the firm. By contrast, according to an economist, the opportunity cost of owning the business

explicit costs
input costs that require an outlay of money by the firm

implicit costs
input costs that do not require an outlay of money by the firm

is still $15 000. The opportunity cost equals the interest on the bank loan (an explicit cost of $10 000) plus the forgone interest on savings (an implicit cost of $5000).

Economic Profit versus Accounting Profit

economic profit
total revenue minus total cost, including both explicit and implicit costs

accounting profit
total revenue minus total explicit cost

Now let's return to the firm's objective—profit. Because economists and accountants measure costs differently, they also measure profit differently. An economist measures a firm's **economic profit** as the firm's total revenue minus all the opportunity costs (explicit and implicit) of producing the goods and services sold. An accountant measures the firm's **accounting profit** as the firm's total revenue minus only the firm's explicit costs.

Figure 13.1 summarizes this difference. Notice that because the accountant ignores the implicit costs, accounting profit is usually larger than economic profit. For a business to be profitable from an economist's standpoint, total revenue must cover all the opportunity costs, both explicit and implicit.

Economic profit is an important concept because it is what motivates the firms that supply goods and services. As we will see, a firm making positive economic profit will stay in business. It is covering all its opportunity costs and has some revenue left to reward the firm owners. When a firm is making economic losses (that is, when economic profits are negative), the business owners are failing to make enough to cover all the costs of production. Unless conditions change, the firm owners will eventually close the business down and exit the industry. To understand how industries evolve, we need to keep an eye on economic profit.

FIGURE 13.1

Economists versus Accountants

Economists include all opportunity costs when analyzing a firm, whereas accountants measure only explicit costs. Therefore, economic profit is smaller than accounting profit.

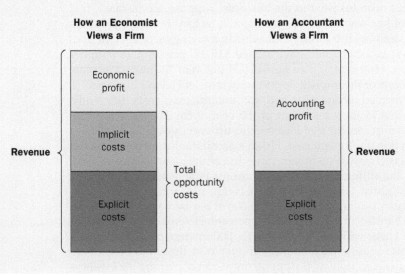

QuickQuiz   Farmer McDonald gives banjo lessons for $20 an hour. One day, he spends 10 hours planting $100 worth of seeds on his farm. What opportunity cost has he incurred? What cost would his accountant measure? If these seeds will yield $200 worth of crops, does McDonald earn an accounting profit? Does he earn an economic profit?

PRODUCTION AND COSTS

Firms incur costs when they buy inputs to produce the goods and services that they plan to sell. In this section we examine the link between a firm's production process and its total cost. Once again, we consider Hungry Helen's Cookie Factory.

In the analysis that follows, we make an important simplifying assumption: We assume that the size of Helen's factory is fixed and that Helen can vary the quantity of cookies produced only by changing the number of workers. This assumption is realistic in the short run, but not in the long run. That is, Helen cannot build a larger factory overnight, but she can do so within a year or so. This analysis, therefore, should be viewed as describing the production decisions that Helen faces in the short run. We examine the relationship between costs and time horizon more fully later in the chapter.

The Production Function

Table 13.1 shows how the quantity of cookies Helen's factory produces per hour depends on the number of workers. As you see in the first two columns, if there are no workers in the factory, Helen produces no cookies. When there is 1 worker, she produces 50 cookies. When there are 2 workers, she produces 90 cookies, and so on. Figure 13.2 presents a graph of these two columns of numbers. The number of workers is on the horizontal axis, and the number of cookies produced is on the vertical axis. This relationship between the quantity of inputs (workers) and quantity of output (cookies) is called the **production function.**

It is again important to emphasize that at this point we are dealing with a *short-run* production function, which allows the number of workers to vary but holds the size of Helen's factory fixed. In the long run, both the number of workers and the size of the factory may be varied. In this case, the relationship between the number of workers, the size of the factory, and the number of cookies produced will be captured by a *long-run* production function. We will return to this distinction later in the chapter. For now we will focus on the short-run production function.

One of the ten principles of economics introduced in Chapter 1 is that rational people think at the margin. As we will see in future chapters, this idea is the key to understanding the decision a firm makes about how many workers to hire and how much output to produce. To take a step toward understanding these decisions, the third column in the table gives the marginal product of a worker. The **marginal product** of any input in the production process is the increase in the quantity of output obtained from one additional unit of that input, holding all other inputs constant. When the number of workers goes from 1 to 2, cookie production increases from 50 to 90, so the marginal product of the second worker is 40 cookies. And when the number of workers goes from 2 to 3, cookie production increases from 90 to 120, so the marginal product of the third worker is 30 cookies. In the table,

production function
the relationship between quantity of inputs used to make a good and the quantity of output of that good

marginal product
the increase in output that arises from an additional unit of input

TABLE 13.1

A Production Function
and Total Cost: Hungry
Helen's Cookie Factory

Number of Workers	Output (quantity of cookies produced per hour)	Marginal Product of Labour	Cost of Factory	Cost of Workers	Total Cost of Inputs (cost of factory + cost of workers)
0	0		$30	$ 0	$30
		50			
1	50		30	10	40
		40			
2	90		30	20	50
		30			
3	120		30	30	60
		20			
4	140		30	40	70
		10			
5	150		30	50	80

FIGURE 13.2

Hungry Helen's Production Function

A production function shows the relationship between the number of workers hired and the quantity of output produced. Here the number of workers hired (on the horizontal axis) is from the first column in Table 13.1, and the quantity of output produced (on the vertical axis) is from the second column. The production function gets flatter as the number of workers increases, which reflects diminishing marginal product.

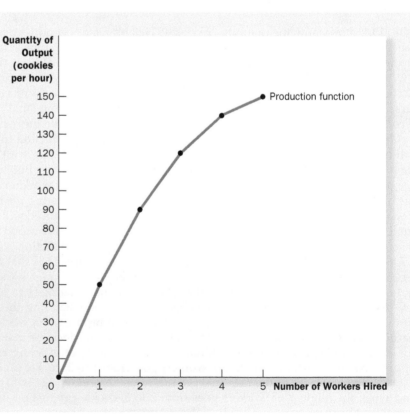

the marginal product is shown halfway between two rows because it represents the change in output as the number of workers increases from one level to another.

Notice that as the number of workers increases, the marginal product declines. The second worker has a marginal product of 40 cookies, the third worker has a marginal product of 30 cookies, and the fourth worker has a marginal product of 20 cookies. This property is called **diminishing marginal product.** At first, when only a few workers are hired, they have easy access to Helen's kitchen equipment. As the number of workers increases, additional workers have to share equipment and work in more crowded conditions. Hence, as more and more workers are hired, each additional worker contributes less to the production of cookies.

Diminishing marginal product is also apparent in Figure 13.2. The production function's slope (rise over run) tells us the change in Helen's output of cookies (rise) for each additional input of labour (run). That is, the slope of the production function measures the marginal product of a worker. As the number of workers increases, the marginal product declines, and the production function becomes flatter.

diminishing marginal product
the property whereby the marginal product of an input declines as the quantity of the input increases

From the Production Function to the Total-Cost Curve

The last three columns of Table 13.1 show Helen's cost of producing cookies. In this example, the cost of Helen's factory is $30 per hour, and the cost of a worker is $10 per hour. If she hires 1 worker, her total cost is $40. If she hires 2 workers, her total cost is $50, and so on. With this information, the table now shows how the number of workers Helen hires is related to the quantity of cookies she produces and to her total cost of production.

Our goal in the next several chapters is to study firms' production and pricing decisions. For this purpose, the most important relationship in Table 13.1 is between quantity produced (in the second column) and total costs (in the sixth column). Figure 13.3 graphs these two columns of data with the quantity produced on the horizontal axis and total cost on the vertical axis. This graph is called the *total-cost curve.*

Now compare the total-cost curve in Figure 13.3 with the production function in Figure 13.2. These two curves are opposite sides of the same coin. The total-cost curve gets steeper as the amount produced rises, whereas the production function gets flatter as production rises. These changes in slope occur for the same reason. High production of cookies means that Helen's kitchen is crowded with many workers. Because the kitchen is crowded, each additional worker adds less to production, reflecting diminishing marginal product. Therefore, the production function is relatively flat. But now turn this logic around: When the kitchen is crowded, producing an additional cookie requires a lot of additional labour and is thus very costly. Therefore, when the quantity produced is large, the total-cost curve is relatively steep.

QuickQuiz If Farmer Jones plants no seeds on his farm, he gets no harvest. If he plants 1 bag of seeds, he gets 3 bushels of wheat. If he plants 2 bags, he gets 5 bushels. If he plants 3 bags, he gets 6 bushels. A bag of seeds costs $100, and seeds are his only cost. Use these data to graph the farmer's production function and total-cost curve. Explain their shapes.

NEL

FIGURE 13.3

Hungry Helen's Total-Cost Curve

A total-cost curve shows the relationship between the quantity of output produced and total cost of production. Here the quantity of output produced (on the horizontal axis) is from the second column in Table 13.1, and the total cost (on the vertical axis) is from the sixth column. The total-cost curve gets steeper as the quantity of output increases because of diminishing marginal product.

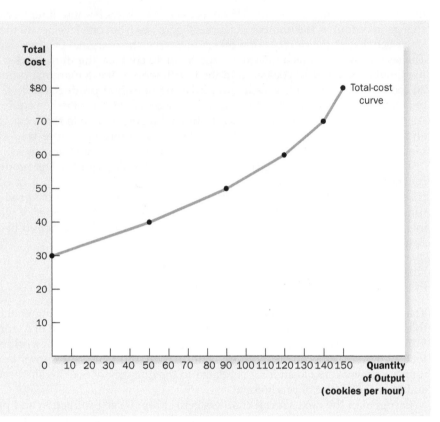

THE VARIOUS MEASURES OF COST

Our analysis of Hungry Helen's Cookie Factory demonstrated how a firm's total cost reflects its production function. From data on a firm's total cost, we can derive several related measures of cost, which will turn out to be useful when we analyze production and pricing decisions in future chapters. To see how these related measures are derived, we consider the example in Table 13.2. This table presents cost data on Helen's neighbour: Thirsty Thelma's Lemonade Stand. Once again we are dealing with the short run, where the size of Thelma's stand is fixed.

The first column of the table shows the number of glasses of lemonade that Thelma might produce, ranging from 0 to 10 glasses per hour. The second column shows Thelma's total cost of producing lemonade. Figure 13.4 plots Thelma's total-cost curve. The quantity of lemonade (from the first column) is on the horizontal axis, and total cost (from the second column) is on the vertical axis. Thirsty Thelma's total-cost curve has a shape similar to Hungry Helen's. In particular, it becomes steeper as the quantity produced rises, which (as we have discussed) reflects diminishing marginal product.

TABLE 13.2

Quantity of Lemonade (glasses per hour)	Total Cost	Fixed Cost	Variable Cost	Average Fixed Cost	Average Variable Cost	Average Total Cost	Marginal Cost
0	$3.00	$3.00	$0.00	—	—	—	
							$0.30
1	3.30	3.00	0.30	$3.00	$0.30	$3.30	
							0.50
2	3.80	3.00	0.80	1.50	0.40	1.90	
							0.70
3	4.50	3.00	1.50	1.00	0.50	1.50	
							0.90
4	5.40	3.00	2.40	0.75	0.60	1.35	
							1.10
5	6.50	3.00	3.50	0.60	0.70	1.30	
							1.30
6	7.80	3.00	4.80	0.50	0.80	1.30	
							1.50
7	9.30	3.00	6.30	0.43	0.90	1.33	
							1.70
8	11.00	3.00	8.00	0.38	1.00	1.38	
							1.90
9	12.90	3.00	9.90	0.33	1.10	1.43	
							2.10
10	15.00	3.00	12.00	0.30	1.20	1.50	

The Various Measures of Cost: Thirsty Thelma's Lemonade Stand

Fixed and Variable Costs

Thelma's total cost can be divided into two types. Some costs, called **fixed costs,** do not vary with the quantity of output produced. They are incurred even if the firm produces nothing at all. Thelma's fixed costs include any rent she pays because this cost is the same regardless of how much lemonade Thelma produces. Similarly, if Thelma needs to hire a full-time bookkeeper to pay bills, regardless of the quantity of lemonade produced, the bookkeeper's salary is a fixed cost. The third column in Table 13.2 shows Thelma's fixed cost, which in this example is $3.00.

Some of the firm's costs, called **variable costs,** change as the firm alters the quantity of output produced. Thelma's variable costs include the cost of lemons, sugar, paper cups, and straws: The more lemonade Thelma makes, the more of these items she needs to buy. Similarly, if Thelma has to hire more workers to make more lemonade, the salaries of these workers are variable costs. The fourth column of the table shows Thelma's variable cost. The variable cost is 0 if she produces nothing, $0.30 if she produces 1 glass of lemonade, $0.80 if she produces 2 glasses, and so on.

A firm's total cost is the sum of fixed and variable costs. In Table 13.2, total cost in the second column equals fixed cost in the third column plus variable cost in the fourth column.

fixed costs
costs that do not vary with the quantity of output produced

variable costs
costs that do vary with the quantity of output produced

FIGURE 13.4

Thirsty Thelma's Total-Cost Curve

Here the quantity of output produced (on the horizontal axis) is from the first column in Table 13.2, and the total cost (on the vertical axis) is from the second column. As in Figure 13.3, the total-cost curve gets steeper as the quantity of output increases because of diminishing marginal product.

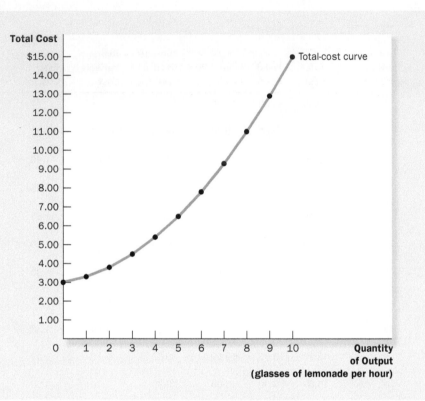

Average and Marginal Costs

As the owner of her firm, Thelma has to decide how much to produce. A key part of this decision is how her costs will vary as she changes the level of production. In making this decision, Thelma might ask her production supervisor the following two questions about the cost of producing lemonade:

- How much does it cost to make the typical glass of lemonade?
- How much does it cost to increase production of lemonade by 1 glass?

average total cost
total cost divided by the quantity of output

average fixed cost
fixed costs divided by the quantity of output

average variable cost
variable costs divided by the quantity of output

Although at first these two questions might seem to have the same answer, they do not. Both answers will turn out to be important for understanding how firms make production decisions.

To find the cost of the typical unit produced, we would divide the firm's costs by the quantity of output it produces. For example, if the firm produces 2 glasses per hour, its total cost is $3.80, and the cost of the typical glass is $3.80/2, or $1.90. Total cost divided by the quantity of output is called **average total cost.** Because total cost is just the sum of fixed and variable costs, average total cost can be expressed as the sum of average fixed cost and average variable cost. **Average fixed cost** is the fixed cost divided by the quantity of output, and **average variable cost** is the variable cost divided by the quantity of output.

Although average total cost tells us the cost of the typical unit, it does not tell us how much total cost will change as the firm alters its level of production. The last column in Table 13.2 shows the amount that total cost rises when the firm increases production by 1 unit of output. This number is called **marginal cost.** For example, if Thelma increases production from 2 to 3 glasses, total cost rises from $3.80 to $4.50, so the marginal cost of the third glass of lemonade is $4.50 minus $3.80, or $0.70.

marginal cost
the increase in total cost that arises from an extra unit of production

It may be helpful to express these definitions mathematically:

$$\text{Average total cost} = \text{Total cost/Quantity}$$
$$ATC = TC/Q$$

and

$$\text{Marginal cost} = \text{Change in total cost/Change in quantity}$$
$$MC = \Delta TC/\Delta Q$$

Here Δ, the Greek letter *delta*, represents the change in a variable. These equations show how average total cost and marginal cost are derived from total cost. *Average total cost tells us the cost of a typical unit of output if total cost is divided evenly over all the units produced. Marginal cost tells us the increase in total cost that arises from producing an additional unit of output.* As we will see more fully in the next chapter, Thelma, our lemonade entrepreneur, will find the concepts of average total cost and marginal cost useful when deciding how much lemonade to produce.

Cost Curves and Their Shapes

Just as in previous chapters we found graphs of supply and demand useful when analyzing the behaviour of markets, we will find graphs of average and marginal cost useful when analyzing the behaviour of firms. Figure 13.5 graphs Thelma's costs using the data from Table 13.2. The horizontal axis measures the quantity the firm produces, and the vertical axis measures marginal and average costs. The graph shows four curves: average total cost *(ATC)*, average fixed cost *(AFC)*, average variable cost *(AVC)*, and marginal cost *(MC)*.

The cost curves shown here for Thirsty Thelma's Lemonade Stand have some features that are common to the cost curves of many firms in the economy. Let's examine three features in particular: the shape of marginal cost, the shape of average total cost, and the relationship between marginal and average total cost.

Rising Marginal Cost   Thirsty Thelma's marginal cost rises with the quantity of output produced. This reflects the property of diminishing marginal product. When Thelma is producing a small quantity of lemonade, she has few workers and much of her equipment is not being used. Because she can easily put these idle resources to use, the marginal product of an extra worker is large, and the marginal cost of an extra glass of lemonade is small. By contrast, when Thelma is producing a large quantity of lemonade, her stand is crowded with workers and most of her equipment is fully utilized. Thelma can produce more lemonade by adding workers, but these new workers have to work in crowded conditions and may have to wait to use the equipment. Therefore, when the quantity of lemonade being produced is already high, the marginal product of an extra worker is low, and the marginal cost of an extra glass of lemonade is large.

FIGURE 13.5

Thirsty Thelma's Average-Cost and Marginal-Cost Curves

This figure shows the average total cost (ATC), average fixed cost (AFC), average variable cost (AVC), and marginal cost (MC) for Thirsty Thelma's Lemonade Stand. All of these curves are obtained by graphing the data in Table 13.2. These cost curves show three features that are typical of many firms: (1) Marginal cost rises with the quantity of output. (2) The average-total-cost curve is U-shaped. (3) The marginal-cost curve crosses the average-total-cost curve at the minimum of average total cost.

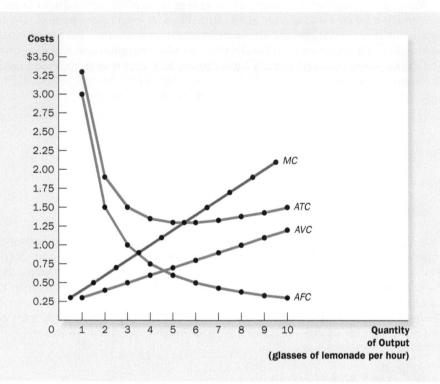

U-Shaped Average Total Cost   Thirsty Thelma's average-total-cost curve is U-shaped. To understand why this is so, remember that average total cost is the sum of average fixed cost and average variable cost. Average fixed cost always declines as output rises because the fixed cost is spread over a larger number of units. Average variable cost typically rises as output increases because of diminishing marginal product.

Average total cost reflects the shapes of both average fixed cost and average variable cost. As shown in Figure 13.5, at very low levels of output, such as 1 or 2 glasses of lemonade per hour, average total cost is very high. Even though average variable cost is low, average fixed cost is high because the fixed cost is spread over only a few units. As output increases, the fixed cost is spread more widely. Average fixed cost declines, rapidly at first and then more slowly. As a result, average total cost also declines until Thirsty Thelma's output reaches 5 glasses of lemonade per hour, when average total cost is $1.30 per glass. When the firm produces more than 6 glasses of lemonade per hour, however, the increase in average variable cost becomes the dominant force, and average total cost starts rising. The tug of war between average fixed cost and average variable cost generates the U-shape in average total cost.

efficient scale
the quantity of output that minimizes average total cost

The bottom of the U-shape occurs at the quantity that minimizes average total cost. This quantity is sometimes called the **efficient scale** of the firm. For Thirsty Thelma, the efficient scale is 5 or 6 glasses of lemonade per hour. If she produces more or less than this amount, her average total cost rises above the minimum of $1.30. At lower levels of output, average total cost is higher than $1.30 because the fixed cost is spread over so few units. At higher levels of output, average total cost is higher than $1.30 because the marginal product of inputs has diminished significantly. At the efficient scale, these two forces are balanced to yield the lowest average total cost.

The Relationship between Marginal Cost and Average Total Cost If you look at Figure 13.5 (or back at Table 13.2), you will see something that may be surprising at first. *Whenever marginal cost is less than average total cost, average total cost is falling. Whenever marginal cost is greater than average total cost, average total cost is rising.* This feature of Thirsty Thelma's cost curves is not a coincidence from the particular numbers used in the example: It is true for all firms.

To see why, consider an analogy. Average total cost is like your cumulative grade point average. Marginal cost is like the grade in the next course you will take. If your grade in your next course is less than your grade point average, your grade point average will fall. If your grade in your next course is higher than your grade point average, your grade point average will rise. The mathematics of average and marginal costs is exactly the same as the mathematics of average and marginal grades.

This relationship between average total cost and marginal cost has an important corollary: *The marginal-cost curve crosses the average-total-cost curve at its minimum.* Why? At low levels of output, marginal cost is below average total cost, so average total cost is falling. But after the two curves cross, marginal cost rises above average total cost. For the reason we have just discussed, average total cost must start to rise at this level of output. Hence, this point of intersection is the minimum of average total cost. As you will see in the next chapter, this point of minimum average total cost plays a key role in the analysis of competitive firms.

Typical Cost Curves

In the examples we have studied so far, the firms exhibit diminishing marginal product and, therefore, rising marginal cost at all levels of output. Yet actual firms are often a bit more complicated than this. In many firms, diminishing marginal product does not start to occur immediately after the first worker is hired. Depending on the production process, the second or third worker might have higher marginal product than the first because a team of workers can divide tasks and work more productively than a single worker. Such firms would first experience increasing marginal product for a while before diminishing marginal product sets in.

Figure 13.6 shows the cost curves for such a firm, including average total cost (*ATC*), average fixed cost (*AFC*), average variable cost (*AVC*), and marginal cost (*MC*). At low levels of output, the firm experiences increasing marginal product, and the marginal-cost curve falls. Eventually, the firm starts to experience diminishing marginal product, and the marginal-cost curve starts to rise. This combination of increasing and then diminishing marginal product also makes the average variable-cost curve U-shaped.

FIGURE 13.6

Cost Curves for a Typical Firm

Many firms experience increasing marginal product before diminishing marginal product. As a result, they have cost curves shaped like those in this figure. Notice that marginal cost and average variable cost fall for a while before starting to rise.

Source: From MANKIW. *Principles of Economics*, 4E. © 2007 South-Western, a part of Cengage Learning, Inc. Reproduced with permission. www.cengage.com/permissions

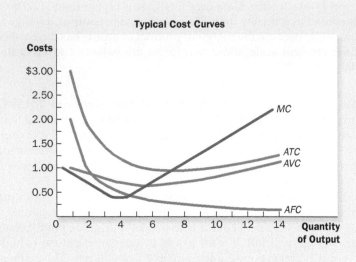

Despite these differences from the Thirsty Thelma example, the cost curves shown here share the three properties that are most important to remember:

1. Marginal cost eventually rises with the quantity of output.
2. The average-total-cost curve is U-shaped.
3. The marginal-cost curve crosses the average-total-cost curve at the minimum of average total cost.

QuickQuiz Suppose Honda's total cost of producing 4 cars is $225 000 and its total cost of producing 5 cars is $250 000. What is the average total cost of producing 5 cars? What is the marginal cost of the fifth car? • Draw the marginal-cost curve and the average-total-cost curve for a typical firm, and explain why these curves cross where they do.

COSTS IN THE SHORT RUN AND IN THE LONG RUN

We noted earlier in this chapter that a firm's costs might depend on the time horizon being examined. Let's examine more precisely why this might be the case.

The Relationship between Short-Run and Long-Run Average Total Cost

For many firms, the division of total costs between fixed and variable costs depends on the time horizon. Consider, for instance, a car manufacturer, such as Ford Motor Company. Over a period of only a few months, Ford cannot adjust the number or sizes of its car factories. The only way it can produce additional cars is to hire more workers at the factories it already has. The cost of these factories is, therefore, a fixed cost in the short run. By contrast, over a period of several years, Ford can expand the size of its factories, build new factories, or close old ones. Thus, the cost of its factories is a variable cost in the long run.

Because many decisions are fixed in the short run but variable in the long run, a firm's long-run cost curves differ from its short-run cost curves. Figure 13.7 shows an example. The figure presents three short-run average-total-cost curves— for a small, medium, and large factory. It also presents the long-run average total-cost curve. As the firm moves along the long-run curve, it is adjusting the size of the factory to the quantity of production.

This graph shows how short-run and long-run costs are related. The long-run average-total-cost curve is a much flatter U-shape than the short-run average-total-cost curve. In addition, all the short-run curves lie on or above the long-run curve. These properties arise because firms have greater flexibility in the long run. In essence, in the long run, the firm gets to choose which short-run curve it wants to use. But in the short run, it has to use whatever short-run curve it chose in the past.

The figure shows an example of how a change in production alters costs over different time horizons. When Ford wants to increase production from 1000 to 1200 cars per day, it has no choice in the short run but to hire more workers at its existing medium-sized factory. Because of diminishing marginal product, average total cost rises from $10 000 to $12 000 per car. In the long run, however, Ford can expand both the size of the factory and its work force, and average total cost returns to $10 000.

FIGURE 13.7

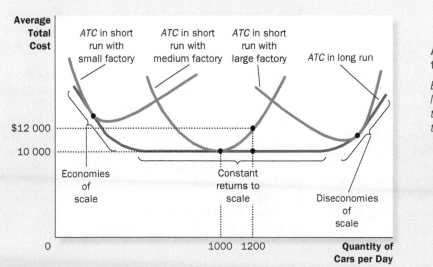

Average Total Cost in the Short and Long Runs

Because fixed costs are variable in the long run, the average-total-cost curve in the short run differs from the average-total-cost curve in the long run.

How long does it take for a firm to get to the long run? The answer depends on the firm. It can take a year or longer for a major manufacturing firm, such as a car company, to build a larger factory. By contrast, a person running a lemonade stand can go and buy a larger pitcher within an hour or less. There is, therefore, no single answer about how long it takes a firm to adjust its production facilities.

Economies and Diseconomies of Scale

economies of scale
the property whereby long-run average total cost falls as the quantity of output increases

diseconomies of scale
the property whereby long-run average total cost rises as the quantity of output increases

constant returns to scale
the property whereby long-run average total cost stays the same as the quantity of output changes

The shape of the long-run average-total-cost curve conveys important information about the technology for producing a good. When long-run average total cost declines as output increases, there are said to be **economies of scale.** When long-run average total cost rises as output increases, there are said to be **diseconomies of scale.** When long-run average total cost does not vary with the level of output, there are said to be **constant returns to scale.** In this example, Ford has economies of scale at low levels of output, constant returns to scale at intermediate levels of output, and diseconomies of scale at high levels of output.

What might cause economies or diseconomies of scale? Economies of scale often arise because higher production levels allow *specialization* among workers, which permits each worker to become better at his or her assigned tasks. For instance, modern assembly-line production requires a large number of workers.

---

i FYI

LESSONS FROM A PIN FACTORY

"Jack of all trades, master of none." This well-known adage helps explain why firms sometimes experience economies of scale. A person who tries to do everything usually ends up doing nothing very well. If a firm wants its workers to be as productive as they can be, it is often best to give each a limited task that he or she can master. But this is possible only if a firm employs many workers and produces a large quantity of output.

In his celebrated book *An Inquiry into the Nature and Causes of the Wealth of Nations*, Adam Smith described a visit he made to a pin factory. Smith was impressed by the specialization among the workers and the resulting economies of scale. He wrote:

One man draws out the wire, another straightens it, a third cuts it, a fourth points it, a fifth grinds it at the top for receiving the head; to make the head requires two or three distinct operations; to put it on is a peculiar business; to whiten it is another; it is even a trade by itself to put them into paper.

Smith reported that because of this specialization, the pin factory produced thousands of pins per worker every day. He conjectured that if the workers had chosen to work separately, rather than as a team of specialists, "they certainly could not each of them make twenty, perhaps not one pin a day." In other words, because of specialization, a large pin factory could achieve higher output per worker and lower average cost per pin than a small pin factory.

The specialization that Smith observed in the pin factory is prevalent in the modern economy. If you want to build a house, for instance, you could try to do all the work yourself. But most people turn to a builder, who in turn hires carpenters, plumbers, electricians, painters, and many other types of workers. These workers specialize in particular jobs, and this allows them to become better at their jobs than if they were generalists. Indeed, the use of specialization to achieve economies of scale is one reason modern societies are as prosperous as they are.

If Ford were producing only a small quantity of cars, it could not take advantage of this approach and would have higher average total cost. Diseconomies of scale can arise because of *coordination problems* that are inherent in any large organization. The more cars Ford produces, the more stretched the management team becomes, and the less effective the managers become at keeping costs down.

This analysis shows why long-run average-total-cost curves are often U-shaped. At low levels of production, the firm benefits from increased size because it can take advantage of greater specialization. Coordination problems, meanwhile, are not yet acute. By contrast, at high levels of production, the benefits of specialization have already been realized, and coordination problems become more severe as the firm grows larger. Thus, long-run average total cost is falling at low levels of production because of increasing specialization and rising at high levels of production because of increasing coordination problems.

QuickQuiz If Bombardier produces 9 jets per month, its long-run total cost is $9.0 million per month. If it produces 10 jets per month, its long-run total cost is $9.5 million per month. Does Bombardier exhibit economies or diseconomies of scale?

CONCLUSION

The purpose of this chapter has been to develop some tools that we can use to study how firms make production and pricing decisions. You should now understand what economists mean by the term *costs* and how costs vary with the quantity of output a firm produces. To refresh your memory, Table 13.3 summarizes some of the definitions we have encountered.

By themselves, of course, a firm's cost curves do not tell us what decisions the firm will make. But they are an important component of that decision, as we will begin to see in the next chapter.

SUMMARY

- The goal of firms is to maximize profit, which equals total revenue minus total cost.

- When analyzing a firm's behaviour, it is important to include all the opportunity costs of production. Some of the opportunity costs, such as the wages a firm pays its workers, are explicit. Other opportunity costs, such as the wages the firm owner gives up by working in the firm rather than taking another job, are implicit.

- A firm's costs reflect its production process. A typical firm's production function becomes flatter as the quantity of an input increases, displaying the property of diminishing marginal

product. As a result, a firm's total-cost curve becomes steeper as the quantity produced rises.

- A firm's total costs can be divided between fixed costs and variable costs. Fixed costs are costs that do not change when the firm alters the quantity of output produced. Variable costs are costs that do change when the firm alters the quantity of output produced.

- From a firm's total cost, two related measures of cost are derived. Average total cost is total cost divided by the quantity of output. Marginal cost is the amount by which total cost rises if output increases by 1 unit.

TABLE 13.3

The Many Types of Cost: A Summary

Term	Definition	Mathematical Description
Explicit costs	Costs that require an outlay of money by the firm	—
Implicit costs	Costs that do not require an outlay of money by the firm	—
Fixed costs	Costs that do not vary with the quantity of output produced	FC
Variable costs	Costs that do vary with the quantity of output produced	VC
Total cost	The market value of all the inputs that a firm uses in production	$TC = FC + VC$
Average fixed cost	Fixed costs divided by the quantity of output	$AFC = FC/Q$
Average variable cost	Variable costs divided by the quantity of output	$AVC = VC/Q$
Average total cost	Total cost divided by the quantity of output	$ATC = TC/Q$
Marginal cost	The increase in total cost that arises from an extra unit of production	$MC = \Delta TC/\Delta Q$

- When analyzing firm behaviour, it is often useful to graph average total cost and marginal cost. For a typical firm, marginal cost rises with the quantity of output. Average total cost first falls as output increases and then rises as output increases further. The marginal-cost curve always crosses the average-total-cost curve at the minimum of average total cost.

- A firm's costs often depend on the time horizon being considered. In particular, many costs are fixed in the short run but variable in the long run. As a result, when the firm changes its level of production, average total cost may rise more in the short run than in the long run.

KEY CONCEPTS

QUESTIONS FOR REVIEW

1. What is the relationship between a firm's total revenue, profit, and total cost?

2. Give an example of an opportunity cost that an accountant might not count as a cost. Why would the accountant ignore this cost?

3. What is marginal product, and what does it mean if it is diminishing?

4. Draw a production function that exhibits diminishing marginal product of labour. Draw the associated total-cost curve. (In both cases, be sure to label the axes.) Explain the shapes of the two curves you have drawn.

5. Define total cost, average total cost, and marginal cost. How are they related?

6. Draw the marginal-cost and average-total-cost curves for a typical firm. Explain why the curves have the shapes that they do and why they cross where they do.

7. How and why does a firm's average-total-cost curve differ in the short run and in the long run?

8. Define *economies of scale* and explain why they might arise. Define *diseconomies of scale* and explain why they might arise.

PROBLEMS AND APPLICATIONS

1. This chapter discusses many types of costs: opportunity cost, total cost, fixed cost, variable cost, average total cost, and marginal cost. Fill in the type of cost that best completes each phrase below:
   a. The true cost of taking some action is its _____.
   b. _____ is falling when marginal cost is below it, and rising when marginal cost is above it.
   c. A cost that does not depend on the quantity produced is a(n) _____.
   d. In the ice-cream industry in the short run, _____ includes the cost of cream and sugar, but not the cost of the factory.
   e. Profits equal total revenue less _____.
   f. The cost of producing an extra unit of output is the _____.

2. Your aunt is thinking about opening a hardware store. She estimates that it would cost $500 000 per year to rent the location and buy the stock. In addition, she would have to quit her $50 000 per year job as an accountant.
   a. Define *opportunity cost*.
   b. What is your aunt's opportunity cost of running a hardware store for a year? If your aunt thought she could sell $510 000 worth of merchandise in a year, should she open the store? Explain.

3. The city government is considering two tax proposals:
   - a lump-sum tax of $300 on each producer of hamburgers
   - a tax of $1 per burger, paid by producers of hamburgers
   a. Which of the following curves—average fixed cost, average variable cost, average total cost, and marginal cost—would shift as a result of the lump-sum tax? Why? Show this in a graph. Label the graph as precisely as possible.
   b. Which of these same four curves would shift as a result of the per-burger tax? Why? Show this in a new graph. Label the graph as precisely as possible.

4. A commercial fisherman notices the following relationship between hours spent fishing and the quantity of fish caught:

Hours	Quantity of Fish (in kilograms)
0	0
1	10
2	18
3	24
4	28
5	30

   a. What is the marginal product of each hour spent fishing?

b. Use these data to graph the fisherman's production function. Explain its shape.

c. The fisherman has a fixed cost of $10 (his pole). The opportunity cost of his time is $5 per hour. Graph the fisherman's total-cost curve. Explain its shape.

5. Nimbus, Inc., makes brooms and then sells them door to door. Here is the relationship between the number of workers and Nimbus's output in a given day:

Workers	Output	Marginal Product	Total Cost	Average Total Cost	Marginal Cost
0	0		—— ——		
		——			——
1	20		—— ——		
		——			——
2	50		—— ——		
		——			——
3	90		—— ——		
		——			——
4	120		—— ——		
		——			——
5	140		—— ——		
		——			——
6	150		—— ——		
		——			——
7	155		—— ——		

a. Fill in the column of marginal products. What pattern do you see? How might you explain it?

b. A worker costs $100 per day, and the firm has fixed costs of $200. Use this information to fill in the column for total cost.

c. Fill in the column for average total cost. (Recall that $ATC = TC/Q$.) What pattern do you see?

d. Now fill in the column for marginal cost. (Recall that $MC = \Delta TC/\Delta Q$.) What pattern do you see?

e. Compare the column for marginal product and the column for marginal cost. Explain the relationship.

f. Compare the column for average total cost and the column for marginal cost. Explain the relationship.

6. A firm has fixed cost of $100 and average variable cost of $5 \times Q$, where Q is the number of units produced.

a. Construct a table showing total cost for Q from 0 to 10.

b. Graph the firm's curves for marginal cost and average total cost.

c. How does marginal cost change with Q? What does this suggest about the firm's production process?

7. Consider the following cost information for a pizzeria:

Q (dozens)	Total Cost	Variable Cost
0	$300	$ 0
1	350	50
2	390	90
3	420	120
4	450	150
5	490	190
6	540	240

a. What is the pizzeria's fixed cost?

b. Construct a table in which you calculate the marginal cost per dozen pizzas using the information on total cost. Also calculate the marginal cost per dozen pizzas using the information on variable cost. What is the relationship between these sets of numbers? Comment.

8. You are thinking about setting up a lemonade stand. The stand itself costs $200. The ingredients for each cup of lemonade cost $0.50.

a. What is your fixed cost of doing business? What is your variable cost per cup?

b. Construct a table showing your total cost, average total cost, and marginal cost for output levels varying from 0 to 45 L. (Hint: There are 4 cups in a litre.) Draw the three cost curves.

9. Your cousin Vinnie owns a painting company with fixed costs of $200 and the following schedule for variable costs:

Quantity of Houses Painted per Month	1	2	3	4	5	6	7
Variable Costs	$10	$20	$40	$80	$160	$320	$640

Calculate average fixed cost, average variable cost, and average total cost for each quantity. What is the efficient scale of the painting company?

10. Healthy Harry's Juice Bar has the following cost schedules:

Q (vats)	Variable Cost	Total Cost
0	$ 0	$ 30
1	10	40
2	25	55
3	45	75
4	70	100
5	100	130
6	135	165

a. Calculate average variable cost, average total cost, and marginal cost for each quantity.

b. Graph all three curves. What is the relationship between the marginal-cost curve and the average-total-cost curve? Between the marginal-cost curve and the average-variable-cost curve? Explain.

11. Consider the following table of long-run total cost for three different firms:

Quantity	1	2	3	4	5	6	7
Firm A	$60	$70	$80	$90	$100	$110	$120
Firm B	11	24	39	56	75	96	119
Firm C	21	34	49	66	85	106	129

Does each of these firms experience economies of scale or diseconomies of scale?

12. You are the chief financial officer for a firm that sells digital music players. Your firm has the following average total cost schedule:

Quantity	Average Total Cost
600 players	$300
601 players	301

Your current level of production is 600 devices, all of which have been sold. Someone calls, desperate to buy one of your music players. The caller offers you $550 for it. Should you accept the offer? Why or why not?

http://   For more study tools, please visit http://www.mankiw5e.nelson.com.

13 The Costs of Production

I. Chapter Overview

A. Context and Purpose

Earlier chapters introduced the workings of the market system (Chapters 1–7), and then explored the role of government in improving efficiency when the market is less than perfect (Chapters 8–12). The focus now returns to the analysis of the market system by examining business structure and operation in the next five chapters (13–17).

This chapter looks at a firm's cost of production and the firm's revenue and profit, and it distinguishes economic cost and profit from accounting cost and profit. The chapter explains that cost and profit take on very specific meanings in economics that differ from the everyday use of the terms. The analysis in this chapter will provide the tools necessary to understand how all firms, from the largest to the smallest, behave under different types of market conditions.

A. Helpful Hints

1. *Economic cost is not the same as accounting cost.* The concept of cost used by economists is not quite the same as that used by accountants. By cost, economists mean "opportunity cost," that is, all those things that must be forgone to acquire an input or the return that a particular resource could get in its best alternative use. Thus, economists include not only the explicit accounting costs, but also implicit costs of production.

2. *The distinction between short run and long run in economics is somewhat arbitrary.* Economists define the short run as a period in which some inputs (typically capital and land) are fixed, while at least one input (typically labour) is variable, and the long run as a period long enough for firms to vary all inputs or even enter or exit the industry. Although arbitrary, it makes a lot of sense: a firm desiring to increase output quickly could expand labour immediately, but it would take a while to build a new factory.

3. *Diminishing marginal product is the rule, not the exception.* As long as only labour can vary, it should not be surprising that output will not rise in proportion with labour input. Imagine growing strawberries in your backyard in a plot that is only 20 × 10 metres. You might be able to pick 3 pints of strawberries in 15 minutes. However, additional workers in the same small plot could not be expected to maintain that level of output per

177

worker. Eventually, the marginal product of an additional worker will fall because land and capital are fixed. With enough workers, the marginal product actually becomes negative when the patch is so crowded that people are getting in each others' way and trampling the berries.

4. *Diminishing marginal product is not the same thing as negative marginal product.* The average person often confuses the two concepts. In the strawberry patch, diminishing marginal product is not bad—even if all workers are identical, not every worker should be expected to add the same amount to output. In addition, hiring more workers adds to total product, albeit at a decreasing rate. Negative marginal product, on the other hand, means that another picker actually reduces total product and should not be hired, or even be allowed to help for free.

5. *Marginal cost always intersects average total cost and average variable costs at their lowest points.* The marginal value contributes to the average, so if marginal is less than average, it pulls the average down, and if marginal is greater than average, it pulls the average up. Think about what happens to the overall GPA (grade point average) of the class when another student adds the course. The marginal GPA of the additional student either raises or lowers the average. Overall, GPA for the class falls as long as the marginal GPA is below the average, and rises when the marginal GPA exceeds the average.

6. *Economies of scale and diseconomies of scale* refer to technological conditions under which long-run average cost decreases or increases, respectively, as output increases.

II. Self-Testing Challenges

A.   True/False Questions

_____1.   Economic profit is typically higher than accounting profit.

_____2.   The marginal product of an input is the last unit of output that it produces.

_____3.   Implicit costs are opportunity costs for which there is no actual money outlay.

_____4.   Whenever marginal cost is less than average variable cost, average variable cost is falling.

_____5.   Average fixed cost does not vary with output.

_____6.   All costs are variable in the short run.

_____7.   Marginal cost is defined as the additional cost incurred as a result of hiring one more unit of input.

_____8.   The average-total-cost curve has the most pronounced U-shape in the short run.

_____9.   Average total cost reaches a minimum where it intersects average variable cost.

_____10.   Diseconomies of scale are caused by problems of coordination and communication that are inherent in large organizations.

_____11.   If marginal product is negative, output decreases whenever one more unit of the variable input is hired.

_____12.   Diminishing marginal product is the property whereby the marginal product of an input declines as the quantity of the input decreases.

B.   Multiple-Choice Questions

1.   Which one of the following costs is variable in the short run?
    a.   wages paid to labour
    b.   payments to suppliers to buy new capital equipment
    c.   rent on land
    d.   interest on business loans to buy capital equipment

2.   Which one of the following costs is variable in the long run?
    a.   wages paid to labour
    b.   grants to suppliers to buy new capital equipment
    c.   purchase price of land
    d.   interest on business loans to buy capital equipment

3.   Which one of the following would an economist say is the definition of the opportunity cost of an input used in production?
    a.   the money paid to acquire that input
    b.   the benefit forgone by not using that input in its best alternative
    c.   the accounting cost of that input
    d.   the benefit forgone by not using that input in its worst alternative

4.   Which one of the following is the point at which marginal cost always equals average total cost?
    a.   at minimum average total cost
    b.   at minimum marginal cost
    c.   at maximum average total cost
    d.   at average variable cost

Use the following data for Jalali's Auto Trader to answer questions 5–11.

Number of automobiles sold per week	Total cost of operation (excluding the value of automobiles)
0	$1000
10	$1400
20	$1600
30	$1700
40	$2000
50	$2600

5. Which one of the following is the variable cost of selling 30 automobiles?
   a. $700
   b. $1400
   c. $1600
   d. $1700

6. Which one of the following is the fixed cost of selling 40 automobiles?
   a. $1000
   b. $1400
   c. $1600
   d. $1700

7. Which one of the following is the marginal cost of the 20th automobile?
   a. $10
   b. $20
   c. $30
   d. $40

8. Which one of the following is the average total cost of selling 40 automobiles?
   a. $25
   b. $30
   c. $32
   d. $50

9. Which one of the following is the average variable cost of selling 20 automobiles?
   a. $25
   b. $30
   c. $32
   d. $50

10. Which one of the following is the average fixed cost of selling 50 automobiles?
    a. $20
    b. $25
    c. $30
    d. $50

11. Which one of the following is the efficient scale of operation for Jalali's Auto Trader?
    a. 20 automobiles sold
    b. 30 automobiles sold
    c. 40 automobiles sold
    d. 50 automobiles sold

12. Which one of the following explains when diminishing marginal product occurs?
    a. whenever business is operating inefficiently, resulting in high per-unit costs
    b. whenever the quality of the available labour pool deteriorates and production costs rise
    c. whenever business becomes so large that it is unwieldy to manage and productivity declines
    d. whenever additional workers add less to output than did the workers who came before

To answer questions 13–16, use the following information for Freischütz's Fabulous Franks, a hot dog stand that has been a downtown institution for 50 years.

Cost of supplies and other materials	$10 000
Rent	$20 000
Wages paid	$25 000
Interest on a $10 000 bank loan	$1000
Freischütz's salary offer from a competitor	$20 000

13. Which one of the following is the total explicit (accounting) cost of running Freischütz's Franks?
    a. $11 000
    b. $36 000
    c. $56 000
    d. $76 000

14.   Which one of the following is the total opportunity (economic) cost of running Freischütz's Franks?
a. $36 000
b. $56 000
c. $75 000
d. $76 000

15.   If Mr. Freischütz pays off the bank loan and invests $10 000 of his own money in the business, thus giving up the chance to earn $1000 in interest elsewhere, which one of the following will occur?
a.   Accounting and economic costs will both rise by $1000.
b.   Accounting and economic costs will both fall by $1000.
c.   Accounting cost will fall by $1000, but economic cost will not change.
d.   Accounting cost will not change, but economic cost will fall by $1000.

16.   If Mr. Freischütz has a job offer of $50 000 per year to manage his competitor's business, which one of the following will occur?
a.   The implicit cost of staying in business will rise.
b.   The explicit cost of staying in business will rise.
c.   The implicit cost of staying in business will fall.
d.   The explicit cost of staying in business will fall.

17.   Which one of the following statements is true?
a.   If fixed costs are positive, the average variable cost and the average total cost move further apart as output increases.
b.   If there are no fixed costs, the average variable cost is constant.
c.   If there are no fixed costs, the average variable cost and the average total cost are the same.

18.   Which one of the following statements is true?
a.   Diseconomies of scale is a short-run concept.
b.   Diminishing marginal product is a short-run concept.
c.   Diminishing marginal product results when the firm doubles in size without doubling output.
d.   Diseconomies of scale results when only one input increases and output fails to keep up.

19.   Which one of the following describes the behaviour of marginal cost when marginal product is rising?
a.   cost is rising
b.   cost is falling
c.   cost is constant

20. With the law of diminishing returns, which of the following occurs as output increases in the short run?
    a. fixed cost will eventually fall
    b. fixed cost will eventually rise
    c. marginal cost will eventually fall
    d. marginal cost will eventually rise

C. Short-Answer Questions

1. Consider the following production function for a pet supply manufacturer, Linh's Lemming Runs.

Number of workers hired	0	1	2	3	4	5	6	7	8	9	10
Output	0	10	25	40	50	59	61	62	62	62	60
Marginal product	—	—	—	—	—	—	—	—	—	—	—

   a. Fill in the missing values for marginal product.

   b. With which worker does diminishing marginal product set in? When does marginal product actually become negative? Compare the two cases in terms of the effect on total output. _____

   _____

   _____

   _____

   _____

2. What is the connection between the U-shaped nature of the average total cost curve and (a) the property of diminishing marginal product, and (b) fixed costs? Explain your answer._____

   _____

   _____

   _____

3. Explain in your own words the difference between accounting profit and economic profit. Include discussion of the distinction between explicit and implicit costs and how they relate to economic cost and opportunity cost.

   _____

   _____

   _____

   _____

   _____

D. Practice Problems

1.   Wendell's Widget Works faces the following cost schedule.

Quantity (Q)	Fixed cost (FC)	Variable cost (VC)	Total cost (TC)	Marginal cost (MC)	Average variable cost (AVC)	Average fixed cost (AFC)	Average total cost (ATC)
0	$46	$ 0	$____	$____	$____	$____	$____
1	$____	$30	$____	$____	$____	$____	$____
2	$____	$50	$____	$____	$____	$____	$____
3	$____	$58	$____	$____	$____	$____	$____
4	$____	$64	$____	$____	$____	$____	$____
5	$____	$84	$____	$____	$____	$____	$____
6	$____	$114	$____	$____	$____	$____	$____
7	$____	$150	$____	$____	$____	$____	$____
8	$____	$190	$____	$____	$____	$____	$____
9	$____	$240	$____	$____	$____	$____	$____

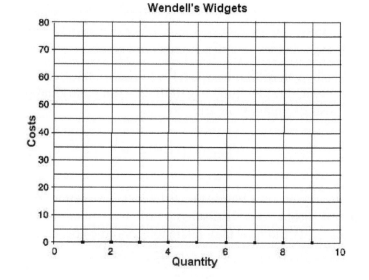

Wendell's Widgets

456

a. Fill in the table and graph the results.

b. Based on these cost curves, where does the diminishing marginal product set in? Explain._____
_____
_____
_____

c. What is the relationship between total cost, variable cost, and fixed cost? Explain._____
_____
_____

d. What is the relationship between average total cost, average variable cost, and AFC? Explain. _____
_____
_____
_____

e. What is the relationship between average total cost and marginal cost? Between average variable cost and marginal cost? Explain.
_____
_____
_____

f. What is Wendell's efficient scale? Explain. _____
_____
_____
_____

2.   Bob's Burger Box has been operating continuously since 1962. The original investment was $100 000, but the business is worth a lot more today. In fact, Bob's chief competitor would like to buy him out and has made a standing offer of $1 million any time that Bob wants to sell. He is also willing to hire Bob for $50 000 per year if Bob sells out. Bob has been tempted because he figures that he could earn 10% on the $1 million if he invests it wisely. You need to help him decide. Currently, Bob figures that he is earning a profit of $100 000 per year based on the following information:

Total Revenue: $200 000 (from 100 000 hamburgers @$2)
Total Money Outlays: $100 000 (wages paid, materials, utilities)

a.   What are his explicit (accounting) costs? What are his implicit costs? What is his total economic (opportunity) cost? Explain. _____
_____
_____

b.   If his goal is to maximize profit, should he stay in business or sell out? Is he earning any money? Would an accountant and an economist give the same answer to the question about how much he is earning? Explain. _____
_____
_____
_____
_____

c.   Would it affect your answer to (b) above if he inherited the business from his uncle and, therefore, had no money of his own invested in the business?
_____
_____

d.   Suppose that instead of owning the business free and clear, Bob owed $1 million to the bank on a 10% loan, or $100 000 per year, in interest. What effect would this have on your answer to (a)? Specifically, would it affect his explicit (accounting) cost? His implicit cost? His total economic (opportunity) cost? How would this affect his economic and accounting profit? Explain. _____
_____
_____
_____
_____
_____

3. Farbod Manufacturing has an opportunity to invest $1500 in Project A or Project B. Project A promises to generate $500 profit at the end of the first year, $550 at the end of two years, $600 at the end of three years, and $625 at the end of four years. Project B promises to generate $25 profit at the end of the first year, $100 at the end of two years, $600 at the end of three years and $1000 at the end of four years. Determine which investment promises to be the better of the two for the company, assuming that Farbod Manufacturing has a weighted average cost of capital of 9%.

E. Advanced Critical Thinking

Your uncle, who farms 1000 hectares in central Manitoba, has always claimed that he is losing money in farming. However, according to his tax returns, he earns a decent profit. Is someone not telling the truth, or does he simply need a better tax accountant? Why do you suppose he stays in agriculture if he is incurring losses as he claims?_____

_____

_____

_____

_____

_____

_____

_____

_____

_____

III. Solutions

A. True/False Questions

1. F; economic profit is accounting profit minus implicit cost.
2. F; the marginal product of an input is the additional output forthcoming from employing an additional unit of that input, other inputs held constant.
3. T
4. T
5. F; average fixed cost always declines as output increases.
6. F; all costs are variable in the *long run*.
7. F; marginal cost is the extra cost incurred as a result of producing an additional unit of output.
8. T
9. F; average total cost reaches a minimum where it intersects *marginal* cost.
10. T
11. T
12. F; it implies that the marginal product of an input declines as more (not less) of an input is employed.

B.   Multiple-Choice Questions

1. a	5. a	9. b	13. c	17. c
2. a	6. a	10. a	14. d	18. b
3. b	7. b	11. c	15. c	19. b
4. a	8. d	12. d	16. a	20. d

C.   Short-Answer Questions

1.   a.   Consider the following production function for a pet supply manufacturer, Linh's Lemming Runs.

Number of workers hired	0	1	2	3	4	5	6	7	8	9	10
Output	0	10	25	40	50	59	61	62	62	62	60
Marginal product	—	10	15	15	10	9	2	1	0	0	−2

    b.   Diminishing returns set in with the 4th worker hired because this is the first drop in marginal product (from 15 to 10). When marginal product begins to decline, total output continues to rise, although at a slower rate. With the 10th worker hired, the marginal product actually becomes negative, which means that *total* product begins to fall.

2.   The U-shaped nature of average total cost arises from the forces of both diminishing marginal product and declining average fixed cost (AFC). Initially, as output increases, the marginal productivity of the variable input rises, causing average variable cost (AVC) to fall. Falling average variable cost and declining AFC cause average total cost (which is the sum of AFC and average variable cost) to fall. Thus, as output increases, marginal productivity of the variable input diminishes, causing average variable cost to rise. Eventually, average variable cost rises faster than average fixed cost falls, causing average total cost to increase.

3.   Accounting profit is based on money flows; it equals the firm's total revenues minus all of the explicit money outlays required to generate those revenues. Economic profit takes into account all opportunity costs, even those that did not result in money outlays. Economic profit equals the firm's total revenues minus the full opportunity cost of earning those revenues, including both money outlays and any implicit opportunity costs of production.

D.   Practice Problems

1.   a.   Wendell's Widget Works faces the following cost schedule:

Quantity (Q)	Fixed cost (FC)	Variable cost (VC)	Total cost (TC)	Marginal cost (MC)	Average variable cost (AVC)	Average fixed cost (AFC)	Average total cost (ATC)
0	$46	$0	$46	—	—	—	—
1	$46	$30	$76	$30	$30	$46	$76
2	$46	$50	$96	$20	$25	$23	$48
3	$46	$58	$104	$8	$19.3	$15.3	$34.7
4	$46	$64	$110	$6	$16	$11.5	$27.5
5	$46	$84	$130	$20	$16.8	$9.2	$26
6	$46	$114	$160	$30	$19	$7.7	$26.7
7	$46	$150	$196	$36	$21.4	$6.6	$28
8	$46	$190	$236	$40	$23.8	$5.8	$29.5
9	46	240	$286	$50	$26.7	$5.1	$31.8

b.   Yes, diminishing marginal product sets in at the output level at which marginal cost begins to rise, with the fifth unit of output. It is diminishing marginal product that causes marginal cost to rise by increasing the labour cost of each additional unit of output.

c.   Costs are either variable or fixed. Therefore, total cost = variable cost + fixed cost.

d.   If TC = VC + FC, then dividing both sides by Q maintains the equality and gives the following identity: ATC = AVC + AFC.

e.   Marginal cost always intersects ATC and average variable cost at their minimum points. In each case, the average is influenced by the marginal value: if MC > ATC or AVC, then the average rises, and if MC < ATC or AVC, then the average is pulled down by the low marginal cost.

f.   Wendell's efficient scale is an output of 5. At this quantity, average total cost reaches a minimum at 26.

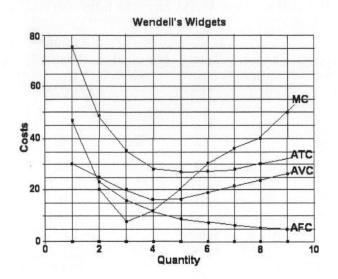

2.   a.   Bob's accounting cost = $100 000. These are the explicit costs or money outlays required to stay in business. His implicit costs include forgone earnings of $50 000 by not accepting the job offer + $100 000 in lost interest by not selling out and investing the $1 million at 10% interest. His total economic cost is the total opportunity cost of staying in business, including both explicit and implicit costs. This opportunity cost equals $250 000 ($100 000 in explicit costs + $50 000 in forgone wages + $100 000 in forgone interest).

b.   To maximize his profit, he should sell out. When he takes into account all of the costs of staying in business, he is losing money. His economic profit is negative: $200 000 in total revenue minus $250 000 in total (opportunity) cost equals a profit (loss) of ($50 000). To an accountant (and the Canada Customs and Revenue Agency), however, he is earning $100 000 ($200 000 in revenues minus $100 000 in explicit cost).

c.   The answer would be unchanged. The opportunity cost of staying in business would still include the interest on the $1 million because, regardless of its source, it is available for him to invest if he sells out.

d.   If Bob owes $1 million to the bank, the $100 000 in interest becomes an explicit cost that would be deducted from accounting profit. However, his economic cost already included the $100 000 in interest as an implicit cost, so his economic profit (in this case a loss) would be unchanged at ($50 000). His accounting profit would be 0 ($200 000 in revenues minus $200 000 in explicit cost).

3. For each project we need to calculate the net present value (NPV).
    Project A

$$NPV_A = -1500 + \frac{500}{1.09} + \frac{550}{(1.09)^2} + \frac{600}{(1.09)^3} + \frac{625}{(1.09)^4}$$

$$= -1500 + 458.72 + 462.18 + 461.54 + 443.26$$

$$= \$325.70$$

Project B

$$NPV_B = -1500 + \frac{25}{1.09} + \frac{100}{(1.09)^2} + \frac{600}{(1.09)^3} + \frac{1000}{(1.09)^4}$$

$$= -1500 + 22.94 + 84.03 + 461.54 + 709.22$$

$$= -\$222.27$$

Project B, having a negative NPV, should not be undertaken. Farbod Manufacturing should invest in Project A.

E. **Advanced Critical Thinking**

This is not inconsistent. His tax returns show his accounting profit equal to total revenue minus total explicit cost. Accounting profit fails to consider any implicit cost of production, such as the value of his time or the interest on his investment in the business. The farmland alone could be worth millions of dollars. If he were not in farming, this money could be invested elsewhere earning hundreds of thousands of dollars per year. His economic profit reflects these implicit costs. If the implicit costs are substantial enough to offset the positive accounting profit, then economic loss will result. If he stays in business in spite of incurring an economic loss, this could mean that he gets enough utility out of working (and owning) the land to make him willing to incur the loss. Another possibility is that he is willing to hold the land as an investment. Every year that the land appreciates in value, it earns a return equal to its rate of appreciation.

Learning Objectives

In this chapter, you will ...

- Learn what characteristics make a market competitive

- Examine how competitive firms decide how much output to produce

- Examine how competitive firms decide when to shut down production temporarily

- Examine how competitive firms decide whether to exit or enter a market

- See how firm behaviour determines a market's short-run and long-run supply curves

If your local gas station raised the price it charges for gasoline by 20 percent, it would see a large drop in the amount of gasoline it sold. Its customers would quickly switch to buying their gasoline at other gas stations. By contrast, if your local water company raised the price of water by 20 percent, it would see only a small decrease in the amount of water it sold. People might water their lawns less often and buy more water-efficient showerheads, but they would be hard-pressed to reduce water consumption greatly and would be unlikely to find another supplier. The difference between the gasoline market and the water market is obvious: Many firms supply gasoline, but only one firm supplies water. As you might expect, this difference in market structure shapes the pricing and production decisions of the firms that operate in these markets.

In this chapter we examine the behaviour of competitive firms, such as your local gas station. You may recall that a market is competitive if each buyer and seller is small compared to the size of the market and, therefore, has little ability to influence market prices. By contrast, if a firm can influence the market price of the good it sells, it is said to have *market power*. Later in the book, we examine the behaviour of firms with market power, such as your local water company.

Our analysis of competitive firms in this chapter will shed light on the decisions that lie behind the supply curve in a competitive market. Not surprisingly, we will find that a market supply curve is tightly linked to firms' costs of production. (Indeed, this general insight should be familiar to you from our analysis in Chapter 7.) But among a firm's various costs—fixed, variable, average, and marginal—which ones are most relevant for its decision about the quantity to supply at any given price? We will see that all these measures of cost play important and interrelated roles.

WHAT IS A COMPETITIVE MARKET?

Our goal in this chapter is to examine how firms make production decisions in competitive markets. As a background for this analysis, we begin by considering what a competitive market is.

The Meaning of Competition

competitive market
a market with many buyers and sellers trading identical products so that each buyer and seller is a price taker

A **competitive market**, sometimes called a *perfectly competitive market*, has two characteristics:

1. There are many buyers and many sellers in the market.
2. The goods offered by the various sellers are largely the same.

As a result of these conditions, the actions of any single buyer or seller in the market have a negligible impact on the market price. Each buyer and seller takes the market price as given.

An example is the market for milk. No single buyer of milk can influence the price of milk because each buyer purchases a small amount relative to the size of the market. Similarly, each seller of milk has limited control over the price because many other sellers are offering milk that is essentially identical. Because each seller can sell all he wants to at the going price, he has little reason to charge less, and if he charges more, buyers will go elsewhere. Buyers and sellers in competitive markets must accept the price the market determines and, therefore, are said to be *price takers*.

In addition to the forgoing two conditions for competition, there is a third condition sometimes thought to characterize perfectly competitive markets:

3. Firms can freely enter or exit the market in the long run.

If, for instance, anyone can decide to start a dairy farm, and if any existing dairy farmer can decide to leave the dairy business, then the dairy industry would satisfy this condition. It should be noted that much of the analysis of competitive firms does not rely on the assumption of free entry and exit, because this condition is not necessary for firms to be price takers. But as we will see later in this chapter, entry and exit are often powerful forces in shaping the long-run outcome in competitive markets.

The Revenue of a Competitive Firm

A firm in a competitive market, like most other firms in the economy, tries to maximize profit, which equals total revenue minus total cost. To see how it does this, we first consider the revenue of a competitive firm. To keep matters concrete, let's consider a specific firm: the Smith Family Dairy Farm.

The Smith farm produces a quantity of milk, Q, and sells each unit at the market price, P. The farm's total revenue is $P \times Q$. For example, if a 4-L jug of milk sells for $6 and the farm sells 1000 jugs, its total revenue is $6000.

Because the Smith farm is small compared to the country's market for milk, it takes the price as given by market conditions. This means, in particular, that the price of milk does not depend on the quantity of output that the Smith farm produces and sells. If the Smiths double the amount of milk they produce, the price of milk remains the same, and their total revenue doubles. As a result, total revenue is proportional to the amount of output.

Table 14.1 shows the revenue for the Smith Family Dairy Farm. The first two columns show the amount of output the farm produces and the price at which it sells its output. The third column is the farm's total revenue. The table assumes that the price of milk is $6 per jug, so total revenue is simply $6 times the number of jugs.

Just as the concepts of average and marginal were useful in the preceding chapter when analyzing costs, they are also useful when analyzing revenue. To see what these concepts tell us, consider these two questions:

1. How much revenue does the farm receive for the typical jug of milk?
2. How much additional revenue does the farm receive if it increases production of milk by 1 jug?

The last two columns in Table 14.1 answer these questions.

The fourth column in the table shows **average revenue**, which is total revenue (from the third column) divided by the amount of output (from the first column). Average revenue tells us how much revenue a firm receives for the typical unit sold. In Table 14.1, you can see that average revenue equals $6, the price of a jug of milk. This illustrates a general lesson that applies not only to competitive firms

average revenue
total revenue divided by the quantity sold

TABLE 14.1

Total, Average, and Marginal Revenue for a Competitive Firm

Quantity	Price	Total Revenue	Average Revenue	Marginal Revenue
(Q)	(P)	(TR = P × Q)	(AR = TR/Q)	(MR = ΔTR/ΔQ)
1 jug	$6	$ 6	$6	
				$6
2	6	12	6	
				6
3	6	18	6	
				6
4	6	24	6	
				6
5	6	30	6	
				6
6	6	36	6	
				6
7	6	42	6	
				6
8	6	48	6	

marginal revenue
the change in total revenue from
an additional unit sold

but to other firms as well. Total revenue is the price times the quantity ($P \times Q$), and average revenue is total revenue ($P \times Q$) divided by the quantity (Q). Therefore, *for all firms, average revenue equals the price of the good.*

The fifth column shows **marginal revenue,** which is the change in total revenue from the sale of each additional unit of output. In Table 14.1, marginal revenue equals $6, the price of a jug of milk. This result illustrates a lesson that applies only to competitive firms. Total revenue is $P \times Q$, and P is fixed for a competitive firm. Therefore, when Q rises by 1 unit, total revenue rises by P dollars. *For competitive firms, marginal revenue equals the price of the good.*

QuickQuiz   When a competitive firm doubles the amount it sells, what happens to the price of its output and its total revenue?

PROFIT MAXIMIZATION AND THE COMPETITIVE FIRM'S SUPPLY CURVE

The goal of a competitive firm is to maximize profit, which equals total revenue minus total cost. We have just discussed the firm's revenue, and in the last chapter we discussed the firm's costs. We are now ready to examine how the firm maximizes profit and how that decision leads to its supply curve.

A Simple Example of Profit Maximization

Let's begin our analysis of the firm's supply decision with the example in Table 14.2. In the first column of the table is the number of 4-L jugs of milk the Smith Family Dairy Farm produces. The second column shows the farm's total revenue, which is $6 times the number of jugs. The third column shows the farm's total cost. Total cost includes fixed costs, which are $3 in this example, and variable costs, which depend on the quantity produced.

The fourth column shows the farm's profit, which is computed by subtracting total cost from total revenue. If the farm produces nothing, it has a loss of $3. If it produces 1 jug, it has a profit of $1. If it produces 2 jugs, it has a profit of $4, and so on. To maximize profit, the Smith farm chooses the quantity that makes profit as large as possible. In this example, profit is maximized when the farm produces 4 or 5 jugs of milk, when the profit is $7.

There is another way to look at the Smith farm's decision: The Smiths can find the profit-maximizing quantity by comparing the marginal revenue and marginal cost from each unit produced. The fifth and sixth columns in Table 14.2 compute marginal revenue and marginal cost from the changes in total revenue and total cost, and the last column shows the change in profit for each additional 4-L jug of milk produced. The first jug of milk the farm produces has a marginal revenue of $6 and a marginal cost of $2; hence, producing that jug increases profit by $4 (from –$3 to $1). The second jug produced has a marginal revenue of $6 and a marginal cost of $3, so that jug increases profit by $3 (from $1 to $4). As long as marginal revenue exceeds marginal cost, increasing the quantity produced raises profit.

| | | | | TABLE 14.2 | | | |

Profit Maximization: A Numerical Example

Quantity	Total Revenue	Total Cost	Profit	Marginal Revenue	Marginal Cost	Change in Profit
(Q)	(TR)	(TC)	(TR − TC)	(MR = $\Delta TR/\Delta Q$)	(MC = $\Delta TC/\Delta Q$)	(MR − MC)
0 jugs	$ 0	$ 3	−$3			
				$6	$2	$4
1	6	5	1			
				6	3	3
2	12	8	4			
				6	4	2
3	18	12	6			
				6	5	1
4	24	17	7			
				6	6	0
5	30	23	7			
				6	7	−1
6	36	30	6			
				6	8	−2
7	42	38	4			
				6	9	−3
8	48	47	1			

Once the Smith farm has reached 5 4-L jugs of milk, however, the situation is very different. The sixth jug would have marginal revenue of $6 and marginal cost of $7, so producing it would reduce profit by $1 (from $7 to $6). As a result, the Smiths would not produce beyond 5 jugs of milk.

One of the ten principles of economics in Chapter 1 is that rational people think at the margin. We now see how the Smith Family Dairy Farm can apply this principle. If marginal revenue is greater than marginal cost—as it is at 1, 2, or 3 jugs—the Smiths should increase the production of milk. If marginal revenue is less than marginal cost—as it is at 6, 7, or 8 jugs—the Smiths should decrease production. If the Smiths think at the margin and make incremental adjustments to the level of production, they are naturally led to produce the profit-maximizing quantity.

The Marginal-Cost Curve and the Firm's Supply Decision

To extend this analysis of profit maximization, consider the cost curves in Figure 14.1. These cost curves have the three features that, as we discussed in the previous chapter, are thought to describe most firms: The marginal-cost curve (MC) is upward sloping. The average-total-cost curve (ATC) is U-shaped. And the marginal-cost curve crosses the average-total-cost curve at the minimum of average total cost. The figure also shows a horizontal line at the market price (P). The price line is horizontal because the firm is a price taker: The price of the firm's output is the same regardless of the quantity that the firm decides to produce.

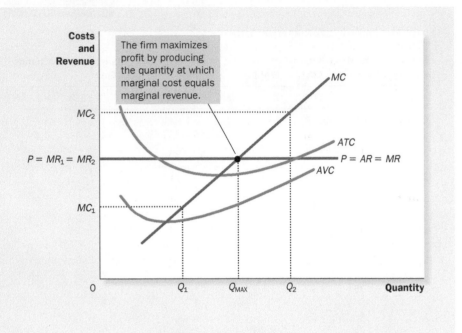

FIGURE 14.1

Profit Maximization for a Competitive Firm

This figure shows the marginal-cost curve (MC), the average-total-cost curve (ATC), and the average-variable-cost curve (AVC). It also shows the market price (P), which equals marginal revenue (MR) and average revenue (AR). At the quantity Q_1, marginal revenue MR_1 exceeds marginal cost MC_1, so raising production increases profit. At the quantity Q_2, marginal cost MC_2 is above marginal revenue MR_2, so reducing production increases profit. The profit-maximizing quantity Q_{MAX} is found where the horizontal price line intersects the marginal-cost curve.

Keep in mind that, for a competitive firm, the firm's price equals both its average revenue (AR) and its marginal revenue (MR).

We can use Figure 14.1 to find the quantity of output that maximizes profit. Imagine that the firm is producing at Q_1. At this level of output, marginal revenue is greater than marginal cost. That is, if the firm raised its level of production and sales by 1 unit, the additional revenue (MR_1) would exceed the additional costs (MC_1). Profit, which equals total revenue minus total cost, would increase. Hence, if marginal revenue is greater than marginal cost, as it is at Q_1, the firm can increase profit by increasing production.

A similar argument applies when output is at Q_2. In this case, marginal cost is greater than marginal revenue. If the firm reduced production by 1 unit, the costs saved (MC_2) would exceed the revenue lost (MR_2). Therefore, if marginal revenue is less than marginal cost, as it is at Q_2, the firm can increase profit by reducing production.

Where do these marginal adjustments to level of production end? Regardless of whether the firm begins with production at a low level (such as Q_1) or at a high level (such as Q_2), the firm will eventually adjust production until the quantity produced reaches Q_{MAX}. This analysis yields three general rules for profit maximization:

1. If marginal revenue is greater than marginal cost, the firm should increase its output.
2. If marginal cost is greater than marginal revenue, the firm should decrease its output.
3. At the profit-maximizing level of output, marginal revenue and marginal cost are exactly equal.

These rules are the key to rational decision making by a profit-maximizing firm. They apply not only to competitive firms but, as we will see in the next chapter, to other types of firms as well.

We can now see how the competitive firm decides the quantity of its good to supply to the market. Because a competitive firm is a price taker, its marginal revenue equals the market price. For any given price, the competitive firm's profit-maximizing quantity of output is found by looking at the intersection of the price with the marginal-cost curve. In Figure 14.1, that quantity of output is Q_{MAX}.

Suppose the price prevailing in this market rises, perhaps because of an increase in market demand. Figure 14.2 shows how a competitive firm responds to an increase in the price. When the price is P_1, the firm produces quantity Q_1, the quantity that equates marginal cost to the price. When the price rises to P_2, the firm finds that marginal revenue is now higher than marginal cost at the previous level of output, so the firm increases production. The new profit-maximizing quantity is Q_2, at which marginal cost equals the new higher price. *In essence, because the firm's marginal-cost curve determines the quantity of the good the firm is willing to supply at any price, it is the competitive firm's supply curve.* There are, however, some caveats to this conclusion, which we examine next.

The Firm's Short-Run Decision to Shut Down

So far we have been analyzing the question of how much a competitive firm will produce. In some circumstances, however, the firm will decide to shut down and not produce anything at all.

Here we should distinguish between a temporary shutdown of a firm and the permanent exit of a firm from the market. A *shutdown* refers to a short-run decision

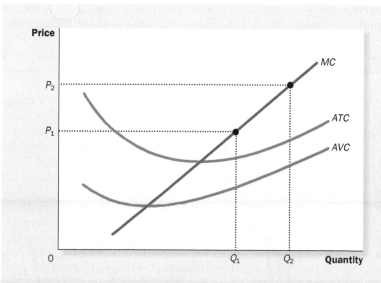

FIGURE 14.2

Marginal Cost as the Competitive Firm's Supply Curve

An increase in the price from P_1 to P_2 leads to an increase in the firm's profit-maximizing quantity from Q_1 to Q_2. Because the marginal-cost curve shows the quantity supplied by the firm at any given price, it is the firm's supply curve.

not to produce anything during a specific period of time because of current market conditions. *Exit* refers to a long-run decision to leave the market. The short-run and long-run decisions differ because most firms cannot avoid their fixed costs in the short run but can do so in the long run. That is, a firm that shuts down temporarily still has to pay its fixed costs, whereas a firm that exits the market saves both its fixed and its variable costs.

For example, consider the production decision that a farmer faces. The cost of the land is one of the farmer's fixed costs. If the farmer decides not to produce any crops one season, the land lies fallow and he cannot recover this cost. When making the short-run decision whether to shut down for a season, the fixed cost of land is said to be a *sunk cost*. By contrast, if the farmer decides to leave farming altogether, he can sell the land. When making the long-run decision whether to exit the market, the cost of land is not sunk. (We return to the issue of sunk costs shortly.)

Now let's consider what determines a firm's shutdown decision. If the firm shuts down, it loses all revenue from the sale of its product. At the same time, it saves the variable costs of making its product (but must still pay the fixed costs). Thus, *the firm shuts down if the revenue that it would get from producing is less than its variable costs of production.*

A small bit of mathematics can make this shutdown criterion more useful. If TR stands for total revenue, and VC stands for variable costs, then the firm's decision can be written as

$$\text{Shut down if } TR < VC$$

The firm shuts down if total revenue is less than variable cost. By dividing both sides of this inequality by the quantity Q, we can write it as

$$\text{Shut down if } TR/Q < VC/Q$$

Notice that this can be further simplified. TR/Q is total revenue divided by quantity, which is average revenue. As we discussed previously, average revenue for any firm is simply the good's price, P. Similarly, VC/Q is average variable cost AVC. Therefore, the firm's shutdown criterion is

$$\text{Shut down if } P < AVC$$

That is, a firm chooses to shut down if the price of the good is less than the average variable cost of production. This criterion is intuitive: When choosing to produce, the firm compares the price it receives for the typical unit to the average variable cost that it must incur to produce the typical unit. If the price doesn't cover the average variable cost, the firm is better off stopping production altogether. Thus, the price that coincides with the minimum point on the average-*variable*-cost curve is sometimes referred to as the *shutdown price*. If the market price is less than the shutdown price, the firm shuts down and ceases production. If conditions change in the future so that the price exceeds the shutdown price, the firm can reopen. Of course we could just as easily refer to it as the *start-up price*.

We now have a full description of a competitive firm's profit-maximizing strategy. If the firm produces anything, it produces the quantity at which marginal cost equals the price of the good. Yet if the price is less than average variable cost

FIGURE 14.3

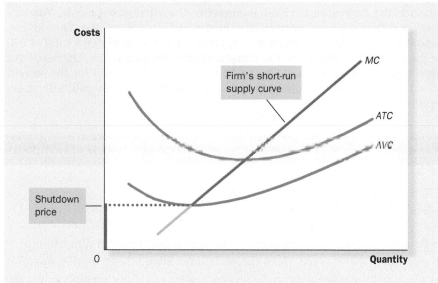

Costs

Firm's short-run
supply curve

MC

ATC

AVC

Shutdown
price

0

Quantity

**The Competitive Firm's Short-Run
Supply Curve**

*In the short run, the competitive firm's supply
curve is its marginal-cost curve (MC) above
average variable cost (AVC). If the price falls
below average variable cost, the firm is
better off shutting down.*

at that quantity, the firm is better off shutting down and not producing anything. These results are illustrated in Figure 14.3.

There are two parts to the competitive firm's short-run supply curve, with a discontinuity at the short-run shutdown price. For prices from zero up to the shut-down price, the firm supplies zero output and the short-run supply curve lies along the vertical axis. For prices above the short-run shutdown price, the competitive firm's *short-run* supply curve is the portion of its marginal-cost curve that lies above average *variable* cost.

Spilt Milk and Other Sunk Costs

Sometime in your life you have probably been told, "Don't cry over spilt milk," or "Let bygones be bygones." These adages hold a deep truth about rational decision making. Economists say that a cost is a **sunk cost** when it has already been committed and cannot be recovered. In a sense, a sunk cost is the opposite of an opportunity cost: An opportunity cost is what you have to give up if you choose to do one thing instead of another, whereas a sunk cost cannot be avoided, regardless of the choices you make. Because nothing can be done about sunk costs, you can ignore them when making decisions about various aspects of life, including business strategy.

Our analysis of the firm's shutdown decision is one example of the irrelevance of sunk costs. We assume that the firm cannot recover its fixed costs by temporarily stopping production. As a result, the firm's fixed costs are sunk in the short run, and the firm can safely ignore these costs when deciding how much to produce. The firm's short-run supply curve is the part of the marginal-cost curve that lies above average variable cost, and the size of the fixed cost does not matter for this supply decision.

sunk cost
a cost that has already been
committed and cannot be recovered

The irrelevance of sunk costs is also important for personal decisions. Imagine, for instance, that you place a $15 value on seeing a newly released movie. You buy a ticket for $10, but before entering the theatre, you lose the ticket. Should you buy another ticket? Or should you now go home and refuse to pay a total of $20 to see the movie? The answer is that you should buy another ticket. The benefit of seeing the movie ($15) still exceeds the opportunity cost (the $10 for the second ticket). The $10 you paid for the lost ticket is a sunk cost. As with spilt milk, there is no point in crying about it.

Case Study

NEAR-EMPTY RESTAURANTS AND OFF-SEASON MINIATURE GOLF

Have you ever walked into a restaurant for lunch and found it almost empty? Why, you might have asked, does the restaurant even bother to stay open? It might seem that the revenue from the few customers could not possibly cover the cost of running the restaurant.

In making the decision whether to open for lunch, a restaurant owner must keep in mind the distinction between fixed and variable costs. Many of a restaurant's costs—the rent, kitchen equipment, tables, plates, silverware, and so on— are fixed. Shutting down during lunch would not reduce these costs. In other words, these costs are sunk in the short run. When the owner is deciding whether to serve lunch, only the variable costs—the price of the additional food and the wages of the extra staff—are relevant. The owner shuts down the restaurant at lunchtime only if the revenue from the few lunchtime customers fails to cover the restaurant's variable costs.

An operator of a miniature-golf course in a summer resort community faces a similar decision. Because revenue varies substantially from season to season, the firm must decide when to open and when to close. Once again, the fixed costs— the costs of buying the land and building the course—are irrelevant. The miniature-golf course should be open for business only during those times of year when its revenue exceeds its variable costs. ●

Staying open can be profitable, even with many tables empty.

The Firm's Long-Run Decision to Exit or Enter a Market

A firm's long-run decision to exit the market is similar to its shutdown decision. If the firm exits, it again will lose all revenue from the sale of its product, but now it saves on both fixed and variable costs of production. Thus, *the firm exits the market if the revenue it would get from producing is less than its total costs.*

We can again make this criterion more useful by writing it mathematically. If *TR* stands for total revenue, and *TC* stands for total cost, then the firm's criterion can be written as

$$\text{Exit if } TR < TC$$

The firm exits if total revenue is less than total cost. By dividing both sides of this inequality by quantity Q, we can write it as

$$\text{Exit if } TR/Q < TC/Q$$

We can simplify this further by noting that TR/Q is average revenue, which equals the price P, and that TC/Q is average total cost ATC. Therefore, the firm's exit criterion is

$$\text{Exit if } P < ATC$$

That is, a firm chooses to exit if the price of the good is less than the average total cost of production. Thus, the price that coincides with the minimum point on the average-*total*-cost curve is sometimes referred to as the *exit price*. The exit price is related to the firm's efficient scale, as discussed in Chapter 13. If the market price is less than the exit price, the firm exits the industry.

It is useful to point out the difference between the exit price, a long-run concept, and the shutdown price, a short-run concept. The exit price coincides with the minimum point on the average-total-cost curve, while the shutdown price coincides with the minimum point on the average-variable-cost curve.

A parallel analysis applies to an entrepreneur who is considering starting a firm. The firm will enter the market if such an action would be profitable, which occurs if the price of the good exceeds the average total cost of production. The entry criterion is

$$\text{Enter if } P > ATC$$

The criterion for entry is exactly the opposite of the criterion for exit.

We can now describe a competitive firm's long-run profit-maximizing strategy. If the firm is in the market, it produces the quantity at which marginal cost equals the price of the good. Yet if the price is less than average total cost at that quantity, the firm chooses to exit (or not enter) the market. These results are illustrated in Figure 14.4 (p. 302).

In this diagram, for simplicity, ATC is drawn as U-shaped, without an extended horizontal portion coinciding with a range of production under constant returns to scale. There are two parts to the competitive firm's long-run supply curve, with a discontinuity at the exit price. For prices from zero up to the exit price, the firm exits (or chooses not to enter) the market, and the long-run supply curve lies along the vertical axis. For prices above the exit price, the competitive firm's *long-run* supply curve is the portion of its marginal-cost curve that lies above average *total* cost.

Measuring Profit in Our Graph for the Competitive Firm

As we analyze exit and entry, it is useful to be able to analyze the firm's profit in more detail. Recall that profit equals total revenue (TR) minus total cost (TC):

$$\text{Profit} = TR - TC$$

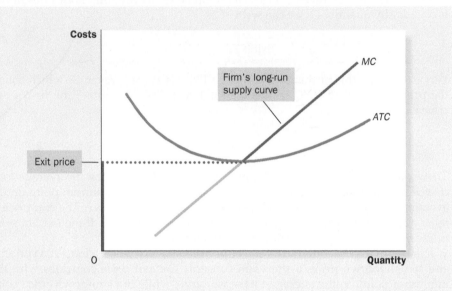

FIGURE 14.4

The Competitive Firm's Long-Run Supply Curve

In the long run, the competitive firm's supply curve is its marginal-cost curve (MC) above average total cost (ATC). If the price falls below average total cost, the firm is better off exiting the market.

We can rewrite this definition by multiplying and dividing the right-hand side by Q:

$$\text{Profit} = (TR/Q - TC/Q) \times Q$$

But note that TR/Q is average revenue, which is the price P, and TC/Q is average total cost ATC. Therefore,

$$\text{Profit} = (P - ATC) \times Q$$

This way of expressing the firm's profit allows us to measure profit in our graphs.

Panel (a) of Figure 14.5 shows a firm earning positive profit. As we have already discussed, the firm maximizes profit by producing the quantity at which price equals marginal cost. Now look at the shaded rectangle. The height of the rectangle is $P - ATC$, the difference between price and average total cost. The width of the rectangle is Q, the quantity produced. Therefore, the area of the rectangle is $(P - ATC) \times Q$, which is the firm's profit.

Similarly, panel (b) of this figure shows a firm with losses (negative profit). In this case, maximizing profit means minimizing losses, a task accomplished once again by producing the quantity at which price equals marginal cost. Now consider the shaded rectangle. The height of the rectangle is $ATC - P$, and the width is Q. The area is $(ATC - P) \times Q$, which is the firm's loss. Because a firm in this situation is not making enough revenue to cover its average total cost, the firm would choose to exit the market.

QuickQuiz How does the price faced by a profit-maximizing competitive firm compare to its marginal cost? Explain. • When does a profit-maximizing competitive firm decide to shut down? When does a profit-maximizing competitive firm decide to exit a market?

FIGURE 14.5

Profit as the Area between Price and Average Total Cost

The area of the shaded box between price and average total cost represents the firm's profit. The height of this box is price minus average total cost (P − ATC), and the width of the box is the quantity of output (Q). In panel (a), price is above average total cost, so the firm has positive profit. In panel (b), price is less than average total cost, so the firm has losses.

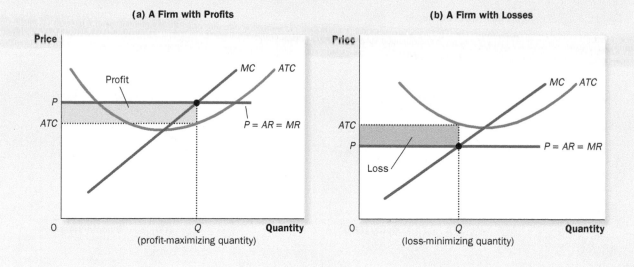

(a) A Firm with Profits

(b) A Firm with Losses

THE SUPPLY CURVE IN A COMPETITIVE MARKET

Now that we have examined the supply decision of a single firm, we can discuss the supply curve for a market. There are two cases to consider. First, we examine a market with a fixed number of firms. Second, we examine a market in which the number of firms can change as old firms exit the market and new firms enter. Both cases are important, for each applies over a specific time horizon. Over short periods of time, it is often difficult for firms to enter and exit, so the assumption of a fixed number of firms is appropriate. But over long periods of time, the number of firms can adjust to changing market conditions.

The Short Run: Market Supply with a Fixed Number of Firms

Consider first a market with 1000 identical firms. For any given price, each firm supplies a quantity of output so that its marginal cost equals the price, as shown in panel (a) of Figure 14.6. That is, as long as price is above average variable cost, each firm's marginal-cost curve is its supply curve. The quantity of output supplied to the market equals the sum of the quantities supplied by each of the 1000 individual firms. Thus, to derive the market supply curve, we add the quantity supplied by each firm in the market. As panel (b) of Figure 14.6 shows, because the firms are identical, the quantity supplied to the market is 1000 times the quantity supplied by each firm.

FIGURE 14.6

Market Supply with a Fixed Number of Firms

In the short run, the number of firms in the market is fixed. As a result, the market supply curve, shown in panel (b), reflects the individual firms' marginal-cost curves, shown in panel (a). Here, in a market of 1000 firms, the quantity of output supplied to the market is 1000 times the quantity supplied by each firm.

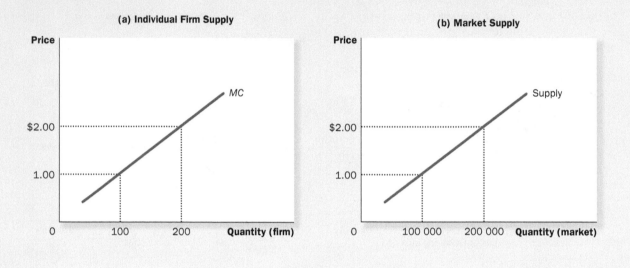

The Long Run: Market Supply with Entry and Exit

Now consider what happens if firms are able to enter or exit the market. Let's suppose that everyone has access to the same technology for producing the good and access to the same markets to buy the inputs into production. Therefore, all firms and all potential firms have the same cost curves.

Decisions about entry and exit in a market of this type depend on the incentives facing the owners of existing firms and the entrepreneurs who could start new firms. If firms already in the market are profitable, then new firms will have an incentive to enter the market. This entry will expand the number of firms, increase the quantity of the good supplied, and drive down prices and profits. Conversely, if firms in the market are making losses, then some existing firms will exit the market. Their exit will reduce the number of firms, decrease the quantity of the good supplied, and drive up prices and profits. *At the end of this process of entry and exit, firms that remain in the market must be making zero economic profit.*

Recall that we can write a firm's profits as

$$\text{Profit} = (P - ATC) \times Q$$

This equation shows that an operating firm has zero profit if and only if the price of the good equals the average total cost of producing that good. If price is above average total cost, profit is positive, which encourages new firms to enter. If price is less than average total cost, profit is negative, which encourages some firms to exit. *The process of entry and exit ends only when price and average total cost are driven to equality.*

This analysis has a surprising implication. We noted earlier in the chapter that competitive firms produce so that price equals marginal cost. We just noted that free entry and exit forces price to equal average total cost. But if price is to equal both marginal cost and average total cost, these two measures of cost must equal each other. Marginal cost and average total cost are equal, however, only when the firm is operating at the minimum of average total cost. Recall from the preceding chapter that the level of production with lowest average total cost is called the firm's *efficient scale.* Therefore, *the long-run equilibrium of a competitive market with free entry and exit must have firms operating at their efficient scale.*

Panel (a) of Figure 14.7 shows a firm in such a long-run equilibrium. In this figure, price *P* equals marginal cost *MC*, so the firm is profit-maximizing. Price also equals average total cost *ATC*, so profits are zero. New firms have no incentive to enter the market, and existing firms have no incentive to leave the market.

From this analysis of firm behaviour, we can determine the long-run supply curve for the market. In a market with free entry and exit, there is only one price consistent with zero profit—the minimum of average total cost. As a result, the long-run market supply curve must be horizontal at this price, as in panel (b) of Figure 14.7. Any price above this level would generate profit, leading to entry and an increase in the total quantity supplied. Any price below this level would generate losses, leading to exit and a decrease in the total quantity supplied. Eventually, the number

FIGURE 14.7

Market Supply with Entry and Exit

Firms will enter or exit the market until profit is driven to zero. Thus, in the long run, price equals the minimum of average total cost, as shown in panel (a). The number of firms adjusts to ensure that all demand is satisfied at this price. The long-run market supply curve is horizontal at this price, as shown in panel (b).

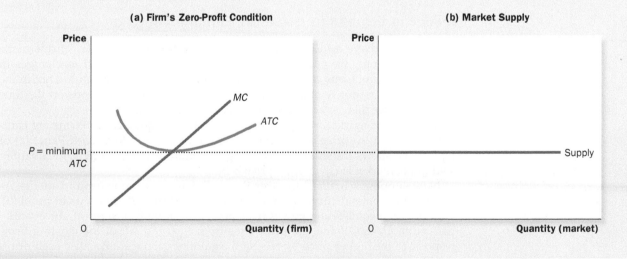

of firms in the market adjusts so that price equals the minimum of average total cost, and there are enough firms to satisfy all the demand at this price.

Why Do Competitive Firms Stay in Business If They Make Zero Profit?

At first, it might seem odd that competitive firms earn zero profit in the long run. After all, people start businesses to make a profit. If entry eventually drives profit to zero, there might seem to be little reason to stay in business.

To understand the zero-profit condition more fully, recall that profit equals total revenue minus total cost, and that total cost includes all the opportunity costs of the firm. In particular, total cost includes the opportunity cost of the time and money that the firm owners devote to the business. In the zero-profit equilibrium, the firm's revenue must compensate the owners for the time and money that they expend to keep their business going.

Consider an example. Suppose that a farmer had to invest $1 million to establish his farm, which otherwise he could have deposited in a bank to earn $50 000 a year in interest. In addition, he had to give up another job that would have paid him $30 000 a year. Then the farmer's opportunity cost of farming includes both the interest he could have earned and the forgone wages—a total of $80 000. Even if his profit is driven to zero, his revenue from farming compensates him for these opportunity costs.

Keep in mind that accountants and economists measure costs differently. As we discussed in the previous chapter, accountants keep track of explicit costs but usually miss implicit costs. That is, they measure costs that require an outflow of money from the firm, but they fail to include opportunity costs of production that do not involve an outflow of money. As a result, in the zero-profit equilibrium, economic profit is zero, but accounting profit is positive. Our farmer's accountant, for instance, would conclude that the farmer earned an accounting profit of $80 000, which is enough to keep the farmer in business.

A Shift in Demand in the Short Run and Long Run

Now that we have a more complete understanding of how many firms make supply decisions, we can better explain how markets respond to changes in demand. Because firms can enter and exit a market in the long run but not in the short run, the response of a market to a change in demand depends on the time horizon. To see this, let's trace the effects of a shift in demand.

Suppose the market for milk begins in long-run equilibrium. Firms are earning zero profit, so price equals the minimum of average total cost. Panel (a) of Figure 14.8 shows the situation. The long-run equilibrium is point A, the quantity sold in the market is Q_1, and the price is P_1.

Now suppose scientists discover that milk has miraculous health benefits. As a result, the demand curve for milk shifts outward from D_1 to D_2, as in panel (b). The short-run equilibrium moves from point A to point B; as a result, the quantity rises from Q_1 to Q_2, and the price rises from P_1 to P_2. All of the existing firms respond to the higher price by raising the amount produced. Because each firm's supply curve reflects its marginal-cost curve, how much they each increase

FIGURE 14.8

An Increase in Demand in the Short Run and Long Run

The market starts in a long-run equilibrium, shown as point A in panel (a). In this equilibrium, each firm makes zero profit, and the price equals the minimum average total cost. Panel (b) shows what happens in the short run when demand rises from D_1 to D_2. The equilibrium goes from point A to point B, price rises from P_1 to P_2, and the quantity sold in the market rises from Q_1 to Q_2. Because price now exceeds average total cost, firms make profits, which over time encourages new firms to enter the market. This entry shifts the short-run supply curve to the right from S_1 to S_2, as shown in panel (c). In the new long-run equilibrium, point C, price has returned to P_1 but the quantity sold has increased to Q_3. Profits are again zero, price is back to the minimum of average total cost, but the market has more firms to satisfy the greater demand.

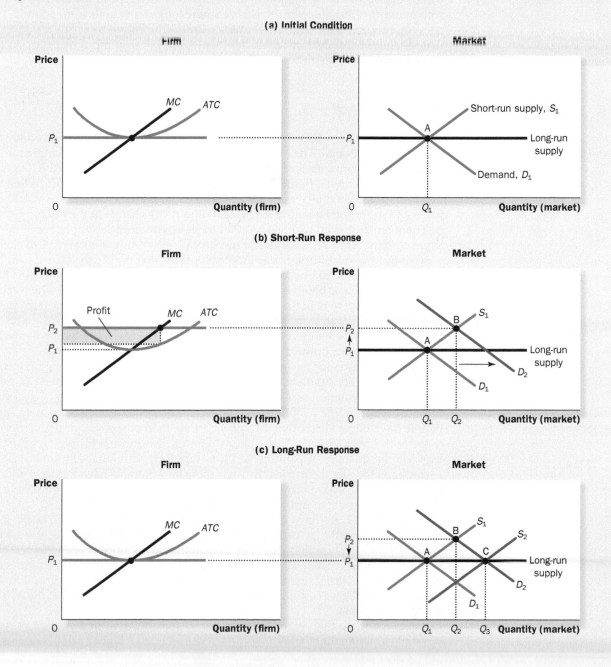

(a) Initial Condition

(b) Short-Run Response

(c) Long-Run Response

CHAPTER 14   FIRMS IN COMPETITIVE MARKETS   307

production is determined by the marginal-cost curve. In the new short-run equilibrium, the price of milk exceeds average total cost, so the firms are making positive profit.

Over time, the profit in this market encourages new firms to enter. Some farmers may switch to milk from other farm products, for example. As the number of firms grows, the short-run supply curve shifts to the right from S_1 to S_2, as in panel (c), and this shift causes the price of milk to fall. Eventually, the price is driven back down to the minimum of average total cost, profits are zero, and firms stop entering. Thus, the market reaches a new long-run equilibrium, point C. The price of milk has returned to P_1, but the quantity produced has risen to Q_3. Each firm is again producing at its efficient scale, but because more firms are in the dairy business, the quantity of milk produced and sold is higher.

Why the Long-Run Supply Curve Might Slope Upward

So far we have seen that entry and exit can cause the long-run market supply curve to be horizontal. The essence of our analysis is that there are a large number of potential entrants, each of which faces the same costs. As a result, the long-run market supply curve is horizontal at the minimum of average total cost. When the demand for the good increases, the long-run result is an increase in the number of firms and in the total quantity supplied, without any change in the price.

There are, however, two reasons that the long-run market supply curve might slope upward. The first is that some resource used in production may be available only in limited quantities. For example, consider the market for farm products. Anyone can choose to buy land and start a farm, but the quantity of land is limited. As more people become farmers, the price of farmland is bid up, which raises the costs of all farmers in the market. Thus, an increase in demand for farm products cannot induce an increase in quantity supplied without also inducing a rise in farmers' costs, which in turn means a rise in price. The result is a long-run market supply curve that is upward sloping, even with free entry into farming.

A second reason for an upward-sloping supply curve is that firms may have different costs. For example, consider the market for painters. Anyone can enter the market for painting services, but not everyone has the same costs. Costs vary in part because some people work faster than others and in part because some people have better alternative uses of their time than others. For any given price, those with lower costs are more likely to enter than those with higher costs. To increase the quantity of painting services supplied, additional entrants must be encouraged to enter the market. Because these new entrants have higher costs, the price must rise to make entry profitable for them. Thus, the market supply curve for painting services slopes upward even with free entry into the market.

Notice that if firms have different costs, some firms earn profit even in the long run. In this case, the price in the market reflects the average total cost of the *marginal firm*—the firm that would exit the market if the price was any lower. This firm earns zero profit, but firms with lower costs earn positive profit. Entry does not eliminate this profit because would-be entrants have higher costs than firms already in the market. Higher-cost firms will enter only if the price rises, making the market profitable for them.

Thus, for these two reasons, the long-run supply curve in a market may be upward sloping rather than horizontal, indicating that a higher price is necessary to induce a larger quantity supplied. Nonetheless, the basic lesson about entry and exit remains true: *Because firms can enter and exit more easily in the long run than in the short run, the long-run supply curve is typically more elastic than the short-run supply curve.*

QuickQuiz In the long run with free entry and exit, is the price in a market equal to marginal cost, average total cost, both, or neither? Explain with a diagram.

CONCLUSION: BEHIND THE SUPPLY CURVE

We have been discussing the behaviour of competitive profit-maximizing firms. You may recall from Chapter 1 that one of the ten principles of economics is that rational people think at the margin. This chapter has applied this idea to the competitive firm. Marginal analysis has given us a theory of the supply curve in a competitive market and, as a result, a deeper understanding of market outcomes.

We have learned that when you buy a good from a firm in a competitive market, you can be assured that the price you pay is close to the cost of producing that good. In particular, if firms are competitive and profit-maximizing, the price of a good equals the marginal cost of making that good. In addition, if firms can freely enter and exit the market, the price also equals the lowest possible average total cost of production.

Although we have assumed throughout this chapter that firms are price takers, many of the tools developed here are also useful for studying firms in less competitive markets. In the next chapter we will examine the behaviour of firms with market power. Marginal analysis will again be useful in analyzing these firms, but it will have quite different implications.

SUMMARY

- Because a competitive firm is a price taker, its revenue is proportional to the amount of output it produces. The price of the good equals both the firm's average revenue and its marginal revenue.

- To maximize profit, a firm chooses a quantity of output such that marginal revenue equals marginal cost. Because marginal revenue for a competitive firm equals the market price, the firm chooses quantity so that price equals marginal cost. Thus, the firm's marginal cost curve is its supply curve.

- In the short run when a firm cannot recover its fixed costs, the firm will choose to shut down temporarily if the price of the good is less than average variable cost. In the long run when the firm can recover both fixed and variable costs, it

- will choose to exit if the price is less than average total cost.

- In a market with free entry and exit, profits are driven to zero in the long run. In this long-run equilibrium, all firms produce at the efficient scale, price equals the minimum of average total cost, and the number of firms adjusts to satisfy the quantity demanded at this price.

- Changes in demand have different effects over different time horizons. In the short run, an increase in demand raises prices and leads to profits, and a decrease in demand lowers prices and leads to losses. But if firms can freely enter and exit the market, then in the long run the number of firms adjusts to drive the market back to the zero profit equilibrium.

KEY CONCEPTS

competitive market, p. 292   marginal revenue, p. 294   sunk cost, p. 299
average revenue, p. 293

QUESTIONS FOR REVIEW

1. What is meant by a competitive firm?

2. Draw the cost curves for a typical firm. For a given price, explain how the firm chooses the level of output that maximizes profit.

3. Under what conditions will a firm shut down temporarily? Explain.

4. Under what conditions will a firm exit a market? Explain.

5. Does a firm's price equal marginal cost in the short run, in the long run, or both? Explain.

6. Does a firm's price equal the minimum of average total cost in the short run, in the long run, or both? Explain.

7. Are market supply curves typically more elastic in the short run or in the long run? Explain.

PROBLEMS AND APPLICATIONS

1. You go out to the best restaurant in town and order a lobster dinner for $40. After eating half of the lobster, you realize that you are quite full. Your date wants you to finish your dinner, because you can't take it home and because "you've already paid for it." What should you do? Relate your answer to the material in this chapter.

2. Bob's lawn-mowing service is a profit-maximizing, competitive firm. Bob mows lawns for $27 each. His total cost each day is $280, of which $30 is a fixed cost. He mows 10 lawns a day. What can you say about Bob's short-run decision regarding shutdown and his long-run decision regarding exit?

3. Consider total cost and total revenue given in the table below:

Quantity	0	1	2	3	4	5	6	7
Total Cost	$8	$9	$10	$11	$13	$19	$27	$37
Total Revenue	0	8	16	24	32	40	48	56

a. Calculate profit for each quantity. How much should the firm produce to maximize profit?

b. Calculate marginal revenue and marginal cost for each quantity. Graph them. (Hint: Put the points between whole numbers.

For example, the marginal cost between 2 and 3 should be graphed at 2.5.) At what quantity do these curves cross? How does this relate to your answer to part (a)?

c. Can you tell whether this firm is in a competitive industry? If so, can you tell whether the industry is in a long-run equilibrium?

4. In 2003 a single case in Alberta of bovine spongiform encephalopathy, also known as mad cow disease, temporarily shut down export markets for Canadian beef.

a. Using firm and industry diagrams, show the short-run effect of declining demand for Canadian beef due to the shutdown of its export markets. Label the diagram carefully and write out in words all of the changes that you can identify.

b. Although export markets eventually began to open up later that same year, the demand for Canadian beef remained low. On a new diagram, show the long-run effect of the declining demand. Explain in words.

5. Suppose the book-printing industry is competitive and begins in a long-run equilibrium.

a. Draw a diagram describing the typical firm in the industry.

b. Hi-Tech Printing Company invents a new process that sharply reduces the cost of printing books. What happens to Hi-Tech's profits and the price of books in the short run when Hi-Tech's patent prevents other firms from using the new technology?

c. What happens in the long run when the patent expires and other firms are free to use the technology?

6. Many small boats are made of fibreglass, which is derived from crude oil. Suppose that the price of oil rises.

a. Using diagrams, show what happens to the cost curves of an individual boat-making firm and to the market supply curve.

b. What happens to the profits of boat makers in the short run? What happens to the number of boat makers in the long run?

7. Suppose that the Canadian textile industry is competitive, and there is no international trade in textiles. In long-run equilibrium, the price per unit of cloth is $30.

a. Describe the equilibrium using graphs for the entire market and for an individual producer.

Now suppose that textile producers in other countries are willing to sell large quantities of cloth in Canada for only $25 per unit.

b. Assuming that Canadian textile producers have large fixed costs, what is the short-run effect of these imports on the quantity produced by an individual producer? What is the short-run effect on profits? Illustrate your answer with a graph.

c. What is the long-run effect on the number of Canadian firms in the industry?

8. Suppose there are 1000 hot-pretzel stands operating in Toronto. Each stand has the usual U-shaped average-total-cost curve. The market demand curve for pretzels slopes downward, and the market for pretzels is in long-run competitive equilibrium.

a. Draw the current equilibrium, using graphs for the entire market and for an individual pretzel stand.

b. Now the city decides to restrict the number of pretzel-stand licences, reducing the number of stands to only 800. What effect will this action have on the market and on an individual stand that is still operating? Use graphs to illustrate your answer.

c. Suppose that the city decides to charge a licence fee for the 800 licences. How will this affect the number of pretzels sold by an individual stand, and the stand's profit? The city wants to raise as much revenue as possible and also wants to ensure that 800 pretzel stands remain in the city. By how much should the city increase the licence fee? Show the answer on your graph.

9. Assume that the gold-mining industry is competitive.

a. Illustrate a long-run equilibrium using diagrams for the gold market and for a representative gold mine.

b. Suppose that an increase in jewellery demand induces a surge in the demand for gold. Using your diagrams from part (a), show what happens in the short run to the gold market and to each existing gold mine.

c. If the demand for gold remains high, what would happen to the price over time? Specifically, would the new long-run equilibrium price be above, below, or equal to the short-run equilibrium price in part (b)? Is it possible for the new long-run equilibrium price to be above the original long-run equilibrium price? Explain.

10. Ball Bearings Inc. faces costs of production as follows:

Quantity	Total Fixed Costs	Total Variable Costs
0	$100	$ 0
1	100	50
2	100	70
3	100	90
4	100	140
5	100	200
6	100	360

a. Calculate the company's average fixed costs, average variable costs, average total costs, and marginal costs.

b. The price of a case of ball bearings is $50. Seeing that she can't make a profit, the chief executive officer (CEO) decides to shut down operations. What are the firm's profits/losses? Was this a wise decision? Explain.

c. Vaguely remembering his introductory economics course, the chief financial officer tells the CEO it is better to produce 1 case of ball bearings, because marginal revenue equals marginal cost at that quantity. What are the firm's profits/losses at that level of production? Was this the best decision? Explain.

11. A firm in a competitive market receives $500 in total revenue and has marginal revenue of $10. What is the average revenue, and how many units were sold?

12. A profit-maximizing firm in a competitive market is currently producing 100 units of output. It has average revenue of $10, average total cost of $8, and fixed costs of $200.
    a. What is profit?
    b. What is marginal cost?
    c. What is average variable cost?
    d. Is the efficient scale of the firm more than, less than, or exactly 100 units?

13. The market for fertilizer is perfectly competitive. Firms in the market are producing output, but are currently experiencing economic losses.

a. How does the price of fertilizer compare to the average total cost, the average variable cost, and the marginal cost of producing fertilizer?
b. Draw two graphs, side by side, illustrating the present situation for the typical firm and in the market.
c. Assuming there is no change in demand or in the firms' cost curves, explain what will happen in the long run to the price of fertilizer, marginal cost, average total cost, the quantity supplied by each firm, and the total quantity supplied to the market.

14. Analyze the two following situations for firms in competitive markets:
    a. Suppose that $TC = 100 + 15Q$, where TC is total cost and Q is the quantity produced. What is the minimum price necessary for this firm to produce any output in the short run?
    b. Suppose that $MC = 4Q$, where MC is marginal cost. The perfectly competitive firm maximizes profits by producing 10 units of output. At what price does it sell these units?

http://   For more study tools, please visit http://www.mankiw5e.nelson.com.

Chapter 14
The Algebra of Perfect Competition

In perfect competition, firms are price takers. Whatever market equilibrium price is, that is the price that firms know they will sell their output for. Marginal revenue equals price in perfect competition, and since profit is maximized where marginal revenue equals marginal cost, that means price equals marginal cost for competitive firms. They take the market price, equate it to their marginal cost and determine how much they will produce.

Example

Market demand is $p = 1020 - Q$. Market supply is $p = .02Q$. A firm has $MC = 2Q$.

First, find market price:

$$1020 - Q = .02Q$$
$$1020 = 1.02Q$$
$$Q = 1000$$
$$P = 1020 - 1000 = \$20$$

Now set $P = MC = 20$:

$$20 = 2Q$$
$$Q = 10$$

Our firm will produce 10 units of output and sell it for $20 per unit for total revenue = $200.

Now suppose that the firm's $ATC = Q + 10/Q$. ATC when $Q = 10$ is $11. Since profit $= (P - ATC)Q$, this firm's profit $= (20 - 11)10 = \$90$.

The firm is making positive economic profit. If this is a representative firm, then the supranormal profits in the industry will attract entry in the long run.

In long run equilibrium, price will equal minimum ATC (which will equal minimum LRAC). For this firm, we are told that ATC is at a minimum at $6.32. *Note to calculus lovers – to find minimum ATC, take the derivative of ATC with respect to Q and set it equal to 0. You'll get Q = 3.16 so that ATC = 6.32 at its minimum. Since this is an introductory course, you are not expected to use calculus and will always be told the value of minimum ATC where required.*

Long run price is therefore $P = 6.32$. If we substitute this into our demand curve, quantity demanded in the long run will be:

$$6.32 = 1020 - Q$$
$$Q = 1013.60$$

If P = 6.32, set MC = 6.32 to see how much each firm will produce in the long run:

$$6.32 = 20Q$$
$$Q = 3.16$$

If each firm produces Q = 3.16 and Qd = 1013.68, there will be 11013.68/.3.16 = 320.79 firms in the long run in equilibrium.

Practice Problems

1. Market demand is given as Qd = 200 – 3P. Market supply is given as Qs = 2P + 100. Each identical firm has MC = .5Q and ATC = .25Q. What quantity of output will a typical firm produce?
    a. 10
    b. 20
    c. 30
    d. 40

2. Market demand is given as Qd = 200 – 3P. Market supply is given as Qs = 2P + 100. Each identical firm has MC = .5Q and ATC = .25Q. What is a firm's average total cost?
    a. $5
    b. $10
    c. $15
    d. $20

3. Market demand is given as Qd = 200 – 3P. Market supply is given as Qs = 2P + 100. Each identical firm has MC = .5Q and ATC = .25Q. What is each firm's profit?
    a. $200
    b. $400
    c. $800
    d. $0

Answers: 1 d   2 b   3 b

CHAPTER 14 Firms in Competitive Markets

I. Chapter Overview

A. Context and Purpose

The previous chapter provided an overview of costs of production. This chapter extends that analysis to cover profit maximization by competitive firms in the short and long run. The next three chapters adapt this model to cover other types of firms.

A. Helpful Hints

1. *The competitive firm's output, price, and profit in the short run is determined by industry supply and demand.* Competitive firms take the price as given and produce the level of output that maximizes profit. In the short run, each competitive firm can earn an economic profit, incur an economic loss as long as loss is less than its fixed cost, or break even.

2. *The competitive firm's output, price, and economic profit in the long run is zero.* In a competitive market with free entry and exit, profits are driven to zero in the long run. All firms produce at the efficient scale, price equals the minimum of average total cost, and the number of firms adjusts to satisfy the quantity demanded at this price.

3. *Sunk costs are sunk.* That is, fixed costs cannot be recovered and, therefore, are irrelevant for future decisions. In the short run, a business cannot avoid its fixed costs even by shutting down. This is why it is rational for a business to continue to produce at a loss in the short run as long as its revenues cover the variable costs. Any revenues in excess of the variable cost will offset part of the fixed cost and reduce losses. However, if the firm shuts down, it will incur losses equal to the full fixed cost.

4. *Sunk costs are really sunk.* This is worth a second hint. Thinking at the margin is what distinguishes economists from noneconomists. Even if you now accept this axiom, its implications still may not be obvious. A business that is maximizing profit ignores fixed costs. This means that in the short run (when there are some fixed costs), a business that just replaced an expensive piece of equipment or made an expensive repair will not find it profitable to raise price even by a slight amount. This is probably counterintuitive, but remember that the firm is already charging whatever the market will bear, up to the point at which MC = MR. Just ask yourself this question: if it is profitable for the firm to raise price now to recoup the cost, why was it not

193

489

profitable to raise price before the big investment just to make more profit? The answer is that if the firm can raise price to make more profit, it would have already done so! If it is rational, however, it will not make the decision based on sunk costs. Similarly, if you go to a concert that turns out to be a waste of time, you should not stay until the end just because you paid $50 for a ticket. The $50 is gone; do not make yourself even more miserable by sitting through a worthless concert.

II. Self-Testing Challenges

A. True/False Questions

_____ 1. A firm earning zero economic profit will exit the industry in the long run.

_____ 2. For all firms, average revenue and marginal revenue equals the price of the good.

_____ 3. A firm facing a price that is less than average total cost will shut down temporarily until the situation improves.

_____ 4. Because a competitive firm's marginal cost curve determines the quantity of the good the firm is willing to supply at any price, it is also the competitive firm's supply curve.

_____ 5. A profit-maximizing competitive firm will produce until $P = MC$.

_____ 6. A firm producing where $MC > MR$ is producing more than the profit-maximizing quantity.

_____ 7. Long-run supply is always horizontal for competitive industries.

_____ 8. For a competitive firm, total revenue is proportional to the amount of output.

_____ 9. A firm that is not covering its variable cost should shut down unless it is at least covering fixed cost.

_____ 10. In the long-run equilibrium, competitive firms must operate at their minimum efficient scale.

_____ 11. The demand curve perceived by an individual competitive firm is perfectly inelastic, while the market demand curve is perfectly elastic.

_____12.   In the long-run equilibrium, the price received by a perfectly competitive firm is equal not only to marginal revenue and marginal cost but also to average total cost.

B. Multiple-Choice Questions

1.   Which one of the following explains why a perfectly competitive firm is **NOT** likely to earn economic profit in the long run?
   a.   because the demand curve for the firm will not remain horizontal in the long run
   b.   because all economic resources are variable in the long run, causing the firm to face uncertainty
   c.   because the existence of economic profit will attract new firms into the industry and reduce the price

2.   Which one of the following is marginal profit equal to?
   a.   marginal revenue minus marginal cost
   b.   marginal revenue plus marginal cost
   c.   marginal cost minus marginal revenue
   d.   marginal cost plus marginal revenue

3.   A profit-maximizing competitive firm will produce up to the point at which
   a.   total revenue is maximized
   b.   marginal revenue is maximized
   c.   total cost is minimized
   d.   marginal revenue equals marginal cost

4.   Bärbel's Bäckerei is a competitive firm producing where MR = $4 and MC = $2. Which one of the following strategies should the firm pursue to maximize profit?
   a.   expand output
   b.   cut back on output
   c.   raise price to increase total revenue
   d.   cut price to increase total revenue

5.   Which one of the following describes the supply curve for a competitive firm?
   a.   the upward-sloping portion of the firm's marginal cost curve
   b.   the portion of the firm's marginal cost curve that lies above the average variable cost
   c.   the portion of the firm's marginal cost curve that lies above the average total cost

6. Which one of the following describes when the long-run market supply curve is likely to slope upward?
   a. if additional firms are attracted into the industry in the long run
   b. if not all firms have the same costs of production
   c. if diminishing marginal product sets in
   d. if there are no barriers to entry into the industry

7. Which one of the following describes how a profit-maximizing competitive firm determines output?
   a. by equating marginal revenue and marginal cost
   b. by equating marginal cost and average revenue
   c. by equating average cost and marginal revenue

8. Which one of the following situations should cause a firm to shut down in the short run?
   a. if it is not covering its variable costs
   b. if it is not covering its fixed costs
   c. if it is not covering its total costs
   d. if it is not covering its money outlays or explicit costs

9. Which one of the following situations should cause a firm to shut down in the long run?
   a. if it is not covering its fixed costs
   b. if it is not covering its accounting costs
   c. if it is not covering its money outlays
   d. if it is not covering its economic costs

10. In a perfectly competitive market, the market price of the product is $10. A firm in this market is producing the output level at which average total cost equals marginal cost, both of which are $8. Which one of the following strategies should the firm pursue in order to maximize profit?
    a.   expand output
    b.   reduce output
    c.   leave output unchanged
    d.   change the price of the product

11. Which one of the following describes when a rational entrepreneur should enter a competitive industry?
    a. only if price exceeds average variable cost
    b. only if price exceeds average total cost
    c. only if price exceeds marginal cost
    d. only if price exceeds average fixed cost

12.   Suppose that demand increases for the output of a competitive industry, thus driving up price. Each of the 1000 current firms is willing to increase quantity supplied by 2 units in response to the higher price. Assuming free entry and exit, which one of the following amounts is the increase in total quantity supplied that the industry will eventually experience?
    a.   less than 2000
    b.   exactly 2000
    c.   more than 2000

13.   Which one of the following is a reason that a perfectly competitive firm will not try to sell more by lowering its price below the market price?
    a.   because its marginal revenue will exceed its price
    b.   because its average total cost will exceed its marginal cost
    c.   because its average variable cost will exceed its marginal cost
    d.   because its demand is perfectly elastic

14.   Which one of the following will be satisfied by a competitive firm in long-run equilibrium?
    a.   P = MR
    b.   MR = MC
    c.   P = AR
    d.   P = AC

Use the following graph for a competitive firm to answer questions 15–17.

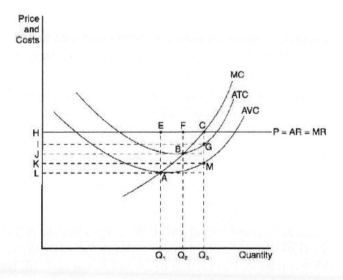

15.   Which one of the following is the output level at which the firm will produce?
    a.   Q$_1$
    b.   Q$_2$
    c.   Q$_3$
    d.   Q$_4$

198 PART 5: Firm Behaviour and the Organization of Industry

16. Which of the following statements represents what the firm is realizing?
    a. profit equal to area HCGI
    b. profit equal to area HCMK
    c. profit equal to area HFBJ
    d. loss equal to area ECMA

17. Which one of the following describes what will happen to this firm in the long run?
    a. More firms will enter the industry, thus driving down price until profit equals zero.
    b. More firms will enter the industry, thus lowering cost and raising profit because of economies of scale.
    c. More firms will enter the industry, thus increasing average total cost but leaving price unchanged until profit equals 0.
    d. Firms will leave the industry, thus increasing price until profit equals zero.

18. The market for maple syrup is perfectly competitive. Currently, each producer is making a profit. Which one of the following can be expected to occur in the long run?
    a. the market demand will increase
    b. the market demand will decrease
    c. the market supply will increase
    d. the market supply will decrease

C. Short-Answer Questions

1. How can the long-run industry supply curve be horizontal even though the short-run supply has a positive slope for both individual firms and the industry?

    _____
    _____
    _____

2. What is the difference between the exit price and the shutdown price?

    _____
    _____

3. A Canadian maple syrup producer knows that an additional carload (120 cases) of its famous Old Recipe Maple Syrup would bring an additional $12 888 in revenue. Production of an additional carload, however, would cost $10 580. Should the producer increase production by one carload? Would selling an additional carload raise or lower the producer's profit from the current $238 000? By how much?

    _____
    _____
    _____

4. If a competitive firm makes zero profit, why does it stay in business?

_____

_____

_____

5. How would a rational, profit-maximizing, competitive firm respond in the short run to an increase in fixed costs? Will there be any change in equilibrium price or quantity in the short run? Why or why not?

_____

_____

_____

6. During the 1990s, most of the major airlines reported large losses. In one year, Air Canada lost more than $400 million. However, Air Canada and other airlines continued their operations despite these losses. Why did these airlines not shut down their operations?

_____

_____

_____

D. Practice Problems

1. The graph below shows a competitive firm maximizing profits. However, the curves are not labelled.

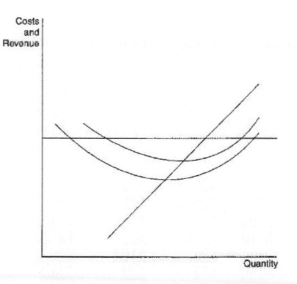

a. Label the following: price (P), AR, marginal revenue (MR), marginal cost (MC), average total cost (ATC), and average variable cost (AVC). Show the equilibrium quantity and price as Q_e and P_e. Label the short-run shutdown point as point A and the breakeven point as point B.

b. Why is it rational for the firm to produce at Q_e? Should it continue to produce temporarily if the price falls below point B but stays above point A? Why or why not? Would your answer be different in the long run? Explain. _____

_____

_____

_____

_____

_____

_____

c. Is the firm in short-run equilibrium? Long-run equilibrium? How can you tell?

_____

_____

_____

d. What is likely to happen to the price in the long run? Why? Show the new price line on the graph and explain what happened in the market to cause this shift.

_____

_____

_____

_____

2. a. In Chapter 13 you calculated production costs for Wendell's Widget Works. Below is the cost schedule.

Quantity (Q)	Variable cost (VC)	Total cost (TC)	Marginal cost (MC)	Average variable cost (AVC)	Average total cost (ATC)	Marginal revenue (MR)	Profit (TR–TC)
0	$0	$46	—	—	—	$___	$___
1	$30	$76	$30	$30	$76	$___	$___
2	$50	$96	$20	$25	$48	$___	$___
3	$58	$104	$8	$19.3	$34.7	$___	$___
4	$64	$110	$6	$16	$27.5	$___	$___
5	$84	$130	$20	$16.8	$26	$___	$___
6	$114	$160	$30	$19	$26.7	$___	$___
7	$150	$196	$36	$21.4	$28	$___	$___
8	$190	$236	$40	$23.8	$29.5	$___	$___
9	$240	$286	$50	$26.7	$31.8	$___	$___

b. Wendell is selling in a competitive market at a price of $40. Fill in the missing blanks for marginal revenue and profit.

c. What is the profit-maximizing output for Wendell? What is his profit or loss? Should he continue to produce in the long run? _____

_____

_____

_____

_____

d. If the price falls to $20, what is Wendell's profit-maximizing output in the short run? What is his profit or loss? What should he do in the long run?

_____

_____

_____

_____

e. If Wendell's price falls to $15, what would be his profit or loss if he continued to produce at a price of $15? What would be his profit or loss if he temporarily shut down in the short run? Which action should he take in the short run? Explain. _____

_____

_____

_____

_____

3. The following graph shows the effects of a tax hike on a competitive industry that shifts the short-run supply curve from Supply$_1$ to Supply$_2$.

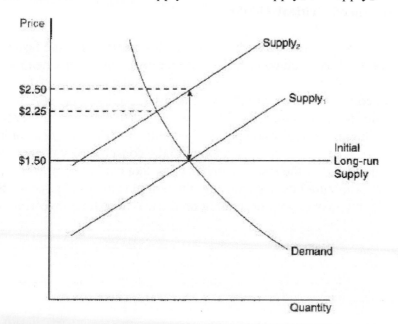

a. How much is the tax? How much will price rise in the short run? (Who pays the tax in the short run?)

_____

_____

b. What happens to quantity in the short run? Identify the initial equilibrium quantity and the new short-run equilibrium quantity after the tax.

_____

_____

_____

c. If the industry was initially in long-run equilibrium at a price of $1.50, what will happen to profit (or loss) in the short run? Explain. _____

_____

_____

_____

d. How will firms respond in the long run? What are the implications for long-run industry supply and the resulting price? Who pays the tax in the long run? Explain. _____

_____

_____

_____

e. Show the new long-run supply curve on the graph.

E. Advanced Critical Thinking

Your campus newspaper has run an editorial attacking the fast-food restaurants in the food court for anticompetitive behaviour when they raised prices simultaneously last week. Demanding equal time, the restaurants responded that the higher prices were necessitated by a rent hike by the university for all restaurants in the food court. They argued further that they were behaving perfectly competitively by raising price because, under competition, all costs are passed along to the consumer. Evaluate both sides of this argument. Are the restaurants behaving like perfect competitors? Should a profit-maximizing business consider the rent in setting the price of its product? Would your answer vary depending on the length of time involved? Explain. __

_____

_____

_____

_____

_____

498

III. Solutions

A. True/False Questions

1. F; zero profit covers all costs of doing business, including a normal return on investment; therefore, there is no reason to enter or exit the industry.
2. F; although average revenue equals the price of the good for all firms, marginal revenue equals the price for competitive firms only.
3. F; a firm facing a price that is less than average *variable* cost will shut down temporarily.
4. T
5. T
6. T
7. F; a competitive market can have an upward-sloping long-run supply curve.
8. T
9. F; a firm that is not covering its variable cost should shut down regardless of fixed cost.
10. T
11. F; the demand faced by a competitive firm is perfectly elastic, while the market demand curve is downward sloping.
12. T

B. Multiple-Choice Questions

1. c	5. c	9. d	13. d	17. a
2. a	6. b	10. a	14. b	18. c
3. d	7. a	11. b	15. c	
4. a	8. a	12. c	16. a	

C. Short-Answer Questions

1. Long-run supply is horizontal if all firms have identical cost curves and there are constant returns to scale. The positive slope of the short-run supply curve results from diminishing returns when some inputs are fixed. In the long run, all inputs are variable.

2. The exit price is a long-run concept, and it coincides with the minimum point on the average total cost curve, while the shutdown price is a short-run concept that coincides with the minimum point on the average variable cost curve.

3. The producer should increase its production by an additional carload. Its profit will increase by $2308 ($12 888 – $10 580).

4.   Profit equals total revenue minus total cost, and total cost includes all the opportunity costs of the firm. That is, total cost includes the opportunity cost of the time and money that the owner(s) of the firm devote to the business. Thus, it is worthwhile for the firm to stay in business, because the owner(s) are doing better than, or at least as well as, they could do in any other activity.

5.   A rational firm would ignore fixed cost in setting its output. Firms maximize profit where MC = MR. Fixed cost affects neither because sunk costs are irrelevant. They do not affect the cost of producing an additional unit of output. Neither price nor quantity will change in the short run.

6.   Many of the airlines' costs are sunk in the short run. The cost of an airplane that an airline has bought and cannot resell is sunk. The opportunity cost of a flight includes only the variable costs of operation, that is, the costs of fuel, the wages and salaries of pilots, flight attendants and the ground crew, among others. As long as the total revenue from flying exceeds these variable costs, the airlines should continue operating.

D. Practice Problems

1.   a.

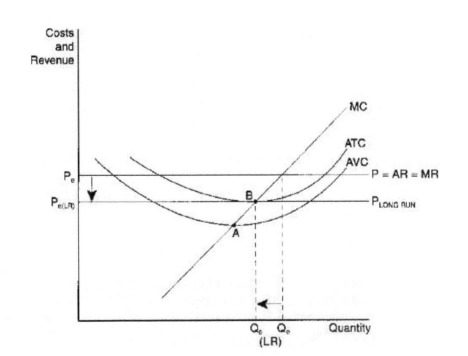

b.   Output level Q_e maximizes profit because it means producing every unit of output that adds more to revenue than it adds to cost. If price falls below point B, the firm will have negative profit (incur a loss). However, in the short run the firm should continue to produce as long as it is above point A, the average variable cost curve. Any price in excess of average variable cost contributes to fixed cost, reducing the losses that result below point B. In the long run, the firm can avoid all costs (nothing is fixed); therefore, it should not produce at a loss (below point B). It can go out of business and avoid all losses.

c. The firm is in short-run equilibrium only. It is earning an economic profit. In long-run equilibrium, entry of new firms will continue until all firms are earning zero economic profits.

d. In the long run, the profit will encourage new firms to enter the industry. The additional industry supply will drive down price until the profit is eliminated. Each firm then will produce at minimum average total cost (its efficient scale) in order to survive. The new price line will be tangent to average total cost (at point B).

2. a. Costs and revenues for Wendell's Widget Works at price $40.

Quantity (Q)	Variable cost (VC)	Total cost (TC)	Marginal cost (MC)	Average variable cost (AVC)	Average total cost (ATC)	Marginal revenue (MR)	Profit (TR–TC)
0	$ 0	$46	—	—	—	—	($46)
1	$30	$76	$30	$30	$76	$40	($36)
2	$50	$96	$20	$25	$48	$40	($16)
3	$58	$104	$8	$19.3	$34.7	$40	$16
4	$64	$110	$6	$16	$27.5	$40	$50
5	$84	$130	$20	$16.8	$26	$40	$70
6	$114	$160	$30	$19	$26.7	$40	$80
7	$150	$196	$36	$21.4	$28	$40	$84
8	$190	$236	$40	$23.8	$29.5	$40	$84
9	$240	$286	$50	$26.7	31.8	$40	$74

b. Wendell maximizes profit by producing up to the point at which MC = MR, or Q = 8. Because the eighth unit adds $40 each to cost and revenue (MC = MR = $40), Wendell is indifferent between stopping with Q = 7 and continuing to Q = 8. Either way, his profit is $84. Because it is greater than zero, he should continue to produce in the long run.

c. At a price (and marginal revenue) of $20, MR = MC at an output of 5. He should produce up to 5 units for a loss of $30 (TR – TC = $100– $130 = -$30). Because it exceeds his average variable cost of $16.80, he is better off producing in the short run to avoid losing his entire fixed cost of $46. A $30 loss is $16 better than a $46 loss. Note that his $20 price exceeds his average variable cost by $3.20, leaving $3.20 times 5 units, or $16, to contribute to fixed cost. In the long run, however, all costs are variable, and Wendell would be better off leaving the widget industry rather than continuing to lose money.

d. At a price of $15, if Wendell continued to produce, his output would be 4 (this is the most he could produce without MC > MR). However, this does not even cover his variable cost. His loss would be $50 (TR – TC = $6 – $110), which is worse than the $46 that he would lose if he shut down. Therefore, he should shut down and lose only his fixed cost.

3. a.   The tax is $1. It will raise the price to $2.25 in the short run, which means that the consumer pays $0.75 ($2.25–$1.50), and the seller pays the remaining $0.25.

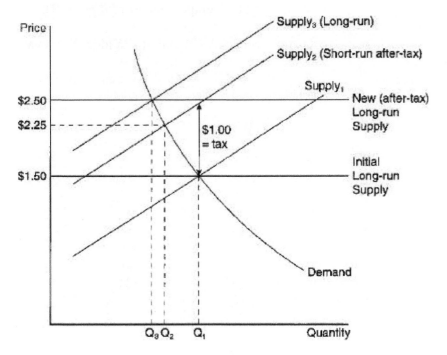

b. Equilibrium quantity falls from Q_1 to Q_2 as a result of the tax.

c. If the industry was in long-run equilibrium, profit was zero. The $0.25 portion of the tax absorbed by the sellers will result in losses in the short run.

d. In the long run, firms will respond to losses by leaving the industry until price rises by the full $1 tax. The long-run industry supply curve will shift upward by $1, which is the price hike required to restore long-run equilibrium at zero profit. Therefore, the consumer pays the full tax in the long run.

e. The new long-run supply curve is Supply3.

E. Advanced Critical Thinking

The fast-food restaurants are not behaving perfectly competitively. Under competition, the consumer ultimately pays all costs of production, but this occurs in the long run through free entry and exit. If competitive firms are losing money, they cannot raise prices to recoup the losses. Some firms eventually go out of business, and price rises because of the reduction in supply in the long run. Profit-maximizing firms do not consider rent and other fixed costs in setting price in the short run because fixed costs are sunk and do not affect marginal cost or marginal revenue.

15

Learning Objectives

In this chapter, you will …

- Learn why some markets have only one seller

- Analyze how a monopoly determines the quantity to produce and the price to charge

- See how the monopoly's decisions affect economic well-being

- See why monopolies try to charge different prices to different customers

- Consider the various public policies aimed at solving the problem of monopoly

If you own a personal computer, it probably uses some version of Windows, the operating system sold by the Microsoft Corporation. When Microsoft first designed Windows many years ago, it applied for and received a copyright from the government. The copyright gives Microsoft the exclusive right to make and sell copies of the Windows operating system. So if a person wants to buy a copy of Windows, he or she has little choice but to give Microsoft the approximately $100 that the firm has decided to charge for its product. Microsoft is said to have a *monopoly* in the market for Windows.

Microsoft's business decisions are not well described by the model of firm behaviour we developed in the previous chapter. In that chapter we analyzed competitive markets, in which there are many firms offering essentially identical products, so each firm has little influence over the price it receives. By contrast, a monopoly such as Microsoft has no close competitors and, therefore, can influence the market price of its product. While a competitive firm is a *price taker*, a monopoly firm is a *price maker*.

In this chapter we examine the implications of this market power. We will see that market power alters the relationship between a firm's costs and the price at which it sells its product to the market. A competitive firm takes the price of its output as given by the market and then chooses the quantity it will supply so that price equals marginal cost. By contrast, the price charged by a monopoly exceeds marginal cost. This result is clearly true in the case of Microsoft's Windows. The marginal cost of Windows—the extra cost that Microsoft would incur by printing one more copy of the program onto a CD—is only a few dollars. The market price of Windows is many times the marginal cost.

It is not surprising that monopolies charge high prices for their products. Customers of monopolies might seem to have little choice but to pay whatever the monopoly charges. But, if so, why does a copy of Windows not cost $1000? Or $10 000? The reason, of course, is that if Microsoft set the price that high, fewer people would buy the product. People would buy fewer computers, switch to other operating systems, or make illegal copies. Monopolies cannot achieve any level of profit they want, because high prices reduce the amount that their customers buy. Although monopolies can control the prices of their goods, their profits are not unlimited.

As we examine the production and pricing decisions of monopolies, we also consider the implications of monopoly for society as a whole. Monopoly firms, like competitive firms, aim to maximize profit. But this goal has very different ramifications for competitive and monopoly firms. As we first saw in Chapter 7, self-interested buyers and sellers in competitive markets are unwittingly led by an invisible hand to promote general economic well-being. By contrast, because monopoly firms are unchecked by competition, the outcome in a market with a monopoly is often not in the best interest of society.

One of the ten principles of economics in Chapter 1 is that governments can sometimes improve market outcomes. The analysis in this chapter will shed more light on this principle. As we examine the problems that monopolies raise for society, we will also discuss the various ways in which government policymakers might respond to these problems. The U.S. government, for example, keeps a close eye on Microsoft's business decisions. In 1994, it prevented Microsoft from buying Intuit, a software firm that sells the leading program for personal finance, on the grounds that the combination of Microsoft and Intuit would concentrate too much market power in one firm. Similarly, in 1998 the U.S. Justice Department objected when Microsoft started integrating its Internet browser into its Windows operating system, claiming that this addition would extend the firm's market power into new areas. To this day, Microsoft continues to wrangle with regulators around the world.

WHY MONOPOLIES ARISE

monopoly
a firm that is the sole seller of a product without close substitutes

A firm is a **monopoly** if it is the sole seller of its product and if its product does not have close substitutes. The fundamental cause of monopoly is *barriers to entry:* A monopoly remains the only seller in its market because other firms cannot enter the market and compete with it. Barriers to entry, in turn, have three main sources:

1. *Monopoly resources:* A key resource is owned by a single firm.
2. *Government-created monopolies:* The government gives a single firm the exclusive right to produce some good or service.
3. *Natural monopolies:* A single firm can produce output at a lower cost than can a large number of producers.

Let's briefly discuss each of these.

Monopoly Resources

The simplest way for a monopoly to arise is for a single firm to own a key resource. For example, consider the market for water in an early Canadian small town. If dozens of town residents have working wells, the competitive model discussed in the preceding chapter describes the behaviour of sellers. As a result, the price of a litre of water is driven to equal the marginal cost of pumping an extra litre. But if there is only one well in town and it is impossible to get water from anywhere else, then the owner of the well has a monopoly on water. Not surprisingly, the monopolist has much greater market power than any single firm in a competitive market. In the case of a necessity like water, the monopolist could command quite a high price, even if the marginal cost is low.

A classic example of a monopoly that arises from the ownership of a key resource is De Beers, the South African diamond company. De Beers controls about 80 percent of the world's production of diamonds. Although the firm's share of the market is not 100 percent, it is large enough to exert substantial influence over the market price of diamonds.

Although exclusive ownership of a key resource is a potential cause of monopoly, in practice, monopolies rarely arise for this reason. Actual economies are large, and resources are owned by many people. Indeed, because many goods are traded internationally, the natural scope of their markets is often worldwide. There are, therefore, few examples of firms that own a resource for which there are no close substitutes.

Government-Created Monopolies

In many cases, monopolies arise because the government has given one person or firm the exclusive right to sell some good or service. Sometimes the monopoly arises from the sheer political clout of the would-be monopolist. Kings, for example, once granted exclusive business licences to their friends and allies. At other times, the government grants a monopoly because doing so is viewed to be in the public interest.

The patent and copyright laws are two important examples of how the government creates a monopoly to serve the public interest. When a pharmaceutical company discovers a new drug, it can apply to the government for a patent. If the government deems the drug to be truly original, it approves the patent, which gives the company the exclusive right to manufacture and sell the drug for 20 years. Similarly, when a novelist finishes a book, she can copyright it. The copyright is a government guarantee that no one can print and sell the work without the author's permission. The copyright makes the novelist a monopolist in the sale of her novel.

The effects of patent and copyright laws are easy to see. Because these laws give one producer a monopoly, they lead to higher prices than would occur under competition. But by allowing these monopoly producers to charge higher prices and earn higher profits, the laws also encourage some desirable behaviour. Drug companies are allowed to be monopolists in the drugs they discover in order to encourage research. Authors are allowed to be monopolists in the sale of their books to encourage them to write more and better books.

Thus, the laws governing patents and copyrights have a benefit and costs. The benefit of the patent and copyright laws is the increased incentive for creative activity. This benefit is offset, to some extent, by the costs of monopoly pricing, which we examine fully later in this chapter.

Natural Monopolies

natural monopoly
a monopoly that arises because a single firm can supply a good or service to an entire market at a smaller cost than could two or more firms

An industry is a **natural monopoly** when a single firm can supply a good or service to an entire market at a lower cost than could two or more firms. A natural monopoly arises when there are economies of scale over the relevant range of output. Figure 15.1 shows the average total costs of a firm with economies of scale. In this case, a single firm can produce any amount of output at least cost. That is, for any given amount of output, a larger number of firms leads to less output per firm and higher average total cost.

An example of a natural monopoly is the distribution of water. To provide water to residents of a town, a firm must build a network of pipes throughout the town. If two or more firms were to compete in the provision of this service, each firm would have to pay the fixed cost of building a network. Thus, the average total cost of water is lowest if a single firm serves the entire market.

We saw other examples of natural monopolies when we discussed public goods and common resources in Chapter 11. We noted in passing that some goods in the economy are excludable but not rival. An example is a bridge used so infrequently that it is never congested. The bridge is excludable because a toll collector can prevent someone from using it. The bridge is not rival because use of the bridge by one person does not diminish the ability of others to use it. Because there is a fixed cost of building the bridge and a negligible marginal cost of additional users, the

FIGURE 15.1

Economies of Scale as a Cause of Monopoly

When a firm's average-total-cost curve continually declines, the firm has what is called a natural monopoly. In this case, when production is divided among more firms, each firm produces less, and average total cost rises. As a result, a single firm can produce any given amount at the smallest cost.

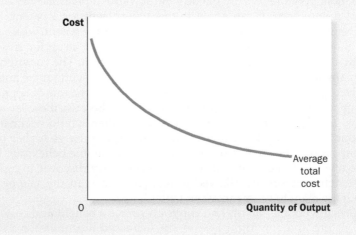

average total cost of a trip across the bridge (the total cost divided by the number of trips) falls as the number of trips rises. Hence, the bridge is a natural monopoly.

When a firm is a natural monopoly, it is less concerned about new entrants eroding its monopoly power. Normally, a firm has trouble maintaining a monopoly position without ownership of a key resource or government protection. The monopolist's profit attracts entrants into the market, and these entrants make the market more competitive. By contrast, entering a market in which another firm has a natural monopoly is unattractive. Would-be entrants know that they cannot achieve the same low costs that the monopolist enjoys because, after entry, each firm would have a smaller piece of the market.

In some cases, the size of the market is one determinant of whether an industry is a natural monopoly. Again, consider a bridge across a river. When the population is small, the bridge may be a natural monopoly. A single bridge can satisfy the entire demand for trips across the river at lowest cost. Yet as the population grows and the bridge becomes congested, satisfying the entire demand may require two or more bridges across the same river. Thus, as a market expands, a natural monopoly can evolve into a competitive market.

QuickQuiz   What are the three reasons that a market might have a monopoly?
• Give two examples of monopolies, and explain the reason for each.

HOW MONOPOLIES MAKE PRODUCTION AND PRICING DECISIONS

Now that we know how monopolies arise, we can consider how a monopoly firm decides how much of its product to make and what price to charge for it. The analysis of monopoly behaviour in this section is the starting point for evaluating whether monopolies are desirable and what policies the government might pursue in monopoly markets.

Monopoly versus Competition

The key difference between a competitive firm and a monopoly is the monopoly's ability to influence the price of its output. A competitive firm is small relative to the market in which it operates and, therefore, takes the price of its output as given by market conditions. By contrast, because a monopoly is the sole producer in its market, it can alter the price of its good by adjusting the quantity it supplies to the market.

One way to view this difference between a competitive firm and a monopoly is to consider the demand curve that each firm faces. When we analyzed profit maximization by competitive firms in the preceding chapter, we drew the market price as a horizontal line. Because a competitive firm can sell as much or as little as it wants at this price, the competitive firm faces a horizontal demand curve, as in panel (a) of Figure 15.2 (p. 318). In effect, because the competitive firm sells a product with many perfect substitutes (the products of all the other firms in its market), the demand curve that any one firm faces is perfectly elastic.

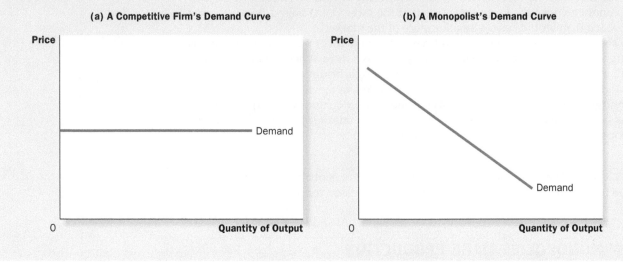

FIGURE 15.2

Demand Curves for Competitive and Monopoly Firms

Because competitive firms are price takers, they in effect face horizontal demand curves, as in panel (a). Because a monopoly firm is the sole producer in its market, it faces the downward-sloping market demand curve, as in panel (b). As a result, the monopoly has to accept a lower price if it wants to sell more output.

(a) A Competitive Firm's Demand Curve

(b) A Monopolist's Demand Curve

By contrast, because a monopoly is the sole producer in its market, its demand curve is the market demand curve. Thus, the monopolist's demand curve slopes downward for all the usual reasons, as in panel (b) of Figure 15.2. If the monopolist raises the price of its good, consumers buy less of it. Looked at another way, if the monopolist reduces the quantity of output it sells, the price of its output increases.

The market demand curve provides a constraint on a monopoly's ability to profit from its market power. A monopolist would prefer, if it were possible, to charge a high price and sell a large quantity at that high price. The market demand curve makes that outcome impossible. In particular, the market demand curve describes the combinations of price and quantity that are available to a monopoly firm. By adjusting the quantity produced (or, equivalently, the price charged), the monopolist can choose any point on the demand curve, but it cannot choose a point off the demand curve.

What point on the demand curve will the monopolist choose? As with competitive firms, we assume that the monopolist's goal is to maximize profit. Because the firm's profit is total revenue minus total costs, our next task in explaining monopoly behaviour is to examine a monopolist's revenue.

A Monopoly's Revenue

Consider a town with a single producer of water. Table 15.1 shows how the monopoly's revenue might depend on the amount of water produced.

TABLE 15.1

Quantity of Water	Price	Total Revenue	Average Revenue	Marginal Revenue	A Monopoly's Total, Average, and Marginal Revenue
(Q)	(P)	(TR = P × Q)	(AR = TR/Q)	(MR = ΔTR/ΔQ)	
0 litres	$11	$ 0	—		
				$10	
1	10	10	$10		
				8	
2	9	18	9		
				6	
3	8	24	8		
				4	
4	7	28	7		
				2	
5	6	30	6		
				0	
6	5	30	5		
				−2	
7	4	28	4		
				−4	
8	3	24	3		

The first two columns show the monopolist's demand schedule. If the monopolist produces 1 L of water, it can sell that litre for $10. If it produces 2 L, it must lower the price to $9 in order to sell both litres. And if it produces 3 L, it must lower the price to $8. And so on. If you graphed these two columns of numbers, you would get a typical downward-sloping demand curve.

The third column of the table presents the monopolist's *total revenue*. It equals the quantity sold (from the first column) times the price (from the second column). The fourth column computes the firm's *average revenue*, the amount of revenue the firm receives per unit sold. We compute average revenue by taking the number for total revenue in the third column and dividing it by the quantity of output in the first column. As we discussed in the previous chapter, average revenue always equals the price of the good. This is true for monopolists as well as for competitive firms.

The last column of Table 15.1 computes the firm's *marginal revenue*, the amount of revenue that the firm receives for each additional unit of output. We compute marginal revenue by taking the change in total revenue when output increases by 1 unit. For example, when the firm is producing 3 L of water, it receives total revenue of $24. Raising production to 4 L increases total revenue to $28. Thus, marginal revenue is $28 minus $24, or $4.

Table 15.1 shows a result that is important for understanding monopoly behaviour: *A monopolist's marginal revenue is always less than the price of its good.* For example, if the firm raises production of water from 3 to 4 L, it will increase total revenue by only $4, even though it will be able to sell each litre for $7. For a monopoly, marginal revenue is lower than price because a monopoly faces a downward-sloping demand curve. To increase the amount sold, a monopoly firm must lower the price of its good. Hence, to sell the fourth litre of water, the monopolist must get $1 less revenue for each of the first three litres. This $3 loss accounts for the difference between the price of the fourth litre ($7) and the marginal revenue of that fourth litre ($4)

Marginal revenue for monopolies is very different from marginal revenue for competitive firms. When a monopoly increases the amount it sells, it has two effects on total revenue ($P \times Q$):

1. *The output effect:* More output is sold, so Q is higher, which tends to increase total revenue.
2. *The price effect:* The price falls, so P is lower, which tends to decrease total revenue.

Because a competitive firm can sell all it wants at the market price, there is no price effect. When it increases production by 1 unit, it receives the market price for that unit, and it does not receive any less for the units it was already selling. That is, because the competitive firm is a price taker, its marginal revenue equals the price of its good. By contrast, when a monopoly increases production by 1 unit, it must reduce the price it charges for every unit it sells, and this cut in price reduces revenue on the units it was already selling. As a result, a monopoly's marginal revenue is less than its price.

Figure 15.3 graphs the demand curve and the marginal-revenue curve for a monopoly firm. (Because the firm's price equals its average revenue, the demand curve is also the average-revenue curve.) These two curves always start at the same point on the vertical axis because the marginal revenue of the first unit sold equals the price of the good. But for the reason we just discussed, the monopolist's marginal revenue on all units after the first is less than the price of the good. Thus, a monopoly's marginal-revenue curve lies below its demand curve.

FIGURE 15.3

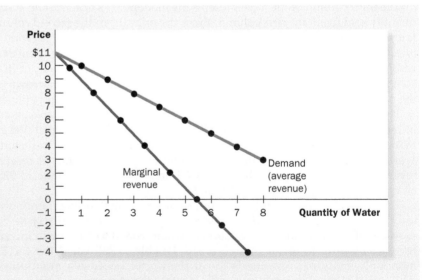

Demand and Marginal-Revenue Curves for a Monopoly

The demand curve shows how the quantity affects the price of the good. The marginal-revenue curve shows how the firm's revenue changes when the quantity increases by 1 unit. Because the price on all units sold must fall if the monopoly increases production, marginal revenue is always less than the price.

You can see in the figure (as well as in Table 15.1) that marginal revenue can even become negative. Marginal revenue is negative when the price effect on revenue is greater than the output effect. In this case, when the firm produces an extra unit of output, the price falls by enough to cause the firm's total revenue to decline, even though the firm is selling more units.

Profit Maximization

Now that we have considered the revenue of a monopoly firm, we are ready to examine how such a firm maximizes profit. Recall from Chapter 1 that one of the ten principles of economics is that rational people think at the margin. This lesson is as true for monopolists as it is for competitive firms. Here we apply the logic of marginal analysis to the monopolist's decision about how much to produce.

Figure 15.4 graphs the demand curve, the marginal-revenue curve, and the cost curves for a monopoly firm. All these curves should seem familiar: The demand and marginal-revenue curves are like those in Figure 15.3, and the cost curves are like those we encountered in the last two chapters. These curves contain all the information we need to determine the level of output that a profit-maximizing monopolist will choose.

Suppose, first, that the firm is producing at a low level of output, such as Q_1. In this case, marginal cost is less than marginal revenue. If the firm increased production by 1 unit, the additional revenue would exceed the additional costs, and profit would rise. Thus, when marginal cost is less than marginal revenue, the firm can increase profit by producing more units.

A similar argument applies at high levels of output, such as Q_2. In this case, marginal cost is greater than marginal revenue. If the firm reduced production

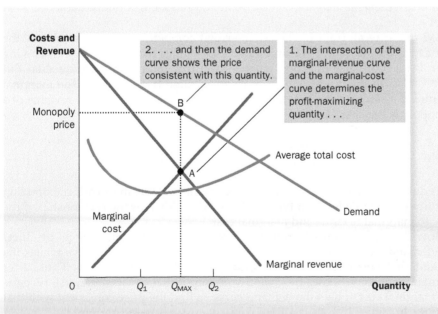

FIGURE 15.4

Profit Maximization for a Monopoly

A monopoly maximizes profit by choosing the quantity at which marginal revenue equals marginal cost (point A). It then uses the demand curve to find the price that will induce consumers to buy that quantity (point B).

WHY A MONOPOLY DOES NOT HAVE A SUPPLY CURVE

You may have noticed that we have analyzed the price in a monopoly market using the market demand curve and the firm's cost curves. We have not made any mention of the market supply curve. By contrast, when we analyzed prices in competitive markets beginning in Chapter 4, the two most important words were always *supply* and *demand.*

What happened to the supply curve? Although monopoly firms make decisions about what quantity to supply (in the way described in this chapter), a monopoly does not have a supply curve. A supply curve tells us the quantity that firms choose to supply at any given price. This concept makes sense when we are analyzing competitive firms, which are price takers. But a monopoly firm is a price maker, not a price taker. It is not meaningful to ask what such a firm would produce at any price because the firm sets the price at the same time it chooses the quantity to supply.

Indeed, the monopolist's decision about how much to supply is impossible to separate from the demand curve it faces. The shape of the demand curve determines the shape of the marginal-revenue curve, which in turn determines the monopolist's profit-maximizing quantity. In a competitive market, supply decisions can be analyzed without knowing the demand curve, but that is not true in a monopoly market. Therefore, we never talk about a monopoly's supply curve.

by 1 unit, the costs saved would exceed the revenue lost. Thus, if marginal cost is greater than marginal revenue, the firm can raise profit by reducing production.

In the end, the firm adjusts its level of production until the quantity reaches Q_{MAX}, at which marginal revenue equals marginal cost. *Thus, the monopolist's profit-maximizing quantity of output is determined by the intersection of the marginal-revenue curve and the marginal-cost curve.* In Figure 15.4, this intersection occurs at point A.

You might recall from the last chapter that competitive firms also choose the quantity of output at which marginal revenue equals marginal cost. In following this rule for profit maximization, competitive firms and monopolies are alike. But there is also an important difference between these types of firm: The marginal revenue of a competitive firm equals its price, whereas the marginal revenue of a monopoly is less than its price. That is,

$$\text{For a competitive firm:} \quad P = MR = MC$$
$$\text{For a monopoly firm:} \quad P > MR = MC$$

The equality of marginal revenue and marginal cost at the profit-maximizing quantity is the same for both types of firm. What differs is the relationship of the price to marginal revenue and marginal cost.

How does the monopoly find the profit-maximizing price for its product? The demand curve answers this question because the demand curve relates the amount that customers are willing to pay to the quantity sold. Thus, after the monopoly firm chooses the quantity of output that equates marginal revenue and marginal cost, it uses the demand curve to find the price consistent with that quantity. In Figure 15.4, the profit-maximizing price is found at point B.

NEL

We can now see a key difference between markets with competitive firms and markets with a monopoly firm: *In competitive markets, price equals marginal cost. In monopolized markets, price exceeds marginal cost.* As we will see in a moment, this finding is crucial to understanding the social cost of monopoly.

A Monopoly's Profit

How much profit does the monopoly make? To see the monopoly's profit, recall that profit equals total revenue (*TR*) minus total costs (*TC*):

$$\text{Profit} = TR - TC$$

We can rewrite this as

$$\text{Profit} = (TR/Q - TC/Q) \times Q$$

TR/Q is average revenue, which equals the price *P*, and *TC/Q* is average total cost *ATC*. Therefore,

$$\text{Profit} = (P - ATC) \times Q$$

This equation for profit (which is the same as the profit equation for competitive firms) allows us to measure the monopolist's profit in our graph.

Consider the shaded box in Figure 15.5. The height of the box (the segment BC) is price minus average total cost, *P – ATC*, which is the profit on the typical unit sold. The width of the box (the segment DC) is the quantity sold, Q_{MAX}. Therefore, the area of this box is the monopoly firm's total profit.

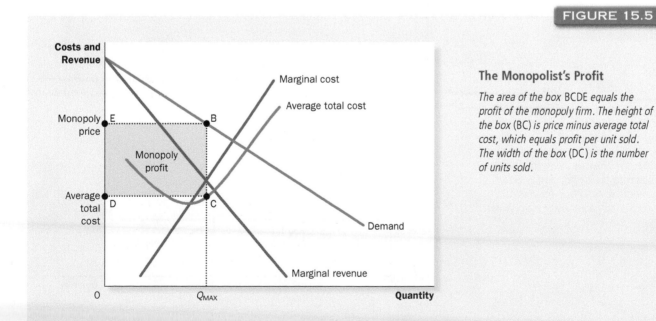

FIGURE 15.5

The Monopolist's Profit

The area of the box BCDE equals the profit of the monopoly firm. The height of the box (BC) is price minus average total cost, which equals profit per unit sold. The width of the box (DC) is the number of units sold.

Case Study
MONOPOLY DRUGS VERSUS GENERIC DRUGS

According to our analysis, prices are determined quite differently in monopolized markets from the way they are in competitive markets. A natural place to test this theory is the market for pharmaceutical drugs, because this market takes on both market structures. When a firm discovers a new drug, patent laws give the firm a monopoly on the sale of that drug. But eventually the firm's patent runs out, and any company can make and sell the drug. At that time, the market switches from being monopolistic to being competitive.

What should happen to the price of a drug when the patent runs out? Figure 15.6 shows the market for a typical drug. In this figure, the marginal-cost of the drug is constant. (This is approximately true for many drugs.)

During the life of the patent, the monopoly firm maximizes profit by producing the quantity at which marginal revenue equals marginal cost and charging a price well above marginal cost. But when the patent runs out, the profit from making the drug should encourage new firms to enter the market. As the market becomes more competitive, the price should fall to equal marginal cost.

Experience is, in fact, consistent with our theory. When the patent on a drug expires, other companies quickly enter and begin selling so-called generic products that are chemically identical to the former monopolist's brand-name product. And just as our analysis predicts, the price of the competitively produced generic drug is well below the price that the monopolist was charging.

FIGURE 15.6

The Market for Drugs

When a patent gives a firm a monopoly over the sale of a drug, the firm charges the monopoly price, which is well above the marginal cost of making the drug. When the patent on a drug runs out, new firms enter the market, making it more competitive. As a result, the price falls from the monopoly price to marginal cost.

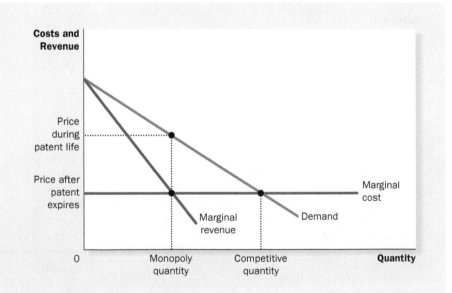

The expiration of a patent, however, does not cause the monopolist to lose all its market power. Some consumers remain loyal to the brand-name drug, perhaps out of fear that the new generic drugs are not actually the same as the drug they have been using for years. As a result, the former monopolist can continue to charge a price at least somewhat above the price charged by its new competitors. ●

QuickQuiz Explain how a monopolist chooses the quantity of output to produce and the price to charge.

THE WELFARE COST OF MONOPOLY

Is monopoly a good way to organize a market? We have seen that a monopoly, in contrast to a competitive firm, charges a price above marginal cost. From the standpoint of consumers, this high price makes monopoly undesirable. At the same time, however, the monopoly is earning profit from charging this high price. From the standpoint of the owners of the firm, the high price makes monopoly very desirable. Is it possible that the benefits to the firm's owners exceed the costs imposed on consumers, making monopoly desirable from the standpoint of society as a whole?

We can answer this question using the tools of welfare economics. Recall from Chapter 7 that total surplus measures the economic well-being of buyers and sellers in a market. Total surplus is the sum of consumer surplus and producer surplus. Consumer surplus is consumers' willingness to pay for a good minus the amount they actually pay for it. Producer surplus is the amount producers receive for a good minus their costs of producing it. In this case, there is a single producer—the monopolist.

You can probably guess the result of this analysis. In Chapter 7 we concluded that the equilibrium of supply and demand in a competitive market is not only a natural outcome but a desirable one. In particular, the invisible hand of the market leads to an allocation of resources that makes total surplus as large as it can be. Because a monopoly leads to an allocation of resources different from that in a competitive market, the outcome must, in some way, fail to maximize total economic well-being.

The Deadweight Loss

We begin by considering what the monopoly firm would do if it were run by a benevolent social planner. The social planner cares not only about the profit earned by the firm's owners but also about the benefits received by the firm's consumers. The planner tries to maximize total surplus, which equals producer surplus (profit) plus consumer surplus. Keep in mind that total surplus equals the value of the good to consumers minus the costs of making the good incurred by the monopoly producer.

Figure 15.7 (p. 326) analyzes what level of output a benevolent social planner would choose. The demand curve reflects the value of the good to consumers, as

FIGURE 15.7

The Efficient Level of Output

A benevolent social planner who wanted to maximize total surplus in the market would choose the level of output where the demand curve and marginal-cost curve intersect. Below this level, the value of the good to the marginal buyer (as reflected in the demand curve) exceeds the marginal cost of making the good. Above this level, the value to the marginal buyer is less than marginal cost.

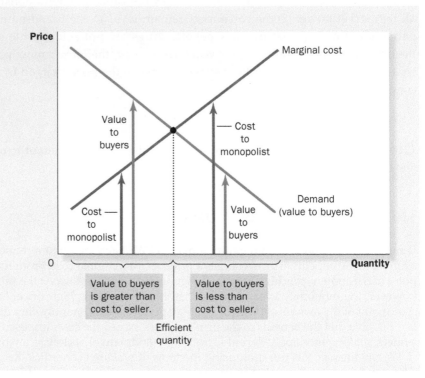

measured by their willingness to pay for it. The marginal-cost curve reflects the costs of the monopolist. *Thus, the socially efficient quantity is found where the demand curve and the marginal-cost curve intersect.* Below this quantity, the value to consumers exceeds the marginal cost of providing the good, so increasing output would raise total surplus. Above this quantity, the marginal cost exceeds the value to consumers, so decreasing output would raise total surplus. At the optimal quantity, the value of an extra unit to consumers exactly equals the marginal cost of production.

If the social planner were running the monopoly, the firm could achieve this efficient outcome by charging the price found at the intersection of the demand and marginal-cost curves. Thus, like a competitive firm and unlike a profit-maximizing monopoly, a social planner would charge a price equal to marginal cost. Because this price would give consumers an accurate signal about the cost of producing the good, consumers would buy the efficient quantity.

We can evaluate the welfare effects of monopoly by comparing the level of output that the monopolist chooses to the level of output that a social planner would choose. As we have seen, the monopolist chooses to produce and sell the quantity of output at which the marginal-revenue and marginal-cost curves intersect; the social planner would choose the quantity at which the demand and marginal-cost curves intersect. Figure 15.8 shows the comparison. *The monopolist produces less than the socially efficient quantity of output.*

We can also view the inefficiency of monopoly in terms of the monopolist's price. Because the market demand curve describes a negative relationship between the price and quantity of the good, a quantity that is inefficiently low is

FIGURE 15.8

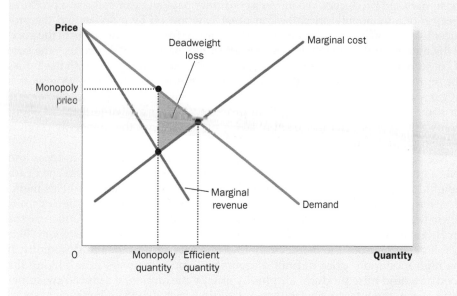

The Inefficiency of Monopoly

Because a monopoly charges a price above marginal cost, not all consumers who value the good at more than its cost buy it. Thus, the quantity produced and sold by a monopoly is below the socially efficient level. The deadweight loss is represented by the area of the triangle between the demand curve (which reflects the value of the good to consumers) and the marginal-cost curve (which reflects the costs of the monopoly producer).

equivalent to a price that is inefficiently high. When a monopolist charges a price above marginal cost, some potential consumers value the good at more than its marginal cost but less than the monopolist's price. These consumers do not end up buying the good. Because the value these consumers place on the good is greater than the cost of providing it to them, this result is inefficient. Thus, monopoly pricing prevents some mutually beneficial trades from taking place.

The inefficiency of monopoly can be measured with a deadweight loss triangle, as illustrated in Figure 15.8. Because the demand curve reflects the value to consumers and the marginal-cost curve reflects the costs to the monopoly producer, the area of the deadweight loss triangle between the demand curve and the marginal-cost curve equals the total surplus lost because of monopoly pricing. It is the reduction in economic well-being that results from the monopoly's use of its market power.

The deadweight loss caused by monopoly is similar to the deadweight loss caused by a tax. Indeed, a monopolist is like a private tax collector. As we saw in Chapter 8, a tax on a good places a wedge between consumers' willingness to pay (as reflected in the demand curve) and producers' costs (as reflected in the supply curve). Because a monopoly exerts its market power by charging a price above marginal cost, it places a similar wedge. In both cases, the wedge causes the quantity sold to fall short of the social optimum. The difference between the two cases is that the government gets the revenue from a tax, whereas a private firm gets the monopoly profit.

The Monopoly's Profit: A Social Cost?

It is tempting to decry monopolies for "profiteering" at the expense of the public. And, indeed, a monopoly firm does earn a higher profit by virtue of its market power. According to the economic analysis of monopoly, however, the firm's profit is not in itself necessarily a problem for society.

Welfare in a monopolized market, like all markets, includes the welfare of both consumers and producers. Whenever a consumer pays an extra dollar to a producer because of a monopoly price, the consumer is worse off by a dollar, and the producer is better off by the same amount. This transfer from the consumers of the good to the owners of the monopoly does not affect the market's total surplus—the sum of consumer and producer surplus. In other words, the monopoly profit itself does not represent a shrinkage in the size of the economic pie; it merely represents a bigger slice for producers and a smaller slice for consumers. Unless consumers are for some reason more deserving than producers—a normative judgement about equity that goes beyond the realm of economic efficiency—the monopoly profit is not a social problem.

The problem in a monopolized market arises because the firm produces and sells a quantity of output below the level that maximizes total surplus. The deadweight loss measures how much the economic pie shrinks as a result. This inefficiency is connected to the monopoly's high price: Consumers buy fewer units when the firm raises its price above marginal cost. But keep in mind that the profit earned on the units that continue to be sold is not the problem. The problem stems from the inefficiently low quantity of output. Put differently, if the high monopoly price did not discourage some consumers from buying the good, it would raise producer surplus by exactly the amount it reduced consumer surplus, leaving total surplus the same as could be achieved by a benevolent social planner.

There is, however, a possible exception to this conclusion. Suppose that a monopoly firm has to incur additional costs to maintain its monopoly position. For example, a firm with a government-created monopoly might need to hire lobbyists to convince lawmakers to continue its monopoly. In this case, the monopoly may use up some of its monopoly profits paying for these additional costs. If so, the social loss from monopoly includes both these costs and the deadweight loss resulting from a price above marginal cost.

QuickQuiz How does a monopolist's quantity of output compare to the quantity of output that maximizes total surplus?

PRICE DISCRIMINATION

So far we have been assuming that the monopoly firm charges the same price to all customers. Yet in many cases firms try to sell the same good to different customers for different prices, even though the costs of producing for the two customers are the same. This practice is called **price discrimination.**

price discrimination
the business practice of selling the same good at different prices to different customers

Before discussing the behaviour of a price-discriminating monopolist, we should note that price discrimination is not possible when a good is sold in a competitive market. In a competitive market, many firms are selling the same good at the market price. No firm is willing to charge a lower price to any customer because the firm can sell all it wants at the market price. And if any firm tried to charge a higher price to a customer, that customer would buy from another firm. For a firm to price-discriminate, it must have some market power.

A Parable about Pricing

To understand why a monopolist would want to price-discriminate, let's consider a simple example. Imagine that you are the president of Readalot Publishing Company. Readalot's best-selling author has just written her latest novel. To keep things simple, let's imagine that you pay the author a flat $2 million for the exclusive rights to publish the book. Let's also assume that the cost of printing the book is zero. Readalot's profit, therefore, is the revenue it gets from selling the book minus the $2 million it has paid to the author. Given these assumptions, how would you, as Readalot's president, decide what price to charge for the book?

Your first step in setting the price is to estimate what the demand for the book is likely to be. Readalot's marketing department tells you that the book will attract two types of readers. The book will appeal to the author's 100 000 die-hard fans. These fans will be willing to pay as much as $30 for the book. In addition, the book will appeal to about 400 000 less enthusiastic readers who will be willing to pay up to $5 for the book.

If Readalot charges a single price to all consumers, what price maximizes profit? There are two natural prices to consider: $30 is the highest price Readalot can charge and still get the 100 000 die-hard fans, and $5 is the highest price it can charge and still get the entire market of 500 000 potential readers. It is a matter of simple arithmetic to solve Readalot's problem. At a price of $30, Readalot sells 100 000 copies, has revenue of $3 million, and makes profit of $1 million. At a price of $5, it sells 500 000 copies, has revenue of $2.5 million, and makes a profit of $500 000. Thus, Readalot maximizes profit by charging $30 and forgoing the opportunity to sell to the 400 000 less enthusiastic readers.

Notice that Readalot's decision causes a deadweight loss. There are 400 000 readers willing to pay $5 for the book, and the marginal cost of providing it to them is zero. Thus, $2 million of total surplus is lost when Readalot charges the higher price. This deadweight loss is the usual inefficiency that arises whenever a monopolist charges a price above marginal cost.

Now suppose that Readalot's marketing department makes an important discovery: These two groups of readers are in separate markets. All the die-hard fans live in Australia, and all the other readers live in Canada. Moreover, it is difficult for readers in one country to buy books in the other.

In response to this discovery, Readalot can change its marketing strategy and increase profits. To the 100 000 Australian readers, it can charge $30 for the book. To the 400 000 Canadian readers, it can charge $5 for the book. In this case, revenue is $3 million in Australia and $2 million in Canada, for a total of $5 million. Profit is then $3 million, which is substantially greater than the $1 million the company could earn charging the same $30 price to all customers. Not surprisingly, Readalot chooses to follow this strategy of price discrimination.

The story of Readalot Publishing is hypothetical, but it describes accurately the business practice of many publishing companies. Textbooks, for example, are often sold at a lower price in Europe than in Canada. Even more important is the price differential between hardcover books and paperbacks. When a publisher has a new novel, it initially releases an expensive hardcover edition and later releases a cheaper paperback edition. The difference in price between these two editions far exceeds the difference in printing costs. The publisher's goal is just as in our example. By selling the hardcover to die-hard fans and the paperback to less enthusiastic readers, the publisher price-discriminates and raises its profit.

The Moral of the Story

Like any parable, the story of Readalot Publishing is stylized. Yet, also like any parable, it teaches some important and general lessons. In this case, there are three lessons to be learned about price discrimination.

The first and most obvious lesson is that price discrimination is a rational strategy for a profit-maximizing monopolist. In other words, by charging different prices to different customers, a monopolist can increase its profit. In essence, a price-discriminating monopolist charges each customer a price closer to that customer's willingness to pay than is possible with a single price.

The second lesson is that price discrimination requires the ability to separate customers according to their willingness to pay. In our example, customers were separated geographically. But sometimes monopolists choose other differences, such as age or income, to distinguish among customers.

A corollary to this second lesson is that certain market forces can prevent firms from price-discriminating. In particular, one such force is *arbitrage,* the process of buying a good in one market at a low price and selling it in another market at a higher price in order to profit from the price difference. In our example, suppose that Australian bookstores could buy the book in Canada and resell it to Australian readers. This arbitrage would prevent Readalot from price-discriminating because no Australian would buy the book at the higher price.

The third lesson from our parable is perhaps the most surprising: Price discrimination can raise economic welfare. Recall that a deadweight loss arises when Readalot charges a single $30 price, because the 400 000 less enthusiastic readers do not end up with the book, even though they value it at more than its marginal cost of production. By contrast, when Readalot price-discriminates, all readers end up with the book, and the outcome is efficient. Thus, price discrimination can eliminate the inefficiency inherent in monopoly pricing.

Note that the increase in welfare from price discrimination shows up as higher producer surplus rather than higher consumer surplus. In our example, consumers are no better off for having bought the book: The price they pay exactly equals the value they place on the book, so they receive no consumer surplus. The entire increase in total surplus from price discrimination accrues to Readalot Publishing in the form of higher profit.

The Analytics of Price Discrimination

Let's consider a bit more formally how price discrimination affects economic welfare. We begin by assuming that the monopolist can price-discriminate perfectly. *Perfect price discrimination* describes a situation in which the monopolist knows exactly the willingness to pay of each customer and can charge each customer a different price. In this case, the monopolist charges each customer exactly his willingness to pay, and the monopolist gets the entire surplus in every transaction. Perfect price discrimination is sometimes referred to as first-degree price discrimination.

Figure 15.9 shows producer and consumer surplus with and without price discrimination. Without price discrimination, the firm charges a single price above marginal cost, as shown in panel (a). Because some potential customers who value the good at more than marginal cost do not buy it at this high price, the monopoly

FIGURE 15.9

Welfare with and without Price Discrimination

Panel (a) shows a monopolist that charges the same price to all customers. Total surplus in this market equals the sum of profit (producer surplus) and consumer surplus. Panel (b) shows a monopolist that can perfectly price-discriminate. Because consumer surplus equals zero, total surplus now equals the firm's profit. Comparing these two panels, you can see that perfect price discrimination raises profit, raises total surplus, and lowers consumer surplus.

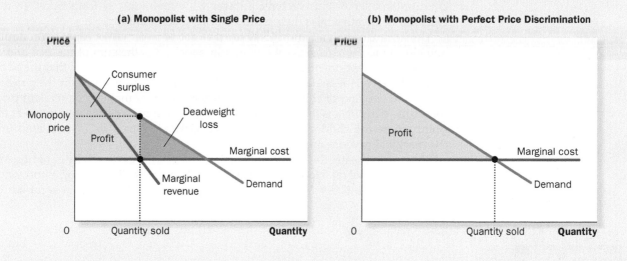

(a) Monopolist with Single Price **(b) Monopolist with Perfect Price Discrimination**

causes a deadweight loss. Yet when a firm can perfectly price-discriminate, as shown in panel (b), each customer who values the good at more than marginal cost buys the good and is charged his willingness to pay. All mutually beneficial trades take place, there is no deadweight loss, and the entire surplus derived from the market goes to the monopoly producer in the form of profit.

In reality, of course, price discrimination is not perfect. Customers do not walk into stores with signs displaying their willingness to pay. Instead, firms price-discriminate by dividing customers into groups: young versus old, weekday versus weekend shoppers, Canadians versus Australians, and so on. Unlike those in our parable of Readalot Publishing, customers within each group differ in their willingness to pay for the product, making perfect price discrimination impossible.

Imperfect price discrimination comes in two forms, referred to as second- and third-degree price discrimination. Second-degree price discrimination involves charging different prices to the same customer for different units that the customer buys. For example, many firms offer lower prices to customers who buy large quantities. A bakery might charge $0.50 for each donut but $5 for a dozen. This is a form of price discrimination because the customer pays a higher price for the first unit bought than for the twelfth. Quantity discounts are often a successful way of price-discriminating because a customer's willingness to pay for an additional unit declines as the customer buys more units.

Third-degree price discrimination can be achieved when the market can be segmented and when the segments have different elasticities of demand. A good example of third-degree price discrimination is movie tickets. Many movie theatres charge a lower price for children and senior citizens than for other patrons. This fact is hard to explain in a competitive market. In a competitive market, price equals marginal cost, and the marginal cost of providing a seat for a child or senior citizen is the same as the marginal cost of providing a seat for anyone else. Yet this fact is easily explained if movie theatres have some local monopoly power and if children and senior citizens have a lower willingness to pay for a ticket. In this case, movie theatres raise their profit by price-discriminating.

This is illustrated in Figure 15.10 for the case of two market segments—adults and children. The total market demand in panel (a) is the sum of the demand of the two market segments, given in panels (b) and (c). It is assumed that the adult demand curve is less elastic than the child demand curve, and that the price at which the demand of children is equal to zero is lower than the equivalent price for adults. This means that there is a kink in the total market-demand curve at the point where the children's demand curve kicks in. This kink is translated into the marginal-revenue curve as well.

The movie theatre decides on the total number of tickets to sell by equating MC with MR in panel (a). However there is not just one price. By drawing a horizontal line through the $MC = MR$ point until it intersects with the MR curves for adults

FIGURE 15.10

Third-Degree Price Discrimination

Panels (b) and (c) show the demand and marginal-revenue curves for the adult and child segment of the market for movie tickets. Panel (a) sums these curves to give the demand and marginal-revenue curves for the total market. The monopolist maximizes profits by setting $MC = MR$ and selling a total quantity of Q_T [panel (a)], but this involves charging different prices in each market: P_A in the adult market [panel (b)] and P_C in the child market [panel (c)], with Q_A tickets sold to adults and Q_C tickets sold to children. The adult price is higher than the child price because the adult demand is less elastic.

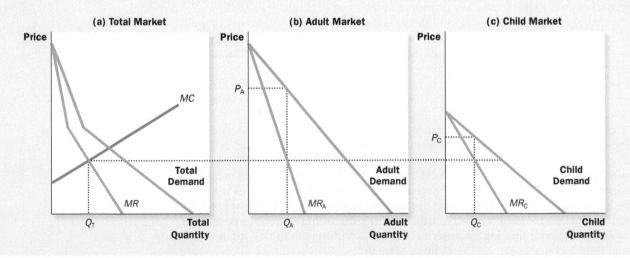

(MR_A) and children (MR_C) and then reading the price off the respective demand curves determines the price in each market segment, P_A and P_C, as well as the number of tickets sold in each market, Q_A and Q_C. Not surprisingly the price in the adult market is higher because the demand curve is less elastic.

How does imperfect price discrimination affect welfare? The analysis of these pricing schemes is quite complicated, and it turns out that there is no general answer to this question. Compared to the monopoly outcome with a single price, imperfect price discrimination can raise, lower, or leave unchanged total surplus in a market. The only certain conclusion is that price discrimination raises the monopoly's profit—otherwise the firm would choose to charge all customers the same price.

Examples of Price Discrimination

Firms in our economy use various business strategies aimed at charging different prices to different customers. We have considered the example of quantity discounts and movie tickets. Now that we understand the economics of price discrimination, let's consider some other examples.

Airline Prices   Seats on airplanes are sold at many different prices. Most airlines charge a lower price for a round-trip ticket between two cities if the traveller stays over a Saturday night. At first this seems odd. Why should it matter to the airline whether a passenger stays over a Saturday night? The reason is that this rule provides a way to separate business travellers and personal travellers. A passenger on a business trip has a high willingness to pay and, most likely, does not want to stay over a Saturday night. By contrast, a passenger travelling for personal reasons has a lower willingness to pay and is more likely to be willing to stay over a Saturday night. Thus, the airlines can successfully price-discriminate by charging a lower price for passengers who stay over a Saturday night.

Discount Coupons   Many companies offer discount coupons to the public in newspapers and magazines. A buyer simply has to clip out the coupon in order to get $0.50 off his next purchase. Why do companies offer these coupons? Why don't they just cut the price of the product by $0.50?

The answer is that coupons allow companies to price-discriminate. Companies know that not all customers are willing to spend the time to clip out coupons. Moreover, the willingness to clip coupons is related to the customer's willingness to pay for the good. A rich and busy executive is unlikely to spend her time clipping discount coupons out of the newspaper, and she is probably willing to pay a higher price for many goods. A person who is unemployed is more likely to clip coupons and has a lower willingness to pay. Thus, by charging a lower price only to those customers who clip coupons, firms can successfully price-discriminate.

Financial Aid   Many colleges and universities give financial aid to needy students. One can view this policy as a type of price discrimination. Wealthy students have greater financial resources and, therefore, a higher willingness to pay than needy students. By charging high tuition and selectively offering financial aid, schools charge prices to customers based on the value they place on going to that school. This behaviour is like that of any price-discriminating monopolist.

Quantity Discounts So far in our examples of price discrimination, the monopolist charges different prices to different customers. Sometimes, however, monopolists price-discriminate by charging different prices to the same customer for different units that the customer buys. For example, many firms offer lower prices to customers who buy large quantities. A bakery might charge $0.50 for each donut but $5 for a dozen. This is a form of price discrimination because the customer pays a higher price for the first unit bought than for the twelfth. Quantity discounts are often a successful way of price-discriminating because a customer's willingness to pay for an additional unit declines as the customer buys more units.

QuickQuiz Give two examples of price discrimination. • How does perfect price discrimination affect consumer surplus, producer surplus, and total surplus?

PUBLIC POLICY TOWARD MONOPOLIES

We have seen that monopolies, in contrast to competitive markets, fail to allocate resources efficiently. Monopolies produce less than the socially desirable quantity of output and, as a result, charge prices above marginal cost. Policymakers in the government can respond to the problem of monopoly in one of four ways:

1. By trying to make monopolized industries more competitive
2. By regulating the behaviour of the monopolies
3. By turning some private monopolies into public enterprises
4. By doing nothing at all

Increasing Competition with Competition Law

One way that the government can respond to the inefficiencies resulting from market power in general, and monopoly in particular, is through legislation designed to encourage competition and discourage the use of monopoly practices. For example, if a merger between two companies would make the industry less competitive and, as a result, reduce the economic well-being of the country as a whole, the government could pass laws that prevent such mergers.

Competition law in Canada is enforced by the Commissioner of Competition of the Competition Bureau, a unit within the federal government's Industry Canada. Lawyers and economists in the bureau investigate anticompetitive practices that fall within the scope of the act. When appropriate, the commissioner may refer cases for criminal prosecution to the attorney general of Canada. In other cases, the commissioner may apply to the Competition Tribunal for review and adjudication.

The tribunal is a quasi-judicial body that is similar to a court. It consists of judges and lay members who are experts from the business, academic, and civil service communities. In most of the cases it deals with, the tribunal must determine whether a particular practice or action has an adverse effect on competition. If it concludes that there is an anticompetitive effect, the tribunal can issue an order to prohibit the practice or action. For example, the tribunal can block a merger or require that a firm divest itself of assets. In 1990, the tribunal ruled that the merger of two of Canada's largest integrated petroleum companies, Imperial Oil and Texaco Canada, would have substantial anticompetitive effects. Although the merger was allowed to proceed, the tribunal ordered that many of the merged entity's assets be given up. This divestiture ultimately involved 414 service stations, 13 terminals, and 1 refinery.

Competition law in Canada prevents other kinds of anticompetitive practices, some of which we will discuss in Chapter 16.

Competition laws have costs as well as benefits. Sometimes companies merge not to reduce competition but to lower costs through more efficient joint production. The benefits of greater efficiency as a result of mergers are called *synergies*. These considerations are particularly important in a global context because some Canadian companies are large and dominant in the domestic market but small in the international market. For example, although the banking market in Canada is dominated by the "Big Five," these banks are small players on the international banking scene. Some bankers have argued that Canadian banks can compete in international markets only by realizing the synergies that would result when operations are combined. Using this argument, four of Canada's largest banks sought permission to merge in 1998: the Royal Bank with the Bank of Montreal, and the Canadian Imperial Bank of Commerce with the Toronto-Dominion Bank. Both merger deals were rejected by the federal government.

If competition laws are to raise social welfare, the government must be able to determine which mergers are desirable and which are not. That is, it must be able to measure and compare the social benefit from synergies with the social cost of reduced competition. However, critics of competition laws are skeptical that the government can perform the necessary cost–benefit analysis with sufficient accuracy.

Regulation

Another way in which the government deals with the problem of monopoly is by regulating the behaviour of monopolists. This solution is common in the case of natural monopolies, such as water and electric companies. These companies are not allowed to charge any price they want. Instead, government agencies regulate their prices.

What price should the government set for a natural monopoly? This question is not as easy as it might at first appear. One might conclude that the price should equal the monopolist's marginal cost. If price equals marginal cost, customers will buy the quantity of the monopolist's output that maximizes total surplus, and the allocation of resources will be efficient.

There are, however, two practical problems with marginal-cost pricing as a regulatory system. The first is illustrated in Figure 15.11 (p. 336). Natural monopolies, by definition, have declining average total cost. As we discussed in Chapter 13, when average total cost is declining, marginal cost is less than average total cost. If regulators are to set price equal to marginal cost, that price will be less than the firm's average total cost, and the firm will lose money. Instead of charging such a low price, the monopoly firm would just exit the industry.

Regulators can respond to this problem in various ways, none of which is perfect. One way is to subsidize the monopolist. In essence, the government picks up the losses inherent in marginal-cost pricing. Yet to pay for the subsidy, the government needs to raise money through taxation, which involves its own deadweight

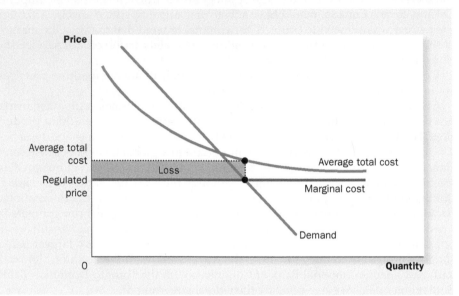

FIGURE 15.11

Marginal-Cost Pricing for a Natural Monopoly

Because a natural monopoly has declining average total cost, marginal cost is less than average total cost. Therefore, if regulators require a natural monopoly to charge a price equal to marginal cost, price will be below average total cost, and the monopoly will lose money.

losses. Alternatively, the regulators can allow the monopolist to charge a price higher than marginal cost. If the regulated price equals average total cost, the monopolist earns exactly zero economic profit. Yet average-cost pricing leads to deadweight losses because the monopolist's price no longer reflects the marginal cost of producing the good. In essence, average-cost pricing is like a tax on the good the monopolist is selling.

The second problem with marginal-cost pricing as a regulatory system (and with average-cost pricing as well) is that it gives the monopolist no incentive to reduce costs. Each firm in a competitive market tries to reduce its costs because lower costs mean higher profits. But if a regulated monopolist knows that regulators will reduce prices whenever costs fall, the monopolist will not benefit from lower costs. In practice, regulators deal with this problem by allowing monopolists to keep some of the benefits from lower costs in the form of higher profit, a practice that requires some departure from marginal-cost pricing.

Public Ownership

The third policy used by the government to deal with monopoly is public ownership. That is, rather than regulating a natural monopoly that is run by a private firm, the government can run the monopoly itself. In contrast to the United States, where there is very little public ownership, this solution is common in many European countries. It is also relatively common in Canada, although somewhat less so in recent years.

In Canada, government ownership occurs at both the federal and the provincial/territorial levels. Government-owned firms are known as Crown corporations. Federal Crown corporations include Canada Post, the Canadian Broadcasting Corporation, and Atomic Energy of Canada Limited. In the past decade, the federal government has privatized some of its Crown corporations, including Petro-Canada, Air Canada, and Canadian National Railway.

At the provincial/territorial level, Crown corporations exist in insurance (Saskatchewan Government Insurance), hydroelectricity (Manitoba Hydro and Hydro-Québec), and telecommunications (Saskatchewan Tel and BC Telephone). Gas and water utilities are also publicly owned in most provinces/territories.

Economists usually prefer private to public ownership of natural monopolies. The key issue is how the ownership of the firm affects the costs of production. Private owners have an incentive to minimize costs as long as they reap part of the benefit in the form of higher profit. If the firm's managers are doing a bad job of keeping costs down, the firm's owners will fire them. By contrast, if the government bureaucrats who run a monopoly do a bad job, the losers are the customers and taxpayers, whose only recourse is the political system. The bureaucrats may become a special-interest group and attempt to block cost-reducing reforms. Put simply, as a way of ensuring that firms are well run, the voting booth is less reliable than the profit motive.

Doing Nothing

Each of the forgoing policies aimed at reducing the problem of monopoly has drawbacks. As a result, some economists argue that it is often best for the government not to try to remedy the inefficiencies of monopoly pricing. Here is the assessment of economist George Stigler, who won the Nobel Prize for his work in industrial organization, writing in the *Fortune Encyclopedia of Economics*:

> A famous theorem in economics states that a competitive enterprise economy will produce the largest possible income from a given stock of resources. No real economy meets the exact conditions of the theorem, and all real economies will fall short of the ideal economy—a difference called "market failure." In my view, however, the degree of "market failure" for the American economy is much smaller than the "political failure" arising from the imperfections of economic policies found in real political systems.

As this quotation makes clear, determining the proper role of the government in the economy requires judgments about politics as well as economics.

QuickQuiz Describe the ways policymakers can respond to the inefficiencies caused by monopolies. List a potential problem with each of these policy responses.

CONCLUSION: THE PREVALENCE OF MONOPOLY

This chapter has discussed the behaviour of firms that have control over the prices they charge. We have seen that these firms behave very differently from the competitive firms studied in the previous chapter. Table 15.2 (p. 339) summarizes some of the key similarities and differences between competitive and monopoly markets.

From the standpoint of public policy, a crucial result is that monopolists produce less than the socially efficient quantity and charge prices above marginal

NEL

IN THE NEWS

PRICE DISCRIMINATION: OPPORTUNITIES FOR ARBITRAGE

In order for a firm to price-discriminate it must be difficult, or costly, for buyers to resell the good at a higher price. If this was not the case, an opportunity for arbitrage arises. Arbitrage occurs when an individual purchases a good at a low price and then immediately (or shortly thereafter) sells it for a higher price.

One common form of price discrimination is for firms to sell the same good for different prices in different countries, with demand conditions dictating the price in each country. Businesses hope that arbitrage will be too costly in this case. As the following article shows, if they are determined enough, arbitragers can take advantage of this.

A Different Kind of Package Holiday

The same Louis Vuitton handbag costs about 40% more in Japan than in France. To economists, this is a market imperfection begging for arbitrage. And Hong Kong, that bastion of entrepreneurship, is obliging. Here is how.

Nine Hong Kong Chinese recently spent a fortnight travelling through Europe. They started in Frankfurt and ended in Rome, passing through one city a day. Early every morning, a van picked them up from their hotel and drove them to the first Louis Vuitton store on the day's agenda. It parked around the corner, and the Chinese entered the store in pairs. They each bought as many Louis Vuitton handbags as they could carry and then returned to the van, in order to be transferred to the next store.

It was gruelling work, complains a girl from the van. She, like the rest in the group, went on the trip because it was an all-expenses-paid way to see Europe. (In fact, those who bought more than their quota of handbags even earned a bonus.) But the itinerary did not allow for any sightseeing at all, and for meals the group are given Chinese takeaway in the van.

The sales staff in the stores tended to be rude; the tour's "boss," says the girl, had expressly asked for bags "with a certain monogram pattern" that is all the rage in Japan, and one shop simply refused to sell her the nine bags she brought to the counter.

The boss never introduced himself to the group, but when his troops returned he stood near the arrivals hall at Hong Kong's airport, watching them claim their luggage. His business seems to be going well—another tour group is apparently already on the way. Savvy Hong Kong tourists claim to know of several competing organisers—an industry, in other words. Nor is Louis

Vuitton the only target: Gucci tours have also taken place.

Should companies whose prices are being arbitraged in this way mind? Louis Vuitton's sales benefit from such tourism, after all. "We definitely do not think that a sale is a sale," complains an irate spokeswoman in Paris. "It took 150 years to build this brand," she says, and losing part of the retail network to a netherworld of shady Asians damages it.

So Louis Vuitton, along with other owners of luxury brands, is working with the authorities to crack down on such tourism. This is tricky, not only because of arbitrageurs tending to pay cash, but also because Louis Vuitton would hate to confuse them with its genuine customers from Asia, who have also been known to binge on bags.

Source: "A Different Kind of Holiday Package," July 2001. © The Economist Newspaper Limited, London 2009.

TABLE 15.2

Competition versus Monopoly: A Summary Comparison

	Competition	Monopoly
Similarities		
Goal of firms	Maximize profits	Maximize profits
Rule for maximizing	$MR = MC$	$MR = MC$
Can earn economic profits in the short run?	Yes	Yes
Differences		
Number of firms	Many	One
Marginal revenue	$MR = P$	$MR < P$
Price	$P = MC$	$P > MC$
Produces welfare-maximizing level of output?	Yes	No
Entry in long run?	Yes	No
Can earn economic profits in long run?	No	Yes
Price discrimination possible?	No	Yes

cost. As a result, they cause deadweight losses. In some cases, these inefficiencies can be mitigated through price discrimination by the monopolist, but other times they call for policymakers to take an active role.

How prevalent are the problems of monopoly? There are two answers to this question.

In one sense, monopolies are common. Most firms have some control over the prices they charge. They are not forced to charge the market price for their goods, because their goods are not exactly the same as those offered by other firms. A Ford Taurus is not the same as a Toyota Camry. Ben & Jerry's ice cream is not the same as Breyers'. Each of these goods has a downward-sloping demand curve, which gives each producer some degree of monopoly power.

Yet firms with substantial monopoly power are quite rare. Few goods are truly unique. Most have substitutes that, even if not exactly the same, are very similar. Ben & Jerry can raise the price of its ice cream a little without losing all its sales; but if the company raises it very much, sales will fall substantially as its customers switch to another brand.

In the end, monopoly power is a matter of degree. It is true that many firms have some monopoly power. It is also true that their monopoly power is usually limited. In these cases, we will not go far wrong assuming that firms operate in competitive markets, even if that is not precisely the case.

SUMMARY

- A monopoly is a firm that is the sole seller in its market. A monopoly arises when a single firm owns a key resource, when the government gives a firm the exclusive right to produce a good, or when a single firm can supply the entire market at a smaller cost than many firms could.

- Because a monopoly is the sole producer in its market, it faces a downward-sloping demand curve for its product. When a monopoly increases production by 1 unit, it causes the price of its good to fall, which reduces the amount of revenue earned on all units produced. As a result, a monopoly's marginal revenue is always below the price of its good.

- Like a competitive firm, a monopoly firm maximizes profit by producing the quantity at which marginal revenue equals marginal cost. The monopoly then chooses the price at which that quantity is demanded. Unlike a competitive firm, a monopoly firm's price exceeds its marginal revenue, so its price exceeds marginal cost.

- A monopolist's profit-maximizing level of output is below the level that maximizes the sum of consumer and producer surplus. That is, when the monopoly charges a price above marginal cost, some consumers who value the good more than its cost of production do not buy it. As a result, monopoly causes deadweight losses similar to the deadweight losses caused by taxes.

- Monopolists often can raise their profits by charging different prices for the same good based on a buyer's willingness to pay. This practice of price discrimination can raise economic welfare by getting the good to some consumers who otherwise would not buy it. In the extreme case of perfect price discrimination, the deadweight losses of monopoly are completely eliminated. More generally, when price discrimination is imperfect, it can either raise or lower welfare compared to the outcome with a single monopoly price.

- Policymakers can respond to the inefficiency of monopoly behaviour in four ways. (1) They can use the antitrust laws to try to make the industry more competitive. (2) They can regulate the prices that the monopoly charges. (3) They can turn the monopolist into a government-run enterprise. (4) Or, if the market failure is deemed small compared to the inevitable imperfections of policies, they can do nothing at all.

KEY CONCEPTS

monopoly, p. 314

natural monopoly, p. 316

price discrimination, p. 328

QUESTIONS FOR REVIEW

1. Give an example of a government-created monopoly. Is creating this monopoly necessarily bad public policy? Explain.

2. Define *natural monopoly*. What does the size of a market have to do with whether an industry is a natural monopoly?

3. Why is a monopolist's marginal revenue less than the price of its good? Can marginal revenue ever be negative? Explain.

4. Draw the demand, marginal-revenue, and marginal-cost curves for a monopolist. Show the profit-maximizing level of output. Show the profit-maximizing price.

5. In your diagram from the previous question, show the level of output that maximizes total surplus. Show the deadweight loss from the monopoly. Explain your answer.

6. What gives the government the power to regulate mergers between firms? From the standpoint of the welfare of society, give a good reason and a bad reason that two firms might want to merge.

7. Describe the two problems that arise when regulators tell a natural monopoly that it must set a price equal to marginal cost.

8. Give two examples of price discrimination. In each case, explain why the monopolist chooses to follow this business strategy.

PROBLEMS AND APPLICATIONS

1. A publisher faces the following demand schedule for the next novel of one of its popular authors:

Price	Quantity Demanded
$100	0
90	100 000
80	200 000
70	300 000
60	400 000
50	500 000
40	600 000
30	700 000
20	800 000
10	900 000
0	1 000 000

The author is paid $2 million to write the book, and the marginal cost of publishing the book is a constant $10 per book.

   a. Compute total revenue, total cost, and profit at each quantity. What quantity would a profit-maximizing publisher choose? What price would it charge?

   b. Compute marginal revenue. (Recall that $MR = \Delta TR/\Delta Q$.) How does marginal revenue compare to the price? Explain.

   c. Graph the marginal-revenue, marginal-cost, and demand curves. At what quantity do the marginal-revenue and marginal-cost curves cross? What does this signify?

   d. In your graph, shade in the deadweight loss. Explain in words what this means.

   e. If the author was paid $3 million instead of $2 million to write the book, how would this affect the publisher's decision regarding the price to charge? Explain.

   f. Suppose the publisher was not profit-maximizing but was concerned with maximizing economic efficiency. What price would it charge for the book? How much profit would it make at this price?

2. Suppose that a natural monopolist was required by law to charge average total cost. On a diagram, label the price charged and the deadweight loss to society relative to marginal-cost pricing.

3. Suppose the Clean Springs Water Company has a monopoly on bottled water sales in British Columbia. If the price of tap water increases, what is the change in Clean Springs' profit-maximizing levels of output, price, and profit? Explain in words and with a graph.

4. A small town is served by many competing supermarkets, which have constant marginal cost.

   a. Using a diagram of the market for groceries, show the consumer surplus, producer surplus, and total surplus.

   b. Now suppose that the independent super-markets combine into one chain. Using a new diagram, show the new consumer surplus, producer surplus, and total surplus. Relative to the competitive market, what is the transfer from consumers to producers? What is the deadweight loss?

5. Johnny Rockabilly has just finished recording his latest CD. His record company's marketing department determines that the demand for the CD is as follows:

Price	Number of CDs
$24	10 000
22	20 000
20	30 000
18	40 000
16	50 000
14	60 000

The company can produce the CD with no fixed cost and a variable cost of $5 per CD.

   a. Find total revenue for quantity equal to 10 000, 20 000, and so on. What is the marginal revenue for each 10 000 increase in the quantity sold?

   b. What quantity of CDs would maximize profit? What would be the price? What would be the profit?

   c. If you were Johnny's agent, what recording fee would you advise Johnny to demand from the record company? Why?

6. A company is considering building a bridge across a river. The bridge would cost $2 million

to build and nothing to maintain. The following table shows the company's anticipated demand over the lifetime of the bridge.

Price per Crossing	Number of Crossings (in thousands)
$8	0
7	100
6	200
5	300
4	400
3	500
2	600
1	700
0	800

a. If the company was to build the bridge, what would be its profit-maximizing price? Would that be the efficient level of output? Why or why not?

b. If the company is interested in maximizing profit, should it build the bridge? What would be its profit or loss?

c. If the government was to build the bridge, what price should it charge?

d. Should the government build the bridge? Explain.

7. Larry, Curly, and Moe run the only saloon in town. Larry wants to sell as many drinks as possible without losing money. Curly wants the saloon to bring in as much revenue as possible. Moe wants to make the largest possible profits. Using a single diagram of the saloon's demand curve and its cost curves, show the price and quantity combinations favoured by each of the three partners. Explain.

8. For many years, both local and long-distance phone services have been provided by provincially owned or regulated monopolies.

a. Explain why long-distance phone service was originally a natural monopoly.

b. Over the past two decades, technological developments have allowed companies to launch communications satellites that can transmit a limited number of calls. How did the growing role of satellites change the cost structure of long-distance phone service?

c. In response to these technological developments, some provinces/territories have deregulated the long-distance market in Canada. Local phone service has remained regulated. Why might it be efficient to have competition in long-distance phone service and regulated monopolies in local phone service?

9. Many schemes for price-discriminating involve some cost. For example, discount coupons take up the time and resources of both the buyer and the seller. This question considers the implications of costly price discrimination. To keep things simple, let's assume that our monopolist's production costs are simply proportional to output, so that average total cost and marginal cost are constant and equal to each other.

a. Draw the cost, demand, and marginal-revenue curves for the monopolist. Show the price the monopolist would charge without price discrimination.

b. In your diagram, mark the area equal to the monopolist's profit and call it X. Mark the area equal to consumer surplus and call it Y. Mark the area equal to the deadweight loss and call it Z.

c. Now suppose that the monopolist can perfectly price-discriminate. What is the monopolist's profit? (Give your answer in terms of X, Y, and Z.)

d. What is the change in the monopolist's profit from price discrimination? What is the change in total surplus from price discrimination? Which change is larger? Explain. (Give your answer in terms of X, Y, and Z.)

e. Now suppose that there is some cost of price discrimination. To model this cost, let's assume that the monopolist has to pay a fixed cost C in order to price-discriminate. How would a monopolist make the decision whether to pay this fixed cost? (Give your answer in terms of X, Y, Z, and C.)

f. How would a benevolent social planner, who cares about total surplus, decide whether the monopolist should price-discriminate? (Give your answer in terms of X, Y, Z, and C.)

g. Compare your answers to parts (e) and (f). How does the monopolist's incentive to price-discriminate differ from the social planner's? Is it possible that the monopolist will price-discriminate even though it is not socially desirable?

10. Consider the relationship between monopoly pricing and price elasticity of demand.
    a. Explain why a monopolist will never produce a quantity at which the demand curve is inelastic. (Hint: If demand is inelastic and the firm raises its price, what happens to total revenue and total costs?)
    b. Draw a diagram for a monopolist, precisely labelling the portion of the demand curve that is inelastic. (Hint: The answer is related to the marginal-revenue curve.)
    c. On your diagram, show the quantity and price that maximizes total revenue.

11. If the government wanted to encourage a monopoly to produce the socially efficient quantity, should it use a per-unit tax or a per-unit subsidy? Explain how this tax or subsidy would achieve the socially efficient level of output. Among the various interested parties—the monopoly firm, the monopoly's consumers, and other taxpayers—who would support the policy and who would oppose it?

12. You live in a town with 300 adults and 200 children, and you are thinking about putting on a play to entertain your neighbours and make some money. This type of play has a fixed cost of $2000, but selling an extra ticket has zero marginal cost. Here are the demand schedules for your two types of customer:

Price	Adults	Children
$10	0	0
9	100	0
8	200	0
7	300	0
6	300	0
5	300	100
4	300	200
3	300	200
2	300	200
1	300	200
0	300	200

a. To maximize profit, what price would you charge for an adult ticket? For a child's ticket? How much profit do you make?
b. The city council passes a law prohibiting you from charging different prices to different customers. What price do you set for a ticket now? How much profit do you make?
c. Who is worse off because of the law prohibiting price discrimination? Who is better off? (If you can, quantify the changes in welfare.)
d. If the fixed cost of the play was $2500 rather than $2000, how would your answers to parts (a), (b), and (c) change?

13. Based on market research, a recording company obtains the following information about the demand and production costs of its new CD:

$$\text{Price} = 1000 - 10Q$$
$$\text{Total Revenue} = 1000Q - 10Q^2$$
$$\text{Marginal Revenue} = 1000 - 20Q$$
$$\text{Marginal Cost} = 100 + 10Q$$

where Q indicates the number of copies sold and P is the price in cents.

a. Find the price and quantity that maximizes the company's profit.
b. Find the price and quantity that would maximize social welfare.
c. Calculate the deadweight loss from monopoly.
d. Suppose, in addition to the costs above, the musician on the album has to be paid. The company is considering four options:
    i. A flat fee of 2000 cents
    ii. 50 percent of the profits
    iii. 150 cents per unit sold
    iv. 50 percent of the revenue

For each option, calculate the profit-maximizing price and quantity. Which, if any, of these compensation schemes would alter the deadweight loss from monopoly? Explain.

http:// For more study tools, please visit http://www.mankiw5e.nelson.com.

Chapter 15
The Algebra of Monopoly

A monopolist maximizes profit by finding the quantity at which marginal revenue equals marginal cost. But marginal revenue is not equal to price in any market but perfect competition (monopoly MR < P), so we need to know equations for MR and MC.

Example

A monopolist faces market demand of $P = 200 - Q$. Its $MR = 200 - 2Q$ and $MC = 2Q$. $ATC = Q$.

The firm sets MR = MC:
$$200 - 2Q = 2Q$$
$$200 = 4Q$$
$$Q = 50$$

To get price substitute $Q = 50$ into the <u>demand</u> curve:
$$P = 200 - 50 = 150$$

ATC when $Q = 50$ is $ATC = 50$

The firm's profit is:
$$Profit = (P - ATC)Q$$
$$= (150 - 50)*50$$
$$= \$5000$$

Because a monopoly produces a lower quantity of output compared to the perfectly competitive outcome, there will be a deadweight loss in total surplus due to monopoly. Let's calculate it for our example. This is what our solution looks like diagrammatically so far:

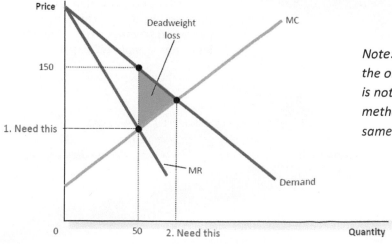

Note: MC = 2Q actually goes through the origin, but in this stock diagram, it is not shown accurately. The algebraic method nonetheless remains the same.

To get #1, substitute Q = 50 into either the MR or MC equation (I'll use the MC equation).

MC = 2Q
MC = 2(50)
MC = 100

To get #2, set demand equal to marginal cost:

200 − Q = 2Q
200 = 3Q
Q = 66.67

Now we can fill in the missing values on our diagram:

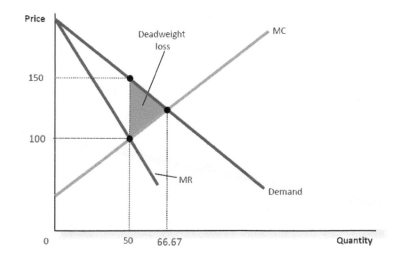

The base of our triangle = 150 − 100 = 50
The height of our triangle = 66.67 − 50 = 16.67

DWL = ½(50)(16.67) = $833.50

Practice Problems

1. A monopolist faces market demand given by P = 60 - Q. It has MR = 60 − 2Q and MC = Q. What quantity of output will the monopolist produce in order to maximize profits?
    a. 20
    b. 30
    c. 40
    d. 50

2. A monopolist faces market demand given by P = 60 - Q. It has MR = 60 – 2Q and MC = Q. What price will the monopolist charge in order to maximize profits?
    a. $20
    b. $30
    c. $40
    d. $50

3. A monopolist faces market demand given by P = 60 - Q. It has MR = 60 – 2Q and MC = Q. What is the deadweight loss due to the monopoly?
    a. $100
    b. $200
    c. $300
    d. $400

Answers: 1 a   2 c   3 a

15 Monopoly

I. Chapter Overview

A. Context and Purpose

The previous chapter introduced market structure by investigating the characteristics of perfect competition. This chapter extends the analysis to monopoly, the case in which barriers to entry protect a single seller from competition. These barriers to entry allow monopolists to earn economic profit in the long run.

A. Helpful Hints

1. *A monopolist is the sole seller of a product without close substitutes.* Monopolies occur because of barriers to entry. Barriers to entry arise for one of the following three reasons:
   (a) *monopoly resources*; that is, control over a key resource
   (b) *government regulation*; that is, government gives a single firm the exclusive right to produce some good (legal monopoly), and
   (c) *the production process* or *economies of scale*; that is, a single firm can produce output at a lower cost than can a large number of producers (natural monopoly).

2. *In general, a monopolist maximizes profit by producing up to, but not beyond, the point at which marginal revenue is equal to marginal cost (MR = MC).* The monopolist then chooses the price at which that quantity is demanded. The primary difference between monopoly and competition is control over price; a monopolist's price exceeds its marginal revenue, so its price exceeds its marginal cost.

3. *No firm, not even a monopoly, can charge whatever it wants (at least not if it cares about the quantity it sells).* Monopolists charge "whatever the market will bear" rather than set price unilaterally. Even monopolists are constrained by the demand curve.

4. *The monopolist must cut price in order to sell more.* If it seems puzzling that price is greater than marginal revenue for monopolists, keep in mind that, unlike the perfect competitor, the monopolist lowers price in order to move along the demand curve and increase sales. Therefore, an extra unit sold adds less than its price to total revenue. Instead, it adds its price minus the loss of revenue caused by cutting price on the earlier units. The net addition to revenue is the marginal revenue. The only reason that this does not hold for competitive firms is that they can sell all that they want at the market price.

5. *Monopoly imposes efficiency costs* on society in the form of deadweight losses from underproduction of the good.

6. *Governments attempt to limit the inefficiency associated with monopoly in a variety of ways.* Policies include making monopolies behave more competitively, regulating monopoly pricing and other behaviour, and converting monopolies into public enterprises (Crown corporations).

7. *Monopolists often charge different prices for the same good based on a buyer's willingness to pay and, therefore, raise their profits.* This practice of price discrimination can increase economic welfare by eliminating part or all (as in the case of perfect price discrimination) the deadweight losses associated with monopoly.

II.   Self-Testing Challenges

A. True/False Questions

_____1.   Unlike competitive producers, a monopolist restricts output below the level at which MR = MC.

_____2.   A monopolist produces the socially efficient quantity of output.

_____3.   For monopoly, price exceeds marginal revenue.

_____4.   A natural monopoly is a single firm that can supply a product to an entire market at a lower cost than could two or more firms.

_____5.   In the long run, a monopolist is guaranteed a positive economic profit.

_____6.   In the short run, a monopolist would never produce where P < ATC.

_____7.   For price discrimination to be effective, a monopolist must be able to separate consumers into different markets.

____8.   Discount coupons are actually irrational behaviour by firms because it would be more efficient for them simply to cut price than to incur the added cost of producing coupons.

____9.   A natural monopolist cannot earn a profit while producing at the competitive output and price levels.

____10. A monopolist has an upward-sloping supply curve.

____11. A monopolist can charge as high a price as it likes.

____12. A monopolist has to accept a lower price if it wants to sell more output.

B. Multiple-Choice Questions

1.   Which one of the following shows where a monopolist produces?
     a.   MC = MR
     b.   MC = P
     c.   P = ATC
     d.   P > ATC

2.   Which one of the following explains why an unregulated monopoly is inefficient?
     a.   because it equates marginal cost with demand, rather than with marginal revenue
     b.   because it equates marginal revenue with demand, rather than with marginal cost
     c.   because it equates marginal revenue with average cost, rather than with marginal cost
     d.   because it equates marginal cost with marginal revenue, rather than with demand

3.   Which one of the following indicates where a monopolist sets price?
     a.   where MC = MR
     b.   from the demand curve at the quantity for which MC = MR
     c.   where supply = demand
     d.   where marginal revenue = demand

4.   Suppose a monopolist is producing at the point where marginal revenue exceeds marginal cost by the greatest amount. Which one of the following should the monopolist do in order to maximize profit?
     a.   increase output and lower price
     b.   decrease output and raise price
     c.   increase both output and price
     d.   decrease both output and price.

5.   Which one of the following makes zero economic profit?
    a.   a monopoly regulated by marginal cost pricing
    b.   a monopoly regulated by average cost pricing
    c.   a monopoly regulated by variable cost pricing
    d.   a monopoly regulated by fixed cost pricing

6.   Which one of the following explains why monopoly occurs?
    a.   because of barriers to entry into the industry
    b.   because of greed by the seller
    c.   because of lack of interest by potential competitors
    d.   because of inadequate regulation by government

7.   As the only seller, which of the following will a monopolist do?
    a.   avoid economic losses
    b.   earn an accounting profit
    c.   earn an economic profit
    d.   Set MR=MC

8.   Which one of the following tends to occur with price discrimination by a monopolist?
    a.   increases in deadweight loss
    b.   decreases in economic efficiency
    c.   leads to output closer to that of the competitive firm
    d.   increases the gap between marginal revenue and price

9.   Which of the following does price discrimination allow a monopolist to do?
    a.   charge more to people based on personal characteristics rather than differences in demand
    b.   take more of the total surplus than they otherwise would have received
    c.   increase their own welfare at the expense of reduced net social welfare
    d.   lower price when costs of production are lower

10.   Which one of the following describes the supply curve of the monopolist?
    a.   It is the whole marginal-cost curve.
    b.   It is the marginal-cost curve above the average variable cost.
    c.   It is the average-total-cost curve.
    d.   It does not exist.

11.   Compared with a perfectly competitive industry with the same cost structure, which one of the following would a monopolist tend toward?
    a.   lower price and output
    b.   lower price and higher output
    c.   higher price and lower output
    d.   higher price and output

12. Suppose a monopolist can sell 20 units of output per week for a price of $30 each, and 21 units of output per week for $29 each. Which one of the following is its marginal revenue for the 21st unit sold?
    a. $1
    b. $9
    c. $29
    d. $30

13. Which one of the following would a price-discriminating monopolist probably produce?
    a. a higher output with average revenue higher than the best single price
    b. a lower output with average revenue higher than the best single price
    c. a higher output with average revenue lower than the best single price
    d. a lower output with average revenue lower than the best single price

Use the following graph to answer questions 14–15.

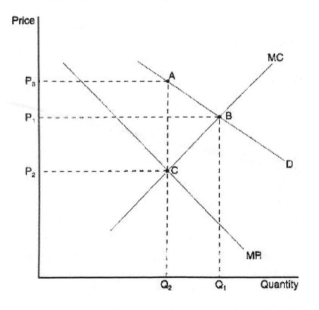

14. Which one of the following describes how the firm would maximize profit?
    a. by producing output Q_1 at price P_1
    b. by producing output Q_2 at price P_2
    c. by producing output Q_2 at price P_3
    d. by producing output Q_2 at price P_1

15. Which one of the following describes deadweight loss from the monopoly?
    a. ABC
    b. P_3ABCP_2
    c. P_3ACP_2
    d. ABQ_1Q_2

Use the graph below to answer questions 16 and 17.

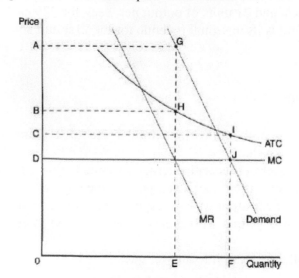

16.   Which one of the following would the profit-maximizing natural monopolist realize?
   a.   AGE0
   b.   AGHB
   c.   DJF0

17.   If the natural monopolist were forced to produce the competitive output and price, which one of the following describes the outcome?
   a.   AGE0
   b.   AGHB
   c.   (CIJD)
   d.   DJF0

18.   If a monopolist produces where its marginal revenue is zero, which of the following has happened?
   a.   maximized its profit
   b.   minimized its cost
   c.   maximized its revenue

19.   Which one of the following statements describes price discrimination in action?
   a.   Movie theatres charge a lower price for children and senior citizens.
   b.   Airlines charge a lower price for a round-trip ticket if the traveller stays over a Saturday night.
   c.   Colleges and universities give financial aid to all students.
   d.   Minimize its average cost.

20.   Which one of the following describes how government policymakers can respond to the problem of monopoly?
    a.   by making monopolies less competitive
    b.   by de-regulating the behaviour of monopolies
    c.   by turning monopolies into public enterprises

C. Short-Answer Questions

1.   Explain why a monopolist produces a lower output than a competitive industry produces, even though both maximize profit by producing where MC = MR.

    _____
    _____
    _____
    _____

2.   What are the advantages and disadvantages of price discrimination for the monopolist and for society as a whole? _____

    _____
    _____
    _____
    _____

3.   What are competition laws and what are their advantages and disadvantages for economic efficiency? _____

    _____
    _____
    _____
    _____

4.   a.   Show equilibrium price and output for the firm in the following graph. Label the profit or loss.

    b.   What type of firm is represented in the diagram? How can you tell? Explain.

    _____
    _____
    _____

    c.   What would happen if this firm produced where price equals marginal cost? Explain. _____

    _____
    _____
    _____

D. Practice Problems

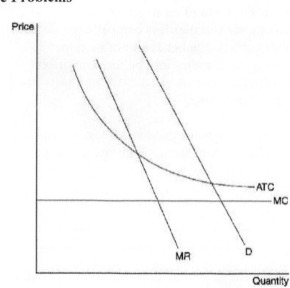

1.   The chart below provides cost and revenue data for Tara's Greenhouse:

Quantity (Q)	Fixed cost (FC)	Variable cost (VC)	Total cost (TC)	Marginal cost (MC)	P	Total revenue (TR)	Marginal revenue (MR)	Average variable cost (AVC)
0	$40	$0	$__	$__	$25	$__	$__	$__
1	$__	$30	$__	$__	$24	$__	$__	$__
2	$__	$50	$__	$__	$23	$__	$__	$__
3	$__	$58	$__	$__	$22	$__	$__	$__
4	$__	$64	$__	$__	$21	$__	$__	$__
5	$__	$70	$__	$__	$20	$__	$__	$__
6	$__	$80	$__	$__	$19	$__	$__	$__
7	$__	$94	$__	$__	$18	$__	$__	$__
8	$__	$114	$__	$__	$17	$__	$__	$__
9	$__	$144	$__	$__	$16	$__	$__	$__

a. Fill in the blanks.

b. Is this firm a competitive firm? How can you tell? _____

_____

_____

c. What price should Tara's Greenhouse charge and what output should it produce? What profit or loss will result? Is this a long-run equilibrium? Explain.

_____

_____

_____

_____

_____

_____

2. Use the following diagram to answer the questions that follow.

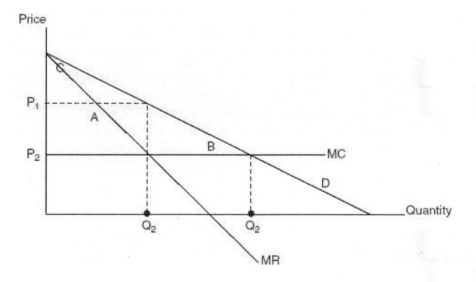

a. What is the equilibrium output under perfect competition and under a monopoly market structure?

b. What is the producer surplus under competition and under monopoly?

c. What is the consumer surplus under competition and under monopoly?

d. What is the deadweight loss under competition and under monopoly?

E. Advanced Critical Thinking

1. The production and distribution of electric power traditionally has been treated as a natural monopoly subject to government regulation of pricing.

    a. Explain clearly why this is so. Would this industry still be a natural monopoly without regulation? _____

    _____
    _____
    _____
    _____
    _____
    _____
    _____
    _____

    b. Recently, there has been a move to deregulate the power industry in some provinces and allow competition among producers, who could buy and sell electricity through a nationwide power grid similar to the pipelines used to transport petroleum or natural gas. How would this affect the industry's status as a natural monopoly? _____

    _____
    _____
    _____
    _____
    _____
    _____
    _____
    _____
    _____
    _____

2. Pharmaceutical companies and their discovery of new drugs can be treated as monopolies.

    a. The laws governing patents on drugs have benefits and costs. Explain the effects of those laws. _____

    _____
    _____
    _____
    _____
    _____
    _____

20.   Which one of the following describes how government policymakers can respond to the problem of monopoly?
    a.   by making monopolies less competitive
    b.   by de-regulating the behaviour of monopolies
    c.   by turning monopolies into public enterprises

C. Short-Answer Questions

1.   Explain why a monopolist produces a lower output than a competitive industry produces, even though both maximize profit by producing where MC = MR.

_____
_____
_____
_____

2.   What are the advantages and disadvantages of price discrimination for the monopolist and for society as a whole? _____

_____
_____
_____
_____

3.   What are competition laws and what are their advantages and disadvantages for economic efficiency? _____

_____
_____
_____
_____

4.   a.   Show equilibrium price and output for the firm in the following graph. Label the profit or loss.

      b.   What type of firm is represented in the diagram? How can you tell? Explain.

_____
_____
_____

      c.   What would happen if this firm produced where price equals marginal cost? Explain. _____

_____
_____
_____

D. Practice Problems

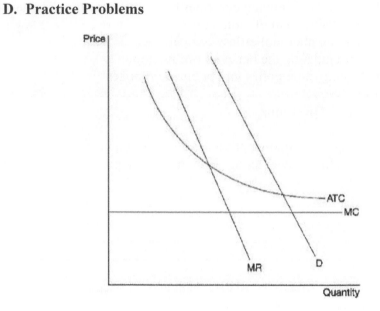

1.   The chart below provides cost and revenue data for Tara's Greenhouse:

Quantity (Q)	Fixed cost (FC)	Variable cost (VC)	Total cost (TC)	Marginal cost (MC)	P	Total revenue (TR)	Marginal revenue (MR)	Average variable cost (AVC)
0	$40	$0	$__	$__	$25	$__	$__	$__
1	$__	$30	$__	$__	$24	$__	$__	$__
2	$__	$50	$__	$__	$23	$__	$__	$__
3	$__	$58	$__	$__	$22	$__	$__	$__
4	$__	$64	$__	$__	$21	$__	$__	$__
5	$__	$70	$__	$__	$20	$__	$__	$__
6	$__	$80	$__	$__	$19	$__	$__	$__
7	$__	$94	$__	$__	$18	$__	$__	$__
8	$__	$114	$__	$__	$17	$__	$__	$__
9	$__	$144	$__	$__	$16	$__	$__	$__

a.   Fill in the blanks.

b.   Is this firm a competitive firm? How can you tell? _____

_____

_____

b. Some patented drugs are quite expensive. The annual cost of AZT, a drug used in the treatment of AIDS, was about $10 000. Wellcome PLC of Britain, the manufacturer of AZT, was forced by AIDS lobby groups to reduce the cost of the drug. Should drug manufacturers be allowed to profit from disease?

_____

_____

_____

_____

_____

_____

_____

III. Solutions

A. True/False Questions

1. F; monopolists produce at MR = MC, below the competitive output where P = MC.
2. F; because a monopolist charges a price above marginal cost, some potential customers who value the product more than its marginal cost but less than the monopolist's price end up not buying the good. Thus, the monopolist produces *less* than the socially efficient quantity of output.
3. T
4. T
5. F; monopolists typically earn economic profits, but only if demand is sufficient to charge a price greater than average total cost.
6. F; in the short run, a monopolist might produce at a loss, as long as variable costs are covered, if demand will not support a higher price.
7. T
8. F; discount coupons are a form of price discrimination that enables firms to capture part or all of consumer surplus; they are a rational strategy whenever the benefit outweighs the cost of the coupons.
9. T
10. F; a monopoly has no supply curve. For a monopolist, the price and amount supplied depend on its demand, and therefore its marginal revenue. Hence, there is no unique relationship between price and quantity supplied.
11. F; no firm, not even a monopoly, can charge what it wants. Monopolists cannot set their prices unilaterally. Rather, they charge whatever the market will bear.
12. T

B. Multiple-Choice Questions

1. a	5. b	9. b	13. a	17. c
2. d	6. a	10. d	14. c	18. c
3. b	7. d	11. c	15. a	19. d
4. a	8. c	12. b	16. b	

C. Short-Answer Questions

1.   A competitive industry will produce the level of output at which that industry's marginal cost curve intersects the demand curve facing the industry, that is, $P = MR = MC$. A monopolist will produce the level of output at which the industry's marginal cost curve intersects the monopoly's marginal revenue curve, that is, $MR = MC$. Because the marginal revenue curve lies below the demand curve (i.e., $MR < P$), this implies a lower level of output in the monopoly industry.

2.   The advantage of price discrimination to the monopolist is that it is a means to capture consumer surplus. This is accomplished by charging different prices for the same good based on a buyer's willingness to pay, that is, charging higher prices to those with low-demand elasticity and lower prices to those with high-demand elasticity. The disadvantage is that it is costly for the monopolist to identify and separate the different groups of consumers. For society, price discrimination can reduce or eliminate the incentive for the monopolist to underproduce because of the price effect of increasing output and moving down the demand curve. Perfect price discrimination would eliminate the deadweight loss from monopoly because marginal revenue would reflect the price paid, leading to output coinciding with society's valuation of the additional product. The discriminating monopolist would be willing to produce whenever the marginal consumer's price is equal to or greater than the cost of producing the additional output.

3.   Competition laws are intended to prevent firms or groups of firms from gaining and using monopoly power. For example, they prohibit price fixing by the firms in an industry. They can be useful in promoting competition, but they can also be detrimental when they protect inefficiency rather than competition. Competition laws have been used, for example, to prevent large chain stores from undercutting small stores on price, even when the large stores were simply more efficient and passing along savings to the consumer.

4.   a.

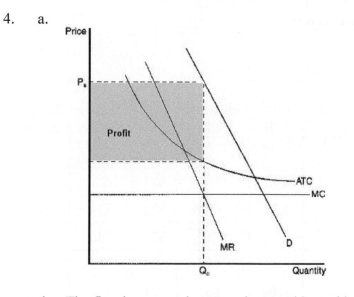

b.   The firm is a natural monopoly, as evidenced by the declining average total cost. The declining average total cost occurs because marginal cost is less than average total cost.

c.   A competitive firm would produce where MC = P. Because MC < ATC, price would be less than average total cost as well. This means that losses are inevitable, and the firm cannot survive in the long run with marginal-cost pricing.

D. Practice Problems

1. a.

Quantity (Q)	Fixed cost (FC)	Variable cost (VC)	Total cost (TC)	Marginal cost (MC)	P	Total revenue (TR)	Marginal revenue(MR)	Average variable cost (AVC)
0	$40	$0	$40	$0	$25	$0	$0	$0
1	$40	$30	$70	$30	$24	$24	$24	$30.00
2	$40	$50	$90	$20	$23	$46	$22	$25.00
3	$40	$58	$98	$8	$22	$66	$20	$19.33
4	$40	$64	$104	$6	$21	$84	$18	$16.00
5	$40	$70	$110	$6	$20	$100	$16	$14.00
6	$40	$80	$120	$10	$19	$114	$14	$13.33
7	$40	$94	$134	$14	$18	$126	$12	$13.43
8	$40	$114	$154	$20	$17	$136	$10	$14.25
9	$40	$144	$184	$30	$16	$144	$8	$16.00

b. No, if it were a competitive firm it would be a price taker. Tara's Greenhouse faces a downward-sloping demand curve from which it can pick the price-quantity combination that it prefers.

c. Tara's Greenhouse should expand output as long as marginal revenue exceeds the increasing portion of marginal cost without going beyond the point at which they are equal. This means producing an output of 6 at a price of $19. Producing 7 units would be less profitable because the marginal revenue of $12 is less than the marginal cost of $14. The firm would lose $2 on the 7th unit of output. The firm will lose $6 (TR – TC = $114 – $120), so this cannot be a long-run equilibrium. In the long run the firm will sell out if business does not improve.

2. a. Q_2 and Q_1, respectively.
   b. Zero under competition; area of the rectangle A under monopoly.
   c. A + B + C under competition; area C under monopoly.
   d. None under competition; area B under monopoly.

E. Advanced Critical Thinking

1. a. The electric power industry has been traditionally characterized by sufficient economies of scale so that one firm has been able to satisfy the market demand at a lower cost than would have been the case with two or more firms. Building more than one power plant for a region would have raised the average total cost. Government regulation of price was a response to natural monopoly, not a cause.

   b. Such a nationwide power grid makes it possible for firms to buy and sell electric power between regions. This means that power companies in different regions can compete even though the market demand within a region is not sufficient to justify building more than one plant. This change means that the production of electric power will no longer fit the natural monopoly case, although the transmission lines remain so. It is still inefficient for competing firms to build multiple transmission lines to serve a specific area.

2. a. Because patents give one producer a monopoly, they lead to higher prices than would occur under competition. Thus, the benefit of these laws is the increased incentive for creative activity. This benefit is offset, to some extent, by the costs of monopoly pricing. Because a monopolist charges a price above marginal cost, it produces less than the socially efficient quantity of output. As a result, some potential consumers who value the good at more than its marginal cost but less than the monopolist's price will not buy the good. Thus, monopoly pricing causes deadweight losses by preventing some mutually beneficial trades from taking place.

   b. If drug manufacturers were not allowed to profit from their inventions and discoveries, would they be interested in developing new drugs? The profits made from the discovery of a new drug are likely to attract new competitors into the field. Where would the sufferers of AIDS and other diseases be without drugs? People respond to incentives. The incentive to improve on existing drugs needs to be present.

MONOPOLISTIC COMPETITION

Learning Objectives

In this chapter, you will ...

- Analyze competition among firms that sell differentiated products

- Compare the outcome under monopolistic competition and under perfect competition

- Consider the desirability of outcomes in monopolistically competitive markets

- Examine the debate over the effects of advertising

- Review the debate over the role of brand names

You walk into a bookstore to buy a book to read during your vacation. On the store's shelves, you find a Kathy Reichs mystery, novels by Michael Ondaatje and Margaret Atwood, and many other choices. When you pick out a book and buy it, what kind of market are you participating in?

On the one hand, the market for books seems competitive. As you look over the shelves at the bookstore, you find many authors and many publishers vying for your attention. A buyer in this market has thousands of competing products from which to choose. And because anyone can enter the industry by writing and publishing a book, the book business is not very profitable. For every highly paid novelist, there are hundreds of struggling ones.

On the other hand, the market for books seems monopolistic. Because each book is unique, publishers have some latitude in choosing what price to charge. The sellers in this market are price makers rather than price takers. And indeed, the price of books greatly exceeds marginal cost. The price of a typical hardcover novel, for instance, is about $25, whereas the cost of printing one additional copy of the novel is less than $5.

The market for novels fits neither the competitive nor the monopoly model. Instead, it is best described by the model of monopolistic competition, the subject of this chapter. The term *monopolistic competition* might at first seem to be an oxymoron, like *jumbo shrimp*. But as we will see, monopolistically competitive industries are monopolistic in some ways and competitive in others. The model describes not only the publishing industry but also the market for many other goods and services.

BETWEEN MONOPOLY AND PERFECT COMPETITION

The previous two chapters analyzed markets with many competitive firms and markets with a single monopoly firm. In Chapter 14, we saw that the price in a perfectly competitive market always equals the marginal cost of production. We also saw that, in the long run, entry and exit drive economic profit to zero, so the price also equals average total cost. In Chapter 15, we saw how monopoly firms can use their market power to keep prices above marginal cost, leading to a positive economic profit for the firm and a deadweight loss for society. Competition and monopoly are extreme forms of market structure. Competition occurs when there are many firms in a market offering essentially identical products; monopoly occurs when there is only one firm in a market.

Although the cases of perfect competition and monopoly illustrate some important ideas about how markets work, most markets in the economy include elements of both these cases and, therefore, are not completely described by either of them. The typical firm in the economy faces competition, but the competition is not so rigorous as to make the firm a price taker like the firms analyzed in Chapter 14. The typical firm also has some degree of market power, but its market power is not so great that the firm can be described exactly by the monopoly model presented in Chapter 15. In other words, many industries fall somewhere between the polar cases of perfect competition and monopoly. Economists call this situation *imperfect competition*.

oligopoly
a market structure in which only a few sellers offer similar or identical products

One type of imperfectly competitive market is an **oligopoly**, which is a market with only a few sellers, each offering a product that is similar or identical to the products offered by other sellers. Economists measure a market's domination by a small number of firms with a statistic called the *concentration ratio*, which is the percentage of total output in the market supplied by the four largest firms. In the Canadian economy, most industries have a four-firm concentration ratio under 50 percent, but in some industries, the biggest firms play a more dominant role. Highly concentrated industries include breakfast cereal (which has a concentration ratio of 83 percent), aircraft manufacturing (85 percent), electric lamp bulbs (89 percent), household laundry equipment (90 percent), and cigarettes (99 percent). These industries are best described as oligopolies.

monopolistic competition
a market structure in which many firms sell products that are similar but not identical

A second type of imperfectly competitive market is called **monopolistic competition**. This describes a market structure in which there are many firms selling products that are similar but not identical. In a monopolistically competitive market, each firm has a monopoly over the product it makes, but many other firms make similar products that compete for the same customers.

To be more precise, monopolistic competition describes a market with the following attributes:

- *Many sellers:* There are many firms competing for the same group of customers.
- *Product differentiation:* Each firm produces a product that is at least slightly different from those of other firms. Thus, rather than being a price taker, each firm faces a downward-sloping demand curve.
- *Free entry and exit:* Firms can enter or exit the market without restriction. Thus, the number of firms in the market adjusts until economic profits are driven to zero.

A moment's thought reveals a long list of markets with these attributes: books, music CDs, movies, computer games, restaurants, piano lessons, cookies, furniture, and so on.

Monopolistic competition, like oligopoly, is a market structure that lies between the extreme cases of competition and monopoly. But oligopoly and monopolistic competition are quite different. Oligopoly departs from the perfectly competitive ideal of Chapter 14 because there are only a few sellers in the market. The small number of sellers makes rigorous competition less likely and strategic interactions among them vitally important. By contrast, under monopolistic competition, there are many sellers, each of which is small compared to the market. A monopolistically competitive market departs from the perfectly competitive ideal because each of the sellers offers a somewhat different product.

Figure 16.1 summarizes the four types of market structure. The first question to ask about any market is how many firms there are. If there is only one firm, the market is a monopoly. If there are only a few firms, the market is an oligopoly. If there are many firms, we need to ask another question: Do the firms sell identical or differentiated products? If the many firms sell differentiated products, the market is monopolistically competitive. If the many firms sell identical products, the market is perfectly competitive.

Because reality is never as clear-cut as theory, at times you may find it hard to decide what structure best describes a market. There is, for instance, no magic number that separates "few" from "many" when counting the number of firms. (Do the approximately dozen companies that now sell cars in the Canada make this market an oligopoly or more competitive? The answer is open to debate.) Similarly, there is no sure way to determine when products are differentiated and when they are identical. (Are different brands of milk really the same? Again, the answer is debatable.) When analyzing actual markets, economists have to keep in mind the lessons learned from studying all types of market structure and then apply each lesson as it seems appropriate.

Now that we understand how economists define the various types of market structure, we can continue our analysis of them. In the next chapter, we analyze oligopoly. In this chapter we examine monopolistic competition.

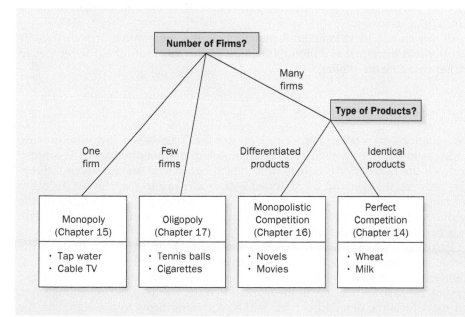

FIGURE 16.1

The Four Types of Market Structure

Economists who study industrial organization divide markets into four types—monopoly, oligopoly, monopolistic competition, and perfect competition.

Source: From MANKIW. *Principles of Economics*, 4E. © 2007 South-Western, a part of Cengage Learning, Inc. Reproduced by permission. www.cengage.com/permissions

QuickQuiz Define *oligopoly* and *monopolistic competition* and give an example of each.

COMPETITION WITH DIFFERENTIATED PRODUCTS

To understand monopolistically competitive markets, we first consider the decisions facing an individual firm. We then examine what happens in the long run as firms enter and exit the industry. Next, we compare the equilibrium under monopolistic competition to the equilibrium under perfect competition that we examined in Chapter 14. Finally, we consider whether the outcome in a monopolistically competitive market is desirable from the standpoint of society as a whole.

The Monopolistically Competitive Firm in the Short Run

Each firm in a monopolistically competitive market is, in many ways, like a monopoly. Because its product is different from those offered by other firms, it faces a downward-sloping demand curve. (By contrast, a perfectly competitive firm faces a horizontal demand curve at the market price.) Thus, the monopolistically competitive firm follows a monopolist's rule for profit maximization: It chooses the quantity at which marginal revenue equals marginal cost and then uses its demand curve to find the price consistent with that quantity.

Figure 16.2 shows the cost, demand, and marginal-revenue curves for two typical firms, each in a different monopolistically competitive industry. In both panels of this figure, the profit-maximizing quantity is found at the intersection of the marginal-revenue and marginal-cost curves. The two panels in this figure show different outcomes for the firm's profit. In panel (a), price exceeds average total cost, so the firm makes a profit. In panel (b), price is below average total cost. In this case, the firm is unable to make a positive profit, so the best the firm can do is to minimize its losses.

All this should seem familiar. A monopolistically competitive firm chooses its quantity and price just as a monopoly does. In the short run, these two types of market structure are similar.

The Long-Run Equilibrium

The situations depicted in Figure 16.2 do not last long. When firms are making profits, as in panel (a), new firms have an incentive to enter the market. This entry increases the number of products from which customers can choose and, therefore, reduces the demand faced by each firm already in the market. In other words, profit encourages entry, and entry shifts the demand curves faced by the incumbent firms to the left. As the demand for incumbent firms' products fall, these firms experience declining profit.

Conversely, when firms are experiencing losses, as in panel (b), firms in the market have an incentive to exit. As firms exit, customers have fewer products from which to choose. This decrease in the number of firms expands the demand faced by those firms that stay in the market. In other words, losses encourage exit, and exit shifts the demand curves of the remaining firms to the right. As the

FIGURE 16.2

Monopolistic Competitors in the Short Run

Monopolistic competitors, like monopolists, maximize profit by producing the quantity at which marginal revenue equals marginal cost. The firm in panel (a) makes a profit because, at this quantity, price is above average total cost. The firm in panel (b) experiences losses because, at this quantity, price is less than average total cost.

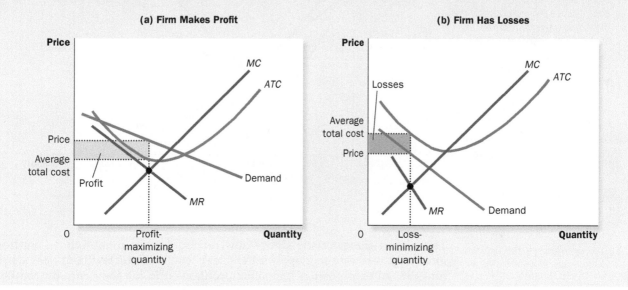

demand for the remaining firms' products rises, these firms experience rising profit (that is, declining losses).

This process of entry and exit continues until the firms in the market are making exactly zero economic profit. Figure 16.3 depicts the long-run equilibrium. Once the market reaches this equilibrium, new firms have no incentive to enter, and existing firms have no incentive to exit.

Notice that the demand curve in this figure just barely touches the average-total-cost curve. Mathematically, we say the two curves are *tangent* to each other. These two curves must be tangent once entry and exit have driven profit to zero. Because profit per unit sold is the difference between price (found on the demand curve) and average total cost, the maximum profit is zero only if these two curves touch each other without crossing.

To sum up, two characteristics describe the long-run equilibrium in a monopolistically competitive market:

1. As in a monopoly market, price exceeds marginal cost. This conclusion arises because profit maximization requires marginal revenue to equal marginal cost and because the downward-sloping demand curve makes marginal revenue less than the price.
2. As in a competitive market, price equals average total cost. This conclusion arises because free entry and exit drive economic profit to zero.

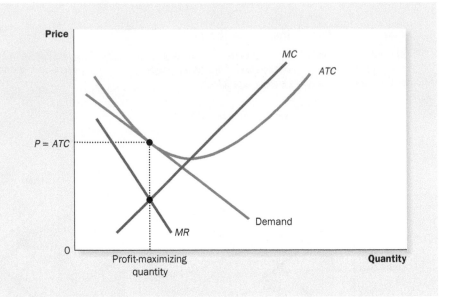

FIGURE 16.3

A Monopolistic Competitor in the Long Run

In a monopolistically competitive market, if firms are making profit, new firms enter, and the demand curves for the incumbent firms shift to the left. Similarly, if firms are experiencing losses, old firms exit, and the demand curves of the remaining firms shift to the right. Because of these shifts in demand, a monopolistically competitive firm eventually finds itself in the long-run equilibrium shown here. In this long-run equilibrium, price equals average total cost, and the firm earns zero profit.

The second characteristic shows how monopolistic competition differs from monopoly. Because a monopoly is the sole seller of a product without close substitutes, it can earn positive economic profit, even in the long run. By contrast, because there is free entry into a monopolistically competitive market, the economic profit of a firm in this type of market is driven to zero.

Monopolistic versus Perfect Competition

Figure 16.4 compares the long-run equilibrium under monopolistic competition to the long-run equilibrium under perfect competition. (Chapter 14 discussed the equilibrium with perfect competition.) There are two noteworthy differences between monopolistic and perfect competition—excess capacity and the markup.

Excess Capacity As we have just seen, entry and exit drive each firm in a monopolistically competitive market to a point of tangency between its demand and average-total-cost curves. Panel (a) of Figure 16.4 shows that the quantity of output at this point is smaller than the quantity that minimizes average total cost. Thus, under monopolistic competition, firms produce on the downward-sloping portion of their average-total-cost curves. In this way, monopolistic competition contrasts starkly with perfect competition. As panel (b) of Figure 16.4 shows, free entry in competitive markets drives firms to produce at the minimum of average total cost.

The quantity that minimizes average total cost is called the *efficient scale* of the firm. In the long run, perfectly competitive firms produce at the efficient scale, whereas monopolistically competitive firms produce below this level. Firms are

FIGURE 16.4

Monopolistic versus Perfect Competition

Panel (a) shows the long-run equilibrium in a monopolistically competitive market, and panel (b) shows the long-run equilibrium in a perfectly competitive market. Two differences are notable: (1) The perfectly competitive firm produces at the efficient scale, where average total cost is minimized. By contrast, the monopolistically competitive firm produces at less than the efficient scale. (2) Price equals marginal cost under perfect competition, but price is above marginal cost under monopolistic competition.

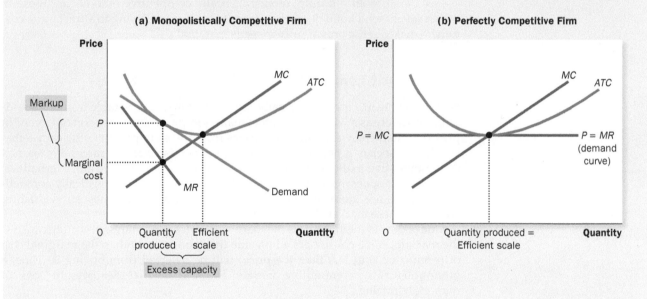

said to have *excess capacity* under monopolistic competition. In other words, a monopolistically competitive firm, unlike a perfectly competitive firm, could increase the quantity it produces and lower the average total cost of production. The firm forgoes this opportunity because it would need to cut its price to sell the additional output. It is more profitable for a monopolistic competitor to continue operating with excess capacity.

Markup over Marginal Cost   A second difference between perfect competition and monopolistic competition is the relationship between price and marginal cost. For a competitive firm, such as that shown in panel (b) of Figure 16.4, price equals marginal cost. For a monopolistically competitive firm, such as that shown in panel (a), price exceeds marginal cost because the firm always has some market power.

How is this markup over marginal cost consistent with free entry and zero profit? The zero-profit condition ensures only that price equals average total cost. It does *not* ensure that price equals marginal cost. Indeed, in the long-run equilibrium, monopolistically competitive firms operate on the declining portion of their average-total-cost curves, so marginal cost is below average total cost. Thus, for price to equal average total cost, price must be above marginal cost.

In this relationship between price and marginal cost, we see a key behavioural difference between perfect competitors and monopolistic competitors. Imagine that you were to ask a firm the following question: "Would you like to see another customer come through your door ready to buy from you at your current price?" A perfectly competitive firm would answer that it didn't care. Because price exactly equals marginal cost, the profit from an extra unit sold is zero. By contrast, a monopolistically competitive firm is always eager to get another customer. Because its price exceeds marginal cost, an extra unit sold at the posted price means more profit.

According to an old quip, monopolistically competitive markets are those in which sellers send holiday greeting cards to the buyers. Trying to attract more customers makes sense only if price exceeds marginal cost.

Monopolistic Competition and the Welfare of Society

Is the outcome in a monopolistically competitive market desirable from the standpoint of society as a whole? Can policymakers improve on the market outcome? In previous chapters, we evaluated markets from the standpoint of efficiency—that is, whether society is getting the most it can out of its scarce resources. We learned that competitive markets lead to efficient outcomes, unless there are externalities, and that monopoly markets lead to deadweight losses. Monopolistically competitive markets are more complex than either of these polar cases, so evaluating welfare in these markets is a more subtle exercise.

One source of inefficiency is the markup of price over marginal cost. Because of the markup, some consumers who value the good at more than the marginal cost of production (but less than the price) will be deterred from buying it. Thus, a monopolistically competitive market has the normal deadweight loss of monopoly pricing.

Although this outcome is clearly undesirable compared to the first-best outcome of price equal to marginal cost, there is no easy way for policymakers to fix the problem. To enforce marginal-cost pricing, policymakers would need to regulate all firms that produce differentiated products. Because such products are so common in the economy, the administrative burden of such regulation would be overwhelming.

Moreover, regulating monopolistic competitors would entail all the problems of regulating natural monopolies. In particular, because monopolistic competitors are making zero profits already, requiring them to lower their prices to equal marginal cost would cause them to make losses. To keep these firms in business, the government would need to help them cover these losses. Rather than raising taxes to pay for these subsidies, policymakers may decide it is better to live with the inefficiency of monopolistic pricing.

Another way in which monopolistic competition may be socially inefficient is that the number of firms in the market may not be the "ideal" one. That is, there may be too much or too little entry. One way to think about this problem is in terms of the externalities associated with entry. Whenever a new firm considers entering the market with a new product, it considers only the profit it would make. Yet its entry would also have two external effects:

1. *The product-variety externality:* Because consumers get some consumer surplus from the introduction of a new product, entry of a new firm conveys a positive externality on consumers.

2. *The business-stealing externality:* Because other firms lose customers and profits from the entry of a new competitor, entry of a new firm imposes a negative externality on existing firms.

Thus, in a monopolistically competitive market, there are both positive and negative externalities associated with the entry of new firms. Depending on which externality is larger, a monopolistically competitive market could have either too few or too many products.

Both of these externalities are closely related to the conditions for monopolistic competition. The product-variety externality arises because a new firm would offer a product different from those of the existing firms. The business-stealing externality arises because firms post a price above marginal cost and, therefore, are always eager to sell additional units. Conversely, because perfectly competitive firms produce identical goods and charge a price equal to marginal cost, neither of these externalities exists under perfect competition.

In the end, we can conclude only that monopolistically competitive markets do not have all the desirable welfare properties of perfectly competitive markets. That is, the invisible hand does not ensure that total surplus is maximized under monopolistic competition. Yet because the inefficiencies are subtle, hard to measure, and hard to fix, there is no easy way for public policy to improve the market outcome.

QuickQuiz List the three key attributes of monopolistic competition. • Draw and explain a diagram to show the long-run equilibrium in a monopolistically competitive market. How does this equilibrium differ from that in a perfectly competitive market?

ADVERTISING

It is nearly impossible to go through a typical day in a modern economy without being bombarded with advertising. Whether you are reading a newspaper, watching television, listening to the radio, or driving down the highway, some firm will try to convince you to buy its product. Such behaviour is a natural feature of monopolistic competition. When firms sell differentiated products and charge prices above marginal cost, each firm has an incentive to advertise in order to attract more buyers to its particular product.

The amount of advertising varies substantially across products. Firms that sell highly differentiated consumer goods, such as over-the-counter drugs, perfumes, soft drinks, razor blades, breakfast cereals, and dog food, typically spend between 10 and 20 percent of revenue for advertising. Firms that sell industrial products, such as drill presses and communications satellites, typically spend very little on advertising. And firms that sell homogeneous products, such as wheat, peanuts, or crude oil, spend nothing at all.

For the economy as a whole, spending on advertising comprises about 2 percent of total firm revenue. This spending takes many forms, including commercials on television and radio, space in newspapers and magazines, direct mail, the Yellow Pages, billboards, and the Internet.

IN THE NEWS

INSUFFICIENT VARIETY AS A MARKET FAILURE

University of Pennsylvania economist Joel Waldfogel argues that, in the presence of large fixed costs, the market may insufficiently service customers with unusual preferences.

If the Shoe Doesn't Fit (Blame the tyranny of the market.)

By Joel Waldfogel

Last week, Nike unveiled a shoe designed specifically for American Indians. The sneaker has both a native-theme design and—more importantly—a wider shape to accommodate the distinctly shaped feet of American Indians. With diabetes and related conditions near epidemic levels in some tribes, American Indian leaders were happy to welcome this comfortable product. If anything, what seems odd is that it took so long. After all, free-market economists have told us for decades that we should rely on market decisions, not the government, to meet our needs, because it's the market that satisfies everyone's every desire.

And yet it turns out that it's the Indian's long wait for a good sneaker that's typical. For small groups with preferences outside the norm, the market often fails to deliver, as I argue in my new book, *The Tyranny of the Market: Why You Can't Always Get What You Want.*

John Stuart Mill pointed out that voting gives rise to a tyranny of the majority. If we vote on what color shirts to make—or whether to make wide or narrow shoes—then the majority gets what it prefers, and the minority does not. The market, on the other hand, is supposed to work differently. As Milton Friedman eloquently put it in 1962, "the characteristic feature of action through political channels is that it tends to require or enforce substantial conformity. The great advantage of the market is that it permits wide diversity. Each man can vote, as it were, for the color of

tie he wants and get it; he does not have to see what color the majority wants and then, if he is in the minority, submit." This is a wonderful argument. Except that for many products and for many people, it's wrong.

Two simple conditions that prevail in many markets mean that individual taste alone doesn't determine individual satisfaction. These conditions are (1) big setup costs and (2) preferences that differ across groups; when they're present, an individual's satisfaction is a function of how many people share his or her tastes. In other words, in these cases, markets share some of the objectionable features of government. They give bigger groups more and better options.

In my research, I've discovered that this phenomenon is widespread. Ten years ago, I started studying radio-station listening patterns. I noticed that people

The Debate over Advertising

Is society wasting the resources it devotes to advertising? Or does advertising serve a valuable purpose? Assessing the social value of advertising is difficult and often generates heated argument among economists. Let's consider both sides of the debate.

The Critique of Advertising Critics of advertising argue that firms advertise in order to manipulate people's tastes. Much advertising is psychological rather

listened to the radio more in metro areas of the United States with relatively large populations. This is not terribly surprising. In larger cities, more stations can attract enough listeners and advertising revenue to cover their costs and stay on the air. With more to choose from on the dial, residents tune in more. So, in this situation of high fixed costs (each station needs a following to keep broadcasting), people help one another by making more options viable.

But who benefits whom? When I looked at black and white listeners separately, I noticed something surprising. Blacks listen more in cities with larger black populations, and whites listen more in cities with larger white populations. Black listening does *not* increase where there's a higher white population, and white listening does not increase with a higher black population. Which means that while overall people help each other by increasing the number of stations on the dial, blacks do not help whites, and whites do not help blacks. Similar patterns arise for Hispanics and non-Hispanics.

A closer look at the data—necessary only because I'm a middle-aged white economist—showed why this was happening. Blacks and whites don't listen to the same radio stations. The black-targeted formats account for about two-thirds of black listening and only 3 percent of white listening. Similarly, the formats that attract the largest white audiences, like country, attract almost no blacks. This means that if you dropped Larry the Cable Guy and a few thousand of his friends from a helicopter (with parachutes) into a metro area, you'd create more demand for country and perhaps album-rock stations, which would be nice for white listeners. But the influx wouldn't help black listeners at all.

In this example, different population groups don't help each other, but they don't hurt each other, either. Sometimes, though, the effect that groups have on each other through the market is actually negative. Industries like daily newspapers offer essentially one product per market. Because the paper can be pitched to appeal to one group or another, the larger one group is, the less the product is tailored to anyone else. This is the tyranny of the majority translated almost literally from politics into markets.

This brings us back to Nike's new shoe. Foot Locker is full of options that fit me and most other Americans. But American Indians make up just 1.5 percent of the U.S. population, and with feet on average three sizes wider, they need different-sized shoes. If we had all voted in a national election on whether the Ministry of Shoes should make wide or typical-width shoes, we surely would

have chosen the latter. That's why Friedman condemned government allocation. And yet the market made the same choice. If Nike's announcement looks like a solution to this problem of ignored minority preference, it really isn't. The company took too many years to bring the shoe on line, and according to the Associated Press, the new sneaker "represents less of a financial opportunity than a goodwill and branding effort."

The tyranny of the market arises elsewhere. With drug development costs near $1 billion, if you are going to be sick, hope that your disease is common enough to attract the interest of drug makers. If you want to fly from your town to Chicago, hope that your city is big enough to fill a plane every day.

When you're not so lucky, you benefit when the government steps in on your behalf, with subsidies for research on drugs for rare diseases or for air service to small locales. For a generation, influential economists have argued for letting the market decide a wide array of questions, to protect your freedom to choose whatever you want. This is true—if everyone agrees with you.

Source: Joel Waldfogel, "If the Shoe Doesn't Fit, Blame the Tyranny of the Market." From *Slate* © October 4, 2007 The Slate Group. All Rights Reserved.

than informational. Consider, for example, the typical television commercial for some brand of soft drink. The commercial most likely does not tell the viewer about the product's price or quality. Instead, it might show a group of happy people at a party on a beach on a beautiful sunny day. In their hands are cans of the soft drink. The goal of the commercial is to convey a subconscious (if not subtle) message: "You too can have many friends and be happy, if only you drink our product." Critics of advertising argue that such a commercial creates a desire that otherwise might not exist.

Critics also argue that advertising impedes competition. Advertising often tries to convince consumers that products are more different than they truly are. By increasing the perception of product differentiation and fostering brand loyalty, advertising makes buyers less concerned with price differences among similar goods. With a less elastic demand curve, each firm charges a larger markup over marginal cost.

The Defence of Advertising   Defenders of advertising argue that firms use advertising to provide information to customers. Advertising conveys the prices of the goods being offered for sale, the existence of new products, and the locations of retail outlets. This information allows customers to make better choices about what to buy and, thus, enhances the ability of markets to allocate resources efficiently.

Defenders also argue that advertising fosters competition. Because advertising allows customers to be more fully informed about all the firms in the market, customers can more easily take advantage of price differences. Thus, each firm has less market power. In addition, advertising allows new firms to enter more easily, because it gives entrants a means to attract customers from existing firms.

Over time, policymakers have come to accept the view that advertising can make markets more competitive. One important example is the regulation of advertising for certain professions, such as lawyers, doctors, and pharmacists. In the past, these groups succeeded in getting governments to prohibit advertising in their fields on the grounds that advertising was "unprofessional." In recent years, however, the courts have concluded that the primary effect of these restrictions on advertising was to curtail competition. They have, therefore, overturned many of the laws that prohibit advertising by members of these professions.

Case Study
ADVERTISING AND THE PRICE OF EYEGLASSES

What effect does advertising have on the price of a good? On the one hand, advertising might make consumers view products as being more different than they otherwise would. If so, it would make markets less competitive and firms' demand curves less elastic, and this would lead firms to charge higher prices. On the other hand, advertising might make it easier for consumers to find the firms offering the best prices. In this case, it would make markets more competitive and firms' demand curves more elastic, and this would lead to lower prices.

In an article published in the *Journal of Law and Economics* in 1972, economist Lee Benham tested these two views of advertising. In the United States during the 1960s, the various state governments had vastly different rules about advertising by optometrists. Some states allowed advertising for eyeglasses and eye examinations. Many states, however, prohibited it. For example, the Florida law read as follows:

It is unlawful for any person, firm, or corporation to . . . advertise either directly or indirectly by any means whatsoever any definite or indefinite price or credit terms on prescriptive or corrective lens, frames, complete prescriptive or corrective glasses, or any optometric service. . . . This section is passed in the interest of public health, safety, and welfare, and its provisions shall be liberally construed to carry out its objects and purposes.

Professional optometrists enthusiastically endorsed these restrictions on advertising.

Benham used the differences in state law as a natural experiment to test the two views of advertising. The results were striking. In those states that prohibited advertising, the average price paid for a pair of eyeglasses was $33. (This number is not as low as it seems, because this price is from 1963, when all prices were much lower than they are today. To convert 1963 prices into today's dollars, you can multiply them by 5.) In those states that did not restrict advertising, the average price was $26. Thus, advertising reduced average prices by more than 20 percent. In the market for eyeglasses, and probably in many other markets as well, advertising fosters competition and leads to lower prices for consumers. ●

Advertising as a Signal of Quality

Many types of advertising contain little apparent information about the product being advertised. Consider a firm introducing a new breakfast cereal. A typical advertisement might have some highly paid actor eating the cereal and exclaiming how wonderful it tastes. How much information does the advertisement really provide?

The answer is: more than you might think. Defenders of advertising argue that even advertising that appears to contain little hard information may in fact tell consumers something about product quality. The willingness of the firm to spend a large amount of money on advertising can itself be a *signal* to consumers about the quality of the product being offered.

Consider the problem facing two firms—Post and Kellogg. Each company has just come up with a recipe for a new cereal that it would sell for $3 a box. To keep things simple, let's assume that the marginal cost of making cereal is zero, so the $3 is all profit. Each company knows that if it spends $10 million on advertising, it will convince 1 million consumers to try its new cereal. And each company knows that if consumers like the cereal, they will buy it not once but many times.

First consider Post's decision. Based on market research, Post knows that its cereal is only mediocre. Although advertising would sell one box to each of 1 million consumers, the consumers would quickly learn that the cereal is not very good and stop buying it. Post decides it is not worth paying $10 million in advertising to get only $3 million in sales. So it does not bother to advertise. It sends its cooks back to the drawing board to find another recipe.

Kellogg, on the other hand, knows that its cereal is great. Each person who tries it will buy a box a month for the next year. Thus, the $10 million in advertising will bring in $36 million in sales. Advertising is profitable here because Kellogg has a good product that consumers will buy repeatedly. Thus, Kellogg chooses to advertise.

Now that we have considered the behaviour of the two firms, let's consider the behaviour of consumers. We began by asserting that consumers are inclined to try a new cereal that they see advertised. But is this behaviour rational? Should a consumer try a new cereal just because the seller has chosen to advertise it?

In fact, it may be completely rational for consumers to try new products that they see advertised. In our story, consumers decide to try Kellogg's new cereal because Kellogg advertises. Kellogg chooses to advertise because it knows that its cereal is quite good, while Post chooses not to advertise because it knows that its cereal is only mediocre. By its willingness to spend money on advertising, Kellogg signals to consumers the quality of its cereal. Each consumer thinks, quite sensibly, "Boy, if the Kellogg Company is willing to spend so much money advertising this new cereal, it must be really good."

What is most surprising about this theory of advertising is that the content of the advertisement is irrelevant. Kellogg signals the quality of its product by its willingness to spend money on advertising. What the advertisements say is not as important as the fact that consumers know ads are expensive. By contrast, cheap advertising cannot be effective at signalling quality to consumers. In our example, if an advertising campaign cost less than $3 million, both Post and Kellogg would use it to market their new cereals. Because both good and mediocre cereals would be advertised, consumers could not infer the quality of a new cereal from the fact that it is advertised. Over time, consumers would learn to ignore such cheap advertising.

This theory can explain why firms pay famous actors large amounts of money to make advertisements that, on the surface, appear to convey no information at all. The information is not in the advertisement's content, but simply in its existence and expense.

Brand Names

Advertising is closely related to the existence of brand names. In many markets, there are two types of firms. Some firms sell products with widely recognized brand names, while other firms sell generic substitutes. For example, in a typical drugstore, you can find Bayer aspirin on the shelf next to a generic aspirin. In a typical grocery store, you can find Pepsi next to less familiar colas. Most often, the firm with the brand name spends more on advertising and charges a higher price for its product.

Just as there is disagreement about the economics of advertising, there is disagreement about the economics of brand names. Let's consider both sides of the debate.

Critics of brand names argue that brand names cause consumers to perceive differences that do not really exist. In many cases, the generic good is almost indistinguishable from the brand-name good. Consumers' willingness to pay more for the brand-name good, these critics assert, is a form of irrationality fostered by advertising. Economist Edward Chamberlin, one of the early developers of the theory of monopolistic competition, concluded from this argument that brand names were bad for the economy. He proposed that the government discourage their use by refusing to enforce the exclusive trademarks that companies use to identify their products.

More recently, economists have defended brand names as a useful way for consumers to ensure that the goods they buy are of high quality. There are two related arguments. First, brand names provide consumers with *information* about quality when quality cannot be easily judged in advance of purchase. Second, brand names give firms an *incentive* to maintain high quality, because firms have a financial stake in maintaining the reputation of their brand names.

FYI

GALBRAITH VERSUS HAYEK

Two of the great economists of the twentieth century were Canadian-born John Kenneth Galbraith and Austrian Friedrich Hayek. They held very different views about advertising, which to a large extent reflected their views about the capitalist system more broadly.

John Kenneth Galbraith's most famous book was *The Affluent Society*, published in 1958. In it, he argued that corporations use advertising to create demand for products that people otherwise do not want or need. The market system should not be applauded, he believed, for satisfying desires that it has itself created. Galbraith was skeptical that economic growth was leading to higher levels of well-being, because people's aspirations were being made to keep pace with their increased material prosperity. He worried that as advertising and salesmanship artificially enhanced the desire for private goods, public spending on such items as better schools and better parks suffered. The end result, according to Galbraith, was "private opulence and public squalor." Galbraith's policy recommendation was clear: Increase the size of government.

Friedrich Hayek's most famous book was *The Road to Serfdom*, published in 1944. It argued that an extensive government role in the economy inevitably means a sacrifice of personal freedoms. Hayek also wrote a well-known critique of Galbraith in 1961, addressing in particular Galbraith's view of advertising. Hayek observed that advertising was merely one example of a broader phenomenon: Many preferences are created by the social environment. Literature, art, and music are all acquired tastes. A person's demand for hearing a Mozart concerto may have been created in a music appreciation class, but this fact does not make the desire less legitimate or the music professor a sinister influence. Hayek concluded, "It is because each individual producer thinks that consumers can be persuaded to like his products that he endeavors to influence them. But though this effort is part of the influences which shape consumers' taste, no producer can in any real sense 'determine' them."

Although these two economists disagreed about the roles of advertising, markets, and government, they did have one thing in common: great acclaim. In 1974, Hayek won the Nobel Prize in Economic Sciences. In 2000, U.S. President Clinton awarded Galbraith (who spent much of his professional life in the United States) the National Medal of Freedom. And even though their most famous works were written many decades ago, they are still well worth reading today.

To see how these arguments work in practice, consider a famous brand name: McDonald's. Imagine that you are driving through an unfamiliar town and want to stop for lunch. You see a McDonald's and a local restaurant next to it. Which do you choose? The local restaurant may in fact offer better food at lower prices, but you have no way of knowing that. By contrast, McDonald's offers a consistent product across many cities. Its brand name is useful to you as a way of judging the quality of what you are about to buy.

The McDonald's brand name also ensures that the company has an incentive to maintain quality. For example, if some customers were to become ill from bad food sold at a McDonald's, the news would be disastrous for the company. McDonald's would lose much of the valuable reputation that it has built up with years of expensive advertising. As a result, it would lose sales and profit not just in the outlet that sold the bad food but in its many outlets throughout the country. By contrast, if some customers were to become ill from bad food at a local restaurant, that restaurant might have to close down, but the lost profits would be much smaller. Hence, McDonald's has a greater incentive to ensure that its food is safe.

The debate over brand names thus centres on the question of whether consumers are rational in preferring brand names over generic substitutes. Critics of brand names argue that brand names are the result of an irrational consumer response to advertising. Defenders of brand names argue that consumers have good reason to pay more for brand-name products because they can be more confident about the quality of these products.

QuickQuiz How might advertising make markets less competitive? How might it make markets more competitive? • Give the arguments for and against brand names.

CONCLUSION

Monopolistic competition is true to its name: It is a hybrid of monopoly and competition. Like a monopoly, each monopolistic competitor faces a downward-sloping demand curve and, as a result, charges a price above marginal cost. As in a perfectly competitive market, there are many firms, and entry and exit drive the profit of each monopolistic competitor toward zero. Table 16.1 summarizes these lessons.

Because monopolistically competitive firms produce differentiated products, each firm advertises in order to attract customers to its own brand. To some extent,

TABLE 16.1

Monopolistic Competition: Between Perfect Competition and Monopoly

	Market Structure		
	Perfect Competition	Monopolistic Competition	Monopoly
Features that all three market structures share			
Goal of firms	Maximize profits	Maximize profits	Maximize profits
Rule for maximizing	$MR = MC$	$MR = MC$	$MR = MC$
Can earn economic profits in the short run?	Yes	Yes	Yes
Features that monopoly and monopolistic competition share			
Price taker?	Yes	No	No
Price	$P = MC$	$P > MC$	$P > MC$
Produces welfare-maximizing level of output?	Yes	No	No
Features that perfect competition and monopolistic competition share			
Number of firms	Many	Many	One
Entry in long run?	Yes	Yes	No
Can earn economic profits in long run?	No	No	Yes

advertising manipulates consumers' tastes, promotes irrational brand loyalty, and impedes competition. To a larger extent, advertising provides information, establishes brand names of reliable quality, and fosters competition.

The theory of monopolistic competition seems to describe many markets in the economy. It is somewhat disappointing, therefore, that the theory does not yield simple and compelling advice for public policy. From the standpoint of the economic theorist, the allocation of resources in monopolistically competitive markets is not perfect. Yet, from the standpoint of a practical policymaker, there may be little that can be done to improve it.

SUMMARY

- A monopolistically competitive market is characterized by three attributes: many firms, differentiated products, and free entry.

- The equilibrium in a monopolistically competitive market differs from that in a perfectly competitive market in two related ways. First, each firm in a monopolistically competitive market has excess capacity. That is, it operates on the downward-sloping portion of the average-total-cost curve. Second, each firm charges a price above marginal cost.

- Monopolistic competition does not have all the desirable properties of perfect competition. There is the standard deadweight loss of monopoly

caused by the markup of price over marginal cost. In addition, the number of firms (and thus the variety of products) can be too large or too small. In practice, the ability of policymakers to correct these inefficiencies is limited.

- The product differentiation inherent in monopolistic competition leads to the use of advertising and brand names. Critics of advertising and brand names argue that firms use them to take advantage of consumer irrationality and to reduce competition. Defenders of advertising and brand names argue that firms use them to inform consumers and to compete more vigorously on price and product quality.

KEY CONCEPTS

oligopoly, p. 346

monopolistic competition, p. 346

QUESTIONS FOR REVIEW

1. Describe the three attributes of monopolistic competition. How is monopolistic competition like monopoly? How is it like perfect competition?

2. Draw a diagram depicting a firm in a monopolistically competitive market that is making profits. Now show what happens to this firm as new firms enter the industry.

3. Draw a diagram of the long-run equilibrium in a monopolistically competitive market. How is price related to average total cost? How is price related to marginal cost?

4. Does a monopolistic competitor produce too much or too little output compared to the most efficient level? What practical considerations make it difficult for policymakers to solve this problem?

5. How might advertising reduce economic well-being? How might advertising increase economic well-being?

6. How might advertising with no apparent informational content in fact convey information to consumers?

7. Explain two benefits that might arise from the existence of brand names.

PROBLEMS AND APPLICATIONS

1. Classify the following markets as perfectly competitive, monopolistic, or monopolistically competitive, and explain your answers.
   a. wooden #2 pencils
   b. bottled water
   c. copper
   d. local telephone service
   e. peanut butter
   f. lipstick

2. For each of the following characteristics, say whether it describes a perfectly competitive firm, a monopolistically competitive firm, both, or neither.
   a. sells a differentiated product from its competitors
   b. has marginal revenue less than price
   c. earns economic profit in the long run
   d. produces at minimum of average total cost in the long run
   e. equates marginal revenue and marginal cost
   f. charges a price above marginal cost

3. For each of the following characteristics, say whether it describes a monopoly firm, a monopolistically competitive firm, both, or neither.
   a. faces a downward-sloping demand curve
   b. has marginal revenue less than price
   c. faces the entry of new firms selling similar products
   d. earns economic profit in the long run
   e. equates marginal revenue and marginal cost
   f. produces the socially efficient quantity of output

4. Sparkle is one firm of many in the market for toothpaste, which is in long-run equilibrium.
   a. Draw a diagram showing Sparkle's demand curve, marginal-revenue curve, average-total-cost curve, and marginal-cost curve. Label Sparkle's profit-maximizing output and price.
   b. What is Sparkle's profit? Explain.
   c. On your diagram, show the consumer surplus derived from the purchase of Sparkle toothpaste. Also show the deadweight loss relative to the efficient level of output.
   d. If the government forced Sparkle to produce the efficient level of output, what would

happen to the firm? What would happen to Sparkle's customers?

5. You are hired as the consultant to a monopolistically competitive firm. The firm reports the following information about its price, marginal cost, and average total cost. Can the firm possibly be maximizing profit? If not, what should it do to increase profit? If the firm is profit-maximizing, is the firm in a long-run equilibrium? If not, what will happen to restore long-run equilibrium?
   a. $P < MC, P < ATC$
   b. $P > MC, P < ATC$
   c. $P = MC, P > ATC$
   d. $P > MC, P = ATC$

6. For each of the following pairs of firms, explain which firm would be more likely to engage in advertising:
   a. a family-owned farm or a family-owned restaurant
   b. a manufacturer of forklifts or a manufacturer of cars
   c. a company that invented a very reliable watch or a company that invented a less reliable watch that costs the same amount to make

7. The makers of Tylenol pain reliever do a lot of advertising and have very loyal customers. In contrast, the makers of generic acetaminophen do no advertising, and their customers shop only for the lowest price. Assume that the marginal costs of Tylenol and generic acetaminophen are the same and constant.
   a. Draw a diagram showing Tylenol's demand, marginal-revenue, and marginal-cost curves. Label Tylenol's price and markup over marginal cost.
   b. Repeat part (a) for a producer of generic acetaminophen. How do the diagrams differ? Which company has the bigger markup? Explain.
   c. Which company has the greater incentive for careful quality control? Why?

8. Sleek Sneakers Co. is one of many firms in the market for shoes.
   a. Assume that Sleek is currently earning short-run economic profits. On a correctly labelled

diagram, show Sleek's profit-maximizing output and price, as well as the area representing profit.

b. What happens to Sleek's price, output, and profit in the long run? Explain this change in words, and show it on a new diagram.

c. Suppose that over time, consumers become more focused on stylistic differences among shoe brands. How would this change in attitude affect each firm's price elasticity of demand? In the long run, how will this change in demand affect Sleek's price, output, and profits?

d. At the profit-maximizing price you identified in part (c), is Sleek's demand curve elastic or inelastic? Explain.

9. In an "In the News" feature in this chapter, economist Joel Waldfogel argues that a free market may fail to serve some customers in the presence of fixed costs. Let's analyze this claim with an example.

a. Suppose that there are N people who might consume a product sold by a monopoly firm. Each person has demand of $q = 2 - P$, so total demand for this product is $Q = Nq = 2N - NP$, or $P = 2 - Q/N$. Graph this market demand curve.

b. For this market demand curve, the equation for marginal revenue is $MR = 2 - 2Q/N$. Add this marginal revenue curve to your graph.

c. To keep things simple, suppose that the marginal cost of producing this product is zero. What quantity would a profit-maximizing monopolist produce? What price would it charge? Show this price on your graph.

d. Ignoring for the moment the fixed costs, calculate profits, consumer surplus, and total surplus at this profit-maximizing price. (These will be functions of N.)

e. Suppose now that before making this product, the firm has to pay fixed costs of research and development equal to $3 000 000. How large does N need to be before the profit-maximizing firm chooses to pay the fixed cost and produce this product? How large does N need to be before it is socially efficient to pay the fixed cost?

f. Discuss how this example relates to Waldfogel's arguments about the inefficiency of free markets.

http://   For more study tools, please visit http://www.mankiw5e.nelson.com.

Chapter 16
The Algebra of Monopolistic Competition

We have seen that a monopolistic competitor behaves just like a monopolist in the short run. It chooses quantity where marginal revenue equals marginal cost and then goes to the demand curve to determine the price of its product. The algebra for solving for quantity, price and profit is exactly the same as for a monopolist. Where they differ is in the long run. In the long run, the firm behaves like a competitive firm. Entry or exit may take place and price will equal average total cost once the industry arrives at equilibrium, Since the firm's demand curve is downward sloping, this will happen when there is a tangency between the demand curve and the average total cost curve at the point where the firm's marginal revenue equals its marginal cost.

Example

A fast food restaurant faces demand for its hamburgers of $P = 10 - 40Q$. Its $MR = 10 - 80Q$. Q is measured in thousands (so add three zeroes to your answer for Q when you are interpreting your results, but don't add the zeroes when you are doing the math). Marginal cost is constant at $2.

To maximize the firm's profit, set MR = MC:

$$10 - 80Q = 2$$
$$8 = 80Q$$
$$Q = .1 \quad (.1 \text{ thousands} = 100 \text{ hamburgers})$$
$$P = 10 - 40(.1) = \$6.00$$

If this firm was in long run equilibrium, then ATC would necessarily equal $6. The ATC would be tangent to the demand curve at P = $6. There would be no entry or exit into the industry.

Practice Problem

1. A monopolistic competitor faces market demand given by $P = 90 - Q$. It has $MR = 90 - 2Q$ and $MC = Q$. ATC is $50 at the current profit-maximizing level of output. Which statement is correct?
    a. The industry is in long run equilibrium.
    b. There will be exit from the industry.
    c. There will be entry into the industry.
    d. None of the above.

Answer: 1 c

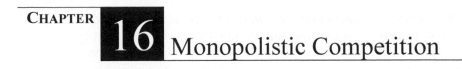
16 Monopolistic Competition

I. Chapter Overview

A. Context and Purpose

Earlier chapters introduced the notion of market structure, which can range from competition, with many buyers and sellers, to monopoly, with a single seller. The extreme cases are useful for analyzing implications of various assumptions about markets, but they may seem unrealistic for the real world, which is rarely that black and white.

We continue our discussion of the grey area between monopoly and competition with Chapter 17, which deals with the market structure of monopolistic competition. This category includes fast-food restaurants, gasoline service stations, and corner markets— in short, most of the businesses that we deal with every day. You will see that monopolistic competition shares some of the characteristics of a monopoly and some of a perfectly competitive industry.

A. Helpful Hints

1. *Monopolistic competition is characterized by three attributes: (i) a great number of firms, (ii) differentiated products, and (iii) free entry into the industry.* Each firm in this market charges a price above its marginal cost of production; this mark-up is associated with the normal deadweight loss of monopoly pricing. Each firm has excess capacity; that is, it operates on the downward-sloping portion of its average-total-cost curve. A monopolistically competitive firm, unlike a perfectly competitive one, could increase the quantity it produces and lower the average total cost of production.

2. *The underproduction of monopolistic competition is a source of inefficiency.* Remember that even though price in monopolistic competition is higher than would be the case in perfect competition, price itself is not the source of inefficiency. Rather, it is the lower quantity that results from the higher price. By itself, the higher price merely redistributes income from buyers to sellers; the efficiency effect occurs because people buy fewer units of the product at the higher price.

225

3. *The product differentiation inherent in monopolistic competition leads to the use of advertising and brand names.* On the one hand, advertising and brand names are defended on the grounds that they inform customers and allow the firms to compete on price and quality. On the other hand, critics argue that firms use advertising and brand names to take advantage of consumer irrationality and to reduce competition.

II.   Self-Testing Challenges

A.   True/False Questions

_____1.   Advertising is inherently inefficient because it adds an additional layer of cost to the product price.

_____2.   Long-run profit disappears under monopolistic competition because new firms enter the industry and drive down price and profit.

_____3.   Monopolistic competitors in the long run produce at minimum average total cost due to free entry into the industry.

_____4.   Monopolistic competitors set output and price at the point where marginal revenue equals marginal cost.

_____5.   Brand names can be advantageous to society by providing an incentive for firms to maintain quality.

_____6.   Policymakers have come to accept the view that advertising can make markets less competitive and that it usually leads to an increase in the price of advertised goods.

_____7.   Excess capacity and mark-up over marginal cost are two noteworthy differences between monopolistic and perfect competition.

_____8.   Monopolistic competitors are able to differentiate their products enough to maintain modest long-run economic profit.

_____9.   Critics of advertising argue that much advertising is psychological rather than informational; firms advertise in order to manipulate people's tastes.

_____10.   Most economists agree that, because of the problem of excess capacity, monopolistic competition is detrimental to society's well-being.

_____11.   Proponents of advertising argue that it fosters competition and would make a firm's demand curve less elastic, which would lead to lower prices.

_____12.   Product differentiations have economic significance whether the differences are real or merely imaginary.

B.   Multiple-Choice Questions

1.   Which one of the following statements is true regarding monopolistic competition?
     a.   Unlike the oligopolist, the monopolistic competitor sells a product that is different from those of other firms.
     b.   Like the perfect competitor, the monopolistic competitor must sell at the prevailing market price.
     c.   Like the monopolist, the monopolistic competitor sells at a price that is greater than marginal cost and marginal revenue.

2.   Which one of the following describes the rivals of firms in monopolistic competition?
     a.   They set their price equal to MR = MC.
     b.   They set their price according to the demand they face.
     c.   They will always match their price increases.
     d.   They will always match their price decreases.

3.   Which one of the following explains why, in the long run, monopolistically competitive firms may earn only zero economic profit?
     a.   because they must lower their price in order to sell a greater quantity
     b.   because profit encourages entry of new firms, which in turn increases the cost of production of incumbent firms
     c.   because of the existence of excess capacity
     d.   profit encourages entry of new firms, which in turn decreases the demand faced by incumbent firms

4.   Which one of the following does excess capacity predict?
     a.   that long-run equilibrium in a monopolistically competitive market occurs with all firms producing at a lower output level than that at which average total costs are minimized
     b.   that monopolistically competitive firms will achieve positive economic profits by restricting output below the economically efficient level
     c.   that profit-maximizing firms in a monopolistically competitive market restrict output to extract positive economic profit
     d.   that there are too many firms producing essentially the same product in a monopolistically competitive market

Use the information below to answer questions 5–7.

Suppose that a monopolistic competitor producing an output of 100 units faces the following revenues and costs: price = $100; marginal revenue = $50; marginal cost = $75, and average total cost = $90.

5.   Which one of the following strategies should the firm use in order to maximize profit?
    a. reduce output and raise price
    b. increase output and raise price
    c. keep output the same but raise price

6.   Which one of the following shows the firm's standing with its current output of 100 units?
    a. realizes a loss of $4000
    b. realizes a loss of $2500
    c. earns a profit of $1000
    d. earns a profit of $2500

7.   If the firm were a competitive firm, with price = $100 and the same cost curves, which one of the following strategies should the firm use?
    a. increase output and keep price the same
    b. increase output and lower price
    c. keep output and price the same
    d. keep output the same but raise price

8.   Which one of the following explains how the monopolistic competitor differs from the competitive firm?
    a. The monopolistic competitor has no demand curve in the traditional sense.
    b. The monopolistic competitor can earn economic profit for long periods of time.
    c. The monopolistic competitor charges a price greater than marginal cost.
    d. The monopolistic competitor exists in an industry without free entry.

9.   Which one of the following statements is true?
    a. Advertising is inherently inefficient because it adds to the cost of production without creating anything of value.
    b. Advertising is inherently valuable because it increases sales and lowers overall average total cost, which leads to lower prices.
    c. Advertising is costly, but it also provides benefits in the form of product information.
    d. Brand names add to the price paid by consumers without providing anything of value.

Use the graphs below to answer questions 11–16.

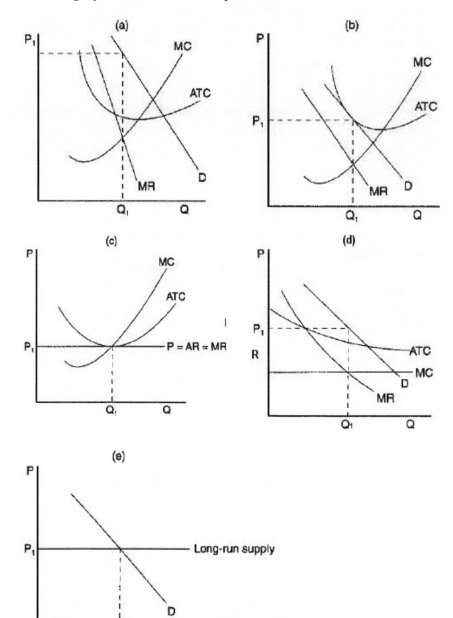

10.   Which one of the following is the diagram that shows a monopolistic competitor in short-run (but not long-run) equilibrium?
    a. (a)
    b. (b)
    c. (c)
    d. (e)

11.   Which one of the following is the diagram that shows a monopolistic competitor in long-run equilibrium?
    a. (a)
    b. (b)
    c. (c)
    d. (d)

12.   Which one of the following is the diagram that shows a competitive firm in long-run equilibrium?
    a. (a)
    b. (b)
    c. (c)
    d. (e)

13.   Which one of the above diagrams is **MOST** likely to represent a monopolist other than a natural monopolist?
    a. (a)
    b. (c)
    c. (d)
    d. (e)

14.   Which one of the following is the diagram that shows a competitive industry in long-run equilibrium?
    a. (a)
    b. (b)
    c. (d)
    d. (e)

15.   Which one of the following is the diagram that shows a natural monopoly in long-run equilibrium?
    a. (a)
    b. (b)
    c. (c)
    d. (d)

16. Which one of the following describes what a monopolistic competitor that is losing money will do in the short run?
   a. continue to produce as long as variable cost is being covered
   b. raise price to reduce its losses
   c. lower price in order to increase sales enough to end the losses
   d. keep price the same and increase output enough to end the losses

17. Which one of the following explains why some economists consider monopolistic competitors to be inefficient?
   a. because they rely heavily on advertising
   b. they produce a limited range of output
   c. they produce an output level for which their average total cost is not at its minimum
   d. they always realize economic profit

18. Which one of the following explains how monopolistic competition differs from monopoly?
   a. monopolists charge whatever the market will bear
   b. monopolists can earn short-run profit
   c. monopolists can earn long-run profit
   d. monopolists produce where marginal revenue = marginal cost but use the demand curve to set price

19. Which one of the following will occur as a result of entry into a monopolistically competitive market?
   a. The industry demand curve will shift to the right.
   b. The industry demand curve will shift to the left.
   c. The demand curve faced by each existing firm will shift to the right.
   d. The demand curve faced by each existing firm will shift to the left.

20. Which one of the following will occur if a monopolistically competitive firm decides to raise its price?
   a. It will increase its profit.
   b. It will increase its revenue.
   c. It will lose all of its customers due to the nature of the demand it faces.
   d. It will lose some, but not all, of its customers due to product differentiation.

B. Short-Answer Questions

1.   How is the mark-up over marginal cost consistent with free entry and zero profit for monopolistically competitive firms? _____

_____

_____

_____

_____

_____

_____

_____

2.   What does monopolistic competition have in common with perfect competition? In what ways does it fall short of the competitive ideal and why? _____

_____

_____

_____

_____

_____

_____

3.   What does monopolistic competition have in common with monopoly? In what ways are the outcomes in a monopolistically competitive industry preferable to those in a monopoly? _____

_____

_____

_____

_____

_____

_____

_____

4.   There are both positive and negative externalities associated with entry of new firms in a monopolistically competitive market. What are they? Explain them.

_____

_____

_____

_____

C. Practice Problems

1. The following table lists characteristics of various types of market structure.

Type of market structure Characteristics	_____	_____	_____	_____
Number of sellers	Very many	Many	One	Few
Type of product	Standardized	Differentiated	Standardized or differentiated	Unique
Barriers to entry	None	Very low	Total	High
Control over price	None	Some	High	Interdependent
Long-run profit	Zero	Zero	Typically positive	Typically positive
Advertising	None	Yes	Limited; often for public relations	Yes, if differentiated
Example:	_____	_____	_____	_____

a. Fill in the blanks for types of market structure and give an example of each.

b. What accounts for the differences in long-run profit between the various market structures? Why is long-run profit listed as "typically positive" rather than simply "positive" for the last two types of market structure listed?

_____
_____
_____
_____
_____
_____

c. Explain why your examples are appropriate.

_____
_____
_____
_____
_____
_____

d. Why do the different market structures vary in their use of advertising?

_____
_____
_____
_____

2. A monopolistically competitive firm produces 50 units of output at a price of $10 each. The firm's average total cost and average variable cost are $8 and $6 respectively. At this level of output, the firm's marginal revenue and marginal cost are both $5 per unit.

a. How much is the firm's profit?

_____

b. Will the firm be able to increase its profit by charging a different price?

_____

c. Is this firm in its long-run equilibrium? Why or why not?

_____

D. Advanced Critical Thinking

A newspaper columnist argued recently that the Canadian economy is much less efficient than it might be because of the large number of virtually identical competing products. He claimed that we would get much more value for our shopping dollars if we had only one brand of toothpaste, for example, rather than the dozens that now exist. Similarly with automobiles, we could produce a high-quality product at a lower price if we concentrated on producing one or two of the best designs currently available. He argues that one advantage of a command system such as the former Soviet Union is that a central planning board can make such decisions in the public interest.

In the form of a Letter to the Editor, respond to the columnist. Your letter should include an economic interpretation of his argument as well as a critique that explains the extent to which you agree or disagree with his argument. _____

_____
_____
_____
_____
_____
_____
_____
_____
_____
_____
_____

III.   **Solutions**

A.   **True/False Questions**

1.   F; advertising adds cost, but it also adds benefits by providing information about product quality and price.
2.   T
3.   F; monopolistic competitors produce at average total cost, but it is above the minimum because of the downward-sloping demand curve.
4.   F; monopolistic competitors set output at the point where marginal revenue equals marginal cost, but price is read from the demand curve.
5.   T
6.   F; they have come to accept the view that advertising fosters more competition and leads to lower prices for consumers.
7.   T
8.   F; monopolistic competitors achieve zero long-run economic profit.
9.   T
10.   F; the excess capacity of monopolistic competition must be weighed against the resulting additional variety available to the consumer.
11.   F; proponents of advertising argue that it enhances competition, which makes the firm's demand curve more, not less, elastic.
12.   T

B.   **Multiple-Choice Questions**

1. a	5. c	9. a	13. a	17. c
2. c	6. c	10. c	14. a	18. d
3. c	7. b	11. b	15. a	19. d
4. a	8. b	12. a	16. b	20. b

C.   **Short-Answer Questions**

1.   Zero-profit condition ensures that price equals average total cost, not marginal cost. In the long-run equilibrium, monopolistically competitive firms operate on the declining portion of their average total cost curve, so marginal cost is below average total cost. Therefore, if price is equal to average total cost, it should be greater than marginal cost.

2.   Both market structures have free entry, resulting in zero long-run profit. However, because monopolistic competitors have some control over price, their marginal revenue is less than the price and their production where MR = MC results in lower output than the socially optimal marginal-cost pricing used by competitors.

3.   Both types of firms face a downward-sloping demand curve and produce where MR = MC, which results in less than the socially optimal marginal-cost pricing of perfect competition. This occurs because both are price setters. However, the monopolistic competitor faces enough competition to eliminate long-run monopoly profits.

4.   They are the product-variety externality and the business-stealing externality. The former arises due to the introduction of a new product as a result of the entry of a new firm. This would convey a positive externality on consumers, as they gain consumer surplus from the new product. The latter, on the other hand, imposes a negative externality on the existing firms, as they lose customers and profits to the new entrants.

D.   Practice Problems

1.   a.

Type of market structure	Perfect competition	Monopolistic competition	Monopoly	Oligopoly
Characteristics:				
Number of sellers	Very many	Many	One	Few
Type of product	Standardized	Differentiated	Standardized or differentiated	Unique
Barriers to entry	None	Very low	Total	High
Control over price	None	Some	High	Interdependent
Long-run profit	Zero	Zero	Typically positive	Typically positive
Advertising	None	Yes	Limited; often for public relations	Yes, if differentiated
Example	Wheat	Convenience marts	Cable television	Automobiles

b.   Freedom of entry accounts for the difference in long-run profitability. Free entry eliminates long-run profits for both competition and monopolistic competition. Both monopoly and oligopoly are characterized by barriers to entry that can permit long-run profit. However, such barriers do not guarantee profit; demand may be insufficient to allow a profit.

c.   Wheat is a good example of perfect competition because there are many sellers, each of whom is a price taker who cannot influence the market price. Convenience marts are monopolistic competitors: each attempts to carve out a market niche in which it has some monopoly power. It can set price within a fairly narrow range. With a government-issued franchise as a single seller, a cable television company is a good example of monopoly. Automobile companies are classic examples of oligopoly, because there are a few interdependent sellers in an industry with high barriers to entry.

d.   Perfect competitors do not advertise because they can already sell all that they produce at the going market price. Monopolistic competitors advertise relatively heavily in order to differentiate their products and gain market share. Monopolists have less incentive to advertise, other than for public relations purposes. Oligopolists with differentiated products tend to advertise heavily in order to build and maintain market share. Those with standardized products, such as the steel industry, are less likely to advertise, other than to provide price information.

2.   a.   The firm's total revenue is TR = P × Q = 10 × 50 = $500.
The firm's total cost of production is TC = ATC × Q = 8 × 50 = $400.
Therefore, the firm's profit is TR − TC = $500 − $400 = $100.

b.   The firm cannot increase its profit by changing its price. It can maximize its profit by producing 50 units of output because MR = MC.

c.   The firm is not in its long-run equilibrium. Its profit will attract new firms into the industry. Entry of new firms will lower the demand faced by this firm. Price will drop until profits are reduced to zero.

E.   Advanced Critical Thinking

The columnist is referring to the well-documented problem of excess capacity under monopolistic competition. Each seller differentiates its product slightly, resulting in a large number of firms, each facing a downward-sloping demand curve. The result is production at less than the efficient scale of output (where average total cost is minimized). The alternative may be worse, however, because of the loss of consumer sovereignty. Under the current system, there are more alternatives available to the consumer; the best will survive in the marketplace. The price may actually be lower because of the effect of competition in pushing firms to cut costs and raise quality as much as possible. A single seller, perhaps operated by the government, would have little incentive to innovate and increase productivity. Without competition, the producers in the former Soviet Union produced products that were less innovative and of lower quality than would have been the case in the presence of competition. If we were to adopt this plan, who would make the decision regarding which toothpaste or which automobile would be produced? Who would push the seller to be more innovative or to increase productivity? Even in the former Soviet Union, sellers were encouraged to use brand names in order to promote accountability for product quality.

OLIGOPOLY

© Chad Mcdermott/Dreamstime.com

Learning Objectives

In this chapter, you will ...

- See what market structures lie between monopoly and competition

- Examine what outcomes are possible when a market is an oligopoly

- Learn about the prisoners' dilemma and how it applies to oligopoly and other issues

- Consider how competition laws try to foster competition in oligopolistic markets

oligopoly
a market structure in which only a few sellers offer similar or identical products

game theory
the study of how people behave in strategic situations

If you go to a store to buy hockey skates, it is likely that you will come home with one of two brands: Nike–Bauer or Reebok–CCM. These two companies make almost all of the skates sold in Canada. Together these firms determine the quantity of skates produced and, given the market demand curve, the price at which skates are sold.

The market for hockey skates is an example of an **oligopoly**. The essence of an oligopolistic market is that there are only a few sellers. As a result, the actions of any one seller in the market can have a large impact on the profits of all the other sellers. Oligopolistic firms are interdependent in a way that competitive firms are not. Our goal in this chapter is to see how this interdependence shapes the firms' behaviour and what problems it raises for public policy.

The analysis of oligopoly offers an opportunity to introduce **game theory**, the study of how people behave in strategic situations. By "strategic," we mean a situation in which a person, when choosing among alternative courses of action, must consider how others might respond to the action that person takes. Strategic thinking is crucial not only in checkers, chess, and tic-tac-toe but in many business decisions. Because oligopolistic markets have only a small number of firms, each firm must act strategically. Each firm knows that its profit depends not only on how much it produces but also on how much the other firms produce. In making its production decision, each firm in an oligopoly should consider how its decision might affect the production decisions of all the other firms.

Game theory is not necessary for understanding competitive or monopoly markets. In a market that is either perfectly competitive or monopolistically competitive, each firm is so small compared to the market that strategic interactions with other firms are not important. In a monopolized market, strategic interactions are absent because the market has only one firm. But, as we will see, game theory is useful for understanding oligopolies and many other situations in which small numbers of players are interacting with one another. Game theory helps explain the strategies that people choose, whether they are playing hockey or selling hockey skates.

MARKETS WITH ONLY A FEW SELLERS

Because an oligopolistic market has only a small group of sellers, a key feature of oligopoly is the tension between cooperation and self-interest. The group of oligopolists is best off cooperating and acting like a monopolist—producing a small quantity of output and charging a price above marginal cost. Yet because each oligopolist cares about only its own profit, there are powerful incentives at work that hinder a group of firms from maintaining the monopoly outcome.

A Duopoly Example

To understand the behaviour of oligopolies, let's consider an oligopoly with only two members, called a *duopoly*. Duopoly is the simplest type of oligopoly. Oligopolies with three or more members face the same problems as oligopolies with only two members, so we do not lose much by starting with the case of duopoly.

Imagine a town in which only two residents—Jack and Jill—own wells that produce water safe for drinking. Each Saturday, Jack and Jill decide how many litres of water to pump, bring the water to town, and sell it for whatever price the market will bear. To keep things simple, suppose that Jack and Jill can pump as much water as they want without cost. That is, the marginal cost of water equals zero.

Table 17.1 shows the town's demand schedule for water. The first column shows the total quantity demanded, and the second column shows the price. If the two

TABLE 17.1

The Demand Schedule for Water

Quantity (in litres)	Price	Total Revenue (and total profit)
0	$120	$ 0
10	110	1100
20	100	2000
30	90	2700
40	80	3200
50	70	3500
60	60	3600
70	50	3500
80	40	3200
90	30	2700
100	20	2000
110	10	1100
120	0	0

NEL

well owners sell a total of 10 L of water, water goes for $110 per litre. If they sell a total of 20 L, the price falls to $100 per litre. And so on. If you graphed these two columns of numbers, you would get a standard downward-sloping demand curve.

The last column in Table 17.1 shows the total revenue from the sale of water. It equals the quantity sold times the price. Because there is assumed to be no cost to pumping water, the total revenue of the two producers equals their total profit.

Let's now consider how the organization of the town's water industry affects the price of water and the quantity of water sold.

Competition, Monopolies, and Cartels

Before considering the price and quantity of water that would result from the duopoly of Jack and Jill, let's discuss briefly what the outcome would be if the water market was either perfectly competitive or monopolistic. If the market for water was perfectly competitive, the production decisions of each firm drive price equal to marginal cost. In the market for water, marginal cost is zero. Thus, under competition, the equilibrium price of water would be zero, and the equilibrium quantity would be 120 L. The price of water would reflect the cost of producing it, and the efficient quantity of water would be produced and consumed.

Now consider how a monopoly would behave. Table 17.1 shows that total profit is maximized at a quantity of 60 L and a price of $60 per litre. A profit-maximizing monopolist, therefore, would produce this quantity and charge this price. As is standard for monopolies, price would exceed marginal cost. The result would be inefficient, because the quantity of water produced and consumed would fall short of the socially efficient level of 120 L.

What outcome should we expect from our duopolists? One possibility is that Jack and Jill get together and agree on the quantity of water to produce and the price to charge for it. Such an agreement among firms over production and price is called **collusion,** and the group of firms acting in unison is called a **cartel.** Once a cartel is formed, the market is in effect served by a monopoly, and we can apply our analysis from Chapter 15. That is, if Jack and Jill were to collude, they would agree on the monopoly outcome because that outcome maximizes the total profit that the producers can get from the market. Our two producers would produce a total of 60 L, which would be sold at a price of $60 per litre. Once again, price exceeds marginal cost, and the outcome is socially inefficient.

A cartel must agree not only on the total level of production but also on the amount produced by each member. In our case, Jack and Jill must agree how to split between themselves the monopoly production of 60 L. Each member of the cartel will want a larger share of the market because a larger market share means larger profit. If Jack and Jill agreed to split the market equally, each would produce 30 L, the price would be $60 per litre, and each would get a profit of $1800.

collusion
an agreement among firms in a market about quantities to produce or prices to charge

cartel
a group of firms acting in unison

The Equilibrium for an Oligopoly

Oligopolists would like to form cartels and earn monopoly profits, but that is often not possible. As we discuss later in this chapter, competition laws prohibit explicit agreements among oligopolists as a matter of public policy. In addition, squabbling among cartel members over how to divide the profit in the market sometimes makes agreement among them impossible. Let's therefore consider what happens if Jack and Jill decide separately how much water to produce.

At first, one might expect Jack and Jill to reach the monopoly outcome on their own, because this outcome maximizes their joint profit. In the absence of a binding agreement, however, the monopoly outcome is unlikely. To see why, imagine that Jack expects Jill to produce only 30 L (half of the monopoly quantity). Jack would reason as follows:

"I could produce 30 L as well. In this case, a total of 60 L of water would be sold at a price of $60 per litre. My profit would be $1800 (30 L × $60 per litre). Alternatively, I could produce 40 L. In this case, a total of 70 L of water would be sold at a price of $50 per litre. My profit would be $2000 (40 L × $50 per litre). Even though total profit in the market would fall, my profit would be higher, because I would have a larger share of the market."

Of course, Jill might reason the same way. If so, Jack and Jill would each bring 40 L to town. Total sales would be 80 L, and the price would fall to $40. Thus, if the duopolists individually pursue their own self-interest when deciding how much to produce, they produce a total quantity greater than the monopoly quantity, charge a price lower than the monopoly price, and earn total profit less than the monopoly profit.

Although the logic of self-interest increases the duopoly's output above the monopoly level, it does not push the duopolists to reach the competitive allocation. Consider what happens when each duopolist is producing 40 L. The price is $40, and each duopolist makes a profit of $1600. In this case, Jack's self-interested logic leads to a different conclusion:

"Right now, my profit is $1600. Suppose I increase my production to 50 L. In this case, a total of 90 L of water would be sold, and the price would be $30 per litre. Then my profit would be only $1500. Rather than increasing production and driving down the price, I am better off keeping my production at 40 L."

The outcome in which Jack and Jill each produce 40 L looks like some sort of equilibrium. In fact, this outcome is called a *Nash equilibrium*. (It is named after economic theorist John Nash, whose life was portrayed in the book and movie *A Beautiful Mind*.) A **Nash equilibrium** is a situation in which economic actors interacting with one another each choose their best strategy given the strategies the others have chosen. In this case, given that Jill is producing 40 L, the best strategy for Jack is to produce 40 L. Similarly, given that Jack is producing 40 L, the best strategy for Jill is to produce 40 L. Once they reach this Nash equilibrium, neither Jack nor Jill has an incentive to make a different decision.

This example illustrates the tension between cooperation and self-interest. Oligopolists would be better off cooperating and reaching the monopoly outcome. Yet because they pursue their own self-interest, they do not end up reaching the monopoly outcome and maximizing their joint profit. Each oligopolist is tempted to raise production and capture a larger share of the market. As each of them tries to do this, total production rises, and the price falls.

At the same time, self-interest does not drive the market all the way to the competitive outcome. Like monopolists, oligopolists are aware that increases in the amount they produce reduce the price of their product. Therefore, they stop short of following the competitive firm's rule of producing up to the point where price equals marginal cost.

In summary, *when firms in an oligopoly individually choose production to maximize profit, they produce a quantity of output greater than the level produced by monopoly and less than the level produced by competition. The oligopoly price is less than the monopoly price but greater than the competitive price (which equals marginal cost).*

Nash equilibrium

a situation in which economic actors interacting with one another each choose their best strategy given the strategies that all the other actors have chosen

How the Size of an Oligopoly Affects the Market Outcome

We can use the insights from this analysis of duopoly to discuss how the size of an oligopoly is likely to affect the outcome in a market. Suppose, for instance, that John and Joan suddenly discover water sources on their property and join Jack and Jill in the water oligopoly. The demand schedule in Table 17.1 remains the same, but now more producers are available to satisfy this demand. How would an increase in the number of sellers from two to four affect the price and quantity of water in the town?

If the sellers of water could form a cartel, they would once again try to maximize total profit by producing the monopoly quantity and charging the monopoly price. Just as when there were only two sellers, the members of the cartel would need to agree on production levels for each member and find some way to enforce the agreement. As the cartel grows larger, however, this outcome is less likely. Reaching and enforcing an agreement becomes more difficult as the size of the group increases.

If the oligopolists do not form a cartel—perhaps because the competition laws prohibit it—they must each decide on their own how much water to produce. To see how the increase in the number of sellers affects the outcome, consider the decision facing each seller. At any time, each well owner has the option to raise production by 1 litre. In making this decision, the well owner weighs two effects:

1. *The output effect:* Because price is above marginal cost, selling 1 more litre of water at the going price will raise profit.
2. *The price effect:* Raising production will increase the total amount sold, which will lower the price of water and lower the profit on all the other litres sold.

If the output effect is larger than the price effect, the well owner will increase production. If the price effect is larger than the output effect, the owner will not raise production. (In fact, in this case, it is profitable to reduce production.) Each oligopolist continues to increase production until these two marginal effects exactly balance, taking the other firms' production as given.

Now consider how the number of firms in the industry affects the marginal analysis of each oligopolist. The larger the number of sellers, the less concerned each seller is about its own impact on the market price. That is, as the oligopoly grows in size, the magnitude of the price effect falls. When the oligopoly grows very large, the price effect disappears altogether, leaving only the output effect. That is, the production decision of an individual firm no longer affects the market price. In this extreme case, each firm takes the market price as given when deciding how much to produce. It increases production as long as price is above marginal cost.

We can now see that a large oligopoly is essentially a group of competitive firms. A competitive firm considers only the output effect when deciding how much to produce: Because a competitive firm is a price taker, the price effect is absent. Thus, *as the number of sellers in an oligopoly grows larger, an oligopolistic market looks more and more like a competitive market. The price approaches marginal cost, and the quantity produced approaches the socially efficient level.*

This analysis of oligopoly offers a new perspective on the effects of international trade. Imagine that Toyota and Honda are the only automakers in Japan, Volkswagen and BMW are the only automakers in Germany, and Ford and General Motors are the only automakers in Canada. If these nations prohibited international trade in autos, each would have an auto oligopoly with only two members, and the market outcome would likely depart substantially from the competitive ideal. With international trade, however, the car market is a world market, and the oligopoly in this example has six members. Allowing free trade increases the number of producers from which each consumer can choose, and this increased competition keeps prices closer to marginal cost. Thus, the theory of oligopoly provides another reason, in addition to the theory of comparative advantage discussed in Chapter 3, why all countries can benefit from free trade.

QuickQuiz If the members of an oligopoly could agree on a total quantity to produce, what quantity would they choose? • If the oligopolists do not act together but instead make production decisions individually, do they produce a total quantity more or less than in your answer to the previous question? Why?

THE ECONOMICS OF COOPERATION

As we have seen, oligopolies would like to reach the monopoly outcome, but doing so requires cooperation, which at times is difficult to maintain. In this section we look more closely at the problems people face when cooperation is desirable but difficult. To analyze the economics of cooperation, we need to learn a little about game theory.

A particularly important "game" is called the **prisoners' dilemma.** This game provides insight into the difficulty of maintaining cooperation. Many times in life, people fail to cooperate with one another even when cooperation would make them all better off. An oligopoly is just one example. The story of the prisoners' dilemma contains a general lesson that applies to any group trying to maintain cooperation among its members.

prisoners' dilemma
a particular "game" between two captured prisoners that illustrates why cooperation is difficult to maintain even when it is mutually beneficial

The Prisoners' Dilemma

The prisoners' dilemma is a story about two criminals who have been captured by the police. Let's call them Bonnie and Clyde. The police have enough evidence to convict Bonnie and Clyde of the minor crime of carrying an unregistered gun, so that each would spend a year in jail. The police also suspect that the two criminals have committed a bank robbery together, but they lack hard evidence to convict them of this major crime. The police question Bonnie and Clyde in separate rooms, and they offer each of them the following deal:

"Right now, we can lock you up for one year. If you confess to the bank robbery and implicate your partner, however, we'll give you immunity and you can go free. Your partner will get 20 years in jail. But if you both confess to the crime, we won't need your testimony and we can avoid the cost of a trial, so you will each get an intermediate sentence of eight years."

If Bonnie and Clyde, heartless bank robbers that they are, care only about their own sentences, what would you expect them to do? Would they confess or remain silent? Figure 17.1 shows their choices. Each prisoner has two strategies: confess or remain silent. The sentence each prisoner gets depends on the strategy he or she chooses and the strategy chosen by his or her partner in crime.

NEL

FIGURE 17.1

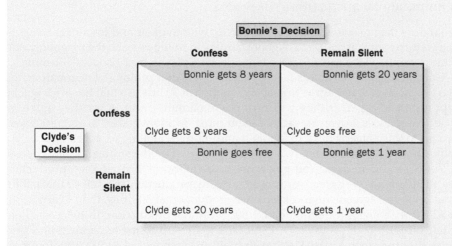

Bonnie's Decision

	Confess	Remain Silent
Confess	Bonnie gets 8 years / Clyde gets 8 years	Bonnie gets 20 years / Clyde goes free
Remain Silent	Bonnie goes free / Clyde gets 20 years	Bonnie gets 1 year / Clyde gets 1 year

Clyde's Decision

The Prisoners' Dilemma

In this game between two criminals suspected of committing a crime, the sentence that each receives depends both on his or her decision whether to confess or remain silent and on the decision made by the other.

Consider first Bonnie's decision. She reasons as follows: "I don't know what Clyde is going to do. If he remains silent, my best strategy is to confess, since then I'll go free rather than spending a year in jail. If he confesses, my best strategy is still to confess, since then I'll spend 8 years in jail rather than 20. So, regardless of what Clyde does, I am better off confessing."

In the language of game theory, a strategy is called a **dominant strategy** if it is the best strategy for a player to follow regardless of the strategies pursued by other players. In this case, confessing is a dominant strategy for Bonnie. She spends less time in jail if she confesses, regardless of whether Clyde confesses or remains silent.

Now consider Clyde's decision. He faces exactly the same choices as Bonnie, and he reasons in much the same way. Regardless of what Bonnie does, Clyde can reduce his time in jail by confessing. In other words, confessing is also a dominant strategy for Clyde.

In the end, both Bonnie and Clyde confess, and both spend eight years in jail. Yet, from their standpoint, this is a terrible outcome. If they had *both* remained silent, both of them would have been better off, spending only one year in jail on the gun charge. By each pursuing his or her own interests, the two prisoners together reach an outcome that is worse for each of them.

You might have thought that Bonnie and Clyde would have foreseen this situation and planned ahead. But even with advance planning, they would still run into problems. Imagine that, before the police captured Bonnie and Clyde, the two criminals had made a pact not to confess. Clearly, this agreement would make them both better off *if* they both live up to it, because they would each spend only one year in jail. But would the two criminals in fact remain silent, simply because they had agreed to? Once they are being questioned separately, the logic of self-interest takes over and leads them to confess. Cooperation between the two prisoners is difficult to maintain, because cooperation is individually irrational.

dominant strategy
a strategy that is best for a player in a game regardless of the strategies chosen by the other players

Oligopolies as a Prisoners' Dilemma

What does the prisoners' dilemma have to do with markets and imperfect competition? It turns out that the game oligopolists play in trying to reach the monopoly outcome is similar to the game that the two prisoners play in the prisoners' dilemma.

Consider again the choices facing Jack and Jill. After prolonged negotiation, the two suppliers of water agree to keep production at 30 litres so that the price will be kept high and together they will earn the maximum profit. After they agree on production levels, however, each of them must decide whether to cooperate and live up to this agreement or to ignore it and produce at a higher level. Figure 17.2 shows how the profits of the two producers depend on the strategies they choose.

Suppose you are Jack. You might reason as follows: "I could keep production low at 30 litres as we agreed, or I could raise my production and sell 40 litres. If Jill lives up to the agreement and keeps her production at 30 litres, then I earn profit of $2000 with high production and $1800 with low production. In this case, I am better off with high production. If Jill fails to live up to the agreement and produces 40 litres, then I earn $1600 with high production and $1500 with low production. Once again, I am better off with high production. So regardless of what Jill chooses to do, I am better off reneging on our agreement and producing at a high level."

Producing 40 litres is a dominant strategy for Jack. Of course, Jill reasons in exactly the same way, and so both produce at the higher level of 40 litres. The result is the inferior outcome (from Jack's and Jill's standpoints) with low profits for each of the two producers.

This example illustrates why oligopolies have trouble maintaining monopoly profits. The monopoly outcome is jointly rational for the oligopoly, but each oligopolist has an incentive to cheat. Just as self-interest drives the prisoners in the prisoners' dilemma to confess, self-interest makes it difficult for the oligopoly to maintain the cooperative outcome with low production, high prices, and monopoly profits.

FIGURE 17.2

Jack and Jill's Oligopoly Game

In this game between Jack and Jill, the profit that each earns from selling water depends on both the quantity he or she chooses to sell and the quantity the other chooses to sell.

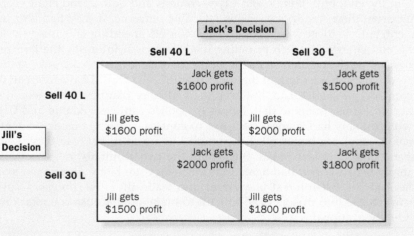

Case Study

OPEC AND THE WORLD OIL MARKET

Our story about the town's market for water is fictional, but if we change water to crude oil, and Jack and Jill to Iran and Iraq, the story is quite close to being true. Much of the world's oil is produced by a few countries, mostly in the Middle East. These countries together make up an oligopoly. Their decisions about how much oil to pump are much the same as Jack and Jill's decisions about how much water to pump.

The countries that produce most of the world's oil have formed a cartel, called the Organization of the Petroleum Exporting Countries (OPEC). As originally formed in 1960, OPEC included Iran, Iraq, Kuwait, Saudi Arabia, and Venezuela. In 2010, Qatar, Indonesia, Libya, the United Arab Emirates, Algeria, Nigeria, Ecuador, and Angola were also members. These countries control more than three-fourths of the world's oil reserves. Like any cartel, OPEC tries to raise the price of its product through a coordinated reduction in quantity produced. OPEC tries to set production levels for each of the member countries.

The problem that OPEC faces is much the same as the problem that Jack and Jill faced in our scenario. The OPEC countries would like to maintain a high price of oil, but each member of the cartel is tempted to increase its production in order to get a larger share of the total profit. OPEC members frequently agree to reduce production but then cheat on their agreements.

OPEC was most successful at maintaining cooperation and high prices in the period from 1973 to 1985. The price of crude oil rose from US$3 per barrel in 1972 to US$11 in 1974 and then to US$35 in 1981. But in the early 1980s member countries began arguing about production levels, and OPEC became ineffective at maintaining cooperation. By 1986 the price of crude oil had fallen back to US$13 per barrel.

In recent years, the members of OPEC have continued to meet regularly, but the cartel has been far less successful at reaching and enforcing agreements. Although the price of oil rose significantly in 2007 and 2008, the primary cause was increased demand in the world oil market, in part from a booming Chinese economy, rather than restricted supply. While this lack of cooperation among OPEC nations has hurt the profits of the oil-producing nations, it has benefited consumers around the world. ●

Other Examples of the Prisoners' Dilemma

We have seen how the prisoners' dilemma can be used to understand the problem facing oligopolies. The same logic applies to many other situations as well. Here we consider two examples in which self-interest prevents cooperation and leads to an inferior outcome for the parties involved: advertising and common resources.

Advertising   When two firms advertise to attract the same customers, they face a problem similar to the prisoners' dilemma. For example, consider the decisions

FIGURE 17.3

An Advertising Game

In this game between firms selling similar products, the profit that each earns depends on both its own advertising decision and the advertising decision of the other firm.

| | | **Molson's Decision** | |
		Advertise	**Don't Advertise**
Labatt's Decision	**Advertise**	Molson gets $3 billion profit / Labatt gets $3 billion profit	Molson gets $2 billion profit / Labatt gets $5 billion profit
	Don't Advertise	Molson gets $5 billion profit / Labatt gets $2 billion profit	Molson gets $4 billion profit / Labatt gets $4 billion profit

facing two beer companies, Molson and Labatt. If neither company advertises, the two companies split the market. If both advertise, they again split the market, but profits are lower, since each company must bear the cost of advertising. Yet if one company advertises while the other does not, the one that advertises attracts customers from the other.

Figure 17.3 shows how the profits of the two companies depend on their actions. You can see that advertising is a dominant strategy for each firm. Thus, both firms choose to advertise, even though both firms would be better off if neither firm advertised.

Common Resources   In Chapter 11 we saw that people tend to overuse common resources. One can view this problem as an example of the prisoners' dilemma.

Imagine that two oil companies—Shell and Esso (Imperial Oil)—own adjacent oil fields. Under the fields is a common pool of oil worth $12 million. Drilling a well to recover the oil costs $1 million. If each company drills one well, each will get half of the oil and earn a $5 million profit ($6 million in revenue minus $1 million in costs).

Because the pool of oil is a common resource, the companies will not use it efficiently. Suppose that either company could drill a second well. If one company has two of the three wells, that company gets two-thirds of the oil, which yields a profit of $6 million. The other company gets one-third of the oil, for a profit of $3 million. Yet if each company drills a second well, the two companies again split the oil. In this case, each bears the cost of a second well, so profit is only $4 million for each company.

Figure 17.4 shows the game. Drilling two wells is a dominant strategy for each company. Once again, the self-interest of the two players leads them to an inferior outcome.

FIGURE 17.4

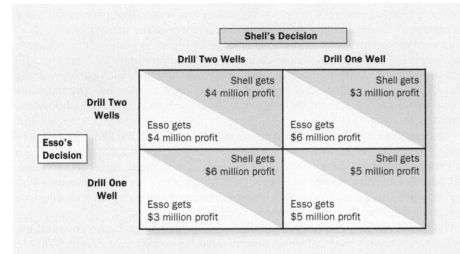

A Common-Resources Game

In this game between firms pumping oil from a common pool, the profit that each earns depends on both the number of wells it drills and the number of wells drilled by the other firm.

The Prisoners' Dilemma and the Welfare of Society

The prisoners' dilemma describes many of life's situations, and it shows that cooperation can be difficult to maintain, even when cooperation would make both players in the game better off. Clearly, this lack of cooperation is a problem for those involved in these situations. But is lack of cooperation a problem from the standpoint of society as a whole? The answer depends on the circumstances.

In some cases, the noncooperative equilibrium is bad for society as well as the players. For example, in the common-resources game in Figure 17.4, the extra wells dug by Shell and Esso are pure waste. Society would be better off if the two players could reach the cooperative outcome.

By contrast, in the case of oligopolists trying to maintain monopoly profits, lack of cooperation is desirable from the standpoint of society as a whole. The monopoly outcome is good for the oligopolists, but it is bad for the consumers of the product. As we first saw in Chapter 7, the competitive outcome is best for society because it maximizes total surplus. When oligopolists fail to cooperate, the quantity they produce is closer to this optimal level. Put differently, the invisible hand guides markets to allocate resources efficiently only when markets are competitive, and markets are competitive only when firms in the market fail to cooperate with one another.

Similarly, consider the case of the police questioning two suspects. Lack of cooperation between the suspects is desirable because it allows the police to convict more criminals. The prisoners' dilemma is a dilemma for the prisoners, but it can be a boon to everyone else.

Why People Sometimes Cooperate

The prisoners' dilemma shows that cooperation is difficult. But is it impossible? Not all prisoners, when questioned by the police, decide to turn in their partners in crime.

Cartels sometimes do manage to maintain collusive arrangements, despite the incentive for individual members to defect. Very often, the reason that players can solve the prisoners' dilemma is that they play the game not once but many times.

To see why cooperation is easier to enforce in repeated games, let's return to our duopolists, Jack and Jill, whose choices were given in Figure 17.2. Jack and Jill would like to agree to maintain the monopoly outcome in which each produces 30 L. Yet if Jack and Jill are to play this game only once, neither has any incentive to live up to this agreement. Self-interest drives each to renege and choose the dominant strategy of 40 L.

Now suppose that Jack and Jill know that they will play the same game every week. When they make their initial agreement to keep production low, they can also specify what happens if one party reneges. They might agree, for instance, that once one of them reneges and produces 40 L, both of them will produce 40 L forever after. This penalty is easy to enforce because if one party is producing at a high level, the other has every reason to do the same.

The threat of this penalty may be all that is needed to maintain cooperation. Each person knows that defecting would raise his or her profit from $1800 to $2000. But this benefit would last for only one week. Thereafter, profit would fall to $1600 and stay there. As long as the players care enough about future profits, they will choose to forgo the one-time gain from defection. Thus, in a game of repeated prisoners' dilemma, the two players may well be able to reach the cooperative outcome.

Case Study
THE PRISONERS' DILEMMA TOURNAMENT

Imagine that you are playing a game of prisoners' dilemma with a person being "questioned" in a separate room. Moreover, imagine that you are going to play not once but many times. Your score at the end of the game is the total number of years in jail. You would like to make this score as small as possible. What strategy would you play? Would you begin by confessing or remaining silent? How would the other player's actions affect your subsequent decisions about confessing?

Repeated prisoners' dilemma is quite a complicated game. To encourage cooperation, players must penalize each other for not cooperating. Yet the strategy described earlier for Jack and Jill's water cartel—defect forever as soon as the other player defects—is not very forgiving. In a game repeated many times, a strategy that allows players to return to the cooperative outcome after a period of noncooperation may be preferable.

To see what strategies work best, political scientist Robert Axelrod held a tournament. People entered by sending computer programs designed to play repeated prisoners' dilemma. Each program then played the game against all the other programs. The "winner" was the program that received the fewest total years in jail.

The winner turned out to be a simple strategy called *tit-for-tat*. According to tit-for-tat, a player should start by cooperating and then do whatever the other player did last time. Thus, a tit-for-tat player cooperates until the other player defects; he then defects until the other player cooperates again. In other words, this strategy starts out friendly, penalizes unfriendly players, and forgives them if warranted. To Axelrod's surprise, this simple strategy did better than all the more complicated strategies that people had sent in.

The tit-for-tat strategy has a long history. It is essentially the biblical strategy of "an eye for an eye, a tooth for a tooth." The prisoners' dilemma tournament suggests that this may be a good rule of thumb for playing some of the games of life. ●

QuickQuiz Tell the story of the prisoners' dilemma. Prepare a table showing the prisoners' choices and explain what outcome is likely. ● What does the prisoners' dilemma teach us about oligopolies?

PUBLIC POLICY TOWARD OLIGOPOLIES

One of the ten principles of economics in Chapter 1 is that governments can sometimes improve market outcomes. The application of this principle to oligopolistic markets is, as a general matter, straightforward. As we have seen, cooperation among oligopolists is undesirable from the standpoint of society as a whole because it leads to production that is too low and prices that are too high. To move the allocation of resources closer to the social optimum, policymakers should try to induce firms in an oligopoly to compete rather than cooperate. Let's consider how policymakers do this and then examine the controversies that arise in this area of public policy.

Restraint of Trade and the Competition Act

Freedom to make contracts is an essential part of a market economy. Businesses and households use contracts to arrange mutually advantageous trades, relying on the court system to enforce those contracts. Yet for many years, Canadian judges have refused to enforce agreements that restrain trade among competitors (reducing quantities and raising prices, or price-fixing) as being against the public interest.

Canada's Competition Act codifies and reinforces this policy. Section 45(1) of the act states:

> Every one who conspires, combines, agrees or arranges with another person
> (a) to limit unduly the facilities for transporting, producing, manufacturing, supplying, storing or dealing in any product,
> (b) to prevent, limit or lessen, unduly, the manufacture or production of a product or to enhance unreasonably the price thereof,
> (c) to prevent or lessen, unduly, competition in the production, manufacture, purchase, barter, sale, storage, rental, transportation or supply of a product, or in the price of insurance on persons or property, or
> (d) to otherwise restrain or injure competition unduly,
> is guilty of an indictable offence and liable to imprisonment for a term not exceeding five years or to a fine not exceeding ten million dollars or both.

The Competition Act contains both civil and criminal provisions. As we discussed in Chapter 15, the Commissioner of Competition, as the head of the Competition Bureau, is responsible for enforcing the act. The commissioner refers criminal cases to the Attorney General of Canada, while civil cases are heard by the Competition Tribunal. Mergers, also discussed in Chapter 15, are governed by the civil provisions of the act. Conspiracies in restraint of trade, such as those described in section 45(1), above, fall under the criminal provisions of the act.

Other activities that are subject to criminal prosecution include bid-rigging, price discrimination, resale price maintenance, and predatory pricing. Bid-rigging occurs when potential bidders agree with other bidders to refrain from bidding on contracts, or rig bids in advance. Price discrimination occurs when a supplier charges different prices for similar quantities of goods sold to firms that compete with one another. Resale price maintenance occurs when a supplier "requires" retailers to sell its product at a specified (or minimum or maximum) price. Predatory pricing involves selling products at unreasonably low prices for the purpose of eliminating or substantially reducing competition. Criminal proceedings must be initiated by the commissioner, but individuals who have been harmed by criminal offences can sue for civil damages. These and other provisions of the Competition Act are used to prevent firms in oligopolistic industries from acting either individually or together in ways that make markets less competitive.

Case Study
COLLUSION IN QUEBEC DRIVING SCHOOLS

Firms in oligopolistic markets have a strong incentive both to collude with one another and to drive one another out of business. The goal of each of these actions is to reduce competition, raise prices, and increase profits. The great eighteenth-century economist Adam Smith was well aware of this potential market failure. With regard to collusion, in his book *The Wealth of Nations* he wrote, "People of the same trade seldom meet together, but the conversation ends in a conspiracy against the public, or in some diversion to raise prices."

A Canadian example of Smith's observation involved driving schools in the province of Quebec. Jacques Perreault was a director in a company that operated driving schools in the Sherbrooke area and the adjoining area of Magog. In 1987, Perreault entered into a conspiracy with several of his competitors to raise and fix the price of driving-school services in the Sherbrooke market. The co-conspirators held approximately 94 percent of the Sherbrooke driving-school market.

Shortly after the conspiracy was implemented, it broke down because several smaller competitors refused to follow the agreed-upon pricing scheme. Perreault made several threats against these renegade competitors in an attempt to restore the conspiracy. He also engaged in selective predatory pricing and drove several noncomplying competitors out of the Sherbrooke and Magog markets, using revenues earned from other regional markets to finance these activities. In 1996, a jury found Perreault and his co-conspirators guilty on numerous counts of price-fixing and predatory pricing. Perreault was sentenced to a prison term of one year, while the other conspirators had to pay fines or carry out community service.

The Perreault case illustrates how firms in an oligopolistic industry can use both collusion and predatory pricing to reduce competition and raise prices. Also of interest is the nature of some of the arguments made by the Crown in its prosecution of the case. In Quebec, everyone who wants to get a driver's licence must pass an accredited driving-school course. As a result of the province's strict guidelines on the standards of training, driving schools offer a relatively homogeneous product. Moreover, Quebec restricts the number of accredited schools within each region of the province. A moratorium on new schools was imposed in 1987; schools leaving the market could sell their licences only to other accredited schools. The Crown argued that the large market share held by Perreault and his co-conspirators, the almost impassable barriers to entry, the virtual nonexistence of substitutes, and the high level of product homogeneity were all evidence of significant market power. The jury's guilty verdict suggests that the Crown's arguments were persuasive. Perhaps if the Quebec government had not restricted entry in the first place, collusion might not have been a problem. ●

IN THE NEWS

AUMANN AND SCHELLING

In 2005, two prominent game theorists won the Nobel Prize.

Economic Work on "Game Theory" Wins Nobel Prize

By Jon E. Hilsenrath

The Cold War was a period of conflict management on a grand, frightening scale, and two researchers who explained how individuals negotiate such conflict won the Nobel Prize in economics for work that grew out of the period.

Thomas Schelling, an 84-year-old retired University of Maryland professor who served long stints as an adviser to the U.S. government, has written on managing the U.S.–Soviet buildup of nuclear arms and extended his theories to subjects such as drug addiction, racial segregation and global warming. Robert Aumann, 75, a mathematician by training and professor at Hebrew

University in Jerusalem, added analytical rigor to the field that both professors helped to create, which has come to be known in economics as "game theory."

The two will share the 10 million kronor prize ($1.3 million) awarded by the Royal Swedish Academy of Sciences. Mr. Schelling is an American citizen, and Mr. Aumann is an American and Israeli citizen.

Game theory is the study of strategy and how people make decisions when interacting in conflict with one another. In a game of chess, two players act not only based on their own strategy, but also on expectations of how their opponent will behave and react. In the 1940s and 1950s, economists began to see their models of individual behavior needed to be less robotic and should reflect the kind of strategic dance found in games like chess.

The movement toward game theory was driven in part by mathematicians like Mr. Aumann and an associate from his days at the Massachusetts Institute of Technology named John Nash, whose life was portrayed in the movie "A Beautiful Mind." Mr. Nash won the economics prize with two others in 1994.

While Messrs. Nash and Aumann used math to give precise formulations to game theory, Prof. Schelling sought to give it practical meaning. He explained, for instance, how decision makers often find it advantageous to limit their own options to get concessions from an opponent. In some cases, for instance, it might be wise for a general to burn bridges behind his troops to send a credible and possibly game-changing message toward his enemy that he has no intention of retreating.

Economists have since applied this idea of "precommitment" to other areas, including business. Some companies, for example, might find it advantageous to build too much capacity, to alert would-be competitors that entering a market will lead them into a price war. . . .

Messrs. Schelling and Aumann both came of age during the Cold War, when fears of a nuclear confrontation between the Soviet Union and the U.S. led scholars to examine the motivations and decision-making of both sides. . . .

Prof. Schelling extended his research beyond the Cold War. For instance, his work has shown how even small differences in preferences between groups of people could lead to large-scale segregation in cities. It also has described drug addiction as a game against oneself. Someone who is trying to quit smoking, for instance, might flush cigarettes down the toilet because he realizes that "some time late at night he won't be able to resist them."

Source: Jon E. Hilsenrath, "Economic Work on 'Game Theory' Wins Nobel Prize," *Wall Street Journal*, October 11, 2005. Reprinted by permission of The Wall Street Journal. Copyright © 2005 Dow Jones & Company, Inc. All Rights Reserved Worldwide. License number 2503651391235.

Controversies over Competition Policy

Over time, much controversy has centred on the question of what kinds of behaviour the competition laws should prohibit. Most commentators agree that price-fixing agreements among competing firms should be illegal. Yet the competition laws have been used to condemn some business practices whose effects are not obvious. Here we consider three examples.

Resale Price Maintenance   One example of a controversial business practice is *resale price maintenance*, also called *fair trade*. Imagine that Superduper Electronics sells DVD players to retail stores for $300. If Superduper requires the retailers to charge customers $350, it is said to engage in resale price maintenance. Any retailer that charged less than $350 would have violated its contract with Superduper.

At first, resale price maintenance might seem anticompetitive and, therefore, detrimental to society. Like an agreement among members of a cartel, it prevents the retailers from competing on price. For this reason, the courts have often viewed resale price maintenance as a violation of the competition laws.

Yet some economists defend resale price maintenance on two grounds. First, they deny that it is aimed at reducing competition. To the extent that Superduper Electronics has any market power, it can exert that power through the wholesale price, rather than through resale price maintenance. Moreover, Superduper has no incentive to discourage competition among its retailers. Indeed, because a cartel of retailers sells less than a group of competitive retailers, Superduper would be worse off if its retailers were a cartel.

Second, economists believe that resale price maintenance has a legitimate goal. Superduper may want its retailers to provide customers with a pleasant showroom and a knowledgeable sales force. Yet, without resale price maintenance, some customers would take advantage of one store's service to learn about the DVD player's special features and then buy the item at a discount retailer that does not provide this service. To some extent, good service is a public good among the retailers that sell Superduper products. As we discussed in Chapter 11, when one person provides a public good, others are able to enjoy it without paying for it. In this case, discount retailers would free-ride on the service provided by other retailers, leading to less service than is desirable. Resale price maintenance is one way for Superduper to solve this free-rider problem.

The example of resale price maintenance illustrates an important principle: *Business practices that appear to reduce competition may in fact have legitimate purposes.* This principle makes the application of the competition laws all the more difficult. The economists, lawyers, and judges in charge of enforcing these laws must determine what kinds of behaviour public policy should prohibit as impeding competition and reducing economic well-being. Often that job is not easy.

Predatory Pricing   Firms with market power normally use that power to raise prices above the competitive level. But should policymakers ever be concerned that firms with market power might charge prices that are too low? This question is at the heart of a second debate over competition policy.

Imagine that a large airline, call it Coyote Air, has a monopoly on some route. Then Roadrunner Express enters and takes 20 percent of the market, leaving Coyote with 80 percent. In response to this competition, Coyote starts slashing its fares. Some competition analysts argue that Coyote's move could be anticompetitive: The price cuts may be intended to drive Roadrunner out of the market so Coyote can recapture its monopoly and raise prices again. Such behaviour is called *predatory pricing.*

Although predatory pricing is a common claim in competition suits, some economists are skeptical of this argument and believe that predatory pricing is rarely, and perhaps never, a profitable business strategy. Why? For a price war to drive out a rival, prices have to be driven below cost. Yet if Coyote starts selling cheap tickets at a loss, it had better be ready to fly more planes, because low fares will attract more customers. Roadrunner, meanwhile, can respond to Coyote's predatory move by cutting back on flights. As a result, Coyote ends up bearing more than 80 percent of the losses, putting Roadrunner in a good position to survive the price war. As in the old Roadrunner–Coyote cartoons, the predator suffers more than the prey.

Economists continue to debate whether predatory pricing should be a concern for anticompetition policymakers. Various questions remain unresolved. Is predatory pricing ever a profitable business strategy? If so, when? Are the courts capable of telling which price cuts are competitive and thus good for consumers and which are predatory? There are no simple answers.

Tying A third example of a controversial business practice is *tying*. Suppose that Makemoney Movies produces two new films—*Spiderman* and *Hamlet*. If Makemoney offers theatres the two films together at a single price, rather than separately, the studio is said to be tying its two products.

The practice of tying is banned under the civil provisions of the Competition Act. The commonly used justification for the ban goes as follows: Imagine that *Spiderman* is a blockbuster, whereas *Hamlet* is an unprofitable art film. By tying, the studio could use the high demand for *Spiderman* to force theatres to buy *Hamlet*. It seems that the studio could use tying as a mechanism for expanding its market power.

Many economists are skeptical of this argument. Imagine that theatres are willing to pay $20 000 for *Spiderman* and nothing for *Hamlet*. Then the most that a theatre would pay for the two movies together is $20 000—the same as it would pay for *Spiderman* by itself. Forcing the theatre to accept a worthless movie as part of the deal does not increase the theatre's willingness to pay. Makemoney cannot increase its market power simply by bundling the two movies together.

Why, then, does tying exist? One possibility is that it is a form of price discrimination. Suppose there are two theatres. City Theatre is willing to pay $15 000 for *Spiderman* and $5000 for *Hamlet*. Country Theatre is just the opposite: It is willing to pay $5000 for *Spiderman* and $15 000 for *Hamlet*. If Makemoney charges separate prices for the two films, its best strategy is to charge $15 000 for each film, and each theatre chooses to show only one film. Yet if Makemoney offers the two movies as a bundle, it can charge each theatre $20 000 for the movies. Thus, if different theatres value the films differently, tying may allow the studio to increase profit by charging a combined price closer to the buyers' total willingness to pay.

The economic theory of tying is even more subtle and complex when considered in the context of vertical integration. This issue arose in a case involving Tele-Direct, a publisher of Yellow Pages directories in Canada. Tele-Direct required that any advertisements placed in its Yellow Pages be designed by its in-house staff. This requirement led to a vertically integrated service, starting with designing the ads, moving to providing advertising space, and ending with producing and distributing the directory. Ads designed by outside agencies were not allowed to appear in Tele-Direct's Yellow Pages. In this case, the provision of advertising space was tied to the design of the ads.

In 1995, the Competition Tribunal ruled that this practice violated the tying provisions of the Competition Act. The Tribunal ordered Tele-Direct to either unbundle its advertising space and design activities and quote separate prices for them, or pay an appropriate commission to outside designers. Yet the efficiency effects of tying in this case are ambiguous. On the one hand, tying in a vertically integrated firm may reduce costs and generate production efficiencies. On the other hand, it excludes competing providers of advertising services from entering the Yellow Pages market. The net effect is uncertain.

Tying remains a controversial business practice. The commonly heard argument that tying allows a firm to extend its market power to other goods is not well founded, at least in its simplest form. Yet economists have proposed more elaborate theories for how tying can impede competition. Given our current economic knowledge, it is unclear whether tying has adverse effects for society as a whole.

IN THE NEWS

DO WE NEED COMPETITION POLICY?

In this chapter we have discussed some of the elements of Canada's competition policy. As the following opinion piece by a York University economist indicates, not everyone believes that we need laws to promote competitive behaviour.

Why Not Dump Competition Policy?

By Fred Lazar

Recently, Terence Corcoran called Sheridan Scott's appointment to head the Competition Bureau an opportunity to kill competition policy reform. I will go one further and argue that the government should seriously consider dismantling most, if not all, of the Competition Act and related regulations.

The foundations for competition policy and this act in general, and the "Abuse of Dominant Position" section in particular, are built on a very flimsy theoretical base.

Joseph Schumpeter, one of the great economists of the 20th century, long ago recognized the importance of the pursuit of monopoly power and economic rents as the primary driver of innovation and risk-taking. For example, he argued that only the incentive of profits led entrepreneurs to take the great risks involved in innovation, and that monopoly power was much more important than competition, as defined by economists, in providing the climate under which innovation occurred. The profits of the monopolist provided the incentives for other people to try to get their share. According to Schumpeter, the process of creative destruction would ensure that no monopoly would last for-

ever. Indeed, few would last very long if they failed to innovate and anticipate their future competition.

Schumpeter's great insights did not permeate the economics mainstream. Fortunately, Professor Michael Porter at the Harvard Business School has demonstrated the critical importance for companies of developing competitive strategies that will create competitive advantages for them, and has argued forcefully about the realities of competitive behaviour and the pursuit of market power.

Innovation and risk-taking and the pursuit of monopoly power and economic profits drive the economy and produce the dramatic improvements in productivity and standards of living.

As Schumpeter recognized, companies that have succeeded in creating a competitive advantage and gaining some degree of market power face a choice. They can defend their advantage through defensive tactics, many of which would be similar to the anti-competitive acts described in the "Abuse of Dominant Position" section of the Competition Act, and thus become fat and lazy and an easy target for competitors; or they can continue to innovate and take risks in order to create new competitive advantages to maintain their market power.

The "Abuse of Dominant Position" provisions in the Competition Act are highly unlikely to encourage the senior management of companies to pursue lean and hungry competitive strategies that produce dynamic efficiency gains.

In Canada, Eaton's was once the leading department store chain. The company has disappeared, overtaken by hungry competitors, not enforcement of competition policy. Similarly, in the United States, Wal-Mart has overtaken Woolworths, Montgomery Ward, Kresge's and even Sears Roebuck, and this dramatic change in the retail sector had nothing to do with the anti-trust laws. The incentive of profits led Sam Walton to take the risks involved in innovation, and he benefited from having easy targets—the old-line retailers who had become fat and lazy.

Did the U.S. Department of Justice case against IBM lead to the creation of Microsoft, Cisco, Sun, Oracle, Dell and others? Not at all. For a time, IBM became fat and lazy, opening up opportunities for dynamic, aggressive and innovative new companies. If IBM had continued to be lean and hungry, several of these new companies, which have become dominant in their own right, would not have been created or survived.

Whatever happened to Stelco in Canada, or U.S. Steel, Ford, the three major broadcast networks, Pan Am, TWA, RCA in consumer electronics and many others in the United States and Canada? The lure of a competitive advantage with its resulting market power and monopoly profits, together with lazy, incumbent "monopolists," produced the dynamic competitive changes in industry after industry.

The lesson: Competition policy does not appear to be a positive force for the process of creative destruction, a process that creates the large, dynamic productivity gains for the economy. Competition policy, in fact, can be a negative force for this process and for the economy as a whole. If companies choose to use competition policy to restrain a major company in order to gain a foothold and expand in an industry—de facto market share regulation—they will most likely become fat and lazy.

Section 1.1 of the Competition Act states: "The purpose of this Act is to maintain and encourage competition in Canada in order to promote the efficiency and adaptability of the Canadian economy, in order to expand the opportunities for Canadian participation in world markets while at the same time recognizing the role of foreign competition in Canada, in order to ensure that small- and medium-sized enterprises have an equitable opportunity to participate in the Canadian economy and in order to provide consumers with competitive prices and product choices."

The act cannot encourage competition. Only the desire to succeed and gain a competitive advantage encourages competition. Further, the act cannot "promote the efficiency and adaptability of the Canadian economy." Here, too, only the actions of senior management can do this, and these actions will succeed only if senior management is properly motivated

and wise enough to recognize the advantages of being lean and hungry. Complacency, which can be encouraged by aggressive application of the competition laws, will be destructive to companies and wasteful for the country.

As Schumpeter has argued, there is no reason to fear the creation of monopolies, unless, of course, the government created them. Monopolies formed through the creation and successful execution of competitive strategies produce long-term economic gains and provide the basis for aggressive competition based on more than just pricing. That then sets the stage for the process of creative destruction so critical to the economy's long-term health.

Fred Lazar is an economist at York University's Schulich School of Business.

Source: Fred Lazar, "Why not dump competition policy?" Reprinted with the permission of the author.

"Me? A monopolist? Now just wait a minute. . . ."

Case Study
THE MICROSOFT CASE

The most important and controversial anticompetition case in recent years has been the U.S. government's suit against the Microsoft Corporation, filed in 1998. Certainly, the case did not lack drama. It pitted one of the world's richest men (Bill Gates) against one of the world's most powerful regulatory agencies (the U.S. Justice Department). Testifying for the government was a prominent economist (MIT professor Franklin Fisher). Testifying for Microsoft was an equally prominent economist (MIT professor Richard Schmalensee). At stake was the future of one of the world's most valuable companies (Microsoft) in one of the economy's fastest-growing industries (computer software).

A central issue in the Microsoft case involved tying—in particular, whether Microsoft should be allowed to integrate its Internet browser into its Windows operating system. The government claimed that Microsoft was bundling these two products together to expand the power it had in the market for computer

NEL

operating systems into an unrelated market (for Internet browsers). Allowing Microsoft to incorporate such products into its operating system, the government argued, would deter other software companies such as Netscape from entering the market and offering new products.

Microsoft responded by pointing out that putting new features into old products is a natural part of technological progress. Cars today include stereos and air conditioners, which were once sold separately, and cameras come with built-in flashes. The same is true with operating systems. Over time, Microsoft has added many features to Windows that were previously stand-alone products. This has made computers more reliable and easier to use because consumers can be confident that the pieces work together. The integration of Internet technology, Microsoft argued, was the natural next step.

One point of disagreement concerned the extent of Microsoft's market power. Noting that more than 80 percent of new personal computers use a Microsoft operating system, the government argued that the company had substantial monopoly power, which it was trying to expand. Microsoft replied that the software market is always changing and that Microsoft's Windows was constantly being challenged by competitors, such as the Apple Mac and Linux operating systems. It also argued that the low price it charged for Windows—about $50 at that time, or only 3 percent of the price of a typical computer—was evidence that its market power was severely limited.

Like many large anticompetition suits, the Microsoft case became a legal morass. In November 1999, after a long trial, Judge Penfield Jackson ruled that Microsoft had great monopoly power and that it had illegally abused that power. In June 2000, after hearings about possible remedies, he ordered that Microsoft be broken up into two companies—one that sold the operating system and one that sold applications software. A year later, an appeals court overturned Jackson's breakup order and handed the case to a new judge. In September 2001, the Justice Department announced that it no longer sought a breakup of the company and wanted to settle the case quickly.

A settlement was finally reached in November 2002. Microsoft accepted some restrictions on its business practices. The government accepted that a browser would remain part of the Windows operating system. But the settlement did not end Microsoft's anticompetition troubles. In recent years, the company has contended with several private anticompetition suits, as well as suits brought by the European Union alleging a variety of anticompetitive behaviours. ●

QuickQuiz What kind of agreement is illegal for businesses to make? • Why are the competition laws controversial?

CONCLUSION

Oligopolies would like to act like monopolies, but self-interest drives them closer to competition. Thus, oligopolies can end up looking either more like monopolies or more like competitive markets, depending on the number of firms in the oligopoly and how cooperative the firms are. The story of the prisoners' dilemma shows why oligopolies can fail to maintain cooperation, even when cooperation is in their best interest.

Policymakers regulate the behaviour of oligopolists through the anticompetition laws. The proper scope of these laws is the subject of ongoing controversy. Although price-fixing among competing firms clearly reduces economic welfare and should be illegal, some business practices that appear to reduce competition may have legitimate if subtle purposes. As a result, policymakers need to be careful when they use the substantial powers of the anticompetition laws to place limits on firms' behaviour.

SUMMARY

- Oligopolists maximize their total profits by forming a cartel and acting like a monopolist. Yet, if oligopolists make decisions about production levels individually, the result is a greater quantity and a lower price than under the monopoly outcome. The larger the number of firms in the oligopoly, the closer the quantity and price will be to the levels that would prevail under competition.

- The prisoners' dilemma shows that self-interest can prevent people from maintaining cooperation, even when cooperation is in their mutual interest. The logic of the prisoners' dilemma applies in many situations, including advertising, common-resource problems, and oligopolies.

- Policymakers use the anticompetition laws to prevent oligopolies from engaging in behaviour that reduces competition. The application of these laws can be controversial, because some behaviour that may seem to reduce competition may in fact have legitimate business purposes.

KEY CONCEPTS

oligopoly, p. 365
game theory, p. 365
collusion, p. 367

cartel, p. 367
Nash equilibrium, p. 368

prisoners' dilemma, p. 370
dominant strategy, p. 371

QUESTIONS FOR REVIEW

1. If a group of sellers could form a cartel, what quantity and price would they try to set?

2. Compare the quantity and price of an oligopoly to those of a monopoly.

3. Compare the quantity and price of an oligopoly to those of a competitive market.

4. How does the number of firms in an oligopoly affect the outcome in its market?

5. What is the prisoners' dilemma, and what does it have to do with oligopoly?

6. Give two examples other than oligopoly to show how the prisoners' dilemma helps to explain behaviour.

7. What kinds of behaviour do the anticompetition laws prohibit?

8. What is resale price maintenance, and why is it controversial?

PROBLEMS AND APPLICATIONS

1. *The New York Times* (Nov. 30, 1993) reported that "the inability of OPEC to agree last week to cut production has sent the oil market into turmoil . . . [leading to] the lowest price for domestic crude oil since June 1990."

   a. Why were the members of OPEC trying to agree to cut production?

   b. Why do you suppose OPEC was unable to agree on cutting production? Why did the oil market go into "turmoil" as a result?

   c. The newspaper also noted OPEC's view "that producing nations outside the organization, like Norway and Britain, should do their share and cut production." What does the phrase "do their share" suggest about OPEC's desired relationship with Norway and Britain?

2. A large share of the world supply of diamonds comes from Russia and South Africa. Suppose that the marginal cost of mining diamonds is constant at $1000 per diamond, and the demand for diamonds is described by the following schedule:

Price	Quantity
$8000	5 000
7000	6 000
6000	7 000
5000	8 000
4000	9 000
3000	10 000
2000	11 000
1000	12 000

   a. If there were many suppliers of diamonds, what would be the price and quantity?

   b. If there was only one supplier of diamonds, what would be the price and quantity?

   c. If Russia and South Africa formed a cartel, what would be the price and quantity? If the countries split the market evenly, what would be South Africa's production and profit? What would happen to South Africa's profit if it increased its production by 1000 while Russia stuck to the cartel agreement?

   d. Use your answer to part (c) to explain why cartel agreements are often not successful.

3. This chapter discusses companies that are oligopolists in the market for the goods they sell. Many of the same ideas apply to companies that are oligopolists in the market for the inputs they buy.

   a. If sellers who are oligopolists try to increase the price of goods they sell, what is the goal of buyers who are oligopolists?

   b. National Hockey League team owners have an oligopoly in the market for hockey players. What is the owners' goal regarding players' salaries? Why is this goal difficult to achieve?

   c. Hockey players went on strike in 2004 because they would not accept the salary cap that the owners wanted to impose. If the owners were already colluding over salaries, why did the owners feel the need for a salary cap?

4. Consider trade relations between Canada and Mexico. Assume that the leaders of the two countries believe the payoffs to alternative trade policies are as follows:

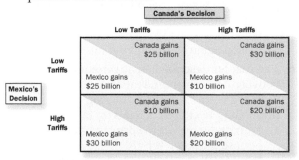

   a. What is the dominant strategy for Canada? For Mexico? Explain.

   b. Define *Nash equilibrium.* What is the Nash equilibrium for trade policy?

   c. In 1993, Parliament ratified the North American Free Trade Agreement (NAFTA), in which Canada, the United States, and Mexico agreed to reduce trade barriers simultaneously. Do the perceived payoffs shown here justify this approach to trade policy?

   d. Based on your understanding of the gains from trade (discussed in Chapters 3 and 9), do you think that these payoffs actually reflect a nation's welfare under the four possible outcomes?

5. Suppose that you and a classmate are assigned a project on which you will receive one combined grade. You each want to receive a good grade,

but you also want to do as little work as possible. The decision box and payoffs are as follows:

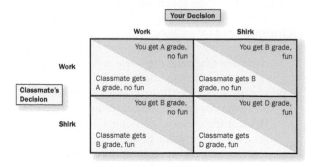

Assume that having fun is your normal state, but having no fun is as unpleasant as receiving a grade that is two letters lower.

a. Write out the decision box that combines the letter grade and the amount of fun you have into a single payoff for each outcome.

b. If neither you nor your classmate knows how much work the other person is doing, what is the likely outcome? Does it matter whether you are likely to work with this person again? Explain your answer.

6. The chapter described an advertising game between Molson and Labatt. Suppose the federal government is considering a law prohibiting beer commercials on television.

a. Would you expect the beer companies to oppose this law? Why?

b. Would you expect beer company profits to rise or fall? Why?

7. Farmer Singh and Farmer Vu graze their cattle in the same field. If there are 20 cows grazing in the field, each cow produces $4000 of milk over its lifetime. If there are more cows in the field, then each cow can eat less grass, and its milk production falls. With 30 cows in the field, each produces $3000 of milk; with 40 cows, each produces $2000 of milk. Cows cost $1000 apiece.

a. Assume that Farmer Singh and Farmer Vu can each purchase either 10 or 20 cows, but that neither knows how many the other is buying when she makes her purchase. Calculate the payoffs of each outcome.

b. What is the likely outcome of this game? What would be the best outcome? Explain.

c. There used to be more common fields than there are today. Why? (For more discussion of this topic, reread Chapter 11.)

8. Little Kona is a small coffee company that is considering entering a market dominated by Big Brew. Each company's profit depends on whether Little Kona enters and whether Big Brew sets a high price or a low price:

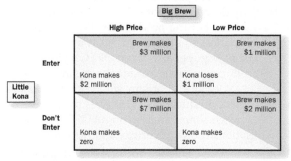

Big Brew threatens Little Kona by saying, "If you enter, we're going to set a low price, so you had better stay out." Do you think Little Kona should believe the threat? Why or why not? What do you think Little Kona should do?

9. Jeff and Steve are playing tennis. Every point comes down to whether Steve guesses correctly whether Jeff will hit the ball to Steve's left or right. The outcomes are:

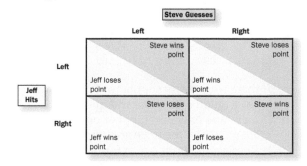

Does either player have a dominant strategy? If Jeff chooses a particular strategy (Left or Right) and sticks with it, what will Steve do? Can you think of a better strategy for Jeff to follow?

10. Let's return to the chapter's discussion of Jack and Jill's water duopoly. Suppose that Jack and Jill are at the duopoly's Nash equilibrium (total

production of 80 L) when a third person, John, discovers a water source and joins the market as a third producer.

a. Jack and Jill propose that the three of them continue to produce a total of 80 L, splitting the market three ways. If John agrees to this, how much profit will he make?

b. After agreeing to the proposed deal, John is considering increasing his production by 10 L. If he does, and Jack and Jill stick to the agreement, how much profit will John make? What does this tell you about the proposed agreement?

c. What is the Nash equilibrium for this market with three producers? How does it compare to the Nash equilibrium with two producers?

http://   For more study tools, please visit http://www.mankiw5e.nelson.com.

Chapter 17
The Algebra of Oligopoly

In this chapter we have seen that firms' profits are impacted by the strategies of other firms. The best strategy for all firms is to split the monopoly outcome and maximize joint profits. But a collusive agreement like this is hard to stick to in practice because an individual firm has incentive to cheat: if it produces more than its agreed share of the monopoly level of output, it can increase its profits. When the other firms realize there has been cheating and their profits have decreased, they will increase their output. What results is that all firms end up producing more than the monopoly outcome, receiving a lower price and earning lower profits than if they had all stuck to the collusive agreement.

Example

There are two firms (a duopoly) facing market demand of $P = 300 - 4Q$. Both firms have a constant marginal cost and average total cost equal to $60 (MC = ATC = 60).

First, suppose the market was served by a monopoly with $MR = 300 - 8Q$ and $MC = 60$.
To maximize profit, the monopoly would set MR = MC and choose P and Q:

$$300 - 8Q = 60$$
$$240 = 8Q$$
$$Q = 30$$
$$P = 300 - 4(30) = \$120$$

Monopoly profit would be $(120 - 60)*30 = \$1800$

If our two firms colluded, they would each produce 15 units of output, and split the monopoly profit for a profit of $900 each.

However, there is incentive to cheat. Suppose Firm 1 decides to cheat and produce 20 units of output. If Firm 2 continues to produce 15 units of output, there will now be 20 + 15 = 35 units in total for sale in the market. If market Q = 35, the market $P = 300 - 4(35) = \$160$.

Firm 1's profit will be $(160 - 60)*20 = \$2000$, $200 more than if it sticks to the agreement

Firm 2's profit will be $(160 - 60)*15 = \$1500$, $300 less than before Firm 1 cheated.

Of course Firm 2 will retaliate. It decides to also produce 20 units of output. Now there will be a total of 40 units of output for sale in the market. If market Q = 40, the market $P = 300 - 4(40) = \$140$.

Firm 1's profit will be (140 – 60)*20 = $1600

Firm 2's profit will be (140 – 60)*20 = $1600

Will either firm cheat again?

Suppose Firm 1 considers increasing its output to 25. The total market output would be 45 and market price would be P = 300 – 4(45) = $120. Firm 1's profit would be (120 – 60)*25 = $1500. Firm 1 has no incentive to produce more than 20 units of output; if it produces more it will see its profit decrease. Similarly, Firm 2 will not produce more than 20 units of output for the same reason. Both firms end up in a sub-optimal Nash equilibrium. Had they stuck to the agreement, each firm would have made $1800 in profit but now they will only make $1600.

Practice Problems

1.   A duopoly faces market demand given by P = 90 – Q and MR = 90 – 2Q. For each firm, MC = ATC = $30? If the two firms agree to split the monopoly outcome, what would be each firm's profit?
   a. $0
   b. $300
   c. $450
   d. $900

2.   A duopoly faces market demand given by P = 90 – Q and MR = 90 – 2Q. For each firm, MC = ATC = $30? If the one firm cheats and produces 5 more units of output than if it had split the monopoly outcome from #1 above, what would be the cheater's profit?
   a. $500
   b. $480
   c. $375
   d. $875

3.   A duopoly faces market demand given by P = 90 – Q and MR = 90 – 2Q. For each firm, MC = ATC = $30? One firm cheats and produces 5 more units of output than if it had split the monopoly outcome from #1 above. If the other firm retaliates and also adds 5 units of output to its previously agreed level of production, what will be the profit of each firm?
   a. $350
   b. $800
   c. $400
   d. $0

Answers: 1 c   2 a   3 c

17 Oligopoly

I. Chapter Overview

A. Context and Purpose

Previous chapters introduced perfect competition and monopoly. These market structures provide useful information about how markets operate, even though most real-world industries are somewhere between the two extremes.

This chapter and the one that follows introduce imperfect competition, which includes the variety of firms between the two extremes. There are two types of imperfectly competitive firms—oligopolies and monopolistic competitors. This chapter deals with oligopoly, which is the market structure with few firms, each of which has a large impact on price and industry output.

A. Helpful Hints

1. *Oligopoly is not a special case with different rules.* All firms maximize profits by producing where marginal revenue equals marginal cost. We can generalize from and extend the oligopoly model to cover most types of firms. The duopoly model with two sellers produces an outcome between competition and monopoly. However, if the two sellers cooperate to maximize their joint profits, the result is the same as the monopoly case. Similarly, as the number of firms increases, the oligopoly case begins to approach the competitive equilibrium.

2. *Game theory is the study of how people behave in strategic situations.* That is, each person or player, in deciding what action to take, must consider how others might respond to that action. In a classic game, the prisoners' dilemma, self-interest can prevent people from maintaining cooperation, even when cooperation is in their mutual interest.

3. *Policymakers use the competition laws to prevent oligopolies from engaging in behaviour that reduces competition, although the application of these laws can be controversial.* Some behaviour that may seem to infringe on competition may, in fact, have legitimate business purposes.

239

II.   Self-Testing Challenges

A.   True/False Questions

_____1.   The prisoners' dilemma shows that people do not always behave rationally.

_____2.   Forming a cartel results in output that approaches the competitive ideal.

_____3.   Most economists believe that resale price maintenance is one way to solve the free-rider problem associated with a public good.

_____4.   Oligopolists maximize profit by holding output below the point at which marginal revenue equals marginal cost.

_____5.   In a game of repeated prisoners' dilemma, the players may well be able to reach a cooperative outcome.

_____6.   Although it is not always attainable, a Nash equilibrium maximizes the well-being of the group.

_____7.   When an oligopolist sets output to maximize profit, the output effect provides an incentive to produce more.

_____8.   The price effect of an increase in production tends to increase profit.

_____9.   As the number of sellers in oligopoly grows larger, the magnitude of the output effect falls.

_____10.   Tit-for-tat strategies are essentially the biblical strategy of "an eye for an eye, a tooth for a tooth."

_____11.   An agreement among firms over production and price is called a cartel.

_____12.   A key feature of oligopoly is the tension between cooperation and self-interest.

B.   Multiple-Choice Questions

1.   Which one of the following occurs in the prisoners' dilemma strategy game?
    a.   Self-interest leads the players to a collectively inferior outcome.
    b.   Players ignore their own self-interest.
    c.   Players operate out of misguided self-interest.
    d.   The good of the many outweighs the desires of the few.

The following table shows the possible outcomes if two oil companies drill in the same spot in the Arctic. Neither company owns the drilling rights to the entire pool of petroleum, so both have an incentive to extract what is essentially a common resource. However, if both companies drill, their overall costs are higher because of the duplication of drilling equipment, but the total amount of oil available is unchanged. Use the data to answer questions 2–4.

Freezoil's decision

		Drill		Do not drill	
Coldzone Oil's decision	Drill	Freezoil	+$5 million	Freezoil	$0
		Coldzone	+$5 million	Coldzone	+$30 million
	Do not drill	Freezoil	+$30 million	Freezoil	$0
		Coldzone	$0	Coldzone	$0

2. Which of the following indicates the game's dominant strategy, if any?
   a. dominant strategy for Freezoil only
   b. dominant strategy for Coldzone Oil only
   c. dominant strategy for both Coldzone Oil and Freezoil
   d. dominant strategy for neither company

3. Which one of the following is the likely outcome of the game?
   a. drilling by either Coldzone Oil or Freezoil, but not both
   b. no drilling by either company
   c. drilling by both companies

4. Which one of the following would be the **MOST** desirable outcome for the two firms combined?
   a. drilling by either Coldzone Oil or Freezoil, but not both
   b. no drilling by either company
   c. drilling by both companies

5. Which one of the following would likely lead to cooperation and the optimal joint outcome?
   a. if both players behaved rationally
   b. if the game were played only once
   c. if the game were played repeatedly, with retaliation against non-cooperative behaviour
   d. if the players split the proceeds evenly

6.   Which one of the following is characteristic of resale price maintenance?
    a.   used by government to maintain price floors
    b.   an illegal restraint of trade by retailers acting in collusion
    c.   establishes a maximum price for resale of items in short supply
    d.   involves minimum retail prices established by manufacturers in order to prevent discounting

7.   Which one of the following best defines tying agreements?
    a.   any requirement that products not be bought or sold in any manner
    b.   used to protect customer goodwill connected with a brand name
    c.   used to diminish a firm's market power

8.   Compared with perfect competition, which of the following do oligopolists tend to do?
    a.   overproduce and overprice
    b.   underproduce and overprice
    c.   overproduce and underprice
    d.   underproduce and underprice

9.   Which one of the following is the **MAIN** reason that cartels such as OPEC tend to fail?
    a.   Self-interest drives individual players to renege on their cooperative agreements.
    b.   There are too many producers for coordination to be feasible.
    c.   The players fail to behave rationally.
    d.   Demand is inadequate, resulting in falling prices in spite of the agreement to hold back output.

10.   Some years ago, parliament banned cigarette advertising on television. Surprisingly, the cigarette companies did not fight the legislation. Which one of the following is the **MOST** likely reason for this inaction by the cigarette companies?
    a.   The companies did not have enough political clout to fight the ban successfully.
    b.   The legislation passed quickly, before the companies could mobilize opposition.
    c.   The ban allowed the companies to concentrate their advertising dollars in more effective media.
    d.   The ban helped the companies cooperate to end advertising that they could not agree to stop on their own.

11. Which one of the following is a dominant strategy?
    a. It is a strategy whereby all players comply with a collusive agreement.
    b. It is a strategy whereby each player takes the best possible action given the strategies chosen by other players.
    c. It is a strategy that is best for a player regardless of the strategies chosen by the other players.

12. Which of the following explains why game theory can help to explain why countries engage in protectionist trade policies?
    a. because when trading partners enact high tariffs, both countries end up better off
    b. because high tariffs represent a dominant strategy for both trading partners
    c. because Nash equilibrium maximizes the joint welfare of the two countries
    d. because totally free trade results in one country winning at the expense of another

13. Raising production will increase the total amount sold, which will decrease the per unit price and lower the profit on all other units sold. Which one of the following is the name of this concept?
    a. the price effect
    b. the output effect
    c. the cost effect
    d. the income effect

14. Which one of the following may make it difficult for oligopolists to collude to set price?
    a. a large number of firms
    b. a standardized product
    c. high barriers to entry
    d. licensing restrictions by government

15. Which one of the following can the prisoners' dilemma help to explain?
    a. nuclear arms races
    b. behaviour by oligopolists
    c. overutilization of natural resources
    d. confessions by criminals who were unlikely to be convicted if they kept quiet

16. Which one of the following describes when Nash equilibrium occurs?
    a. when all players comply with a collusive agreement
    b. when each player takes the best possible action given the strategies chosen by other players
    c. when a player selects the best strategy regardless of the strategies chosen by the other players

17. In a prisoners' dilemma game, which one of the following makes the attainment of a cooperative outcome more likely?
    a. Players realize that the mutual interest is served best by cooperating.
    b. The game is played repeatedly, with the threat of retaliation against those who refuse to cooperate.
    c. The game is played only once, and players know that there will be devastating retaliation if they fail to cooperate.
    d. Players realize that if they fail to cooperate, so will others.

18. Which one of the following defines predatory pricing?
    a. pricing above cost to drive competitors out of business
    b. pricing at cost to drive competitors out of business
    c. pricing below cost to drive competitors out of business

19. Which one of the following does concentration ratio measure?
    a. the number of firms in an industry
    b. the number of firms in a country
    c. the proportion of the owners that is concentrated in the four largest industries
    d. the proportion of the total output in the market supplied by the four largest firms

20. Suppose that a cartel consisting of two firms is in collusion to maximize profit. Each firm employs a tit-for-tat strategy, and the game is repeated indefinitely. Which one of the following describes when equilibrium occurs?
    a. when one firm cheats and the other adheres to the agreement
    b. when both firms adhere to the agreement
    c. when both firms produce the same amount of output
    d. when each firm produces its maximum output possible

C. Short-Answer Questions

1. Suppose that mergers in the auto industry resulted in only two surviving firms, Canadian Automotive Manufacturing and European Motor Works. Both firms are considering developing an electric automobile. Each is afraid that the other firm will develop the new automobile first, giving it a competitive edge. Even worse, the firm that fails to develop an electric automobile will lose reputation and sales in other markets as well. However, because the market is quite limited, if both companies develop an electric automobile, they will lose money. Collectively, they would be better off if neither firm develops the new technology. The table below shows the options and profits for Canadian and European.

2.

Canadian's decision

		Develop	Do not develop
European's decision	Develop	Canadian —$5 million European –$5 million	Canadian –$30 million European +$20 million
	Do not develop	Canadian +$20million European –$30million	Canadian $0 European $0

a. Is there a dominant strategy for Canadian? For European? Explain.

_____

_____

_____

_____

b. If the firms act independently out of individual self-interest, what
outcome will result? Is it in their joint interest? Explain. _____

_____

_____

_____

_____

c. If the firms cooperate, what outcome is likely? Explain. _____

_____

_____

_____

3.   What are tying agreements and what is their status under the Competition
Act? Why would sellers use them? What are the arguments for and against
tying agreements? Can you think of a product that you bought subject to a
tying agreement? _____

_____

_____

_____

_____

_____

4. Evaluate resale price maintenance or fair trade practices. What are they, and what are the arguments pro and con? _____

_____

_____

_____

_____

_____

5. Oligopolists face a conflict between self-interest and group interest. Self-interest tends to make them compete, even though cooperation would be more beneficial for the group. Which behaviour would be more in society's best interest, cooperation or competition, and how does society accomplish this goal? Explain. _____

_____

_____

_____

_____

_____

D. Practice Problems

1. The data below apply to the market for widgets, which has only two firms, Will's Widget Works and Wendell's Widget Wonderland.

The Market for Widgets						
Quantity (market)	Price (P)	Total revenue (TR) (mkt.)	Marginal revenue (MR) (mkt.)	Total revenue (TR) (firm)	Quantity (firm)	Average total cost (ATC) (firm)
1000	$500	$_____	$_____	$_____	_____	$110
1200	450	$_____	$_____	$_____	_____	$110
1400	400	$_____	$_____	$_____	_____	$110
1600	350	$_____	$_____	$_____	_____	$110
1800	300	$_____	$_____	$_____	_____	$110
2560	110	$_____	$_____	$_____	_____	$110

a. Suppose that the two widget makers divide up the market so that each firm has an equal share. Fill in the missing values in the table. If they jointly set output and price to maximize their combined profit (and they must produce in multiples of 200), how much will they each produce and at what price? How much profit will each firm realize?

b. What will be the industry output, price, and profit? How does this compare with the output, price, and profit with only one firm in the market? Explain. _____

_____

_____

_____

_____

_____

_____

_____

_____

_____

c. If Will believes that he can cheat on the agreement without Wendell knowing, would he have any incentive to change his level of output? What would happen to his total revenue and profit if he expanded output by 200 and Wendell did not respond? What if he expanded by 400? By 600? What level of output would maximize Will's profit if Wendell does not respond? Is it likely that Wendell would ignore Will's behaviour? Explain. If Wendell responds the same way, what would be the new level of output and the resulting price for both firms combined? _____

_____

_____

_____

_____

_____

_____

d. Does your answer to (b) help to explain the long-term prospects for survival of cartels? What is likely to happen to such agreements in the long run and why? Would the agreement be more likely to survive if the game were run repeatedly with cheating consistently subject to retaliation and cooperation rewarded by the other player? _____

_____

_____

_____

_____

_____

_____

e. Given that the average total cost is constant at $110, what is the marginal cost of each additional widget? What would happen to output and price if the number of firms continued to expand until there were many competitors? _____

_____

_____

_____

_____

_____

2. Two firms at the city's International Airport have licences to carry passengers downtown. These two firms, Airport Limo and Airport Taxi, cannot compete with price, but can compete through advertising. The table below shows the options and profits for these two companies.

Airport limo

		Advertise		Do not Advertise	
Airport	Advertise	Limo	$30	Limo	$0
		Taxi	$50	Taxi	$60
Taxi	Do not advertise	Limo	$40	Limo	$10
		Taxi	$30	Taxi	$80

a. Does each company have a dominant strategy and if so, what is it?

b. Is there a Nash equilibrium?

E. Advanced Critical Thinking

Some economists have argued that competition policy has done more harm than good. They believe that monopoly power is more likely to be created than cured by government action, and that competition laws are often aimed toward protecting competitors rather than competition. They believe that the market provides the best protection against inappropriate restraint of trade. Do you agree? Write a short essay in which you give the arguments for and against competition laws. Be specific, including, at a minimum, discussion of resale price maintenance, tying agreements, and price fixing. _____

_____

_____

_____

_____

_____

_____

_____

_____

III.   Solutions

A.   True/False Questions

1.   F; the prisoners' dilemma shows that rational self-interest may not always maximize joint interest.
2.   F; forming a cartel results in monopoly output.
3.   T
4.   F; oligopolists maximize profit by setting output where marginal revenue equals marginal cost.
5.   T
6.   F; a Nash equilibrium often fails to maximize the group's interests.
7.   T
8.   F; the price effect decreases profit.
9.   F; as oligopoly grows in size, the magnitude of price effect falls.
10.   T
11.   F; it is called collusion. A cartel is a group of firms acting in unison.
12.   T

B.   Multiple-Choice Questions

1. a	5. c	9. a	13. a	17. b
2. c	6. d	10. d	14. a	18. c
3. c	7. b	11. c	15. a	19. d
4. a	8. b	12. b	16. b	

C.   Short-Answer Questions

1.   a.   Yes, both firms have "develop" as a dominant strategy because, whatever choice the competition makes, developing the electric automobile makes the firm better off. For example, if Canadian decides not to develop, then European can gain $20 million by developing, but nothing for not developing. If Canadian decides to develop, then European loses either way, but the loss is less ($5 million vs. $30 million) if European develops.

b.   Both firms will develop electric autos because this is a dominant strategy that maximizes each firm's individual gain regardless of the other's choice. It is not in their joint interest, however, because both firms lose $5 million, which they could have avoided if neither developed an electric car.

c.   As explained in (b), both firms could cooperate and agree not to produce an electric automobile, resulting in neither a gain nor a loss. This outcome is their best collective choice.

2.   Tying agreements are business practices under which sellers bundle two products for sale so that buyers are forced to purchase both if they want either one. This practice has been banned under the civil provisions of the Competition Act, because it can be used as a form of price discrimination, making it easier for sellers to capture part of consumer surplus without charging separate prices to different buyers. Manufacturers can also protect against inferior accessories or replacement parts by tying lease agreements to the purchase of original equipment supplies and parts. Although they do restrict consumers' options, they also protect the seller. A good example is the operating system that is bundled with new personal computers—nearly all new PC-platform machines come with Microsoft software.

3.   Resale price maintenance practices allow the manufacturer to set a minimum retail price for the product. Critics argue that they prevent competition and subsidize inefficient, high-cost retailers at the expense of big discount stores. Supporters argue that discounters get a free ride when full-service stores offer product information and advice that the discounters do not offer. Customers get advice from the full-service stores, then buy from a discounter. Also, some manufacturers prefer to avoid having their brand name associated with a discount image.

4.   Competition is better for society because it leads to price and output that are closer to the competitive ideal. Competition laws are used to limit cooperation by oligopolists in setting price and other production and sales decisions.

D. Practice Problems

1.   The data below apply to the market for widgets, which has only two firms, Will's Widget Works and Wendell's Widget Wonderland.

The Market for Widgets

Quantity (market)	Price (P)	Total revenue (TR) (mkt.)	Marginal revenue (MR) (mkt.)	Total revenue (TR) (firm)	Quantity (firm)	Average total cost (ATC) (firm)
1000	$500	$500 000	—	$250 000	$500	$110
1200	$450	$540 000	$200	$270 000	$600	$110
1400	$400	$560 000	$100	$280 000	$700	$110
1600	$350	$560 000	$0	$280 000	$800	$110
1800	$300	$540 000	–$100	$270 000	$900	$110
2560	$110	$281 600	—	—	—	$110

628

a. If the firms cooperate to maximize joint profit, they will jointly produce the monopoly output and charge the monopoly price (and earn monopoly profit). They will produce as long as marginal revenue exceeds marginal cost for the industry. Output will be 600 each at a price of $450. Each firm will earn a profit of $204 000. Industry output will be 1200 at a price of $450. Industry profit will be $408 000.

b. Will would earn a greater profit if he could increase output while Wendell continues to produce 600. If he expanded output by 200, his total output would be 800 and industry output would be 1400 at a price of $400. His revenue would be $320 000 (800 × $400), and his total cost would be $88 000 (800 × $110), for a profit of $232 000. If Will increased output to 1000, his profit would be $240 000 (1000 × $350 less 1000 × $110). However, if he increased output to 1200, his profit would fall to $228 000 (1200 × 300 less 1200 × $110). Therefore, Will would maximize profit at output = 1000. However, Wendell is likely to do the same thing, resulting in combined output of 2000 at a price of $250. Combined profit would fall to $280 000 (2000 × $250 less 2000 × $110).

c. Yes, the answer demonstrates the strong incentive for firms to cheat on their agreements to limit output. Each firm finds it profitable to increase output beyond the agreed-upon amount. If the game is repeated and there is the possibility of rewards for cooperation and penalties for cheating, there is a higher chance that the agreement will be honoured.

d. If average total cost is constant at $110, then marginal cost must also be $110. With many competitors, there would be no price effect, and marginal revenue would be the same as price. Output would expand until price equals marginal cost. This occurs at an output of 2560 and a price of $110.

2. a. Airport Taxi does not have a dominant strategy. If Airport Limo advertises, then Taxi does best by advertising, but if Limo does not advertise, then Taxi should not advertise. Airport Limo, on the other hand, has a dominant strategy, and it should advertise.

    b. The Nash equilibrium is for both companies to advertise. Each company does best by advertising, given what the other firm does.

E.   Advanced Critical Thinking

It is true that results under competition policy have been mixed. Some policies have actually restrained competition: for example, resale price maintenance laws that permit the manufacturer to set a minimum retail price. However, without such laws, full-service retailers would be at a disadvantage relative to discount stores that may "free ride" on the full-service stores as providers of production information and service. Similarly, tying agreements can restrict voluntary exchange, but manufacturers may need to protect their reputations by controlling the quality of supplies and accessories used along with their products. Also criticized are restrictions against predatory pricing— selling below cost just long enough to drive competitors out of business, then raising price even higher than before. Critics argue that potential competitors are available to undercut the predatory firm as soon as price rises. Perhaps the strongest case can be made for restrictions on collusion to fix prices.

© TedNad/iStockphoto.com

6

THE ECONOMICS OF
LABOUR MARKETS

THE MARKETS FOR THE FACTORS OF PRODUCTION

18

Learning Objectives

In this chapter, you will ...

* Analyze the labour demand of competitive, profit-maximizing firms

* Consider the household decisions that lie behind labour supply

* Learn why equilibrium wages equal the value of the marginal product of labour

* Consider how the other factors of production—land and capital—are compensated

* Examine how a change in the supply of one factor alters the earnings of all the factors

When you finish school, your income will be determined largely by the kind of job you take. If you become a computer programmer, you will earn more than if you become a gas station attendant. This fact is not surprising, but it is not obvious why it is true. No law requires that computer programmers be paid more than gas station attendants. No ethical principle says that programmers are more deserving. What then determines which job will pay you the higher wage?

Your income, of course, is a small piece of a larger economic picture. In 2009, the total income of all Canadian residents was about $1.1 trillion. People earned this income in various ways. Workers earned about three-fourths of it in the form of wages and fringe benefits. The rest went to landowners and to the owners of *capital*—the economy's stock of equipment and structures—in the form of rent, profit, and interest. What determines how much goes to workers? To landowners? To the owners of capital? Why do some workers earn higher wages than others, some landowners higher rental income than others, and some capital owners greater profit than others? Why, in particular, do computer programmers earn more than gas station attendants?

The answers to these questions, like most in economics, hinge on supply and demand. The supply and demand for labour, land, and capital determine the prices paid to workers, landowners, and capital owners. To understand why some people have higher incomes than others, therefore, we need to look more deeply at the markets for the services they provide. That is our job in this and the next two chapters.

factors of production
the inputs used to produce goods and services

This chapter provides the basic theory for the analysis of factor markets. As you may recall from Chapter 2, the **factors of production** are the inputs used to produce goods and services. Labour, land, and capital are the three most important factors of production. When a computer firm produces a new software program, it uses programmers' time (labour), the physical space on which its offices sit (land), and an office building and computer equipment (capital). Similarly, when a gas station sells gas, it uses attendants' time (labour), the physical space (land), and the gas tanks and pumps (capital).

Although in many ways factor markets resemble the goods markets we have analyzed in previous chapters, they are different in one important way: The demand for a factor of production is a *derived demand*. That is, a firm's demand for a factor of production is derived from its decision to supply a good in another market. The demand for computer programmers is inextricably tied to the supply of computer software, and the demand for gas station attendants is inextricably tied to the supply of gasoline.

In this chapter we analyze factor demand by considering how a competitive, profit-maximizing firm decides how much of any factor to buy. We begin our analysis by examining the demand for labour. Labour is the most important factor of production, for workers receive most of the total income earned in the Canadian economy. Later in the chapter, we see that the lessons we learn about the labour market apply directly to the markets for the other factors of production.

The basic theory of factor markets developed in this chapter takes a large step toward explaining how the income of the Canadian economy is distributed among workers, landowners, and owners of capital. Chapter 19 will build on this analysis to examine in more detail why some workers earn more than others. Chapter 20 will examine how much inequality results from this process and then consider what role the government should and does play in altering the distribution of income.

THE DEMAND FOR LABOUR

Labour markets, like other markets in the economy, are governed by the forces of supply and demand. This is illustrated in Figure 18.1. In panel (a) the supply and demand for apples determine the price of apples. In panel (b) the supply and demand for apple pickers determine the price, or wage, of apple pickers.

As we have already noted, labour markets are different from most other markets because labour demand is a derived demand. Most labour services, rather than being final goods ready to be enjoyed by consumers, are inputs into the production of other goods. To understand labour demand, we need to focus on the firms that hire the labour and use it to produce goods for sale. By examining the link between the production of goods and the demand for labour, we gain insight into the determination of equilibrium wages.

The Competitive, Profit-Maximizing Firm

Let's look at how a typical firm, such as an apple producer, decides the quantity of labour to demand. The firm owns an apple orchard and each week must decide how many apple pickers to hire to harvest its crop. After the firm makes its hiring

FIGURE 18.1

The Versatility of Supply and Demand

The basic tools of supply and demand apply to goods and to labour services. Panel (a) shows how the supply and demand for apples determine the price of apples. Panel (b) shows how the supply and demand for apple pickers determine the wage of apple pickers.

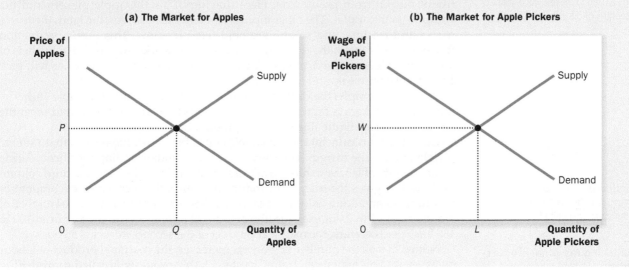

decision, the workers pick as many apples as they can. The firm then sells the apples, pays the workers, and keeps what is left as profit.

We make two assumptions about our firm. First, we assume that our firm is *competitive* both in the market for apples (where the firm is a seller) and in the market for apple pickers (where the firm is a buyer). A competitive firm is a price taker. Because there are many other firms selling apples and hiring apple pickers, a single firm has little influence over the price it gets for apples or the wage it pays apple pickers. The firm takes the price and the wage as given by market conditions. It has to decide only how many workers to hire and how many apples to sell.

Second, we assume that the firm is *profit-maximizing*. Thus, the firm does not directly care about the number of workers it has or the number of apples it produces. It cares only about profit, which equals the total revenue from the sale of apples minus the total cost of producing them. The firm's supply of apples and its demand for workers are derived from its primary goal of maximizing profit.

The Production Function and the Marginal Product of Labour

To make its hiring decision, the firm must consider how the size of its work force affects the amount of output produced. In other words, it must consider how the number of apple pickers affects the quantity of apples it can harvest and sell.

production function
the relationship between the quantity of inputs used to make a good and the quantity of output of that good

Table 18.1 gives a numerical example. In the first column is the number of workers. In the second column is the quantity of apples the workers harvest each week.

These two columns of numbers describe the firm's ability to produce. As we noted in Chapter 13, economists use the term **production function** to describe the relationship between the quantity of the inputs used in production and the quantity of output from production. Here the "input" is the apple pickers and the "output" is the apples. The other inputs—the trees themselves, the land, the firm's trucks and tractors, and so on—are held fixed for now. This firm's production function shows that if the firm hires 1 worker, that worker will pick 100 bushels of apples per week. If the firm hires 2 workers, the two workers together will pick 180 bushels per week, and so on.

Figure 18.2 graphs the data on labour and output presented in Table 18.1. The number of workers is on the horizontal axis, and the amount of output is on the vertical axis. This figure illustrates the production function.

One of the ten principles of economics introduced in Chapter 1 is that rational people think at the margin. This idea is the key to understanding how firms decide what quantity of labour to hire. To take a step toward this decision, the third column in Table 18.1 gives the **marginal product of labour**, the increase in the amount of output from an additional unit of labour. When the firm increases the number of workers from 1 to 2, for example, the amount of apples produced rises from 100 to 180 bushels. Therefore, the marginal product of the second worker is 80 bushels.

marginal product of labour
the increase in the amount of output from an additional unit of labour

Notice that as the number of workers increases, the marginal product of labour declines. As you may recall from Chapter 13, this property is called **diminishing marginal product.** At first, when only a few workers are hired, they can pick the low-hanging fruit. As the number of workers increases, additional workers have

diminishing marginal product
the property whereby the marginal product of an input declines as the quantity of the input increases

TABLE 18.1

How the Competitive Firm Decides How Much Labour to Hire

Labour	Output	Marginal Product of Labour	Value of the Marginal Product of Labour	Wage	Marginal Profit
L (number of workers)	Q (bushels per week)	$MPL = \Delta Q/\Delta L$ (bushels per week)	$VMPL = P \times MPL$	W	$\Delta Profit = VMPL - W$
0	0				
		100	$1000	$500	$500
1	100				
		80	800	500	300
2	180				
		60	600	500	100
3	240				
		40	400	500	−100
4	280				
		20	200	500	−300
5	300				

FIGURE 18.2

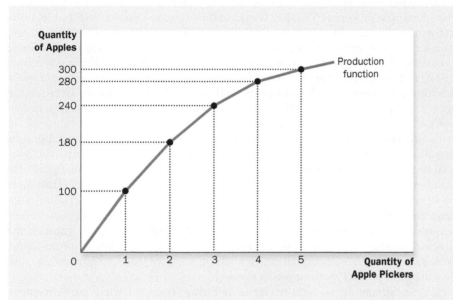

The Production Function

The production function is the relationship between the inputs into production (apple pickers) and the output from production (apples). As the quantity of the input increases, the production function gets flatter, reflecting the property of diminishing marginal product.

to climb higher up the ladders to find apples to pick. Hence, as more and more workers are hired, each additional worker contributes less to the production of apples. For this reason, the production function in Figure 18.2 becomes flatter as the number of workers rises.

The Value of the Marginal Product and the Demand for Labour

Our profit-maximizing firm is concerned more with money than with apples. As a result, when deciding how many workers to hire to pick apples, the firm considers how much profit each worker would bring in. Because profit is total revenue minus total cost, the profit from an additional worker is the worker's contribution to revenue minus the worker's wage.

To find the worker's contribution to revenue, we must convert the marginal product of labour (which is measured in bushels of apples) into the *value* of the marginal product (which is measured in dollars). We do this using the price of apples. To continue our example, if a bushel of apples sells for $10 and if an additional worker produces 80 bushels of apples, then the worker produces $800 of revenue.

The **value of the marginal product** of any input is the marginal product of that input multiplied by the market price of the output. The fourth column in Table 18.1 shows the value of the marginal product of labour in our example, assuming the price of apples is $10 per bushel. Because the market price is constant for a competitive firm, the value of the marginal product (like the marginal product itself) diminishes as the number of workers rises. Economists sometimes call this column of numbers the firm's *marginal revenue product:* It is the extra revenue the firm gets from hiring an additional unit of a factor of production.

value of the marginal product
the marginal product of an input times the price of the output

Now consider how many workers the firm will hire. Suppose that the market wage for apple pickers is $500 per week. In this case, as you see in Table 18.1, the first worker that the firm hires is profitable: The first worker yields $1000 in revenue, or $500 in profit. Similarly, the second worker yields $800 in additional revenue, or $300 in profit. The third worker produces $600 in additional revenue, or $100 in profit. After the third worker, however, hiring workers is unprofitable. The fourth worker would yield only $400 of additional revenue. Because the worker's wage is $500, hiring the fourth worker would mean a $100 reduction in profit. Thus, the firm hires only three workers.

It is instructive to consider the firm's decision graphically. Figure 18.3 graphs the value of the marginal product. This curve slopes downward because the marginal product of labour diminishes as the number of workers rises. The figure also includes a horizontal line at the market wage. To maximize profit, the firm hires workers up to the point where these two curves cross. Below this level of employment, the value of the marginal product exceeds the wage, so hiring another worker would increase profit. Above this level of employment, the value of the marginal product is less than the wage, so the marginal worker is unprofitable. Thus, *a competitive, profit-maximizing firm hires workers up to the point where the value of the marginal product of labour equals the wage.*

Having explained the profit-maximizing hiring strategy for a competitive firm, we can now offer a theory of labour demand. Recall that a firm's labour demand curve tells us the quantity of labour that a firm demands at any given wage. We have just seen in Figure 18.3 that the firm makes that decision by choosing the quantity of labour at which the value of the marginal product equals the wage. As a result, *the value-of-marginal-product curve is the labour demand curve for a competitive, profit-maximizing firm.*

FIGURE 18.3

The Value of the Marginal Product of Labour

This figure shows how the value of the marginal product (the marginal product times the price of the output) depends on the number of workers. The curve slopes downward because of diminishing marginal product. For a competitive, profit-maximizing firm, this value-of-marginal-product curve is also the firm's labour demand curve.

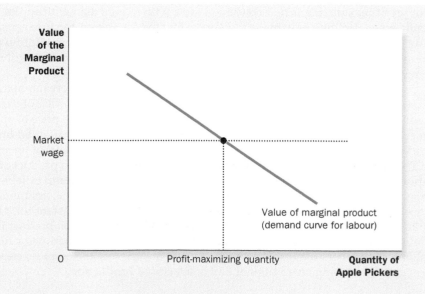

INPUT DEMAND AND OUTPUT SUPPLY: TWO SIDES OF THE SAME COIN

In Chapter 14 we saw how a competitive, profit-maximizing firm decides how much of its output to sell: It chooses the quantity of output at which the price of the good equals the marginal cost of production. We have just seen how such a firm decides how much labour to hire: It chooses the quantity of labour at which the wage equals the value of the marginal product. Because the production function links the quantity of inputs to the quantity of output, you should not be surprised to learn that the firm's decision about input demand is closely linked to its decision about output supply. In fact, these two decisions are two sides of the same coin.

To see this relationship more fully, let's consider how the marginal product of labour (MPL) and marginal cost (MC) are related. Suppose an additional worker costs $500 and has a marginal product of 50 bushels of apples. In this case, producing 50 more bushels costs $500; the marginal cost of a bushel is $500/50, or $10. More generally, if W is the wage, and an extra unit of labour produces MPL units of output, then the marginal cost of a unit of output is $MC = W/MPL$.

This analysis shows that diminishing marginal product is closely related to increasing marginal cost. When our apple orchard becomes crowded with workers, each additional worker adds less to the production of apples (MPL falls). Similarly, when the apple firm is producing a large quantity of apples, the orchard is already crowded with workers, so it is more costly to produce an additional bushel of apples (MC rises).

Now consider our criterion for profit maximization. We determined earlier that a profit-maximizing firm chooses the quantity of labour so that the value of the marginal product ($P \times MPL$) equals the wage (W). We can write this mathematically as

$$P \times MPL = W$$

If we divide both sides of this equation by MPL, we obtain

$$P = W/MPL$$

We just noted that W/MPL equals marginal cost MC. Therefore, we can substitute to obtain

$$P = MC$$

This equation states that the price of the firm's output is equal to the marginal cost of producing a unit of output. *Thus, when a competitive firm hires labour up to the point at which the value of the marginal product equals the wage, it also produces up to the point at which the price equals marginal cost.* Our analysis of labour demand in this chapter is just another way of looking at the production decision we first saw in Chapter 14.

What Causes the Labour Demand Curve to Shift?

We now understand the labour demand curve: It reflects the value of the marginal product of labour. With this insight in mind, let's consider a few of the things that might cause the labour demand curve to shift.

The Output Price   The value of the marginal product is marginal product times the price of the firm's output. Thus, when the output price changes, the value of the marginal product changes, and the labour demand curve shifts. An increase in the price of apples, for instance, raises the value of the marginal product of each worker who picks apples and, therefore, increases labour demand from the firms that supply apples. Conversely, a decrease in the price of apples reduces the value of the marginal product and decreases labour demand.

Technological Change   Between 1976 and 2000, the amount of output a typical Canadian worker produced in an hour rose by 27 percent. Why? The most important reason is technological progress: Scientists and engineers are constantly figuring out new and better ways of doing things. This has profound implications for the labour market. Technological advance typically raises the marginal product of labour, which in turn increases the demand for labour, which in turn shifts the labour demand curve to the right.

It is also possible for technological change to reduce labour demand. The invention of a cheap industrial robot, for instance, could conceivably reduce the marginal product of labour, shifting the labour demand curve to the left. Economists call this *labour-saving* "technological change." History suggests, however, that most technological progress is instead *labour-augmenting*. Such technological advance explains persistently rising employment in the face of rising wages: Even though wages (adjusted for inflation) increased by over 100 percent during the last four decades of the twentieth century, firms nonetheless increased by over 50 percent the amount of labour they employed.

The Supply of Other Factors   The quantity available of one factor of production can affect the marginal product of other factors. A fall in the supply of ladders, for instance, will reduce the marginal product of apple pickers and thus the demand for apple pickers. We consider this linkage among the factors of production more fully later in the chapter.

QuickQuiz Define *marginal product of labour* and *value of the marginal product of labour.* • Describe how a competitive, profit-maximizing firm decides how many workers to hire.

THE SUPPLY OF LABOUR

Having analyzed labour demand in detail, let's turn to the other side of the market and consider labour supply. A formal model of labour supply is included in Chapter 21, where we develop the theory of household decision making. Here we discuss briefly and informally the decisions that lie behind the labour supply curve.

The Tradeoff between Work and Leisure

One of the ten principles of economics in Chapter 1 is that people face tradeoffs. Probably no tradeoff is more obvious or more important in a person's life than the tradeoff between work and leisure. The more hours you spend working, the fewer hours you have to watch TV, enjoy dinner with friends, or pursue your favourite hobby. The tradeoff between labour and leisure lies behind the labour supply curve.

Another of the ten principles of economics is that the cost of something is what you give up to get it. What do you give up to get an hour of leisure? You give up an hour of work, which in turn means an hour of wages. Thus, if your wage is $15 per hour, the opportunity cost of an hour of leisure is $15. And when you get a raise to $20 per hour, the opportunity cost of enjoying leisure goes up.

The labour supply curve reflects how workers' decisions about the labour–leisure tradeoff respond to a change in that opportunity cost. An upward-sloping labour supply curve means that an increase in the wage induces workers to increase the quantity of labour they supply. Because time is limited, more hours of work means that workers are enjoying less leisure. That is, workers respond to the increase in the opportunity cost of leisure by taking less of it.

It is worth noting that the labour supply curve need not be upward sloping. Imagine you got that raise from $15 to $20 per hour. The opportunity cost of leisure is now greater, but you are also richer than you were before. You might decide that with your extra wealth you can now afford to enjoy more leisure. That is, at the higher wage, you might choose to work fewer hours. If so, your labour supply curve would slope backward. In Chapter 21, we discuss this possibility in terms of conflicting effects on your labour supply decision (called *the income and substitution effects*). For now, we ignore the possibility of backward-sloping labour supply and assume that the labour supply curve is upward sloping.

What Causes the Labour Supply Curve to Shift?

The labour supply curve shifts whenever people change the amount they want to work at a given wage. Let's now consider some of the events that might cause such a shift.

Changes in Tastes   In 1950, 34 percent of women were employed at paid jobs or looking for work. In 2000, the number had risen to 60 percent. There are, of course, many explanations for this development, but one of them is changing attitudes toward work. A generation or two ago, it was the norm for women to stay at home while raising children. Today, family sizes are smaller, and more mothers choose to work. The result is an increase in the supply of labour.

Changes in Alternative Opportunities   The supply of labour in any one labour market depends on the opportunities available in other labour markets. If the wage earned by pear pickers suddenly rises, some apple pickers may choose to switch occupations. The supply of labour in the market for apple pickers falls.

Immigration   Movement of workers from region to region, or country to country, is an obvious and often important source of shifts in labour supply. When immigrants come to Canada, for instance, the supply of labour in Canada increases and the supply of labour in the immigrants' home countries contracts. In fact, much of the policy debate about immigration centres on its effect on labour supply and, thereby, equilibrium in the labour market.

QuickQuiz Who has a greater opportunity cost of enjoying leisure—a janitor or a brain surgeon? Explain. Can this help explain why doctors work such long hours?

EQUILIBRIUM IN THE LABOUR MARKET

So far we have established two facts about how wages are determined in competitive labour markets:

1. The wage adjusts to balance the supply and demand for labour.
2. The wage equals the value of the marginal product of labour.

At first, it might seem surprising that the wage can do both these things at once. In fact, there is no real puzzle here, but understanding why there is no puzzle is an important step to understanding wage determination.

Figure 18.4 shows the labour market in equilibrium. The wage and the quantity of labour have adjusted to balance supply and demand. When the market is in this equilibrium, each firm has bought as much labour as it finds profitable at the equilibrium wage. That is, each firm has followed the rule for profit maximization: It has hired workers until the value of the marginal product equals the wage. Hence, the wage must equal the value of the marginal product of labour once it has brought supply and demand into equilibrium.

This brings us to an important lesson: *Any event that changes the supply or demand for labour must change the equilibrium wage and the value of the marginal product by the same amount, because these must always be equal.* To see how this works, let's consider some events that shift these curves.

Shifts in Labour Supply

Suppose that immigration increases the number of workers willing to pick apples. As Figure 18.5 shows, the supply of labour shifts to the right from S_1 to

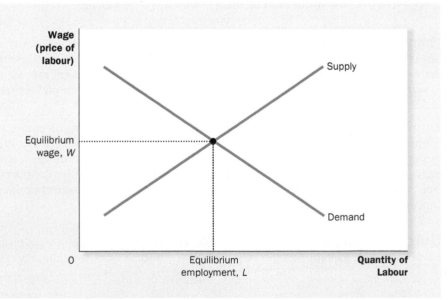

FIGURE 18.4

Equilibrium in a Labour Market

Like all prices, the price of labour (the wage) depends on supply and demand. Because the demand curve reflects the value of the marginal product of labour, in equilibrium, workers receive the value of their marginal contribution to the production of goods and services.

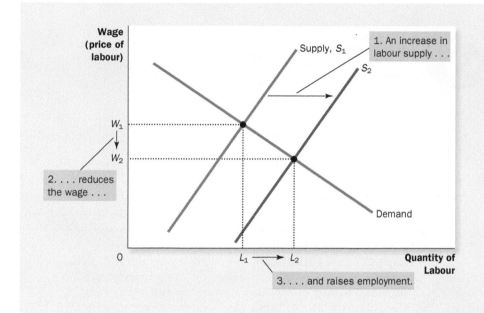

FIGURE 18.5

A Shift in Labour Supply

When labour supply increases from S_1 to S_2, perhaps because of an immigration of new workers, the equilibrium wage falls from W_1 to W_2. At this lower wage, firms hire more labour, so employment rises from L_1 to L_2. The change in the wage reflects a change in the value of the marginal product of labour: With more workers, the added output from an extra worker is smaller.

S_2. At the initial wage W_1, the quantity of labour supplied now exceeds the quantity demanded. This surplus of labour puts downward pressure on the wage of apple pickers, and the fall in the wage from W_1 to W_2 in turn makes it profitable for firms to hire more workers. As the number of workers employed in each apple orchard rises, the marginal product of a worker falls, and so does the value of the marginal product. In the new equilibrium, both the wage and the value of the marginal product of labour are lower than they were before the influx of new workers.

An episode in Israel illustrates how a shift in labour supply can alter the equilibrium in a labour market. During most of the 1980s, many thousands of Palestinians regularly commuted from their homes in the Israeli-occupied West Bank and Gaza Strip to jobs in Israel, primarily in the construction and agriculture industries. In 1988, however, political unrest in these occupied areas induced the Israeli government to take steps that, as a byproduct, reduced this supply of workers. Curfews were imposed, work permits were checked more thoroughly, and a ban on overnight stays of Palestinians in Israel was enforced more rigorously. The economic impact of these steps was exactly as theory predicts: The number of Palestinians with jobs in Israel fell by half, while those who continued to work in Israel enjoyed wage increases of about 50 percent. With a reduced number of Palestinian workers in Israel, the value of the marginal product of the remaining workers was much higher.

Shifts in Labour Demand

Now suppose that an increase in the popularity of apples causes their price to rise. This price increase does not change the marginal product of labour for any given

IN THE NEWS

IMMIGRATION AND GROWTH

Immigrants make up a growing part of Canada's population, which has important implications for labour markets.

Immigrants Account for Our Growth: Trend Will Continue

By Joseph Brean

Until this census, and ever since the mid-1990s, the journalistic shorthand for how much of Canada's population growth was due to immigration was "more than half."

As of today, it is "almost two-thirds."

"Never before happened," said Dan Hiebert, a professor of geography at the University of British Columbia, who studies the immigrant experience of labour and housing markets.

Stats Can will not give the exact number until their December immigration report, but yesterday's census numbers show Canada's population growth rate of 5.4%—the highest of any G8 nation—is "almost two-thirds" due to immigration.

"That ratio will continue to grow, and within about 25 years, it will grow to 100%," said Prof. Hiebert.

This is a trend that continues to distinguish Canada from the United States, where 60% of growth is "natural increase."

Canada plans to admit between 240,000 and 265,000 immigrants in 2007. Of those, about 60% are to be economic class, meaning skilled workers, 25% family class, and 15% protected persons.

Prof. Hiebert said there is a "very high propensity" for these immigrants to settle in "the big three and a half" of Toronto, Montreal, Vancouver, and sort of Calgary, which explains why four out of five immigrants settle in urban areas, and roughly 90% of the national growth was in cities, according to the census.

"The population growth in Alberta has more of a dimension of the shifting around of the Canadian population than it does to immigration," Prof. Hiebert said.

Of the 1.2-million international immigrants over the five-year census period, fully half went to Ontario.

Roughly 44% of immigrants to Canada are female, a proportion that has been increasing by about one percentage point a year. The 10 largest source countries are, in order: China, India, Philippines, Pakistan, United States, Colombia, United Kingdom, South Korea, Iran and France.

In Quebec, which regulates its own immigration, the population grew three times as fast in this census period as in the previous, which is partly due to increased immigration, but also to smaller net losses to other provinces.

Gord Steeves, acting president of the Federation of Canadian Municipalities and a Winnipeg city councillor, said cities are increasingly overwhelmed by the new responsibilities posed by immigrants. He said cities are finding that people from opposite sides of foreign ethnic and national conflicts—once Eastern European, now increasingly African—are finding themselves living side-by-side in Canadian cities, with inevitable problems of integration.

"We're having to resolve those issues at a community level in Winnipeg," he said. "We deal with any problems through our police service, which, you know, is trying to fit a square peg into a round hole."

Don Devoretz, a professor of economics at Simon Fraser University in B.C. and co-director with Prof. Hiebert of Vancouver's Centre of Excellence for the study of immigration, said it is possible to examine whether, over their lifetime, immigrants put more money into Canada than they take from it, and the answer is yes.

"Although we're not sure the present group will do that, every predecessor group has," he said.

He rejects what he calls the "UN argument, that you need immigrants because you don't have enough people," and says the Canadian immigration system is vulnerable to a sort of abuse from people who come and leave as soon as they can, leaving behind in some cases what he calls "citizenship restaurants."

This has created a "growing diaspora" of Canadians around the globe, with long-term effects that are hard to predict, as the recent evacuation of war-ravaged Lebanon proved.

Herbert Grubel, professor emeritus of economics at Simon Fraser University

number of workers, but it does raise the *value* of the marginal product. With a higher price of apples, hiring more apple pickers is now profitable. As Figure 18.6 shows, when the demand for labour shifts to the right from D_1 to D_2, the equilibrium wage rises from W_1 to W_2, and equilibrium employment rises from L_1 to L_2. Once again, the wage and the value of the marginal product of labour move together.

This analysis shows that prosperity for firms in an industry is often linked to prosperity for workers in that industry. When the price of apples rises, apple producers make greater profit, and apple pickers earn higher wages. When the price of apples falls, apple producers earn smaller profit, and apple pickers earn lower wages. This lesson is well known to workers in industries with highly volatile

FIGURE 18.6

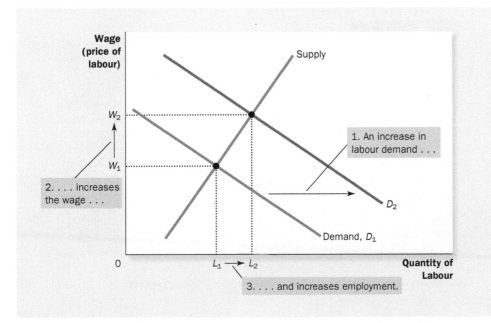

A Shift in Labour Demand

When labour demand increases from D_1 to D_2, perhaps because of an increase in the price of the firms' output, the equilibrium wage rises from W_1 to W_2, and employment rises from L_1 to L_2. Again, the change in the wage reflects a change in the value of the marginal product of labour: With a higher output price, the added output from an extra worker is more valuable.

prices. Workers in oil fields, for instance, know from experience that their earnings are closely linked to the world price of crude oil.

From these examples, you should now have a good understanding of how wages are set in competitive labour markets. Labour supply and labour demand together determine the equilibrium wage, and shifts in the supply or demand curve for labour cause the equilibrium wage to change. At the same time, profit maximization by the firms that demand labour ensures that the equilibrium wage always equals the value of the marginal product of labour.

Case Study
PRODUCTIVITY AND WAGES

One of the ten principles of economics in Chapter 1 is that our standard of living depends on our ability to produce goods and services. We can now see how this principle works in the market for labour. In particular, our analysis of labour demand shows that wages equal productivity as measured by the value of the marginal product of labour. Put simply, highly productive workers are highly paid, and less productive workers are less highly paid.

This lesson is key to understanding why workers today are better off than workers in previous generations. Table 18.2 presents some data on growth in productivity and growth in real wages in Canada (that is, wages adjusted for inflation). From 1961 to 2007, productivity as measured by output per hour of

TABLE 18.2

Productivity and Wage Growth in Canada

Time Period	Growth Rate of Productivity	Growth Rate of Real Wages
1961–2007	1.73%	1.67%
1961–1973	3.00	3.87
1973–1981	1.29	1.38
1981–1989	1.15	0.28
1989–2000	1.54	0.79
2000–2007	1.03	1.24

Note: Sub-periods are chosen to be cyclically neutral (peak to peak). Real wages and labour share are calculated with the labour compensation series from the Canadian Productivity Accounts.

Source: Reprinted by permission of the Centre for the Study of Living Standards.

MONOPSONY

On the preceding pages, we built our analysis of the labour market with the tools of supply and demand. In doing so, we assumed that the labour market was competitive. That is, we assumed that there were many buyers of labour and many sellers of labour, so each buyer or seller had a negligible effect on the wage.

Yet imagine the labour market in a small town dominated by a single large employer. That employer can exert a large influence on the going wage, and it may well use that market power to alter the outcome. Such a market in which there is a single buyer is called a *monopsony*.

A monopsony is in many ways similar to a monopoly (a market with one seller). Recall from Chapter 15 that a monopoly firm produces less of the good than would a competitive firm; by reducing the quantity offered for sale, the monopoly firm moves along the product's demand curve, raising the price and also its profits. Similarly, a monopsony firm in a labour market hires fewer workers than would a competitive firm; by reducing the number of jobs available, the monopsony firm moves along the labour supply curve, reducing the wage it pays and raising its profits. Thus, both monopolists and monopsonists reduce economic activity in a market below the socially optimal level. In both cases, the existence of market power distorts the outcome and causes deadweight losses.

This book does not present the formal model of monopsony because, in the real world, monopsonies are rare. In most labour markets, workers have many possible employers, and firms compete with one another to attract workers. In this case, the model of supply and demand is the best one to use.

work grew 1.73 percent per year. Real wages grew at 1.67 percent—almost exactly the same rate, just as standard theory predicts. With a growth rate of 1.7 percent per year, productivity and real wages double about every 40 years.

Productivity growth varies over time. Table 18.2 also shows the data for several shorter periods that economists have identified as having very different productivity experiences. Around 1973, the Canadian economy experienced a significant slowdown in productivity growth that has lasted, to varying degrees, up to today. The cause of this productivity slowdown is not well understood. Moreover, it is evident that during this period of declining productivity, the link between productivity and real wages was broken. From 1981 to 2000, productivity growth outstripped real wage growth by a significant margin. From 2000 to 2007, the link was reestablished, although with real wage growth slightly higher than productivity growth. The reasons for short-term differences between growth rates in productivity and real wages are not completely understood; however, the longer term relationship is quite stable and consistent with our theory. ●

QuickQuiz How does an immigration of workers affect labour supply, labour demand, the marginal product of labour, and the equilibrium wage?

THE OTHER FACTORS OF PRODUCTION: LAND AND CAPITAL

We have seen how firms decide how much labour to hire and how these decisions determine workers' wages. At the same time that firms are hiring workers, they are also deciding about other inputs to production. For example, our apple-producing firm might have to choose the size of its apple orchard and the number of ladders to make available to its apple pickers. We can think of the firm's factors of production as falling into three categories: labour, land, and capital.

The meaning of the terms *labour* and *land* is clear, but the definition of *capital* is somewhat tricky. Economists use the term **capital** to refer to the stock of equipment and structures used for production. That is, the economy's capital represents the accumulation of goods produced in the past that are being used in the present to produce new goods and services. For our apple firm, the capital stock includes the ladders used to climb the trees, the trucks used to transport the apples, the buildings used to store the apples, and even the trees themselves.

capital
the equipment and structures used to produce goods and services

Equilibrium in the Markets for Land and Capital

What determines how much the owners of land and capital earn for their contribution to the production process? Before answering this question, we need to distinguish between two prices: the purchase price and the rental price. The *purchase price* of land or capital is the price a person pays to own that factor of production indefinitely. The *rental price* is the price a person pays to use that factor for a limited period of time. It is important to keep this distinction in mind because, as we will see, these prices are determined by somewhat different economic forces.

Having defined these terms, we can now apply the theory of factor demand that we developed for the labour market to the markets for land and capital. The wage is, after all, simply the rental price of labour. Therefore, much of what we have learned about wage determination applies also to the rental prices of land and capital. As Figure 18.7 illustrates, the rental price of land, shown in panel (a), and the rental price of capital, shown in panel (b), are determined by supply and demand. Moreover, the demand for land and capital is determined just like the demand for labour. That is, when our apple-producing firm is deciding how much land and how many ladders to rent, it follows the same logic as when deciding how many workers to hire. For both land and capital, the firm increases the quantity hired until the value of the factor's marginal product equals the factor's price. Thus, the demand curve for each factor reflects the marginal productivity of that factor.

We can now explain how much income goes to labour, how much goes to landowners, and how much goes to the owners of capital. As long as the firms using the factors of production are competitive and profit-maximizing, each factor's rental price must equal the value of the marginal product for that factor. *Labour, land, and capital each earn the value of their marginal contribution to the production process.*

Now consider the purchase price of land and capital. The rental price and the purchase price are obviously related: Buyers are willing to pay more for a piece of land or capital if it produces a valuable stream of rental income. And, as we have just seen, the equilibrium rental income at any point in time equals the value of that factor's marginal product. Therefore, the equilibrium purchase price of a piece of land or capital depends on both the current value of the marginal product and the value of the marginal product expected to prevail in the future.

FIGURE 18.7

The Markets for Land and Capital

Supply and demand determine the compensation paid to the owners of land, as shown in panel (a), and the compensation paid to the owners of capital, as shown in panel (b). The demand for each factor, in turn, depends on the value of the marginal product of that factor.

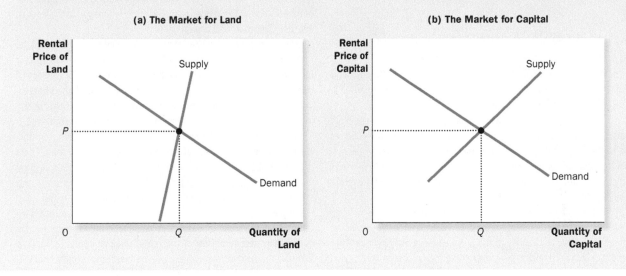

Linkages among the Factors of Production

We have seen that the price paid to any factor of production—labour, land, or capital—equals the value of the marginal product of that factor. The marginal product of any factor, in turn, depends on the quantity of that factor that is available. Because of diminishing marginal product, a factor in abundant supply has a low marginal product and thus a low price, and a factor in scarce supply has a high marginal product and a high price. As a result, when the supply of a factor falls, its equilibrium factor price rises.

When the supply of any factor changes, however, the effects are not limited to the market for that factor. In most situations, factors of production are used together in a way that makes the productivity of each factor dependent on the quantities of the other factors available to be used in the production process. As a result, a change in the supply of any one factor alters the earnings of all the factors.

For example, suppose a hurricane destroys many of the ladders that workers use to pick apples from the orchards. What happens to the earnings of the various factors of production? Most obviously, the supply of ladders falls and, therefore, the equilibrium rental price of ladders rises. Those owners who were lucky enough to avoid damage to their ladders now earn a higher return when they rent out their ladders to the firms that produce apples.

Yet the effects of this event do not stop at the ladder market. Because there are fewer ladders with which to work, the workers who pick apples have a

WHAT IS CAPITAL INCOME?

Labour income is an easy concept to understand: It is the paycheque that workers receive from their employers. The income earned by capital, however, is less obvious.

In our analysis, we have been implicitly assuming that households own capital—ladders, drill presses, warehouses, and so on—and rent it to the firms that use it. This assumption has simplified our analysis of how capital owners are compensated, but it is not very realistic. In fact, most firms own the capital they use, and therefore they receive the earnings from this capital.

These earnings eventually are paid by firms to households in various ways. Some of the earnings are paid in the form of *interest* to households who have lent money to the firms, either directly by investing in company bonds, or indirectly by depositing their money in banks, which in turn lend it to businesses. Thus, when you receive interest on your bank account, that income is part of the economy's capital income.

Capital income may be distributed to households in two other ways. First, some of the earnings from capital are paid to households in the form of dividends. *Dividends* are payments by a firm to its shareholders. A shareholder is a person who has bought a share in the ownership of the firm and, therefore, is entitled to a share in the firm's profits.

Second, shareholders may receive income through the companies they own through capital gains. A *capital gain* occurs when the value of a company's stock increases. A firm does not have to pay out all of its earnings to shareholders in the form of dividends. Instead, it can retain some of those earnings and use them to buy additional capital. Although the earnings retained by the firm are not paid out to shareholders, shareholders benefit from them nonetheless. This is because retained earnings increase the amount of capital the firm owns, which increases future earnings, which increase the value of the firm's shares, which generate a capital gain.

So, in a sense, rather than renting capital to firms and receiving the capital income in the form of rental payments, households can be viewed as renting money to firms, which in turn use this money to purchase capital. The rental payments on this money take the form of interest, dividends, and capital gains.

What determines the interest rate required by debtholders and the rate of return required by shareholders? The answer to this question is beyond the scope of this chapter, but it is related to the concept of opportunity cost. Debtholders must earn interest and shareholders must earn dividends and capital gains to compensate them for the income they could have earned by investing their money elsewhere.

These institutional details are interesting and important, but they do not alter our conclusion about the income earned by the owners of capital. Capital is paid according to the value of its marginal product, regardless of whether this income is transmitted to the shareholders in the form of interest, dividends, or capital gains.

However, the fact that capital income is derived as a return on financial investments in businesses does have implications for the equilibrium determination of the rental price of capital. Canada's financial markets are very small compared with the world's financial markets, so the savings and investment decisions of Canadians have very little impact on world interest rates or rates of return. Canada's financial markets are also very open, in that Canadians can invest in companies anywhere in the world and residents of other countries are free to invest in Canadian companies.

These two market characteristics—small and open—mean that interest rates and rates of return on investments in Canadian companies are, to a large extent, independent of the amount of financial capital provided by Canadians. For a small open economy like Canada's, then, the supply curve for capital can be viewed as perfectly horizontal, or perfectly elastic, at the rental rate implied by the world interest rate, at least as a first approximation. As a result, changes in either the demand or the supply of capital in Canada have no impact on the rental price of capital.

smaller marginal product. Thus, the reduction in the supply of ladders reduces the demand for the labour of apple pickers, and this causes the equilibrium wage to fall.

This story shows a general lesson: An event that changes the supply of any factor of production can alter the earnings of all the factors. The change in earnings of any factor can be found by analyzing the impact of the event on the value of the marginal product of that factor.

QuickQuiz   What determines the income of the owners of land and capital? •
How would an increase in the quantity of capital affect the incomes of those who
already own capital? How would it affect the incomes of workers?

CONCLUSION

This chapter explained how labour, land, and capital are compensated for the
roles they play in the production process. The theory developed here is called the
neoclassical theory of distribution. According to the neoclassical theory, the amount
paid to each factor of production depends on the supply and demand for that
factor. The demand, in turn, depends on that particular factor's marginal productivity. In equilibrium, each factor of production earns the value of its marginal
contribution to the production of goods and services.

The neoclassical theory of distribution is widely accepted. Most economists
begin with the neoclassical theory when trying to explain how the Canadian
economy's $1 trillion of income is distributed among the economy's various mem-
bers. In the following two chapters, we consider the distribution of income in
more detail. As you will see, the neoclassical theory provides the framework for
this discussion.

Even at this point you can use the theory to answer the question that began this
chapter: Why are computer programmers paid more than gas station attendants?
It is because programmers can produce a good of greater market value than can a
gas station attendant. People are willing to pay dearly for a good computer game,
but they are willing to pay little to have their gas pumped and their windshield
washed. The wages of these workers reflect the market prices of the goods or services they produce. If people suddenly got tired of using computers and decided
to spend more time driving, the prices of these goods and services would change,
and so would the equilibrium wages of these two groups of workers.

SUMMARY

- The economy's income is distributed in the
  markets for the factors of production. The three
  most important factors of production are labour,
  land, and capital.

- The demand for factors, such as labour, is a
  derived demand that comes from firms that
  use the factors to produce goods and services.
  Competitive, profit-maximizing firms hire
  each factor up to the point at which the value
  of the marginal product of the factor equals
  its price.

- The supply of labour arises from individuals'
  tradeoff between work and leisure. An upward-
  sloping labour supply curve means that people

  respond to an increase in the wage by enjoying
  less leisure and working more hours.

- The price paid to each factor adjusts to balance
  the supply and demand for that factor. Because
  factor demand reflects the value of the marginal product of that factor, in equilibrium, each
  factor is compensated according to its marginal
  contribution to the production of goods and
  services.

- Because factors of production are used together,
  the marginal product of any one factor depends
  on the quantities of all factors that are available.
  As a result, a change in the supply of one factor
  alters the equilibrium earnings of all the factors.

KEY CONCEPTS

factors of production, p. 394
production function, p. 396
marginal product of
    labour, p. 396

diminishing marginal
    product, p. 396
value of the marginal
    product, p. 397

capital, p. 408

QUESTIONS FOR REVIEW

1. Explain how a firm's production function is related to its marginal product of labour, how a firm's marginal product of labour is related to the value of its marginal product, and how a firm's value of marginal product is related to its demand for labour.

2. Give two examples of events that could shift the demand for labour.

3. Give two examples of events that could shift the supply of labour.

4. Explain how the wage can adjust to balance the supply and demand for labour while simultaneously equalling the value of the marginal product of labour.

5. If the population of Canada suddenly grew because of a large immigration, what would happen to wages? What would happen to the rents earned by the owners of land and capital?

PROBLEMS AND APPLICATIONS

1. Suppose that the prime minister proposes a new law aimed at reducing heath care costs: All Canadians are to be required to eat one apple daily.
   a. How would this apple-a-day law affect the demand and equilibrium price of apples?
   b. How would the law affect the marginal product and the value of the marginal product of apple pickers?
   c. How would the law affect the demand and equilibrium wage for apple pickers?

2. Show the effect of each of the following events on the market for labour in the computer manufacturing industry.
   a. The government buys personal computers for all college and university students.
   b. More postsecondary students major in engineering and computer science.
   c. Computer firms build new manufacturing plants.

3. Your enterprising uncle opens a sandwich shop that employs 7 people. The employees are paid $6 per hour, and a sandwich sells for $3. If your uncle is maximizing his profit, what is the value

of the marginal product of the last worker he hired? What is that worker's marginal product?

4. Suppose a freeze in British Columbia destroys part of the apple crop.
   a. Explain what happens to the price of apples and the marginal product of apple pickers as a result of the freeze. Can you say what happens to the demand for apple pickers? Why or why not?
   b. Suppose the price of apples doubles and the marginal product falls by 30 percent. What happens to the equilibrium wage of apple pickers?
   c. Suppose the price of apples rises by 30 percent and the marginal product falls by 50 percent. What happens to the equilibrium wage of apple pickers?

5. During the 1980s and 1990s Canada experienced a significant inflow of capital from other countries.
   a. Using a diagram of the Canadian capital market, show the effect of this inflow on the rental price of capital in Canada and on the quantity of capital in use.

b. Using a diagram of the Canadian labour market, show the effect of the capital inflow on the average wage paid to Canadian workers.

6. Suppose that labour is the only input used by a perfectly competitive firm that can hire workers for $50 per day. The firm's production function is as follows:

Days of Labour	Units of Output
0	0
1	7
2	13
3	19
4	25
5	28
6	29

Each unit of output sells for $10. Plot the firm's demand for labour. How many days of labour should the firm hire? Show this point on your graph.

7. This chapter has assumed that labour is supplied by individual workers acting competitively. In some markets, however, the supply of labour is determined by a union of workers.
   a. Explain why the situation faced by a labour union may resemble the situation faced by a monopoly firm.
   b. The goal of a monopoly firm is to maximize profits. Is there an analogous goal for labour unions?
   c. Now extend the analogy between monopoly firms and unions. How do you suppose that the wage set by a union compares to the wage in a competitive market? How do you suppose employment differs in the two cases?
   d. What other goals might unions have that make unions different from monopoly firms?

8. Leadbelly Co. sells pencils in a perfectly competitive product market and hires workers in a perfectly competitive labour market. Assume that the market wage rate for workers is $150 per day.
   a. What rule should Leadbelly follow to hire the profit-maximizing amount of labour?
   b. At the profit-maximizing level of output, the marginal product of the last worker hired is 30 boxes of pencils per day. Calculate the price of a box of pencils.
   c. Draw a diagram of the labour market for pencil workers (as in Figure 18.4) next to a diagram of the labour supply and demand for Leadbelly Co. (as in Figure 18.3). Label the equilibrium wage and quantity of labour for both the market and the firm. How are these diagrams related?
   d. Suppose some pencil workers switch to jobs in the growing computer industry. On the side-by-side diagrams you prepared in part (c), show how this change affects the equilibrium wage and quantity of labour for both the pencil market and for Leadbelly. How does this change affect the marginal product of labour at Leadbelly?

9. Smiling Cow Dairy can sell all the milk it wants for $4 a litre, and it can rent all the robots it wants to milk the cows at a capital rental price of $100 a day. It faces the following production schedule:

Number of Robots	Total Product
0	0 litres
1	50
2	85
3	115
4	140
5	150
6	155

   a. In what kind of market structure does the firm sell its output? How can you tell?
   b. In what kind of market structure does the firm rent robots? How can you tell?
   c. Calculate the marginal product and the value of the marginal product for each additional robot.
   d. How many robots should the firm rent? Explain.

http://   For more study tools, please visit http://www.mankiw5e.nelson.com.

18 The Markets for the Factors of Production

I. Chapter Overview

A. Context and Purpose

Previous chapters provided a framework for analysis of product markets. This chapter and the following analyze the operation of input markets—markets for the factors of production. Chapter 18 explains the behaviour of labour markets, followed in Chapter 19 by an in-depth look at how wages are determined in the Canadian economic system.

A. Helpful Hints

1. *The demand for a factor of production is a derived demand.* A firm's demand for a factor of production is derived from its decision to supply a good in another market. For example, the demand for bakers is directly tied to the supply of bread.

2. *The price paid to a factor input is determined by the demand for and supply of that factor.* Factor demand reflects the value of the marginal product of that factor, and, in competitive markets, each factor is compensated according to its marginal contribution to the production of goods and services. In a competitive bread industry, the baker would be paid according to his value of marginal product, which is (price of the bread) × (marginal product of the baker).

3. *The profit-maximizing firm hires additional workers until it breaks even on the last worker hired.* If it seems counterintuitive that employers would hire workers until they just break even on the last worker hired, remember that this is a *marginal* decision. They are not breaking even on the *average* worker. By hiring every worker who can produce more than enough to pay his or her wage, the firm is maximizing its net gain or profit. It breaks even on the marginal worker, but it keeps the gains from all of the workers who were hired before.

II. Self-Testing Challenges

A.   True/False Questions

_____1.   An increase in the demand for oranges will cause an increase in the value of the marginal product of orange pickers.

_____2.   A technological breakthrough that raises the productivity of apple pickers will have no effect on the value of the marginal product of apple pickers, although it will raise the value of the marginal product of capital.

_____3.   The demand for a factor of production by a competitive firm is the value of its marginal product.

_____4.   When a firm hires labour up to the point at which the wage equals the value of the marginal revenue product, it is producing up to the point at which price exceeds marginal cost by the greatest amount.

_____5.   The demand for a factor of production is called a derived demand because it is derived from the marginal product of that factor.

_____6.   An increase in the supply of electricians will lead to a decrease in the value of the marginal product of electricians.

_____7.   An increase in capital leads to an increase in the value of the marginal product of both capital and labour.

_____8.   The demand for labour is independent of the price of the product.

_____9.   A competitive profit-maximizing firm chooses the quantity of labour at the point at which the wage equals the marginal cost of production.

_____10.   An event that changes the supply of one factor of production alters the earning of that factor alone.

_____11.   Any event that changes the supply and demand for labour must change the equilibrium wage and the marginal product by the same amount, because these must always be equal.

_____12.   A monopsony is a market in which a single firm is the only buyer of labour.

B. Multiple-Choice Questions

1. Which one of the following is reflected by the demand for labour?
   a. the marginal product of labour
   b. the average product of labour
   c. the value of the average product of labour
   d. the value of the marginal product of labour

2. Which one of the following describes the outcome of an increase in the supply of labour in a competitive market?
   a. It will increase the wage rate and the value of the marginal product.
   b. It will increase the wage rate and decrease the value of the marginal product.
   c. It will decrease the wage rate and the value of the marginal product.
   d. It will decrease the wage rate and increase the value of the marginal product.

3. Which one of the following will result from an increase in the demand for apples?
   a. A decrease in apple pickers' wages
   b. a decrease in the value of the marginal product of apple pickers
   c. higher short-run profits for apple growers
   d. a decrease in the number of apple pickers employed

4. Which one of the following is **NOT** the ultimate source of the difference in productivity, wages, and standard of living?
   a. human capital
   b. physical capital
   c. technological knowledge

5. As the wage rate increases due to a decrease in labour supply, which one of the following will occur?
   a. The value of the marginal product will fall.
   b. The value of the marginal product will rise.
   c. A shortage of labour will result.
   d. A surplus of labour will result.

6. Which one of the following is **NOT** an example of a factor of production?
   a. steelworkers used to produce sheet metal
   b. foundries used to produce steel
   c. iron ore used to produce steel
   d. share of stock in a steel company

7.   Which one of the following causes a shift in the supply of labour?
     a.   changes in labour laws
     b.   changes in government
     c.   immigration

Ken's Kamera Kiosk sells film in small booths in shopping centres. Ken must decide how many people to hire, based on the data below. Use the following table to answer questions 8–12.

Labour hired	Output	Marginal product	Product price
0	0	—	—
1	5	___	$5
2	12	___	$5
3	17	___	$5
4	19	___	$5
5	20	___	$5
6	19	___	$5

8.   Which one of the following is the marginal product of the 4th unit of labour hired?
     a.   2
     b.   5
     c.   19

9.   Which one of the following is the value of the marginal product of the 3rd unit of labour hired?
     a. $5.00
     b. $8.67
     c. $25.00
     d. $85.00

10. If Ken wants to maximize profit, up to how many workers should he hire if the wage is $5.00?
     a.   1
     b.   2
     c.   4
     d.   5

11. Which one of the following is the number of workers Ken should hire if the wage rises to $5.50?
     a.   1
     b.   2
     c.   3
     d.   4

12.   Which one of the following is the quantity of labour at which diminishing returns set in?
        a. 2
        b. 3
        c. 5
        d. 6

13.   Suppose that an influenza pandemic killed one-third of Earth's human population. Which one of the following would be the **MOST** likely economic effect on the survivors?
        a. Wages would rise, and the returns to capital and land would fall.
        b. Returns to all factors of production would fall.
        c. Returns to all factors of production would rise.
        d. Wages would fall, but the returns to capital and land would rise.

14.   Which one of the following categories of Canadians is **MOST** likely to support immigration restrictions to reduce the supply of labour?
        a. workers
        b. employers
        c. landlords
        d. owners of capital

Use the following information to answer questions 15–17.
Suppose that Bob's Burger Box is maximizing profit by hiring workers at $6 per hour. Bob sells hamburgers in a competitive market for $2 each. He currently employs 18 people.

15.   Which one of the following is the value of the marginal product of the 18th worker?
        a. $0.11
        b. $0.33
        c. $3.00
        d. $6.00

16.   Which one of the following is the marginal product of the 18th worker?
        a. 1
        b. 2
        c. 4
        d. 5

17.   If the price of hamburgers rises to $3, the value of the marginal product will _____ and the number of workers hired will _____.
        a. rise to $9, increase
        b. rise to $18, increase
        c. fall to $6, decrease
        d. fall to $3, decrease

18.   Which one of the following can workers who augment their stock of human capital expect to receive?
   a. higher wages that reflect an increase in the worker's value of marginal product
   b. the same wages but increase the worker's value of marginal product
   c. higher wages that reflect a decrease in the worker's value of marginal product
   d. the same wages but decrease the worker's value of marginal product

19.   As a result of an increase in the rental price of capital, _____ capital will be used in production, the marginal product of labour will _____, and the equilibrium wage will _____
   a. less, increase, fall
   b. more, decrease, rise
   c. more, increase, fall
   d. less, decrease, fall

20.   In a perfectly competitive labour market for an industry, which one of the following will result from a decrease in wages elsewhere in the economy?
   a. an increase in wages and employment in this industry
   b. a decrease in wages and employment in this industry
   c. a decrease in wages and an increase in employment in this industry
   d. an increase in wages and a decrease in employment in this industry

C. Short-Answer Questions

1.   A competitive firm's value of the marginal product is sometimes called that firm's marginal revenue product. Why? _____
_____
_____
_____

2.   Among the owners of the factors of production, who would win and who would lose from increasing the restrictions on immigration into Canada? Explain in terms of marginal productivity theory. _____
_____
_____
_____
_____

3.   Explain the relationship between the equilibrium wage and the value of the marginal product. _____
_____
_____
_____

4.   Should professors be concerned about the increasing demand for online
     and computer-based learning? _____

     _____

     _____

     _____

D. Practice Problems

1.   The data below show the relationship between number of workers hired
     and costs and revenues for a small Italian restaurant in Hamilton, Enrico's
     Eggplant Emporium.

Quantity of labour (L)	Output (Q)	Marginal product (MP_{labour})	Price (P)	Value of the marginal product (VMP_{labour})	Wage (W)	Marginal profit (Δ_{profit})
0	0	____	$10	____	$11	____
1	5	____	$10	____	$11	____
2	10	____	$10	____	$11	____
3	14	____	$10	____	$11	____
4	17	____	$10	____	$11	____
5	19	____	$10	____	$11	____
6	20	____	$10	____	$11	____
7	20	____	$10	____	$11	____
8	19	____	$10	____	$11	____

a.   Fill in the blanks in the table.

b.   At what point do diminishing returns set in? Explain. _____

     _____

     _____

c.   How many workers should be hired? Explain. _____

     _____

     _____

d.   If the fixed cost is $100 and labour is the only variable factor, what is
     the firm's profit? Explain. _____

     _____

     _____

     _____

     _____

e. If the price of the product increases to $12, how many workers should
    be hired? Explain. If the wage increases to $15 after the price hike,
    how many workers should be hired? Explain. _____

    _____
    _____
    _____
    _____

2. A case study in the text describes the economic effects of the Black Death
    in 14th century Europe.

    a. Below , show graphically the effects of the plague that destroyed about
        one-third of the population within a few years. Indicate clearly which
        curves shift and in which direction, as well as the direction of the
        changes in factor prices and equilibrium quantities.

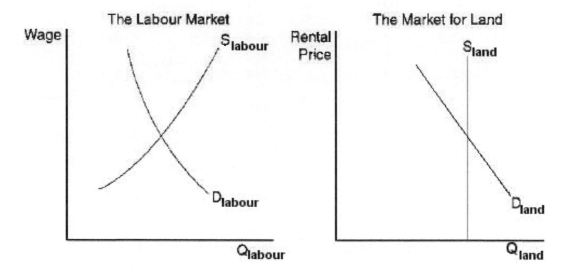

    b. Explain the unusual shape of the supply curve for land. Is this
        reasonable? Can you think of any way that the supply curve might
        have a positive slope?

        _____
        _____
        _____
        _____

    c. Explain the shifts that you identified in part (a), and include a
        discussion of the effects on the value of the marginal product of each
        of the factors of production.

        _____
        _____
        _____
        _____

662

E. Advanced Critical Thinking

Critics of the minimum wage argue that it causes unemployment by putting a floor under the price of labour in competitive labour markets, and that it hurts those whom it is designed to help—workers with the least amount of experience and job skills. Supporters of the minimum wage argue that the minimum wage has little or no negative impact on employment, because it has been kept at a very low level, typically less than half of the average wage paid by manufacturing firms. In addition, they claim that labour markets do not behave competitively; rather, they assert that big employers set wages with little regard for supply and demand. They argue further that even if the minimum wage reduces employment, the lost jobs would be the least productive, lowest paid jobs in the economy, so that society would not gain much by keeping them anyway.

1. Evaluate the opposing arguments. What are the advantages and disadvantages of the minimum wage? Who gains and who loses under a minimum wage?

_____

_____

_____

_____

_____

_____

_____

2. If you wanted to measure the negative impact of the minimum wage on employment, why would it be a bad idea to look at the overall level of employment in the economy before and after a change in the minimum wage? Can you think of any specific groups of workers whose employment experience before and after a minimum wage change might be a better indicator of the effects of the minimum wage? Explain. _____

_____

_____

_____

_____

_____

_____

_____

III.   Solutions

A.   True/False Questions

1.   T
2.   F; a technological breakthrough that raises the productivity of apple pickers will raise the value of the marginal product of apple pickers and raise the value of the marginal product of capital.
3.   T
4.   F; when a firm hires labour up to the point at which the wage equals the value of the marginal revenue product, it is producing up to the point at which price equals marginal cost.
5.   F; the derived demand for a factor of production means that it is derived from the decision to supply a product in another market.
6.   T
7.   F; an increase in capital leads to an increase in the value of the marginal product of labour, but a decrease in the value of the marginal product of capital.
8.   F; the demand for labour is dependent on the price of the product and the marginal product of labour.
9.   F; a profit-maximizing employer will hire labour up to the point that the value of the marginal product equals the wage rate.
10.   F; such an event can alter the earnings of *all* factors of production.
11.   T
12.   T

B.   Multiple-Choice Questions

1. d	5. b	9. c	13. a	17. a
2. c	6. d	10. d	14. a	18. a
3. c	7. c	11. d	15. d	19. d
4. c	8. a	12. b	16. c	20. c

C.   Short-Answer Questions

1.   The value of the marginal product of an input is the marginal product of that input times the price of the output, i.e., $VMP = P \times MP$. The marginal revenue product is the extra revenue the firm gets from the sale of output created by the use of one additional unit of an input, i.e., $MRP = MR \times MP$. Because marginal revenue equals the price of the product, $P = MR$, for competitive firms, it follows that their VMP and MRP are the same.

2. The reduction in the supply of labour would raise the wage and value of the marginal product for current workers. With less labour available, the value of the marginal product of capital and land would fall because of a fall in the marginal product of both capital and land. As a result, the rental price of both capital and land would fall. Owners of capital and landlords would lose, although workers would gain.

3. The equilibrium wage must equal the value of the marginal product in competitive markets. This occurs because employers will hire additional workers as long as the wage exceeds the value of the marginal product.

4. In the short run, the increase in demand for these types of courses may displace labour and cause a temporary decline in the demand for professors. This decrease in demand may drive professors' salaries downward. However, the enhanced use of online and computer-based learning, along with innovations in teaching, will create job opportunities for instructors with experience in these areas. There is not enough information to assess the net effect.

D. Practice Problems

1. a.

Quantity of labour (L)	Output (Q)	Marginal product (MP$_{labour}$)	Price (P)	Value of the marginal product (VMP$_{labour}$)	Wage (W)	Marginal profit (Δ_{profit})
0	0	—	$10	—	$11	—
1	5	5	$10	$50	$11	$39
2	10	5	$10	$50	$11	$39
3	14	4	$10	$40	$11	$29
4	17	3	$10	$30	$11	$19
5	19	2	$10	$20	$11	$9
6	20	1	$10	$10	$11	($ 1)
7	20	0	$10	0	$11	($11)
8	19	(1)	$10	($10)	$11	($21)

b. The third unit of labour hired results in diminishing returns; the marginal product of the third worker is only 4, down from the marginal product of 5 for the second worker.

c. The firm should hire five workers, following the marginal rule that they should add workers as long as additional workers add more to revenue than they add to cost. The fifth worker has a VMP of $20, but costs the firm a wage of only $11, for a marginal profit of $9 on that worker. Another worker would cost the firm $11 but add only $10 to revenues for a marginal loss of $1.

d. The firm will earn a profit of $35. The variable cost is the wage bill of $55 (5 workers @ $11). Total cost is $155 (fixed cost of $100 plus variable cost of $55). Total revenue is $190 (19 units @ $10). The difference (TR − TC) is $35.

e. At a price of $12, the firm should hire a sixth worker. The VMP will be $12 (MP × P = 1 × $12). The wage is still $11, so the firm makes a $1 marginal profit on the sixth worker. However, if the wage increases to $15, the sixth worker is not worth the cost ($15 > $12). The fifth worker, however, costs $15 and adds $24 (2 × $12), and should be hired.

2. a.

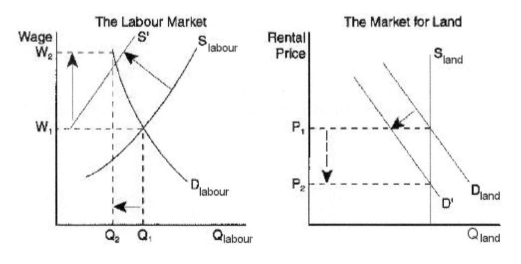

b. The vertical slope of the supply curve for land suggests that it is totally inelastic, because it is in fixed supply. This is reasonable, unless it is possible to respond to higher land rental prices by retrieving unusable land such as swamps or land that had been under water. In the latter case, the supply curve would have a positive slope.

c. The supply of labour shifts to the left because of the high death rate. The wage increases because of the decreased supply. The value of the marginal product of labour rises until it is equal to the new wage rate, because in equilibrium, employment will adjust until the last worker hired has a VMP just equal to his or her wage. The drop in the number of workers will reduce the productivity of land, causing a shift to the left in its VMP curve. The rental price of land will drop as a result of the drop in demand.

E.   Advanced Critical Thinking

1. The minimum wage can put a floor under income for the working poor. It can provide more dignity than welfare for those who need assistance. However, it can lead to unemployment, particularly among groups with few job skills and little experience. Teenagers just entering the labour force are particularly susceptible to the negative impact of the minimum wage on their employability. An employer who might have hired an untested young worker for $4 per hour may decline to take a chance at $6/hour. The winners are those who keep their jobs and realize higher wages. The losers are those who lose their jobs or fail to be hired as a result of the minimum wage.

2. The overall level of employment would probably hide the effect of the minimum wage on employment among the relatively hard-to-employ, such as teenagers or those with relatively low education levels. A better measure of the impact of the minimum wage would be to look at employment among teenagers, especially minorities, and others who may be at a disadvantage in the labour market. With a few exceptions, those studies generally have shown a negative effect on employment due to the minimum wage.

EARNINGS AND DISCRIMINATION

Learning Objectives

In this chapter, you will ...

- Examine how wages compensate for differences in job characteristics

- Learn and compare the human-capital and signalling theories of education

- Examine why in some occupations a few superstars earn tremendous incomes

- Learn why wages rise above the level that balances supply and demand

- Consider why it is difficult to measure the impact of discrimination on wages

- See when market forces can and cannot provide a natural remedy for discrimination

- Consider the debate over comparable worth as a system for setting wages

In Canada today, the typical physician earns about $200 000 per year, the typical police officer about $50 000, and the typical farm worker about $20 000. These examples illustrate the large differences in earnings that are so common in our economy. They also explain why some people live in mansions, ride in limousines, and vacation on the French Riviera, while other people live in small apartments, ride the bus, and vacation in their own backyards.

Why do earnings vary so much from person to person? Chapter 18, which developed the basic neoclassical theory of the labour market, offers an answer to this question. There we saw that wages are governed by labour supply and labour demand. Labour demand, in turn, reflects the marginal productivity of labour. In equilibrium, each worker is paid the value of his or her marginal contribution to the economy's production of goods and services.

This theory of the labour market, although widely accepted by economists, is only the beginning of the story. To understand the wide variation in earnings that we observe, we must go beyond this general framework and examine more precisely what determines the supply and demand for different types of labour. That is our goal in this chapter.

SOME DETERMINANTS OF EQUILIBRIUM WAGES

Workers differ from one another in many ways. Jobs also have differing characteristics—both in terms of the wage they pay and in terms of their nonmonetary attributes. In this section we consider how the characteristics of workers and jobs affect labour supply, labour demand, and equilibrium wages.

Compensating Differentials

When a worker is deciding whether to take a job, the wage is only one of many job attributes that the worker takes into account. Some jobs are easy, fun, and safe; others are hard, dull, and dangerous. The better the job as gauged by these non-monetary characteristics, the more people there are who are willing to do the job at any given wage. In other words, the supply of labour for easy, fun, and safe jobs is greater than the supply of labour for hard, dull, and dangerous jobs. As a result, "good" jobs will tend to have lower equilibrium wages than "bad" jobs.

For example, imagine you are looking for a summer job in a local beach community. Two kinds of jobs are available. You can take a job as a beach-badge checker, or you can take a job as a garbage collector. The beach-badge checkers take leisurely strolls along the beach during the day and check to make sure the tourists have bought the required beach permits. The garbage collectors wake up before dawn to drive dirty, noisy trucks around town to pick up garbage. Which job would you want? Most people would prefer the beach job if the wages were the same. To induce people to become garbage collectors, the town has to offer higher wages to garbage collectors than to beach-badge checkers.

Economists use the term **compensating differential** to refer to a difference in wages that arises from nonmonetary characteristics of different jobs. Compensating differentials are prevalent in the economy. Here are some examples:

compensating differential
a difference in wages that arises to offset the nonmonetary characteristics of different jobs

- Coal miners are paid more than other workers with similar levels of education. Their higher wage compensates them for the dirty and dangerous nature of coal mining, as well as the long-term health problems that coal miners experience.
- Workers who work the night shift at factories are paid more than similar workers who work the day shift. The higher wage compensates them for having to work at night and sleep during the day, a lifestyle that most people find undesirable.
- Professors are paid less than lawyers and doctors, who have similar amounts of education. Professors' lower wages compensate them for the great intellectual and personal satisfaction that their jobs offer. (Indeed, teaching economics is so much fun that it is surprising that economics professors are paid anything at all!)

Human Capital

As we discussed in the previous chapter, the word *capital* usually refers to the economy's stock of equipment and structures. The capital stock includes the farmer's tractor, the manufacturer's factory, and the teacher's chalkboard. The essence of capital is that it is a factor of production that itself has been produced.

human capital
the accumulation of investments in people, such as education and on-the-job training

There is another type of capital that, while less tangible than physical capital, is just as important to the economy's production. **Human capital** is the accumulation of investments in people. The most important type of human capital is education. Like all forms of capital, education represents an expenditure of resources at one point in time to raise productivity in the future. But, unlike an investment in other forms of capital, an investment in education is tied to a specific person, and this linkage is what makes it human capital.

Not surprisingly, workers with more human capital on average earn more than those with less human capital. University graduates in Canada, for example, earn about 60 percent more than workers who end their education with a high-school diploma. This large difference has been documented in many countries around the world. It tends to be even larger in less-developed countries, where educated workers are in scarce supply.

It is easy to see why education raises wages from the perspective of supply and demand. Firms—the demanders of labour—are willing to pay more for the highly educated because highly educated workers have higher marginal products. Workers—the suppliers of labour—are willing to pay the cost of becoming educated only if there is a reward for doing so. In essence, the difference in wages between highly educated workers and less educated workers may be considered a compensating differential for the cost of becoming educated.

Case Study
THE VALUE OF SKILLS

"The rich get richer and the poor get poorer." Like many adages, this one is not always true, but has it been true in Canada? We'll talk more about income distribution in the next chapter, but at this point we will address what many feel is an important determinant of the distribution of income in an economy: the wage gap between workers with high skills and workers with low skills. Numerous studies have documented and tried to explain movements in this wage gap, or "premium," over time.

Figure 19.1 (p. 418) shows the ratio of the median earnings of university graduates to the median earnings of high-school graduates without any additional education; the data are for males in Canada and the United States from 1980 to 2000. The figure shows that in the United States the ratio has grown steadily over time. In 1980, U.S. university graduates earned about 40 percent more than high-school graduates; in 2000 they earned about 80 percent more. The situation has been somewhat different in Canada. Although the relative wages of Canadian university graduates are clearly higher than the wages of high-school graduates, the wage premium has not grown over time. In 1980, Canadian university graduates earned about 60 percent more than high-school graduates; in 2000, they still earned about 60 percent more.

What explains these different trends in the earnings gap between skilled and unskilled workers? No one knows the full explanation, but economists have proposed various hypotheses. One explanation relies on the supply and demand of skilled labour relative to the supply and demand of unskilled labour in the two countries to explain differences in relative wages.

One explanation for the rising wage premium in the United States is that demand for skilled labour there increased more quickly than the relative supply. With the relative demand curve for skilled labour shifting outward faster than the relative supply curve, there has been a corresponding increase in relative wages, which in turn has contributed to greater wage inequality in the United States.

Economists have offered two hypotheses for the U.S. trend. The first explanation is that international trade has increased the relative demand for skilled

FIGURE 19.1

Ratio of Earnings of University Graduates to High-School Graduates, 1980–2000

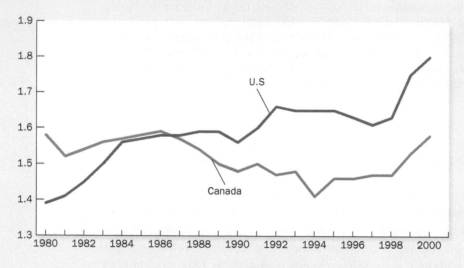

Source: Adapted from J. Burbidge, L. MaGee, and A. Robb, "The Education Premium in Canada and the United States," *Canadian Public Policy*, Vol. XXVIII, No. 2, 2002.

labour. In recent years, the amount of trade between the United States and other countries has increased dramatically. Because unskilled labour is plentiful and cheap in many foreign countries, the United States tends to import goods produced with unskilled labour and to export goods produced with skilled labour. Thus, the expansion in international trade has increased the domestic (relative) demand for skilled labour.

The second hypothesis is that changes in technology have altered the relative demand for skilled and unskilled labour. Consider the growing use of computers. Computers raise the demand for skilled workers who can use the new machines and reduce the demand for unskilled workers whose jobs are replaced by computers. For example, many companies now rely more on computer databases and less on filing cabinets to keep business records. This change raises the demand for computer programmers and reduces the demand for filing clerks. Thus, with increased computerization, the demand for skilled labour rises and the demand for unskilled labour falls.

Economists have found it difficult to gauge the validity of these two hypotheses. It is possible, perhaps even likely, that both are true: Increasing international trade and technological change may both be responsible for the growing U.S. wage gap.

But why haven't we observed a similar increase in the relative earnings of Canadian skilled workers? Canada's trade with other countries has also grown significantly, and Canadian companies have access to the same technologies as U.S. companies. Yet the wage gap in Canada has remained relatively constant over time. Are Canadian labour markets not subject to similar influences?

Several possible explanations have been offered. One possibility is that in Canada the supply of skilled labour relative to unskilled labour has increased at about the same rate as the relative demand. As a result, the gap between the earnings of skilled workers and the earnings of unskilled workers has remained roughly unchanged over this 20-year period. On the other hand, in the United States, the relative supply of skilled labour has not kept up with the rise in relative demand, which explains the increase in the earnings of skilled workers relative to those of unskilled workers in the United States.

Another explanation is that Canadian companies have lagged U.S. companies in investment in capital equipment over this period. If investment in equipment makes skilled workers relatively more productive than unskilled workers, this too could explain the relatively flat skill premium in Canada relative to the United States. ●

Ability, Effort, and Chance

Why do NHL hockey players get paid more than those in the minor leagues? Certainly, the higher wage is not a compensating differential. Playing in the NHL is not a less pleasant task than playing in the minor leagues; in fact, the opposite is true. The NHL does not require more years of schooling or more experience. To a large extent, players in the NHL earn more just because they have greater natural ability.

Natural ability is important for workers in all occupations. Because of heredity and upbringing, people differ in their physical and mental attributes. Some people are strong, others weak. Some people are smart, others less so. Some people are outgoing, others awkward in social situations. These and many other personal characteristics determine how productive workers are and, therefore, play a role in determining the wages they earn.

Closely related to ability is effort. Some people work hard, others are lazy. We should not be surprised to find that those who work hard are more productive and earn higher wages. To some extent, firms reward workers directly by paying people on the basis of what they produce. Salespeople, for instance, are often paid as a percentage of the sales they make. At other times, hard work is rewarded less directly in the form of a higher annual salary or a bonus.

Chance also plays a role in determining wages. If a person attended a trade school to learn how to repair televisions with vacuum tubes and then found this skill was made obsolete by the invention of solid-state electronics, he or she would end up earning a low wage compared to others with similar years of training. The low wage of this worker is due to chance—a phenomenon that economists recognize but do not shed much light on.

How important are ability, effort, and chance in determining wages? It is hard to say, because ability, effort, and chance are hard to measure. But indirect evidence suggests that they are very important. When labour economists study wages, they relate a worker's wage to those variables that can be measured—years of schooling, years of experience, age, and job characteristics. Although all of these measured variables affect a worker's wage as theory predicts, they account for less than half of the variation in wages in our economy. Because so much of the variation in wages is left unexplained, omitted variables, including ability, effort, and chance, must play an important role.

Case Study
THE BENEFITS OF BEAUTY

People differ in many ways. One difference is in how attractive they are. The actress Keira Knightley, for instance, is a beautiful woman. In part for this reason, her movies attract large audiences. Not surprisingly, the large audiences mean a large income for Knightley.

How prevalent are the economic benefits of beauty? Labour economists Daniel Hamermesh and Jeff Biddle tried to answer this question in a study published in the December 1994 issue of *The American Economic Review*. Hamermesh and Biddle examined data from surveys of individuals in the United States and Canada. The interviewers who conducted the survey were asked to rate each respondent's physical appearance. Hamermesh and Biddle then examined how much the wages of the respondents depended on the standard determinants—education, experience, and so on—and how much they depended on physical appearance.

Hamermesh and Biddle found that beauty pays. People who are deemed to be more attractive than average earn 5 percent more than people of average looks. People of average looks earn 5 to 10 percent more than people considered less attractive than average. Similar results were found for men and women.

What explains these differences in wages? There are several ways to interpret the "beauty premium."

One interpretation is that good looks are themselves a type of innate ability determining productivity and wages. Some people are born with the attributes of a movie star; other people are not. Good looks are useful in any job in which workers present themselves to the public—such as acting, sales, and waiting on tables. In this case, an attractive worker is more valuable to the firm than an unattractive worker. The firm's willingness to pay more to attractive workers reflects its customers' preferences.

A second interpretation is that reported beauty is an indirect measure of other types of ability. How attractive a person appears depends on more than just heredity. It also depends on dress, hairstyle, personal demeanour, and other attributes that a person can control. Perhaps a person who successfully projects an attractive image in a survey interview is more likely to be an intelligent person who succeeds at other tasks as well.

A third interpretation is that the beauty premium is a type of discrimination, a topic to which we return later. ●

Good looks pay.

An Alternative View of Education: Signalling

Earlier we discussed the human-capital view of education, according to which schooling raises workers' wages because it makes them more productive. Although this view is widely accepted, some economists have proposed an alternative theory, which emphasizes that firms use educational attainment as a way of sorting between high-ability and low-ability workers. According to this alternative view, when people earn a college or university degree, for instance, they do not become more productive, but they do *signal* their high ability to prospective employers. Because it is easier for high-ability people to earn a college or university degree than it is for low-ability people, more high-ability people get post-secondary degrees. As a result, it is rational for firms to interpret a postsecondary degree as a signal of ability.

The signalling theory of education is similar to the signalling theory of advertising discussed in Chapter 16. In the signalling theory of advertising, the advertisement itself contains no real information, but the firm signals the quality of its product to consumers by its willingness to spend money on advertising. In the signalling theory of education, schooling has no real productivity benefit, but the worker signals his innate productivity to employers by his willingness to spend years at school. In both cases, an action is being taken not for its intrinsic benefit but because the willingness to take that action conveys private information to someone observing it.

Thus, we now have two views of education: the human-capital theory and the signalling theory. Both views can explain why better-educated workers tend to earn more than less-educated workers. According to the human-capital view, education makes workers more productive; according to the signalling view, education is correlated with natural ability. But the two views have radically different predictions for the effects of policies that aim to increase educational attainment. According to the human-capital view, increasing educational levels for all workers would raise all workers' productivity and thereby their wages. According to the signalling view, education does not enhance productivity, so raising all workers' educational levels would not affect wages.

Most likely, truth lies somewhere between these two extremes. The benefits to education are probably a combination of the productivity-enhancing effects of human capital and the productivity-revealing effects of signalling. The open question is the relative size of these two effects.

The Superstar Phenomenon

Although most singers earn very little and often have to take other jobs to support themselves, singer Sarah McLachlan has earned millions of dollars making music. Similarly, although most people who play hockey do it for free as a hobby, Sidney Crosby earns millions as an NHL hockey player. Sarah McLachlan and Sidney Crosby are superstars in their fields, and their great public appeal is reflected in high incomes.

Why do Sarah McLachlan and Sidney Crosby earn so much? It is not surprising that there are differences in incomes within occupations. Good carpenters earn more than mediocre carpenters, and good plumbers earn more than mediocre plumbers. People vary in ability and effort, and these differences lead to differences in income. Yet the best carpenters and plumbers do not earn the many millions that are common among the best performers and athletes. What explains the difference?

To understand the tremendous incomes of Sarah McLachlan and Sidney Crosby, we must examine the special features of the markets in which they sell their services. Superstars arise in markets that have two characteristics:

1. Every customer in the market wants to enjoy the good supplied by the best producer.
2. The good is produced with a technology that makes it possible for the best producer to supply every customer at low cost.

If Sarah McLachlan is one of the best singers around, then everyone will want to buy her next CD; buying twice as many CDs by a singer half as good is not a good substitute. Moreover, it is *possible* for everyone to enjoy the singing of Sarah McLachlan. Because it is easy to make multiple copies of a CD, Sarah McLachlan can provide her service to millions of people simultaneously. Similarly, because hockey games are broadcast on television, millions of fans can enjoy the extraordinary athletic skills of Sidney Crosby.

We can now see why there are no superstar carpenters and plumbers. Other things equal, everyone prefers to employ the best carpenter, but a carpenter, unlike a musician, can provide his services to only a limited number of customers. Although the best carpenter will be able to command a somewhat higher wage than the average carpenter, the average carpenter will still be able to earn a good living.

Above-Equilibrium Wages: Minimum-Wage Laws, Unions, and Efficiency Wages

Most analyses of wage differences among workers are based on the equilibrium model of the labour market—that is, wages are assumed to adjust to balance labour supply and labour demand. But this assumption does not always apply. For some workers, wages are set above the level that brings supply and demand into equilibrium. Let's consider three reasons why this might be so.

One reason for above-equilibrium wages is minimum-wage laws, as we first saw in Chapter 6. Most workers in the economy are not affected by these laws because their equilibrium wages are well above the legal minimum. But for some workers, especially the least skilled and least experienced, minimum-wage laws raise wages above the level they would earn in an unregulated labour market.

A second reason that wages might rise above their equilibrium level is the market power of labour unions. A **union** is a worker association that bargains with employers over wages and working conditions. Unions often raise wages above the level that would prevail without a union, perhaps because they can threaten to withhold labour from the firm by calling a **strike**. Studies suggest that union workers earn about 10 to 20 percent more than similar nonunion workers.

A third reason for above-equilibrium wages is suggested by the theory of **efficiency wages.** This theory holds that a firm can find it profitable to pay high wages because doing so increases the productivity of its workers. In particular, high wages may reduce worker turnover, increase worker effort, and raise the quality of workers who apply for jobs at the firm. If this theory is correct, then some firms may choose to pay their workers more than they would normally earn.

Above-equilibrium wages, whether caused by minimum-wage laws, unions, or efficiency wages, have similar effects on the labour market. In particular, pushing

union
a worker association that bargains with employers over wages and working conditions

strike
the organized withdrawal of labour from a firm by a union

efficiency wages
above-equilibrium wages paid by firms in order to increase worker productivity

a wage above the equilibrium level raises the quantity of labour supplied and reduces the quantity of labour demanded. The result is a surplus of labour, or unemployment. The study of unemployment and the public policies aimed to deal with it is usually considered a topic within macroeconomics, so it goes beyond the scope of this chapter. But it would be a mistake to ignore these issues completely when analyzing earnings. Although most wage differences can be understood while maintaining the assumption of equilibrium in the labour market, above-equilibrium wages play a role in some cases.

QuickQuiz Define *compensating differential* and give an example. • Give two reasons why more-educated workers earn more than less-educated workers.

THE ECONOMICS OF DISCRIMINATION

Another source of differences in wages is discrimination. **Discrimination** occurs when the marketplace offers different opportunities to similar individuals who differ only by race, ethnic group, sex, age, or other personal characteristics. Discrimination reflects some people's prejudice against certain groups in society. Although discrimination is an emotionally charged topic that often generates heated debate, economists try to study the topic objectively in order to separate myth from reality.

discrimination
the offering of different opportunities to similar individuals who differ only by race, ethnic group, sex, age, or other personal characteristics

Measuring Labour-Market Discrimination

How much does discrimination in labour markets affect the earnings of different groups of people? This question is important, but answering it is not easy.

It might seem natural to gauge the amount of discrimination in labour markets by looking at the average wages of different groups. For example, Canadian studies show that women who are members of ethnic minorities receive lower wages than white women and that men who are members of ethnic minorities are paid less than white men. The average wage of female workers is about 80 percent of the average wage of male workers. Studies have found that Aboriginal people living off reserves earn about 10 percent less than non-Aboriginal people. There is also some evidence that earnings differences exist among workers of different language origins. In particular, some studies find a significant unilingual-francophone earnings disadvantage, although more recent evidence suggests that the size of the disadvantage is decreasing. These wage differentials are sometimes presented as evidence that many employers discriminate against minority groups and women.

Yet there is a potential problem with this inference. Even in a labour market that is free of discrimination, different people earn different wages. People differ in the amount of human capital they have and in the kinds of work they are able and willing to do. People also differ in the amount of experience they have and the extent to which that experience is continuous or uninterrupted. The wage differences we observe in the economy may be, to a large extent, attributable to the determinants of equilibrium wages we discussed in the previous section. Simply observing differences in wages among broad groups—minorities and nonminorities, women and men—does not prove that employers discriminate.

Consider, for example, the role of human capital. The proportion of individuals with high-school, college, and university degrees differs substantially across various groups. For example, the proportion of white males and females with high-school, college, and university degrees in Canada exceeds the proportion of Aboriginal people with these degrees. Moreover, a greater proportion of males than females have college and university degrees, although this is changing as more females than males are now enrolled in Canadian universities. With the sizable wage gap between skilled and unskilled labour discussed earlier in this chapter, no doubt some of the wage differences between groups can be attributed to differences in education levels.

Differences in human capital may themselves be a function of discrimination of a more subtle form. "Pre-market differences" in productive characteristics, such as schooling, may be influenced by various social factors, and these social influences may themselves be the result of systemic pre-market discrimination that affects people's choices and opportunities. For example, for many years schools directed girls away from science and math courses even though these subjects may have had greater value in the marketplace than some of the alternatives.

Human capital acquired in the form of job experience can also help explain wage differences. In particular, women tend to have less job experience on average than men. One reason is that female labour-force participation has increased over the past several decades. Because of this historic change, the average female worker today is younger than the average male worker. In addition, women are more likely to interrupt their careers to raise children. For both reasons, the experience of the average female worker is less than the experience of the average male worker. (Of course, this still doesn't explain the wage gap between women and men of the same age and with the same experience.)

Yet another source of wage differences is compensating differentials. Men and women do not always choose the same type of work, and this fact may help explain some of the earnings differential between men and women. For example, women are more likely to be administrative assistants, and men are more likely to be truck drivers. The relative wages for these jobs depend in part on the working conditions of each job. Because these nonmonetary aspects are hard to measure, it is difficult to gauge the practical importance of compensating differentials in explaining the wage differences that we observe.

In the end, the study of wage differences among groups does not establish any clear conclusion about the prevalence of discrimination in Canadian labour markets. Most economists believe that some of the observed wage differentials are attributable to discrimination, but there is no consensus about how much. The only conclusion about which economists are in consensus is a negative one: *Because the differences in average wages among groups in part reflect differences in human capital and job characteristics, they do not by themselves say anything about how much discrimination there is in the labour market.*

Discrimination by Employers

Let's now turn from measurement to the economic forces that lie behind discrimination in labour markets. If one group in society receives a lower wage than another group, even after controlling for human capital and job characteristics, who is to blame for this differential?

The answer is not obvious. It might seem natural to blame employers for discriminatory wage differences. After all, employers make the hiring decisions that determine labour demand and wages. If some groups of workers earn lower wages than they should, then it seems that employers are responsible. Yet many economists are skeptical of this easy answer. They believe that competitive, market economies provide a natural antidote to employer discrimination. That antidote is called the *profit motive*.

Imagine an economy in which workers are differentiated by their hair colour. Blondes and brunettes have the same skills, experience, and work ethic. Yet, because of discrimination, employers prefer not to hire workers with blonde hair. Thus, the demand for blondes is lower than it otherwise would be. As a result, blondes earn a lower wage than brunettes.

How long can this wage differential persist? In this economy, there is an easy way for a firm to beat out its competitors: It can hire blonde workers. By hiring blondes, a firm pays lower wages and thus has lower costs than firms that hire brunettes. Over time, more and more "blonde" firms enter the market to take advantage of this cost advantage. The existing "brunette" firms have higher costs and, therefore, begin to lose money when faced with the new competitors. These losses induce the brunette firms to go out of business. Eventually, the entry of blonde firms and the exit of brunette firms cause the demand for blonde workers to rise and the demand for brunette workers to fall. This process continues until the wage differential disappears.

Put simply, business owners who care only about making money are at an advantage when competing against those who also care about discriminating. As a result, firms that do not discriminate tend to replace those that do. In this way, competitive markets have a natural remedy for employer discrimination.

Case Study
EXPLAINING THE GENDER WAGE GAP

Table 19.1 illustrates ratios of female-to-male wages in Canada by selected occupation groups for 1997 and 2006. Over all occupations, the ratio increased slightly from 1997 to 2006, from 80.7 to 84.0. This was also true, for the most part,

TABLE 19.1

Ratio of Female-to-Male Wages by Occupation, 1997 and 2006

Occupation	1997	2006
All occupations	80.7	84.0
Management	77.3	84.4
Clerical	92.0	95.8
Sciences	85.0	86.0
Teachers	88.7	88.1
Sales	76.6	78.3
Construction	84.0	63.1

Source: Adapted from Statistics Canada, CANSIM database http://cansim2.statcan.gc.ca, 282-0070.

for different occupations. There was also quite a bit of variation across occupations, with a low of 63.1 in construction in 2006 and a high of 95.8 in clerical occupations.

As discussed previously, unadjusted (gross) data can be misleading. The size and variability of the earnings gap across age groups, educational levels, and occupations suggest that many factors are at work, and it is important to attempt to identify and control for those factors. Economists typically do this by using data on individual workers and accounting for individual characteristics that would be expected to influence earnings: education, experience, occupation or industry, hours of work, and so on. Statistical techniques are then used to divide the gross female–male earnings gap into two components: the part that is explained by differences in individual worker characteristics, and the part that is unexplained. The unexplained component is typically attributed to discrimination.

An example of this approach, based on a Statistics Canada study, is shown in Table 19.2. This table shows the percentage of the female–male wage gap that is explained by differences in various worker characteristics and the percentage that is then left unexplained. Fifty-one percent of the wage gap is unexplained and could therefore be attributed to discrimination of some kind. Of the factors that help to explain the wage gap, the most important are the industry that a person works in, the person's occupation, and his or her full-year, full-time equivalent (FYFTE) on-the-job experience. ●

TABLE 19.2

Fraction of the Female-to-Male Wage Gap Explained by Various Factors

Source: Adapted from Statistics Canada, Analytical Studies Branch Research Paper Series: *The Persistent Gap: New Evidence on the Canadian Gender Wage Gap*, 11F0019MWE 2001157 No. 157, released January 20, 2001.

Factors Explaining Gap	Fraction of Gap Explained
Education	4.5
FYFTE*	10.1
Tenure	2.8
Age of youngest family member	0.7
Marital status	0.8
Part-time status	3.6
Region	0.0
Urban size	−0.6
Union status	0.8
Firm size	0.9
Duties	4.3
Influence on budget and staffing decisions	1.3
Industry	11.2
Occupation	8.6
Total explained	49.0
Total unexplained	51.0

*FYFTE is full-year, full-time equivalent experience.

MORE WOMEN ON CAMPUS

Females now outnumber males at Canadian postsecondary institutions. This has implications for labour markets and for male–female earnings differentials.

Gender Revolution Transforms Canadian Campuses

By Don Butler

OTTAWA—A "revolution" has transformed the gender makeup of Canadian universities over the past 30 years. Where once males dominated, females are now almost everywhere in the majority.

Setareh Ziai never doubted she would go to university. "It wasn't an option for me not to go, personally or culturally," the third-year medical student at the University of Ottawa cheerfully admits.

"Growing up, the idea of education never ended after high school," says the 25-year-old, who has her sights set on a career as a surgical specialist. "If you wanted to make the most of your life, your best way of doing that would be to continue school past high school."

Lynn Wolfson is just 20, but already she is making a mark in her math and physics program at Carleton University. Last month, the second-year student won a national award valued at $33,000 that gives her summer work at the National Research Council for the next three years.

"I can't remember a time when I didn't think I would go to university," she says. "It was just kind of an expectation in my household."

The young women are part of what University of Ottawa vice-rector David Mitchell calls an "amazing revolution." This revolution has been driven by seismic social change—most notably, the flood of women into the work-force—the marketplace's growing demand for post-secondary credentials, and the strong academic performance of many young women in high school.

It has also been nudged along by programs aimed at raising women's participation in fields where they traditionally have been absent or underrepresented, such as engineering and the sciences.

Nevertheless, the extent to which women now outnumber men on campus is startling and, for some, a cause for concern. Consider the following:

- Women accounted for 57 per cent of all university students in the fall of 2001, the latest year for which system-wide gender breakdowns are available. There were 75,000 more women than men in full-time undergraduate programs and as many women as men in full-time graduate studies. Excluding the only two male-dominated fields—engineering and applied sciences, and mathematics and physical sciences—nearly two out of every three university students are female.

- Women have made enormous strides in a range of formerly male-dominated fields. In law, where male grads once outnumbered women seven to one, women now constitute 55 per cent of graduates. Veterinary medicine was once 90-percent male; now two women graduate for every man.

  Ratios in biology and journalism favour women two to one. As many women as men are graduating in medicine, commerce and political science. And nearly as many women as men are graduating in architecture and chemical engineering.

- In the decade ending in 2001, women accounted for 90 per cent of full-time enrolment growth at Canadian universities. Since 1981, women have driven three-quarters of enrolment growth.

- Since its inception, the Canada Millennium Scholarship Foundation has awarded 420,000 bursaries to post-secondary students worth $1.5 billion. Sixty-one per cent have gone to women.

- More women now have university degrees than men. And since women are earning about 60 per cent of undergraduate degrees, the spread is widening. Women also account for 6 in 10 graduates of community colleges, where they have long been in the majority.

- Women are quickly catching up to men in the most highly qualified segment of the working age population. In 1991, only 288,190 Canadian women had credentials above the bachelor level. By 2001, that had risen to 509,440. By contrast, the number of men with such qualifications rose much more slowly, from 462,000 in 1991 to 618,340 a decade later.

- Even in the handful of disciplines where men still dominate, female enrolment is growing more rapidly. For example, about 80 per cent of engineering students are still male. But between 1997 and 2000, female enrolment in engineering and applied sciences grew at nearly three times the rate of male enrolment.

Nor is this revolution confined to Canada; it is mirrored in virtually every other industrialized country.

"There's an engine charging along and nothing seems to get in their way," says Thomas Mortenson, a senior scholar at the Pell Institute for the Study of Opportunity in Higher Education in Washington, D.C. "They've left the boys really in the dust."

Is this good news or bad news? It depends on your perspective.

"There's really two stories here," says Mortenson. "One is the glorious success of women expanding opportunities and taking advantage of them.

"But the concern that I have is that the boys haven't been brought along with the girls on this wonderful acceleration of educational opportunity."

"The biggest change over the last century has been the rise of women in the world," says Mitchell. "Universities have reflected that in spades. Will that pendulum that swung towards female dominance in universities and related disciplines continue to swing? Will it go past 60 per cent? Will it go past 70 per cent?

"We have no way of knowing," he admits, "except that the momentum seems to suggest that it will continue for some time yet."

Alan Harrison, Carleton's vice-president academic, says the exponential increase in the number of educated women is something most people would regard as positive.

"The question is, at what point does it stop being good?" he asks. "When you have a balance, roughly 50–50, should we stop?"

Even if universities wanted to stem the rising tide of female enrolment, it's not at all clear that they could.

Unstoppable societal forces have been driving the change in gender mix.

One was the casting off of the shackles of expectation and social role that constrained women until the late 1960s.

As women began to enter the workforce in large numbers in the 1970s, they quickly realized that post-secondary education was vital if they wanted to avoid the pink-collar ghettoes to which most working women had been consigned in the past.

While a university degree is associated with higher pay for both genders, males with no degree have more options than females; they can get jobs with decent pay in male-dominated fields like the trades, heavy manufacturing, resource industries and construction, though opportunities in those fields are static or contracting.

"For men, there are reasonable jobs out there if you just have high school," says Lynn Barr-Telford, chief of survey development and analysis at the Centre for Education Statistics. "For women, there are not-so-reasonable jobs, part-time jobs and staying at home with family."

Census data bear this out. In 2000, men with high school degrees and full-time jobs earned about $41,000 on average; equivalent female high school grads averaged barely $30,000. And 100,000 more women than men in the full-time labour force worked in jobs paying less than $20,000 a year, even though about a million more men are employed than women.

Young women are also winning the competition for university admission because, overall, they get better marks in high school, says Fen Hampson, director of Carleton's Norman Paterson School of International Affairs, where women comprise 70 per cent of the students.

"All the evidence is that girls are outperforming boys in high school, and that's why more of them are getting into university in a highly competitive environment."

According to a 2003 Statistics Canada report, a gender gap exists in exposure to books and reading among four-year-olds: 79 per cent of girls looked at books daily, compared with only 64 per cent of boys. And two-thirds of parents encourage their young daughters to write daily; barely half do so for boys.

This literacy advantage persists throughout elementary and high school.

There are scant signs that the gender balance pendulum is set to reverse course any time soon.

One of the few may be in Quebec, where male university enrolment grew last fall at a slightly faster rate than female enrolment. Gender breakdowns for the current school year aren't available yet from other provinces, so it's impossible to know whether the Quebec numbers represent a real change or merely a brief detour.

If female domination of universities continues to expand, the implications for society may be profound, says David Mitchell.

"The future may well look like a place where the options for women are far greater for the good jobs," he says. "We may have service-sector jobs, low-paying jobs and minimum-wage jobs filled mostly by men. We might have professional positions or executive positions filled more often by women."

But women shouldn't feel too gleeful about their educational ascendancy, cautions Monique Frize, a professor of biomedical engineering at Carleton and the University of Ottawa. Unless more men start going to university, she says, "I think there'll be a lot of resentment, a lot of misogyny.

"There is enough of that already," she says wearily. "I think it's going to aggravate it, and the boys will resent the girls."

Source: Don Butler, "An 'amazing' revolution is happening at university," *The Ottawa Citizen*, February 9, 2004. Material reprinted with the express permission of Ottawa Citizen Group Inc., A CanWest Partnership.

Discrimination by Customers and Governments

The profit motive is a strong force acting to eliminate discriminatory wage differentials, but there are limits to its corrective abilities. Here we consider two of the most important limits: *customer preferences* and *government policies*.

To see how customer preferences for discrimination can affect wages, consider again our imaginary economy with blondes and brunettes. Suppose that restaurant owners discriminate against blondes when hiring servers. As a result, blonde servers earn lower wages than brunette servers. In this case, a restaurant could open up with blonde servers and charge lower prices. If customers cared only about the quality and price of their meals, the discriminatory firms would be driven out of business, and the wage differential would disappear.

On the other hand, it is possible that customers prefer being served by brunettes. If this preference for discrimination is strong, the entry of blonde restaurants need not succeed in eliminating the wage differential between brunettes and blondes. That is, if customers have discriminatory preferences, a competitive market is consistent with a discriminatory wage differential. An economy with such discrimination would contain two types of restaurants: Blonde restaurants hire blondes, have lower costs, and charge lower prices. Brunette restaurants hire brunettes, have higher costs, and charge higher prices. Customers who did not care about the hair colour of their servers would be attracted to the lower prices at the blonde restaurants. Bigoted customers would go to the brunette restaurants. They would pay for their discriminatory preference in the form of higher prices.

Another way for discrimination to persist in competitive markets is for the government to mandate discriminatory practices. If, for instance, the government passed a law stating that blondes could wash dishes in restaurants but could not work as servers, then a wage differential could persist in a competitive market. For example, before South Africa abandoned its system of apartheid, blacks were prohibited from working in some jobs. Discriminatory governments pass such laws to suppress the normal equalizing force of free and competitive markets.

To sum up: *Competitive markets contain a natural remedy for employer discrimination. The entry into the market of firms that care only about profit tends to eliminate discriminatory wage differentials. These wage differentials persist in competitive markets only when customers are willing to pay to maintain the discriminatory practice or when the government mandates it.*

Case Study
DISCRIMINATION IN SPORTS

As we have seen, measuring discrimination is difficult. To determine whether one group of workers is discriminated against, a researcher must correct for differences in productivity between that group and other workers in the economy. Yet, in most firms, it is difficult to measure a particular worker's contribution to the production of goods and services.

One type of firm in which measurement is easier is the sports team. Professional teams have many objective measures of productivity. In baseball, for example, we can measure a player's batting average, home runs, stolen bases, and so on. In hockey, we can measure a player's goals, assists, and plus–minus statistics.

Economists focus on three main types of potential discrimination in sports: (1) salary discrimination; (2) position segregation, where certain positions are systematically assigned to certain groups; and (3) hiring, or entry, discrimination, where only the most productive elements of the discriminated group are hired.

U.S. studies have tended to focus on wage discrimination on racial grounds. These studies suggest that racial discrimination has indeed existed in sports teams, and that much of the blame may lie with customers. For example, a study published in the *Journal of Labor Economics* in 1988 (6:1) found that black basketball players earned 20 percent less than white players of comparable ability. The study also found that attendance at basketball games was larger for teams with a greater proportion of white players. A similar situation also existed for baseball players, although more recent studies of salaries have found no evidence of discriminatory wage differentials. One interpretation of these findings is that customer discrimination makes black players less profitable than white players for team owners. In the presence of such customer discrimination, a discriminatory wage gap can persist, even if team owners care only about profit.

A series of studies that appeared in *Canadian Public Policy* between 1987 and 1995 examined the existence of discrimination against francophone hockey players in the NHL. Early work focused on hiring discrimination. Using various performance measures for NHL players, it was determined that francophone players are underrepresented in the NHL and have tended to outperform their anglophone counterparts. One interpretation of this evidence is that francophones have been subjected to hiring discrimination. As a result of discrimination, francophones must outperform anglophones by a significant margin to get into the league in the first place.

Subsequent studies have questioned this interpretation. For example, an alternative interpretation is that the inability of marginal francophone players to communicate well in English impedes their ability to adapt to the needs of the team. Thus, for marginal players, selecting partially on the basis of language maximizes the success of the team both on and off the ice.

Other work has emphasized differences in playing styles between junior hockey teams in Quebec (the primary providers of francophone players to the NHL) and junior hockey teams in English-speaking provinces. In particular, the Quebec-based teams tend to favour smaller players with offensive abilities, whereas NHL teams tend to favour bigger players with defensive abilities, especially for marginal or "role" players. This suggests that the underrepresentation of francophones in the NHL is not due to hiring discrimination but to different preferences in playing styles. Yet another study, using updated data, has found no evidence of either hiring or wage discrimination against francophones.

A recent salvo in the debate introduces the role of the location of NHL cities. The premise of this study is that the historic tensions between English Canadians and French Canadians suggests that francophones playing for teams based in English Canada may face salary discrimination, while francophones playing for teams based in the United States, where no such tensions exist, do not. Using this approach, the study finds evidence that francophones playing in English Canada do indeed suffer significant salary discrimination. •

QuickQuiz   Why is it hard to establish whether a group of workers is being discriminated against? • Explain how profit-maximizing firms tend to eliminate discriminatory wage differentials. • How might a discriminatory wage differential persist?

CONCLUSION

In competitive markets, workers earn a wage equal to the value of their marginal contribution to the production of goods and services. Many things, however, affect the value of the marginal product. Firms pay more for workers who are more talented, more diligent, more experienced, and more educated because these workers are more productive. Firms pay less to those workers against whom customers discriminate because these workers contribute less to revenue.

The theory of the labour market we have developed in the last two chapters explains why some workers earn higher wages than other workers. The theory does not say that the resulting distribution of income is equal, fair, or desirable in any way. That is the topic we take up in Chapter 20.

SUMMARY

- Workers earn different wages for many reasons. To some extent, wage differentials compensate workers for job attributes. Other things equal, workers in hard, unpleasant jobs get paid more than workers in easy, pleasant jobs.

- Workers with more human capital get paid more than workers with less human capital. The return to accumulating human capital is high and has increased over the past two decades.

- Although years of education, experience, and job characteristics affect earnings as theory predicts, there is much variation in earnings that cannot be explained by things that economists can measure. The unexplained variation in earnings is largely attributable to natural ability, effort, and chance.

- Some economists have suggested that more-educated workers earn higher wages not because education raises productivity but because workers with high natural ability use education as a way to signal their high ability to employers. If this signalling theory is correct, then increasing the educational attainment of all workers would not raise the overall level of wages.

- Wages are sometimes pushed above the level that brings supply and demand into balance. Three reasons for above-equilibrium wages are minimum-wage laws, unions, and efficiency wages.

- Some differences in earnings are attributable to discrimination on the basis of race, sex, or other factors. Measuring the amount of discrimination is difficult, however, because one must correct for differences in human capital and job characteristics.

- Competitive markets tend to limit the impact of discrimination on wages. If the wages of a group of workers are lower than those of another group for reasons not related to marginal productivity, then nondiscriminatory firms will be more profitable than discriminatory firms. Profit-maximizing behaviour, therefore, can reduce discriminatory wage differentials. Discrimination persists in competitive markets, however, if customers are willing to pay more to discriminatory firms or if the government passes laws requiring firms to discriminate.

KEY CONCEPTS

compensating differential, p. 416
human capital, p. 416

union, p. 422
strike, p. 422

efficiency wages, p. 422
discrimination, p. 423

QUESTIONS FOR REVIEW

1. Why are coal miners paid more than other workers with similar amounts of education?

2. In what sense is education a type of capital?

3. How might education raise a worker's wage without raising the worker's productivity?

4. What conditions lead to economic superstars? Would you expect to see superstars in dentistry? In economics? Explain.

5. Give three reasons why a worker's wage might be above the level that balances supply and demand.

6. What difficulties arise in deciding whether a group of workers has a lower wage because of discrimination?

7. Do the forces of economic competition tend to exacerbate or ameliorate discrimination on the basis of race?

8. Give an example of how discrimination might persist in a competitive market.

PROBLEMS AND APPLICATIONS

1. University and college students sometimes work as summer interns for private firms or the government. Many of these positions pay little or nothing.
   a. What is the opportunity cost of taking such a job?
   b. Explain why students are willing to take these jobs.
   c. If you were to compare the earnings later in life of workers who had worked as interns and those who had taken summer jobs that paid more, what would you expect to find?

2. As explained in Chapter 6, a minimum-wage law distorts the market for low-wage labour. To reduce this distortion, some economists advocate a two-tiered minimum-wage system, with a regular minimum wage for adult workers and a lower, "sub-minimum" wage for teenaged workers. Give two reasons why a single minimum wage might distort the labour market for teenaged workers more than it would the market for adult workers.

3. A basic finding of labour economics is that workers who have more experience in the labour force are paid more than workers who have less experience (holding constant the amount of formal education). Why might this be so? Some studies have also found that experience at the

same job (called "job tenure") has an extra positive influence on wages. Explain.

4. At some colleges and universities, economics professors receive higher salaries than professors in some other fields.
   a. Why might this be true?
   b. Some other colleges and universities have a policy of paying equal salaries to professors in all fields. At some of these schools, economics professors have lighter teaching loads than professors in some other fields. What role do the differences in teaching loads play?

5. Sara works for Steve, whom she dislikes because of his snobbish attitude. Yet when she looks for other jobs, the best she can do is find a job paying $10 000 less than her current salary. Should she take the job? Analyze Sara's situation from an economic point of view.

6. Imagine that someone offers you a choice: You could spend four years studying at the world's best university, but you would have to keep your attendance there a secret. Or you could be awarded an official degree from the world's best university, but you couldn't actually attend. Which choice do you think would enhance your future earnings more? What does your answer say about the debate over signalling versus human capital in the role of education?

7. When recording devices were first invented almost 100 years ago, musicians could suddenly supply their music to large audiences at low cost. How do you suppose this development affected the income of the best musicians? How do you suppose it affected the income of average musicians?

8. A case study in this chapter described how customer discrimination in sports seems to have an important effect on players' earnings. Note that this is possible because sports fans know the players' characteristics, including their race. Why is this knowledge important

for the existence of discrimination? Give some specific examples of industries where customer discrimination is and is not likely to influence wages.

9. Suppose that all young women were channelled into careers as secretaries, nurses, and teachers; at the same time, young men were encouraged to consider these three careers and many others as well.
   a. Draw a diagram showing the combined labour market for secretaries, nurses, and teachers. Draw a diagram showing the combined labour market for all other fields. In which market is the wage higher? Do men or women receive higher wages on average?
   b. Now suppose that society changed and encouraged both young women and young men to consider a wide range of careers. Over time, what effect would this change have on the wages in the two markets you illustrated in part (a)? What effect would the change have on the average wages of men and women?

10. Economist June O'Neill argues that "until family roles are more equal, women are not likely to have the same pattern of market work and earnings as men." What does she mean by the "pattern" of market work? How do these characteristics of jobs and careers affect earnings?

11. This chapter considers the economics of discrimination by employers, customers, and governments. Now consider discrimination by workers. Suppose that some brunette workers did not like working with blonde workers. Do you think this worker discrimination could explain lower wages for blonde workers? If such a wage differential existed, what would a profit-maximizing entrepreneur do? If there were many such entrepreneurs, what would happen over time?

http://   For more study tools, please visit http://www.mankiw5e.nelson.com.

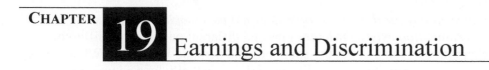

19 Earnings and Discrimination

I. Chapter Overview

A. Context and Purpose

The previous chapter introduced markets for the factors of production, with an emphasis on the labour market. Chapter 19 explores wage patterns in Canada, looking at the factors that explain differences in wages. It extends the supply and demand analysis of Chapter 18 to investigate in more depth the factors that affect the supply of and demand for labour. This chapter provides the background for a discussion of the distribution of income in Chapter 20. Understanding the factors that determine wages will help to explain why some people are rich and some are poor.

A. Helpful Hints

1. *A person's earnings depend on the supply and demand for that person's labour*, which in turn depends on natural ability, human capital, compensating differentials, discrimination, and so on.

2. *Human capital refers to the accumulation of investments in people*, for example, in the form of education, training, or health care.

3. *Compensating differential refers to a difference in wages that arises to offset the nonmonetary characteristics of different jobs.* Some jobs are more desirable than others; these typically need not pay as much as less attractive jobs in order to attract the same number of workers.

4. Sidney Crosby earned US$8.7 million in the 2007–2008 season, and he may be worth it. People often react in horror to high salaries by sports superstars. Upon learning that Crosby earned a salary of $8.7 million for playing hockey for the Pittsburgh Penguins, a common reaction is that he is overpaid, that "nobody deserves that much." Marginal productivity theory, however, tells another story: if Crosby is paid $8.7 million a year, it is because he is worth at least that much to the team. Suppose that he brings in US$18 million in additional ticket sales and advertising revenues to the Penguins during the contract year. Is he overpaid or underpaid? There is no easy answer, but remember that in this case he would be earning only about half of the value of his marginal product! Superstars can earn super salaries to a large extent because they can provide a service to many fans simultaneously through television. They earn a lot because we have made them valuable productive factors.

267

5.   *Different pay for different people does not necessarily mean that discrimination exists.* Different jobs and different people have different characteristics that affect the supply of and demand for labour. What seems to be a discriminatory wage differential may actually be a compensating differential that offsets a nonmonetary aspect of the job.

II. Self-Testing Challenges

A. True/False Questions

____1.   The rate of return to higher education in Canada has grown steadily in recent decades.

____2.   Employer discrimination is hard to eliminate, because if one employer discriminates, competition forces others to follow suit.

____3.   Efficiency wages theory holds that above-equilibrium wages arise because firms find it profitable to pay high wages in order to increase the profitability of their workers.

____4.   The best evidence of continuing discrimination against women by employers is the wage gap in the market: women still earn roughly three-fourths of what men earn.

____5.   The signalling theory helps to explain why wages have not risen over time in Canada as the average educational level has risen.

____6.   The wage gap between men and women has actually increased in recent years, although this appears to be due mostly to changing job characteristics, rather than discrimination.

____7.   Empirical and indirect evidence suggests that ability, effort and chance, although hard to measure, are likely to be significant contributors to wage differences.

____8.   Profit-maximizing competitive firms cannot discriminate in the hiring of workers, unless consumers are willing to pay to maintain the discriminatory practice.

____9.   The return to investments in human capital has increased over the past decade.

____10.   Differences in earnings can be explained completely by differences in investment in human capital.

____11.   International trade and technological change may bring about the growing wage inequality between skilled and unskilled labour.

____12.   According to the human-capital view of education, increasing educational levels would not affect wages.

B. Multiple-Choice Questions

1.   If two jobs require the same amount of knowledge, skills, and experience, which one of the following is the likely description of the lower paying of the two jobs?
   a. more pleasant
   b. more unpleasant
   c. more risky
   d. more routine

2.   Which one of the following is an example of human capital?
   a. basic population
   b. on-the-job training
   c. higher consumption

3.   Which one of the following would provide evidence favouring human-capital theory over the signalling theory regarding the effect of education on earnings?
   a. High-school dropouts earn less than high-school graduates.
   b. University graduates earn more than high-school graduates.
   c. Earnings are higher for students who stayed in school longer because of compulsory attendance laws.
   d. Technical school graduates earn more than workers who did not attend technical school.

4.   Which one of the following defines a labour union?
   a. an association of workers working in the same industry, but in different jobs
   b. an association of workers that bargains with employers over wages and working conditions for its members
   c. an association of workers that tries to increase employment
   d. an association of workers formed to restrain wage increases

5.   Which one of the following types of discrimination is the labour market **MOST** likely to cure?
   a. employer discrimination
   b. discrimination by customers
   c. discrimination caused by government mandates
   d. discrimination caused by racism

6.   Which one of the following is **NOT** a form of discrimination?
   a.   employers' preferences for employees with certain characteristics
   b.   customers who prefer to deal only with certain racial or ethnic groups
   c.   government mandates that some jobs are not available to people with certain characteristics
   d.   lower demand for the labour of certain groups with lower value of marginal product

The following graphs show the markets for autoworkers and steelworkers. Workers in the two markets have similar skills, so they can move freely between the two. In both markets the initial equilibrium is at the intersection of S_1 and D_1. Use the graphs to answer questions 7–10.

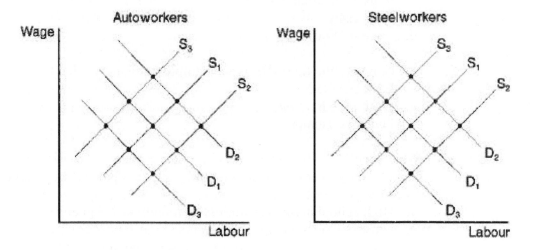

7.   A new study shows that steelworkers are much more at risk of injury on the job than was previously thought to be the case. Which one of the following is the likely result in the market for steelworkers?
   a.   Demand will increase and supply will fall, thus raising wages and employment.
   b.   Demand will increase, thus leading to higher wages and higher employment.
   c.   Supply will decrease, thus leading to higher wages and lower employment.
   d.   Supply will increase, thus leading to lower wages and higher employment.

8.   Referring back to the previous question, which one of the following describes what the change in the market for steelworkers will do to the market for autoworkers?
   a.   Demand will increase and supply will fall, thus increasing the wage rate and employment.
   b.   Demand will increase, thus increasing the wage rate and employment.

    c. Supply will decrease, thus increasing the wage rate and reducing employment.

    d. Supply will increase, thus decreasing the wage rate and increasing employment.

9.   Suppose that Canadian automakers hire American autoworkers who work in Canada but live (and spend their incomes) in the United States. Which one of the following describes what will happen to the markets for autoworkers in Canada?

    a. Both the supply of and the demand for autoworkers will increase in the same proportion, thus leaving the wage rate unchanged.

    b. The supply of autoworkers will rise, thus leading to higher employment but a lower wage rate; demand will not change.

    c. The demand for autoworkers will decrease, thus driving down the wage rate and employment; supply will not change.

    d. Both the supply of and the demand for autoworkers will decrease in the same proportion, thus leaving the wage rate unchanged.

10.   Assuming that workers can easily change jobs between the auto industry and the steel industry, what impact will the changes in the auto industry have (explained in the previous question) on the market for steelworkers in Canada?

    a. The supply of steelworkers would increase to S_2, demand would not change, employment would rise, and the wage rate would fall.

    b. The supply of steelworkers would decrease to S_2, demand would not change, and employment and the wage rate would decrease.

    c. The demand for steelworkers will fall to D_3, and employment and the wage rate will fall.

    d. The demand for steelworkers will rise to D_2, and employment and the wage rate will rise.

11.   Which one of the following will result in a wage differential between males and females?

    a. discrimination against females by employers

    b. differences in job choice by males only

    c. differences in job choice by females only

    d. clustering by workers into certain traditionally low-paying occupations

Use the following graphs to answer questions 12 and 13.

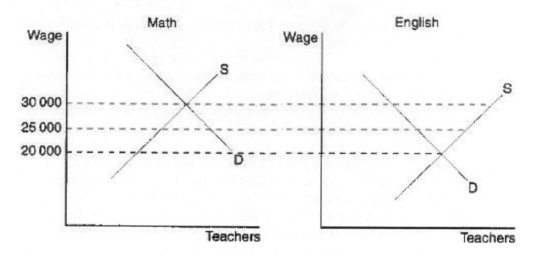

12.   If the government passes a law that all teachers with the same seniority must receive the same pay, and the salaries are set at $25 000 for both math and English teachers, which one of the following would be the result?
   a. a surplus of math teachers and a shortage of English teachers
   b. a shortage of math teachers and a surplus of English teachers
   c. just enough teachers, because on average the wage is at equilibrium
   d. an incentive for more teachers to become math teachers, because of the shortage

13.   Which one of the following would be the **MOST** likely outcome of equalizing salaries in the previous question?
   a. a reduction in the quality of teachers in both math and English
   b. an increase in the quality of teachers in both math and English
   c. the hiring of English teachers with better credentials than those hired in math
   d. the hiring of math teachers with better credentials than those hired in English

14.   Which one of the following is the immediate effect of immigration?
   a. an increase in the supply of labour
   b. a decrease in the supply of labour
   c. a decrease in the demand for labour
   d. an increase in the number of workers who cannot find jobs at any wage

15. Given the two characteristics of markets that give rise to superstars, the satellite broadcasting technology that allows millions of fans to enjoy the athletic skills of Jarome Iginla most likely _____ the cost of broadcasting Calgary Flames' hockey games to large audiences, _____ the income of Jarome Iginla, and _____ the incomes of average hockey players.
   a. increases, increases, increases
   b. decreases, increases, decreases
   c. increases, increases, decreases
   d. decreases, decreases, decreases.

16. Which one of the following terms refers to differences in wages that compensate for unpleasant working conditions, or riskiness of certain jobs?
   a. wage premiums
   b. employer discrimination
   c. compensating wage differentials
   d. signalling wage differentials

17. Which one of the following groups of workers is likely to receive the **HIGHEST** pay as a result of a compensating wage differential?
   a. garbage collectors
   b. waiters at ski resorts
   c. dish washers
   d. maids

18. Which one of the following defines the efficiency wage?
   a. It is higher than the market-clearing wage to reward workers for informing on others who shirk.
   b. It is lower than the market-clearing wage to allow managers the resources to monitor labour productivity.
   c. It is lower than the market-clearing wage because of workers who shirk.
   d. It is higher than the market-clearing wage to increase worker productivity.

19. Which one of the following refers to the natural antidote that many economists believe competitive market economies provide to employer discrimination?
   a. cost minimization
   b. revenue maximization
   c. profit motive
   d. wage differentials

20.   From the perspective of an economist, which one of the following is a type of potential discrimination in professional sports?
   a. salary consistency
   b. position fluctuation
   c. hiring discrimination

C. Short-Answer Questions

1. According to a letter to the *New York Times* several years ago, garbage collectors in New York City earned more than assistant professors at Yale University. The letter writer attributed this to powerful unions in New York City. Do you think that the letter writer was correct about the cause, or could there be other reasons for the garbage collectors to earn more?

   _____
   _____
   _____
   _____

2. Debate continues over whether the free market can cure labour market discrimination without government intervention. What do you think? To what extent can the market solve problems of discrimination without government intervention? What problem areas are likely to remain without intervention?

   _____
   _____
   _____
   _____

D. Practice Problems

1. A positive relationship exists between education (or training) and earnings. Workers with higher educational attainment earn more than those with lesser amounts of education or training. In fact, this wage gap has grown in recent years.

   a. In economic terms, how do you explain the relationship between education and earnings? What are the two theories that might help to explain the relationship, and why is it difficult to determine which view is correct? Why is the wage gap growing between the educated and the less educated?

   _____
   _____
   _____
   _____
   _____
   _____

b. Why is experience also correlated with earnings?

_____

_____

_____

_____

2. A study by labour economists D. Hamermesh and J. Biddle (Source:
    American Economic Review, December 1994) found that people who are
    perceived as good-looking earn an average of 10 percent more than those
    who are perceived as homely, and 5 percent more than people of average
    looks.

    a. What do these findings indicate? _____

    _____

    _____

    _____

    _____

    b. Do these findings mean that there is a beauty premium or beauty
        discrimination?

    _____

    _____

    _____

E. Advanced Critical Thinking

1. According to a columnist for the *Edmonton Times*:

    "Comparable worth legislation is long overdue. Women are paid less than
    80% of the wages paid to men, and improvement is coming at a glacially slow
    pace. Until the law recognizes that women are equal to men and should receive
    equal pay for equal work, there will be no justice in the workplace. Female
    English teachers, for example, earn less than male economics teachers with the
    same training. A simple act of Parliament could solve this problem by requiring
    job evaluation and comparable pay for comparable occupations."

    Write a letter to the editor critiquing this column, explaining why you agree
    or disagree. Whether you agree or disagree, acknowledge the arguments on both
    sides of the issue and then explain your position.

    _____

    _____

    _____

    _____

    _____

    _____

    _____

2. Does attending school increase wages because it increases productivity, or does it appear to increase productivity because high-ability people are more likely to stay in school? Discuss.

_____

_____

_____

_____

_____

_____

III. Solutions

A. True/False Questions

1. F; there has been no tendency for the wage premium to grow over time in Canada over the past decade.
2. F; employer discrimination puts the employer at a competitive disadvantage, because other competitors who hire the best person for the job will have lower costs of production and be able to undercut the discriminator on price.
3. T
4. F; even though women still earn less than men, it is difficult to determine how much of the differential is due to discrimination.
5. F; signalling theory works only to explain *relative* wages, because relatively more education by one person suggests relatively more ability or effort; if everyone has more education, then higher earnings must be due to increased productivity.
6. F; the wage gap between men and women continues to narrow.
7. T
8. T
9. T
10. F; not entirely: differences in earnings are also attributable to luck, ability, effort, and discrimination.
11. T
12. F; according to the human-capital view, education enhances productivity and thereby raises wages.

B. Multiple-Choice Questions

1. a	5. a	9. b	13. c	17. a
2. b	6. d	10. a	14. a	18. d
3. c	7. c	11. a	15. b	19. c
4. b	8. d	12. b	16. c	20. c

C. Short-Answer Questions

1. Although the unions could help to explain such a wage differential, it is more likely that New York garbage collectors receive a compensating wage differential that more than offsets the effect of their lower human capital. Even for a higher wage, it is doubtful that Yale's assistant professors would quit their jobs in order to collect garbage in New York City. In fact, a position at Yale is so desirable that lesser universities may even have to pay compensating wage differentials to compete with the nonmonetary aspects of a position at Yale.

2. The labour market is likely to deal effectively with employer discrimination. Those employers with tastes for discrimination will be at a competitive disadvantage relative to employers who hire the best person for the job without regard for irrelevant personal characteristics. At least under competition, long-run profit is zero; there is no room for an employer to hire anyone other than the best person for the position without losing money. In the case of discrimination by customers, however, the employer may find it profitable to discriminate. If customers do not like to deal with certain ethnic groups, for example, a profit-maximizing employer will respond accordingly. Until attitudes change, the problem may well require government intervention to ban such discrimination, because the market will not take care of it.

D.   Practice Problems

1. a. Education or training raises the value of the marginal product of the worker. It represents an increase in human capital that makes the worker more productive, just as a piece of physical capital increases workers' productivity. An alternative to the human capital theory is the signalling theory, which states that additional educational attainment tells the employer something about the ability and effort of the potential employee. Even if the education does not increase the value of the marginal product to the employer, it suggests that the employee is somehow superior to those who did not receive comparable education. This helps to explain why college graduates may find good-paying jobs outside of their areas of academic expertise: the degree itself signals something to potential employers. Both theories lead to similar conclusions, namely that better educated workers earn more. This makes it hard to

distinguish the signalling effect from the human capital effect. The education wage gap has grown as the demand for skilled workers has increased relative to the demand for unskilled workers in an increasingly technological society.

   b. Experience is a form of human capital. Workers can gain skills through training or through on-the-job experience and training. Therefore, with experience, the value of the marginal product of the worker rises, at least up to a certain point. As a result, earnings tend to rise with age, and then peak and fall somewhat as the worker nears retirement, when productivity may be slowing down.

2.   a. These findings suggest that good-looking individuals are paid more. This may be interpreted that good looks are directly related to productivity and wages. Good looks are useful for workers who have to deal with customers, such as salespeople, and those who have to present themselves to the public, such as actors. In these cases, attractive workers are more valuable to firms and may command higher wages. These findings may also suggest that appearance correlates with higher self-esteem, which leads to higher productivity.

   b. These findings do not necessarily mean that there is a beauty discrimination. However, further investigation might reveal evidence of discrimination such as customers' discriminatory preferences for good-looking salesclerks, actors, and waitstaff.

E.   Advanced Critical Thinking

1. On the positive side, comparable worth is an attempt to deal with discrimination that the free market has been unable to eliminate. Competitive labour markets can stop employer discrimination, but not all labour markets behave competitively. Employers with preferences for discrimination may be able to indulge those tastes if they can afford somewhat higher costs. Comparable worth laws can stop such discrimination without waiting generations for attitudes to change.

   Unfortunately, comparable worth laws often have unintended consequences. At first glance, it seems desirable: women are paid less than men when they cluster into occupations that pay less. However, those wage differentials reflect differences in relative supply and demand. Some occupations may seem more demanding, or less appealing in some other nonmonetary aspect. Without a financial incentive to go into that industry, not enough people will choose that occupation. As a result, there will be shortages. Also problematic is the loss of the incentives for little girls and

little boys to reach for nonstereotypical jobs. Those pay differentials between traditionally male and traditionally female jobs have helped to break down the cultural barriers. More girls are growing up to become doctors, economists, and computer programmers today, rather than nurses, English teachers, and elementary school teachers, thanks in part to salaries that have encouraged them to take the chance. The irony of comparable worth legislation is that, however well-meaning it is, it would actually slow down this change and perpetuate the inefficiency of people clustering into occupations that may not be those most in demand by society.

2. According to human-capital theory, education makes workers more productive. Increasing educational levels for all workers, therefore, would raise all workers' productivity and thus their wages. Signalling theory, on the other hand, holds that education is correlated with natural ability. Education does not necessarily make a worker more productive, but it signals the worker's high ability to prospective employers. Thus, raising all workers' educational levels would not affect wages.

    Both theories can explain why better-educated workers tend to earn more than less-educated ones. But the two views offer different predictions for the effects of education policies. The benefits to education are a combination of the productivity-enhancing effects of human capital and the productivity-revealing effects of signalling.

© Sean Gladwell/GetStock.com

TOPICS FOR FURTHER STUDY

THE THEORY OF CONSUMER CHOICE 21

© Sean Gladwell/GetStock.com

When you walk into a store, you are confronted with thousands of goods that you might buy. Of course, because your financial resources are limited, you cannot buy everything that you want. You therefore consider the prices of the various goods being offered for sale and buy a bundle of goods that, given your resources, best suits your needs and desires.

In this chapter we develop the theory that describes how consumers make decisions about what to buy. So far throughout this book, we have summarized consumers' decisions with the demand curve. As we discussed in Chapters 4 through 7, the demand curve for a good reflects consumers' willingness to pay for it. When the price of a good rises, consumers are willing to pay for fewer units, so the quantity demanded falls. We now look more deeply at the decisions that lie behind the demand curve. The theory of consumer choice presented in this chapter provides a more complete understanding of demand, just as the theory of the competitive firm in Chapter 14 provides a more complete understanding of supply.

One of the ten principles of economics discussed in Chapter 1 is that people face tradeoffs. The theory of consumer choice examines the tradeoffs that people face in their role as consumers. When a consumer buys more of one good, he can afford less of other goods. When he spends more time enjoying leisure and less time working, he has lower income and can afford less consumption. When he spends more of his income in the present and saves less of it, he must accept a lower level of consumption in the future. The theory of consumer choice examines how consumers facing these tradeoffs make decisions and how they respond to changes in their environment.

After developing the basic theory of consumer choice, we apply it to three questions about household decisions. In particular, we ask:

1. Do all demand curves slope downward?
2. How do wages affect labour supply?
3. How do interest rates affect household saving?

At first, these questions might seem unrelated. But, as we will see, we can use the theory of consumer choice to address each of them.

THE BUDGET CONSTRAINT: WHAT THE CONSUMER CAN AFFORD

Most people would like to increase the quantity or quality of the goods they consume—to take longer vacations, drive fancier cars, or eat at better restaurants. People consume less than they desire because their spending is *constrained*, or limited, by their income. We begin our study of consumer choice by examining this link between income and spending.

To keep things simple, we examine the decision facing a consumer who buys only two goods: Pepsi and pizza. Of course, real people buy thousands of different kinds of goods. Yet assuming there are only two goods greatly simplifies the problem without altering the basic insights about consumer choice.

We first consider how the consumer's income constrains the amount he spends on Pepsi and pizza. Suppose that the consumer has an income of $1000 per month and that he spends his entire income each month on Pepsi and pizza. The price of a litre of Pepsi is $2, and the price of a pizza is $10.

The table in Figure 21.1 shows some of the many combinations of Pepsi and pizza that the consumer can buy. The first line in the table shows that if the consumer spends all his income on pizza, he can eat 100 pizzas during the month, but he would not be able to buy any Pepsi at all. The second line shows another possible consumption bundle: 90 pizzas and 50 L of Pepsi. And so on. Each consumption bundle in the table costs exactly $1000.

The graph in Figure 21.1 illustrates the consumption bundles that the consumer can choose. The vertical axis measures the number of litres of Pepsi, and the horizontal axis measures the number of pizzas. Three points are marked on this figure. At point A, the consumer buys no Pepsi and consumes 100 pizzas. At point B, the consumer buys no pizza and consumes 500 L of Pepsi. At point C, the consumer buys 50 pizzas and 250 L of Pepsi. Point C, which is exactly at the middle of the line from A to B, is the point at which the consumer spends an equal amount ($500) on Pepsi and pizza. Of course, these are only three of the many combinations of Pepsi and pizza that the consumer can choose. All the points on the line from A to B are possible. This line, called the **budget constraint**, shows the consumption bundles that the consumer can afford. In this case, it shows the tradeoff between Pepsi and pizza that the consumer faces.

The slope of the budget constraint measures the rate at which the consumer can trade one good for the other. Recall from the appendix to Chapter 2 that the slope between two points is calculated as the change in the vertical distance divided by the change in the horizontal distance (rise over run). From point A to point B, the

budget constraint
the limit on the consumption bundles that a consumer can afford

FIGURE 21.1

The Consumer's Budget Constraint

The budget constraint shows the various bundles of goods that the consumer can afford for a given income. Here the consumer buys bundles of Pepsi and pizza. The table and graph show what the consumer can afford if his income is $1000, the price of Pepsi is $2 per litre, and the price of a pizza is $10.

Litres of Pepsi	Number of Pizzas	Spending on Pepsi	Spending on Pizza	Total Spending
0	100	$ 0	$1000	$1000
50	90	100	900	1000
100	80	200	800	1000
150	70	300	700	1000
200	60	400	600	1000
250	50	500	500	1000
300	40	600	400	1000
350	30	700	300	1000
400	20	800	200	1000
450	10	900	100	1000
500	0	1000	0	1000

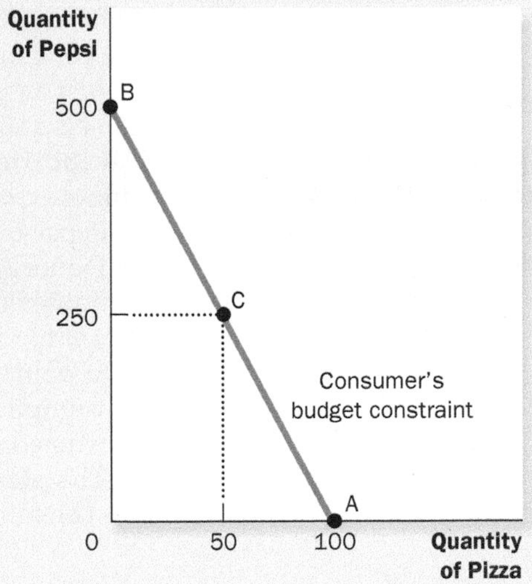

vertical distance is 500 L, and the horizontal distance is 100 pizzas. Thus, the slope is 5 L per pizza. (Actually, because the budget constraint slopes downward, the slope is a negative number. But for our purposes we can ignore the minus sign.)

Notice that the slope of the budget constraint equals the *relative price* of the two goods—the price of one good compared to the price of the other. A pizza costs 5 times as much as a litre of Pepsi, so the opportunity cost of a pizza is 5 L of Pepsi. The budget constraint's slope of 5 reflects the tradeoff the market is offering the consumer: 1 pizza for 5 L of Pepsi.

QuickQuiz Draw the budget constraint for a person with income of $1000 if the price of Pepsi is $5 per litre and the price of a pizza is $10. What is the slope of this budget constraint?

PREFERENCES: WHAT THE CONSUMER WANTS

Our goal in this chapter is to see how consumers make choices. The budget constraint is one piece of the analysis: It shows what combination of goods the consumer can afford given his income and the prices of the goods. The consumer's choices, however, depend not only on his budget constraint but also on his preferences regarding the two goods. Therefore, the consumer's preferences are the next piece of our analysis.

Representing Preferences with Indifference Curves

The consumer's preferences allow him to choose among different bundles of Pepsi and pizza. If you offer the consumer two different bundles, he chooses the bundle that best suits his tastes. If the two bundles suit his tastes equally well, we say that the consumer is *indifferent* between the two bundles.

Just as we have represented the consumer's budget constraint graphically, we can also represent his preferences graphically. We do this with indifference curves. An **indifference curve** shows the bundles of consumption that make the consumer equally happy. In this case, the indifference curves show the combinations of Pepsi and pizza with which the consumer is equally satisfied.

Figure 21.2 shows two of the consumer's many indifference curves. The consumer is indifferent among combinations A, B, and C because they are all on the same curve. Not surprisingly, if the consumer's consumption of pizza is reduced, say from point A to point B, consumption of Pepsi must increase to keep him equally happy. If consumption of pizza is reduced again, from point B to point C, the amount of Pepsi consumed must increase yet again.

The slope at any point on an indifference curve equals the rate at which the consumer is willing to substitute one good for the other. This rate is called the

indifference curve
a curve that shows consumption bundles that give the consumer the same level of satisfaction

FIGURE 21.2

The Consumer's Preferences

The consumer's preferences are represented with indifference curves, which show the combinations of Pepsi and pizza that make the consumer equally satisfied. Because the consumer prefers more of a good, points on a higher indifference curve (I_2 here) are preferred to points on a lower indifference curve (I_1). The marginal rate of substitution (MRS) shows the rate at which the consumer is willing to trade Pepsi for pizza.

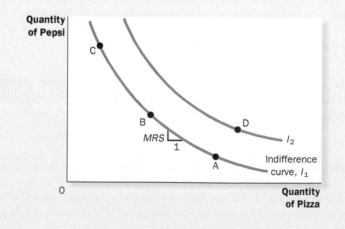

marginal rate of substitution (*MRS*). In this case, the marginal rate of substitution measures how much Pepsi the consumer requires in order to be compensated for a one-unit reduction in pizza consumption (as indicated by the numeral "1" in Figure 21.2). Notice that because the indifference curves are not straight lines, the marginal rate of substitution is not the same at all points on a given indifference curve. The rate at which a consumer is willing to trade one good for the other depends on the amounts of the goods he is already consuming. That is, the rate at which a consumer is willing to trade pizza for Pepsi depends on whether he is more hungry or more thirsty, which in turn depends on how much pizza and Pepsi he is consuming.

The consumer is equally happy at all points on any given indifference curve, but he prefers some indifference curves to others. Because he prefers more consumption to less, higher indifference curves are preferred to lower ones. In Figure 21.2, any point on curve I_2 is preferred to any point on curve I_1.

A consumer's set of indifference curves gives a complete ranking of the consumer's preferences. That is, we can use the indifference curves to rank any two bundles of goods. For example, the indifference curves tell us that point D is preferred to point A because point D is on a higher indifference curve than point A. (That conclusion may be obvious, however, because point D offers the consumer both more pizza and more Pepsi.) The indifference curves also tell us that point D is preferred to point C because point D is on a higher indifference curve. Even though point D has less Pepsi than point C, it has more than enough extra pizza to make the consumer prefer it. By seeing which point is on the higher indifference curve, we can use the set of indifference curves to rank any combinations of Pepsi and pizza.

> **marginal rate of substitution**
> the rate at which a consumer is willing to trade one good for another

Four Properties of Indifference Curves

Because indifference curves represent a consumer's preferences, they have certain properties that reflect those preferences. Here we consider four properties that describe most indifference curves:

- *Property 1: Higher indifference curves are preferred to lower ones.* People usually prefer more of something to less of it. This preference for greater quantities is reflected in the indifference curves. As Figure 21.2 shows, higher indifference curves represent larger quantities of goods than lower indifference curves. Thus, the consumer prefers being on higher indifference curves.
- *Property 2: Indifference curves are downward sloping.* The slope of an indifference curve reflects the rate at which the consumer is willing to substitute one good for the other. In most cases, the consumer likes both goods. Therefore, if the quantity of one good is reduced, the quantity of the other good must increase in order for the consumer to be equally happy. For this reason, most indifference curves slope downward.
- *Property 3: Indifference curves do not cross.* To see why this is true, suppose that two indifference curves did cross, as in Figure 21.3 (p. 464). Then, because point A is on the same indifference curve as point B, the two points would make the consumer equally happy. In addition, because point B is on the same indifference curve as point C, these two points would make the consumer equally happy. But these conclusions imply that points A and C would also make the consumer equally happy, even though point C has more of both goods. This

NEL

The Impossibility of Intersecting Indifference Curves

A situation like this can never happen. According to these indifference curves, the consumer would be equally satisfied at points A, B, and C, even though point C has more of both goods than point A.

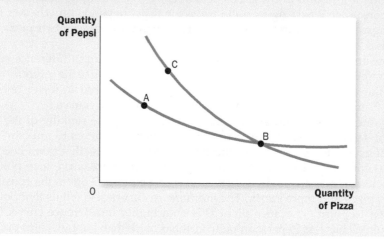

contradicts our assumption that the consumer always prefers more of both goods to less. Thus, indifference curves cannot cross.

- *Property 4: Indifference curves are bowed inward.* The slope of an indifference curve is the marginal rate of substitution—the rate at which the consumer is willing to trade off one good for the other. The marginal rate of substitution (*MRS*) usually depends on the amount of each good the consumer is currently consuming. In particular, because people are more willing to trade away goods that they have in abundance and less willing to trade away goods of which they have little, the indifference curves are bowed inward. As an example, consider Figure 21.4. At point A, because the consumer has a lot of Pepsi and only a little pizza, he is very hungry but not very thirsty. To induce the consumer to give up 1 pizza, the consumer has to be given 6 L of Pepsi: The marginal rate of substitution is 6 L per pizza. By contrast, at point B, the consumer has little Pepsi and a lot of pizza, so he is very thirsty but not very hungry. At this point, he would be willing to give up 1 pizza to get 1 L of Pepsi: The marginal rate of substitution is 1 L per pizza. Thus, the bowed shape of the indifference curve reflects the consumer's greater willingness to give up a good that he already has in large quantity.

Two Extreme Examples of Indifference Curves

The shape of an indifference curve tells us about the consumer's willingness to trade one good for the other. When the goods are easy to substitute for each other, the indifference curves are less bowed; when the goods are hard to substitute, the indifference curves are very bowed. To see why this is true, let's consider the extreme cases.

FIGURE 21.4

Bowed Indifference Curves

Indifference curves are usually bowed inward. This shape implies that the marginal rate of substitution (MRS) depends on the quantity of the two goods the consumer is consuming. At point A, the consumer has little pizza and much Pepsi, so he requires a lot of extra Pepsi to induce him to give up one of the pizzas: The marginal rate of substitution is 6 L of Pepsi per pizza. At point B, the consumer has much pizza and little Pepsi, so he requires only a little extra Pepsi to induce him to give up one of the pizzas: The marginal rate of substitution is 1 L of Pepsi per pizza.

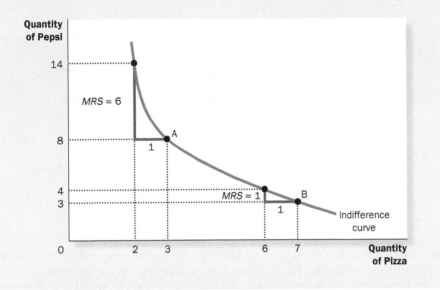

Perfect Substitutes   Suppose that someone offered you bundles of nickels and dimes. How would you rank the different bundles?

Most likely, you would care only about the total monetary value of each bundle. If so, you would judge a bundle based on the number of nickels plus twice the number of dimes. In other words, you would always be willing to trade 1 dime for 2 nickels, regardless of the number of nickels and dimes in the bundle. Your marginal rate of substitution between nickels and dimes would be a fixed number: 2.

We can represent your preferences about nickels and dimes with the indifference curves in panel (a) of Figure 21.5. Because the marginal rate of substitution is constant, the indifference curves are straight lines. In this extreme case of straight indifference curves, we say that the two goods are **perfect substitutes.**

Perfect Complements   Suppose now that someone offered you bundles of shoes. Some of the shoes fit your left foot, others your right foot. How would you rank these different bundles?

In this case, you might care only about the number of pairs of shoes. In other words, you would judge a bundle based on the number of pairs you could

perfect substitutes
two goods with straight-line indifference curves

FIGURE 21.5

Perfect Substitutes and Perfect Complements

When two goods are easily substitutable, such as nickels and dimes, the indifference curves are straight lines, as shown in panel (a). When two goods are strongly complementary, such as left shoes and right shoes, the indifference curves are right angles, as shown in panel (b).

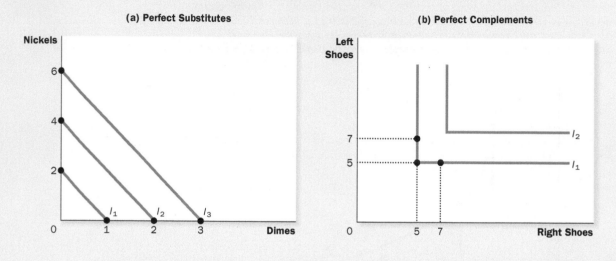

assemble from it. A bundle of 5 left shoes and 7 right shoes yields only 5 pairs. Getting 1 more right shoe has no value if there is no left shoe to go with it.

We can represent your preferences for right and left shoes with the indifference curves in panel (b) of Figure 21.5. In this case, a bundle with 5 left shoes and 5 right shoes is just as good as a bundle with 5 left shoes and 7 right shoes. It is also just as good as a bundle with 7 left shoes and 5 right shoes. The indifference curves, therefore, are right angles. In this extreme case of right-angle indifference curves, we say that the two goods are **perfect complements.**

perfect complements
two goods with right-angle
indifference curves

In the real world, of course, most goods are neither perfect substitutes (like nickels and dimes) nor perfect complements (like right shoes and left shoes). More typically, the indifference curves are bowed inward, but not so bowed as to become right angles.

QuickQuiz Draw some indifference curves for Pepsi and pizza. Explain the four properties of these indifference curves.

OPTIMIZATION: WHAT THE CONSUMER CHOOSES

The goal of this chapter is to understand how a consumer makes choices. We have the two pieces necessary for this analysis: the consumer's budget constraint and the consumer's preferences. Now we put these two pieces together and consider the consumer's decision about what to buy.

The Consumer's Optimal Choices

Consider once again our Pepsi and pizza example. The consumer would like to end up with the best possible combination of Pepsi and pizza—that is, the combination on the highest possible indifference curve. But the consumer must also end up on or below his budget constraint, which measures the total resources available to him.

Figure 21.6 shows the consumer's budget constraint and three of his many indifference curves. The highest indifference curve that the consumer can reach (I_2 in the figure) is the one that just barely touches the budget constraint. The point at which this indifference curve and the budget constraint touch is called the *optimum*. The consumer would prefer point A, but he cannot afford that point because it lies above his budget constraint. The consumer can afford point B, but that point is on a lower indifference curve and, therefore, provides the consumer less satisfaction. The optimum represents the best combination of consumption of Pepsi and pizza available to the consumer.

Notice that, at the optimum, the slope of the indifference curve equals the slope of the budget constraint. We say that the indifference curve is *tangent* to the budget constraint. The slope of the indifference curve is the marginal rate of substitution between Pepsi and pizza, and the slope of the budget constraint is the relative price of Pepsi and pizza. Thus, *the consumer chooses consumption of the two goods so that the marginal rate of substitution equals the relative price.*

In Chapter 7 we saw how market prices reflect the marginal value that consumers place on goods. This analysis of consumer choice shows the same result in another way. In making his consumption choices, the consumer takes as given the relative price of the two goods and then chooses an optimum at which his marginal rate of substitution equals this relative price. The relative price is the rate at which the *market* is willing to trade one good for the other, whereas the marginal rate of substitution is the rate at which the *consumer* is willing to trade one good for the other. At the consumer's optimum, the consumer's valuation of the two goods (as measured by the marginal rate of substitution) equals the market's valuation

FIGURE 21.6

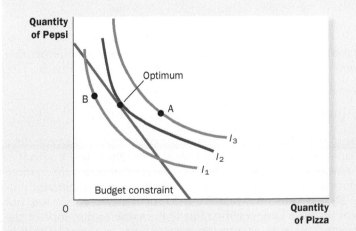

The Consumer's Optimum

The consumer chooses the point on his budget constraint that lies on the highest indifference curve. At this point, called the optimum, *the marginal rate of substitution equals the relative price of the two goods. Here the highest indifference curve the consumer can reach is I_2. The consumer prefers point A, which lies on indifference curve I_3, but the consumer cannot afford this bundle of Pepsi and pizza. By contrast, point B is affordable, but because it lies on a lower indifference curve, the consumer does not prefer it.*

UTILITY: AN ALTERNATIVE WAY TO DESCRIBE PREFERENCES AND OPTIMIZATION

We have used indifference curves to represent the consumer's preferences. Another common way to represent preferences is with the concept of *utility*. Utility is an abstract measure of the satisfaction or happiness that a consumer receives from a bundle of goods. Economists say that a consumer prefers one bundle of goods to another if the first provides more utility than the second.

Indifference curves and utility are closely related. Because the consumer prefers points on higher indifference curves, bundles of goods on higher indifference curves provide higher utility. Because the consumer is equally happy with all points on the same indifference curve, all these bundles provide the same utility. You can think of an indifference curve as an "equal-utility" curve.

The *marginal utility* of any good is the increase in utility that the consumer gets from an additional unit of that good. Most goods are assumed to exhibit *diminishing marginal utility:* The more of the good the consumer already has, the lower the marginal utility provided by an extra unit of that good.

The marginal rate of substitution between two goods depends on their marginal utilities. For example, if the marginal utility of good X is twice the marginal utility of good Y, then a person would need 2 units of good Y to compensate for losing 1 unit of good X, and the marginal rate of substitution equals 2. More generally, the marginal rate of substitution (and thus the slope of the indifference curve) equals the marginal utility of one good divided by the marginal utility of the other good.

Utility analysis provides another way to describe consumer optimization. Recall that at the consumer's optimum, the marginal rate of substitution equals the ratio of prices. That is,

$$MRS = P_X/P_Y$$

Because the marginal rate of substitution equals the ratio of marginal utilities, we can write this condition for optimization as

$$MU_X/MU_Y = P_X/P_Y$$

Now rearrange this expression to become

$$MU_X/P_X = MU_Y/P_Y$$

This equation has a simple interpretation: At the optimum, the marginal utility per dollar spent on good X equals the marginal utility per dollar spent on good Y. (Why? If this equality did not hold, the consumer could increase utility by spending less on the good that provided lower marginal utility per dollar and more on the good that provided higher marginal utility per dollar.)

When economists discuss the theory of consumer choice, they might express the theory using different words. One economist might say that the goal of the consumer is to maximize utility. Another economist might say that the goal of the consumer is to end up on the highest possible indifference curve. The first economist would conclude that at the consumer's optimum, the marginal utility per dollar is the same for all goods, whereas the second would conclude that the indifference curve is tangent to the budget constraint. In essence, these are two ways of saying the same thing.

(as measured by the relative price). As a result of this consumer optimization, market prices of different goods reflect the value that consumers place on those goods.

How Changes in Income Affect the Consumer's Choices

Now that we have seen how the consumer makes the consumption decision, let's examine how consumption responds to changes in income. To be specific, suppose that income increases. With higher income, the consumer can afford more of both goods. The increase in income, therefore, shifts the budget constraint outward, as in Figure 21.7. Because the relative price of the two goods has not changed, the slope of the new budget constraint is the same as the slope of the initial budget constraint. That is, an increase in income leads to a parallel shift in the budget constraint.

FIGURE 21.7

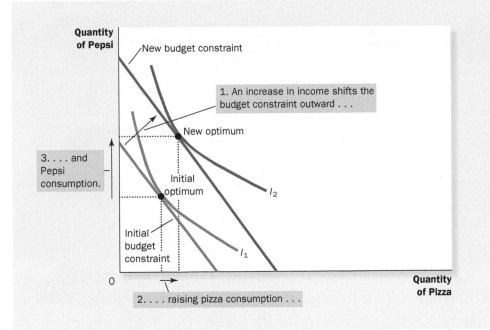

Quantity of Pepsi

New budget constraint

1. An increase in income shifts the budget constraint outward . . .

New optimum

3. . . . and Pepsi consumption.

Initial optimum

I_2

Initial budget constraint

I_1

0

Quantity of Pizza

2. . . . raising pizza consumption . . .

An Increase in Income

When the consumer's income rises, the budget constraint shifts out. If both goods are normal goods, the consumer responds to the increase in income by buying more of both of them. Here the consumer buys more pizza and more Pepsi.

The expanded budget constraint allows the consumer to choose a better combination of Pepsi and pizza. In other words, the consumer can now reach a higher indifference curve. Given the shift in the budget constraint and the consumer's preferences as represented by his indifference curves, the consumer's optimum moves from the point labelled "Initial optimum" to the point labelled "New optimum."

Notice that, in Figure 21.7, the consumer chooses to consume more Pepsi and more pizza. Although the logic of the model does not require increased consumption of both goods in response to increased income, this situation is the most common one. As you may recall from Chapter 4, if a consumer wants more of a good when his income rises, economists call it a **normal good**. The indifference curves in Figure 21.7 are drawn under the assumption that both Pepsi and pizza are normal goods.

Figure 21.8 shows an example in which an increase in income induces the consumer to buy more pizza but less Pepsi. If a consumer buys less of a good when his income rises, economists call it an **inferior good**. Figure 21.8 (p. 470) is drawn under the assumption that pizza is a normal good and Pepsi is an inferior good.

Although most goods are normal goods, there are some inferior goods in the world. One example is bus rides. High-income consumers are more likely to own cars and less likely to ride the bus than low-income consumers. Bus rides, therefore, are an inferior good.

How Changes in Prices Affect the Consumer's Choices

Let's now use this model of consumer choice to consider how a change in the price of one of the goods alters the consumer's choices. Suppose, in particular, that the

normal good
a good for which, other things equal, an increase in income leads to an increase in demand

inferior good
a good for which, other things equal, an increase in income leads to a decrease in demand

FIGURE 21.8

An Inferior Good

A good is an inferior good if the consumer buys less of it when his income rises. Here Pepsi is an inferior good: When the consumer's income increases and the budget constraint shifts outward, the consumer buys more pizza but less Pepsi.

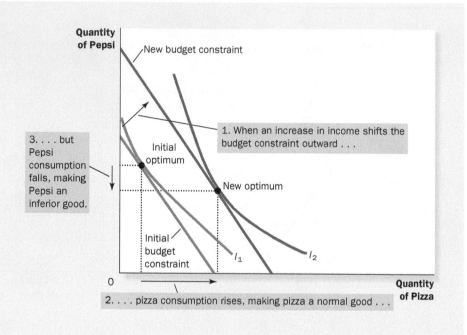

Quantity of Pepsi

New budget constraint

3. . . . but Pepsi consumption falls, making Pepsi an inferior good.

Initial optimum

1. When an increase in income shifts the budget constraint outward . . .

New optimum

Initial budget constraint

I_1

I_2

0

Quantity of Pizza

2. . . . pizza consumption rises, making pizza a normal good . . .

price of Pepsi falls from $2 to $1 per litre. It is no surprise that the lower price expands the consumer's set of buying opportunities. In other words, a fall in the price of any good shifts the budget constraint outward.

Figure 21.9 considers more specifically how the fall in price affects the budget constraint. If the consumer spends his entire $1000 income on pizza, then the price of Pepsi is irrelevant. Thus, point A in the figure stays the same. Yet if the consumer spends his entire income of $1000 on Pepsi, he can now buy 1000 rather than only 500 L. Thus, the end point of the budget constraint moves from point B to point D.

Notice that in this case the outward shift in the budget constraint changes its slope. (This differs from what happened previously when prices stayed the same but the consumer's income changed.) As we have discussed, the slope of the budget constraint reflects the relative price of Pepsi and pizza. Because the price of Pepsi has fallen to $1 from $2, while the price of pizza has remained at $10, the consumer can now trade a pizza for 10 rather than 5 L of Pepsi. As a result, the new budget constraint is more steeply sloped.

How such a change in the budget constraint alters the consumption of both goods depends on the consumer's preferences. For the indifference curves drawn in this figure, the consumer buys more Pepsi and less pizza.

Income and Substitution Effects

The impact of a change in the price of a good on consumption can be decomposed into two effects: an **income effect** and a **substitution effect.** To see what these two

income effect
the change in consumption that results when a price change moves the consumer to a higher or lower indifference curve

substitution effect
the change in consumption that results when a price change moves the consumer along a given indifference curve to a point with a new marginal rate of substitution

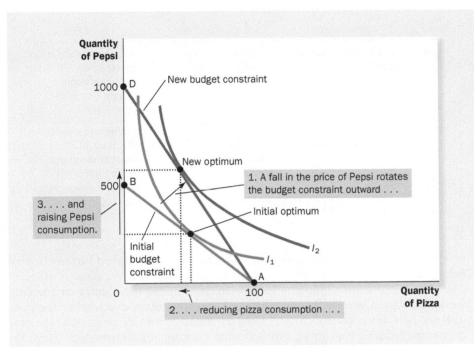

FIGURE 21.9

A Change in Price

When the price of Pepsi falls, the consumer's budget constraint shifts outward and changes slope. The consumer moves from the initial optimum to the new optimum, which changes his purchases of both Pepsi and pizza. In this case, the quantity of Pepsi consumed rises, and the quantity of pizza consumed falls.

effects are, consider how our consumer might respond when he learns that the price of Pepsi has fallen. He might reason in the following ways:

- "Great news! Now that Pepsi is cheaper, my income has greater purchasing power. I am, in effect, richer than I was. Because I am richer, I can buy both more Pepsi and more pizza." (This is the income effect.)
- "Now that the price of Pepsi has fallen, I get more litres of Pepsi for every pizza that I give up. Because pizza is now relatively more expensive, I should buy less pizza and more Pepsi." (This is the substitution effect.)

Which statement do you find more compelling?

In fact, both of these statements make sense. The decrease in the price of Pepsi makes the consumer better off. If Pepsi and pizza are both normal goods, the consumer will want to spread this improvement in his purchasing power over both goods. This income effect tends to make the consumer buy more pizza and more Pepsi. Yet, at the same time, consumption of Pepsi has become less expensive relative to consumption of pizza. This substitution effect tends to make the consumer choose more Pepsi and less pizza.

Now consider the end result of these two effects. The consumer certainly buys more Pepsi, because the income and substitution effects both act to raise purchases of Pepsi. But it is ambiguous whether the consumer buys more pizza, because the income and substitution effects work in opposite directions. This conclusion is summarized in Table 21.1 (p. 472).

We can interpret the income and substitution effects using indifference curves. *The income effect is the change in consumption that results from the movement to a higher*

TABLE 21.1

Income and Substitution Effects When the Price of Pepsi Falls

Good	Income Effect	Substitution Effect	Total Effect
Pepsi	Consumer is richer, so he buys more Pepsi.	Pepsi is relatively cheaper, so consumer buys more Pepsi.	Income and substitution effects act in same direction, so consumer buys more Pepsi.
Pizza	Consumer is richer, so he buys more pizza.	Pizza is relatively more expensive, so consumer buys less pizza.	Income and substitution effects act in opposite directions, so the total effect on pizza consumption is ambiguous.

indifference curve. The substitution effect is the change in consumption that results from being at a point on an indifference curve with a different marginal rate of substitution.

Figure 21.10 shows graphically how to decompose the change in the consumer's decision into the income effect and the substitution effect. When the price of Pepsi falls, the consumer moves from the initial optimum, point A, to the new optimum, point C. We can view this change as occurring in two steps. First, the consumer moves *along* the initial indifference curve I_1 from point A to point B. The consumer is equally happy at these two points, but at point B, the marginal rate of substitution reflects the new relative price. (The dashed line through point B reflects the new relative price by being parallel to the new budget constraint.) Next, the consumer *shifts* to the higher indifference curve I_2 by moving from point B to point C. Even though point B and point C are on different indifference curves, they have the same marginal rate of substitution. That is, the slope of the indifference curve I_1 at point B equals the slope of the indifference curve I_2 at point C.

Although the consumer never actually chooses point B, this hypothetical point is useful to clarify the two effects that determine the consumer's decision. Notice that the change from point A to point B represents a pure change in the marginal rate of substitution without any change in the consumer's welfare. Similarly, the change from point B to point C represents a pure change in welfare without any change in the marginal rate of substitution. Thus, the movement from A to B shows the substitution effect, and the movement from B to C shows the income effect.

Deriving the Demand Curve

We have just seen how changes in the price of a good alter the consumer's budget constraint and, therefore, the quantities of the two goods that he chooses to buy. The demand curve for any good reflects these consumption decisions. Recall that a demand curve shows the quantity demanded of a good for any given price. We can view a consumer's demand curve as a summary of the optimal decisions that arise from his budget constraint and indifference curves.

For example, Figure 21.11 considers the demand for Pepsi. Panel (a) shows that when the price of a litre falls from $2 to $1, the consumer's budget constraint shifts outward. Because of both income and substitution effects, the consumer increases his purchases of Pepsi from 250 to 750 L. Panel (b) shows the demand curve that

FIGURE 21.10

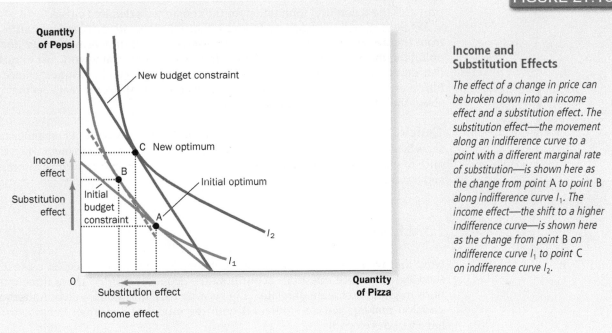

Income and Substitution Effects

The effect of a change in price can be broken down into an income effect and a substitution effect. The substitution effect—the movement along an indifference curve to a point with a different marginal rate of substitution—is shown here as the change from point A to point B along indifference curve I_1. The income effect—the shift to a higher indifference curve—is shown here as the change from point B on indifference curve I_1 to point C on indifference curve I_2.

FIGURE 21.11

Deriving the Demand Curve

Panel (a) shows that when the price of Pepsi falls from $2 to $1, the consumer's optimum moves from point A to point B, and the quantity of Pepsi consumed rises from 250 to 750 L. The demand curve in panel (b) reflects this relationship between the price and the quantity demanded.

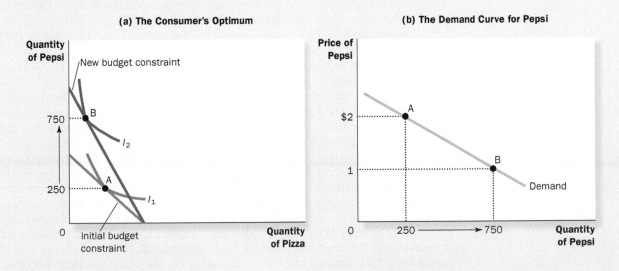

results from this consumer's decisions. In this way, the theory of consumer choice provides the theoretical foundation for the consumer's demand curve.

While it may be comforting to know that the demand curve arises naturally from the theory of consumer choice, this exercise by itself does not justify developing the theory. There is no need for a rigorous, analytic framework just to establish that people respond to changes in prices. The theory of consumer choice is, however, very useful in studying various decisions that people make as they go about their lives, as we see in the next section.

QuickQuiz Draw a budget constraint and indifference curves for Pepsi and pizza. Show what happens to the budget constraint and the consumer's optimum when the price of pizza rises. In your diagram, decompose the change into an income effect and a substitution effect.

THREE APPLICATIONS

Now that we have developed the basic theory of consumer choice, let's use it to shed light on three questions about how the economy works. These three questions might at first seem unrelated. But because each question involves household decision making, we can address it with the model of consumer behaviour we have just developed.

Do All Demand Curves Slope Downward?

Normally, when the price of a good rises, people buy less of it. Chapter 4 called this usual behaviour the *law of demand*. This law is reflected in the downward slope of the demand curve.

As a matter of economic theory, however, demand curves can sometimes slope upward. In other words, consumers can sometimes violate the law of demand and buy *more* of a good when the price rises. To see how this can happen, consider Figure 21.12. In this example, the consumer buys two goods—meat and potatoes. Initially, the consumer's budget constraint is the line from point A to point B. The optimum is point C. When the price of potatoes rises, the budget constraint shifts inward and is now the line from point A to point D. The optimum is now point E. Notice that a rise in the price of potatoes has led the consumer to buy a larger quantity of potatoes.

Why is the consumer responding in a seemingly perverse way? The reason is that potatoes here are a strongly inferior good. When the price of potatoes rises, the consumer is poorer. The income effect makes the consumer want to buy less meat and more potatoes. At the same time, because the potatoes have become more expensive relative to meat, the substitution effect makes the consumer want to buy more meat and less potatoes. In this particular case, however, the income effect is so strong that it exceeds the substitution effect. In the end, the consumer responds to the higher price of potatoes by buying less meat and more potatoes.

Giffen good
a good for which an increase in the price raises the quantity demanded

Economists use the term **Giffen good** to describe a good that violates the law of demand. (The term is named for economist Robert Giffen, who first noted this possibility.) In this example, potatoes are a Giffen good. Giffen goods are inferior goods for which the income effect dominates the substitution effect. Therefore, they have demand curves that slope upward.

NEL

FIGURE 21.12

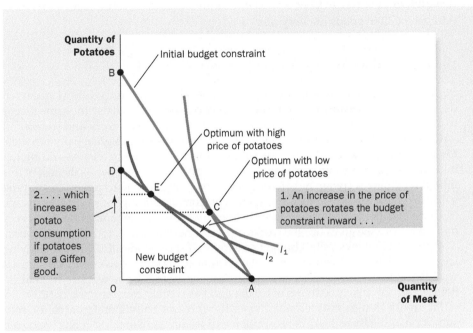

A Giffen Good

In this example, when the price of potatoes rises, the consumer's optimum shifts from point C to point E. In this case, the consumer responds to a higher price of potatoes by buying less meat and more potatoes.

Case Study
THE SEARCH FOR GIFFEN GOODS

Have any actual Giffen goods ever been observed? Some historians suggest that potatoes were a Giffen good during the Irish potato famine of the nineteenth century. Potatoes were such a large part of people's diet that when the price of potatoes rose, it had a large income effect. People responded to their reduced living standard by cutting back on the luxury of meat and buying more of the staple food of potatoes. Thus, it is argued that a higher price of potatoes actually raised the quantity of potatoes demanded.

A 2007 study by Robert Jensen and Nolan Miller (*Giffen Behavior: Theory and Evidence*) produced similar but more concrete evidence for the existence of Giffen goods. These two economists conducted a field experiment for five months in the Chinese province of Hunan. They gave randomly selected households vouchers that subsidized the purchase of rice, a staple in local diets, and used surveys to measure how consumption of rice responded to changes in the price. They found strong evidence that poor households exhibited Giffen behaviour. Lowering the price of rice with the subsidy voucher caused households to reduce their consumption of rice, and removing the subsidy had the opposite effect. Jensen and Miller wrote, "To the best of our knowledge, this is the first rigorous empirical evidence of Giffen behavior."

Thus, the theory of consumer choice allows demand curves to slope upward, and sometimes that strange phenomenon actually occurs. As a result, the law of demand we first saw in Chapter 4 is not completely reliable. It is safe to say, however, that Giffen goods are very rare. ●

How Do Wages Affect Labour Supply?

So far we have used the theory of consumer choice to analyze how a person decides how to allocate his income between two goods. We can use the same theory to analyze how a person decides to allocate his time between work and leisure.

Consider the decision facing Sally, a freelance software designer. Sally is awake for 100 hours per week. She spends some of this time enjoying leisure—riding her bike, watching television, studying economics, and so on. She spends the rest of this time developing software at her computer. For every hour she spends developing software, she earns $50, which she spends on consumption goods. Thus, her wage ($50) reflects the tradeoff Sally faces between leisure and consumption. For every hour of leisure she gives up, she works one more hour and gets $50 of consumption.

Figure 21.13 shows Sally's budget constraint. If she spends all 100 hours enjoying leisure, she has no consumption. If she spends all 100 hours working, she earns a weekly consumption of $5000 but has no time for leisure. If she works a normal 40-hour week, she enjoys 60 hours of leisure and has weekly consumption of $2000.

Figure 21.13 uses indifference curves to represent Sally's preferences for consumption and leisure. Here consumption and leisure are the two "goods" between which Sally is choosing. Because Sally always prefers more leisure and more consumption, she prefers points on higher indifference curves to points on lower ones. At a wage of $50 per hour, Sally chooses a combination of consumption and leisure represented by the point labelled "optimum." This is the point on the budget constraint that is on the highest possible indifference curve, which is curve I_2.

Now consider what happens when Sally's wage increases from $50 to $60 per hour. Figure 21.14 shows two possible outcomes. In each case, the budget constraint, shown

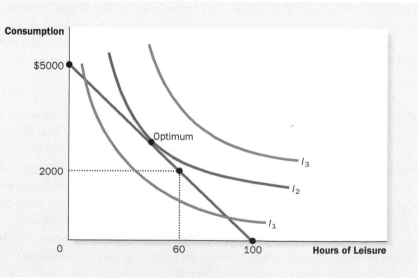

FIGURE 21.13

The Work–Leisure Decision

This figure shows Sally's budget constraint for deciding how much to work, her indifference curves for consumption and leisure, and her optimum.

FIGURE 21.14

An Increase in the Wage

The two sets of panels of this figure show how a person might respond to an increase in the wage. The graphs on the left show the consumer's initial budget constraint BC_1 and new budget constraint BC_2, as well as the consumer's optimal choices over consumption and leisure. The graphs on the right show the resulting labour supply curve. Because hours worked equal total hours available minus hours of leisure, any change in leisure implies an opposite change in the quantity of labour supplied. In panel (a), when the wage rises, consumption rises and leisure falls, resulting in a labour supply curve that slopes upward. In panel (b), when the wage rises, both consumption and leisure rise, resulting in a labour supply curve that slopes backward.

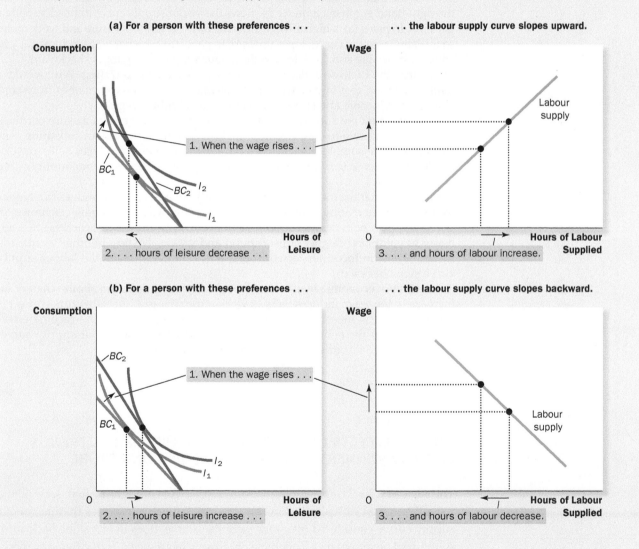

(a) For a person with these preferences . . .   **. . . the labour supply curve slopes upward.**

1. When the wage rises . . .

2. . . . hours of leisure decrease . . .

3. . . . and hours of labour increase.

(b) For a person with these preferences . . .   **. . . the labour supply curve slopes backward.**

1. When the wage rises . . .

2. . . . hours of leisure increase . . .

3. . . . and hours of labour decrease.

in the left-hand graph, shifts outward from BC_1 to BC_2. In the process, the budget constraint becomes steeper, reflecting the change in relative price. At the higher wage, Sally gets more consumption for every hour of leisure that she gives up.

Sally's preferences, as represented by her indifference curves, determine the resulting responses of consumption and leisure to the higher wage. In both panels, consumption rises. Yet the response of leisure to the change in the wage is different in the two cases. In panel (a), Sally responds to the higher wage by enjoying less leisure. In panel (b), Sally responds by enjoying more leisure.

Sally's decision between leisure and consumption determines her supply of labour because the more leisure she enjoys, the less time she has left to work. In each panel, the right-hand graph in Figure 21.14 shows the labour supply curve implied by Sally's decision. In panel (a), a higher wage induces Sally to enjoy less leisure and work more, so the labour supply curve slopes upward. In panel (b), a higher wage induces Sally to enjoy more leisure and work less, so the labour supply curve slopes "backward."

At first, the backward-sloping labour supply curve is puzzling. Why would a person respond to a higher wage by working less? The answer comes from considering the income and substitution effects of a higher wage.

Consider first the substitution effect. When Sally's wage rises, leisure becomes more costly relative to consumption, and this encourages Sally to substitute consumption for leisure. In other words, the substitution effect induces Sally to work harder in response to higher wages, which tends to make the labour supply curve slope upward.

Now consider the income effect. When Sally's wage rises, she moves to a higher indifference curve. She is now better off than she was. As long as consumption and leisure are both normal goods, she tends to want to use this increase in well-being to enjoy both higher consumption and greater leisure. In other words, the income effect induces her to work less, which tends to make the labour supply curve slope backward.

In the end, economic theory does not give a clear prediction about whether an increase in the wage induces Sally to work more or less. If the substitution effect is greater than the income effect for Sally, she works more. If the income effect is greater than the substitution effect, she works less. The labour supply curve, therefore, could be either upward or backward sloping.

Case Study

INCOME EFFECTS ON LABOUR SUPPLY: HISTORICAL TRENDS, LOTTERY WINNERS, AND THE CARNEGIE CONJECTURE

The idea of a backward-sloping labour supply curve might at first seem like a mere theoretical curiosity, but in fact it is not. Evidence indicates that the labour supply curve, considered over long periods of time, does in fact slope backward. A hundred years ago many people worked six days a week. Today five-day workweeks are the norm. At the same time that the length of the workweek has been falling, the wage of the typical worker (adjusted for inflation) has been rising.

Here is how economists explain this historical pattern: Over time, advances in technology raise workers' productivity and, thereby, the demand for labour. The increase in labour demand raises equilibrium wages. As wages rise, so does the reward for working. Yet rather than responding to this increased incentive by working more, most workers choose to take part of their greater prosperity in the form of more leisure. In other words, the income effect of higher wages dominates the substitution effect.

Further evidence that the income effect on labour supply is strong comes from a very different kind of data: winners of lotteries. Winners of large prizes in a lottery see large increases in their incomes and, as a result, large outward shifts in their budget constraints. Because the winners' wages have not changed, however, the *slopes* of their budget constraints remain the same. There is, therefore, no substitution effect. By examining the behaviour of lottery winners, we can isolate the income effect on labour supply.

The results from studies of lottery winners are striking. Of those winners who win more than $50 000, almost 25 percent quit working within a year, and another 9 percent reduce the number of hours they work. Of those winners who win more than $1 million, almost 40 percent stop working. The income effect on labour supply of winning such a large prize is substantial.

Similar results were found in a study, published in the May 1993 issue of the *Quarterly Journal of Economics,* of how receiving a bequest affects a person's labour supply. The study found that a single person who inherits more than $150 000 is four times as likely to stop working as a single person who inherits less than $25 000. This finding would not have surprised the nineteenth-century American industrialist Andrew Carnegie. Carnegie warned that "the parent who leaves his son enormous wealth generally deadens the talents and energies of the son, and tempts him to lead a less useful and less worthy life than he otherwise would." That is, Carnegie viewed the income effect on labour supply to be substantial and, from his paternalistic perspective, regrettable. During his life and at his death, Carnegie gave much of his vast fortune to charity. ●

"No more 9-to-5 for me."

How Do Interest Rates Affect Household Saving?

An important decision that every person faces is how much income to consume today and how much to save for the future. We can use the theory of consumer choice to analyze how people make this decision and how the amount they save depends on the interest rate their savings will earn.

Consider the decision facing Sam, a worker planning ahead for retirement. To keep things simple, let's divide Sam's life into two periods. In the first period, Sam is young and working. In the second period, he is old and retired. When young, Sam earns $100 000. He divides this income between current consumption and saving. When he is old, Sam will consume what he has saved, including the interest that his savings have earned.

Suppose that the interest rate is 10 percent. Then, for every dollar that Sam saves when young, he can consume $1.10 when old. We can view "consumption when young" and "consumption when old" as the two goods that Sam must choose between. The interest rate determines the relative price of these two goods.

FIGURE 21.15

The Consumption–Saving Decision

This figure shows the budget constraint for a person deciding how much to consume in the two periods of his life, the indifference curves representing his preferences, and the optimum.

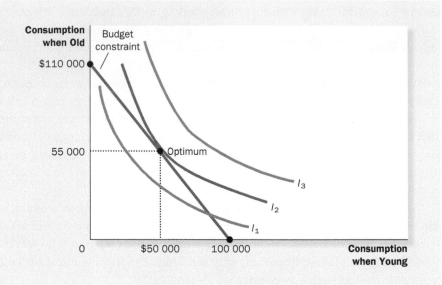

Figure 21.15 shows Sam's budget constraint. If he saves nothing, he consumes $100 000 when young and nothing when old. If he saves everything, he consumes nothing when young and $110 000 when old. The budget constraint shows these and all the intermediate possibilities.

Figure 21.15 uses indifference curves to represent Sam's preferences for consumption in the two periods. Because Sam prefers more consumption in both periods, he prefers points on higher indifference curves to points on lower ones. Given his preferences, Sam chooses the optimal combination of consumption in both periods of life, which is the point on the budget constraint that is on the highest possible indifference curve. At this optimum, Sam consumes $50 000 when young and $55 000 when old.

Now consider what happens when the interest rate increases from 10 percent to 20 percent. Figure 21.16 shows two possible outcomes. In both cases, the budget constraint shifts outward and becomes steeper. At the new higher interest rate, Sam gets more consumption when old for every dollar of consumption that he gives up when young.

The two panels show different preferences for Sam and the resulting response to the higher interest rate. In both cases, consumption when old rises. Yet the response of consumption when young to the change in the interest rate is different in the two cases. In panel (a), Sam responds to the higher interest rate by consuming less when young. In panel (b), Sam responds by consuming more when young.

Sam's saving, of course, is his income when young minus the amount he consumes when young. In panel (a), consumption when young falls when the interest rate rises, so saving must rise. In panel (b), Sam consumes more when young, so saving must fall.

The case shown in panel (b) might at first seem odd: Sam responds to an increase in the return to saving by saving less. Yet this behaviour is not as peculiar as it might seem. We can understand it by considering the income and substitution effects of a higher interest rate.

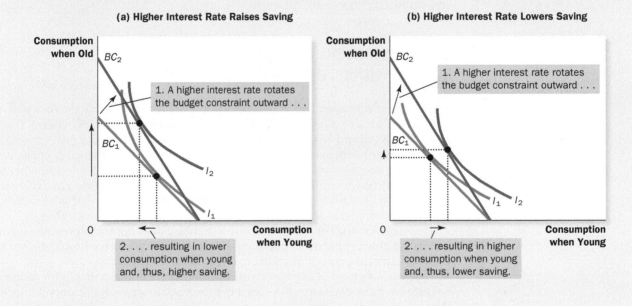

FIGURE 21.16

An Increase in the Interest Rate

In both panels, an increase in the interest rate shifts the budget constraint outward. In panel (a), consumption when young falls, and consumption when old rises. The result is an increase in saving when young. In panel (b), consumption in both periods rises. The result is a decrease in saving when young.

Consider first the substitution effect. When the interest rate rises, consumption when old becomes less costly relative to consumption when young. Therefore, the substitution effect induces Sam to consume more when old and less when young. In other words, the substitution effect induces Sam to save more.

Now consider the income effect. When the interest rate rises, Sam moves to a higher indifference curve. He is now better off than he was. As long as consumption in both periods consists of normal goods, he tends to want to use this increase in well-being to enjoy higher consumption in both periods. In other words, the income effect induces him to save less.

The end result, of course, depends on both the income and substitution effects. If the substitution effect of a higher interest rate is greater than the income effect, Sam saves more. If the income effect is greater than the substitution effect, Sam saves less. Thus, the theory of consumer choice says that an increase in the interest rate could either encourage or discourage saving.

Although this ambiguous result is interesting from the standpoint of economic theory, it is disappointing from the standpoint of economic policy. It turns out that an important issue in tax policy hinges in part on how saving responds to interest rates. Some economists have advocated reducing the taxation of interest and other capital income, arguing that such a policy change would raise the after-tax interest rate that savers can earn and would thereby encourage people to save more. Other economists have argued that because of offsetting income and substitution effects, such a tax change might not increase saving and could even reduce it. Unfortunately, research has not led to a consensus about how interest rates affect saving. As a result, there remains disagreement among economists about whether changes in tax policy aimed to encourage saving would, in fact, have the intended effect.

QuickQuiz Explain how an increase in the wage can potentially decrease the amount that a person wants to work.

CONCLUSION: DO PEOPLE REALLY THINK THIS WAY?

The theory of consumer choice describes how people make decisions. As we have seen, it has broad applicability. It can explain how a person chooses between Pepsi and pizza, work and leisure, consumption and saving, and on and on.

At this point, however, you might be tempted to treat the theory of consumer choice with some skepticism. After all, you are a consumer. You decide what to buy every time you walk into a store. And you know that you do not decide by writing down budget constraints and indifference curves. Doesn't this knowledge about your own decision making provide evidence against the theory?

The answer is no. The theory of consumer choice does not try to present a literal account of how people make decisions. It is a model. And, as we first discussed in Chapter 2, models are not intended to be completely realistic.

The best way to view the theory of consumer choice is as a metaphor for how consumers make decisions. No consumer (except an occasional economist) goes through the explicit optimization envisioned in the theory. Yet consumers are aware that their choices are constrained by their financial resources. And, given those constraints, they do the best they can to achieve the highest level of satisfaction. The theory of consumer choice tries to describe this implicit, psychological process in a way that permits explicit, economic analysis.

The proof of the pudding is in the eating. And the test of a theory is in its applications. In the last section of this chapter we applied the theory of consumer choice to three practical issues about the economy. If you take more advanced courses in economics, you will see that this theory provides the framework for much additional analysis.

SUMMARY

- A consumer's budget constraint shows the possible combinations of different goods he can buy given his income and the prices of the goods. The slope of the budget constraint equals the relative price of the goods.

- The consumer's indifference curves represent his preferences. An indifference curve shows the various bundles of goods that make the consumer equally happy. Points on higher indifference curves are preferred to points on lower

indifference curves. The slope of an indifference curve at any point is the consumer's marginal rate of substitution—the rate at which the consumer is willing to trade one good for the other.

- The consumer optimizes by choosing the point on his budget constraint that lies on the highest indifference curve. At this point, the slope of the indifference curve (the marginal rate of substitution between the goods) equals the slope of the budget constraint (the relative price of the goods).

- When the price of a good falls, the impact on the consumer's choices can be broken down into an income effect and a substitution effect. The income effect is the change in consumption that arises because a lower price makes the consumer better off. The substitution effect is the change in consumption that arises because a price change encourages greater consumption of the good that has become relatively cheaper. The income effect is reflected in the movement from a lower to a higher indifference curve, whereas the substitution effect is reflected by a movement along an indifference curve to a point with a different slope.

- The theory of consumer choice can be applied in many situations. It can explain why demand curves can potentially slope upward, why higher wages could either increase or decrease the quantity of labour supplied, and why higher interest rates could either increase or decrease saving.

KEY CONCEPTS

budget constraint, p. 460
indifference curve, p. 462
marginal rate of
  substitution, p. 463

perfect substitutes, p. 465
perfect complements, p. 466
normal good, p. 469
inferior good, p. 469

income effect, p. 470
substitution effect, p. 470
Giffen good, p. 474

QUESTIONS FOR REVIEW

1. A consumer has income of $3000. Wine costs $3 per glass, and cheese costs $6 per kilogram. Draw the consumer's budget constraint. What is the slope of this budget constraint?

2. Draw a consumer's indifference curves for wine and cheese. Describe and explain four properties of these indifference curves.

3. Pick a point on an indifference curve for wine and cheese and show the marginal rate of substitution. What does the marginal rate of substitution tell us?

4. Show a consumer's budget constraint and indifference curves for wine and cheese. Show the optimal consumption choice. If the price of wine is $3 per glass and the price of cheese is $6 per kilogram, what is the marginal rate of substitution at this optimum?

5. A person who consumes wine and cheese gets a raise, so his income increases from $3000 to $4000. Show what happens if both wine and cheese are normal goods. Now show what happens if cheese is an inferior good.

6. The price of cheese rises from $6 to $10 per kilogram, while the price of wine remains $3 per glass. For a consumer with a constant income of $3000, show what happens to consumption of wine and cheese. Decompose the change into income and substitution effects.

7. Can an increase in the price of cheese possibly induce a consumer to buy more cheese? Explain.

PROBLEMS AND APPLICATIONS

1. Jennifer divides her income between coffee and croissants (both of which are normal goods). An early frost in Brazil causes a large increase in the price of coffee in Canada.
   a. Show the effect of the frost on Jennifer's budget constraint.

   b. Show the effect of the frost on Jennifer's optimal consumption bundle, assuming that the substitution effect outweighs the income effect for croissants.
   c. Show the effect of the frost on Jennifer's optimal consumption bundle, assuming that

the income effect outweighs the substitution effect for croissants.

2. Compare the following two pairs of goods:

   • Coke and Pepsi
   • Skis and ski bindings

   In which case do you expect the indifference curves to be fairly straight, and in which case do you expect the indifference curves to be very bowed? In which case will the consumer respond more to a change in the relative price of the two goods?

3. Mario consumes only cheese and crackers.
   a. Could cheese and crackers both be inferior goods for Mario? Explain.
   b. Suppose that cheese is a normal good for Mario while crackers are an inferior good. If the price of cheese falls, what happens to Mario's consumption of crackers? What happens to his consumption of cheese? Explain.

4. Jim buys only milk and cookies.
   a. In 2009, Jim earns $100, milk costs $2 per litre, and cookies cost $4 per dozen. Draw Jim's budget constraint.
   b. Now suppose that all prices increase by 10 percent in 2010 and that Jim's salary increases by 10 percent as well. Draw Jim's new budget constraint. How would Jim's optimal combination of milk and cookies in 2010 compare to his optimal combination in 2009?

5. Consider your decision about how many hours to work.
   a. Draw your budget constraint assuming that you pay no taxes on your income. On the same diagram, draw another budget constraint assuming that you pay a 15 percent tax.
   b. Show how the tax might lead to more hours of work, fewer hours, or the same number of hours. Explain.

6. Sarah is awake for 100 hours per week. Using one diagram, show Sarah's budget constraints if she earns $6 per hour, $8 per hour, and $10 per hour. Now draw indifference curves such that Sarah's labour supply curve is upward sloping when the wage is between $6 and $8 per hour,

and backward sloping when the wage is between $8 and $10 per hour.

7. Draw the indifference curve for someone deciding how much to work. Suppose the wage increases. Is it possible that the person's consumption would fall? Is this plausible? Discuss. (Hint: Think about income and substitution effects.)

8. Suppose you take a job that pays $30 000 and set some of this income aside in a savings account that pays an annual interest rate of 5 percent. Use a diagram with a budget constraint and indifference curves to show how your consumption changes in each of the following situations. To keep things simple, assume that you pay no taxes on your income.
   a. Your salary increases to $40 000.
   b. The interest rate on your bank account rises to 8 percent.

9. As discussed in the text, we can divide an individual's life into two hypothetical periods: "young" and "old." Suppose that the individual earns income only when young and saves some of that income to consume when old. If the interest rate on savings falls, can you tell what happens to consumption when young? Can you tell what happens to consumption when old? Explain.

10. The welfare system provides income to some needy families. Typically, the maximum payment goes to families that earn no income; then, as families begin to earn income, the welfare payment declines gradually and eventually disappears. Let's consider the possible effects of this program on a family's labour supply.
    a. Draw a budget constraint for a family assuming that the welfare system did not exist. On the same diagram, draw a budget constraint that reflects the existence of the welfare system.
    b. Adding indifference curves to your diagram, show how the welfare system could reduce the number of hours worked by the family. Explain, with reference to both the income and substitution effects.

c. Using your diagram from part (b), show the effect of the welfare system on the well-being of the family.

11. Economist George Stigler once wrote that, according to consumer theory, "if consumers do not buy less of a commodity when their incomes rise, they will surely buy less when the price of the commodity rises." Explain this statement.

12. A college student has two options for meals: eating at the dining hall for $6 per meal, or eating a Cup O' Soup for $1.50 per meal. His weekly food budget is $60.
   a. Draw the budget constraint showing the tradeoff between dining hall meals and Cups O' Soup. Assuming that he spends equal amounts on both goods, draw an indifference curve showing the optimum choice. Label the optimum as point A.
   b. Suppose the price of a Cup O' Soup now rises to $2. Using your diagram from part (a), show the consequences of this change in price. Assume that our student now spends only 30 percent of his income on dining hall meals. Label the new optimum as point B.
   c. What happened to the quantity of Cups O' Soup consumed as a result of this price change? What does this result say about the income and substitution effects? Explain.
   d. Use points A and B to draw a demand curve for Cup O' Soup. What is this type of good called?

13. Consider a couple's decision about how many children to have. Assume that over a lifetime a couple has 200 000 hours of time to either work

or raise children. The wage is $10 per hour. Raising a child takes 20 000 hours of time.
   a. Draw the budget constraint showing the tradeoff between lifetime consumption and number of children. (Ignore the fact that children come only in whole numbers!) Show indifference curves and an optimum choice.
   b. Suppose the wage increases to $12 per hour. Show how the budget constraint shifts. Using income and substitution effects, discuss the impact of the change on number of children and lifetime consumption.
   c. We observe that, as societies get richer and wages rise, people typically have fewer children. Is this fact consistent with this model? Explain.

14. Five consumers have the following marginal utility of apples and pears:

	Marginal Utility of Apples	Marginal Utility of Pears
Jerry	12	6
George	6	6
Elaine	6	3
Kramer	3	6
Newman	12	3

The price of an apple is $2, and the price of a pear is $1. Which, if any, of these consumers are optimizing over their choice of fruit? For those who are not, how should they change their spending?

http://   For more study tools, please visit http://www.mankiw5e.nelson.com.

Chapter 21
The Algebra of Consumer Choice

We have seen that a consumer choosing a bundle of two goods, good X and good Y, will maximize her total utility by choosing quantities of X and Y such that her marginal utility per dollar spent on X (MU_x/P_x) equals the marginal utility per dollar spent on Y (MU_y/P_y). Diagrammatically this is the same as choosing quantities of X and Y such that the |slope of the budget constraint| (P_x/P_y) equals the |slope of the highest possible indifference curve|. The slope of an indifference curve at any point is the marginal rate of substitution (MRS) and is calculated as MU_x/MU_y. The point of tangency where the slopes of the two curves are equal occurs when $MU_x/MU_y = P_x/P_y$. If we rearrange this tangency condition we get $MU_x/P_x = MU_y/P_y$. In other words, the tangency condition is the same as equating the marginal utility per dollar spent on each good.

Example

Aaron is attending a special reception hosted by his employer. One of the main events at the reception is a beer and wine tasting, and Aaron likes both beverages (he is not driving and does not work the next day). It is a cash bar (the employer is donating all proceeds to charity). The price of a small glass of beer is $5 and the price of a glass of wine is $7. He has brought $35 with him - $6 to tip the server and $29 to spend on beverages. Aaron knows his total utility for various amounts of beer and wine and these are listed in the table below:

Aaron's Total Utility from Glasses of Beer or Glasses of Wine

Quantity	Beer	Wine
1	5	10
2	17	14
3	27	21

How many glasses of beer and glasses of wine should Aaron have if he wants to maximize his total utility?

We need to find the marginal utility per dollar spent for each quantity of each beverage.

Quantity	TU Beer	MU Beer	MU/P for Beer	TU Wine	MU Wine	MU/P for Wine
1	5	5	1	10	10	1.4
2	17	12	2.4	24	14	2
3	27	10	2	32	8	1.1

The marginal utilities per dollar spent on beer and wine are equal at a value of 2. These correspond to 3 glasses of beer and 2 glasses of wine; this is Aaron's optimal consumption bundle of beer and wine. At the given prices, Aaron spends $15 on beer and $14 on wine for a total expenditure of $29.

This is exactly equal to the income he has allocated to spend on beverages. We know that Aaron is maximizing his total utility, given his budget constraint.

We also know that the |slope of his budget constraint| when beer is on the x-axis is 5/7. If we knew what his indifference curve looked like, we could draw it so it was just tangent to his budget constraint at 3 beer and 2 wine. We know the |slope of the indifference curve| at that point is 5/7, equal to the |slope of his budget constraint|, because he is maximizing his total utility.

Practice Problems

Jordy has a budget of $420 which he can allocate to buying tickets for either baseball games or hockey games. The price of a baseball game ticket is $60 and the price of a hockey ticket is $120. His total utilities from different quantities of games are given in the table below. Use the information in the table to answer the following questions.

# of Games	TU Baseball	TU Hockey
1	21	60
2	46	100
3	66	130
4	81	150

1. What is Jordy's marginal utility per dollar spent when he buys 4 baseball tickets?
   a. 4
   b. 15
   c. .25
   d. 81

2. What is Jordy's optimal consumption bundle of baseball and hockey games?
   a. 2 baseball games and 2 hockey games
   b. 1 baseball game and 3 hockey games
   c. 4 baseball games and 1 hockey game
   d. 3 baseball games and 2 hockey games

3. What is the highest level of total utility Jordy can currently obtain?
   a. 231 utils
   b. 166 utils
   c. 216 utils
   d. 196 utils

Answers: 1 c   2 d   3 b

21 The Theory of Consumer Choice

I. Chapter Overview

A. Context and Purpose

The previous chapters analyzed the supply of and demand for productive resources and explored the resulting distribution of income in Canada. The section concluded with a critique of Canadian antipoverty programs. This chapter returns to the earlier discussion of consumer choice, using indifference curve analysis to analyze consumer maximization of utility and its implications for demand.

B. Helpful Hints

1. *Budget constraint shows the different combinations of goods and services that are affordable.* The opportunity cost of consuming more of one good is the reduced amount of the other good that can be purchased. The slope of budget constraint is equal to the relative price of the goods.

2. *The indifference curve is used to measure consumer's relative preference between two goods.* It shows the bundles of consumption that make a consumer equally happy.

3. *The marginal rate of substitution (MRS)* is the rate at which the consumer is willing to substitute one good for another; it is equal to the slope of the indifference curve.

4. *Optimization* refers to the process of utility-maximizing consumers rearranging their consumption patterns until their marginal rate of substitution between the goods equals the relative price of the goods. At this point, the slope of the indifference curve equals the slope of budget constraint.

5. *It is easy to get tripped up on the slopes of the curves.* The slope of the budget constraint is the P_x/P_y, where x is on the horizontal axis and y on the vertical. This may seem backwards, because slope is normally $\Delta y/\Delta x$. Remember, however, that the formula uses the *price* of x, not the quantity. The higher the price, the lower the quantity that can be purchased.

293

II. Self-Testing Challenges

A. True/False Questions

_____1.   For a demand curve to slope upward, the substitution effect must outweigh the income effect.

_____2.   The main problem with indifference curve analysis is that people do not actually calculate utility when making choices.

_____3.   The marginal rate of substitution (MRS) of good X for good Y is the relative price of good X versus good Y.

_____4.   A Giffen good must be an inferior good, but not all inferior goods are Giffen goods.

_____5.   For a normal good, the income effect of an increase in price leads to decreased consumption.

_____6.   The substitution effect of a price increase always leads to lower consumption.

_____7.   The indifference curve between Molson and Labatt beer is likely to be straighter than the indifference curve between Molson and Coca-Cola.

_____8.   It is not possible for every good to be an inferior good for a consumer.

_____9.   The substitution effect of a price change is the change in consumption that results from a change in the marginal rate of substitution.

_____10.   The income effect of a price change is the change in consumption that results from movement to a higher or lower indifference curve without any change in relative price.

B. Multiple-Choice Questions

1.   If a rational consumer likes cranberry juice twice as much as she likes orange juice, which one of the following would the consumer do?
    a.   buy only cranberry juice
    b.   buy cranberry juice until, at the margin, she is indifferent between the two juices
    c.   buy twice as much cranberry juice as orange juice
    d.   buy whichever juice gives her the most utility per dollar spent

2. Which one of the following will be the shape of the indifference curves for two goods that are perfect substitutes?
    a. straight lines
    b. right angles
    c. bowed inward
    d. bowed outward

3. Which one of the following will be the shape of the indifference curves for two goods that are perfect complements?
    a. straight lines
    b. right angles
    c. bowed inward
    d. bowed outward

4. A consumer maximizes utility by choosing consumption bundles that have which one of the following characteristics?
    a. maximize the marginal rate of substitution (MRS)
    b. maximize the gap between the MRS and the relative price
    c. set the MRS equal to the relative price
    d. maximize consumption of the lower-priced good

5. Suppose a consumer decreases her consumption of good X when the price of good Y rises. Which one of the following is the most likely explanation for this behaviour?
    a. Good X is an inferior good.
    b. Good Y is an inferior good.
    c. The income effect dominates the substitution effect for good X.
    d. The substitution effect dominates the income effect for good X.

6. Which of the following would be the most likely reason for a backward-bending labour supply curve?
    a. the income effect dominates the substitution effect
    b. the substitution effect dominates the income effect
    c. both income and substitution effects are quite weak

7. Which of the following characterizes leisure?
    a. it's a normal good
    b. it's an inferior good
    c. it's a Giffen good
    d. it's not an economic good

8. Which one of the following is the reason for the bowed shape of the typical indifference curve?
    a. people typically preferring one good to another
    b. diminishing marginal utility
    c. increased average utility
    d. diminishing relative utility

9. Which one of the following would be suggested by the intersection of two indifference curves?
    a. consumers were inconsistent or irrational
    b. one of the goods must be inferior
    c. both goods must be inferior
    d. at least one of the goods must be normal

10. Which one of the following is indicated by the fact that winners of large lottery prizes often quit their jobs?
    a. irrational behaviour
    b. a strong income effect
    c. a strong substitution effect
    d. leisure as an inferior good

11. In the labour market, which one of the following occurs when wages increase?
    a. substitution effect encourages more work, but the income effect discourages work
    b. income and substitution effects both encourage more work
    c. income and substitution effects both discourage work
    d. income effect encourages more work, but the substitution effect discourages work

12. Suppose that Luigi prefers pizza to fried chicken 2:1. If pizza costs $9 and chicken costs $3, which one of the following should Luigi buy?
    a. More chicken and less pizza, until the prices are equal and the marginal utilities are equal.
    b. More pizza and less chicken, until the marginal utilities are equal to the relative price.
    c. More chicken and less pizza, until another pizza is worth three times as much as another order of chicken is worth to him.
    d. The same quantities of pizza and chicken as before.

Use the graph below to answer questions 13–17. The diagram shows the equilibrium for goods X and Y, starting at an equilibrium at point A. The consumer's income is $60.

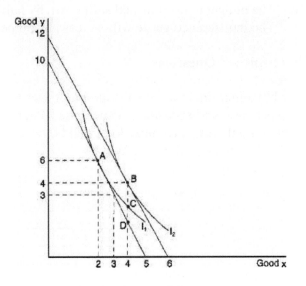

13.   What is the price of good X in the graph?
        a. $2
        b. $5
        c. $12
        d. $30

14.   Which one of the following statements is true?
        a.   Both X and Y are normal goods.
        b.   Both X and Y are inferior goods.
        c.   Good X is inferior and good Y is normal.
        d.   Good X is normal and good Y is inferior.

15.   What is the equilibrium MRS?
        a.   ½
        b.   2
        c.   3
        d.   ⅓

16.   Between which two points is the consumer indifferent?
        a.   A and B
        b.   A and C
        c.   A and D
        d.   C and D

17.   Which one of the following will occur if income is cut in half?
    a.   The marginal rate of substitution will be cut in half.
    b.   The indifference curve will shift down by half.
    c.   The budget constraint will shift down by half.
    d.   The indifference curve will increase by 50 percent.

C. Short-Answer Questions

1.   Joe has a marginal rate of substitution of beer for soda of 1/5. Beer costs $10 per case, and soda costs $5 per case. What should Joe do, and why? Can you tell how much beer Joe should buy? How much soda? What will his MRS be in equilibrium? Why?

    _____

    _____

    _____

    _____

    _____

    _____

    _____

2.   Explain what could make a labour supply curve backward-bending.

    _____

    _____

    _____

    _____

    _____

    _____

D. Practice Problems

1.   The indifference curve diagram below shows the tradeoff between ice cream and brownies for Ben.

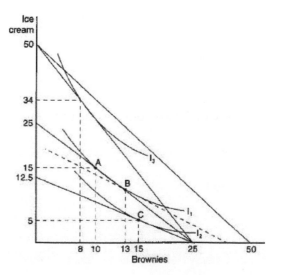

a. The prices of ice cream and brownies are initially $1 each, and Ben can buy 25 brownies if he spends his entire budget on brownies. How much ice cream and how many brownies will Ben buy? Explain. What will happen if the price of ice cream doubles? What is his new indifference curve? How much ice cream will Ben buy now? How many brownies will he buy? _____

_____

_____

_____

_____

_____

b. Separate the effect of raising the price of ice cream into a substitution and an income effect. Illustrate on the diagram and explain in your own words.

_____

_____

_____

_____

_____

_____

c. Can you tell what Ben's income is? Show the effect of a 100 percent increase in income from the original budget constraint, due to a fabulous new job. Label the new curve(s) with '. What will happen to his consumption of ice cream? Of brownies? Label the new equilibrium as E'. Can you tell from the diagram if brownies are a normal or an inferior good? How can you tell? _____

_____

_____

_____

_____

_____

III. Solutions

A. True/False Questions

1. F; for a demand curve to slope upward, the income effect must be dominant (and the good must be inferior).
2. F; people do not need to calculate utility in making choices for the model to predict behaviour and describe the outcome accurately.
3. F; the marginal rate of substitution (MRS) of good X for good Y is the rate at which the consumer is willing to trade X for y; only in equilibrium is it equal to the relative price.
4. T
5. T
6. T
7. T
8. T
9. T
10. T

B. Multiple-Choice Questions

1. d	5. c	9. a	13. c	17. c
2. a	6. a	10. b	14. d	
3. b	7. a	11. a	15. b	
4. c	8. b	12. c	16. b	

C. Short-Answer Questions

1. Buy more beer! Joe should cut back on soda and buy more beer, because beer is worth five times as much as soda to him, but it costs only twice as much. He can get more utility per dollar by buying more beer, until the marginal utility of beer falls and the marginal utility of soda rises enough to change the MRS of beer for soda to ½, which equals the relative price. We do not know, however, how much beer and soda he will actually purchase when he reaches that equilibrium, without knowing the exact shape of his indifference curve as well as his income.

2. As wages rise, the substitution effect encourages more work effort. At the same time, the higher wages make the worker feel richer, causing an income effect. Because people demand more leisure at higher incomes (leisure is a normal good), the income effect of a wage increase discourages work effort. If this effect is stronger than the substitution encouraging work, the net effect will be less labour supplied at higher wages: a backward-bending supply curve.

D. Practice Problems

1.   The indifference curve diagram below shows the trade-off between ice cream and brownies for Ben.

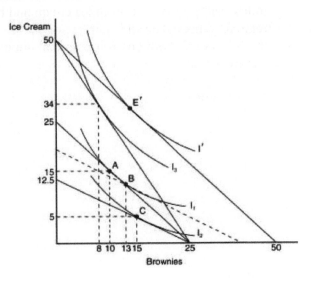

a.   Ben will buy 15 servings of ice cream and 10 brownies. This maximizes his utility at the current prices of $1 each. He must be on indifference curve I_1, because this is the only indifference curve that is tangent to a budget line with a relative price of one ice cream to one brownie. If the price of ice cream doubles, then the budget constraint will pivot around its intercept point with the brownie axis: maximum possible brownie consumption will not change, but potential ice cream consumption will be halved, from 25 to 12.5. At this new equilibrium on I_2, Ben will buy 15 brownies and only 5 ice creams.

b.   When the price of ice cream increases from $1 to $2, the budget constraint pivots from 25 to 12.5 ice creams. Ben cuts back on ice cream consumption for two reasons: first, brownies have become a better buy (the budget constraint slope has decreased), and, second, his income has fallen in real terms (he feels poorer because of the price hike). The first effect, the substitution effect, is the movement along I_1 from A to B, reflecting only a change in relative price. The second effect, the income effect, is the movement from B to C, which is a parallel shift in the budget constraint showing a drop in real income. The dashed line tangent to I_1 at point B is a hypothetical budget constraint reflecting the change in relative price while holding real income constant (utility has not changed from I_1). The combined effect is A to C.

c. Ben's income must be $25, because his initial budget constraint allowed him to purchase either 25 ice creams or 25 brownies when the price was $1 for either. A 100 percent increase in income would double his budget constraint. The new equilibrium would be at E', on indifference curve I'. If both ice cream and brownie consumption rise relative to his old equilibrium at point A (as shown on the graph at E'), this shows that both goods are normal goods (consumption rises as income rises).

FRONTIERS OF MICROECONOMICS

Learning Objectives

In this chapter, you will ...

- Learn how to examine problems caused by asymmetric information
- Examine the market solutions to asymmetric information
- Consider why democratic voting systems may not represent the preferences of society
- Realize why people may not always behave as rational maximizers

Economics is a study of the choices that people make and the resulting interactions they have with one another. This study has many facets, as we have seen in the preceding chapters. Yet it would be a mistake to think that all the facets we have seen make up a finished jewel, perfect and unchanging. Like all scientists, economists are always on the lookout for new areas to study and new phenomena to explain. This final chapter on microeconomics offers an assortment of three topics at the discipline's frontier to see how economists are trying to expand their understanding of human behaviour and society.

The first topic is the economics of *asymmetric information*. Many times in life, some people are better informed than others, and this difference in information can affect the choices they make and how they deal with one another. Thinking about this asymmetry can shed light on many aspects of the world, from the market for used cars to the custom of gift giving.

The second topic we examine in this chapter is *political economy*. Throughout this book we have seen many examples where markets fail and government policy can potentially improve matters. But "potentially" is a needed qualifier: Whether this potential is realized depends on how well our political institutions work. The field of political economy applies the tools of economics to understand the functioning of government.

The third topic in this chapter is *behavioural economics*. This field brings some of the insights from psychology into the study of economic issues. It offers a view of human behaviour that is more subtle and complex than that found in conventional economic theory, but this view may also be more realistic.

This chapter covers a lot of ground. To do so, it offers not a full helping of these three topics but, instead, a taste of each. One goal is to show a few of the directions economists are heading in their effort to expand knowledge of how the economy works. Another goal is to whet your appetite for more courses in economics.

ASYMMETRIC INFORMATION

"I know something you don't know." This statement is a common taunt among children, but it also conveys a deep truth about how people sometimes interact with one another. Many times in life, one person knows more about what is going on than another. A difference in access to relevant knowledge is called an *information asymmetry.*

Examples abound. A worker knows more than his employer about how much effort he puts into his job. A seller of a used car knows more than the buyer about the car's condition. The first is an example of a *hidden action*, whereas the second is an example of a *hidden characteristic*. In each case, the party in the dark (the employer, the car buyer) would like to know the relevant information, but the informed party (the worker, the car seller) may have an incentive to conceal it.

Because asymmetric information is so prevalent, economists have devoted much effort in recent decades to studying its effects. And, indeed, the 2001 Nobel Prize in economics was awarded to three economists (George Akerlof, Michael Spence, and Joseph Stiglitz) for their pioneering work on this topic. Let's discuss some of the insights that this study has revealed.

Hidden Actions: Principals, Agents, and Moral Hazard

moral hazard
the tendency of a person who is imperfectly monitored to engage in dishonest or otherwise undesirable behaviour

agent
a person who is performing an act for another person, called the principal

principal
a person for whom another person, called the agent, is performing some act

Moral hazard is a problem that arises when one person, called the **agent,** is performing some task on behalf of another person, called the **principal.** If the principal cannot perfectly monitor the agent's behaviour, the agent tends to undertake less effort than the principal considers desirable. The phrase *moral hazard* refers to the risk, or "hazard," of inappropriate or otherwise "immoral" behaviour by the agent. In such a situation, the principal tries various ways to encourage the agent to act more responsibly.

The employment relationship is the classic example. The employer is the principal, and the worker is the agent. The moral-hazard problem is the temptation of imperfectly monitored workers to shirk their responsibilities. Employers can respond to this problem in various ways:

- *Better monitoring:* Parents hiring nannies have been known to plant hidden video cameras in their homes to record the nanny's behaviour when the parents are away. The aim is to catch irresponsible behaviour.
- *High wages:* According to *efficiency-wage theories* (discussed in Chapter 19), some employers may choose to pay their workers a wage above the level that equilibrates supply and demand in the labour market. A worker who earns an above-equilibrium wage is less likely to shirk, because if she is caught and fired, she might not be able to find another high-paying job.
- *Delayed payment:* Firms can delay part of a worker's compensation, so if the worker is caught shirking and is fired, he suffers a larger penalty. One example of delayed compensation is the year-end bonus. Similarly, a firm may choose to pay its workers more later in their lives. Thus, the wage increases that workers

get as they age may reflect not just the benefits of experience but also a response to moral hazard.

Employers can use any combination of these various mechanisms to reduce the problem of moral hazard.

There are many other examples of moral hazard beyond the workplace. A homeowner with fire insurance will likely buy too few fire extinguishers because the homeowner bears the cost of the extinguisher while the insurance company receives much of the benefit. A family may live near a river with a high risk of flooding because the family enjoys the scenic views, while the government bears the cost of disaster relief after a flood. Many regulations are aimed at addressing the problem: An insurance company may require homeowners to buy fire extinguishers, and the government may prohibit building homes on land with high

CORPORATE MANAGEMENT

Much production in the modern economy takes place within corporations. Like other firms, corporations buy inputs in markets for the factors of production and sell their output in markets for goods and services. Also, like other firms, they are guided in their decisions by the objective of profit maximization. But a large corporation has to deal with some issues that do not arise in, say, a small family-owned business.

What is distinctive about a corporation? From a legal standpoint, a corporation is an organization that is granted a charter recognizing it as a separate legal entity, with its own rights and responsibilities, distinct from those of its owners and employees. From an economic standpoint, the most important feature of the corporate form of organization is the separation of ownership and control. One group of people, called the shareholders, own the corporation and share in its profits. Another group of people, called the managers, are employed by the corporation to make decisions about how to deploy the corporation's resources.

The separation of ownership and control creates a principal–agent problem. In this case, the shareholders are the principals, and the managers are the agents. The chief executive officer and other managers are in the best position to know the business opportunities that are available, and they are charged with the task of maximizing profit for the shareholders. But ensuring that they carry out this task is not always easy. The managers may have goals of their own, such as taking life easy, having a plush office and a private jet, throwing lavish parties, or enjoying the prestige of presiding over a large business empire. The managers' goals may not always coincide with the goal of profit maximization.

The corporation's board of directors is responsible for hiring and firing top management. The board monitors the managers' performance, and it designs their compensation packages. These packages often include incentives aimed at aligning the interest of shareholders with the interest of management. Managers might be given bonuses based on performance or options to buy the company's stock, which are more valuable if the company performs well.

Note, however, that the directors are themselves agents of the shareholders. The existence of a board overseeing management only shifts the principal–agent problem. The issue then becomes how to ensure that the board of directors fulfills its own legal obligation of acting in the best interest of the shareholders. If the directors become too friendly with management, they may not provide the required oversight.

The corporation principal–agent problem has been in the news in recent years. The top managers of several prominent companies, such as Enron, Tyco, and WorldCom, were found to be engaging in activities that enriched themselves at the expense of their shareholders. In these cases, the actions were so extreme that they were criminal, and the corporate managers were not just fired but also sent to prison. In some cases, shareholders sued directors for failing to monitor management sufficiently.

Fortunately, criminal activity by corporate managers is rare. But in some ways, it is only the tip of the iceberg. Whenever ownership and control are separated, as they are in most large corporations, there is an inevitable tension between the interests of shareholders and the interests of management.

risk of flooding. But the insurance company does not have perfect information about how cautious homeowners are, and the government does not have perfect information about the risk that families undertake when choosing where to live. As a result, the problem of moral hazard persists.

Hidden Characteristics: Adverse Selection and the Lemons Problem

adverse selection
the tendency for the mix of unobserved attributes to become undesirable from the standpoint of an uninformed party

Adverse selection is a problem that arises in markets where the seller knows more about the attributes of the good being sold than the buyer does. As a result, the buyer runs the risk of being sold a good of low quality. That is, the "selection" of goods being sold may be "adverse" from the standpoint of the uninformed buyer.

The classic example of adverse selection is the market for used cars. Sellers of used cars know their vehicles' defects while buyers often do not. Because owners of the worst cars are more likely to sell them than are the owners of the best cars, buyers are apprehensive about getting a "lemon." As a result, many people avoid buying vehicles in the used-car market. This lemons problem can explain why a used car only a few weeks old sells for thousands of dollars less than a new car of the same type. A buyer of the used car might surmise that the seller is getting rid of the car quickly because the seller knows something about it that the buyer does not.

A second example of adverse selection occurs in the labour market. According to another efficiency-wage theory, workers vary in their abilities, and they may know their own abilities better than do the firms that hire them. When a firm cuts the wage it pays, the more talented workers are more likely to quit, knowing they are better able to find other employment. Conversely, a firm may choose to pay an above-equilibrium wage to attract a better mix of workers.

A third example of adverse selection occurs in markets for insurance. For example, buyers of life insurance know more about their own health problems than do insurance companies. Because people with greater hidden health problems are more likely to buy life insurance than are other people, the price of life insurance reflects the costs of a sicker-than-average person. As a result, people in average health may be discouraged from buying life insurance by the high price.

When markets suffer from adverse selection, the invisible hand does not necessarily work its magic. In the used-car market, owners of good cars may choose to keep them rather than sell them at the low price that skeptical buyers are willing to pay. In the labour market, wages may be stuck above the level that balances supply and demand, resulting in unemployment. In insurance markets, buyers with low risk may choose to remain uninsured because the policies they are offered fail to reflect their true characteristics. Advocates of government-provided insurance sometimes point to the problem of adverse selection as one reason not to trust the private market to provide the right amount of insurance on its own.

Signalling to Convey Private Information

signalling
an action taken by an informed party to reveal private information to an uninformed party

Although asymmetric information is sometimes a motivation for public policy, it also motivates some individual behaviour that otherwise might be hard to explain. Markets respond to problems of asymmetric information in many ways. One of them is **signalling**, which refers to actions taken by an informed party for the sole purpose of credibly revealing his private information.

We have seen examples of signalling in previous chapters. As we saw in Chapter 16, firms may spend money on advertising to signal to potential customers that they have high-quality products. As we saw in Chapter 19, students may earn postsecondary and postgraduate degrees to signal to potential employers that they are high-ability individuals. Recall that the signalling theory of education contrasts with the human-capital theory, which asserts that education increases a person's productivity, rather than merely conveying information about innate talent. These two examples of signalling (advertising, education) may seem very different, but below the surface they are much the same: In both cases, the informed party (the firm, the student) is using the signal to convince the uninformed party (the customer, the employer) that the informed party is offering something of high quality.

What does it take for an action to be an effective signal? Obviously, it must be costly. If a signal were free, everyone would use it, and it would convey no information. For the same reason, there is another requirement: The signal must be less costly, or more beneficial, to the person with the higher-quality product. Otherwise, everyone would have the same incentive to use the signal, and the signal would reveal nothing.

Consider again our two examples. In the advertising case, a firm with a good product reaps a larger benefit from advertising because customers who try the product once are more likely to become repeat customers. Thus, it is rational for the firm with the good product to pay for the cost of the signal (advertising), and it is rational for the customer to use the signal as a piece of information about the product's quality. In the education case, a talented person can get through school more easily than a less talented one. Thus, it is rational for the talented person to pay for the cost of the signal (education), and it is rational for the employer to use the signal as a piece of information about the person's talent.

The world is replete with instances of signalling. Magazine ads sometimes include the phrase "as seen on TV." Why does a firm selling a product in a magazine choose to stress this fact? One possibility is that the firm is trying to convey its willingness to pay for an expensive signal (a spot on television) in the hope that you will infer that its product is of high quality. For the same reason, graduates of elite schools are always sure to put that fact on their résumés.

Case Study
GIFTS AS SIGNALS

A man is debating what to give his girlfriend for her birthday. "I know," he says to himself, "I'll give her cash. After all, I don't know her tastes as well as she does, and with cash, she can buy anything she wants." But when he hands her the money, she is offended. Convinced he doesn't really love her, she breaks off the relationship.

What's the economics behind this story?

In some ways, gift giving is a strange custom. As the man in our story suggests, people typically know their own preferences better than others do, so we might

"Now we'll see how much he loves me."

© Ariel Skelley/Corbis

screening
an action taken by an uninformed party to induce an informed party to reveal information

expect everyone to prefer cash to in-kind transfers. If your employer substituted merchandise for your paycheque, you would likely object to the means of payment. But your reaction is very different when someone who (you hope) loves you does the same thing.

One interpretation of gift giving is that it reflects asymmetric information and signalling. The man in our story has private information that the girlfriend would like to know: Does he really love her? Choosing a good gift for her is a signal of his love. Certainly, picking out a gift has the right characteristics to be a signal. It is costly (it takes time), and its cost depends on the private information (how much he loves her). If he really loves her, choosing a good gift is easy because he is thinking about her all the time. If he doesn't love her, finding the right gift is more difficult. Thus, giving a gift that suits the girlfriend is one way for him to convey the private information of his love for her. Giving cash shows that he isn't even bothering to try.

The signalling theory of gift giving is consistent with another observation: People care most about the custom when the strength of affection is most in question. Thus, giving cash to a girlfriend or boyfriend is usually a bad move. But when students receive a cheque from their parents, they are less often offended. The parents' love is less likely to be in doubt, so the recipient probably won't interpret the cash gift as a signal of lack of affection. ●

Screening to Induce Information Revelation

When an informed party takes actions to reveal his private information, the phenomenon is called *signalling*. When an uninformed party takes actions to induce the informed party to reveal private information, the phenomenon is called **screening**.

Some screening is common sense. A person buying a used car may ask that it be checked by an auto mechanic before the sale. A seller who refuses this request reveals his private information that the car is a lemon. The buyer may decide to offer a lower price or to look for another car.

Other examples of screening are more subtle. For example, consider a firm that sells car insurance. The firm would like to charge a low premium to safe drivers and a high premium to risky drivers. But how can it tell them apart? Drivers know whether they are safe or risky, but the risky ones won't admit to it. A driver's history is one piece of information (which insurance companies in fact use), but because of the intrinsic randomness of car accidents, history is an imperfect indicator of future risks.

The insurance company might be able to sort out the two kinds of drivers by offering different insurance policies that would induce them to separate themselves. One policy would have a high premium and cover the full cost of any accidents that occur. Another policy would have low premiums but would have, say, a $1000 deductible. (That is, the driver would be responsible for the first $1000 of damage, and the insurance company would cover the remaining risk.) Notice that the deductible is more of a burden for risky drivers because they are more likely to have an accident. Thus, with a large enough deductible, the low-premium policy with a deductible would attract the safe drivers, while the high-premium policy without a deductible would attract the risky drivers. Faced with these two policies, the two kinds of drivers would reveal their private information by choosing different insurance policies.

Asymmetric Information and Public Policy

We have examined two kinds of asymmetric information—moral hazard and adverse selection. And we have seen how individuals may respond to the problem with signalling or screening. Now let's consider what the study of asymmetric information suggests about the proper scope of public policy.

The tension between market success and market failure is central in microeconomics. We learned in Chapter 7 that the equilibrium of supply and demand is efficient in the sense that it maximizes the total surplus that society can obtain in a market. Adam Smith's invisible hand seemed to reign supreme. This conclusion was then tempered with the study of externalities (Chapter 10), public goods (Chapter 11), imperfect competition (Chapters 15 through 17), and poverty (Chapter 20). These examples of market failure showed that government can sometimes improve market outcomes.

The study of asymmetric information gives us new reason to be wary of markets. When some people know more than others, the market may fail to put resources to their best use. People with high-quality used cars may have trouble selling them because buyers will be afraid of getting a lemon. People with few health problems may have trouble getting low-cost health insurance because insurance companies lump them together with those who have significant (but hidden) health problems.

Although asymmetric information may call for government action in some cases, three facts complicate the issue. First, as we have seen, the private market can sometimes deal with information asymmetries on its own, using a combination of signalling and screening. Second, the government rarely has more information than the private parties. Even if the market's allocation of resources is not first-best, it may be second-best. That is, when there are information asymmetries, policymakers may find it hard to improve upon the market's admittedly imperfect outcome. Third, the government is itself an imperfect institution—a topic we take up in the next section.

QuickQuiz A person who buys a life insurance policy pays a certain amount per year and receives for his family a much larger payment in the event of his death. Would you expect buyers of life insurance to have higher or lower death rates than the average person? How might this be an example of moral hazard? Of adverse selection? How might a life insurance company deal with these problems?

Case Study

ASYMMETRIC INFORMATION AND THE 2007–2009 FINANCIAL CRISIS

In 2007, the world economy entered an economic and financial contraction, the likes of which had not been experienced since the Great Depression of the 1930s. Dubbed by many as the *Second Great Contraction* (the first being the Great Depression), the resulting worldwide recession left virtually no country unscathed. Canada entered recession in the fourth quarter of 2008 and emerged in the third quarter of 2009. While Canada weathered the storm much better than many other countries, over this period, gross domestic product (the total value of goods and services produced in Canada) fell by over 7 percent.

It is widely agreed that the Second Great Contraction started as a financial crisis, triggered by the subprime mortgage market in the United States. Subprime mortgages are risky mortgages issued to individuals with poor credit histories who have a high probability of default. As the crisis spread across financial institutions around the world, credit dried up and countries entered a severe recession. At the time this book was written, it seemed that the world, and in particular Canada, was slowly emerging from the recession; however, the effects of the crisis are expected to last for a long time.

While analysis of the crisis is complex, and indeed is ongoing, the presence of asymmetric information in financial markets is thought by many economists to have been an important factor exacerbating the crisis.

Indeed, the presence of asymmetric information explains in large part the very existence of financial intermediaries, such as banks. While banks offer many services—a place to safely keep your funds, along with their many other useful functions—in large part, they exist because of their ability to reduce the risks associated with asymmetric information. For example, borrowers know more about their financial condition and ability to repay loans than lenders do, which can give rise to both adverse selection (where those least able to pay back a loan are more likely to seek a loan) and moral hazard (where borrowers engage in excessive risk-taking). This makes lending money directly to borrowers a risky proposition. Banks and other financial intermediaries possess specialized expertise in analyzing and assessing risk and in monitoring lenders, which reduces both adverse selection and moral hazard in financial markets. That is why you might be more inclined to give your money to a bank, which in turn lends the money to consumers and companies, rather than lending the money directly to borrowers yourself.

While the underlying causes of the financial crisis are still being debated, some economists have argued that, leading up to the crisis, the financial sector did not manage very well the risks associated with asymmetric information. The argument is that the emergence of several innovations in the financial sector and the growth of so-called "shadow banking institutions" (such as investment banks and hedge funds), which were heavily involved in them, resulted in a weakening of the traditional assessment and monitoring activities of financial institutions.

One such innovation, called *securitization* or *asset-backed securities*, involves the bundling together of loans, such as mortgages, into a security that is then sold to a third party, who can in turn sell it to another party or bundle it with other securities to form yet another security, and on and on. In the recent financial crisis, as the mortgages underlying these securities became farther removed from the original face-to-face lender–borrower arrangement, it is argued that the problem of asymmetric information concerning the risk associated with the underlying assets became worse. Many of these asset-backed securities were backed by high-risk subprime mortgages.

Leading in to the crisis, investment banks such as Bear Stearns and Lehman Brothers in the United States were heavily involved in asset-backed securities. Investment banks are nondeposit-taking institutions that underwrite and trade

NEL

securities, and issue financial advice to companies and governments, among other things. These institutions are not subject to the same regulatory scrutiny as deposit-taking banks. In 2008, after receiving an emergency loan from the U.S. Federal Reserve (the U.S. central bank), Bear Stearns was bought by JPMorgan Chase for a fraction of its pre-crisis value; Lehman Brothers went bankrupt. The collapse of Bear Stearns and Lehman Brothers has come to epitomize the financial crisis.

It has also been argued that financial institutions faced strong incentives to engage in risky behaviour because of the nature of the compensation schemes for their employees: a type of moral hazard. For example, financial sector bonuses tied to returns with no downside in the event of default encouraged riskier and riskier behaviour on the part of employees. As a result of this, some analysts have called for greater, and better, regulation of financial institutions, their activities, and their compensation schemes.

Finally, it has also been strongly suggested that the reaction of governments to the crisis—and in particular the bailout of financial institutions and, in the United States and Canada, car manufacturers—generated a type of moral hazard. The idea here is that knowing that the government will bail you out gives you little incentive to manage your risks prudently. The unprecedented government bailouts associated with the crisis may thus have set the stage for problems down the road as companies and financial institutions that are considered "too big to fail" engaged in riskier behaviour.

The repercussions of the financial and economic crisis are likely to be long-lasting. While there is some disagreement over the form that subsequent policies should take to minimize the chance of similar events in the future, an understanding of the role of asymmetric information will be front and centre. ●

POLITICAL ECONOMY

As we have seen, markets left on their own do not always reach a desirable allocation of resources. When we judge the market's outcome to be either inefficient or inequitable, there may be a role for the government to step in and improve the situation. Yet before we embrace an activist government, we need to consider one more fact: The government is also an imperfect institution. The field of *political economy* (sometimes called the field of *public choice*) applies the methods of economics to study how government works.

The Condorcet Voting Paradox

Most advanced societies rely on democratic principles to set government policy. When a city is deciding between two locations to build a new park, for example, we have a simple way to choose: The majority gets its way. Yet, for most policy issues, the number of possible outcomes far exceeds two. A new park, for instance, could be placed in many possible locations. In this case, as the eighteenth-century French political theorist Marquis de Condorcet famously noted, democracy might run into some problems trying to choose one of the outcomes.

TABLE 22.1

The Condorcet Paradox

If voters have these preferences over outcomes A, B, *and* C, *then in pairwise majority voting,* A *beats* B, B *beats* C, *and* C *beats* A.

	Voter Type		
	Type 1	Type 2	Type 3
Percent of electorate	35	45	20
First choice	A	B	C
Second choice	B	C	A
Third choice	C	A	B

For example, suppose there are three possible outcomes, labelled A, B, and C, and there are three voter types with the preferences shown in Table 22.1. The mayor of our town wants to aggregate these individual preferences into preferences for society as a whole. How should she do it?

At first, she might try some pairwise votes. If she asks voters to choose first between B and C, voter types 1 and 2 will vote for B, giving B the majority. If she then asks voters to choose between A and B, voter types 1 and 3 will vote for A, giving A the majority. Observing that A beats B, and B beats C, the mayor might conclude that A is the voters' clear choice.

But wait: Suppose the mayor then asks voters to choose between A and C. In this case, voter types 2 and 3 vote for C, giving C the majority. That is, under pairwise majority voting, A beats B, B beats C, and C beats A. Normally, we expect preferences to exhibit a property called *transitivity:* If A is preferred to B, and B is preferred to C, then we would expect A to be preferred to C. The **Condorcet paradox** is that democratic outcomes do not always obey this property. Pairwise voting might produce transitive preferences for a society, depending on the pattern of individual preferences, but as our example in the table shows, it cannot be counted on to do so.

One implication of the Condorcet paradox is that the order in which things are voted on can affect the result. If the mayor suggests choosing first between A and B and then comparing the winner to C, the town ends up choosing C. But if the voters choose first between B and C and then compare the winner to A, the town ends up with A. And if the voters choose first between A and C and then compare the winner to B, the town ends up with B.

There are two lessons to be learned from the Condorcet paradox. The narrow lesson is that when there are more than two options, setting the agenda (that is, deciding the order in which items are voted) can have a powerful impact on the outcome of a democratic election. The broad lesson is that majority voting by itself does not tell us what outcome a society really wants.

Condorcet paradox
the failure of majority rule to produce transitive preferences for society

Arrow's Impossibility Theorem

Since political theorists first noticed Condorcet's paradox, they have spent much energy studying voting systems and proposing new ones. For example, as an alternative to pairwise majority voting, the mayor of our town could ask each voter to rank the possible outcomes. For each voter, we could give 1 point for last place, 2 points for second to last, 3 points for third to last, and so on. The outcome that receives the most total points wins. With the preferences in Table 22.1, outcome B is the winner. (You can do the arithmetic yourself.) This voting method is called a *Borda count,* for the eighteenth-century French mathematician and political scientist who devised it. It is often used in polls that rank sports teams.

Is there a perfect voting system? Economist Kenneth Arrow took up this question in his 1951 book, *Social Choice and Individual Values.* Arrow started by defining what a perfect voting system would be. He assumes that individuals in society have preferences over the various possible outcomes: A, B, C, and so on. He then assumes that society wants a voting scheme to choose among these outcomes that satisfies several properties:

- *Unanimity:* If everyone prefers A to B, then A should beat B.
- *Transitivity:* If A beats B, and B beats C, then A should beat C.
- *Independence of irrelevant alternatives:* The ranking between any two outcomes A and B should not depend on whether some third outcome C is also available.
- *No dictators:* No person always gets his or her way, regardless of everyone else's preferences.

These all seem like desirable properties for a voting system to have. Yet Arrow proved, mathematically and incontrovertibly, that *no voting system can satisfy all of these properties.* This amazing result is called **Arrow's impossibility theorem.**

The mathematics needed to prove Arrow's theorem is beyond the scope of this book, but we can get some sense of why the theorem is true from a couple of examples. We have already seen the problem with the method of majority rule. The Condorcet paradox shows that majority rule fails to produce a ranking among the outcomes that always satisfies transitivity.

As another example, the Borda count fails to satisfy the independence of irrelevant alternatives. Recall that, using the preferences in Table 22.1, outcome B wins with a Borda count. But suppose that suddenly C disappears as an alternative. If the Borda count method is applied only to outcomes A and B, then A wins. (Once again, you can do the arithmetic on your own.) Thus, eliminating alternative C changes the ranking between A and B. The reason for this change is that the result of the Borda count depends on the number of points that A and B receive, and the number of points depends on whether the irrelevant alternative, C, is also available.

Arrow's impossibility theorem is a deep and disturbing result. It doesn't say that we should abandon democracy as a form of government. But it does say that, no matter what voting scheme society adopts for aggregating the preferences of its members, in some way it will be flawed as a mechanism for social choice.

Arrow's impossibility theorem
a mathematical result showing that, under certain assumed conditions, there is no scheme for aggregating individual preferences into a valid set of social preferences

The Median Voter Is King

Despite Arrow's theorem, voting is how most societies choose their leaders and public policies, often by majority rule. The next step in studying government is to examine how governments run by majority rule work. That is, in a democratic society, who determines what policy is chosen? In some cases, the theory of democratic government yields a surprisingly simple answer.

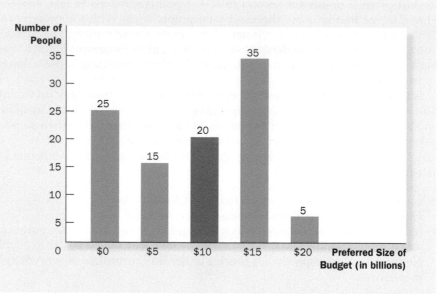

FIGURE 22.1

The Median Voter Theorem: An Example

This bar chart shows how 100 voters' most-preferred budget is distributed over five options, ranging from zero to $20 billion. If society makes its choice by majority rule, the median voter (who here prefers $10 billion) determines the outcome.

median voter theorem
a mathematical result showing that if voters are choosing a point along a line and each voter wants the point closest to his most preferred point, then majority rule will pick the most preferred point of the median voter

Let's consider an example. Imagine that society is deciding on how much money to spend on some public good, such as the CBC. Each voter has his own most preferred budget, and he always prefers outcomes closer to his most preferred value to outcomes further away. Thus, we can line up voters from those who prefer the smallest budget to those who prefer the largest. Figure 22.1 is an example. Here there are 100 voters, and the budget size varies from zero to $20 billion. Given these preferences, what outcome would you expect democracy to produce?

According to a famous result called the **median voter theorem,** majority rule will produce the outcome most preferred by the median voter. The *median voter* is the voter exactly in the middle of the distribution. In this example, if you take the line of voters ordered by their preferred budgets and count 50 voters from either end of the line, you will find that the median voter wants a budget of $10 billion. By contrast, the average preferred outcome (calculated by adding the preferred outcomes and dividing by the number of voters) is $9 billion, and the modal outcome (the one preferred by the greatest number of voters) is $15 billion.

The median voter rules the day because his preferred outcome beats any other proposal in a two-way race. In our example, more than half of the voters want $10 billion or more, and more than half want $10 billion or less. If someone proposes, say, $8 billion instead of $10 billion, everyone who prefers $10 billion or more will vote with the median voter. Similarly, if someone proposes $12 billion instead of $10 billion, everyone who wants $10 billion or less will vote with the median voter. In either case, the median voter has more than half of the voters on his side.

What about the Condorcet voting paradox? It turns out that when the voters are picking a point along a line and each voter aims for his own most preferred point, the Condorcet paradox cannot arise. The median voter's most preferred outcome beats all comers.

One implication of the median voter theorem is that if each of two political parties is trying to maximize its chance of election, they will both move their positions toward the median voter. Suppose, for example, that the Liberal party advocates a budget of $15 billion, while the Conservative party advocates a budget of $10 billion. The Liberal position is more popular in the sense that $15 billion has more proponents than any other single choice. Nonetheless, the Conservative party gets more than 50 percent of the vote: It will attract the 20 voters who want $10 billion, the 15 voters who want $5 billion, and the 25 voters who want zero. If the Liberals want to win, they will move their platform toward the median voter. Thus, this theory can explain why the parties in a two-party system are similar to each other: They are both moving toward the median voter.

Another implication of the median voter theorem is that minority views are not given much weight. Imagine that 40 percent of the population wants a lot of money spent on the national parks, and 60 percent wants nothing spent. In this case, the median voter's preference is zero, regardless of the intensity of the minority's view. Such is the logic of democracy. Rather than reaching a compromise that takes into account everyone's preferences, majority rule looks only to the person in the exact middle of the distribution.

Politicians Are People, Too

When economists study consumer behaviour, they assume that consumers buy the bundle of goods and services that gives them the greatest level of satisfaction. When economists study firm behaviour, they assume that firms produce the quantity of goods and services that yields the greatest level of profits. What should they assume when they study people involved in the practice of politics?

Politicians also have objectives. It would be nice to assume that political leaders are always looking out for the well-being of society as a whole, that they are aiming for an optimal combination of efficiency and equity. Nice, perhaps, but not realistic. Self-interest is as powerful a motive for political actors as it is for consumers and firm owners. Some politicians are motivated by desire for reelection and are willing to sacrifice the national interest when doing so solidifies their base of voters. Other politicians are motivated by simple greed. If you have any doubt, you should look at the world's poor nations, where corruption among government officials is a common impediment to economic development.

This book is not the place to develop a theory of political behaviour. That topic is best left to the political scientists. But when thinking about economic policy, remember that this policy is made not by a benevolent king, but by real people with their own all-too-human desires. Sometimes they are motivated to further the national interest, but sometimes they are motivated by their own political and financial ambitions. We shouldn't be surprised when economic policy fails to resemble the ideals derived in economics textbooks.

QuickQuiz A school district is voting on the school budget and the resulting student–teacher ratio. A poll finds that 35 percent of the voters want a ratio of 9:1, 25 percent want a ratio of 10:1, and 40 percent want a ratio of 12:1. What outcome would you expect the district to end up with?

BEHAVIOURAL ECONOMICS

Economics is a study of human behaviour, but it is not the only field that can make that claim. The social science of psychology also sheds light on the choices that people make in their lives. The fields of economics and psychology usually proceed independently, in part because they address a different range of questions. But recently a field called *behavioural economics* has emerged in which economists are making use of basic psychological insights. Let's consider some of these insights here.

People Aren't Always Rational

Economic theory is populated by a particular species of organism, sometimes called *Homo economicus*. Members of this species are always rational. As firm managers, they maximize profits. As consumers, they maximize utility (or, equivalently, pick the point on the highest indifference curve). Given the constraints they face, they rationally weigh all the costs and benefits and always choose the best possible course of action.

Real people, however, are *Homo sapiens*. Although in many ways they resemble the rational, calculating people assumed in economic theory, they are far more complex. They can be forgetful, impulsive, confused, emotional, and shortsighted. These imperfections of human reasoning are the bread-and-butter of psychologists, but until recently, economists have neglected them.

Herbert Simon, one of the first social scientists to work at the boundary of economics and psychology, suggested that humans should be viewed not as rational maximizers but as *satisficers*. Rather than always choosing the best course of action, they make decisions that are merely good enough. Similarly, other economists have suggested that humans are only "near rational" or that they exhibit "bounded rationality."

Studies of human decision making have tried to detect systematic mistakes that people make. Here are a few of the findings:

- *People are overconfident.* Imagine that you were asked some numerical questions, such as the number of African countries in the United Nations, the height of the tallest mountain in North America, and so on. Instead of being asked for a single estimate, however, you were asked to give a 90 percent confidence interval—a range such that you were 90 percent confident the true number falls within it. When psychologists run experiments like this, they find that most people give ranges that are too small: The true number falls within their intervals far less than 90 percent of the time. That is, most people are too sure of their own abilities.
- *People give too much weight to a small number of vivid observations.* Imagine that you are thinking about buying a car of brand X. To learn about its reliability, you read *Consumer Reports,* which has surveyed 1000 owners of car X. Then you run into a friend who owns car X, and she tells you that her car is a lemon. How do you treat your friend's observation? If you think rationally, you will realize that she has increased your sample size only from 1000 to 1001, which does not provide much new information. But because your friend's story is so vivid, you may be tempted to give it more weight in your decision making than you should.

- *People are reluctant to change their minds.* People tend to interpret evidence to confirm beliefs they already hold. In one study, subjects were asked to read and evaluate a research report on whether capital punishment deters crime. After reading the report, those who initially favoured the death penalty said they were more sure in their view, and those who initially opposed the death penalty also said they were more sure in their view. The two groups interpreted the same evidence in exactly opposite ways.

Think about decisions you have made in your own life. Do you exhibit some of these traits?

Why, you might ask, is economics built on the rationality assumption when psychology and common sense cast doubt on it? One answer is that the assumption, even if not exactly true, is still a good approximation. For example, when we studied the differences between competitive and monopoly firms, the assumption that firms rationally maximize profit yielded many important and valid insights. Recall from Chapter 2 that economic models are not meant to replicate reality but are supposed to show the essence of the problem at hand as an aid to understanding.

Another reason that economists so often assume rationality may be that economists are themselves not rational maximizers. Like most people, they are overconfident, and they are reluctant to change their minds. Their choice among alternative theories of human behaviour may exhibit excessive inertia. Moreover, economists may be content with a theory that is not perfect but is good enough. The model of rational man may be the theory of choice for a satisficing social scientist.

People Care About Fairness

Another insight about human behaviour is best illustrated with an experiment called the *ultimatum game.* The game works like this: Two volunteers (who are otherwise strangers to each other) are told that they are going to play a game and could win a total of $100. Before they play, they learn the rules. The game begins with a coin flip, which is used to assign the volunteers to the roles of player A and player B. Player A's job is to propose a division of the $100 prize between himself and the other player. After player A makes his proposal, player B decides whether to accept or reject it. If he accepts it, both players are paid according to the proposal. If player B rejects the proposal, both players walk away with nothing. In either case, the game then ends.

Before proceeding, stop and think about what you would do in this situation. If you were player A, what division of the $100 would you propose? If you were player B, what proposals would you accept?

Conventional economic theory assumes in this situation that people are rational wealth-maximizers. This assumption leads to a simple prediction: Player A should propose that he gets $99 and player B gets $1, and player B should accept the proposal. After all, once the proposal is made, player B is better off accepting it as long as he gets something out of it. Moreover, because player A knows that accepting the proposal is in player's B interest, player A has no reason to offer him more than $1. In the language of game theory (discussed in Chapter 17), the 99–1 split is the Nash equilibrium.

Yet when experimental economists ask real people to play the ultimatum game, the results are very different from this prediction. People in the role of player B usually reject proposals that give them only $1 or a similarly small amount. Knowing this, people in the role of player A usually propose giving player B much more than $1. Some people will offer a 50–50 split, but it is more common for player A to propose giving player B an amount such as $30 or $40, keeping the larger share for himself. In this case, player B usually accepts the proposal.

What's going on here? The natural interpretation is that people are driven in part by some innate sense of fairness. A 99–1 split seems so wildly unfair to many people that they reject it, even to their own detriment. By contrast, a 70–30 split is still unfair, but it is not so unfair that it induces people to abandon their normal self-interest.

IN THE NEWS

THIS IS YOUR BRAIN ON ECONOMICS

Research is increasingly focused on the intersection of economics and neuroscience.

Enter the Neuro-Economists: Why Do Investors Do What They Do?

By Tyler Cowen

Las Vegas uses flashing lights and ringing bells to create an illusion of reward and to encourage risk taking. Insurance company offices present a more somber mood to remind us of our mortality. Every marketer knows that context and presentation influence our decisions.

For the first time, economists are studying these phenomena scientifically. The economists are using a new technology that allows them to trace the activity of neurons inside the brain and thereby study how emotions influence our choices, including economic choices like gambles and investments.

For instance, when humans are in a "positive arousal state," they think about prospective benefits and enjoy the feeling of risk. All of us are familiar with the giddy excitement that accompanies a triumph. Camelia Kuhnen and Brian Knutson, two researchers at Stanford University, have found that people are more likely to take a foolish risk when their brains show this kind of activation.

But when people think about costs, they use different brain modules and become more anxious. They play it too safe, at least in the laboratory. Furthermore, people are especially afraid of ambiguous risks with unknown odds. This may help explain why so many investors are reluctant to seek out foreign stock markets, even when they could diversify their portfolios at low cost.

If one truth shines through, it is that people are not consistent or fully rational decision makers. Peter L. Bossaerts, an economics professor at the California Institute of Technology, has found that brains assess risk and return separately, rather than making a single calculation of what economists call expected utility.

Researchers can see on the screen how people compartmentalize their choices into different parts of their brains. This may not always sound like economics but neuro-economists start with the insight—borrowed from the economist Friedrich Hayek—that resources are scarce within the brain and must be allocated to competing uses. Whether in economies or brains, well-functioning systems should not be expected to exhibit centralized command and control.

Throughout our study of household and firm behaviour, the innate sense of fairness has not played any role. But the results of the ultimatum game suggest that perhaps it should. For example, in Chapters 18 and 19 we discussed how wages were determined by labour supply and labour demand. Some economists have suggested that the perceived fairness of what a firm pays its workers should also enter the picture. Thus, when a firm has an especially profitable year, workers (like player B) may expect to be paid a fair share of the prize, even if the standard equilibrium does not dictate it. The firm (like player A) might well decide to give workers more than the equilibrium wage for fear that the workers might otherwise try to punish the firm with reduced effort, strikes, or even vandalism.

Neuro-economics is just getting started. The first major empirical paper was published in 2001 by Kevin McCabe, Daniel Houser, Lee Ryan, Vernon Smith and Theodore Trouard, all economics professors. A neuro-economics laboratory at Cal Tech, led by Colin F. Camerer, a math prodigy and now an economics professor, has assembled the foremost group of interdisciplinary researchers. Many of the early entrants, who have learned neurology as well as economics, continue to dominate the field.

Investors are becoming interested in the money-making potential of these ideas. Imagine training traders to set their emotions aside or testing their objectivity in advance with brain scans. Futuristic devices might monitor their emotions on the trading floor or in a bargaining session and instruct them how to compensate for possible mistakes.

Are the best traders most adept at reading the minds of others? Or is trading skill correlated with traits like the ability to calculate and ignore the surrounding caldron of human emotions?

More ambitiously, future research may try to determine when a short-term price bubble will collapse. Does the market tide turn when people stop smiling, adjust to their adrenalin levels or make different kinds of eye contact?

Not all of neuro-economics uses brain scans. Andrew W. Lo, a professor at the Sloan School of Management at the Massachusetts Institute of Technology, applied polygraph-like techniques to securities traders to show that anxiety and fear affect market behavior. Measuring eye movements, which is easy and cheap, helps the researcher ascertain what is on a mind. Other researchers have opened up monkey skulls to measure individual neurons; monkey neurons fire in proportion to the amount and probability of rewards. But do most economists care? Are phrases like "nucleus accumbens"—referring to a sub-cortical nucleus of the brain associated with reward—welcome in a profession caught up in interest rates and money supply? Skeptics question whether neuro-economics explains real-world phenomena.

The neuro-economists admit that their endeavor is in its infancy. It is difficult to identify brain modules and their roles. Even if one part of the brain is active at a particular moment, how is that incorporated into a person's broader method for making decisions?

The number of people scanned in any study is typically small, if only because the hookups cost about $500 an hour and require access to an expensive machine.

Furthermore, the setting may matter. Perhaps we cannot equate choices made on the New York Stock Exchange trading floor with choices made under a hospital scanner, where the subject must lie on his back, remain motionless and endure a loud whirring, all the while calculating a trading strategy.

That said, neuro-economics will make huge strides as technology allows researchers to identify more brain regions and read brains more accurately and at lower cost. It is a growth area in a profession that knows human feelings matter, but does not always know what to do with them.

What is the next step? Perhaps neuro-economics should turn its attention to political economy. Do people use the same part of their brains to vote as to trade? Is voting governed by fear, disgust or perhaps the desire to gain something new and exciting?

Tyler Cowen is a professor of economics at George Mason University and is co-author of a blog, www.marginalrevolution.com.

People Are Inconsistent over Time

Imagine some dreary task, such as doing your laundry, shovelling snow off your driveway, or filling out your income tax forms. Now consider the following questions:

1. Would you prefer (A) to spend 50 minutes doing the task immediately or (B) to spend 60 minutes doing the task tomorrow?
2. Would you prefer (A) to spend 50 minutes doing the task in 90 days or (B) to spend 60 minutes doing the task in 91 days?

When asked questions like these, many people choose B to question 1 and A to question 2. When looking ahead to the future (as in question 2), they minimize the amount of time spent on the dreary task. But faced with the prospect of doing the task immediately (as in question 1), they choose to put it off.

In some ways, this behaviour is not surprising: Everyone procrastinates from time to time. But from the standpoint of the theory of rational man, it is puzzling. Suppose that, in response to question 2, a person chooses to spend 50 minutes in 90 days. Then, when the 90th day arrives, we allow him to change his mind. In effect, he then faces question 1, so he opts for doing the task the next day. But why should the mere passage of time affect the choices he makes?

Many times in life, people make plans for themselves, but then they fail to follow through. A smoker promises herself that she will quit, but within a few hours of smoking her last cigarette, she craves another and breaks her promise. A person trying to lose weight promises that he will stop eating dessert, but when the waiter brings the dessert cart, the promise is forgotten. In both cases, the desire for instant gratification induces the decision maker to abandon his own past plans.

Some economists believe that the consumption–saving decision is an important instance where people exhibit this inconsistency over time. For many people, spending provides a type of instant gratification. Saving, like passing up the cigarette or the dessert, requires a sacrifice in the present for a reward in the distant future. And just as many smokers wish they could quit and many overweight individuals wish they ate less, many consumers wish they saved more. According to one survey, more than 50 percent of Canadians were concerned that they were not saving enough for retirement.

An implication of this inconsistency over time is that people should try to find ways to commit their future selves to following through on their plans. A smoker trying to quit may throw away her cigarettes, and a person on a diet may put a lock on the refrigerator. What can a person who saves too little do? He should find some way to lock up his money before he spends it. Some retirement accounts, such as retirement saving plans, do exactly that. A worker can agree to have some money taken out of his paycheque before he ever sees it. The money is deposited in an account that can be used before retirement only with a penalty. Perhaps that is one reason why these retirement accounts are so popular: They protect people from their own desires for instant gratification.

QuickQuiz Describe at least three ways in which human decision making differs from that of the rational individual of conventional economic theory.

CONCLUSION

This chapter has examined the frontier of microeconomics. You may have noticed that we have sketched out ideas rather than fully developing them. This is no accident. One reason is that you might study these topics in more detail in advanced courses. Another reason is that these topics remain active areas of research and, therefore, are still being fleshed out.

To see how these topics fit into the broader picture, recall the ten principles of economics from Chapter 1. One principle states that markets are usually a good way to organize economic activity. Another principle states that governments can sometimes improve market outcomes. As you study economics, you can more fully appreciate the truth of these principles as well as the caveats that go with them. The study of asymmetric information should make you more wary of market outcomes. The study of political economy should make you more wary of government solutions. And the study of behavioural economics should make you wary of any institution that relies on human decision making—including both the market and the government.

If there is a unifying theme to these topics, it is that life is messy. Information is imperfect, government is imperfect, and people are imperfect. Of course, you knew this long before you started studying economics, but economists need to understand these imperfections as precisely as they can if they are to explain, and perhaps even improve, the world around them.

SUMMARY

- In many economic transactions, information is asymmetric. When there are hidden actions, principals may be concerned that agents suffer from the problem of moral hazard. When there are hidden characteristics, buyers may be concerned about the problem of adverse selection among the sellers. Private markets sometimes deal with asymmetric information with signalling and screening.

- Although government policy can sometimes improve market outcomes, governments are themselves imperfect institutions. The Condorcet paradox shows that majority rule fails to produce transitive preferences for society, and Arrow's impossibility theorem shows that no voting

scheme will be perfect. In many situations, democratic institutions will produce the outcome desired by the median voter, regardless of the preferences of the rest of the electorate. Moreover, the individuals who set government policy may be motivated by self-interest rather than the national interest.

- The study of psychology and economics reveals that human decision making is more complex than is assumed in conventional economic theory. People are not always rational, they care about the fairness of economic outcomes (even to their own detriment), and they can be inconsistent over time.

KEY CONCEPTS

moral hazard, p. 488
agent, p. 488
principal, p. 488
adverse selection, p. 490

signalling, p. 490
screening, p. 492
Condorcet paradox, p. 496

Arrow's impossibility
theorem, p. 497
median voter theorem, p. 498

QUESTIONS FOR REVIEW

1. What is moral hazard? List three things an employer might do to reduce the severity of this problem.

2. What is adverse selection? Give an example of a market in which adverse selection might be a problem.

3. Define *signalling* and *screening*, and give an example of each.

4. What unusual property of voting did Condorcet notice?

5. Explain why majority rule respects the preferences of the median voter rather than the average voter.

6. Describe the ultimatum game. What outcome from this game would conventional economic theory predict? Do experiments confirm this prediction? Explain.

PROBLEMS AND APPLICATIONS

1. Each of the following situations involves moral hazard. In each case, identify the principal and the agent, and explain why there is asymmetric information. How does the action described reduce the problem of moral hazard?
   a. Landlords require tenants to pay security deposits.
   b. Firms compensate top executives with options to buy company stock at a given price in the future.
   c. Car insurance companies offer discounts to customers who install antitheft devices in their cars.

2. Suppose that the Acme Life Insurance Company charges $5000 annually for an insurance policy. The company's president suggests that the company raise the annual price to $6000 in order to increase its profits. If the firm followed this suggestion, what economic problem might arise? Would the firm's pool of customers tend to become more or less healthy on average? Would the company's profits necessarily increase?

3. A case study in this chapter describes how a boyfriend can signal to a girlfriend that he loves her by giving an appropriate gift. Do you think saying "I love you" can also serve as a signal? Why or why not?

4. Some AIDS activists believe that life insurance companies should not be allowed to ask applicants if they are infected with the HIV virus that causes AIDS. Would this rule help or hurt those who are HIV-positive? Would it help or hurt those who are not HIV-positive? Would it exacerbate or mitigate the problem of adverse selection in the market for life insurance? Do you think it would increase or decrease the number of people without life insurance? In your opinion, would this be a good policy?

5. The government is considering two ways to help the needy: giving them cash, or giving them free meals at soup kitchens. Give an argument for giving cash. Give an argument, based on asymmetric information, for why the soup kitchen may be better than the cash handout.

6. Ken walks into an ice-cream parlour.

   WAITER: We have vanilla and chocolate today.
   KEN: I'll take vanilla.
   WAITER: I almost forgot. We also have strawberry.
   KEN: In that case, I'll take chocolate.

   What standard property of decision making is Ken violating? (Hint: Reread the section on Arrow's impossibility theorem.)

7. Why might a political party in a two-party system choose not to move toward the median voter? (Hint: Think about abstentions from voting and political contributions.)

8. Two ice-cream stands are deciding where to locate along a one-kilometre beach. Each person

sitting on the beach buys exactly one ice-cream cone per day from the stand nearest to him. Each ice-cream seller wants the maximum number of customers. Where along the beach will the two stands locate?

9. After a widely reported earthquake in California, many people call their insurance company to apply for earthquake insurance. Might this reaction reflect some deviation from rationality? Discuss.

10. Three friends are choosing a restaurant for dinner. Here are their preferences:

	Rachel	Ross	Joey
First choice	Italian	Italian	Chinese
Second choice	Chinese	Chinese	Mexican
Third choice	Mexican	Mexican	French
Fourth choice	French	French	Italian

  a. If the three friends use a Borda count to make their decision, where do they go to eat?
  b. On their way to their chosen restaurant, they see that the Mexican and French restaurants are closed, so they use a Borda count again to decide between the remaining two restaurants. Where do they decide to go now?
  c. How do your answers to parts (a) and (b) relate to Arrow's impossibility theorem?

11. Three friends are choosing a TV show to watch. Here are their preferences:

	Chandler	Phoebe	Monica
First choice	Lost	Heroes	Scrubs
Second choice	Heroes	Scrubs	Lost
Third choice	Scrubs	Lost	Heroes

  a. If the three friends try using a Borda count to make their choice, what would happen?
  b. Monica suggests a vote by majority rule. She proposes that first they choose between Lost and Heroes, and then they choose between the winner of the first vote and Scrubs. If they all vote their preferences honestly, what outcome would occur?
  c. Should Chandler agree to Monica's suggestion? What voting system would he prefer?

  d. Phoebe and Monica convince Chandler to go along with Monica's proposal. In round one, Chandler dishonestly says he prefers Heroes over Lost. Why might he do this?

12. Five roommates are planning to spend the weekend in their dorm room watching movies, and they are debating how many movies to watch. Here is their willingness to pay:

	Quentin	Spike	Ridley	Martin	Steven
First film	$7	$5	$4	$2	$1
Second film	6	4	2	1	0
Third film	5	3	1	0	0
Fourth film	3	1	0	0	0
Fifth film	1	0	0	0	0

A video costs $8 to rent, which the roommates split equally, so each pays $1.60 per movie.

  a. What is the efficient number of movies to watch (that is, the number that maximizes total surplus)?
  b. From the standpoint of each roommate, what is the preferred number of movies?
  c. What is the preference of the median roommate?
  d. If the roommates held a vote on the efficient outcome versus the median voter's preference, how would each person vote? Which outcome would get a majority?
  e. If one of the roommates proposed a different number of movies, could his proposal beat the winner from part (d) in a vote?
  f. Can majority rule be counted on to reach efficient outcomes in the provision of public goods?

13. A group of athletes are competing in a multi-day triathlon. They have a running race on day one, a swimming race on day two, and a biking race on day three. You know the order in which the athletes finish each of the three components. From this information, you are asked to rank the athletes in the overall competition. You are given the following conditions:

  a. The ordering of athletes should be transitive: If athlete A is ranked above athlete B, and athlete B is ranked above athlete C, then athlete A must rank above athlete C.
  b. If athlete A beats athlete B in all three races, athlete A should rank higher than athlete B.

c. The rank ordering of any two athletes should not depend on whether a third athlete drops out of the competition just before the final ranking.

According to Arrow's theorem, there are only three ways to rank the athletes that satisfy these properties. What are they? Are these desirable? Why or why not? Can you think of a better ranking scheme? Which of the three properties above does your scheme not satisfy?

http://

For more study tools, please visit http://www.mankiw5e.nelson.com.

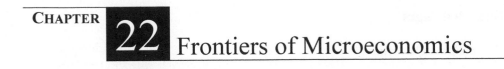

22 Frontiers of Microeconomics

I.   Chapter Overview

A.   Context and Purpose

Chapter 22 is the last chapter in the microeconomics portion of the text. It is the second of two unrelated chapters that introduce some advanced topics in microeconomics. These two chapters are intended to whet the appetite for further study in economics.

The purpose of Chapter 22 is to provide a taste of three topics on the frontier of microeconomics research. The first topic is *asymmetric information*, a situation when one person in an economic relationship has more relevant knowledge than the other person. The second topic is *political economy*, the application of economic tools to the understanding of the functioning of government. The third topic we address is *behavioural economics*, the introduction of psychology into the study of economic issues.

B.   Helpful Hints

1. *The market for insurance demonstrates many of the problems and market solutions generated by asymmetric information.* For auto insurance, firms first screen prospective customers to reduce *adverse selection*—the problem of selling insurance to worse-than-average drivers. After the sale of the insurance, auto insurance companies require a deductible or co-payment on collision insurance. This reduces *moral hazard*—the problem of insured drivers driving more recklessly once they are insured.

2. *No method of economic decision-making is always perfect.* Markets may not maximize total surplus due to externalities, public goods, imperfect competition, and asymmetric information. In addition, people and firms may not always rationally maximize their own well-being. But government may not be able to improve upon the situation because governments may not have any better information than markets; all voting schemes are imperfect, and politicians may choose to maximize their own well-being instead of the well-being of society.

303

II.   Self-Testing Challenges

A.   True/False Questions

_____1.   Asymmetric information is a problem that occurs when one person in a transaction knows more about what is going on than the other.

_____2.   In the principal–agent relationship, the principal performs a task on behalf of the agent.

_____3.   Signals to convey high quality are most effective when they are costless to all firms in the industry.

_____4.   The Condorcet paradox shows that majority-rule voting always reveals the outcome that society really wants.

_____5.   Arrow's Impossibility Theorem shows that no voting system can satisfy the properties required of a perfect voting system.

_____6.   According to the Median Voter Theorem, majority rule will produce the average preferred outcome.

_____7.   Politicians do not always choose the ideal economic policy because some politicians are corrupt and greedy, and others are willing to sacrifice the national interest for local popularity.

_____8.   In the real world, people always behave rationally when making economic decisions.

_____9.   Because people tend to care about fairness, firms may give bonuses during particularly profitable years to be fair and to avoid retaliation from the workers.

_____10.   People seem to naturally engage in delayed gratification, and they tend to follow through on plans made today to do something unpleasant in the future.

_____11.   To avoid the problem of adverse selection, health insurance companies screen their prospective customers to discover hidden health problems.

_____12.   The ultimate game demonstrates that people will always make choices according to their self-interest.

B.   **Multiple-Choice Questions**

1.   John's car is in need of repair, therefore John decides to sell it to avoid the repair bill. Unaware of the problem, Susan buys the car. Which one of the following is this is an example of?
a.   adverse selection
b.   moral hazard
c.   efficiency wages
d.   hidden actions

2.   Judy wants to avoid buying a car that is a lemon. She takes a car she would like to buy to her mechanic to be inspected before she purchases it. Which one of the following is this is known as?
a.   moral hazard
b.   adverse selection
c.   signaling
d.   screening

3.   Chris is a travelling sales representative for an apparel company. Which one of the following is Chris's role in this employment relationship?
a.   principal
b.   agent
c.   screener
d.   monitor

4.   Which one of the following must be true about a signal that is used to reveal private information in order for the signal to be effective?
a.   It must be free to the informed party.
b.   It must be costly to the informed party but less costly to the party with the higher-quality product.
c.   It must be applied to an expensive product.
d.   It must be less beneficial to the party with the higher-quality product.

5.   Which one of the following is an example of a signal that is used to reveal private information?
a.   Pierre randomly chooses a gift for Monique.
b.   Lexus advertises its cars during the Grey Cup.
c.   Consuela lived close to, so attended, the Richard Ivey School of Business.

6.   Which one of the following is **NOT** a method firms use to avoid the moral hazard problem in the employment relationship?
a.   Pay above equilibrium wages.
b.   Put hidden video cameras in the workplace.
c.   Buy life insurance on their workers.
d.   Pay employees with delayed compensation such as a year-end bonus.

7. Which one of the following **BEST** demonstrates the problem of moral hazard?
   a. Karen does not buy health insurance because it is too expensive and she is healthy.
   b. Kyoko chooses to attend a well-respected college.
   c. Namdar drives more recklessly after he buys auto insurance.
   d. A life insurance company forces Teemu to have a physical examination prior to selling insurance to him.

8. Under pairwise majority voting, if A is preferred to B, and B is preferred to C, then A should be preferred to C. Which one of the following is the name of this relationship?
   a. the property of unanimity
   b. the property of transitivity
   c. the property of independence
   d. the property of efficiency

9. Which one of the following is **NOT** a property required of a perfect voting system?
   a. the median voter always wins
   b. transitivity
   c. no dictators
   d. unanimity

10. Suppose that 40 percent of the voting population wish to spend $1000 for artwork in City Hall, 25 percent wish to spend $20 000, and 35 percent wish to spend $22 000. Which one of the following options contains the median preferred outcome, the average preferred outcome, and the modal preferred outcome?
    a. $1000, $14 333, $1000
    b. $20 000, $20 000, $22 000
    c. $20 000, $13 100, $1000
    d. $1000, $20 000, $22 000

11. Which one of the following is true under pairwise majority rule if people vote for the outcome closest to their **MOST** preferred outcome?
    a. The average preferred outcome wins.
    b. The outcome preferred by the median voter wins.
    c. The outcome preferred by the greatest number of voters wins.
    d. There is no clear winner due to Arrow's Impossibility Theorem.

12. Which one of the following is **NOT** true about how people make decisions?
    a. People are sometimes too sure of their own abilities.
    b. People are reluctant to change their minds in the face of new information.
    c. People give too much weight to a small number of vivid observations.
    d. People are always rational maximizers.

13. In the *ultimatum game*, which one of the following splits would be rational for both the person proposing the split and the person who must accept or reject the split?
    a. 99/1
    b. 75/25
    c. 50/50
    d. 1/99

14. Which one of the following helps explain why firms pay bonuses to workers during particularly profitable years in order to prevent workers from becoming disgruntled?
    a. People are rational maximizers.
    b. People are inconsistent over time.
    c. People care about fairness.
    d. People are reluctant to change their minds.

15. John's friend dies of a sudden heart attack. John rushes to his doctor for an expensive physical examination. Which one of the following is demonstrated by John's response?
    a. People give too much weight to a small number of vivid observations.
    b. People easily change their minds when confronted with new information.
    c. People enjoy going to the doctor.
    d. People lack confidence.

16. Which one of the following is a response to people's inconsistent behaviour over time?
    a. efficiency wages
    b. year-end bonuses
    c. forced contributions to a retirement plan

Use the following set of voter preferences to answer questions 17–20.

	Voter type		
	Type 1	Type 2	Type 3
Percent of electorate	35	25	40
First choice	C	A	B
Second choice	A	B	C
Third choice	B	C	A

17. When the choice is between A and B, which one of the following is the portion of the population that votes for A?
    a. 25 percent
    b. 35 percent
    c. 40 percent
    d. 60 percent

18. Under pairwise majority voting, which one of the following outcomes wins?
    a. A
    b. B
    c. C
    d. These preferences suffer from the Condorcet Paradox, so there is no clear winner.

19. If A is first compared to C, and then the winner is compared to B, which one of the following outcomes is the winner?
    a. A
    b. B
    c. C
    d. These preferences suffer from the Condorcet Paradox, so there is no clear winner.

20. If a Borda count is used, which one of the following outcomes is preferred?
    a. A
    b. B
    c. C
    d. These preferences do not exhibit transitivity, so there is no clear winner.

C.   **Short-Answer Questions**

1.   Would the buyers of auto insurance be expected to have a higher or lower than average probability of having an auto accident? Why? How does the insurance company address the adverse selection in this market? How does it address the moral hazard in this market? _____

    _____

    _____

    _____

    _____

2.   To reduce adverse selection, firms signal high quality with expensive advertising. What are the necessary characteristics of an effective signal? Why do firms producing low-quality goods not use expensive advertising to falsely signal high quality?

    _____

    _____

    _____

    _____

    _____

3.   Suppose that 30 percent of the voters want to spend $10 000 on a new park, 30 percent want to spend $11 000, and 40 percent wish to spend $25 000. How much does the average voter want to spend? How much does the median voter want to spend? If each voter chooses the point closest to his most preferred choice, what will be the final choice between these three choices of a majority rule? Does the Condorcet paradox arise? _____

    _____

    _____

    _____

    _____

4.   Do politicians always choose policies that maximize the well-being of society? Why or why not?_____

    _____

    _____

    _____

5.   The most popular major on campus is economics. One student takes an introductory economics class and tells her friend that it was the worst class she has ever taken. The friend avoids taking any economics. Is this rational? Explain.

    _____

    _____

    _____

    _____

6. Why does choosing a good gift qualify as a signal of love and concern to the recipient?

_____

_____

_____

D.   Practice Problems

1. For each of the following situations, identify the principal and the agent, describe the information asymmetry involved, and explain how moral hazard has been reduced.

    a. Dental insurance companies offer free annual checkups. _____

    _____

    _____

    _____

    b. Firms compensate travelling sales representatives with commissions (a percent of the value of the sales). _____

    _____

    _____

    _____

    c. McDonald's pays twice the minimum wage to high school students.

    _____

    _____

    _____

    d. Farmers in Ontario's Niagara Peninsula pay Mexican migrant workers bonuses if they pick fruit and vegetables for the entire summer rather than only part of the summer._____

    _____

    _____

    _____

2. For each of the following statements, describe the information asymmetry involved, name the type of action that has been taken to reduce adverse selection (signalling or screening), and explain how adverse selection has been reduced.

    a. McDonald's only hires high school students with good grades.

    _____

    _____

    _____

    _____

b. Hyundai provides a 100 000-km warranty on its new cars. _____

_____

_____

_____

c. A life insurance company requires prospective customers to take a physical examination. _____

_____

_____

_____

d. Labatt's sponsors the Grey Cup half-time show. _____

_____

_____

_____

3. Answer the following questions regarding the Condorcet paradox for the two sets of voting preferences below.

Case 1

Voter type

	Type 1	Type 2	Type 3
Percent of electorate	15	40	45
First choice	C	A	B
Second choice	A	B	C
Third choice	B	C	A

a. If voters must choose between A and B, what are the percentages of votes that each outcome receives, and which outcome wins? _____

_____

_____

_____

_____

b. If voters must choose between B and C, what are the percentages of votes that each outcome receives, and which outcome wins? _____

_____

_____

_____

c. If voters must choose between C and A, what are the percentages of votes that each outcome receives and which outcome wins? _____

_____

_____

_____

d. Do these preferences exhibit transitivity? Explain.

_____

_____

_____

e. If the voters choose between A and B and then compare with C, which outcome wins? _____

_____

_____

_____

f. If the voters choose between B and C and then compare with A, which outcome wins? _____

_____

_____

_____

g. If the voters choose between A and C and then compare with B, which outcome wins? _____

_____

_____

_____

h. Does the order in which items are voted on matter in this case? Why or why not?

_____

_____

_____

Case 2

	Voter type		
	Type 1	Type 2	Type 3
Percent of electorate	30	15	55
First choice	A	B	C
Second choice	B	C	A
Third choice	C	A	B

a. If voters must choose between A and B, what are the percentages of votes that each outcome receives, and which outcome wins? _____

_____

_____

_____

b. If voters must choose between B and C, what are the percentages of votes that each outcome receives, and which outcome wins? _____

_____

_____

_____

c. If voters must choose between C and A, what are the percentages of votes that each outcome receives, and which outcome wins? _____

_____

_____

_____

d. Do these preferences exhibit transitivity? Explain. _____

_____

_____

_____

e. If the voters choose between A and B and then compare with C, which outcome wins? _____

_____

_____

_____

f. If the voters choose between B and C and then compare with A, which outcome wins? _____

_____

_____

_____

g. If the voters choose between A and C and then compare with B, which outcome wins? _____

_____

_____

_____

h. Does the order in which items are voted on matter in this case? Why or why not?

_____

_____

_____

4. a. For Case 1 in problem 3 above, which outcome wins if a Borda count is used to determine the winner among outcomes A, B, and C, and what are the scores for each outcome? _____

_____

_____

_____

b. For Case 1 in problem 3 above, eliminate outcome C and use a Borda count to find the winner from the remaining choices of A and B. What property required of a perfect voting system has been violated? Explain. _____

_____

_____

_____

c. Compare the results of Case 1 in problem 3 under simple majority rule, a Borda count with three choices, and a Borda count with two choices. What conclusion can be drawn from these results? _____

_____

_____

_____

E.   Advanced Critical Thinking

Pavel and Hamid are watching a television news story about lung cancer. Hamid says to Pavel, "I think it is terrible that people with cancer often can't buy supplemental health insurance. People who are ill are the ones who really need supplemental health insurance. Even worse, once someone gets supplemental health insurance, they often have to pay a deductible equal to 20 percent of the first $3000 of their medical bills each year. Only then does the insurance company cover the remainder of the medical bills."

1. What problem caused by asymmetric information are insurance companies trying to avoid when they deny coverage to someone who may already be ill? What would happen if the insurance companies did not deny coverage to people who are already ill? _____

_____

_____

_____

2. What problem does charging a deductible help solve? What might happen if insurance companies did not require a deductible? _____

_____

_____

_____

3. How might public policy address the problems in the market for supplemental health insurance? What are some of the shortcomings of a public policy solution?

_____

_____

_____

III. Solutions

A. True/False Questions

1. T
2. F; the agent performs a task on behalf of the principal.
3. F; signals must be costly, yet less costly to the person with the higher-quality product.
4. F; it shows that the order in which items are voted on can determine the outcome; therefore majority-rule voting does not always reveal what society wants.
5. T
6. F; it will produce the outcome preferred by the median voter.
7. T
8. F; there is evidence that people are only "near rational."
9. T
10. F; people tend to seek instant gratification and fail to follow through on unpleasant tasks.
11. T.
12. F; conventional economic theory assumes that people are rational wealth-maximizers. However, people are also driven, in part, by some innate sense of fairness.

B. Multiple-Choice Questions

1. a	5. c	9. a	13. a	17. d
2. d	6. c	10. c	14. c	18. d
3. b	7. c	11. b	15. a	19. b
4. b	8. b	12. d	16. c	20. c

C. Short-Answer Questions

1.   Higher, because buyers of insurance know more about their probability of an accident, and those with a high probability of having accidents will need insurance. An insurance company checks a driver's driving history and offer policies that appeal differently to risky and safe drivers, and then it charges higher premiums to risky drivers. The insurance company requires a deductible to avoid moral hazard.

2.   It must be costly, but less costly to the individual with the higher-quality product. Because low-quality firms will not generate repeat purchases from their advertising, it is not cost effective for them to engage in expensive advertising.

3.   The average voter wants to spend $16 300 [0.3($10 000) + 0.3($11 000) + 0.4($25 000) = $16 300]. The median voter wants to spend $11 000. The final choice will be $11 000. No, the Condorcet paradox does not arise. For any pair, find the winner, and then compare it with the remaining choice— $11 000 always wins.

4.   No. Some politicians may act out of greed and others may sacrifice the national interest to improve their local popularity.

5.   No. People give too much weight to a small number of vivid observations. In this case, the friend's comment is just one additional observation out of thousands.

6.   It takes time; that is, it is costly, to choose a good gift, and it also provides information that the gift giver is knowledgeable about the recipient.

D. Practice Problems

1.   a.   The insurance company is the principal; the insured is the agent. Only the agent knows how well he takes care of his teeth. By checking the insured's teeth each year, the insurance company can better monitor the behaviour of the insured and reduce major future claims.

b. The firm is the principal; the sales representative is the agent. The firm does not know how hard the sales rep works. By paying the sales rep only a commission, the firm is able to better monitor the sales representative's work habits, and the worker is less likely to shirk.

c. McDonald's is the principal; the student is the agent. McDonald's does not know how hard the student works. By paying above-market wages, McDonald's increases the cost of shirking and the cost of being fired. The worker is less likely to shirk.

d. Niagara farmers are the principal; Mexican migrant workers are the agent. Farmers do not know how hard workers work. By paying them large bonuses for working an entire season, farmers raise the cost of shirking and the cost of being fired. The result is that workers are less likely to shirk.

2. a. McDonald's does not know the abilities of the potential workers as well as the workers do. McDonald's *screens* potential workers using past educational performance, and it is able to select high-ability workers.

b. Buyers do not know the quality of Hyundai cars because these cars are relatively new to the Canadian market. Hyundai *signals* high quality with a long warranty, and buyers are able to select high-quality cars.

c. The life insurance company does not know as much about the health of the insurance buyer as the buyer does. The insurance company *screens* prospective customers with a physical exam to find hidden health problems so its insurance pool is not sicker than average.

d. Beer buyers do not know the quality of Labatt's beer as well as the Labatt Brewing Company does. Labatt's *signals* high quality with expensive advertising because it could only afford to do so if it could generate repeat buyers. Customers are able to choose a high-quality beer.

3. **Case 1**

    a. A = 15 + 40 = 55, B = 45. A beats B.

    b. B = 40 + 45 = 85, C = 15. B beats C.

    c. C = 15 + 45 = 60, A = 40. C beats A.

    d. No. A beats B and B beats C, so transitivity requires that A beats C but, in fact, C beats A.

    e. A beats B, so compare A with C and C wins.

    f. B beats C, so compare B with A and A wins.

    g. C beats A, so compare C with B and B wins.

    h. Yes, because these preferences do not exhibit transitivity.

Case 2

    a. A = 30 + 55 = 85, B = 15. A beats B.

    b. B = 30 + 15 = 45, C = 55. C beats B.

    c. A = 30, C = 15 + 55 = 70. C beats A.

    d. Yes. C beats A and A beats B. Transitivity requires that C beats B and it does.

    e. A beats B, so compare B with C and C wins.

    f. C beats B, so compare C with A and C wins.

    g. C beats A, so compare C with B and C wins.

    h. No, because these preferences exhibit transitivity.

4.   a. If choosing between A, B, and C, A = 30 + 120 + 45 = 195, B = 15 + 80 + 135 = 230, C = 45 + 40 + 90 = 175, and B wins.

      b. If choosing between only A and B, A = 30 + 80 + 45 = 155, B = 15 + 40 + 90 = 145, and A wins. Independence of irrelevant alternatives: the rankings of A and B should not change when C is removed, but the ranking did change.

      c. A wins, then B wins, then A wins. Thus, majority voting does not necessarily reveal what society wants, and deciding the order on which items are voted may affect the outcome.

E. Advanced Critical Thinking

1.   Adverse selection. People who are already ill would seek to buy supplemental health insurance. Their medical bills would be far higher than average, causing premiums to rise. At the artificially high price for supplemental insurance, fewer healthy people would buy this insurance because the cost would exceed their expected bills. When healthy people drop out of the market, the price rises even further for the remaining participants, thus further reducing the size of the supplemental health insurance market.

2.   Moral hazard. Without a deductible, people might go to the doctor even if they do not really need medical attention. They also have little incentive to take care of themselves to avoid illness because they bear no cost of the illness. As above, this raises the cost of supplemental insurance above the expected bills of healthy people and many will fail to buy insurance.

3.   Some people advocate government-provided, supplemental health insurance where everyone, whether sick or healthy, would be forced to participate. Majority-rule democratic institutions may not generate the amount of supplemental health care that people want. Self-interested politicians may choose to provide an amount of supplemental health care that is different from what people actually want.

GLOSSARY

ability-to-pay principle the idea that taxes should be levied on a person according to how well that person can shoulder the burden

absolute advantage the comparison among producers of a good according to their productivity

accounting profit total revenue minus total explicit cost

adverse selection the tendency for the mix of unobserved attributes to become undesirable from the standpoint of an uninformed party

agent a person who is performing an act for another person, called the *principal*

Arrow's impossibility theorem a mathematical result showing that, under certain assumed conditions, there is no scheme for aggregating individual preferences into a valid set of social preferences

average fixed cost fixed costs divided by the quantity of output

average revenue total revenue divided by the quantity sold

average tax rate total taxes paid divided by total income

average total cost total cost divided by the quantity of output

average variable cost variable costs divided by the quantity of output

benefits principle the idea that people should pay taxes based on the benefits they receive from government services

budget constraint the limit on the consumption bundles that a consumer can afford

budget deficit an excess of government spending over government receipts

budget surplus an excess of government receipts over government spending

business cycle fluctuations in economic activity, such as employment and production

capital the equipment and structures used to produce goods and services

cartel a group of firms acting in unison

circular-flow diagram a visual model of the economy that shows how dollars flow through markets among households and firms

Coase theorem the proposition that if private parties can bargain without cost over the allocation of resources, they can solve the problem of externalities on their own

collusion an agreement among firms in a market about quantities to produce or prices to charge

common resources goods that are rival in consumption but not excludable

comparative advantage the comparison among producers of a good according to their opportunity cost

compensating differential a difference in wages that arises to offset the nonmonetary characteristics of different jobs

competitive market a market in which there are many buyers and many sellers so that each has a negligible impact on the market price

complements two goods for which an increase in the price of one leads to a decrease in the demand for the other

Condorcet paradox the failure of majority rule to produce transitive preferences for society

constant returns to scale the property whereby long-run average total cost stays the same as the quantity of output changes

consumer surplus a buyer's willingness to pay minus the amount the buyer actually pays

corrective taxes taxes enacted to correct the effects of negative externalities

cost the value of everything a seller must give up to produce a good

cost–benefit analysis a study that compares the costs and benefits to society of providing a public good

cross-price elasticity of demand a measure of how much the quantity demanded of one good responds to a change in the price of another good, computed as the percentage change in quantity demanded of the first good divided by the percentage change in the price of the second good

deadweight loss the fall in total surplus that results from a market distortion, such as a tax

demand curve a graph of the relationship between the price of a good and the quantity demanded

demand schedule a table that shows the relationship between the price of a good and the quantity demanded

diminishing marginal product the property whereby the marginal product of an input declines as the quantity of the input increases

discrimination the offering of different opportunities to similar individuals who differ only by race, ethnic group, sex, age, or other personal characteristics

diseconomies of scale the property whereby long-run average total cost rises as the quantity of output increases

dominant strategy a strategy that is best for a player in a game regardless of the strategies chosen by the other players

economic profit total revenue minus total cost, including both explicit and implicit costs

economics the study of how society manages its scarce resources

economies of scale the property whereby long-run average total cost falls as the quantity of output increases

efficiency the property of a resource allocation of maximizing the total surplus received by all members of society

efficiency wages above-equilibrium wages paid by firms in order to increase worker productivity

efficient scale   the quantity of output that minimizes average total cost

elasticity   a measure of the responsiveness of quantity demanded or quantity supplied to one of its determinants

equilibrium   a situation in which the price has reached the level where quantity supplied equals quantity demanded

equilibrium price   the price that balances quantity supplied and quantity demanded

equilibrium quantity   the quantity supplied and the quantity demanded at the equilibrium price

equity   the fairness of the distribution of well-being among the members of society

excludability   the property of a good whereby a person can be prevented from using it

explicit costs   input costs that require an outlay of money by the firm

exports   goods and services produced domestically and sold abroad

externality   the uncompensated impact of one person's actions on the well-being of a bystander

factors of production   the inputs used to produce goods and services

fixed costs   costs that do not vary with the quantity of output produced

free rider   a person who receives the benefit of a good but avoids paying for it

game theory   the study of how people behave in strategic situations

Giffen good   a good for which an increase in the price raises the quantity demanded

horizontal equity   the idea that taxpayers with similar abilities to pay taxes should pay the same amount

human capital   the accumulation of investments in people, such as education and on-the-job training

implicit costs   input costs that do not require an outlay of money by the firm

imports   goods and services produced abroad and sold domestically

incentive   something that induces a person to act

income effect   the change in consumption that results when a price change moves the consumer to a higher or lower indifference curve

income elasticity of demand   a measure of how much the quantity demanded of a good responds to a change in consumers' income, computed as the percentage change in quantity demanded divided by the percentage change in income

indifference curve   a curve that shows consumption bundles that give the consumer the same level of satisfaction

inferior good   a good for which, other things equal, an increase in income leads to a decrease in demand

inflation   an increase in the overall level of prices in the economy

in-kind transfers   transfers to the poor given in the form of goods and services rather than cash

internalizing the externality   alter incentives so that people take account of the external effects of their actions

law of demand   the claim that, other things equal, the quantity demanded of a good falls when the price of the good rises

law of supply   the claim that, other things equal, the quantity supplied of a good rises when the price of the good rises

law of supply and demand   the claim that the price of any good adjusts to bring the quantity supplied and the quantity demanded for that good into balance

liberalism   the political philosophy according to which the government should choose policies deemed to be just, as evaluated by an impartial observer behind a "veil of ignorance"

libertarianism   the political philosophy according to which the government should punish crimes and enforce voluntary agreements but not redistribute income

life cycle   the regular pattern of income variation over a person's life

lump-sum tax   a tax that is the same amount for every person

macroeconomics   the study of economy-wide phenomena, including inflation, unemployment, and economic growth

marginal changes   small incremental adjustments to a plan of action

marginal cost   the increase in total cost that arises from an extra unit of production

marginal product   the increase in output that arises from an additional unit of input

marginal product of labour   the increase in the amount of output from an additional unit of labour

marginal rate of substitution   the rate at which a consumer is willing to trade one good for another

marginal revenue   the change in total revenue from an additional unit sold

marginal tax rate   the extra taxes paid on an additional dollar of income

market   a group of buyers and sellers of a particular good or service

market economy   an economy that allocates resources through the decentralized decisions of many firms and households as they interact in markets for goods and services

market failure   a situation in which a market left on its own fails to allocate resources efficiently

market power   the ability of a single economic actor (or small group of actors) to have a substantial influence on market prices

maximin criterion the claim that the government should aim to maximize the well-being of the worst-off person in society

median voter theorem a mathematical result showing that if voters are choosing a point along a line and each voter wants the point closest to his most preferred point, then majority rule will pick the most preferred point of the median voter

microeconomics the study of how households and firms make decisions and how they interact in markets

monopolistic competition a market structure in which many firms sell products that are similar but not identical

monopoly a firm that is the sole seller of a product without close substitutes

moral hazard the tendency of a person who is imperfectly monitored to engage in dishonest or otherwise undesirable behaviour

Nash equilibrium a situation in which economic actors interacting with one another each choose their best strategy given the strategies that all the other actors have chosen

natural monopoly a monopoly that arises because a single firm can supply a good or services to an entire market at a smaller cost than could two or more firms

negative income tax a tax system that collects revenue from high-income households and gives transfers to low-income households

normal good a good for which, other things equal, an increase in income leads to an increase in demand

normative statements claims that attempt to prescribe how the world should be

oligopoly a market structure in which only a few sellers offer similar or identical products

opportunity cost whatever must be given up to obtain some item

perfect complements two goods with right-angle indifference curves

perfect substitutes two goods with straight-line indifference curves

permanent income a person's normal income

positive statements claims that attempt to describe the world as it is

poverty line an absolute level of income set by the federal government for each family size, below which a family is deemed to be in poverty

poverty rate the percentage of the population whose family income falls below an absolute level called the *poverty line*

price ceiling a legal maximum on the price at which a good can be sold

price discrimination the business practice of selling the same good at different prices to different customers

price elasticity of demand a measure of how much the quantity demanded of a good responds to a change in the price of that good, computed as the percentage change in quantity demanded divided by the percentage change in price

price elasticity of supply a measure of how much the quantity supplied of a good responds to a change in the price of that good, computed as the percentage change in quantity supplied divided by the percentage change in price

price floor a legal minimum on the price at which a good can be sold

principal a person for whom another person, called the *agent*, is performing some act

prisoners' dilemma a particular "game" between two captured prisoners that illustrates why cooperation is difficult to maintain even when it is mutually beneficial

private goods goods that are both excludable and rival in consumption

producer surplus the amount a seller is paid for a good minus the seller's cost

production function the relationship between quantity of inputs used to make a good and the quantity of output of that good

production possibilities frontier a graph that shows the combinations of output that the economy can possibly produce given the available factors of production and the available production technology

productivity the quantity of goods and services produced from each hour of a worker's time

profit total revenue minus total cost

progressive tax a tax for which high-income taxpayers pay a larger fraction of their income than do low-income taxpayers

property rights the ability of an individual to own and exercise control over scarce resources

proportional tax a tax for which high-income and low-income taxpayers pay the same fraction of income

public goods goods that are neither excludable nor rival in consumption

quantity demanded the amount of a good that buyers are willing and able to purchase

quantity supplied the amount of a good that sellers are willing and able to sell

rational people people who systematically and purposefully do the best they can to achieve their objectives

regressive tax a tax for which high-income taxpayers pay a smaller fraction of their income than do low-income taxpayers

rival in consumption the property of a good whereby one person's use diminishes other people's use

scarcity the limited nature of society's resources

screening an action taken by an uninformed party to induce an informed party to reveal information

shortage a situation in which quantity demanded is greater than quantity supplied

signaling an action taken by an informed party to reveal private information to an uninformed party

strike the organized withdrawal of labour from a firm by a union

substitutes two goods for which an increase in the price of one leads to an increase in the demand for the other

substitution effect the change in consumption that results when a price change moves the consumer along a given indifference curve to a point with a new marginal rate of substitution

sunk cost a cost that has already been committed and cannot be recovered

supply curve a graph of the relationship between the price of a good and the quantity supplied

supply schedule a table that shows the relationship between the price of a good and the quantity supplied

surplus a situation in which quantity supplied is greater than quantity demanded

tariff a tax on goods produced abroad and sold domestically

tax incidence the manner in which the burden of a tax is shared among participants in a market

total cost the market value of the inputs a firm uses in production

total revenue (for a firm) the amount a firm receives for the sale of its output

total revenue (in a market) the amount paid by buyers and received by sellers of a good, computed as the price of the good times the quantity sold

Tragedy of the Commons a parable that illustrates why common resources get used more than is desirable from the standpoint of society as a whole

transaction costs the costs that parties incur in the process of agreeing and following through on a bargain

union a worker association that bargains with employers over wages and working conditions

utilitarianism the political philosophy according to which the government should choose policies to maximize the total utility of everyone in society

utility a measure of happiness or satisfaction

value of the marginal product the marginal product of an input times the price of the output

variable costs costs that vary with the quantity of output produced

vertical equity the idea that taxpayers with a greater ability to pay taxes should pay larger amounts

welfare government programs that supplement the incomes of the needy

welfare economics the study of how the allocation of resources affects economic well-being

willingness to pay the maximum amount that a buyer will pay for a good

world price the price of a good that prevails in the world market for that good

INDEX

Note: Page numbers in **boldface** refer to pages where key terms are defined. Page numbers followed by "f" or "t" refer to figures or tables.